CANADIAN
MARKETING in action→

SEVENTH EDITION

Keith J. Tuckwell
St. Lawrence College

PEARSON
Prentice
Hall

Toronto

Library and Archives Canada Cataloguing in Publication

Tuckwell, Keith J. (Keith John), 1950–
     Canadian marketing in action / Keith J. Tuckwell. — 7th ed.

Includes index.
ISBN 0-13-127779-0

1. Marketing—Textbooks.   2. Marketing—Canada—Textbooks.   I. Title.

HF5415.12.C3T75 2007 658.8   C2005-907644-5

ISBN 0-13-127779-0

Vice-President, Editorial Director: Michael J. Young
Editor-in-Chief: Gary Bennett
Acquisitions Editor: Laura Paterson Forbes
Marketing Manager: Eileen Lasswell
Developmental Editor: Pamela Voves
Production Editor: Cheryl Jackson
Copy Editor: Kelli Howey
Proofreader: Susan McNish
Production Coordinator: Patricia Ciardullo
Page Layout: Debbie Kumpf
Permissions Manager: Susan Wallace-Cox
Permissions Researcher: Lisa Brant
Art Director: Mary Opper
Cover and Interior Design: Michelle Bellemare
Cover image: First Light/Getty Images/Veer Incorporated

1 2 3 4 5   11 10 09 08 07

Printed and bound in United States of America

Statistics Canada information is used with the permission of the Minister of Industry, as Minister responsible for Statistics Canada. Information on the availability of the wide range of data from Statistics Canada can be obtained from Statistics Canada's Regional Offices, its World Wide Web site at http://www.statcan.ca, and its toll-free access number 1-800-263-1136.

To Esther . . . and our children, Marnie, Graham, and Gordon

Contents

Preface

Before we made any changes to the new seventh edition, we asked faculty reviewers to identify the major challenges they face when teaching an introductory marketing course. Four were identified:

- It is difficult getting today's students to read a textbook.
- Multicultural classes present language problems.
- It is difficult to cover content in the time allocated.
- Certain topics are more difficult than others for students to comprehend.

Since its inception, readability has been the primary strength of *Canadian Marketing in Action*. The new edition is no different. The writing style is clear and concise; there is good balance between theories and practical application of concepts, and there is a host of examples that students can quickly relate to. More difficult topics like marketing research, business-to-business marketing, distribution strategy and management, and online marketing have been streamlined, with key concepts presented in an easy-to-understand manner. As the reviewers say, "Students read Tuckwell books!" The seventh edition maintains this tradition.

Reviewers also identified three important issues challenging marketing organizations today: the influence of technology on various aspects of marketing practice; the design and implementation of customer relationship management programs to attract, retain, and maximize the potential of customers; and the burgeoning role and impact of social responsibility on marketing practices. These topics are given special attention in the early chapters where fundamental marketing concepts are presented, and they have been included in appropriate chapters throughout the textbook.

The manuscript for the seventh edition was reviewed thoroughly. Every time I prepare a new edition I am amazed at how quickly things change in marketing. This edition contains an abundance of new material embedded in chapter content; it was an extensive revision process. Most of the **Marketing in Action** vignettes are brand new. The vignettes feature well-known Canadian companies and show how they apply essential marketing concepts successfully.

While much of the content has changed, the original concept of the book has not. This book originated because there was a demand for a good, wholly Canadian resource for teaching marketing. Faculty were looking for a textbook that offered better balance between theory and practice, and they wanted the material presented in a clear, concise style. A readable format that students could appreciate was also demanded. This textbook continues to meet all of these needs.

In terms of organization and sequencing of chapters, the seventh edition has not changed. However, material within chapters has changed considerably. There is some resequencing of material in Chapters 1 and 2 in order to simplify the presentation of the marketing mix and the external environments that impact marketing.

The market for an introductory marketing textbook is very competitive: several longstanding and successful books are readily available to teachers and students, and I would like to think that *Canadian Marketing in Action*, now into its seventh edition, is one of those books.

My personal goal is to always produce the most up-to-date text possible—a text that not only reflects the state of current marketing practice, but also indicates the future direction of marketing practice in Canada. When you review the features of the book described in the next sections, I am confident you will find it unique and worthy of consideration.

Critical Issues

This edition focuses on essential issues that are shaping contemporary marketing practice. Among these issues are customer relationship management (database management techniques and customer retention strategies); electronic commerce and Internet-based marketing practices; strategic alliances and partnering among companies; socially responsible marketing; the impact of technology on marketing strategy; and integrated marketing communications.

New Features

As in previous editions, the seventh edition is presented in a practical, student-oriented style and provides good balance between theory and practice. It is written from a Canadian perspective, while considering the influences on marketing from all over the world. All essential marketing concepts that are important to today's business organizations are presented in an applied manner. All marketing concepts are considered in the context of consumer marketing, business-to-business marketing, and services and not-for-profit marketing.

Input from reviewers has resulted in significant changes to the seventh edition. Among the more important and exciting changes and additions are the following:

- In Chapter 1, **Contemporary Marketing,** formal discussion of the marketing mix is now front and centre. Understanding this concept right away is essential and it sets the stage for discussing factors that impact the marketing mix later in the text. The "Issues" section that appeared in previous editions has been dropped. In its place is expanded discussion of customer relationship marketing and database marketing concepts. Technology is fuelling marketing practice today, so expanded coverage of these topics is necessary. Chapter content has changed dramatically with very new examples and illustrations added.

- Chapter 2, **The External Marketing Environment,** is now completely focused on the external environments that influence the practice of marketing. With so many new examples and illustrations added, it now reads like a completely new chapter. This chapter is much clearer in terms of presentation and much easier to read than before.

- Chapter 3, **Marketing Research,** was perceived as a difficult chapter for students. This chapter has been streamlined somewhat, but many new applied examples were added to demonstrate and clarify key research concepts. Online marketing research concepts were also added to the chapter.

- In Chapter 4, **Consumer Buying Behaviour,** some re-sequencing of material was implemented. The discussion flows better now and the presentation of key buying behaviour concepts is more consistent. All of the ads in this chapter are new and there are more of them to demonstrate how knowledge of consumer buying behaviour is applied.

- In Chapter 5, **Business-to-Business Marketing and Organizational Buying Behaviour,** there is new discussion of e-procurement procedures and electronic supply chain management practices. A new vignette featuring **Dell Corporation** shows how these business practices are applied.

- In Chapter 6, **Market Segmentation and Target Marketing,** some content has been re-sequenced or streamlined in order to more clearly explain essential segmentation and targeting concepts. New examples embedded in the chapter along with a complete range of new visuals aptly portray how marketers apply these concepts. The concept of direct (one-to-one) segmentation is given more attention given the influence of technology on marketing practice today.

- In Chapter 8, **Product Strategy,** more emphasis is placed on branding and brand strategies. Effective branding is pivotal to the success of a product. A new vignette titled **Brand Crafting** aptly demonstrates the role and importance of an effective brand name. No major changes were made in Chapter 9, **Product Management.** Both chapters include new visuals that demonstrate brand strategy and brand management decisions.

- The quantitative aspects of price strategy are often the most difficult for students to comprehend. In Chapter 10, **Price Strategy and Determination,** the section dealing with pricing methods was streamlined and explanations of specific pricing methods are now explained in a more concise manner. In Chapter 11, **Price Management,** greater attention is paid to price incentives, mainly due to their popularity in so many industries, and newer concepts such as price bundling, a phenomenon of the telecommunications industry. These issues along with many new visuals give both chapters a fresh, new look.

- Distribution is another challenging topic for students, but it is an area of marketing that organizations are concentrating on today. Chapter 12, **Distribution Channels and Physical Distribution** now includes much more discussion on supply chain management and multi-channel concepts. As well, there is new discussion on information technology and its influence on distribution decisions. A new vignette titled **Supply Chain Management Is Key to Success** presents new perspectives on the role and importance of distribution decisions.

- Chapter 13, **Wholesaling and Retailing,** identifies the latest trends affecting channel members. Issues such as retail co-branding, the "blurring" of competition, the growth of power malls and big-box stores, the emergence of "lifestyle" malls, and the latest information about e-tailing are presented in detail.

- Part 7 includes the three chapters that focus on integrated marketing communications. Chapter 14, **Advertising and Public Relations,** initially starts with a discussion of the role and importance of an integrated communications plan. Each element of IMC is briefly discussed and then the rest of the chapter focuses on advertising and public relations. A completely new range of visuals has been added to demonstrate the application of advertising and public relations concepts.

- Chapter 15, **Direct Response and Interactive Communications,** examines the increasing roles that direct response and interactive communications play in the marketing communications mix. These forms of communications effectively respond to an organization's demand for accountability and measurement of the dollars invested in communications. Organizations moving in the direction of direct response and online communications are clearly identified and their strategies are discussed.

- Chapter 16, **Sales Promotion, Personal Selling, and Event Marketing and Sponsorships,** rounds out the discussion of integrated marketing communications. A new vignette titled **Hallmark Promotion Builds Sales** effectively portrays the impact of sales promotion strategies. An interesting vignette titled **Olympic Dreams!** discusses the benefits and drawbacks of Olympic event sponsorship, a hot topic considering the 2010 Winter Olympics will be hosted by Vancouver.

- Chapter 17 is dedicated to **Internet Marketing.** While e-marketing concepts are presented throughout the text, it is essential for the student to appreciate the potential of e-marketing in the future. This topic has proven difficult for students to master, so content is presented in a clear, easy-to-understand style. The intent of the chapter is to show how online marketing strategies are integrated with traditional marketing strategies. New vignettes focus on Internet-based marketing research applications and **Dell Corporation's** success with online marketing programs.

- Throughout, many new illustrations have been added to give the text a fresh, new look. New ads from Toyota, Gillette, General Motors, Scott Paper, Harvey's, Procter & Gamble, Unilever, Coca-Cola, Bell Canada, and many other companies aptly demonstrate important marketing concepts.

- Virtually all of the Marketing in Action vignettes are new. These vignettes feature the marketing strategies employed by organizations such as Reebok, Telus, Hallmark, Dell, Maple Leaf Sports and Entertainment, General Motors, Major League Baseball, Harley-Davidson, Cara Restaurants, Toyota, Sony, and many others that are familiar to students.

Pedagogy

Objective-Based Learning   Each chapter starts with a list of learning objectives directly related to the key concepts presented in the chapter. As each objective is covered in the body of the text, a reference in the margin identifies the concepts linked to that objective.

Photos, Figures, Charts, and Advertisements   Throughout each chapter, key concepts and applications are illustrated with strong visual material. Sample advertisements and statistical-oriented charts augment the Canadian perspective.

Key Terms   Key terms are highlighted within the text and listed at the end of each chapter with page references. Many are defined in the glossary at the end of the text.

Weblinks   Helpful Internet sites are provided throughout the text and are easily identifiable by URLs that appear in the margins.

Chapter Summaries   The summary at the end of each chapter helps reinforce main points and concepts.

Review Questions; Discussion and Application Questions   These two sets of questions allow students to review material and apply the concepts learned in the chapter.

E-Assignments   Each chapter includes one or two exercises that involve the student in using the Internet or evaluating the role of the Internet in developing marketing strategies.

Appendices   Appendix A, **The Financial Implications of Marketing Practice,** is a marketing mathematics section, expanding on the content presented in the pricing chapters. Appendix B provides a complete list of the **Canadian Marketing Cases.** (See the description below.)

Glossary   A glossary of the principal key terms and definitions appears at the end of the textbook.

Video Cases A new selection of videos is available with the seventh edition. The video cases are available on CD and the Companion Website. The videos were selected from two CBC shows: *Venture,* and *Marketplace.* Details of how to use the videos in class discussion are included in the Instructor's Manual. Each video illustrates an important element of marketing discussed in the textbook. Each case is described briefly, and a short series of questions is included to stimulate discussion.

Canadian Marketing Cases

Accompanying the textbook, posted at the Companion Website (**www.pearsoned.ca/ tuckwell**), and included in the Instructors' Manual are 16 cases. Some of the companies featured in the new cases include The Hockey Company/Reebok Canada, Wendy's Restaurants, Nick-N-Willy's, Ben & Jerry's, and Mercedes-Benz. Popular cases from the last edition have been retained and updated where necessary. Among this group are Cineplex Odeon Theatres, Beiersdorf (Nivea for Men), Toronto Blue Jays, and the Running Room. All cases are ideal for in-class discussion, presentations, or take-home assignments. A complete list of the cases can be found in Appendix B of the textbook and in the Instructor's Manual.

Supplements

INSTRUCTOR'S RESOURCE CD-ROM

The *Instructor's Resource CD-ROM* (0-13-201977-9) includes the following instructor supplements:

- **Instructor's Manual.** Prepared by the author, the manual includes learning objectives, chapter summaries, answers to chapter questions, additional illustrations of key concepts, 16 Canadian marketing cases, guideline answers to case questions, a synopsis of video cases, and an extensive listing of topics suitable for term papers and class presentations.

- **Pearson TestGen.** More than 1900 test questions, including multiple-choice, true/false, matching, and short answer questions, are provided in TestGen format. TestGen is a testing software that enables instructors to view and edit the existing questions, add questions, generate tests, and distribute the tests in a variety of formats. Powerful search and sort functions make it easy to locate questions and arrange them in any order desired. TestGen also enables instructors to administer tests on a local area network, have the tests graded electronically, and have the results prepared in electronic or printed reports. TestGen is compatible with Windows and Macintosh operating systems, and can be downloaded from the TestGen website located at www.pearsoned.com/testgen. Contact your local sales representative for details and access.

- **PowerPoints.** A collection of 340 transparencies, culled from the textbook or specifically designed to complement chapter content, is also available electronically in PowerPoint software on the Instructor's Resource CD-ROM.

- **Image Library.** Selected full-colour ads published in the text are available for viewing in the Image Library included on this CD.

Most of these instructor supplements are also available for download from a password-protected section of Pearson Education Canada's online catalogue (vig.pearsoned. ca). Navigate to your book's catalogue page to view a list of those supplements that are available. See your local sales representative for details and access.

CBC/PEARSON EDUCATION CANADA VIDEO LIBRARY (0-13-129061-4)

The videos that accompany the seventh edition cover a broad range of marketing topics and feature well-known Canadian and international companies. The problems and opportunities faced by these companies and the strategic direction they might consider can be the focal point of student discussion or assignments.

COMPANION WEBSITE

The Companion Website at **www.pearsoned.ca/tuckwell** is a handy reference for students. The site provides video resources and an online study guide that includes chapter quizzes and application and Internet exercises. The Virtual Marketing Library lists annotated weblinks organized by key areas of marketing, providing a great source of valuable information right at the user's fingertips. The website also provides access to the Canadian Marketing Cases.

PEARSON CUSTOM PUBLISHING (WWW.PRENHALL.COM/CUSTOMBUSINESS)

Pearson Custom Publishing can provide you and your students with texts, cases, and articles to enhance your course. Choose material from Darden, Ivey, Harvard Business School Publishing, NACRA, and Thunderbird to create your own custom casebook. Contact your Pearson sales representative for details.

ONLINE LEARNING SOLUTIONS

Pearson Education Canada supports instructors interested in using online course management systems. We provide text-related content in WebCT and Blackboard. To find out more about creating an online course using Pearson content in one of these platforms, contact your Pearson sales representative.

NEW! PEARSON ADVANTAGE PROGRAM

Pearson Education is proud to introduce the Pearson Advantage program, the first integrated Canadian service program committed to meeting the customization, training, and support needs for your course. Ask your Pearson sales representative for details!

YOUR PEARSON SALES REPRESENTATIVE

Your Pearson sales rep is always available to ensure you have everything you need to teach a winning course. Armed with experience, training, and product knowledge, your Pearson rep will support your assessment and adoption of any of the products, services, and technology outlined here to ensure our offerings are tailored to suit your individual needs and the needs of your students. Whether it's getting instructions on TestGen software or specific content files for your new online course, your Pearson sales representative is there to help.

MASTERING MARKETING CD-ROM (0-13060011-3)

This self-paced, interactive software helps reinforce marketing principles by linking theory to practice. It features 12 video episodes, bringing key marketing concepts to life. Students watch as employees at CanGo, a fictional Internet company, are faced with various realistic marketing issues. Interactive exercises accompany each video segment, challenging students to analyze the issue and develop new marketing strategies. Available for a small extra charge in a value-package.

MARKETING PLAN PRO 6.0 CD-ROM (0-13-148526-1)

Available at a modest extra charge in a value-package, this highly acclaimed software enables students to build a marketing plan from scratch. Marketing Plan Pro also includes sample marketing plans.

THE MARKETING PLAN: A HANDBOOK WITH CD-ROM BY MARIAN BURKE WOOD, 2E (0-13-164149-2)

This brief paperback, which includes Marketing Plan Pro software (described above), is the ideal companion for any course in which students will create a marketing plan.

LEMONADE MARKET SIM (0-13-197547-1)

This simple to use excel based simulation has students working in teams and exploring the four P's of marketing: product, price, place and promotion. For more details, please contact your Pearson Sales representative.

INTERPRETIVE SIMULATIONS

Pearson Education has partnered with Interpretive to provide a wide range of web based simulations. Bundle a simulation with a Pearson text and save your students some money! To learn more about marketing simulations such as New Shoes, Market Share and StratSim Marketing, please visit **www.interpretive.com** or ask your Pearson Education Canada sales representative for more information.

Organization of the Text

The book is divided into eight sections:

PART 1—MARKETING TODAY

The initial section presents an overview of contemporary marketing, its processes, and practices. It introduces the concept of the marketing mix and presents external influences on the planning and implementation of marketing programs. Special topics include relationship marketing and the role of customer relationship management programs and the importance of ethics and social responsibility in contemporary business practice.

PART 2—INPUTS FOR MARKETING PLANNING

This section examines the inputs a manager considers prior to developing a marketing plan. The initial emphasis is on various marketing research techniques used to collect information and data about customers and the marketplace. The discussion then shifts to essential marketing concepts in the areas of consumer buying behaviour and business buying behaviour.

PART 3—MARKETING PLANNING

With appropriate background information available, the marketing manager now shifts attention to identifying and selecting target markets and the development of marketing plans to reach and influence those targets. Marketing plans are influenced by a variety of factors, the main influence being the direction a company wants to take. The links between corporate plans and marketing plans are discussed in detail in this section.

PART 4—PRODUCT

In this section, the text examines the first element of the marketing mix. How products are developed, marketed, and managed is the focus of the product chapters. This part includes coverage of branding strategy, package design, new-product development and innovation, and rejuvenation strategies for established products.

PART 5—PRICE

This section explores the role of price in the marketing mix. The discussion deals with pricing strategies, the role of pricing in achieving corporate objectives, and methods of determining prices. Also discussed is how the price function is managed in business organizations.

PART 6—DISTRIBUTION

This section concentrates on the roles of distribution planning and physical distribution, wholesaling, and retailing. The role and impact of the Internet and other emerging technologies on the distribution of goods and services is a major topic of discussion.

PART 7—INTEGRATED MARKETING COMMUNICATIONS

This section is organized so that three distinct chapters examine the components of integrated marketing communications. The initial chapter covers advertising and public relations. The second chapter covers direct response and interactive communications. The third concentrates on sales promotion, personal selling, and event marketing and sponsorships. The intent is to show how communications strategies are integrated in order to achieve marketing objectives.

PART 8—EMERGING DIRECTIONS IN MARKETING

The practice of marketing is constantly evolving. With this in mind, this section retains the standalone chapter on electronic marketing. While electronic marketing concepts are integrated throughout the text, it is important for a student to understand the fundamentals of electronic marketing while appreciating that it is an addition to, and not a replacement of, traditional marketing practices. The unique considerations of services and not-for-profit marketing and the importance of global marketing are also presented in this section.

Acknowledgments

Many organizations and individuals have contributed to the development of this text-book. I would like to thank the following organizations sincerely for their cooperation and contribution.

Adams Brands Canada
Apple Canada
Autobytel.com
Beiersdorf Canada Inc.
Bell Canada
Bluenotes
BMW Canada
Calloway Golf
Canadian Business
Canadian Geographic
Canadian National
    Railways
Canadian Tourism
    Commission
Cara Restaurants
Clover Leaf Seafoods
Coca-Cola Canada
Courtyard Marriott Hotel
    Toronto
Crowne Plaza Hotels
CTV Network
Dell Corporation
Desjardins Financial
eBay.ca
FedEx
General Motors
Grand & Toy

Hallmark Canada
Harley-Davidson
Harvey's Restaurants
Honda Canada
Honda Canada, Acura
    Division
Intrawest Corporation
Jaguar Canada
KAO Brands Canada
Kimberly Clark
KitchenAid
Kodak Canada
Kraft Canada Inc.
L'Oreal Canada
La Senza
Labatt Breweries of
    Canada
Mark's Work Wearhouse
MasterCard Canada
Mazda Canada
Mercedes-Benz Canada
Millward Brown Goldfarb
MSN Autos Canada
Nestlé Canada
Novartis Consumer
    Health Canada
Philips Electronics

Procter & Gamble
Reckitt Benkeiser Canada
    Inc.
Resolve Corporation
Rolex Canada
Scott Paper
Sears Canada Inc.
Shell Canada Limited
Statistics Canada
TD Canada Trust
The Ford Motor Company
    of Canada
The Gillette Company
The Globe and Mail
Toyota Motor Company of
    Canada
Unilever Inc.
United Way of Toronto
UPS Canada
Via Rail
Viking Kitchen Appliances
VISA Canada Association
Wendy's Restaurants
    Canada
Xerox Canada Ltd.
Yahoo.ca

For undertaking the tedious task of reviewing the textbook at various stages of development, I am indebted to my colleagues. The input provided by each of you was appreciated. I would like to sincerely thank the following reviewers:

William Clymer (Durham College)

George Dracopoulos (Vanier College)

Daniel Duyck (Bishop's University)

Steve Janisse (St. Clair College)

Cyri Jones (Capilano College School of Business)

Stefan Kuch (Vanier College)

William Bradford MacDonald (Nova Scotia Community College)

Judith Nash (SAIT)

Robert Soroka (Dawson College)

From Pearson Education Canada, I would like to sincerely thank Laura Forbes, Eileen Lasswell, Pamela Voves, Cheryl Jackson, Kelli Howey, Susan McNish, Lisa Brant, Patricia Ciardullo, Michelle Bellemare, and Debbie Kumpf for their dedication to producing another terrific edition of *Canadian Marketing in Action*.

The tedious and time-consuming task of writing another book is complete! For their support once again I must sincerely thank my family. To Marnie, Graham, and Gord ... thank you! As always, a very special thank you to my wife, Esther.

Keith J. Tuckwell   *2005*

A Great Way to Learn and Instruct Online

The Pearson Education Canada Companion Website is easy to navigate and is organized to correspond to the chapters in this textbook. Whether you are a student in the classroom or a distance learner you will discover helpful resources for in-depth study and research that empower you in your quest for greater knowledge and maximize your potential for success in the course.

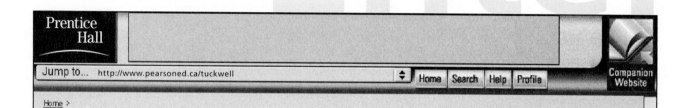

[www.pearsoned.ca/tuckwell]

Prentice Hall

Jump to... http://www.pearsoned.ca/tuckwell   Home Search Help Profile

Companion Website

Home >

PH Companion Website

Canadian Marketing in Action, Seventh Edition, by Keith J. Tuckwell

Student Resources

The modules in this section provide students with tools for learning course material. These modules include:
- Chapter Objectives
- Chapter Quiz
- Application Exercises
- Internet Exercises
- PowerPoint Presentations
- Canadian Marketing Cases
- Additional marketing resources

In the self-study modules, students can send answers to the grader and receive instant feedback on their progress through the Results Reporter. Coaching comments and references to the textbook may be available to ensure that students take advantage of all available resources to enhance their learning experience.

Instructor Resources

A link to the protected Instructor's Central site provides instructors with additional teaching tools. Downloadable PowerPoint Presentations and an Instructor's Manual are just some of the materials that may be available in this section. Where appropriate, this section will be password protected. To get a password, simply contact your Pearson Education Canada Representative or call Faculty Sales and Services at 1-800-850-5813.

Marketing Today

The purpose of this book is to examine what is involved in the practice and management of marketing. Part 1 presents an overview of contemporary marketing, its processes, and its practices.

Chapter 1 shows how marketing has evolved to become the focal point of business activity. Emphasis is placed on the role of marketing in contemporary business and the decision variables that comprise the marketing mix.

Chapter 2 examines the external environment by taking a look at a series of uncontrollable variables that influence marketing decisions and the development of marketing strategy.

© Kevin Dodge/Masterfile.

Contemporary Marketing

Learning Objectives

After studying this chapter, you will be able to

1. Define marketing and describe its role and importance in contemporary organizations.

2. Describe how marketing has evolved to become the driving force of business growth.

3. Explain the variety of activities that contemporary marketing practice embraces.

4. Explain the concept of the marketing mix.

5. Describe the decision-making processes associated with marketing mix elements.

6. Explain relationship marketing and the role of customer relationship management programs in relationship marketing.

The Importance of Marketing

One of the toughest challenges facing a business today is trying to anticipate where the business is going and how it will get there. No company can accurately foresee what the future will bring. What any company does know for sure is that change is occurring rapidly, and if it clings to traditional products and services and traditional practices it will be heading for failure.

Change is occurring everywhere. Technology today is faster, cheaper, and better, and it has changed the way people live and work. Sophisticated notebook computers, cellular phones, and personal digital assistants (sophisticated communications devices that combine Internet, email and voice messaging) play key roles in day-to-day business practices. The presence of the Internet and the World Wide Web, allowing businesses to communicate and do business with individual customers, is a testimony to technological advancements.

Populations are getting older, so marketing organizations now face the prospect of attracting new, younger customers while retaining older ones. Satisfying the needs of diverse age groups poses a challenge. Emerging countries, such as China, Indonesia, and Russia, have large populations and growing middle classes. Their presence on the world stage presents new opportunities for North American–based companies.

Where does marketing fit in all of this? Simply put, marketing is an agent of change. In other words, the role of marketing is twofold. It provides a means for companies to constantly assess changing conditions, and then provides the expertise to develop appropriate strategies so that an organization will be able to take advantage of the changes. Business organizations create and market products and services for unique customer groups within a population.

Marketing is a vital cog in the corporate wheel! Without good marketing companies would not grow and prosper. One of Canada's most successful companies is Tim Hortons. In an independent survey conducted by research firm The Strategic Counsel Tim Hortons was ranked as Canada's best-managed brand, and the reasons are all marketing related. These reasons include:[1]

- strong customer service
- popular products
- prolific community involvement
- a large number of locations

1. Define marketing and describe its role and importance in contemporary organizations.

The Strategic Counsel
www.thestrategiccounsel.com

- implementation of an efficient business system to deliver products
- consistent delivery of brand promise

Other Canadian companies and brands cited for management excellence in the study included President's Choice, WestJet, Canadian Tire, Loblaws, Cirque du Soleil, and Shoppers Drug Mart. Companies and brands such as these demonstrate marketing initiative. They don't sit still or rest on their laurels. They recognize the need to stay sharp and change with the times in order to always be a step or two ahead of their competitors. To do so, they constantly monitor their respective business environments and put marketing plans into place that meet the ever-changing needs of customers. That's why they are respected leaders that hold dominant positions in their industries.

Marketing Defined

This brings us to the point where we can try to define marketing; that is, try to explain what this activity involves. Think for a minute about what your reply would be if someone asked you the question, "What is marketing?"

The simplest way of defining marketing would be to call it a process that identifies a need and then offers a means (a good or service) of satisfying it. This definition focuses on two very important steps in the marketing process—identification (on the part of the organization) and satisfaction (on the part of the customer)—and suggests that all marketing activity is focused on a kind of transaction or exchange between the organization and the customer.

American Marketing Association
www.marketingpower.com

marketing

exchange

benefit

In an attempt to convey the full complexity of modern marketing activity, the American Marketing Association (AMA), an international association of academics and marketing professionals, has formulated its own definition. **Marketing** is the process of planning and executing the conception, pricing, promotion, and distribution of ideas, goods, and services to create exchanges that satisfy individual and organizational objectives.[2]

A key word in the definition is "exchange." **Exchange** involves the transfer of something of value (a benefit) from the organization in return for something else from the customer so that both parties benefit in the process. Exchange occurs when a customer presents her cash, credit card, or debit card for a pair of Nike running shoes at the Bay or Athlete's World. **Benefit** is based on the discovery and satisfaction of a customer's needs and the building of an ongoing relationship with the customer. Customer satisfaction and relationship marketing are the cornerstones of contemporary marketing and, as such, will be discussed throughout the text.

Dell Computer Inc. provides an example of how the definition of marketing is applied. Prior to the launch of Dell, all computer companies marketed computers the same way. A young entrepreneur by the name of Michael Dell decided to market custom-designed computers (made to customer specifications) directly to consumers. Eliminating expensive distribution costs provides savings and convenience to customers. Dell introduced a new form of exchange and new benefits. Dell is now a leading brand of computers (US$41 billion in annual sales), with a solid reputation for quality products at lower cost. Dell established an entirely new way of marketing computers.[3]

The task of marketing today is to collect, analyze, and apply information about customers in order to develop total marketing programs, including products, prices, distribution, and communications, that respond to changing needs and preferences. A truly market-driven company recognizes that being oriented toward the customer is not enough. To grow and prosper, a company requires knowledge of its competitors' products and how customers view them. This is how McDonald's remains number one

2. Describe how marketing has evolved to become the driving force of business growth.

in fast-food retailing, Nike number one in athletic shoes, and Wal-Mart number one in department stores. The goal of the company is to stay one step ahead of the competition by offering goods and services that provide customers with value, all the time.

Marketing Past and Present

We have seen that contemporary marketing is a complex process based on a simple idea: to identify a need and then satisfy it. To understand how a simple thought has grown into such a complex process, it would be helpful to look at the evolution of marketing, for marketing is a philosophy or way of thinking in an organization. Business organizations have moved through several stages of thinking with regard to how they approach customers. Initially the emphasis was on production, then on sales, then on marketing, and finally on societal or socially responsible marketing. It should not be assumed, however, that all companies share the same philosophy about marketing or that they are at the same stage in terms of how they think about it. In fact, all four orientations described below are alive and well.

PRODUCTION ORIENTATION

Organizations following a **production orientation** pay little attention to what customers need. Instead, they concentrate on what they are capable of producing. The basic premise of a production orientation is quite simple: if a company builds a quality product at an affordable price, the product will eventually sell itself. Businesses realize profits by producing and distributing only a limited variety of products as efficiently as possible. Henry Ford's classic statement "They can have any colour of car as long as it's black" illustrates the philosophy behind the production orientation. Ford's efficient assembly line reduced the cost of a vehicle to the point where efficient transportation was available to the public. Even today, some companies try to survive using this kind of outdated approach.

production orientation

SELLING ORIENTATION

As manufacturers added new product lines and as more and more competitors entered the market, customers had a greater selection of products. Consequently, customers had to be convinced to buy products. The emphasis shifted from production to selling. Companies adopting a **selling orientation** believed the more they sold the more profit they would make. The "hard sell" became the basic philosophy of doing business. But companies that paid little attention to costs found that this was not always the case. At the same time, consumers became increasingly demanding of a product's quality, performance, and dependability.

selling orientation

This stage was the earliest attempt to match potential customers' needs with products or services. In the automobile industry, competing firms, such as Ford and General Motors, offered automobiles at different price points and then searched for a consumer market that would buy those models. For example, GM offered the Chevrolet and Pontiac in a lower price range, Buick and Oldsmobile in a mid price range, and Cadillac in a high price range. The idea was to get customers into the GM family and move them up. The fact that more variety was available meant these companies had to "sell" their goods—their efforts focused on advertising and promotions to get customers into the dealer showrooms.

MARKETING ORIENTATION

When a marketing orientation exists, all business planning revolves around the customer. This organizational philosophy has been appropriately coined the **marketing**

marketing concept

concept and is expressed as follows: the essential task of the organization is to determine the needs and wants of a target market and then to deliver a set of satisfactions in such a way that the organization's product is perceived to be a better value than a competing product. The resources of the entire firm are directed at determining and satisfying customer needs and building ongoing relationships. The marketing concept has been expressed in unique ways by marketers. For example, "Make what you can sell instead of trying to sell what you can make," or "Love the customer and not the product." Perhaps Burger King said it best with its famous advertising slogan: "Have it your way."

Firms applying the marketing concept realize profits by staying one step ahead of competitors in the delivery of desired satisfactions to customers. In order to do so, they must first implement sound marketing research programs to determine customer needs. Marketing research is an essential component of the marketing process (see Chapter 3 for details). Then they must concentrate on operating their production, sales, and distribution systems efficiently. There must be a close working relationship among the various departments of a business, and each must contribute to achieve common company goals.

Sony and Harley-Davidson are good examples of companies that practise the marketing concept. Among Sony's inventions are the VCR, a product that literally changed our lives, and the Walkman (more recently the Discman), a product that allows us to listen to ear-splitting music without disturbing anyone. Sony builds products of the highest quality, and the company's reputation is such that consumers willingly pay more for their products. According to brand consultant Tim Munoz, "Sony consistently brings to market products that delight people, products that capture their imagination. Sony's products stop you in your tracks. A company that creates products like this can effectively position itself as 'the best' and easily fend off the competition."[4]

Harley-Davidson was just about bankrupt at one time but resurrected itself by capturing the imagination of an entirely new customer base. The brand's image, reputation, and association were legendary, but Japanese competitors such as Honda, Suzuki, and Yamaha were capturing the hearts and minds of mainstream North Americans. Harley reversed its fortune by focusing on its core customer group while simultaneously expanding its appeal to an unexpected market—CEOs, lawyers, doctors, and other professionals. It seems that the Harley name resonates in the heart, soul, and mind of its customer. It's a unique bike—it's a Harley! New customers bought into the Harley image.[5] See the illustration in Figure 1.1.

If there is a lesson to be learned from these examples, it is that business organizations must adopt the marketing concept and reflect it in all their operations. If you give customers what they want you are well on your way to operating a business profitably.

SOCIALLY RESPONSIBLE MARKETING ORIENTATION

socially responsible
marketing

Progressive business organizations are now at the stage where consideration for the environment and other worthwhile social causes has come to the forefront of strategic planning and decision making. This trend will continue. The essence of **socially responsible marketing** is that business should conduct itself in the best interests of consumers and society (see Figure 1.2).

Philosophically, conducting business in a socially responsible manner should be natural for all business organizations; after all, the planet's well-being is in everyone's best interests. But pressured business executives in today's hectic environment find it difficult to balance the demands of operating competitively, producing profits, increasing shareholder values, and preserving the environment. The importance of being socially responsible is reinforced by the results of a study conducted by the Canadian

1.1   Harley-Davidson rejuvenated its business by appealing to and satisfying the needs of a professional target market

When was the first time you heard the calling?
How long have you ignored it?

It's time to ride.
The 2004 FLSTC Heritage Softail® Classic.

Find your retailer at 1-800-LUV2RIDE or www.harleycanada.com.

Democracy and Corporate Accountability Commission. The study found that 70 percent of consumers felt that business executives have a responsibility to take into consideration the impact their decisions have on employees, local communities, and the country, as well as making profits.[6] Therefore, the societal marketing concept insists that managers do balance the various demands mentioned above.

Consumer and environmental groups will continue to challenge companies and ultimately force them to adopt an environmentally minded corporate culture. Toyota has shown initiative in this regard and has developed the first mass-produced and -marketed hybrid vehicle. The Toyota Prius is the first hybrid vehicle that provides the comfort, features, and performance of a mid-sized sedan, so it competes effectively with conventional 4-cylinder mid-sized sedans (the marketing concept). However, in terms of fuel efficiency and emissions performance the Prius sedan is in a class by itself. The Prius has the best fuel efficiency rating of any mid-sized vehicle sold in North America (the societal marketing concept).[7] See the illustration in Figure 1.3.

Socially responsible marketing can be divided into two main areas: (1) programs designed to conserve, preserve, and protect the environment, as in the case of the Toyota example above, and (2) programs designed to support causes of benefit to society (e.g., AIDS research). The latter is referred to as **cause marketing.** Cause-related marketing allows companies to meet both social responsibility and business goals. Even though

cause marketing

FIGURE
1.2   **Elements of Socially Responsible Marketing**

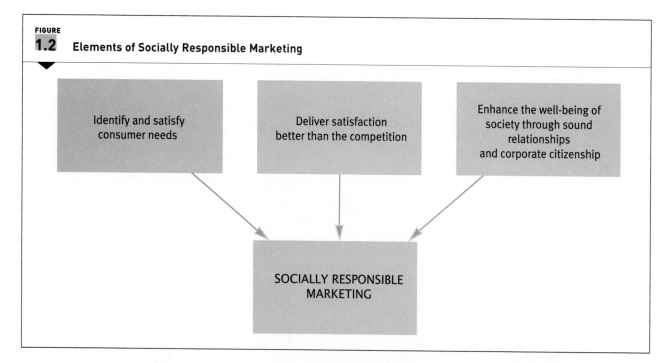

| Identify and satisfy consumer needs | Deliver satisfaction better than the competition | Enhance the well-being of society through sound relationships and corporate citizenship |

SOCIALLY RESPONSIBLE MARKETING

FIGURE
1.3

Toyota's investment in hybrid automobile engines reflects the intention of the societal marketing concept

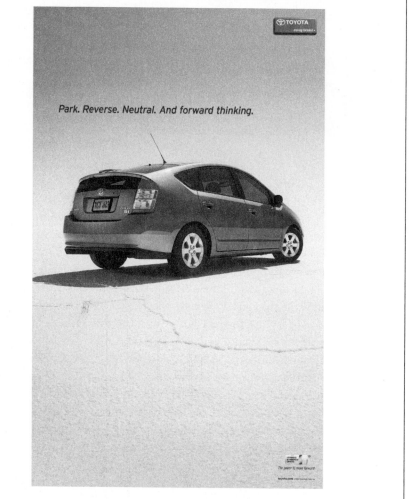

Park. Reverse. Neutral. And forward thinking.

cause marketing is in its infancy, marketers are rapidly becoming aware that aligning their business activities with consumer cause concerns has sales potential.

KitchenAid Canada, a marketer of large and small appliances, has formed a partnership with the Canadian Breast Cancer Society. The program encourages consumers across Canada to host cooking parties at home to raise funds (instead of bringing a hostess gift, people donate money), and enlists guests to become "cure ambassadors." The program is supported by a website, television and print advertising, and public relations activities.[8] As part of Toyota's commitment to "environmental stewardship," Toyota Canada has joined with Earth Day Canada in offering the Toyota Earth Day Scholarship program, which provides entry scholarships to students who have demonstrated outstanding achievement in academics and environmental community service. (see Figure 1.4). The growth and interest in socially responsible marketing is a major factor influencing the practice of marketing today.

Marketing has evolved through a series of stages with a different philosophy taking hold in each stage. For a summary of the evolution of marketing refer to Figure 1.5.

For more insight into how an organization applies the marketing concept and the societal marketing concept read the Marketing in Action vignette **Harley-Davidson Rides On**.

KitchenAid Canada
cookforthecure.ca

FIGURE
1.4

Toyota implements cause marketing programs to help achieve social and business objectives

FIGURE
1.5

Evolution of Marketing

Phase	Characteristics
Production Orientation	• Sell what you can produce • Limited or no choice for customer • Profit from production efficiency
Selling Orientation	• Products matched to customer needs (e.g., quality, variety, etc.) • Choices more readily available • Profits based on expanded sales
Marketing Orientation	• All activity revolves around customers and their satisfaction • Extremely competitive since the customer has a wide choice of goods and services • Profits from efficient production marketing
Socially Responsible Marketing Orientation	• Fulfill society's expectations (e.g., for a safe environment) • Be a good corporate citizen • Higher short-term costs accepted in return for long-term profit • Both efficient production and marketing to an informed consumer in a rapidly changing environment contribute to profit • Relationship between marketer and customer crucial to profit (implement customer relationship management programs)

The Marketing Process

The fundamental principle on which marketing programs are designed is that an organization anticipates unmet needs in the market and then develops products to meet those needs. It sounds very simple when put into words, yet when put into practice it is a very complex process.

market

Before proceeding, the term "market" should be defined. A **market** may be the ultimate consumer, an organizational buyer, or both. In consumer market terms, a market is a group of people who have a *similar need* for a product or service, the *resources* to purchase the product or service, and the *willingness* and *ability* to buy it. In *business-to-business* market terms, a market is an organizational buyer—such as an industry, wholesaler, or retailer—that buys goods and services for its own use or for resale.

So far, we have seen how the marketing concept gradually evolved from several distinct stages of organizational thinking. But a question remains: Why has marketing been so successful in revolutionizing the way business is carried on today? Perhaps the best answer to this question is that the marketing theory has capitalized on a basic psychological truth: people experience pleasure when they are able to satisfy a need. The follow-up to this proposition is that people also seek to repeat pleasurable experiences.

For these reasons, marketing professionals try to design products that are innovative and able to satisfy one or more of their customers' needs. To illustrate, consider a segment of modern-day consumers who are pressed for time: households with two

MARKETING IN ACTION

Harley-Davidson Rides On

Just who rides a Harley-Davidson motorcycle? Is it a rebellious gang member or the chief accountant for a large corporation? The Harley-Davidson motorcycle does have a rebellious reputation, but perhaps surprisingly the bikes appeal to an upscale target market—and their appeal to that group has helped the company retain its position in the motorcycle market. In fact, Harley-Davidson is considered a text-book case of a company that does everything right.

In marketing parlance, the key to Harley's success is marketing that drives right to the heart of the buyer. Owning and riding a Harley is an emotional experience. Of course, it all starts with the product. The typical Harley may look old (that's part of the bike's mystique) but underneath the 1930s styling are fuel-injected, computerized engine-management systems, cruise control, and CD players.

Harley knows how to market, and the company firmly believes that everything it does starts and ends with the customer. The people who ride Harleys look the part, but it's simply a role they play—the truth is they are doctors, lawyers, accountants, engineers, and construction workers. They trade their pinstriped suits in for motorcycle regalia on the weekends and enjoy the ride. The average buyer in the United States and Canada is a 45-year-old man with a household income of $78 000 in the U.S. and about $85 000 in Canada.

To get to know its customers and what they want, Harley doesn't do that much research. The company prefers to send its executives out onto the road—to mingle with riders, to listen to their compliments and complaints, and to look for the next big trend. They talk to a very narrow group: 40- to 50-year-old males who want to recover their youth.

Willie G. Davidson, grandson of the company's founder, is the chief designer. Willie gets his ideas from the customers. He walks around with notebook in hand looking for ideas that will find their way into a new model. The Fat Boy, for example (a $30 000 bike) was first spied at a Montreal bike show.

Another aspect of Harley's success relates to the bike's fan club, a group of owners the company affectionately refers to as HOGs—for Harley Owners Group—a group that is 700 000 strong around the world. Members who pay a membership fee each year enroll in local chapters, take part in club rides, attend regional and national events, raise money for charities, and, most importantly, build loyalty for the brand. Who better to promote the brand than your customers?

Charity rides give something back to the community. Each year thousands of riders collect toys for children and cash for muscular dystrophy, the blind, and homeless teenagers. Harley has raised $40 million for muscular dystrophy, $2 million of which was generated by Canadian riders.

So now that you have read about Harley-Davidson, perhaps your image of the company is quite different. This marketing-oriented company works directly with its customers to design the bikes they want. It also understands the importance of being a good corporate citizen. Creating goodwill is good for business!

Adapted from Oliver Bertin, "Harley-Davidson's great ride to the top," *Globe and Mail*, July 14, 2004, pp. B1, B4.

Courtesy of Larter Advertising

working adults. These families are looking for convenience and ease of use with the products they buy. The Campbell Soup Company answers this demand with Soup at Hand, a microwavable cup of soup that can be sipped anytime, anywhere. Campbell's also offers Supper Bakes, a microwavable meal kit that is ready in five minutes. Nestlé offers a ready-to-drink breakfast called Breakfast Anytime. The flavoured beverage offers all of the energy and nutrition a person needs to start the day—a perfect fit for busy people who tend to skip breakfast!

The cost of getting a consumer to make an initial purchase is very high. Some researchers suggest that it is five times more costly to get a new customer to buy than to keep an old one. Therefore, in accordance with the marketing concept, it is in the firm's best financial interests to keep its current customers satisfied. The goods and services provided by a firm must live up to the expectations created by its own marketing efforts; otherwise, the firm will lose not only its credibility but also its customer base.

Meeting customers' expectations consistently is problematic for a variety of reasons. In the automobile industry, for example, cost-cutting programs over an extended period have negatively affected the quality (actual and perceived) of domestically produced cars made by DaimlerChrysler, General Motors, and Ford. As recently as 1995 these companies controlled 73 percent of the retail market, but by 2003 their share dropped below 50 percent. Japanese brands such as Toyota, Honda, Nissan, and Mazda are preferred by Canadian consumers. This trend is occurring despite interest-free financing, free DVD players, and thousands of dollars in rebates being offered by domestic manufacturers. To halt this trend North American manufacturers have no choice but to put the quality back in their automobiles—and quickly![9]

J. D. Power and Associates
www.jdpower.com

Toyota knows that the level of present customer satisfaction can influence the decisions made by new customers. According to the J. D. Power and Associates annual Vehicle Dependability Study, several Toyota models consistently lead the rankings. The study is based on actual responses from 48 000 original owners. The latest study, released in June 2004, shows several Toyota models leading their respective segments: Corolla (compact car), Avalon (premium mid-size), Lexus ES 300 (entry luxury), Lexus LS 430 (premium luxury), MR2 Spyder (sports car), Toyota 4Runner (mid-size SUV), and Lexus RX 300 (entry luxury SUV). At the nameplate level, Lexus ranked highest overall for the tenth consecutive year.[10] Refer to Figure 1.6 for a visual illustration.

3. Explain the variety of activities that contemporary marketing practice embraces.

Marketing in Practice

Marketing in practice embraces a host of activities designed to attract, satisfy, and retain customers. The essential elements of this process involve:

1. Assessing customer needs by doing marketing research. The purpose of research is to discover unmet needs among consumers and to determine the potential for new products.
2. Identifying and selecting a target market to pursue.
3. Developing a strategic marketing plan that embraces the various elements of the marketing mix.
4. Evaluating the marketing strategy to ensure that goals set out in the plan are achieved.

The following section illustrates the essential elements of the marketing process and provides examples of these activities. Refer to Figure 1.7 for a visual illustration of these elements.

> **FIGURE**
> ## 1.6   Toyota has an excellent reputation for quality and dependability

THE RELENTLESS PURSUIT OF PERFECTION   LEXUS

**OUR EARS ARE BURNING.
OR IS THAT JUST THE ASPHALT?**

In our relentless pursuit of perfection, we've picked up some admirers along the way. We don't let it go to our heads. Instead it goes straight back into our cars.

RX 330
"Highest Ranked Entry Luxury Sport Utility Vehicle in Initial Quality in the U.S."
J.D. POWER AND ASSOCIATES

GS 430
"Highest Ranked Mid Luxury Car in Initial Quality Two Years in a Row in the U.S."
J.D. POWER AND ASSOCIATES

SC 430
"Highest Ranked Premium Luxury Car in Initial Quality in the U.S."
J.D. POWER AND ASSOCIATES

LX 470
"Highest Ranked Premium Luxury Sport Utility Vehicle in Initial Quality in the U.S."
J.D. POWER AND ASSOCIATES

Courtesy of Lexus Canada

ASSESSING CUSTOMER NEEDS

A needs assessment is the first stage in an organization's marketing planning process. In a **needs assessment,** an organization collects appropriate information about consumer needs to determine if a market is worth pursuing. To do so, the company will use a variety of research techniques and check various sources of information. Typically, a company conducts a market analysis and a consumer analysis. When an organization conducts a **market analysis,** the factors it considers include market demand, sales volume potential, production capabilities, and the availability of the resources necessary to produce and market the product or service. Beiersdorf Canada, maker of Elastoplast bandages, identified a new opportunity when it introduced Elastoplast Spray Bandage. The company calls it "a significant advancement in first aid." Designed to be sprayed onto wounds and then gradually disappear with no residue, the Spray Bandage offers a "quick and convenient" solution to wound care and is perfect for areas that are hard to cover with traditional bandages.[11]

Unilever, an established company in the personal care packaged goods business, identified a new opportunity when it introduced Dove Cleansing Cloths. Dove is an established brand leader in the hand-soap market. Cleansing Cloths are designed to meet the convenience and efficiency needs of busy women. Consumers' reactions to the product have been positive: they cite the convenience of not having to turn on a tap, the

needs assessment

market analysis

FIGURE
1.7

Elements of the Marketing Process

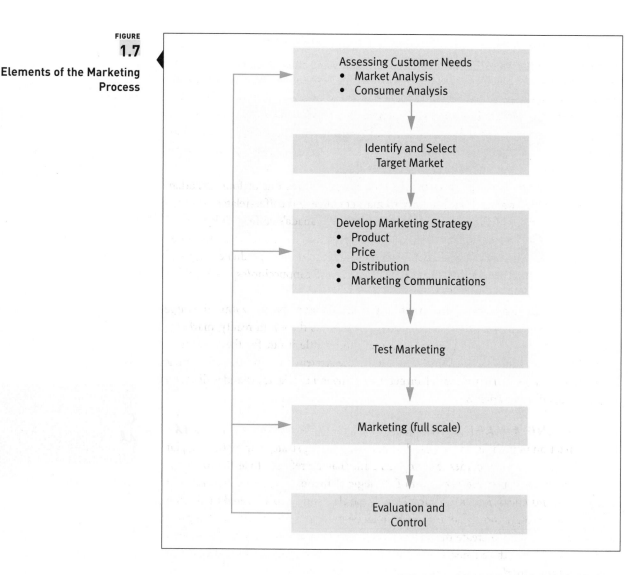

gentle cleaning nature of the product, the ease with which the package can be handled, less mess, and less laundry (face towels) as primary benefits.[12] Unilever appears to be on the right track with this new product.

consumer analysis

When an organization conducts a **consumer analysis,** it monitors demographic and behaviour changes within Canadian society. Business organizations use marketing research procedures to evaluate changes in consumers' tastes and preferences, attitudes, and lifestyles so that marketing strategies can be adjusted accordingly. To illustrate the importance of assessing customer needs, consider what Starbucks is doing to market coffee to diverse age groups. Kitty-corner to each other on a busy Vancouver street, Starbucks opened two distinctly different cafés. One café imposes itself on the streetscape in an arc of glass and steel. On a patio sit young people wearing trendy black clothing. The second café nestles tastefully in a brick heritage building. It has a cozy wood interior and is softly lit. The patrons are older, wealthier, and more subdued. One café is for Generation X (19- to 35-year-olds), while the other is for baby boomers (36- to 50-year-olds). By design, the stores are worlds apart—different decor, different atmosphere, different demographics. Starbucks' strategy may seem odd on the surface, but when examined more closely it demonstrates a way to offer a common grouping of products to diverse targets with different expectations of what a café should be.[13]

IDENTIFYING AND SELECTING A TARGET MARKET

An organization cannot satisfy the needs of all consumers, so it concentrates its efforts on a segment of the population that offers the most promise. That specific segment of the population is referred to as a target market. A **target market** is a group of people to which a company markets its products. Typically, members of a target group have something in common (e.g., they fall within a certain age range, they have similar educational backgrounds or occupations, they live in the same area, or they share a common interest or activity).

To illustrate the concept of targeting, consider that three out of four Canadians drink coffee. Therefore, it should be easy to market coffee and coffee-related products. Further examination of the market reveals that half of Canada's coffee drinkers are 35 to 64 years old, and those drinkers who own their own cappuccino/espresso maker are highly educated (college diploma, university degree, and post-graduate degree).[14] Therefore, the target description of potential buyers of cappuccino/espresso makers becomes quite narrow.

In theory, the similarity of the target should mean that all people within the target would respond to a similar marketing strategy. But that is theory. In reality, marketing is extremely competitive, and numerous competitors battle it out for the same set of customers. The competitor with the best strategy, the strategy that has the most impact on the target market, wins the battle! Target marketing is a crucial topic and is discussed in greater detail in Chapter 6.

DEVELOPING A MARKETING STRATEGY—THE MARKETING MIX

An organization now shifts its focus to devising a marketing strategy or marketing plan. A well-defined strategy includes four key elements that are referred to as the marketing mix. The **marketing mix** refers to a set of strategic elements comprising *product, price, distribution,* and *marketing communications.* These elements are considered in planning a marketing strategy, and any one of them may be enhanced, deducted, or changed to some degree in order to create the strategy necessary to efficiently and effectively market a product. When the elements are combined the resulting strategy should satisfy the needs of a target market and achieve organizational objectives.

An additional factor, *public image,* also has an influence on the purchase intentions of customers. Generally speaking, if someone views a company positively there is a stronger likelihood they will buy its products. Therefore, companies strive to implement marketing strategies that enhance their image and reputation. These strategies are often implemented at the corporate level of an organization rather than at the brand level. Let us examine the four primary decision areas of the marketing mix along with the influence of public image. Refer to Figure 1.8 for a summary of the marketing mix.

PRODUCT STRATEGY   **Product strategy** embraces a variety of decisions. The most critical decision a firm faces is determining what products or services to market. Once that decision is made, subsequent decisions may involve the setting of quality standards, sizes, brand name, packaging, guarantees, and level of service.

Product strategy can be further divided on the basis of *tangibility* (characteristics perceptible by touch, or any of the other senses) and *intangibility* (characteristics not perceptible by the senses). For example, a brand of beer such as Molson Canadian or Coors Light is, by and large, not that distinguishable from competing products on the basis of tangible characteristics, such as taste and appearance, or on the basis of price and distribution. As a result, product strategy for Molson Canadian will touch on subtle differences in taste (tangibility) but rely heavily on intangible factors, such as heritage

target market

4. Explain the concept of the marketing mix

marketing mix

product strategy

5. Describe the decision-making processes associated with marketing mix elements.

FIGURE
1.8

The Marketing Mix

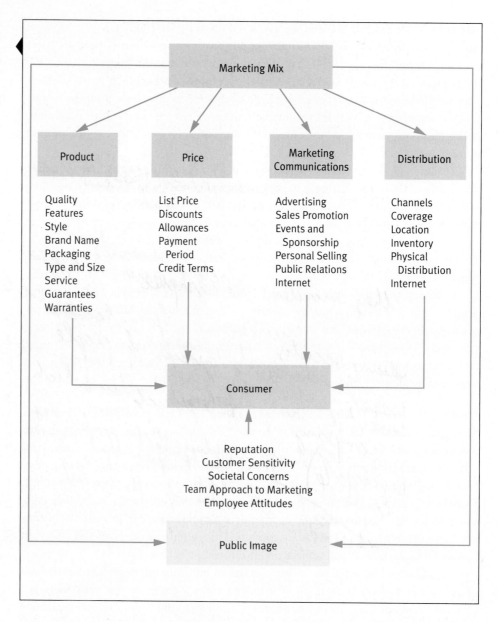

or lifestyle associations, to distinguish it from competitive brands. Molson Canadian is a leading brand, the result of effective advertising campaigns that use popular slogans such as "I Am Canadian" to associate the brand to an attractive lifestyle.

product differentiation

Product strategy involves **product differentiation,** which is defined as a strategy that focuses marketing practice on unique attributes, or differential advantages, of a product that are of value to customers in order to distinguish it from all other brands. With so many brands offering similar benefits it is important for a brand to get an edge on the competition. The goal is innovation—to invest considerable sums of money in developing products, resulting in a breakthrough product that will move the company forward. See Figure 1.9 for an illustration.

Minute Maid Simply Orange is an innovative product for several reasons: the product tastes good, the bottle is easy to hold and pour, and the carafe-shaped bottle sets it apart from other juices (see the illustration in Figure 1.9).

Product strategy and product management issues are discussed in detail in Chapters 8 and 9.

"Minute Maid" and "Simply Orange" trademarks appear courtesy of the Coca-Cola® Company.

FIGURE
1.9

This advertisement clearly indicates the unique attributes and benefits offered

PRICE STRATEGY   **Price strategy** involves the development of a pricing structure that is fair and equitable for the consumer while still profitable for the organization. Since most products are sold in a competitive market, organizations are free to establish prices according to what the market will bear. A host of factors are considered when a price strategy is established, including the cost of manufacturing the product, the location of the customer, the desired profit level, and the degree of competition. Generally, the less distinguishable a product is among its competitors (a condition referred to as *low differential advantage*), the less flexibility there is with price, since the product has no outstanding qualities to make it worth spending more on it than on its competitors. The inverse is also true.

It should be pointed out that price is subject to regulation in certain markets and service sectors. In situations where a monopoly or near-monopoly exists, any planned increases in price must be approved by governments or government agencies. For example, prices are controlled in some provinces for hydroelectric power, telephone rates, cable television, and beer, wine, and other alcoholic beverages.

In addition to setting individual product prices, businesses can also establish comprehensive price policies that set company guidelines relating to trade allowances,

price strategy

discount programs, and credit terms. Businesses can provide these additional incentives, and customers can evaluate them while making their purchase decisions. A retailer like Wal-Mart, for example, buys the goods it resells in very large quantities. Therefore it qualifies for larger discounts and allowances from suppliers, and in turn can pass on the savings to its customers. Wal-Mart's price strategy is to offer the lowest possible prices on a regular basis. Wal-Mart's slogan is "We sell for less. Everyday."

Pricing strategy and pricing management issues are discussed in detail in Chapters 10 and 11.

distribution strategy

marketing channel

DISTRIBUTION STRATEGY **Distribution strategy** refers to the selection and management of marketing channels and the physical distribution of products. A **marketing channel** is a series of firms or individuals that participate in the flow of goods and services from producer to final users or consumers, so decisions are based on the transactions between the various members of the channel. A product, such as peanut butter, jam, or any similar packaged food product, moves from a manufacturer such as Kraft Canada to a wholesaler such as National Grocers to a retailer such as IGA, which, in turn, sells it to the consumer. These products may also bypass wholesalers entirely and be shipped directly to individual warehouse outlets, such as Costco.

Distribution decisions must be made as to which type of channel to use, the degree of market coverage desired (i.e., how intense the coverage will be), the location and availability of the product, inventory (the amount of product stored at manufacturing or warehousing facilities), and transportation modes (air, rail, or water transport, or pipeline). Developing effective and efficient distribution systems requires that an organization work closely and develop a harmonious relationship with distributors (wholesalers and retailers) who resell a product along the channel.

Progressive-oriented companies are adding direct channels of distribution as they figure out ways to take advantage of Internet business transactions. The Ford Motor Company, for example, has an e-commerce initiative that allows consumers to order cars over the Internet without setting foot inside a dealership. The customer can "spec out" a vehicle and actually have the vehicle delivered without having to haggle about price. Vehicles are custom ordered from the Ford website. The e-price that is available is ultimately what the dealer would sell for after the usual buyer–seller negotiations at a dealership.[15] As indicated at the start of the chapter, the success of Dell Computer Inc. is primarily based on its method of distribution. Competitors have not been able to duplicate Dell's success in distributing products directly to customers.

Operating a distribution system is a complex task, and as a result companies are turning the task over to external distribution specialists. A specialist analyzes a company's existing distribution and warehousing operation or builds them a new one from scratch, promising to run it better and cheaper, for a fee. Grocery chain Safeway Canada and Wal-Mart Canada, two leaders in their respective markets, each employ a specialist to operate their warehouse and distribution networks.

Distribution strategy and distribution management are presented in detail in Chapters 12 and 13.

marketing communications strategy

MARKETING COMMUNICATIONS STRATEGY **Marketing communications strategy** involves another group of mix elements; it is the blending of advertising, public relations, direct response and interactive communications, sales promotion, personal selling, and event marketing and sponsorship. Typically, marketing communications is the most visible aspect of an organization's marketing strategy. Since there are various methods of communications, it is important that a company or product present a clear and consistent message in each medium to achieve the highest possible impact. This premise is referred to as **integrated marketing communications.**

integrated marketing communications

Advertising   **Advertising** is a persuasive form of marketing communications designed to stimulate a positive response (usually a purchase) in a defined target market. In advertising, decisions are made about the content, style, and tone of the message (i.e., what to say and how to say it). For some products a humorous appeal may be used, while in other cases celebrities may be used to endorse the product. Professional golfers, such as Tiger Woods (Nike, Titleist, American Express, and Buick), or NHL star Jarome Iginla (Campbell's Chunky Soup and Cheerios), for example, play prominent roles in print and broadcast advertising for the products they endorse and use professionally. Companies may also place advertisements focusing on the entire company, rather than just one of its products, to improve their public image.

advertising

A company must also make decisions about what media to use to deliver the message. Should the organization attempt to reach the masses through network television advertising, or should it target a selective audience through a specialized magazine or the Internet? The Internet is a relatively new medium to send messages through. Unlike traditional print or broadcast media, the Internet is a two-way medium. Experts anticipate that within the next 10 years interactive television, electronic media (e.g., the Internet), and wireless media (e.g., cell phones and personal digital assistants) will play a more important role; and traditional media, such as magazines, newspapers, and commercial television, will have a less important role. Prominent newspapers, magazines, and television networks are already available online and, in most cases, are free of charge to visitors.

Advertising has become advertising *ad nauseam,* and since people are forever being pitched to, marketers are looking at new, more effective ways of delivering the message. A new strategy called **undercover marketing** or **buzz marketing** is quickly becoming popular, particularly for reaching younger target markets. One aspect of buzz marketing involves trendsetting individuals going undercover to promote products in a variety of social settings (bars, street corners, parks, and so on). When the unsuspecting public starts asking questions about the product, the pitch begins. It could simply be part of a conversation between two or more people.

undercover marketing (buzz marketing)

Advertising strategy is discussed in detail in Chapters 14 and 15.

Sales Promotion   **Sales Promotion** is divided into two areas: consumer promotion and trade promotion. Consumer promotion involves using coupons, cash refunds, contests, and other incentives designed to encourage consumers to make immediate purchases. Depending upon the nature of the promotion, a particular activity is designed either to attract new customers or to encourage current customers to buy more of a product. Something as simple as a coupon distributed in a magazine or at shelf level in a supermarket will encourage new customers to buy a product. Trade promotion includes rebates, trade allowances, and performance allowances designed to encourage distributors to carry and resell a product. An illustration of an effective sales promotion activity appears in Figure 1.10.

sales promotion

Sales promotion strategy is discussed in detail in Chapter 16.

Event Marketing   **Event marketing** involves supporting an event with integrated communications. Typically, event marketing is coordinated with advertising and public relations communications to maximize the benefits of sponsorship participation. Event marketing and sponsorships fall into three categories: sports, entertainment, and arts and cultural events. Reebok recently agreed to a five-year partnership with the Canadian

event marketing

Football League to help it connect with the 18- to 24-year-old age group. The deal involves a new line of lifestyle apparel that will be available at retailers such as Sportchek and Foot Locker. The CFL will get royalties from the sale of the merchandise.[16]

Being involved with events is a natural fit for many of Canada's leading companies. Familiar names such as RBC Financial Group, Molson, Labatt, Shell Oil, and Nike are associated with countless events across Canada. These and other companies recognize the public awareness and public image benefits that sponsorship relationships offer. Event marketing is presented in detail in Chapter 16.

personal selling

Personal selling **Personal selling** involves face-to-face or other direct forms of communication (e.g., telemarketing) between marketing organizations and potential buyers. Personal selling plays a key role in business-to-business marketing situations (e.g., suppliers of component parts selling to companies producing consumer electronics products or automobiles). Participating in trade shows is another important means of communicating with customers in a personal way.

The linking of various marketing communications efforts is vital for the success of the organization. For example, advertising is designed to create awareness and interest, and sales promotion is designed to encourage trial purchases. When both activities are combined, the desired action among consumers may occur faster. In business-to-business marketing, advertising will create company and product awareness but professionally trained sales people create the desire and opportunity to obtain the product; it is the lat-

FIGURE
1.10 **An illustration of a sales promotion offer that attracts new and current customers**

The Gillette Company

ter activity that "closes deals" or achieves sales. Sales people play a key role in customer relationship management programs. Personal selling is presented in detail in Chapter 16.

Public Relations   **Public relations** concern a firm's relationships and communications with its various publics. These include not only customers but also other groups, such as shareholders, employees, governments, suppliers, and distributors. Generally, public relations communications are intended to complement an organization's other marketing strategies. Public relations is a useful tool for building or enhancing a company's or brand's image.

public relations

More recently, public relations has become the main means of communication in times of crisis, and crisis can strike at a moment's notice. RBC Financial Group faced a crisis situation when a computer glitch prevented 2.5 million clients from accessing their cash. The incident quickly snowballed into a public relations nightmare for Canada's largest bank. In assessing how RBC handled the situation one public relations expert stated, "RBC's biggest sin was not being more aggressive. They took too long to communicate with their clients and the public. When they did respond they said they understood what a tremendous inconvenience it was going to be, but they took far too long.[17] The moral to this story is clear—it is important for an organization to take action quickly and to provide reassurance to distressed clients. When used properly public relations does help resolve business problems. Public relations communications is discussed in detail in Chapter 14.

For insight into how a unique hamburger restaurant uses the marketing mix, read the Marketing in Action vignette **Webers—A Cottage Country Tradition**.

Webers
www.webersrestaurants.com

PUBLIC IMAGE AND ITS INFLUENCE   For any business, large or small, a good reputation is an important asset. Nevertheless, business organizations, particularly large ones, have often neglected their corporate image as they become engrossed in the image of individual brands, product lines, or services. That situation is changing, and businesses are now placing greater emphasis on socially responsible marketing. As a result, **public image** is now an integral part of an organization's corporate strategy and marketing strategy. A firm's reputation is important enough to require special attention.

public image

In an effort to develop a better public image, many firms are showing greater sensitivity to their customers. As a result, firms have implemented more comprehensive customer service programs and customer relationship management programs. Organizations today recognize that the attitude of all employees toward customers plays a significant role in influencing customer satisfaction and building a better company image.

At the corporate level, companies are enhancing their image by getting involved with issues important to customers. Through **corporate advertising** campaigns they let the public know how they stand on environmental issues and social issues. Corporate advertising is not intended to directly sell a product, but, since the objective is to enhance the image of the company and create goodwill, there could be some long-term and indirect effect on sales. See Figure 1.11 for an illustration.

corporate advertising

EVALUATING MARKETING ACTIVITY

Products and marketing strategies are usually tested for acceptance in a small area of the market prior to a full-scale launch. **Test marketing** involves placing a product for sale in one or more geographic areas and observing its performance under conditions similar to the ones proposed in the marketing plan. Once the product and the marketing plan have been evaluated, a regional or national "rollout" follows.

test marketing

Webers—A Cottage Country Tradition

The sight of very long lineups extending halfway into a parking lot might deter some people from stopping for a hamburger, but for travellers heading north to Ontario's cottage country those lineups are an attraction. Webers' charbroiled burger is the true smell of summer. It is a delight that people pine for!

This now-famous landmark had humble beginnings and a very shaky start. Paul Weber Sr., the original owner, lost $3000 in the first year and his son Paul remembers throwing stones at garbage cans to pass the time while waiting for customers to come in. Business was slow! But when the customers started coming, they never stopped!

As one drives up Highway 11 past Orillia it is impossible to miss the billowing smoke, the orange pedestrian crossway stretching above the highway, the jammed parking lot, and the long lineups outside the small restaurant. Speak to anyone in line and you hear the same story. "My parents brought me here as a kid, and now I bring my kids."

If location is important in retailing then Webers has it in spades. Located en route to some of the prettiest cottage country in Ontario, Webers is an ideal pit stop. For many, the stop at Webers is the best part of the journey. Paul Weber's little hamburger stand has grown into a cottage-country landmark.

The location is good, but it's the product that brings people back. Unlike typical fast-food restaurants that dabble in all kinds of items, Webers has stuck to what it does best—charbroiled burgers, fries, soft drinks, and chocolate milkshakes (the only flavour served). That's what the customers wanted years ago, and it's what they want today.

Perhaps nobody knows the restaurant and the customers better than Mike McParland, who has been flipping burgers since day one. Customers gave him the nickname "Key Man" because he seemed to always be around. He believes the legendary burger joint is situated in the perfect place—for many travellers it's the halfway spot, where the kids start to get antsy and it's time to get out of the car. Over his 40 years of service he's seen families grow up.

In 1983 the business faced a setback. That year, Highway 11 was made a divided highway. Southbound traffic could no longer stop at the restaurant and sales dropped 25 percent. Weber's solution was to buy an old pedestrian bridge that once linked Front Street to the CN Tower in Toronto, and erect it across the highway. Yes, people thought he was nuts—but now the bridge is a looming beacon that you are about to arrive at Webers. The first day the bridge was operational the restaurant was swamped. The lineups were so long that by Sunday afternoon they had to close—no food left!

Service also plays a key role in Webers' success. While long lineups and good service seem contradictory, the Webers system moves people through the line quickly. Ordering and paying for goods is done while standing in line. By the time the customer reaches the counter her order is ready, with only the condiments to be added. Customers enjoy eating outside, so the grounds and parking lot are kept immaculate.

Mike "Key Man" McParland offers some good perspective on why Webers is so successful. He says, "People love the smell of the smoke from the grill. They can smell it for miles away." He adds, "I don't cook fast food. I cook good food as fast as I can."

Webers serves more than 6000 burgers on the average Friday in the summer. The biggest of the fast-food restaurants can only dream of such volume. Good product, good service, good location, and good buzz—it's a combination that makes Webers successful.

Adapted from Susan Hiller, "A whiff of tradition," *Financial Post*, August 5, 2003, p. A9.

Courtesy of The Weber Co. Ltd.

This pedestrian bridge purchased by Webers allows customers travelling in both directions on a divided highway to stop in.

To complete the marketing cycle, research is usually conducted periodically so that the organization is certain that the product continues to meet the changing needs (tastes, preferences, habits, and lifestyles) of a volatile marketplace. The organization will also measure the results a product achieves (through its marketing plan) against the objectives that were established. Such objectives usually focus on sales revenue, market share, and profit. By constantly staying in touch with customers and adjusting the marketing plans when necessary, an organization will prosper. Research is normally conducted through surveys that are implemented by telephone, personal interview, mail, or online.

The Relationship Marketing Era

From the discussion in this chapter thus far, it is certain that marketing practice will directly consider the interests of consumers being served, and that more attention will be given to the interests of society. Marketing now finds itself in an era of **relationship marketing,** or **customer relationship marketing.** Relationship marketing is, essentially, an extension of the marketing concept.

6. Explain relationship marketing and the role of customer relationship management programs in relationship marketing.

relationship marketing (customer relationship marketing)

FIGURE
1.11

Some advertising is designed to build an image and create goodwill

A million tons of garbage makes a wonderful chocolate cake.

What a delicious idea. Capture the methane rising from an old garbage dump and turn it into power. At EPCOR's Cloverbar facility, that's exactly what we're doing, creating enough power for 4500 homes for the next ten years. Now that's a lot of baking.

This is just one more way EPCOR is harnessing nature to provide the power and water you need in the most responsible and reliable way. See epcor.ca for more. **It's doing the right thing.**

EPCOR

EPCOR Utilities Inc.

Marketing today is all about relationships, and these relationships go beyond just focusing on the ultimate consumer. Marketing involves managing relationships with consumers and relationships with other members of the channel of distribution. Customer relationship management embraces the entire channel—from supplier to producer to distributor to consumer. It looks at activities along this chain and leads to an emphasis on the long-term value of customer relationships in addition to short-term sales and profit.

In a marketing context, **customer relationship management (CRM)** is the partnering of organizations in a chain of distribution—from the supplier of raw materials to the ultimate consumer who purchases the end product—which then conduct business in such a way that all participants benefit. Marketing strategies are developed that are in the best interests of everyone in the entire channel of distribution. A relationship, therefore, may involve numerous businesses that cooperatively work together, or it may involve only one company and its consumers.

Relationship management is concerned not with individual transactions, but with establishing, maintaining, and enhancing long-term relationships. It's about customer satisfaction, plain and simple. It calls for teamwork and open communication within an organization and among all participants in the chain. It is a flexible system of planning that involves the identification of needs, the establishment of joint objectives, and the breaking down of traditional roles (see Figure 1.12).

For relationship marketing to be successful, an organization has to adopt an internal attitude that gives the customer the first and final say. Business organizations exist, above all, to serve their customers, and all employees must recognize that they contribute to this effort. This attitude, often referred to as the **corporate culture,** is defined as the values, norms, and practices shared by all the employees of an organization. Such thinking puts the customer on a pedestal above all others in the organization.

To understand the application of a customer relationship management program, consider the recent plan implemented by Fairmont Hotels & Resorts. This luxury hotel chain combined deep customer insights with product and service configuration changes to build its presence in the business travel segment of the market. Business travellers tend to be diverse and demanding. Marketing research revealed that travellers weren't interested in earning extra nights in a Fairmont Hotel (the typical perk offered by many competitors) as a reward for their loyalty. Their priorities focused on rectifying problems when they occurred, recognition of individual preferences, and flexibility regarding arrival and checkout times.

customer relationship management (CRM)

corporate culture

Fairmont Hotels & Resorts
www.fairmont.com

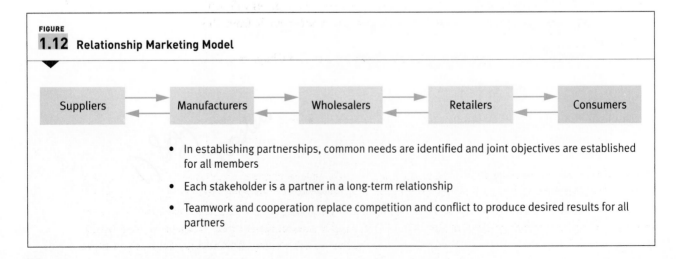

FIGURE
1.12 Relationship Marketing Model

Suppliers → Manufacturers → Wholesalers → Retailers → Consumers

- In establishing partnerships, common needs are identified and joint objectives are established for all members
- Each stakeholder is a partner in a long-term relationship
- Teamwork and cooperation replace competition and conflict to produce desired results for all partners

Based on this information, Fairmont examined each step in the guest experience—from check-in and valet parking to checkout—and set a standard of performance for each activity. The goal was to always satisfy customers with each and every thing they did. Internal systems were changed and the management structure was changed so that each hotel had someone available to ensure the hotel consistently met its customer commitments. After implementing these changes, Fairmont's share of the Canadian business travel market jumped 16 percent in a flat market.[18] The hotel's investment in better customer relationship management paid dividends!

To implement effective customer relationship management programs an organization must invest in technology. Information technology and database marketing and management techniques are the root source of customer information—the information needed about customers to devise better marketing strategies. Database management practices are discussed in more detail in Chapters 2 and 3.

In caring for customers, marketers face two problems all the time: *how to get customers,* and *how to hold on to them.* Traditionally, marketers placed greater emphasis on attracting customers and made much use of the mass media, which is very expensive. Contemporary marketers who believe in relationship marketing strike a balance between attracting and maintaining customers. Loyalty-oriented programs, such as HBC Rewards, Air Miles, and Canadian Tire money, keep current customers coming back.

Another aspect of relationship marketing involves companies in related or unrelated markets working cooperatively to achieve objectives. Such cooperative arrangements are referred to as strategic alliances, or simply partnerships. A **strategic alliance** is a partnering process whereby two firms combine their resources in a marketing venture for the purpose of satisfying the customers they share. Toyota and Nissan, archrivals in the automotive market, decided to work together on new gasoline–electric hybrid vehicles in order to speed the development of more affordable environmentally friendly cars. They see working together as a more practical means of recovering the massive development costs of such projects.[19]

Relationship marketing programs are also effective when companies in different markets share common target markets. In this situation, two or more companies can save money in all aspects of their operations by working cooperatively. Laura Secord and Hallmark Cards have combined forces and operate stores together. Laura Secord feeds off Hallmark's customers and vice-versa. In similar fashion, Canadian Tire and Budget Canada have struck a five-year deal that will see Budget Car and Truck rental kiosks set up at more than 100 Canadian Tire stores. As part of the agreement Budget will purchase gasoline from Canadian Tire, and Canadian Tire's Automotive Centres will service Budget's vehicles. Both organizations and their customers will benefit from this partnership.[20]

Customer relationship management is discussed in more detail in Chapters 3, 4, 5, and 15.

strategic alliance

SUMMARY

The text defines marketing as the process of planning and executing the conception, pricing, promotion, and distribution of ideas, goods, and services to create exchanges that satisfy individual and organizational objectives.

In today's competitive marketplace, it is the quality of an organization's marketing activity that determines the success, even the survival, of that organization. Given this situation, businesses are adopting a marketing-oriented corporate culture whereby all the employees of an organization, in every activity they perform, must consider the satisfaction of customer needs as the main priority.

Marketing practice has evolved over time. Early Canadian business development saw much of the organization's profit-making activities centred on creating production efficiency. Gradually, business philosophy shifted to an emphasis on selling, and for the first time, business organizations started to look at the needs of consumers and offered a greater selection of products. Now, the emphasis is on the marketing concept, which is the belief that business must focus directly on satisfying consumer needs.

Marketing has now reached the stage where consideration for the environment and social responsibility are at the forefront of strategic planning. The result has been increased customer service and a more caring business environment. Companies that lag behind in contemporary marketing thinking or that fail to adapt to changes that are occurring risk financial trouble.

Marketing in practice embraces many activities that culminate in an overall plan to build long-term relationships with customers. These activities include needs assessment, identifying and selecting a target market, developing the marketing strategy by using elements of the marketing mix, and then evaluating the strategy for effectiveness.

As marketing has become more technology-driven, organizations have embraced the concept of relationship marketing. Marketing today—and in the future—involves managing the relationship between a marketing organization and its customers and the marketing organizations that comprise the channel of distribution. The concept of relationship marketing is fairly simple: each member of the channel devises marketing strategies that are mutually beneficial to all channel members. Member firms recognize the value of managing customer relationships in order to maximize the buying potential of customers. This way of marketing has spawned activities and initiatives that include loyalty programs, strategic alliances, and partnerships. The goal of relationship marketing and customer relationship management programs is to produce more effective and efficient marketing strategies.

KEY TERMS

advertising   19

benefit   4

cause marketing   7

consumer analysis   14

corporate advertising   21

corporate culture   24

customer relationship management (CRM)   24

distribution strategy   18

event marketing   19

exchange   4

integrated marketing communications   19

market   10

market analysis   13

marketing   4

marketing channel   18

marketing communications strategy   18

marketing concept   5

marketing mix   15

needs assessment   13

personal selling   20

price strategy   17

product differentiation   16

product strategy   15

production orientation   5

public image   21

public relations   21

relationship marketing (customer relationship marketing)   23

sales promotion   19

selling orientation   5

socially responsible marketing   6

strategic alliance   25

target market   15

test marketing   21

undercover marketing (buzz marketing)   19

REVIEW QUESTIONS

1. What is the basic premise on which marketing is built?
2. Briefly compare the operating philosophies of companies that have a: production orientation, selling orientation, marketing orientation.
3. A key term in the chapter is "marketing concept." Briefly explain this term and provide an illustration of how it is applied.
4. When a company "assesses customer needs," it conducts a market analysis and consumer analysis. Briefly describe what is involved in each area.

5. What is a target market?
6. Identify the four key elements of the marketing mix.
7. What is relationship marketing, and what role does it play in contemporary marketing?
8. Briefly explain the importance of social responsibility in the practice of contemporary marketing. Provide some new examples that demonstrate social responsibility marketing.

DISCUSSION AND APPLICATION QUESTIONS

1. How do colleges and universities implement the marketing concept? Cite some examples of marketing activities at your college or university.

2. Coca-Cola is the best-selling soft drink in the world. What marketing factors have contributed to the success of this brand?

3. What elements of the marketing mix are most important to each of the following companies or brands?

   a) Federal Express

   b) Toronto Raptors (or any other professional sports team)

   c) Canadian Tire

   d) McDonald's

   e) Pepsi-Cola

4. The text mentions several examples of strategic alliances. Can you identify any other alliances that have made the business news recently? What are the benefits to each company in the alliances you identified?

5. Select a prominent retail, service, or manufacturing organization in your own hometown, and analyze how it has made use of socially responsible marketing practice.

E-ASSIGNMENT

Visit the website of a worldwide brand, such as Coca-Cola or BMW. Analyze the site, and determine how the company uses the Internet to communicate information about relationship marketing and socially responsible marketing. Does the site communicate useful information about the company? Was the site easy to navigate?

ENDNOTES

1. Timothy Woolstencroft and Nette Hanna, "The best of Canada's brands," *Marketing*, June 14, 2004, p. 13.

2. American Marketing Association, "AMA Board approves new definition," *Marketing News*, March 1, 1985, p. 4.

3. Bill Robinson, "Five best companies," *Forbes* (www.forbes.com), August 1, 2002.

4. Ibid.

5. Ibid.

6. Ellen Roseman, "Most want socially responsible companies," *Toronto Star*, February 1, 2002, p. E2.

7. Toyota Canada Inc., press release, August 25, 2003.

8. Michelle Warren, "Cause commotion," *Marketing*, October 6/13, 2003, p. 21.

9. Greg Keenan, "Drivers deserting Detroit," *Globe and Mail*, October 4, 2003, pp. B1, B5.

10. J. D. Power and Associates, press release, June 29, 2004.

11. "Cut care in a can," *Marketing*, March 22, 2004, p. 6.

12. Lesley Young, "New and approved," *Marketing*, April 5/12, 2004, pp. 10–11.

13. "One café for Yuppies another for Gen X," *Financial Post*, October 31, 1998, p. D6.

14. "A marketing profile of coffee drinkers," *Marketing*, September 5, 2000, p. 13.

15. Keith McArthur, "Ford gears up online buying project," *Globe and Mail*, May 13, 2000, pp. B1, B2.

16. Maya Bahar, "CFL inks five-year partnership with Reebok," *Strategy*, May 17, 2004, p. 5.

17. "It's a tech thing," *Marketing*, June 28, 2004, p. 7.

18. George S. Day, "No two customers are alike," *Financial Post*, June 16, 2003, p. FE5.

19. Todd Zaun, "Toyota, Nissan to co-operate," *Globe and Mail*, September 2, 2002, p. B11.

20. "Budget parks in Canadian Tire," *Marketing*, March 3, 2003, p. 2.

CHAPTER

2

The External Marketing Environment

After studying this chapter, you will be able to

1. Identify and explain the impact of the economy and economic cycles on marketing practices.

2. Explain the influence of various competitive influences that have an impact on the development of marketing strategies.

3. Determine how social and demographic trends shape marketing strategies now and in the future.

4. Explain how lifestyle trends and environmental concerns influence the development of marketing strategies.

5. Identify and explain the influence of various technologies on how marketing is practised now and in the future.

6. Identify the role that laws and regulations play in the practice of marketing in Canada.

The environment that marketing operates in is constantly changing. Problems, opportunities, successes, and failures are largely dependent on an organization's ability to adapt to changing conditions. In this regard, a business must anticipate change and how it will affect its operations. To be successful, new strategies must evolve. To foresee and adjust to change, a company reviews and analyzes certain external conditions that influence the nature of its marketing strategies. Trends that occur in the economy, competition, technology, laws and other regulations, and the consumer must be considered when developing a marketing strategy. While trends in all of these areas are important, it is technology and the rapid of pace of change in technology that will have the most impact on marketing practice in the next decade. Each of these external influences is examined in detail in this chapter. See Figure 2.1 for a visual illustration of the external marketing influences.

> 1. Identify and explain the impact of the economy and economic cycles on marketing practices.

Economic Influences

The economy has a significant impact on an organization's marketing activity. Canada's economic situation is measured by such variables as the gross domestic product (GDP), inflation, employment levels, real income, and interest rates. How these indicators interact helps determine how conservative or how aggressive an organization's marketing efforts will be. Let us briefly define each of these economic variables:

- **Gross Domestic Product**—The GDP is the total value of goods and services produced in a country on an annual basis. Positive growth in GDP from year to year would reflect a productive economy and plentiful jobs. `gross domestic product (GDP)`

- **Inflation**—Inflation refers to a general rising price level for goods and services, resulting in reduced purchasing power. For example, if inflation rises significantly next year we can buy less with the money we have. `inflation`

- **Employment**—Employment refers to the number of people with jobs from year to year. A high level of employment reflects a vibrant economy and vice-versa. `employment`

- **Real Income**—This is income adjusted for inflation over time. `real income`

The relationships among these economic variables are dynamic. For example, if during a given period widespread cost increases drive prices up beyond, for instance, the

Forces ⊕/⊖

* Always having
to be willing
to change *

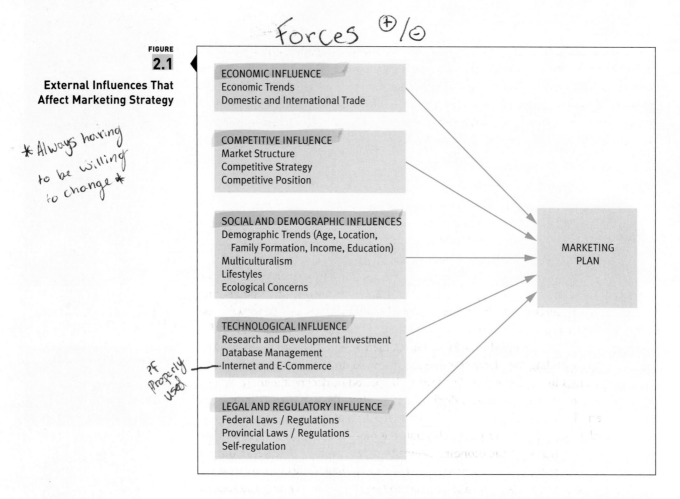

If
Properly
used

means of lower-income and middle-income groups, the purchasing of goods and services will decrease. The result is reduced purchasing power for consumers and less money available for discretionary or optional purchases. Inflation will slow down the economy, and as fewer workers are required the employment level will shrink. Inflation also shrinks real income. Real income indicates the volume of goods and services that money will buy (that is, if inflation rises, a $40 000 income in 2006 will be worth less than a $40 000 income in 2005 or previous years because it will purchase less).

INCOME

disposable income

Disposable income refers to actual income after taxes and other expenses—it is income available for optional purchases. Throughout the 1990s and in recent years there was a consistent decline in disposable income. Canadians were working hard but the rising costs of basic necessities and services such as rent, hydro, gas, telephone, and so on meant there was less available for optional purchases such as vacations and sports and recreational activities. Feeling stretched financially, the average Canadian family was concentrating on purchases for necessities only.

VALUE OF THE CANADIAN DOLLAR

The state of the economy also affects the value of the Canadian dollar, which in turn has a special impact on the activities of Canadian organizations that export internationally. When, for instance, the Canadian dollar is worth less than the American dollar, Canadian-produced goods become more attractive to and marketable among American buyers, since the prices of our goods in their market are lower than those of their own goods. Conversely, if the Canadian dollar were higher in value than the American dollar, our goods would become less attractive because the prices of Canadian goods would be higher than the American ones in their market. In this case, exports to the United States would probably decline. Since the Canadian dollar is historically worth much less than the American dollar, Canada enjoys a favourable balance of trade with the United States. Approximately 83 percent of Canada's exports go to the United States, while only 70 percent of our imports come from the United States.[1]

BUSINESS CYCLES

Economic growth in Canada is measured by real growth in gross domestic product from year to year or the percentage increase in the per capita real GDP. Over the long term Canada has experienced high rates of economic growth. In the most recent five-year period where statistics are available (1999 to 2003), Canada's average annual rate of growth for GDP has been 2.5 percent. Such a figure reflects an economy that is stable.[2]

The economy of a country either contracts or expands and goes through various stages in the process: recession, depression, recovery, and prosperity. Contraction occurs when an economy reaches a peak—the economy is booming but there is no growth. The future is unknown and often predicted by extending current trends. Therefore, if a downward trend is predicted (that is, lower GDP), there will be lower spending by consumers. Lower spending then leads to more reductions in output, and negative growth in GDP continues in a spiral effect. The longer the period of decline the more serious the consequences for the economy. A decline in real output that lasts for six months or more is referred to as a **recession**. A long and harsh period of decline is a **depression**.

recession
depression

Eventually the decline in output (GDP) bottoms out—it is at its lowest value in the business cycle. At this point the economy begins to expand. Initial increases in output and consumer spending lead to optimistic forecasts for growth. Consumers react positively and begin to spend more. Businesses react to the consumer spending and start to invest more in their operations (perhaps expanding a manufacturing facility, or building a new facility). The initial phase of expansion is referred to as **recovery**. When growth is sustained at significant levels for an extended period, the economy is experiencing **prosperity**.

recovery

prosperity

Since so many factors combine to have an influence on an economy, predicting the state of an economy for business planning purposes is always difficult, even for economists. That said, an organization must stay abreast of key economic trends and adjust its business planning and investments in marketing activities accordingly. To demonstrate, the post-9/11 era was devastating to various sectors of the economy. The fallout in the short term has been devastating for companies in the travel industry: airlines, hotels, and car rental companies. Other industries were not hurt by the terrorist attacks at all, but were affected by other economic factors that resulted in falling profits. In Canada, for example, in 2002, the major domestic automobile manufacturers (General Motors, Ford, and DaimlerChrysler) laid off 5000 workers to reduce costs and restore profitability despite the fact that automobile sales reached record levels.

RATIONALIZATION

When the economy turns sour many companies evaluate the efficiency of their operations and begin a process called rationalization. **Rationalization** is defined as the restructuring, downsizing, and—if necessary—closing of operations that are not economically justified. With many Canadian companies being owned by companies based in foreign countries, it is sometimes an easy decision to close a Canadian facility. All things being equal, if wages are lower in another country the decision to reduce production or move production out of Canada makes economic sense.

rationalization

Camco, a Canadian appliance manufacturer that is 51 percent owned by General Electric (U.S.) recently closed its manufacturing plant in Hamilton, Ontario. Two economic factors were key in the decision: a recent sharp increase in the Canadian dollar that affected exports to the United States (a short-term effect), and lower wage rates in Mexico and Korea (a long-term effect). The Hamilton plant manufactured a variety of well-known brand names including General Electric, Westinghouse, Moffat, McClary, and Hotpoint.[3]

FREE TRADE

Canada is part of a North American free trade market that includes the United States and Mexico. The agreement represents an opportunity for Canadian businesses. Companies from all three countries are adjusting to the larger market and are implementing programs to achieve economies in production and marketing. On the positive side, the potential for Canadian industries seems huge. A single market of 360 million people with an annual output of US$10 trillion gives Canada and its free trade partners greater clout in world trading.

A potential negative consequence of free trade is the corporate downsizing that could occur (the process of rationalization just described), especially if the economy in North America were to take a downturn. The lower land costs, taxes, and labour rates in Mexico are attractive to new industries or those industries considering relocation. When all costs are considered, the cost of manufacturing tends to be lower in both the United States and Mexico—a distinct disadvantage for Canada.

Competitive Influences

2. Explain the influence of various competitive influences that have an impact on the development of marketing strategies.

The activity of competitors is probably the most thoroughly analyzed aspect of marketing practice, as competitors are constantly striving to find new and better ways of appealing to similar target markets. The competitive environment that an organization operates in must be defined and analyzed, and the strategies of direct and indirect competitors must be monitored and evaluated.

MARKET STRUCTURES

In Canada, a business operates in one of four different types of market structure: monopoly, oligopoly, monopolistic competition, and pure competition. Each has a different impact on marketing strategy.

monopoly

In a **monopoly**, one firm serves the entire market (there are no close substitutes) and therefore theoretically controls most of the marketing mix elements: product, price, distribution, and marketing communications. In Canada, government regulates monopolies so market control is limited. Examples of monopolistic but regulated markets include cable television within geographic areas, electricity, water, and alcoholic beverages in some regions. In Ontario, for example, alcohol and wine are sold only in government-controlled liquor stores. Since consumers do not have a choice in matters such as these, governments at all levels must regulate price and service availability, ensuring that customers are treated fairly.

Parmalat Canada
www.parmalat.ca

To illustrate, consider what could happen in Canada's milk industry. The collapse of Italian dairy Parmalat Finanziaria is sending ripples through the Canadian dairy industry. More than 70 percent of all milk produced in Canada is processed and sold by Parmalat Canada, Saputo Inc., and Agropur Cooperative. Dairy farmers fear that milk prices will be at the mercy of a new dairy behemoth if Parmalat Canada (producers of Beatrice-brand milk) disappears or if its assets are bought up by one of the other two companies.[4]

The airline industry in Canada was heading toward monopoly as a result of the merger of Canadian Airlines with Air Canada. At the time of the merger, Air Canada controlled 80 percent of domestic air travel. The introduction of WestJet and some other regional air carriers in the post-merger period provided consumers with alternatives, and the market remained competitive. Since the merger, Air Canada's share of domestic air travel has actually decreased.

In an **oligopoly**, a few large firms dominate the market. The beer industry is a good example of an oligopoly in Canada. The two major companies, Molson and Labatt, control about 88 percent of the market, with the country's craft brewers and imported premium brands splitting the rest. It is very difficult for others to enter the market and be successful, unless they are satisfied with a very small piece of the action. Small breweries simply do not have the marketing budgets to compete in terms of advertising and promotion.

In an oligopoly, firms generally compete on the basis of product differentiation and brand image. In the beer industry, subtle differences in taste may not be all that important, but the image of the brand that marketing creates could be a vital factor in the consumer's purchase decision. As well, there tends to be a "follow the leader" mindset. That is, one company does something and its archrival immediately responds. Molson launches Canadian Light; Labatt follows with Blue Light. Molson drops prices on several key brands temporarily; Labatt follows suit with its key brands. With such responses so fast and predictable, it's difficult to get an edge on your competitor.

In a market characterized by **monopolistic competition**, there are many firms, large and small, each offering a unique marketing mix. Marketers use any of the mix elements to differentiate the product or service from competitors. Products are clearly distinguished by brand names. In effect, each competitor is striving to build its market share, but due to the presence of strong competition there are always substitute products for consumers to turn to.

In the restaurant market, for example, the quick-serve segment is served by brand names such as McDonald's, Harvey's, A&W, Burger King, Dairy Queen, Subway, KFC, and others. McDonald's remains the dominant brand and controls 28 percent of the market in Canada. Subway is a contender with 7.2 percent of the market, but all other brands listed here are 5 percent or lower. McDonald's ongoing success is a tribute to its good marketing: the company offers products that its customers want at prices they are willing to pay, outspends its competitors on advertising and promotions, and has locations virtually everywhere. The other brands do the best they can to compete using the financial resources that are available.

Most Canadian industries are highly concentrated and best described as oligopolies or as monopolistically competitive.

In a market where **pure competition** exists, all firms market a uniform product—no single buyer or seller has much effect on the price. There are many buyers and sellers. In effect, the advantage of one product over another is not that clear to consumers. Pure competition is common in the agriculture industry and in markets for financial assets such as stocks, bonds, and mutual funds. In the financial services market there is an endless array of companies, so it is often very difficult for customers to make decisions about which ones to deal with. Very often the deciding factor is performance and level of service provided. Consequently, financial services firms tend to differentiate themselves by marketing their success—their investment track record or reputation in the industry.

COMPETITIVE STRATEGIES

Once an organization has identified the type of competition it faces, its attention shifts to the strategies of competitors. It must monitor competition from direct and indirect

oligopoly

monopolistic competition

pure competition

direct competition

Pantene Pro V
www.pantene.com

sources. **Direct competition** is competition from alternative products and services that satisfy the needs of a common target market. For example, in the shampoo market Pantene Pro V (Procter & Gamble) is a market leader, with a 14.5-percent market share. It competes directly with Head & Shoulders and Herbal Essences (other P&G brands), Dove, Suave, Thermasilk, and Finesse (all Unilever brands), and Garnier Fructus (a L'Oreal brand), among many others that are on the market. Pantene has been successful in protecting its leadership position by lowering prices slightly and presenting a better value proposition to consumers.[5] Other brands present alternative propositions to consumers.

In the digital camera market, brands such as Sony, Kodak, Canon, Olympus, Fuji, and Nikon compete directly with each other. The brand leaders are Sony and Kodak. Both brands take a different approach in terms of marketing strategy. Sony's position is based on its legacy of quality technology and cutting-edge design. In contrast, Kodak taps its heritage and focuses on ease of use and getting to the picture. Kodak's theme is, "The best part of photography is the prints." Both brands are competing for the leadership position in the digital camera market. Sony owns 22 percent of the market to Kodak's 18 percent. The consumer will decide if Kodak's strong heritage in photography is a better strategy than Sony's cool style and technology approach.[6] Refer to the illustration in Figure 2.2.

indirect competition

Firms must also consider indirect competition. **Indirect competition** is competition from substitute products that offer customers the same benefit. For example, when someone is thirsty, they may reach for a soft drink—such as Coca-Cola or Pepsi-Cola, two products that are direct competitors with each other. However, the consumer has a broader choice. They could choose a purified water beverage, such as Dasani or Aquafina. They could also select a fruit juice (Fruitopia), an iced tea (Nestea or Brisk), or an energy-replacement drink (Gatorade or Powerade). When Coca-Cola develops its marketing strategies, it must look beyond traditional soft drinks and consider the activities of other beverages. Coca-Cola is in the beverage business, not just the soft drink business.

Mentioned earlier was the fact that the nature of competition is changing. Consequently, the difference between direct and indirect competition is becoming blurred. Pharmacies—such as Shoppers Drug Mart, Jean Coutu, and London Drugs—used to be concerned about each other. Now, Zellers, Wal-Mart, and Loblaws all offer pharmacy services. There are so many more competitors to consider. Tim Hortons at one time sold only doughnuts, muffins, and coffee. Now they offer an expanded menu and compete with McDonald's, KFC, Subway, and a host of other fast-food restaurants. In fact, Tim Hortons is now the largest quick-serve restaurant in Canada, ahead of McDonald's in sales revenue.

Technology is changing the nature of competition in many markets. Book stores such as Indigo Books & Music have to compete with online retailers such as Amazon.com. Because consumers are attracted to the convenience offered by Amazon, Indigo has established an online presence to serve customers better.

For additional insight into the influence of competition and changes in consumer preferences, see the Marketing in Action vignette **McDonald's Protects Its Lead.**

THE COMPETITIVE POSITION

market share

A firm's market share indicates its competitive position in the marketplace. **Market share** is the sales volume of one competing company or product expressed as a percentage of the total market sales volume. Competing products are classified in many ways. Author Philip Kotler describes and classifies competitors as leaders, challengers, followers, and nichers.[7]

FIGURE
2.2

Advertising helps differentiate Kodak from other brands of digital cameras

A **market leader** is the largest firm in the industry and is a leader in strategic actions (e.g., new-product innovation, pricing and price increases, and aggressive promotion activity). Examples of leaders include Tim Hortons (which controls 67.8 percent of the market among coffee shop chains), McDonald's (28.4 percent of the market among fast-food chains), and Colgate toothpaste (40.8 percent of the toothpaste market). McDonald's market share is greater than the sum of Subway, Burger King, A&W, Wendy's, and Dairy Queen.[8] In the soft drink market, Coca-Cola is the undisputed leader worldwide. When Coke says "Always Coca-Cola," it means it!

A **market challenger** is a firm or firms (product or products) attempting to gain market leadership through aggressive marketing efforts. Perhaps the best example is the battle between Pepsi-Cola (the challenger) and Coca-Cola (the leader). While Coca-Cola retains leadership, Pepsi-Cola implements more aggressive marketing strategies. Advertising slogans such as "The Choice of a New Generation" and "It's the Cola" grab the attention of potential customers in younger age groups. Even in a market like dish

market leader

market challenger

McDonald's Protects Its Lead

Even though McDonald's is a dominant leader in the quick-serve restaurant market, the company realizes it can never be complacent. Its business, like any other business, must evolve with changes that occur in the economy, the competition, and the consumer. McDonald's excels at what it does because the company is usually the first to identify change, and by taking appropriate action it retains a solid leadership position.

In today's fast-paced society the demands of the consumer can be overwhelming. McDonald's is a fast-food restaurant and has always prided itself on delivering the goods quickly to customers. But McDonald's observes that gratification is now becoming increasingly instantaneous—people hardly want to stop their cars to grab their food. As well, consumers are demanding healthier food choices, the by-product of the low-carbohydrate craze popularized by the Atkins and South Beach diets.

How does McDonald's react to these changes? The company now generates 60 percent of its sales from drive-through operations. That's up from 40 percent only five years ago. Any marketing manager following that kind of sales trends realizes that any improvement in providing more convenience in the drive-through could generate significant profit. McDonald's initially raised the convenience bar with a two-window drive-through—order at one window and pick up your order at another. The company followed that with a 30-second drive-through guarantee supported by a national advertising campaign: "Thirty seconds from the time you pay till you're on your way." Customers forced to wait longer receive a coupon for free fries or a breakfast sandwich.

Just recently, McDonald's added the two-lane, two-speaker drive-through in outlets where adequate space is available. This way the person with the 5-dollar order doesn't have to wait for the person with the 20-dollar order. CEO of McDonald's Canada Bill Johnson says that "people on the go want things quicker." The trick is to make sure customers are in the right lane!

In response to the demand for healthier food choices, McDonald's launched a "Healthy Lifestyles" program in 2004. Under the sub-brand "Go Active," the program includes a selection of premium salads targeted at women; milk and juice options with kids' Happy Meals instead of pop; market trials of fruits and vegetables, such as sliced apples with dip; and "Happy Meals for adults" that include salads and bottled water. In addition, order takers have stopped prompting customers to "super size" their meal. Nutritional information for all meals is being posted near the order counter.

On the service front, McDonald's is test marketing touch-screen kiosks in various U.S. locations. The kiosks allow customers to place their orders and pay for them by bill or credit card—a process that takes about one minute. Once perfected, the technology will lead to shorter wait times, labour cost savings, and, ultimately, higher average cheques.

Michael Newman/PhotoEdit

In an attempt to tie all marketing initiatives together, McDonald's is using a global advertising campaign for the first time in its history. The new campaign features teenage heartthrob Justin Timberlake and is built around the theme "I'm lovin' it." When the campaign was unveiled it garnered a screaming response from McDonald's largely teenaged workforce—CEO Johnson quickly knew they were onto something with the new campaign.

McDonald's primary focus remains on its 1200 outlets across Canada that generate annual sales revenue of $2.5 billion. It also retains focus on what it does best: selling hamburgers quickly. But the chain—which serves 3 million people, or 10 percent of the population daily—must adapt to a new breed of consumers looking for more than just a burger. "We can't be all things to all people," says Johnson. As the uncertain future unfolds, McDonald's must find ways to constantly tweak its menu to offer more choices while still holding true to the fast-food concept. Thus far, McDonald's is doing a very good job at it!

Adapted from Dana Flavelle, "McDonald's to wage war on obesity," *Toronto Star*, January 20, 2004, pp. D1, D11; Deborah Cohen, "Taking the server out of service," *Financial Post*, June 21, 2004, p. FP13; Natalie Williams, "Salad days," *Strategy*, May 31, 2004, pp. 4, 5; Jason Chow, "McDonald's windows of growth," *Financial Post*, December 17, 2003, pp. FP1, 10; and Zena Olijnyk, "McLatte with those fries?" *Canadian Business*, March 18, 2002 (online version).

detergent the battle for leadership can be intense. Palmolive currently leads the category with a 36.5-percent market share, but is followed closely by Sunlight at 36.0 percent;[9] during the previous year Sunlight was the market leader. Both brands are battling each other for market supremacy with no real winner emerging to date.

A **market follower** is generally satisfied with its market share position. Often, it has entered the market late and has not incurred the research and development costs that innovators do. As a result, it is content to follow the leaders on product, price, distribution, and other marketing actions. From the toothpaste market example cited above, Colgate is the leader (40.8-percent share) and Crest is the challenger (28.4-percent share). Remaining brands, such as Aquafresh, Arm & Hammer, Close Up, Oral-B, Aim, and Pepsodent, all of which have less than 5-percent market share, are followers. Brands like these do not have the financial resources to compete with the leaders.

market follower

A **market nicher** practises "niche marketing." **Niche marketing** refers to the concentration of resources in one or more distinguishable market segments. They specialize in serving niches that larger competitors overlook or are simply not interested in. A market nicher is the big fish in a small pond, as opposed to the little fish in a big pond. In order to niche market, a firm differentiates itself on the basis of specialization or an area of strength.

market nicher
niche marketing

Mott's is well known for brands such as Hawaiian Punch and Clamato, but the company dabbles in the soft drink business as well. Mott's will never compete with Coca-Cola or Pepsi-Cola, but is quite satisfied with its niche in the gourmet soft drink segment of the market. The gourmet segment is characterized by brands with higher prices and quirky images. Mott's markets IBC sodas (originally developed and sold by Independent Breweries Company as far back as 1920) in a variety of popular and unique flavours—including root beer, black cherry, cream soda, and tangerine cream soda—that are are not part of Coke's and Pepsi's product mix.

The subject of niche marketing is discussed in more detail in the "Market Segmentation" section of Chapter 4.

3. Determine how social and demographic trends shape marketing strategies now and in the future.

demographics

Social and Demographic Influences

Consumers are another of the unpredictable variables that influence marketing strategies. To keep abreast of the changing consumer, market planners analyze demographic and social trends. **Demographics** is the study of the characteristics of a population. These characteristics include size, growth rates, age, location, gender, income, education, marital status, and ethnic background. Among these characteristics several trends have emerged: the population is aging, household formations are changing, ethnic groups are forming a larger percentage of the population, and the size of the middle class is shrinking. Let us examine some of these trends.

SIZE AND AGE

The age distribution of Canada's population is changing. As of 2004, Canada's population totalled 31 825 416.[10] The average annual growth rate of the population over the past 25 years has been around 1.3 percent, but in the past 5 years it has dropped to 0.8 percent annually, an all-time low.[11] In comparison, the rate of population growth in the United States was 1.0 percent, and only 0.4 percent in Europe. Much of Canada's population growth comes from immigration.

Canada's population is aging. In 1991 the median age was 33.5; in 2001 it was 37.6, a 12.2-percent increase over a decade. Refer to Figure 2.3 for a visual illustration of Canada's population by age.

FIGURE 2.3   **Canada's Population by Age**

Source: Age Pyramid of Population of Canada July 1, 1901–2001, adapted from the Statistics Canada publication *Profile of the Canadian population by age and sex: Canada ages*, 2001 Census, Catalogue 96F0030, July 16, 2002 available at http://www12.statcan.ca/english/census01/Products/Analytic/companion/age/cda01pymd.cfm

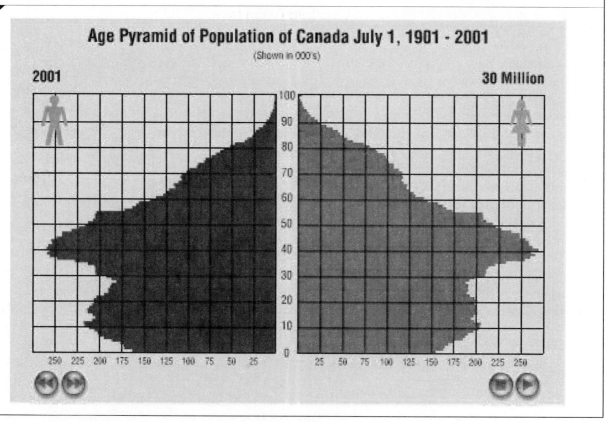

Certain age groups are growing much faster than average. Changes in the age distribution of the population are due to variations in the birth rates in recent years; the baby boom from 1946 to 1964 was followed by a "baby bust" in the late 1960s and the 1970s; a "mini-boom" then occurred in the late 1980s. The latter group is often referred to as the "echo-boom" generation, or Generation Y.

Because of the baby boom, the bulk of the Canadian population is maturing. In 2001, it was estimated that 29 percent of the population would be over age 50. By 2011, the figure is projected to increase to 35.4 percent, and by 2021 to 40 percent.[12] The aging population will challenge marketing organizations. Since in the future there will be fewer new customers in younger age categories, marketers will have to adjust their strategies to make their products attractive to older age groups, otherwise they will not experience any sales growth. Currently there is a tendency for marketers to target the youth market and the 20-something market. This is a generation that has grown up with brands such as Tommy Hilfiger, Gap, and Guess. The long-term outlook for these brands is dim if their respective marketing strategies are not adjusted according to age trends.

Since baby boomers and seniors will play a dominant role, there is a bright future for products that encourage healthier lifestyles, security services and products, and products that extend vitality and longevity. Recently launched products such as Viagra, Levitra, and Cialis have certainly tapped into the needs of the aging male population. See Figure 2.4 for details on age trends in Canada.

LOCATION

More Canadians than ever before live in cities. According to the 2001 Census data, 79.4 percent of the population lives in urban areas. Both Ontario and British Columbia exceed the national average for urban population. As well, 51 percent of the population lives in four major urban areas: metropolitan Montreal; the Golden Horseshoe area in southern Ontario, which includes metropolitan Toronto; the Edmonton–Calgary corridor; and British Columbia's Lower Mainland.[13] A **census metropolitan area (CMA)** encompasses all urban and rural areas that are linked to a city's urban core, either socially or economically. The CMA with the strongest rate of growth in Canada is Calgary. Between 1996 and 2001 the population of Calgary soared by 15.8 percent to reach 951 400.[14] In order for products and services to succeed in the future, there will have to be a greater concentration of marketing strategies in key urban centres. The trend toward urban living is expected to continue.

census metropolitan area (CMA)

FIGURE
2.4   Age Trends in the Canadian Population (thousands)

Source: "Age Trends in Canadian Population (Thousands)," adapted from the Statistics Canada CANSIM database ‹http://cansim2.statcan.ca›, Tables 051-0001 and 052-0001.

Age	2001	%	2111	%	2021	%
0–9	3 742.5	12.1	3 370.2	10.1	3 518.4	9.9
10–19	4 157.6	13.4	4 038.6	12.1	3 688.7	10.4
20–34	6 449.8	20.8	6 797.9	20.4	6 821.1	19.3
35–49	7 685.7	24.8	7 330.1	22.0	7 184.8	20.3
50+	8 966.8	28.9	11 812.9	35.5	14 168.7	40.1

FAMILY FORMATION

The nature of Canadian families is changing. Essentially, families are getting smaller and they are less traditional in structure. The traditional family was a married couple with a few children. Many Canadians now postpone marriage or dispense with it altogether. Common-law unions are increasing, while people who do marry are doing so later in life. Now, married couples comprise only 68 percent of the population, and common-law couples 13 percent. The latter is a jump of 10 percentage points in the past 20 years. Lone-parent families comprise the remaining 19 percent of the population.[15]

More and more children are born and raised outside marriage or experience the breakdown of their parents' marriage. As a result, we are witnessing an evolution in cultural values where there is a difference between younger and older people in their attitudes, values, expectations, and taken-for-granted assumptions. Canadians, many of whom have children, now have relatively high rates of separation and divorce. New forms of cohabitation have produced the **blended family**, which brings together children of previous marriages, and where kids may move back and forth between parents.

In the past decade, there was a back-to-the-family-unit trend as baby boomers, who had previously delayed marriage to pursue careers, started forming families. In fact, the baby boomers created a mini boom. What has emerged is the so-called **sandwich generation**, in which people are simultaneously trying to assume responsibility for dependent children and care for aging relatives. Such a trend is placing an added burden on family finances. The burden is magnified by the fact that young adults between 20 and 29 years of age have decided to extend the period in which they live with their families. Unlike their parents, who were eager to leave home when they were young, this generation prefers the comfort, security, and convenience of their parents' home. The latest Census reveals that 41 percent of 20- to 29-year-olds lived with their parents, a large increase from 27 percent in 1981.[16]

Canadian households continue to shrink in size. The average family size in 2001 fell to 2.6 from 2.9 in 1981. One- and two-person households have increased in the past decade. The character of the family has changed for economic reasons. With each passing decade there are more women in the work force. Two wage earners per household has become the norm, so it is expected that the number of members within each household will remain small.

Same-sex marriages are forming a new kind of household. It is estimated that as much as 10 percent of the population is gay or lesbian, so these households will become more interesting to marketers in the future (see the advertising illustration in Figure 2.5). Marketers will face the challenge of trying to attract gay customers without alienating any of their core customers. Recent marketing research conducted by the Print Measurement Bureau reveals that gays and lesbians are more attentive to personal improvement. They are three times more likely to use a hair gel daily, 75 percent more likely to use a face moisturizer, and twice as likely to use bath additives.[17] This type of information should pique the interest of companies marketing personal-care products: Gillette, Procter & Gamble, Unilever, L'Oreal, and others.

SPENDING POWER AND WEALTH

In the past decade, slower productivity growth has meant that prices in Canada have risen faster than incomes. In other words, the spending power of the dollar has shrunk. When other factors such as increases in federal and provincial taxes are considered, the relative wealth or spending power of the middle- and lower-income groups has dropped. Real wealth is becoming concentrated in the upper-income groups. To refer to an old expression, "the rich are getting richer, and the poor are getting poorer." Others refer to this situation as the "disappearing of the middle class."

blended family

sandwich generation

Print Measurement Bureau
www.pmb.ca

Reprinted by permission of the Marriott Hotels of Canada

FIGURE
2.5

The Courtyard Marriott hotel advertises to attract a gay target audience

These expressions refer to income distribution trends. **Income distribution** refers to the trends in income among various income groups: upper class, middle class, and lower class. Census data verify a polarization of incomes at the upper and lower end of the spectrum. Statistics Canada reports that 2.7 percent of the population earns more than $100 000 annually. Ten years earlier, this group accounted for only 1.8 percent of the population. Average earnings have gone up in Canada and the reason is the big gains at the upper end. At the other end of the scale, workers who earned $20 000 or less accounted for 17.3 percent of the population.[18]

As a result of these income trends the demand for upscale goods has been strong. Marketers of luxury automobiles, jewellery, and expensive property benefit. The luxury segment is the fastest growing segment of the automobile market. Retailers such as Wal-Mart that focus on lower prices while offering reasonable quality (value) are also experiencing growth. Middle- and lower-income groups are stretching their incomes as far as possible by shopping at discount outlets. An irony here is that upper-income people do buy luxury cars, but they also buy their everyday necessities at Wal-Mart and other discount outlets.

income distribution

How people spend their income and what they spend it on varies with the state of the economy. For example, in the 1980s the economy was booming, so consumers in all income groups were spending wildly—it was an era of "conspicuous consumption." A recession in the early 1990s put a damper on spending, so consumers shopped for better value. This period was characterized as an era of "strategic consumption." Nonetheless, baby boomers were entering their prime wage-earning years and younger families were headed by dual-income workers. These targets were demanding better quality and service and had the financial resources to pay for them. Refer to Figure 2.6 for an illustration.

At the same time, lower- and middle-income groups were more financially challenged and pulled back on their spending. Marketers began stressing value in their marketing strategies. By the late 1990s Wal-Mart, a retailer known for everyday low prices, secured the outright lead among all department stores and discount department stores in Canada. Wal-Mart is a store that appeals to all income groups.

EDUCATION

New jobs in North America have higher entry requirements than ever and are largely based on technology. More than ever before, education and training are key issues if Canada is to compete globally. It is imperative that Canadians possess the necessary

FIGURE 2.6   **The Audi A8 appeals directly to upscale baby boomers**

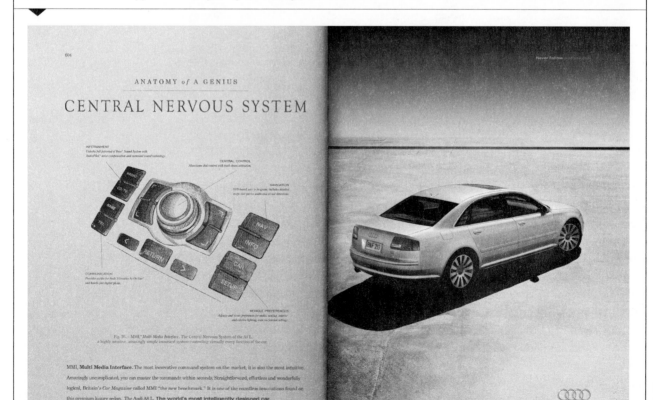

Audi of America, Inc.

skills to cope with ever-changing technology. Shortages in the basic skills would adversely affect Canada's ability to compete; so that we may have a well-trained workforce in the future, it is expected that governments and industries will have to cooperate to increase spending on "quality" education.

The Canadian population is now better educated than ever. Canada ranks highest among countries who are members of the Organisation for Economic Co-operation and Development (OECD) in terms of the proportion of its working-age population having college or university education. Currently, 20 percent of our working population has a university degree, and 21 percent has a college education. The trend toward university and college education was evident in the 1990s. More and more jobs required postsecondary education, so young men and women were more likely to extend their stay in the parents' home and delay marriage and family while getting the desired level of education.[19]

Organisation for Economic
Co-operation and Development
www.oecd.org

From a marketing perspective, customers are now more informed and they take more time deliberating on purchases. With such a high level of education, Canadians have accepted innovative electronic products at a much faster pace than people in many other developed countries. Consumers are using the Internet to search for goods and services that provide better value. In fact, the number of Canadian households surfing the Internet continues to grow. An estimated 7.9 million (64 percent) of the 12.3 million Canadian households had at least one member who used the Internet regularly in 2003. Households with high income, with members active in the labour force, with children living at home, and with people with higher levels of education have been in the forefront of Internet adoption.[20]

MULTICULTURALISM

Canada is emerging as a very culturally diverse country. The population is continuing to shift from one of a predominantly European background. Immigration trends indicate that Asians are becoming a major ethnic group in Canada. Existing within Canadian culture are many diverse **subcultures**—subgroups within a larger cultural context that have distinctive lifestyles based on religious, racial, and geographic differences.

subcultures

Currently, Canada's foreign-born population represents 18.4 percent of the total population. When Canadian children of the foreign-born population are factored in, about one-third of the population reports an ethnic background other than British or French (2001 Census). Canada's subcultures are evident in urban and suburban areas of cities where large ethnic populations occupy neighbourhoods. See Figure 2.7 for details regarding the ethnic population of Canada.

Canadian companies have been relatively slow in taking advantage of Canada's ethnic population, but with its proportion rising steadily those marketing organizations that successfully target and meet the needs of various ethnic groups stand to profit the most. To demonstrate, consider the Chinese population—more than 1 million strong in Canada. Apparently the Chinese love to buy luxury brands "to show off, to astonish others, to stand out from others," says Joseph Chen, a research executive at Millward Brown Goldfarb. The Chinese identify with Canadian culture but they prefer the Chinese culture. Says Chen, "They like to display wealth in the form of luxury brands to show their economic advancement." The Goldfarb study showed that 63 percent of Chinese owned luxury brands, compared to only 17 percent for whites.[21] Data such as these strongly suggest that marketers develop unique marketing programs for ethnic targets where practical.

Staying abreast of demographic trends is crucial if brands expect to grow. For insight into how marketers respond to demographic trends, read the Marketing in Action vignette **Doritos Capitalizes on Adolescent Expansion.**

FIGURE
2.7

Canada's Ethnic Population: Percentage of each market's population

Source: "Canada's Ethnic Population," adapted from the Statistics Canada website ‹http://www40.statcan.ca/101/cst01/demo46b.htm›

Market	1991	2001
Toronto	38.0	43.7
Montreal	16.4	18.4
Vancouver	30.1	37.5
Ottawa-Hull	14.7	17.6
Edmonton	18.3	17.8
Calgary	20.3	20.9
Winnipeg	17.4	16.5
Hamilton	23.5	23.6
Kitchener	21.5	22.1
St. Catharines-Niagara	18.9	17.8

Source: Statistics Canada, 2001 Census, www.statcan.ca/english/Pgdb/demo46b.htm.

Some Regional Data about Canada's Ethnic Population

British Columbia

One in every three people in Vancouver is Asian. Thirty-seven percent of Greater Vancouver residents are members of a visible minority group. Abbotsford has Canada's third highest proportion of visible minorities after Toronto and Vancouver.

The Prairies

Calgary has the fourth highest proportion of visible minorities in Canada. Five percent of the city's population identified themselves as Chinese.

Ontario

Toronto is the most multicultural city in the world, with 44 percent of its people born outside of Canada.

Quebec

Montreal has Canada's third largest population of visible minorities. Blacks are the largest visible minority in Quebec, representing 4.1 percent of the total population.

The Maritimes

Halifax has the highest proportion of Canadian-born blacks in Canada. Blacks account for 4 percent of the population (twice the national average).

Source: Adapted from "The New Canada," *Strategy*, February 24, 2003, p. 21.

4. Explain how lifestyle trends and environmental concerns influence the development of marketing strategies.

Lifestyles and Environmental Influences

The 1990s saw a shift in Canadians' attitudes toward work, lifestyles, and consumption. Generally speaking, we are now a society that places a greater emphasis on quality of life rather than work. That said, work is essential to sustain the desired quality of life, and Canadians are working harder than ever. In fact, a study conducted by Health Canada reveals that one in four Canadians works more than 50 hours a week, compared to one in ten a decade ago. The traditional 40-hour workweek is a myth. The 2001 National Work–Life Survey reinforces how hard Canadians are working. The study shows that managers and professionals cannot meet the expectations of their jobs in a nine-to-five day. Regardless of their home situation (kids to tend to or not) they choose to work longer to get ahead. Balancing work and family lives is a serious challenge for most people.[22]

These findings strongly suggest that today's consumers are pressed for time. Therefore, goods and services that provide convenience will grab their attention. Prepared convenience foods have capitalized on this trend. AC Nielsen Canada, a

MARKETING IN ACTION

Doritos Capitalizes on Adolescent Expansion

For the past decade, marketers have focused on the youth segment of the market. There was a desire to be cool with kids and for good reason—they influence nearly $20 billion in household purchases annually.

Over the next decade things will change. The preschool population is shrinking and the 5- to 12-year-olds group will shrink by 14 percent. The 13- to 24-year-olds segment is expected to increase a bit more going forward. This population shift is unique to Canada, so marketers that look at the entire North American market as a single market are perplexed. Marketing and advertising strategies used south of the border aren't working here.

Frito-Lay Canada has started to focus on the 20-year-plus segment and is experiencing good results. The Doritos brand had always focused squarely on teens and had reached $122 million in sales by 1999. The brand controlled 83 percent of the flavoured tortilla chip market. Suddenly the business hit a brick wall. The company immediately thought the brand had fallen out of favour with teens. Marketing research indicated otherwise. It was simply a case of demographics—there were fewer teens out there buying the brand.

So focused on teens, Doritos was also ignoring those teens and former customers who had graduated to young adulthood. Advertising depicted teen boys harassing librarians with the earth-shattering crunch of Doritos. The message wasn't resonating with the older group.

Insights from the marketing research led to some changes. Both teens and the older age group perceived Doritos to be more of a social brand. Brand attributes were described by terms such as "pioneer,

unique, social, fun, and youthful in spirit." This information spawned a new advertising campaign aimed directly at 21- to 23-year-olds. The new tagline was "Bold taste you can play with." This was considered an aspirational adage for both age groups. The 20-somethings reminisced about their college and university days, and the 16-year-olds had visions of the days when they would be moving out on their own.

Doritos' marketers have discovered that aiming a bit higher in terms of age is one of the keys to continued success. The strategy of spanning teen and young adult demos is working better than ever before, thanks to a new phenomenon called "adolescent expansion." Adolescent expansion is based on the notion that today's consumer takes more time to grow up. The number of 20- to 29-year-olds staying at home and remaining single tends to confirm this notion.

The shift in direction paid handsome dividends. Doritos' dollar market share increased to 88.4 percent, and sales of the base Nachos brand, including the baked products, increased 24 percent between 2002 and 2003.

Adapted from Lisa D'Innocenzo, "The disappearing kid," *Strategy*, December 15, 2003, pp. 1, 6.

Daniel Acker/Bloomberg News/Landov

marketing research company, reports that annual sales for refrigerated ready-made meals increased by 46 percent, for salad greens in a bag increased by 21 percent, and for frozen and refrigerated pizza increased by 25 percent in 2002.[23] Mother's cooking at home for the family isn't what it used to be!

There is also a stronger concern for health and welfare. A good diet, the aging process, and the effects of the environment on health all are hot topics, creating a widespread desire for general "wellness." As a result, people will continue to spend more for products and services related to a healthy lifestyle. Attitudes about the ingredients in food products are changing, and there is a trend toward natural foods and herbal remedies.

In the early 2000s the low-carbohydrate, high-protein diet craze began to sweep across North America. Companies in the food business had to quickly adapt to survive. Marketers of doughnuts (Krispy Kreme), frozen french fries (McCain) and bread (Weston Bakeries) were among the first companies to feel the impact. Sales of their regular products dropped significantly and profits suffered. On a more positive note, many new products were brought to market. Subway now offers an Atkins wrap (the Atkins Diet helped spawn the low-carb craze) and McDonald's added a Lighter Choices menu and a protein platter, which does not include bread. Low-carb beers such as Sleeman Clear and Labatt Sterling were introduced. Pepsi-Cola launched Pepsi Edge, and promoted it as "full-flavoured taste with half the sugar, carbs, and calories of regular colas." An advertisement appealing to people wanting to eat healthier appears in Figure 2.8.

FIGURE
2.8

A new product that appeals to consumers seeking a healthier lifestyle

Courtesy of Wendy's International, Inc.

As discussed in Chapter 1, socially responsible marketing and a genuine concern for the environment is now in vogue. A shift in consumers' attitudes on social and environmental issues has played a role in changing the way a company views its marketing programs. They are moving toward cause-related marketing and are operating on the premise that the emotional attributes associated with cause-linked brands differentiate them from their rivals. If brand cost and quality are perceived as equal, a customer will choose to buy the product associated with the cause. As well, companies are implementing programs that help to preserve the environment.

Kraft Canada (a food company) is fully committed to a worthy cause—hunger. Each year Kraft provides significant amounts of food to Canada's food banks. It also runs an advertising campaign designed to change the stigma associated with using food banks. PepsiCo is a company that firmly believes in the 3R's: reduce, reuse, and recycle. Using scientific research and new technology, the company continually improves performance through conservation, source reduction, recycling, and product packaging design. In the "reduce" area alone, Pepsi has reduced the use of plastic in 2-litre bottles by 28 percent, the use of aluminum in cans by 37 percent, and the use of glass by 25 percent. PepsiCo's goal is to be a good corporate citizen.[24]

Social marketers say that their efforts are designed to build a social identity linked to their company or brands—it's not about generating publicity. They believe consumers will buy brands and support companies that reflect their own social values.

Technological Influences

5. Identify and explain the influence of various technologies on how marketing is practised now and in the future.

The technological environment consists of the discoveries, inventions, and innovations that provide for marketing opportunities. New products, new packaging, cost-reduced materials and substitute materials for existing products, and the emergence of e-learning are all the result of technological advancement. In the next decade, advances in electronics, biotechnology, and the information technologies of computing and telecommunications will be the driving force for change and growth. By all accounts, the telecommunications world will be wireless by 2010.

Technological advances are having a dramatic impact on marketing, and they will be the single most important influence in the future. From how a company collects and uses information, to the development of new products, to improvement of production and distribution processes, all are affected by technology. Perhaps the areas of marketing affected most involve how customers will be managed to maximize revenue and profit and how companies will communicate with customers.

DATABASE MANAGEMENT

Today's technology allows companies to deal with customers on an individual basis; that is, unique marketing strategies can be developed for each customer. This capability is referred to as **database marketing**. In database marketing companies collect a mountain of information about customers, analyze it to predict how likely the customer is to buy, and then develop a marketing strategy precisely designed to meet the needs of the customer. The **database** is a customer information file that a company continuously updates.

database marketing

database

Customer relationship management programs (discussed in Chapter 1) are based on database technology. Companies such as IBM, Microsoft, Apple, Procter & Gamble, and the Hudson's Bay Company realize the importance of customer relationship management and have successful database programs in place. These companies and many others employ 1-800 telephone numbers, telemarketing, and online communications to target messages directly to individual customers. The concept of relationship marketing is based on the belief that it is less expensive and more profitable to hold on to current customers than to attract new ones.

TECHNOLOGY AND MARKETING COMMUNICATIONS

Traditionally marketers relied on the mass media (television, radio, newspaper, magazine, and outdoor advertising) to deliver messages to large audiences. Today's technology allows for direct communications with individuals by media such as the Internet, cell phones, and personal digital assistants. In fact, marketers are now capable of communicating with customers and conducting a paid transaction through wireless communications devices. The science of marketing has come a long way in the past few years!

Online and interactive communications offer a high degree of personalization. These new media offer the ability to listen to customers and to learn from them, and to deliver content and services tailored to their responses and actions. While many companies are still in the exploratory stage in terms of how to use them, General Motors has figured things out. The leading advertiser in North America has repositioned its marketing budget to place more money into relationship marketing and online communications. GM is looking for better ways to target customers, and has determined it is a lot easier to identify prospects when they visit its GM websites than when they view television commercials;[25] refer to Figure 2.9 for an illustration. If GM is heading in this direction, competitors and companies in other industries won't be far behind.

THE INTERNET AND E-COMMERCE

The Internet has had an overwhelming and rapid impact on marketing and commerce. Many companies jumped into the world of e-commerce (conducting business online) without proper knowledge of how to do things. Internet commerce offers great potential, but too many companies have had unrealistic expectations. Companies were being guided—or should we say *mis*guided—by the "create a website and they will come" mentality.

FIGURE 2.9

Interactive communications lead to direct links with potential customers

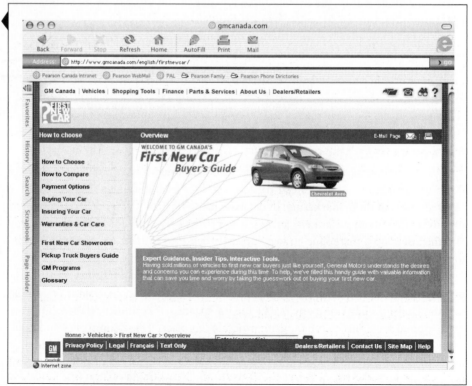

General Motors of Canada Limited

Companies are gradually learning how to integrate Web-based activities with other traditional marketing activities, but the learning process has been painful for some. For example, Canadian Tire and Future Shop entered the e-commerce arena early only to encounter countless customer relationship and fulfillment problems. Fulfillment refers to an organization's capability to deliver the goods. The retailers also discovered that they weren't adding to sales, but merely taking away sales from stores. Both companies realized there had to be a better way to integrate e-commerce into their businesses, and have since refined their online operations considerably.[26]

E-commerce in Canada is starting to take off and it will take off even further when consumers have greater access to high-speed Internet service. In 2003, the latest year that statistics are available, online sales in Canada totalled $19.1 billion, a 40-percent increase over 2002. Online sales account for only 1 percent of revenues among firms doing business online. In the consumer market, the dollar value of business-to-consumer sales rose 51 percent to $5.5 billion, with online retailers accounting for $1.7 billion in consumer sales. Business-to-business sales (a business selling goods to another business) rose 35 percent to $13.1 billion.[27]

The Internet has forever changed the speed of business time by eliminating walls, bricks, and mortar. Companies that communicate directly and frequently with customers now have the ability to develop and market new products much more quickly. Startup organizations can become instant and serious threats to long-established businesses. For example, ING Direct is a bank that operates without walls (i.e., a branchless bank) and now has a strong presence in Canada. Canadian consumers' receptiveness to new banking technology is one reason why the ING Group chose to launch an Internet banking service in Canada. Finally, consumers can complete worldwide searches for information about products in minutes, compared to days, months, or even years before the Internet. The Internet has great potential to become the main focal point for commercial transactions, but when this will occur is difficult to predict.

ING Direct
www.ingdirect.ca

Legal and Regulatory Influences

Yes, Canada is a free-enterprise society, but in any society of this nature the consumer can be subjected to unscrupulous business practices—practices that serve only the needs of the business using them. WestJet, for example, was caught electronically spying on Air Canada—a practice that cost the CEO of WestJet his job. Consequently, numerous laws and regulations (some voluntary and some involuntary) have been put into place to protect consumer rights and the rights of corporations and to ensure that organizations conduct business in a competitive manner. Ignorance of the law is not a defence for business; companies must act according to the law or face the perils of the judicial system.

6. Identify the role that laws and regulations play in the practice of marketing in Canada.

The legal environment for marketing and other business practices in Canada is the domain of **Industry Canada**. Its principal responsibility is to administer the **Competition Act**, an act that brought together a number of related laws to help consumers and businesses function in Canada. The purpose of the Competition Act is threefold:

Industry Canada
Competition Act

1. To maintain and encourage competition in Canada.
2. To ensure that small- and medium-sized businesses have an equitable opportunity to participate in the Canadian economy.
3. To provide consumers with product choice and competitive prices.

Within the Ministry of Industry, there are three distinct bureaus that influence business and marketing activity: the Bureau of Competition Policy, the Bureau of

Consumer Affairs, and the Bureau of Corporate Affairs. The federal government and numerous provincial governments are currently revamping consumer protection laws to reflect the explosive growth in e-commerce and the surge of complaints by people and small businesses doing business on the Internet.

Canadian consumers are protected by various privacy laws, the Privacy Act, and the Personal Information Protection and Electronic Documents Act (PIPEDA). The Privacy Act respects the rights of Canadians by placing limits on the collection, use, and disclosure of personal information. It gives Canadians the right to access and correct any personal information about them held by government organizations.

PIPEDA sets the ground rules for how private-sector organizations may collect, use, or disclose personal information. As of January 2004, this Act covers information collected by commercial organizations in all provinces. The law requires organizations to obtain your consent when they collect, use, or disclose your personal information.[28] Such a law has direct implications for marketing organizations that accumulate data about their customers. It also has implications for the direct marketing industry, which relies heavily on direct-mail lists and email marketing lists to send offers to prospective customers. New strategies will be replacing the old ways of doing business! For more information about privacy laws, see the Privacy Commissioner of Canada website.

Privacy Commissioner of Canada
www.privcom.gc.ca

BUREAU OF COMPETITION POLICY

This bureau enforces the rules that govern and promote the efficiency of a competitive Canadian marketplace. Its chief instrument for carrying out these functions is the Competition Act. Among the trade practices that it routinely reviews are mergers and acquisitions. The bureau seeks to ensure that monopolies are not created, that competition is not affected negatively, that no price fixing or other pricing infractions occur, and that advertising does not misrepresent a product or mislead the consumer. Its role was illustrated in a June 2003 decision in which Suzy Shier Inc. was ordered to pay a $1-million penalty for marking clothing on sale when it had not been sold at a regular price for any length of time. The fine was levied under the "ordinary selling price" provision of competition legislation. This was the second such penalty for Suzy Shier. In 1995 it was fined $300 000 for a similar violation.[29]

Companies can contact the Bureau for information about the regulations and interpretation of the Act.

BUREAU OF CONSUMER AFFAIRS

This bureau promotes a safe, orderly, and fair marketplace for consumers and businesses. In consultation with other government agencies and organizations that represent business groups, it establishes and enforces regulations and programs that protect the interests of consumers. The bureau also ensures that dangerous products are identified and that certain products that cause injury are removed from the market. The legislation under the jurisdiction of the federal Office of Consumer Affairs includes the Consumer Packaging and Labelling Act, the Textile Labelling Act, and the Weights and Measures Act.

Recently, the government established new regulations for food packaging that allow manufacturers to make one of five generic health claims on their products. For example, Becel margarine will be allowed to say it helps prevent heart disease. There is some fear that the new legislation will lead to misleading claims, giving consumers the impression that certain foods are a magic bullet to better health. For example, a milk producer could encourage women to consume a high-calcium product to reduce osteoporosis, not mentioning that because the product is also high in saturated fat such consumption could increase the incidence of heart disease.[30] While the new legislation has good intentions, it could create controversy.

BUREAU OF CORPORATE AFFAIRS

This bureau provides a regulatory framework for the business community in Canada. Its intent is to ensure orderly conduct among businesses across the country, to encourage economic development, and to promote creativity, innovation, and the exploitation of technology. It is also responsible for laws governing industrial design, patents, trademarks, and copyright. Legislation administered by Corporate Affairs includes the Bankruptcy and Insolvency Act, the Canada Corporations Act, the Patent Act, and the Copyright Act.

The following example illustrates one aspect of this bureau's responsibilities. The U.S.–based Intel Corp. sued Kelowna-based Intel Financial Inc., a 10-person financial services company, for trademark infringement. The suit claimed that Intel Financial was confusing customers and "infringing the exclusive rights of Intel Corp. in the trademark Intel." Intel believes that intellectual property laws require companies to take a proactive approach to defending their logos and slogans. If a company does not contest firms that violate its brand rights, its trademark becomes diluted. A third person could come along and adopt a similar trademark, and argue that there are already two companies using the same brand name, so why can't a third? Intel must protect its brand names and logos.[31]

As noted earlier in this chapter, companies must understand and operate within the legal and regulatory environment or face the perils of the court system. That said, laws and regulations are not uniform across Canada. For this reason, a company may find it necessary to be knowledgeable about any provincial legislation that may affect it. Regulations governing the marketing of securities, insurance, and liquor, for example, vary from province to province. A product like margarine cannot be the same colour as butter in the province of Quebec. In all other provinces, colour is not an issue. Therefore Unilever, a maker of margarine, has to produce and market separate product lines for the Quebec market.[32]

Self-regulation is an alternative to government regulation. In the advertising industry, Advertising Standards Canada (a group that represents advertisers and advertising agencies) established the Canadian Code of Advertising Standards for its members to follow. Within this code are specific guidelines governing such issues as how the genders are portrayed in advertising, accuracy and clarity of product claims, price claims, comparative advertising, and advertising to children, to name a few. Organizations such as the Canadian Marketing Association (CMA) and the Canadian Bankers Association have established policies and guidelines that their member companies agree to follow.

As a conclusion to this chapter, refer to Figure 2.10. This chart provides a visual summary of the various elements that must be considered in an organization's quest to satisfy customers.

self-regulation

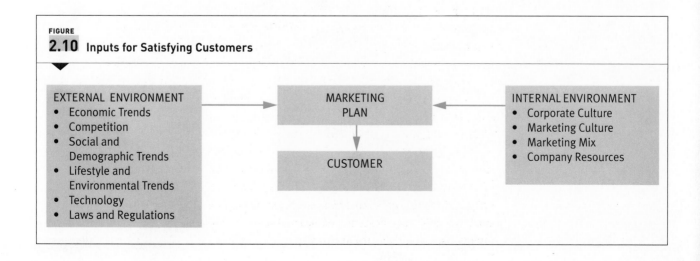

FIGURE
2.10 Inputs for Satisfying Customers

SUMMARY

The environment that marketing operates in is dynamic, and organizations must therefore constantly anticipate and react to change. How an organization handles change is a key factor in its success or failure in the marketplace.

Decisions about the marketing mix are influenced by conditions that exist beyond the company. Essentially, there are five key external influences: the economy, competition, social and demographic trends, technology, and laws and regulations.

The general state of the economy will influence how aggressive or how conservative an organization's marketing strategy may be. An organization must react to changes in the economy and recognize that the economy experiences various business cycles such as recession, depression, recovery, and prosperity. The nature of the market a firm competes in also influences marketing strategy. How an organization uses the marketing mix differs from one market structure (monopoly, oligopoly, monopolistic competition, and pure competition) to another. An organization's position or relative strength in a market (leader, challenger, follower, or nicher) also has an impact on marketing strategy.

Social and demographic trends must be monitored closely. Canada's population is aging, household formations are changing, the population is now more ethnic in nature, and there is a trend toward living in urban areas. These trends will influence marketing strategy today and in the future.

Quality of life and environmental concerns must also be considered when developing marketing strategies. Healthier lifestyles and a societal desire for preservation will continue to impact marketing strategies. Marketing initiatives that demonstrate a sense of social responsibility will be widely accepted and lead to better profits for firms that show leadership in this area.

Technology will have a strong and direct impact on marketing. As more and more organizations adopt database management techniques they will be better equipped to communicate and market directly to customers, and to implement customer relationship management programs. All firms must anticipate that the Internet and online marketing strategies will play a stronger role in the future.

Finally, an organization must operate within the laws and regulations established by various government bodies and by organizations and associations that establish self-regulating policies within particular industries. Laws and regulations are designed to protect consumers and corporations and to ensure a healthy, competitive environment in which to market goods and services.

When analyzed, the conditions that are present, though beyond the control of the organization, have a significant influence on the direction of its marketing practice.

KEY TERMS

blended family   40

census metropolitan area (CMA)   39

Competition Act   49

database   47

database marketing   47

demographics   38

depression   31

direct competition   34

disposable income   30

employment   29

gross domestic product (GDP)   29

income distribution   41

indirect competition   34

Industry Canada   49

inflation   29

market challenger   35

market follower   37

market leader   35

market nicher (niche marketing)   37

market share   34

monopolistic competition   33

monopoly   32

oligopoly   33

prosperity   31

pure competition   33

rationalization   31

real income   29

recession   31

recovery   31

sandwich generation   40

self-regulation   51

subcultures   43

REVIEW QUESTIONS

1. Briefly explain the difference between the following business cycles and indicate how each cycle influences marketing strategy: recession, recovery, and prosperity.
2. When a firm rationalizes its operations what is it doing?
3. Describe the basic components of the following markets and identify a new example of each: monopoly, oligopoly, monopolistic competition, and pure competition.
4. Briefly describe the four classifications of competitors.
5. What is the difference between direct competition and indirect competition? Provide a new example to demonstrate the difference between the two forms of competition.
6. How do the marketing strategies differ between a market leader and a market challenger?
7. Explain what niche marketing is and briefly describe two examples of the concept in practice.
8. Briefly explain how social and demographic trends affect marketing activity. What demographic trends will become more important in the future?
9. Briefly describe how lifestyle and environmental concerns have influenced marketing strategy.
10. How important is technology, and what impact will it have on marketing organizations in the future?
11. Briefly explain the roles of the Bureau of Competition Policy, the Bureau of Consumer Affairs, and the Bureau of Corporate Affairs.

DISCUSSION AND APPLICATION QUESTIONS

1. Canadian Tire remains a highly successful company despite competition from American retailers. Analyze Canadian Tire's marketing mix. Which elements of the marketing mix have contributed to the success of this company? Be specific.
2. Provide some examples of companies that have a good corporate image. What marketing activities have helped these companies achieve their image?
3. Identify a company or product (good or service) that you would characterize as a market leader. Briefly describe the nature of its marketing practice. Identify the challenger in the same market and briefly describe its marketing practice. What makes the leader the leader?
4. With reference to the vignette "McDonald's Protects Its Lead," what new marketing strategies can you recommend to McDonald's in order to fend off competitors and keep it in the forefront of the fast-food marketplace? Consider the bigger picture when analyzing who McDonald's competitors really are.

E-ASSIGNMENTS

1. Conduct some Internet-based secondary research to compile recent statistics about Internet growth. Identify the variables that are considered when determining growth (e.g., number of websites, number of users, value of transactions, etc.).
2. Visit the Statistics Canada website (www.statcan.ca) and determine the following:
   - What are the components of population growth, and what are the basic trends in each area for the past five years?
   - What five areas from around the world comprise the largest source of immigrants entering Canada?
   - What percentage of the Canadian population has a university degree? What percentage has some form of postsecondary education?
   - How many households are there in Canada and what is the average expenditure per household?

ENDNOTES

1. Statistics Canada, Imports and Exports of Goods on a Balance-of-Payments Basis, www.statscan.ca.

2. Statistics Canada, Real Gross Domestic Product, Expenditure-Based, www.statcan.ca.

3. Dana Flavelle, "Camco to shut Hamilton plant as profit, sales fall," *Toronto Star*, October 18, 2003, pp. D1, D4.

4. Michelle DaCruz, "Milk money," *Financial Post*, January 7, 2004, p. FP2.

5. Jack Neff, "Hair brand gets fortified," *Advertising Age*, September 1, 2003, p. 6.

6. Beth Snyder Bulik, "Sony, Kodak lead U.S. battle for share in digital cameras," *Advertising Age*, May 31, 2004, p. 12.

7. Philip Kotler and Gary Armstrong, *Principles of Marketing*, 10th edition (Upper Saddle River, New Jersey: Prentice-Hall, 2004), p. 56.

8. "Report on market shares," *Marketing*, May 27, 2002, www.marketingmag.ca.

9. Ibid.

10. Statistics Canada, August 2004, www.statcan.ca.

11. Jane Armstrong, "Canada is 30 million, but will that last?" *Globe and Mail*, March 13, 2002, www.globeandmail.com.

12. Statistics Canada, CANSIM, Matrix 6900.

13. Statistics Canada, www.geodepot.statcan.ca/Diss/Highlights, 2004.

14. Ibid.

15. "Update on families," *Canadian Social Trends*, Summer 2003, pp. 11–13.

16. Ibid., p. 12.

17. Andrea Zoe Aster, "Defining pink consumers," *Marketing*, April 19, 2004, p. 4.

18. Nancy Carr, "More Canadians earning $100,000-plus," *Globe and Mail*, March 12, 2003, p. 11.

19. "Update on Education," *Canadian Social Trends*, Winter 2003, pp. 19–22.

20. "Household Internet use survey," Statistics Canada, *The Daily*, July 8, 2004, www.statcan.ca.

21. Chris Daniels, "Shopping mosaic," *Marketing*, May 17/24, 2004, pp. 13, 14.

22. Kathryn May, "Nine-to-five work week a myth: Study," *National Post*, August 24, 2002, p. A4.

23. Prepared convenience food sales soaring in supermarkets," News Blast, Kostuch Publications, December 10, 2002.

24. www.pepsico.com.citizenship/health-wellness.

25. "GM shows way toward the new mix," *Advertising Age*, January 20, 2003, p. 20.

26. Marina Strauss and Patrick Brethour, "Consumers shy away from Web shopping," *Globe and Mail*, December 15, 2001, pp. B1, B4.

27. Terry Weber, "Online sales up 40% in 2003," *Globe and Mail*, April 16, 2004, www.globeandmail.com.

28. "Privacy Legislation in Canada," a fact sheet published by the Office of the Privacy Commissioner, www.privcom.gc.ca.

29. Marina Strauss, "Suzy Shier's fake bargains bring $1-million dressing down," *Globe and Mail*, June 14, 2003, pp. B1, B4.

30. Marina Strauss, "Appetite for health claims growing," *Globe and Mail*, November 27, 2002, p. B4.

31. Sahm Adrangi, "B.C. firm in pricey bout of name calling," *Globe and Mail*, August 22, 2003, p. B7.

32. Konrad Yakabusli, "Unilever loses margarine case," *Globe and Mail*, May 27, 1999, p. B3.

Inputs for Marketing Planning

This section presents topics that are classified as inputs for marketing planning. Prior to striking a marketing plan, the marketing manager must have a thorough understanding of the customer, be it a consumer or business organization. Understanding customers frequently involves the collection of data and information through marketing research.

Chapter 3 examines in detail the role and process of marketing research and shows how organizations collect information that assists in the planning of their marketing activities.

Chapter 4 presents the elements of consumer behaviour, the purchase decision process, and the factors that influence it.

Chapter 5 focuses on the behavioural tendencies of business, industry, and governments, and the steps involved in their decisions to purchase goods and services.

PART

2

CHAPTER

3

Marketing Research

Since a considerable amount of money is invested in the design, development, and marketing of goods and services, a marketing organization is very concerned about protecting its investment. In addition, its desire to remain competitive and be knowledgeable about consumers' changing needs makes it necessary to collect appropriate information before and after critical decisions are made. Carefully planned marketing research is the tool that provides organizations with the insight necessary to take advantage of new opportunities. This chapter will discuss the marketing research process and the impact it has on making business decisions and planning marketing strategies.

Marketing Research: Role and Scope

Research provides an organization with data. The data do not guarantee that the firm will take proper decisions and actions since data are always open to interpretation. The old saying that "some information is better than no information" puts the role of marketing research into perspective. A vital marketing tool, it is used to help reduce or eliminate the uncertainty and risk associated with making business decisions.

In many ways, marketing research is a form of insurance—it ensures that the action a company might take is the right action. To demonstrate, consider the decision Ikea made when it opened a new store in Vaughan (on the outskirts of Toronto). Ikea is well known for its maze-like layout—people must follow a set pattern and see all of the merchandise before they reach the checkout counters. Such a pattern encourages impulse buying, which means that customers frequently leave the store with far more than they intended to buy. Why would Ikea change this winning formula? Research among customers revealed a more conventional layout was preferred. Shoppers indicated they wanted an environment that was less confusing. "If it was less confusing we would return more frequently," was a common response. So, Ikea evaluated impulse buying and its traditional layout against a more conventional layout that would generate more store visits. Deciding on the latter option, Ikea implemented a conventional layout that features a central corridor that opens onto aisles set at right angles every few metres.[1]

The moral of this story is simple: research provides useful information to develop an effective marketing strategy. It's all about keeping the customer satisfied!

The American Marketing Association defines **marketing research** as the function that links the consumer/customer/public to the marketer through information—information used to define marketing opportunities and problems; to generate, refine, and evaluate marketing actions; to monitor marketing performance; and to improve the understanding of marketing as a process.

marketing research

Marketing research specifies the information required to address these issues; designs the method for collecting information; manages and implements the information collection process; analyzes the results; and communicates the findings and their implications.[2]

THE SCOPE OF MARKETING RESEARCH

market analysis

product research

consumer analysis

Generally speaking, marketing research covers three main areas: **market analysis**, which produces information about the marketplace; **product research**, which produces information about how people perceive product attributes; and **consumer analysis**, which produces information about the needs and motivations of consumers.

The testing of new product concepts is the single most common task asked of market research firms by their clients. Other uses of marketing research include testing advertising for impact and effectiveness; conducting surveys to measure customer satisfaction; tracking brand awareness versus the competition; pre-testing of advertising strategies; and measuring the influence of pricing tests. Regardless of the nature of the research study, the information obtained will assist managers in their decision making.

How do managers go about collecting information? Prudent marketing decision makers combine their intuition and judgment with all other information sources available. They use the scientific method, which implies that the data generated are reliable and valid.

reliability

validity

scientific method

Reliability refers to similar results being achieved if another study were undertaken under similar conditions. **Validity** refers to the research procedure's ability to actually measure what it was intended to. The key elements of the **scientific method** are:

1. The awareness of a problem is reached through exploratory investigations.
2. Information sources and methodologies of collecting information are implemented properly.
3. Alternative solutions are thoroughly evaluated.
4. Data are properly analyzed and interpreted.
5. Specific actions taken are based on research findings.

Here's a quick illustration of how proper research influenced a decision at Wal-Mart Canada. A research study was undertaken to analyze how customers navigate Wal-Mart stores. The research involved one-hour, videotaped "shop-along" interviews with 20 recruited female customers from various demographic backgrounds. From the interviews Wal-Mart learned that shoppers wanted better signage. They thought the placement of signs could be better and there could be a lot less clutter. Signs should be at eye level and their design should be more eye-catching. Wal-Mart implemented the suggested changes in a test store and then did the same research again. Customers indicated they were aware of the new signs (since they were different from other Wal-Mart stores) and were generally quite happy with what they saw. Wal-Mart is implementing the sign changes nationwide.[3]

The Marketing Research Process

2. Outline the basic stages in the marketing research process.

The research process is a systematic one with many steps: problem awareness, exploratory research, secondary data collection, primary research, data transfer and processing, data analysis and interpretation, and recommendations and implementation (Figure 3.1).

PROBLEM AWARENESS

In the problem awareness stage, an attempt is made to specify the nature of the difficulty. For example, a company or product may be experiencing declining sales, but the decline itself is not the problem. Instead, it is a symptom that makes people aware that there is a deeper problem within the organization that must be identified. Many practitioners of marketing research state that the proper identification of a problem is the first

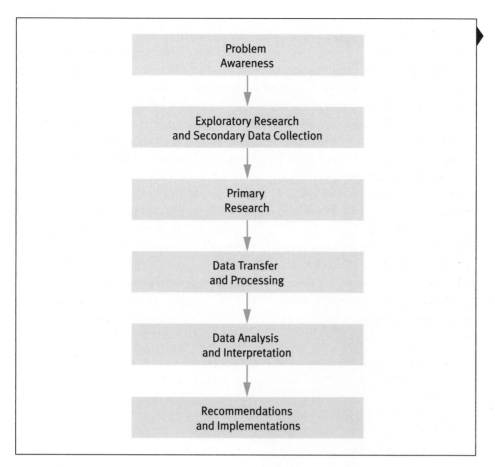

FIGURE
3.1

**Marketing Research
Process**

step in finding its solution. Therefore, it is essential that a problem be precisely defined. After all, a business organization does not want to waste valuable time and money collecting information that will not lead to action. Currently, market research projects are usually commissioned to address a specific decision that has to be made, and good research projects are designed to address that decision alone. Once such data are available, they may be linked to other research projects at a later date.

Defining a problem involves developing a clearly worded statement that provides direction for further research on the topic to be investigated. To define a problem precisely, a company usually performs some form of exploratory research.

EXPLORATORY RESEARCH

Exploratory research is research that helps define the precise nature of a problem through the use of informal analysis. This informal analysis is often referred to as the funnelling process. **Funnelling** is the process of dividing a subject into manageable variables and thereby narrowing down the field so that specifically directed research can be conducted. Funnelling is accomplished by means of a thorough situation analysis. In a **situation analysis**, the researcher collects information from knowledgeable people inside and outside the organization and from secondary sources such as government reports, studies on related issues, and census data. Many variables are analyzed as potential problem areas, and through the funnelling process areas that appear to be unrelated are eliminated.

Figure 3.2 illustrates exploratory research and the funnelling process. Let us assume that the sales of a product are declining. This indicates that there is a problem. To find

exploratory research

funnelling

situation analysis

FIGURE
3.2

**Exploratory Research and
Funnelling Process**

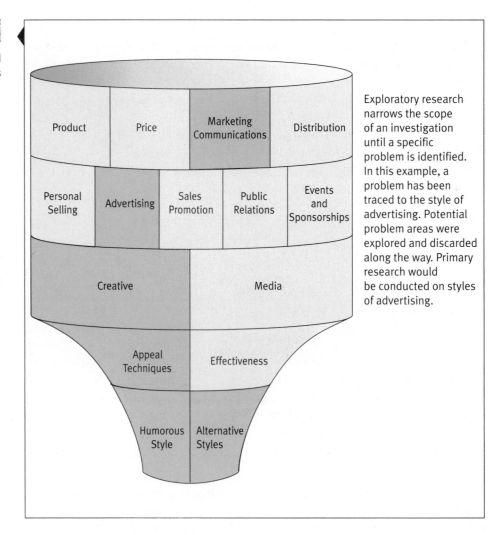

Exploratory research narrows the scope of an investigation until a specific problem is identified. In this example, a problem has been traced to the style of advertising. Potential problem areas were explored and discarded along the way. Primary research would be conducted on styles of advertising.

the cause of the decline would be to identify the problem. Identifying the true nature of the problem is the task of exploratory research. As the diagram demonstrates, the company could follow several routes in order to pinpoint the problem. The researcher investigates a number of matters: product and product quality issues, marketing communication strategies, pricing strategies, availability, and distribution. In this case, the problem is narrowed down to marketing communications. From there, the researcher looks into possible areas of marketing communications where the real problem might be, rejects some, and further pursues others—advertising, in our example. As this analysis unfolds, it should become apparent which elements are contributing to the sales decline. The eventual isolation of a "creative" problem in this illustration (a problem with the advertising message) assumes that other areas have been evaluated, at least informally, and rejected as the source of the problem.

Sometimes the problem is both pinpointed and resolved through discussions held with people knowledgeable in the area of concern or through the collection and consideration of secondary data. Or, new information may be uncovered that changes the focus of the issue under investigation. If it turns out that primary research is required (that is, if the problem is not resolved through secondary research), it can be conducted only if the problem is specific in nature or narrow in scope. The exploratory process narrows the scope of the problem until it becomes resolvable.

SECONDARY DATA COLLECTION

Exploratory research usually involves the use of secondary data. **Secondary data** are data that have been compiled and published for purposes unrelated to the specific problem under investigation, yet they may have some significance in its resolution. They are available from sources both internal and external to the company.

secondary data

INTERNAL DATA SOURCES   Internal data sources are those that are available within the organization. Such information includes customer profiles (e.g., size and frequency of purchase), sales analysis reports (e.g., sales by region, nation, customer, or product), inventory analysis, production reports, cost analyses, marketing budgets (e.g., actual spending versus planned spending), and profit-and-loss statements. This information is incorporated into a company's database and is updated continuously for use in planning and decision making.

3. Describe the methodologies for collecting secondary and primary research data.

As discussed in Chapter 1, a database management system or management information system is a vital tool for marketing. A **database management system** consists of people and equipment organized to provide a continuous, orderly collection and exchange of information (internal and external) needed in a firm's decision-making process. Refer to Figure 3.3 for a sample model of a database management system. With so much information now available, the emphasis has shifted from the generation of information to the shaping and evaluation of information to make it useful to the decision maker. What has evolved is the decision support system. A **decision support system (DSS)** is an interactive, personalized marketing information system designed in such a manner that it can be initiated and controlled by individual decision makers.[4]

database management system

decision support system (DSS)

Marketing research information contained in a decision support system is useful for both control purposes and planning purposes. Control information includes routine

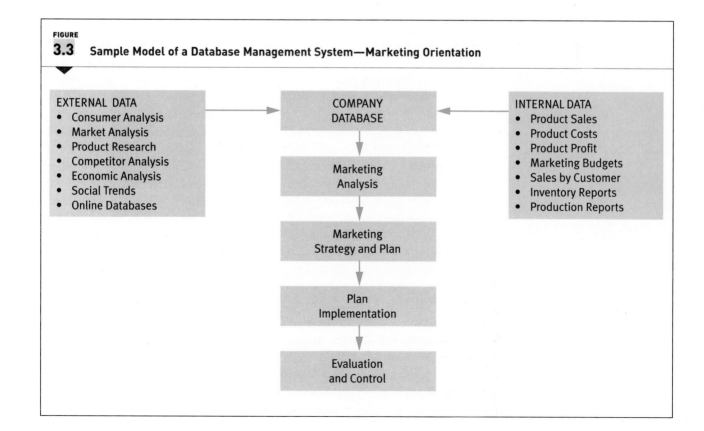

FIGURE 3.3   **Sample Model of a Database Management System—Marketing Orientation**

EXTERNAL DATA
- Consumer Analysis
- Market Analysis
- Product Research
- Competitor Analysis
- Economic Analysis
- Social Trends
- Online Databases

COMPANY DATABASE

INTERNAL DATA
- Product Sales
- Product Costs
- Product Profit
- Marketing Budgets
- Sales by Customer
- Inventory Reports
- Production Reports

Marketing Analysis

Marketing Strategy and Plan

Plan Implementation

Evaluation and Control

reports that indicate what has happened in an organization, such as sales reports, inventory reports, budget reports, and cost reports. Such information is continuously updated and distributed to managers through the management information system and will influence the marketing strategy during the course of an operating year. For example, if raw material costs or packaging costs rise unexpectedly, a price increase will have to go into effect if profit levels are to be maintained.

The decision support systems that exist today are interactive, flexible, discovery-oriented, and easy to learn and use. A good decision support system not only allows managers to ask "what if" questions but also enables them to manipulate the data any way they want. It is a useful tool for sales forecasting, planning marketing budgets, and financial analysis.

geographical information systems

The information collected by marketing research on such matters as economic, demographic, psychographic, and geographic patterns is valuable for planning purposes. Many companies now use mapping software—known as **geographical information systems**—to help make business decisions and get a competitive edge. Williams-Sonoma, an American kitchen retailer, used mapping software to determine the best location for a new store in Toronto. The software determined that the Eaton Centre was a good fit because it attracted well-educated consumers in their mid-40s, with household incomes of $140 000 or more, and who spend a lot on home furnishings. That's the customer Williams-Sonoma wants to reach. In this case, the decision about where to locate was clear.[5]

data mining

The electronic era has resulted in an information explosion that now allows for the storage and transfer of great amounts of business data in a short time. What has emerged is a new concept called **data mining**. In a marketing context, data mining is the analysis of information that establishes relationships between pieces of information so that more effective marketing strategies can be identified and implemented. Rather than looking at an entire data set, data mining techniques attempt to locate informational patterns and nuggets within that database.[6]

Data mining is a useful technique to employ when developing and implementing a customer relationship management program. The goal of data mining is to produce lower marketing costs and increased efficiency by identifying prospects most likely to buy, or buy in large volume, and the availability of smarter software programs provides this opportunity. A firm's competitive advantage will depend increasingly on knowing the situation better than the competition and being able to take action quickly, based on knowing what's going on.[7]

Wal-Mart is a company adept at data mining. Don't be fooled by the folksy greeters: Wal-Mart controls one of the largest data collection systems anywhere in the world with the capability of tracking sales on a minute-by-minute basis. It can also quickly detect regional and local market trends. Such knowledge allows Wal-Mart to customize each store's offerings while keeping suppliers abreast of how well their products are selling.

For additional insight into how professional baseball teams use information technology, read the Marketing in Action vignette **Technology, Business, and Major League Baseball**.

EXTERNAL DATA SOURCES   An organization refers to external sources when internal information does not resolve the problem at hand. The primary sources of external data are government, business, and academia. As well, the Internet can provide a wealth of valuable information to marketing organizations.

Federal, provincial, and municipal governments have an abundance of information that marketing organizations can examine. The major source of government information

MARKETING IN ACTION

Technology, Business, and Major League Baseball

When it comes to keeping track of statistics, no sport does it better than baseball. But in today's competitive market baseball has gone a step further and automated its scouting operations. The goal for each team is clear: to make better decisions about the players it drafts (young prospects are selected by each team every year), and to follow more closely the development of young players on their minor league teams.

Typically, a team now operates an amateur scouting database and a professional scouting database. Every run, every hit, and every error will accumulate, along with the team's collective wisdom on a prospect's future.

Only a few years ago teams approached the amateur draft with mounds of paper to shuffle through. Scouts from all across the country would consult by telephone about who the best prospects were. These days, all the scouts are in one conference room scrolling through scouting reports on their laptops. Video clips of the players in action may also be available.

It's a different world—the reports are up-to-the-minute and the databases are synchronized so everyone's on the same page. They can analyze the records, even plug in test scenarios to forecast future player development outcomes. Automation provides speed and accuracy, which officials say increases the odds of getting the right players initially and getting the most out of the players they have. Further, all key people in the organization are in the loop, with up-to-date snapshots of their players.

For a baseball team, the cost of entry into automation is minuscule when one considers what major league players earn. For a mere $200 000 a team can automate its entire scouting and player records system. In research terms the scouting systems are simply data warehouses and decision support systems. The team's records are merged with other records provided by the Major League Baseball Scouting Bureau and other services.

In addition to hard and fast baseball statistics, the database includes information about a player's speed, coordination, strength, hitting, throwing, alertness, ailments, and the like. Even specific strengths are noted, such as a pitcher's ability to hold runners on base or if a batter can hit certain pitches. Anything of importance is in the system!

It seems ironic that a game that hasn't changed in a century has embraced the latest technology to improve its product. It also seems odd that computer automation will make a difference on the field. But sometimes all it takes to make a difference is the addition of one or two players at the right time—and that's what the owners are hoping for. In the end a real person makes the decisions but it's hoped the decisions will be better ones!

Adapted from Ted Smalley Bowen, "IT scores a hit with baseball scouts," *Globe and Mail*, July 11, 2002, p. B11.

Pat Sullivan/CP Photo Archive

63

is Statistics Canada, which provides census information (population and household trends, income, education, and occupation trends) and information on all aspects of the economy (employment, inflation, interest rates, domestic production, and international trade, to name a few) for free or a small fee. Much of this information is published in *The Market Research Handbook* and *The Canada Yearbook*, and it is readily available in summary form online from the Statistics Canada website. At the federal and provincial levels, the department or ministry involved with industry, trade, and commerce is the most common source of business information. At the municipal level, the departments of economic development publish reports relevant to their municipalities. For a summary of other sources of secondary information, refer to Figure 3.4.

Basic data can also be obtained from a variety of commercial sources. One of the more prominent commercial providers of secondary information is AC Nielsen Canada. Through a service called MarketTrack, AC Nielsen sells information to business clients on a subscription basis, meaning it provides ongoing reports where data are being continuously updated. MarketTrack provides packaged-goods marketing organizations with brand market share data, distribution data, inventory data, and retail price data from data AC Nielsen collects from national grocery, pharmacy, and mass merchandising

AC Nielsen
www.acnielsen.com

FIGURE
3.4

A Selection of Secondary Information Sources of Interest to Marketers

Source	Examples
Governments	Statistics Canada; *Marketing Research Handbook* (published by Statistics Canada); *Canada Yearbook*; Industry Canada
Newspapers and Business Periodicals	*Globe and Mail Report on Business*; *Report on Business Magazine*; *National Post* (*Financial Post* section); *National Post Business*; *Canadian Business*
Handbooks and Surveys	*The Handbook of Canadian Consumer Markets* published by the Conference Board of Canada; *FP Markets— Canadian Demographics*
Commercial Directories	Dun & Bradstreet (various reports available on financial and credit information); *The Canadian Key Business Directory*; *The Guide to Canadian Manufacturers*; *Fraser's Canadian Trade Index* (directories provide statistical information about manufacturers in Canada)
Industry and Trade Journals	*Canadian Grocer*; *Grocer Today*; *L'Epicier* (high-profile industries usually have a few publications that provide current trend information)
Commercial Research Companies	AC Nielsen Canada, Environics Research Group, The Strategic Counsel (these companies provide syndicated surveys and customized research studies for clients); Print Measurement Bureau, NADbank, BBM Bureau of Measurement (these companies provide media usage and trend data)
Online Data Sources	Company websites; government websites (Statistics Canada data and Industry Canada data); news websites; business periodicals websites (*Marketing* magazine and *Strategy* magazine publish various marketing reports); Internet search engines (Yahoo! Google, etc. facilitate a search of websites)

chains. This service, which is based on scanning technology at point-of-purchase, allows marketers to understand trends and identify market opportunities. The information is available nationally, regionally, and by key markets within some regions.[8]

Environics Research Group is another Canadian research company that conducts several syndicated surveys of interest to marketing organizations. A **syndicated survey** is one where the findings are offered for sale to any organization that has an interest in them. Environics' *Focus Canada Report* is a comprehensive survey of attitudes toward public policy issues and political, economic, and social trends. Published quarterly, the report consists of in-home interviews with 2 000 adult Canadians. The *3SC Social Values Monitor* is an internationally recognized business planning tool that maps the changing values, attitudes, and behaviour of consumers. Organizations can include their own questions on this survey (for a fee). Information obtained from this survey allows an organization to position its products and services in relation to the trends.[9]

A sound understanding of the social values of a specific target market often has a direct impact on the nature and style of a new advertising campaign. The message will appeal to the values held by the target. To demonstrate, consider the situation that Labatt Blue faced. Among young beer drinkers Blue had an image for being "dad's beer." Its "Out of the Blue" advertising strategy wasn't resonating with 21- to 25-year-old males. Blue conducted some lifestyle research and discovered what guys do with their friends, to their friends, or for their friends. The information set the stage for a new campaign using the theme "Cheers. To Friends."

A series of Blue commercials were aired showing what guys are up to, such as tying a naked pal to a telephone pole on his birthday, giving each other wedgies, playing a series of pranks, or just hanging out. Viewers are meant to relate to the antics and call their friends to go for a beer. "This is a very real part of what guys do together," says Andrew Howard, senior director of marketing at Labatt Breweries of Canada.[10]

ONLINE DATABASES   In the past, collecting information from the external data sources listed above was a time-consuming and tedious task. The rapid development of online databases means that information now can be transferred almost instantaneously. An **online database** is a public information database accessible to anyone with electronic communication facilities.

Online databases are available from public and commercial sources. Among public sources available electronically is the federal government's census data (Statistics Canada). Census data are collected every five years. The information collected is very detailed and covers dozens of demographic and socioeconomic topics, such as family and household structures, occupation, income, education, ethnicity, age, marital status, and so on.

From commercial sources such as Dun & Bradstreet, organizations can access **directory databases**. These databases provide a quick picture of a company and its products and services. Typical information includes ownership, size (dollar sales), and location of the company; number of employees; identification of key management personnel and officers; and basic profit data. Examples of directories that are available electronically include *The Canadian Key Business Directory* and *The Canadian Trade Index*. Dun & Bradstreet also provides direct-mail lists and telemarketing lists to companies that want to reach companies with specific characteristics. These particular directories are of interest to business-to-business marketing organizations.

A host of commercial websites also offer information for a fee. Among this group are industry associations, news and information companies, and business publications. When searching for information online, one quickly determines that there are so many sites it is difficult to find the right one. Among the popular news journals that marketers frequently refer to are the *Globe and Mail* and the *National Post*.

Environics Research Group
http://erg.environics.net
syndicated survey

online database

directory databases

FIGURE
3.5 Secondary Data and Online Database Information

Secondary Data

Advantages
1. Information is inexpensive or obtainable at no cost.
2. Information is readily available.
3. Possibly the only source of information (e.g., census data).
4. Useful in exploratory research stage where information is assessed to identify a problem.

Disadvantages
1. The data do not resolve the specific problem under investigation (e.g., data were compiled for another problem or purpose).
2. Reliability and accuracy of data are questionable.
3. Information can be outdated, even obsolete, for the intended situation.

Information from an Online Database

Advantages
1. Data are available very quickly (on the spot).
2. Identification of relevant data occurs quickly.

Disadvantages
1. Amount of data available is overwhelming (discourages use of data).
2. Hidden costs associated with retrieval and distribution of data (e.g., cost per hour for computer time).

Secondary data offer the marketing organization numerous advantages and disadvantages. For a list of these advantages and disadvantages, see Figure 3.5.

PRIMARY RESEARCH

primary research

If secondary research does not resolve the problem, the research process moves to another stage: the collection of primary data. **Primary research** refers to the process of collecting and recording new data, called primary data, in order to resolve a specific problem, usually at a high cost to the sponsoring organization. Primary research is custom designed and focuses on resolving a particular question or obtaining specified information. A procedure is developed and a research instrument designed to perform the specific task. In directing the primary research, the marketing organization identifies the precise nature of the problem, the objectives of the study, and the hypotheses associated with it. **Research objectives** are statements that outline what the research is to accomplish, while **hypotheses**, which are statements of predicted outcomes, are confirmed or refuted by the data collected. Consider the following example:

research objectives

hypotheses

> **Research Objective:** To determine the impact of an emotional style of advertising on adults 25 to 49 years of age.

> **Research Hypothesis:** An emotional style of advertising will generate significantly higher recognition and recall scores than other types of message appeal techniques.

In this case, the findings of the research will be compared to the norms achieved in similar studies for other products using other styles of advertising. Such comparisons will determine the effectiveness or ineffectiveness of emotional messages. Research companies have access to such data and provide this type of comparison when needed.

The outcome of the research often leads to certain actions by the marketing organization. In the above-mentioned example, if the hypothesis is proven the client may adopt a new style of advertising. Refer to Figure 3.6 for a summary of the steps involved in primary research.

Conducting a marketing research study is beyond the scope and expertise of most marketing organizations in Canada. Consequently, independent market research firms are hired to perform the task. Usually, a marketing research manager from the sponsoring organization is responsible for supervising the research study and works directly with the marketing research firm in designing the project.

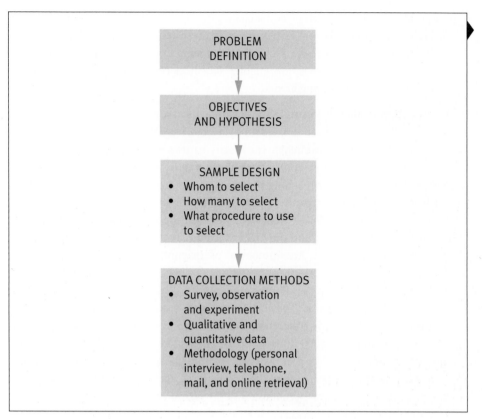

FIGURE
3.6
Primary Research Steps

SAMPLE DESIGN   Prior to implementing a research study, the researchers identify the characteristics of the people they would like to participate in the study. This process is referred to as *sample designing*. A **sample** is defined as a representative portion of an entire population that is used to obtain information about that population. A sample must form an accurate representation of the population if the information gathered is to be considered reliable. Some basic steps have to be taken to develop a representative sample:

sample

1. ***Define the Population (Universe)***—It should be first pointed out that the terms "population" and "universe" are interchangeable in research terminology. A **population** is a group of people with certain specific age, gender, or other demographic characteristics. Defining a population involves identifying its basic characteristics. For the purposes of primary research, a description of a population might be "male golfers between the ages of 21 and 45 years living in cities with over 500 000 residents." A proper research procedure will screen potential respondents for these characteristics.

population

2. ***Identify the Sampling Frame***—The **sampling frame** refers to a listing that can be used for reaching a population. The telephone directory could be used as a sampling frame for the golf population described above, as could a subscription list from *Score* or *Golf* magazines. If Sears wanted to conduct research among its current customers, it could use its credit card account holder list as a means of access. Membership lists from various associations are often useful for identifying potential respondents.

sampling frame

3. ***Determine the Type of Sample***—The researcher has the option of using a probability sample or a non-probability sample. If a **probability sample** is used, the

probability sample

respondents have a known or equal chance of selection and are randomly selected from across the population. For example, the researcher may use a predetermined and systematic procedure for picking respondents through a telephone directory. The known chance of selection enables statistical procedures to be used in the results to estimate sampling errors.

non-probability sample

In a **non-probability sample**, the respondents have an unknown chance of selection, and their being chosen is based on such factors as convenience for the researcher or the judgment of the researcher. The researcher uses his or her experience to determine who would be most appropriate. For example, an independent retailer may conduct a survey by approaching potential customers who visit the store. Factors such as cost and timing are other reasons for using non-probability samples.

4. *Determine the Sample Size*—Generally, the larger the sample, the greater the accuracy of the data collected and the higher the cost. The nature of the research study is a determining factor in the number of participants required. Some researchers use a 1-percent rule (1 percent of the defined population or universe), while others state absolute minimums of 200 respondents. To illustrate the concept of sample size, consider the Environics *Social Values Monitor* research study referred to earlier in the chapter. This study collects data on social values and trends in Canada each year using a sample of 2000 households, but the data gathered are projected across the entire population. The accuracy of the sample is usually calculated statistically and stated in the research report. Therefore, a researcher takes into consideration the margin of error that is acceptable and the degree of certainty required.

DATA COLLECTION METHODS   There are three primary methods a researcher can use to collect data: surveys, observation, and experiments (Figure 3.7), and the data collected can be either qualitative or quantitative in nature.

survey research

Survey Research   For **survey research**, data are collected systematically through some form of communication with a representative sample by means of a questionnaire that records responses. Most surveys include predetermined questions and a selection of responses that are easily filled in by the respondent. This technique is referred to as

fixed-response questioning

fixed-response questioning. Survey research is conducted by personal interview, telephone, and mail, and online through company websites.

A survey is usually designed to be structured or unstructured. In a structured survey, the questionnaire follows a planned format: screening questions at the beginning,

---

FIGURE
3.7   **Data Collection Methods**

Survey
- A systematic collection of data made by communicating with a representative sample, usually by using a questionnaire
- Disguised or undisguised, structured or unstructured formats are used

Observation
- Behaviour of respondent is observed by personal, mechanical, or electronic means

Experiments
- The manipulation of variables under controlled conditions to observe respondents' reactions
- Good for testing marketing influences (e.g., product formula changes, package design alternatives, advertising copy tests)

central-issue questions (those dealing with the nature of the research) in the middle, and classification (demographic) questions at the end. In the case of questions dealing with the specific nature of the issue, a funnelling technique is used. **Funnelling** (of questions) refers to the use of general questions initially, progressing to more specific questions as the respondent proceeds through the questionnaire. As described above, fixed-response questions that list possible answers (e.g., tick-off or multiple-choice questions) are the most popular. They permit the data to be easily transferred to a computer for tabulation and subsequent analysis.

Observation Research   In **observation research**, the behaviour of the respondent is observed and recorded. In this form of research a person knowingly or unknowingly can participate in a study. To illustrate, the purchase behaviour of people in a supermarket can be observed in person or by electronic means. The behaviour of a shopper accepting or rejecting a product could be the focus of such a study. In other situations, respondents are usually aware of being observed, perhaps through a two-way mirror, by a hidden camera while being interviewed, by agreeing to be followed, or by electronic measurement of impulses. See the illustration in Figure 3.8.

Observation research in retail stores using hidden cameras is growing in popularity in the United States, but its use is somewhat restricted in Canada due to privacy laws. The goal of electronic observation is to determine why some products sell well and others fail. By following individual shoppers and analyzing traffic patterns it is possible to determine a store's "hot zones and cold zones." Some soft drink companies use such data to determine best locations for displays; beer companies use the data to determine if beer in a refrigerator sells better than beer sitting on a shelf at room temperature. Since a natural shopping environment is being observed, companies place high value in what they observe.[11]

Many companies now hire anthropologists to gather deeper consumer insight. What they discover can enhance positioning strategies and assist with new-product launches. Anthropologists go on "cultural digs," excavating the lives of real people. They will go shopping with people, follow them around, and watch how they interact with others. Scott Paper placed an anthropologist in selected homes to observe women 25 to 54 years old. The goal was to build a brand idea by finding out what *really* goes on in the bathroom. Scott discovered that women view the bathroom as a place where they can have a moment of solitude and privacy. For many women, the bathroom is a shrine.[12]

From such knowledge a marketing idea was born! Cashmere Cottonelle toilet paper was positioned as a luxury brand. It was aligned with the idea that solitude can be a luxury in a hectic life. One of Cashmere's print ads shows a roll of toilet paper unfurling into a cashmere scarf (see the advertising illustration in Figure 3.9).

Electronic observation on the Internet tracks people's surfing and purchase behaviour. Electronic observation is achieved through cookies. A **cookie** is an electronic identification tag sent from a web server to a user's browser to track surfing patterns, such as ads clicked, products purchased, and sites visited, and to determine the user's origin. Cookies help companies personalize marketing messages for web users.

Experimental Research   In **experimental research**, one or more factors are manipulated under controlled conditions while other elements remain constant, so that respondents' reactions can be evaluated. With this type of research the test market is the acid test for a new product or service. **Test marketing** involves placing a product for sale in one or more limited markets that are representative of the whole in order to observe the product's performance under a proposed marketing plan. Good test marketing

funnelling (of questions)

observation research

Scott Paper
www.scottpaper.ca

cookie

experimental research

test marketing

**FIGURE
3.8**

A person's shopping
behaviour can be observed
personally or electronically

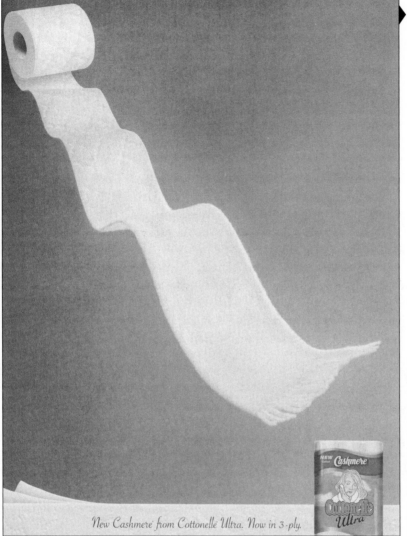

New Cashmere from Cottonelle Ultra. Now in 3-ply.

Company: Scott Paper Limited. Agency: john st.

FIGURE
3.9

Insights collected from observation research helped position Cashmere as a luxury brand. It was aligned with the idea that solitude can be a luxury in a hectic life

provides a marketing organization with three main benefits: it allows the organization to observe consumers' reactions to the product; it enables alternative marketing strategies to be evaluated (e.g., different strategies can be tested in different geographic markets); and it provides experience prior to an expensive regional or national launch.

Information gained from test marketing is useful for planning. For example, actual trend data for sales and market share can be used to forecast similar data should a product be launched regionally or nationally. As well, the effect that a new product will have on the sales of current similar products can be considered. Such an effect is often referred to as **cannibalization** or **cannibalization rate**—the rate at which a new product reduces the sales of an existing product. Finally, a company can determine the characteristics of consumers who will buy the product (i.e., knowledge of demographic and psychographic characteristics will help define pricing and promotion strategies).

The case of Dairy Queen illustrates test marketing in action. Ice cream typically comes to mind when Dairy Queen is mentioned—not hamburgers. But in several Canadian locations, including Fredericton and Vancouver, Dairy Queen is test marketing a new concept called Dairy Queen Grill and Chill. The concept includes updated store décor, table service, a premium burger patty, a new style of bun, and new grilled sandwiches—a dramatic change from traditional Dairy Queen outlets. Dairy Queen has

cannibalization
(cannibalization rate)

determined that the casual restaurant business is growing and that consumers are willing to pay more for a high-quality offering. The test markets will prove or disprove this notion. If the stores are a success, then more will be opened across Canada.[13]

In contemporary marketing, there are those who believe test marketing is absolutely essential and those who believe it is a stage that can be skipped. Information Resources Inc., a large provider of test market services, recommends that at least two markets be tested, not only to compare the impact of different demographics but also to cancel out the potential effects of natural disasters, plant closings, or other purely local factors.[14] The opposite view is that competition is so intense today that a test market tips off the competition as to what a company is doing and gives them time to react. As well, advancing technology is shortening the life cycles of many products. If a product stays too long in the test market, a competitor could launch its product first. The product in the test market would then look like a follower rather than a leader.

A company is well advised to assess the pros and cons of test marketing and make a decision to use it or not on a case-by-case basis. For example, products that involve a high financial risk should be tested initially. Products considered to be fads would not have time to be tested before the financial opportunity would be lost. On the world stage Canada is becoming known as a hotbed for new-product launches—in effect, Canada is perceived by global marketers to be an ideal testing ground prior to expansion to other countries. For more details, read the Marketing in Action vignette **Pfizer Tests in Canada**.

QUALITATIVE DATA VERSUS QUANTITATIVE DATA   According to the nature of the information sought, research data are classified as qualitative or quantitative. There are significant differences between these classifications.

qualitative data

Qualitative Data   **Qualitative data** are usually collected from small samples in a controlled environment. They result from questions concerned with "why" and from in-depth probing of the participants. Typically, such data are gathered from focus group interviews. A **focus group** is a small group of people (8 to 10) with common characteristics (e.g., a target market profile), brought together to discuss issues related to the marketing of a product or service.

focus group

The word "focus" implies that the discussion concentrates on one topic or concept. A trained moderator usually conducts the interview. The role of the moderator is to get the participants to interact fairly freely in order to uncover the reasons and motivations underlying their remarks. Probing uncovers the hidden interplay of psychological factors that drive a consumer to buy one brand rather than another. The major drawback of using focus groups concerns the reliability of the data. The sample size is too small to be representative of the entire population, and most people in a focus group do not like to show disagreement with a prevailing opinion. For that reason interviews are held in several locations.

A typical session lasts about two hours and costs between $3500 and $4500. High-volume marketers like breweries, banks, and packaged-goods companies hold sessions weekly or more often. A major packaged-goods company can spend $30 000 for one eight-session study, which is considered the minimum needed to find out anything important. Sessions are typically planned in various regions and cities to obtain a cross-section of perspectives.

Marketing decisions involving considerable sums of money are very risky if based on such limited research. But while most marketers acknowledge that focus groups aren't scientific, the participant's offhand reactions regularly produce major changes to product and promotional strategies. The Oland Specialty Beer Company recently mothballed a

MARKETING IN ACTION

Pfizer Tests in Canada

If it works in Canada, it's bound to work elsewhere—or so many packaged-goods marketers believe. In recent years several large companies have used Canada as a test market for products with global aspirations. What is the logic behind this strategy?

There are several reasons why Canada is viewed as an ideal test market. First, we have an increasingly diverse population that enables marketers to isolate various consumer segments. Second, a product's performance can be monitored in urban versus suburban, or east versus west markets.

The urban versus suburban capability is of interest to products ultimately going to the United States. Urban success is crucial there. For a global launch, testing in Canada can reduce the risk and give marketers better insights due to the ethnicity of the market.

Pfizer Consumer Healthcare (Canada) tested its Listerine PocketPaks in Canada. The rationale for selecting Canada is clearly stated by Graham Robertson, category manager oral care products: "If you compare Canada to other countries on the map, it seems big enough to make an impact and to see how the product really does. Yet it's still small enough to make any changes if need be. That's why it makes such a great test market."

For Pfizer, Canada also offered low-cost media alternatives that reach a very urban population. Urban response to the product was critical before going to the United States. Testing a product in a small market like Canada enables companies to smooth out the wrinkles on the production and marketing side of things. Pfizer knew that Listerine PocketPaks would be a tricky product to manufacture, so it was imperative to have a good handle on what the demand would be before going to the United States.

Sleek translucent packaging combined with *Matrix*-inspired advertising starring a female action hero who destroys hideous aliens made PocketPaks a hit with the 15- to 30-year-old target in Canada. It is now the number-one brand in the portable breath freshener category. When the product was launched in the United States the only change in marketing strategy was the advertising. The action hero theme used for all Listerine products in Canada is unique. U.S. marketing managers went with an entirely different advertising strategy.

Pfizer Consumer Healthcare (Canada) is now testing Listerine mouthwash with fluoride. In summing up the Canadian test-market situation, Brand Manager Tanya Willer states: "This is an educated market that is marketing sensitive. People here are smart consumers, so that challenges you to come up with the right marketing strategy. If you could win here, you could probably win elsewhere in the world with some local customization."

Procter & Gamble also chose Canada to test market the Swiffer WetJet largely due to our demographic composition. The success of Swiffer WetJet in Canada led to a strong launch in the United States and Europe. In fact, the brand is now a $350-million business.

Adapted from Lisa D'Inocenzo, "America's testing ground," *Strategy*, March 10, 2003, pp. 1, 9.

Pfizer Canada Inc.

successful, long-running ad campaign for Alexander Keith's beer after hearing calls for a fresh approach from respondents in a single round of focus groups. As Rob McCarthy, Keith's national marketing manager, said "You have to trust your judgement and experience in these situations."[15]

In the automobile market, DaimlerChrylser initially received a mixed reaction from focus groups for its PT Cruiser. Some people said the car was too toy-like. The company responded by adding bigger fenders, a smaller rear window, and a sloping roofline. The retooled Cruiser received a positive response in focus groups. The vehicle became one of Chrysler's all-time bestsellers. In contrast, General Motors is placing less emphasis on focus groups. Vice-chairman Robert Lutz wants to limit consumer input on car design, saying, "It's like trying to drive by looking in the rearview mirror."[16] Perhaps the customer will decide if such a viewpoint is appropriate.

Marketers should be aware that focus groups are exploratory in nature. A follow-up quantitative survey is required to establish numbers, which costs organizations additional money and time. On the positive side, attitudes that are revealed in a focus group can be used as a foundation for formulating questions and questionnaires if and when quantitative research is required. The attitudes uncovered can be expressed as answers for closed-ended questions in a questionnaire.

Qualitative research also reinforces the beliefs, attitudes, and convictions of marketing managers. For example, unsubstantiated beliefs or attitudes that a marketing manager may have had prior to the research (e.g., that the perceived quality of the product is not as high as expected) can be confirmed in the discussion among participants. Hearing responses in a focus group has greater impact than an impersonal and voluminous statistical study. Qualitative research is best applied to exploratory topics—detailing processes, building hypotheses, and refining ideas. It can be used to set the direction for further in-depth studies.[17]

quantitative data

Quantitative Data **Quantitative data** provide answers to questions concerned with "what," "when," "who," "how many," and "how often." This research attempts to put feelings, attitudes, and opinions into numbers and percentages. The data are gathered from structured questionnaires and a large sample to ensure accuracy and reliability. The interpretation of results is based on the numbers compiled, not on the judgment of the researcher. For this reason, it is a tool that is used for measuring and evaluating rather than investigating and exploring. Quantitative research will statistically confirm the attitudes and feelings that arose in qualitative research, and for this reason a marketer can have more confidence in the decisions that are made based on the research. A brief comparison of qualitative and quantitative research is provided in Figure 3.10

In today's marketplace, the respective roles of qualitative research and quantitative research are changing. There is a tendency for companies to do more qualitative research. Not to diminish the value of quantitative research, the numbers are included in a report to support the actions taken by marketers. At Molson, for example, there is a vice-president accountable for marketing research. Molson does focus groups and qualitative research but it also does quantitative research on all television ads before production of the ad takes place. Each ad must hit a specific persuasion level. "We do not shoot ads until we know they will persuade beer drinkers to drink that brand," says Michael Downey, Molson senior vice-president, global marketing.[18]

SURVEY METHODOLOGY   There are four primary means of contacting consumers when conducting surveys to collect quantitative data: personal interviews, telephone interviews, mail interviews, and the Internet. **Personal interviews** involve face-to-face

personal interviews

FIGURE
3.10 Comparing Qualitative and Quantitative Research

Qualitative Research	Quantitative Research
• Collected from a small sample group • Question format is unstructured • Questions deal with why people act, do, purchase, etc. • Small sample poses reliability (of data) problems	• Collected data from a truly representative sample (e.g., 200–300 people who represent a specified target market) • Structured format (e.g., questionnaire with pre-determined responses) is common • Questions deal with what, when, who, how many, and how often • Data are statistically reliable; degree of error can be calculated

communication with groups (e.g., focus groups) or with individuals and are usually done through quantitative questionnaires. Popular locations for interviews are busy street corners, shopping malls, and the homes of respondents. Trained interviewers provide guidance and explain difficult questions to respondents if necessary.

Telephone interviews involve communication with individuals via the telephone. Usually, the interviews are conducted from central locations (e.g., one central location can reach all Canadian markets), and consequently there is supervised control over the interview process. Generally speaking, telephone interviews yield higher response rates than the other data collection methods.

telephone interviews

Market researchers are finding it increasingly difficult to find Canadians who are willing and available to take part in telephone surveys. A recent survey by the Professional Marketing Research Society found that 78 percent of people whom market researchers reach on the phone refuse to participate. A reason for the high refusal rate is consumer confusion between marketing research and telemarketing. Some companies pitch products under the guise of marketing research and such a practice has negatively impacted the research business.[19]

Professional Marketing Research Society
www.pmrs-aprm.com

Mail interviews are a silent process of collecting information. Using the mail to distribute a survey means that a highly dispersed sample is reached in a cost-efficient manner. In a mail interview there is no interviewer present, so there is a tendency for respondents to provide more honest answers. The main drawbacks are the lack of control and the amount of time required to implement and retrieve the surveys. As a result, response rates tend to be lower.

mail interviews

Online surveys on the Internet allow an organization to be much less invasive in collecting information. Some companies have actually found that consumers seem more willing to divulge information over the Internet compared with the more traditional means of surveying. As well, it takes less time to get results.

online surveys

When McCain Foods launched its new Roasters brand of frozen potato products, it used online research to survey 1 000 consumers. The turnaround time from start to finish was two months, a time frame impossible to duplicate by any other research method. Coca-Cola used online concept testing to determine what new flavours to add to the Fruitopia single-serving product line. A **concept test** is a test to determine what new-product ideas are worth pursuing before a significant investment is made in development. In the Fruitopia test, more than 3000 respondents took part. So accurate were the results that Fruitopia sales volume grew by 30 percent in the market.[20]

concept test

Compared to traditional data collection methods, online research provides information more quickly and at a much lower cost. Since marketers will be able to make decisions more quickly in an ever-changing marketplace, it is expected that online research techniques will grow in importance. It is a tool marketers will use to gain competitive advantage. On the downside, recruiting participation can be a lot like fishing—participation is left up to the fish. Therefore, the validity of the information is questionable. The information collected may not truly represent the feelings of the target market the company is trying to reach.

The fact that more than 60 percent of Canadians aged 15 and over currently have access to the Internet at home, at work, or at some other location, with that number increasing each year, bodes well for the future of online research.

The decision about which of these survey techniques to use is based on three primary factors:

1. *Nature of Information Sought*—The amount of information to be collected and the time it will take to complete the survey are considerations. For example, if discussion is necessary to get the answers needed, personal interviews in a focus group may be best. If large amounts of information are required, the best option may be the mail.

2. *Cost and Time*—When time is critical, certain options are eliminated. The telephone and the Internet are the best means of obtaining quick, cost-efficient information. Costs must also be weighed against benefits. The net financial gains expected to result from the research may determine which method is to be used.

3. *Respondent*—The selection of a survey method can be influenced by the location of the respondents and how easily they can be reached. For example, if the participant is to be reached at home, any method—personal interview, telephone, mail, or online—can be used. Responding online is very convenient for people. In contrast, if the participant has to be reached in a central location, such as a shopping mall, a personal interview is the only choice.

Refer to Figure 3.11 for a summary of the advantages and disadvantages of each survey method.

DATA TRANSFER AND PROCESSING

editing

data transfer

Once the data have been collected, editing, data transfer, and tabulation take place. In the **editing** stage, completed questionnaires are reviewed for consistency and completeness. Whether to include questionnaires with incomplete or seemingly contradictory answers is left to the discretion of the researcher. In the **data transfer** stage, answers to questions are transferred to a computer. On quantitative questionnaires, most questions are closed ended (require fixed-response answers), and all answers are pre-coded to facilitate the transfer. In the case of telephone surveys, it is now common to enter the responses directly into the computer as the questions are being asked.

tabulation

frequency distribution

cross-tabulation

Once the survey results have been entered into a computer, the results are tabulated. **Tabulation** is the process of counting the various responses for each question and arriving at a frequency distribution. A **frequency distribution** shows the number of times each answer was chosen for a question. Numerous cross-tabulations are also made. **Cross-tabulation** is the comparison and contrasting of the answers of various subgroups or of particular subgroups and the total response group. For example, a question dealing with brand awareness could be analyzed by the age, gender, or income of respondents. Computer software is used to produce tabulated results in a presentable format (rows and columns of numbers).

FIGURE
FIGURE
3.11   **Survey Methodology for Collecting Quantitative Data**

PERSONAL INTERVIEW

Advantages

- Higher rates of participation
- Visual observations possible by interviewer
- Flexibility (e.g., inclusion of visuals possible)
- Large amounts of data collected

Disadvantages

- Higher cost (time needed)
- Reluctance to respond to certain questions
- Interviewer bias is possible

TELEPHONE INTERVIEW

Advantages

- Convenience and control
- Costs less
- Timely responses
- Geographic flexibility

Disadvantages

- Lack of observation
- Short questions and questionnaire
- Can be viewed as an invasion of privacy

MAIL SURVEYS

Advantages

- Geographic flexibility in selecting target
- Cost-efficient
- Large sample obtainable
- Respondent in relaxed environment
- Impersonality results in more accurate responses

Disadvantages

- Lack of control
- The time between distribution and return is long
- Potential for misinterpretation by respondent
- Low response rates

ONLINE RESEARCH

Advantages

- Efficient and inexpensive reach (elimination of telephone and humans)
- Less intrusive than traditional methods
- Convenient for respondent
- Fast turnaround of information (2–3 days versus 4–5 weeks)

Disadvantages

- Respondent voluntarily participates, so respondent authenticity is questioned
- Limited sample frame (Internet users only)
- Research via bulk e-mail associated with spam (Internet junk mail)
- Reliability of information is questionable

DATA ANALYSIS AND INTERPRETATION

Data analysis refers to the evaluation of responses on a question-by-question basis, a process that gives meaning to the data. At this point, the statistical data for each question are reviewed, and the researcher makes observations about them. Typically, a researcher makes comparisons between responses of subgroups on a percentage or ratio basis.

data analysis

Data interpretation, on the other hand, involves relating the accumulated data to the problem under review and to the objectives and hypotheses of the research study. The process of interpretation uncovers solutions to the problem. The researcher draws conclusions that state the data's implications for managers. For example, Nestlé Canada conducted extensive consumer research before it reintroduced its Coffee Crisp brand. The research was designed to learn how chocolate and snacks fit into consumers' lives. Brand manager Mark Wilson jokingly acknowledges that "We found out, surprise, surprise, that Coffee Crisp is about the taste of coffee, not a dark rich taste but a light, fun taste." The research determined that Coffee Crisp owns the coffee position. It is a unique attribute that creates equity for the brand. Ultimately, the research was the impetus for launching two new flavours: Triple Mocha and French Vanilla.[21]

data interpretation

FIGURE
3.12 Applying Marketing Research: Research Leads to New Advertising Campaign for Kraft Dinner

---

Advantages

Kraft Dinner is the country's number-one-selling grocery item with a 75-percent share of its category and Kraft Canada's biggest volume business. Despite such a lofty status sales were flat and had been for some time.

Problem

To discover just what was ailing this powerhouse brand. It was hypothesized that erosion in brand confidence among consumers was due to the fact there was no communication with people to find out what they love about Kraft Dinner.

Marketing Research Procedure

A methodology was employed that would create a personality profile for the brand. There would be an exclusive focus on the emotional aura around the brand. The notion of a brand carrying human traits is nearly as old as advertising itself, but it is only lately that psychiatric profiling has been gaining momentum.

To determine Kraft Dinner's personality profile, two specific exercises were undertaken by research participants:

1. "Kraft Dinner has died. You have to write the obituary that goes in your local newspaper."
2. "You're a psychiatrist and Kraft Dinner has come to see you. Analyze the problem and tell him a solution."

Research Findings

From the obituary pages

- "Tragically yesterday the hero of many a Canadian meal died accidentally."
- "He was affectionately known as KD by his many friends."
- "There was an easy way about him that was both knowing and comforting."
- "KD valued his time with friends."

From the psychiatrist's couch

- "Kraft has low self-esteem and insecurity."

- "Kraft Dinner is feeling guilt and anxiety about his image."
- "Kraft has low self-esteem, is old, lethargic, and withdrawn."

Analysis and Interpretation

Kraft Dinner is

- Dependable
- Comfortable
- A friend
- Nonjudgmental
- Easy-going
- Unpretentious
- Trustworthy
- Loved by all

Recommended Therapy

- Build self-confidence
- Remember and promote the immortal place he holds in our hearts
- Raise self-esteem
- Get across the point that you are worth more

Actions Taken

Kraft raised the price of Kraft Dinner, redesigned the packaging, launched a new KD Web site and created a series of television commercials targeting young people who grew up eating the product. The ads touched on a person's relationships with Kraft Dinner.

Results

Testing of the commercials revealed that the spots outperformed all others in the category in North America. Already the biggest seller on the grocery shelves, Kraft Dinner experienced a significant increase in base brand sales.

Source: Adapted from Peter Vamos, "Psychological profiling gets inside a brand's head," *Strategy*, August 27, 2000, p. 2.

> 4. Explain what uses are made of secondary and primary research data in resolving marketing problems.

RECOMMENDATIONS AND IMPLEMENTATION

The recommendations outline suggested courses of action that the sponsoring organization should take in view of the data collected. Once a research project is complete, the research company will present its findings in a written report. Frequently, an oral presentation of the key findings is also made to the client. Very often senior management is informed of the data as it becomes known, so that the managers are better prepared for possible actions or changes in strategic direction. Preparing senior managers in this way is important, particularly if the proposed actions are in conflict with their personal views and feelings. The managers most likely to implement research findings are those who participate in research design, have the flexibility to make decisions, and see research findings that confirm their intentions.

These days, thanks to changing technology and faster turnaround times, market research is more streamlined, with clients expecting solid decision-making results—yesterday. Voluminous research reports, often referred to as "doorstoppers" are being replaced by personal presentations using PowerPoint or the like to display succinct objectives and results, rather than extensive tables and numbers.

For a more complete look at how marketing research influences the direction of marketing strategy refer to Figure 3.12. The figure identifies a problem faced by Kraft Dinner, outlines the research procedures used to obtain information, and shows the actions taken as a result of the information.

SUMMARY

Marketing research must be viewed as a tool that assists the manager in the decision-making process. It is a systematic procedure that, if used properly, will produce reliable and valid data. Most organizational research falls into three key categories: market analysis, product analysis, and consumer analysis.

The research process begins with a firm's becoming aware of a problem situation. From there, exploratory research is conducted to narrow the scope of the investigation. To do so requires the consultation of knowledgeable people and secondary data sources. Advancing computer technology and the availability of online database information now provide a company with the information it needs, quickly. A database is the nucleus of the organization's management information system. This system ensures the continuous and orderly flow of information to the decision makers, who use the information to develop marketing strategies.

The integration of interactive decision support systems now allows managers to evaluate "what if" situations. Progressive-minded companies are now involved in a new procedure called data mining. Data mining provides an organization with a means of converting raw data into useful information that can be used to identify and implement more effective marketing strategies. Information for the database is collected from in-house sources, external secondary sources, and online database sources.

If the problem is not resolved at this stage, the next step is primary research. The initial phase of primary research involves clearly defining the problem and establishing research objectives and hypotheses. Primary research is the gathering of new data from a representative sample. The process requires the determination of whom and how many should participate in the sample. These decisions are part of the sample design process.

Primary data are collected from surveys, observation, and experiments. Survey data are qualitative or quantitative in nature. Qualitative data are collected by focus group interviews or by one-on-one interviews and answer the question "why." Quantitative data are obtained by questionnaires through personal interview, telephone, and mail or online surveys and involve translating thoughts and feelings into measurable numbers. Once the data are secured, they are computer processed for analysis and interpretation by the researcher.

Experimental research involves testing a marketing mix activity within a controlled situation in order to measure the effectiveness of the activity. Test marketing is an example of experimental research. In a test market, a product is placed in a representative market so that its performance under a proposed marketing plan can be observed.

The research process is complete when the marketing research company presents its findings to the client. In a written report and verbal presentation the research company interprets the data and makes recommendations based on the problem that the research study was addressing.

KEY TERMS

REVIEW QUESTIONS

1. In the context of marketing research, what is the relationship between the following sets of terms?
   a) Secondary data and primary data
   b) Research objectives and hypotheses
   c) Observational and experimental techniques
   d) Population and sampling frame
   e) Qualitative data and quantitative data
   f) Probability sample and non-probability sample
   g) Frequency distribution and cross-tabulation
   h) Tabulation and cross-tabulation
   i) Data analysis and data interpretation

2. What is the "problem awareness" stage of the marketing research process?

3. What is the difference between funnelling and situation analysis in the exploratory research stage?

4. What is a decision support system? What are its uses?

5. What is data mining, and what advantages does it offer a marketing organization?

6. What are the advantages and disadvantages of secondary data sources?

7. Briefly explain the four steps in the sample design process.

8. What is the difference between survey research and observation research?

9. What purpose does a test market serve?

10. What is a "focus group?" What are the benefits of focus group research?

11. Under what circumstances would you use the telephone for collecting survey data? When would you use the personal interview?

DISCUSSION AND APPLICATION QUESTIONS

1. "Decisions based on qualitative data are not risky." Discuss this statement by examining the nature of information collected by qualitative research.

2. Many experts doubt the reliability and validity of online research surveys, but many marketing organizations see online research as a quick and convenient means of securing information from customers. Conduct some secondary research on the usefulness of online surveys and form a position on the issue. Will online surveys continue to grow in importance?

3. You are about to devise a new advertising strategy (a message strategy) for the Porsche Boxster. You do not know how to present the automobile to potential customers and would like to find out more about them. What information would you like to obtain, and what procedure would you recommend to obtain it?

E-ASSIGNMENTS

1. Visit the Molson "I AM" website (**www.IAM.ca**). Proceed through the registration procedure. In terms of marketing research, what is the value of the information that Molson is requesting? How do you think Molson will use this information? Reassess the situation over a period of time; that is, after you have received some communications from this website.

2. Select a market where there is a clear brand leader and brand challenger (e.g., Colgate and Crest toothpastes, Coca-Cola and Pepsi-Cola, Gillette and Schick razors). Visit the website for each brand with the objective to document relevant marketing information. Is the website a useful source of competitive information? What is your opinion? Do any of the sites attempt to collect information about you? What is the value of the information they are collecting?

ENDNOTES

1. Dana Flavelle, "New store shortens exit trek," *Toronto Star*, July 24, 2003, pp. C1, C12.

2. "New definition of marketing research approved," *Marketing News*, January 22, 1987, p. 1.

3. Michelle Warren, "Caution! Floss ahead," *Marketing*, April 5/12, 2004, p. 4.

4. Carl McDaniel and Roger Gates, *Marketing Research Essentials* (St. Paul, MN: West Publishing company, 1995), p. 89.

5. Shirley Won, "Unconventional road maps gives retailers an edge," *Globe and Mail*, May 25, 2004, p. B11.

6. Ross Waring, "The promise and reality of data mining," *Strategy*, June 7, 1999, p. D9.

7. Kevin Marron, "Tools for taming data chaos," *Globe and Mail*, September 6, 2002, p. T1.

8. www.acnielsen.ca/ProductsandServices.

9. www.erg.environics.net/services/default.asp.

10. Michelle Warren, "Labatt smiling over new Blue work," *Marketing*, March 3, 2003, p. 3.

11. John Heinzl, "Some retailers watching every move," *Globe and Mail*, May 3, 2002, p. B10.

12. Andrea Zoe Aster, "Digging deeper," *Marketing*, November 22, 2004, p. 31.

13. Shawna Richer, "Dairy Queen tests tasty new brands in Maritimes," *Globe and Mail*, July 23, 2003, p. B21.

14. Jack Neff, "White Bread, USA," *Advertising Age*, July 9, 2001, pp. 1, 12.

15. Matthew McKinnon, "Focus pocus," *National Post Business*," August 2002, pp. 56–63.

16. Matthew McKinnon, "Dates in Focus: A brief history of talking to consumers," *National Post Business*, August 2002, p. 61.

17. George Stalk and Jill Black, "Consistent mistakes plague customer research," *Globe and Mail*, July 24, 1998, p. B21.

18. Wendy Cuthbert, "Hold the numbers," *Strategy*, June 4, 2001, pp. B6, B7.

19. Colin Flint, "Marketing researchers facing a lot of hang-ups," *Financial Post*, March 26, 2004, p. FP4.

20. Andrea Zoe Aster, "Consumer research goes online," *Marketing*, June 7, 2004, p. 13.

21. Sarah Dobson, "Coffee Crisp targets caffeine crowd," *Marketing*, February 10, 2003, p. 3.

© Don Mason/CORBIS

Consumer Buying Behaviour

The behaviour of Canadian consumers is in a constant state of flux. The expression "the only constant in life is change" holds true here. It is this change that marketing organizations must recognize and act on. Organizations must anticipate changes among consumers and develop the appropriate marketing strategies to meet the challenges of a dynamic marketplace. To keep abreast of change, an organization will implement many of the research procedures that were discussed in the previous chapter.

Marketers must also keep close watch on the various external trends that were presented in Chapter 2 since they also have an impact on consumers' behaviour. To refresh your memory, these key trends included an aging population, changing household formations, an increase in ethnic households particularly in urban areas, advancing technology that is changing the way people buy products, and the cyclical economic trends that impact lifestyles.

This chapter will discuss the dynamics of consumer behaviour and illustrate how marketing organizations use information about behaviour to develop marketing strategies.

What Is Consumer Behaviour?

Consumer behaviour is defined as "the acts of individuals in obtaining goods and services, including the decision processes that precede and determine these acts."[1] An organization must have a firm understanding of how and why consumers make purchase decisions so that appropriate marketing strategies are planned and implemented.

To quickly understand how companies react to behaviour, consider the impact of the low-carbohydrate phenomenon that swept North America in late 2003 and 2004. With the sale of regular products falling in many food categories, companies quickly launched low-carbohydrate line extensions (e.g., low-carb Special K, Pepsi Edge, and Campbell's Carb Request ready-to-serve soup). The low-carbohydrate products were priced higher than regular products. In the rush to capitalize on the trend marketers quickly discovered that consumers were reluctant to pay a premium for poor-tasting products, and the anticipated sales of the new lines did not materialize. If there is a moral to this illustration it is a simple one: what people say (they want) and what people do (actually buy) are often in conflict. This confuses the hell out of marketers.

From a purely competitive viewpoint, marketers must have access to information on consumer buying motivation in order to develop persuasive strategies for getting consumers to buy or use a product. Consequently, large sums of money are allocated to marketing research in order to determine who makes the buying decision and what factors play a role in making the decision.

Prior to examining the factors that influence buying decisions, one should appreciate the steps involved in the decision-making process.

consumer behaviour

1. Explain the role and importance of consumer behaviour with respect to the development of marketing strategies.

2. Describe the steps in the consumer purchase decision process.

The Consumer Purchase Decision Process

Knowing exactly how purchase decisions are made is difficult. While we know that certain variables influence behaviour, there are so many contributing variables that we cannot be certain which ones actually trigger a response. The purchase of a particular brand of product could be the result of an endorsement by a celebrity or a friend; it could be based on past experience with the product; or it could be due to the delivery of a free sample. Every purchase situation is unique. Sometimes, too, a consumer may be governed by rational (logical) behaviour for one purchase and at other times by irrational (emotional) behaviour.

Despite these difficulties, a generic model of the buying decision process may be offered. Essentially, there are five steps in the consumer purchase decision process (Figure 4.1). These steps are problem recognition, information search, evaluating alternatives, purchase decision, and post-purchase evaluation.

Let us examine each step in the decision-making process in detail.

PROBLEM RECOGNITION

problem recognition

The process begins with **problem recognition**. At this stage, a consumer discovers a need or an unfulfilled desire; for example, the muffler on the family station wagon goes, the engine of a 10-year-old automobile finally gives out, or a child outgrows a pair of ice skates. In each case, there is a need to replace the product. A person could also simply decide they want something, like a new plasma-screen television, laptop computer, or cell phone. In this case the purchase process is based more on impulse.

INFORMATION SEARCH

information search

Once the problem or need has been defined, the individual conducts an **information search** to solve the problem. The extent of the search varies with the nature of the purchase. If it is a routine purchase, no information may be sought. If it is a complex

FIGURE
4.1

The Consumer Purchase Decision Process

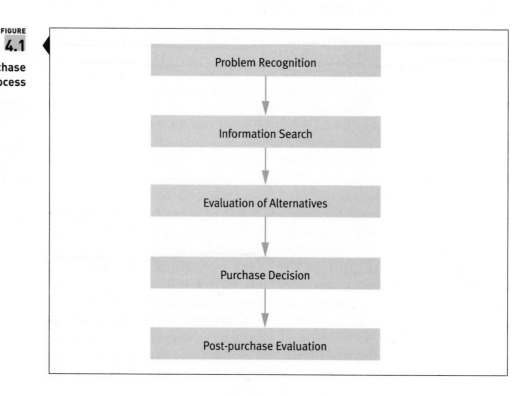

decision, numerous sources of information may be investigated. Generally, as the risk increases (i.e., as the price increases), the extent of the search for information also increases.

Sources of information may be internal or external. For example, your personal experiences with a product may be sufficient to make a new decision. A person will spend little time on the decision to replace a tube of toothpaste or bottle of mouthwash. However, if a person wanted to buy a new car, numerous external sources would be consulted. External sources of information include personal sources (e.g., relatives and friends), public sources (e.g., ratings organizations such as Consumer Reports or the Canadian Automobile Association), and commercial sources (e.g., the marketing activities of companies, including their websites where an abundance of information is available).

It is now very common for consumers to use the Internet to search for information about products they may purchase. Statistics Canada reports that 79 percent of men and 70 percent of women searched the Internet for information on goods and services, by far the most popular activity reported after emailing.[2] Ernst & Young and Maritz Automotive Research Group research shows that 25 percent of people who are in the market to buy a new car use the Internet in their buying process. A majority (83 percent) of this group will use it to search out information, and 13 percent will conduct the transaction online.[3]

The importance of the purchase plays a key role in the time and effort a consumer will spend searching the marketplace for information. Purchase decisions are classified as routine, limited, or complex. ***Routine purchases*** do not involve much money and take little time. Products that are routinely purchased include items subject to brand preference, such as toothpaste, coffee, cigarettes, and deodorant.

In contrast, ***complex*** purchase decisions require a lot of time, effort, money, and a proper evaluation of alternatives. In this case, consumers are more receptive to advertising information and, as indicated above, will visit websites to track down information that may assist them. Products that fall into this category are housing, automobiles, televisions and other electronics equipment, and major household appliances. For example, a young married couple in the midst of decorating their first home (their first big decision) have all kinds of decisions to make about furnishings. For the kitchen, do they purchase traditional-looking white appliances or do they opt for something more contemporary and more expensive such as stainless steel? The couple's lifestyle and how much they are willing to pay for that lifestyle will influence the decision. Regardless, the couple will seek information on brands they may purchase. Refer to Figure 4.2 for an illustration of the purchase decision continuum.

With information in hand, the consumer will move to the next stage.

EVALUATION OF ALTERNATIVES

Let us pursue the example of the purchase of a new automobile. At this stage, a consumer will establish some kind of criteria against which the attributes of the automobile will be evaluated. For a marketer, this is a crucial stage, since the quality of a marketing strategy is being tested. Will the advertising deliver the right message? Will the message be convincing and actually motivate an individual to act on it?

To illustrate the concept of **evaluation**, let us assume that someone is contemplating the purchase of an entry-level luxury car. With such a car, they are looking for a certain amount of value along with prestige, an interesting combination. On the value side, the criteria may include safety, comfort, durability, and price. On the prestige side, the criteria may include the look of the car and its trendy image, performance, and responsiveness. The criteria place the makes of cars in the consumer's **evoked set**. The evoked set is a group of brands that a person would consider acceptable among competing

evaluation ③

evoked set

FIGURE
4.2
The Purchase Decision
Continuum

Factors	Routine Decision	Limited Decision	Complex Decision
Time	Low	Limited	Extensive (Rigid Process)
Evaluation	Minimal	Some	Significant
Preference	Existing Product	Open to New Product	Very Open to New Product Information
Purchase Frequency	Frequent	Moderate	Low
Risk	Low	Moderate	High
Experience	High	Some	Low

brands in a class of products. In this case, the evoked set may include a moderately priced BMW, Mercedes-Benz, Jaguar X-Type, and the Infiniti G35. Manufacturers refer to these cars as downscale luxury cars and price them in the $40 000 to $50 000 range.

PURCHASE DECISION

purchase decision

Once the best alternative has been selected, a consumer is ready to make the **purchase decision**. In the case of the car purchase, the consumer will visit a few dealers and more than likely test-drive the model that is under consideration.

Now, the consumer will go through another decision-making process, as he or she must decide who to buy the car from and when to buy it. These decisions will be based on such factors as price, availability of credit, the level and quality of service, and dealer reputation.

The simultaneous evaluation of the car and the dealer influences the final decision. For example, the customer may forgo his or her first choice—say, the BMW—to take advantage of an extended warranty, better service, and maintenance package offered by the Mercedes dealer.

The decision on when to purchase the car could be based on such circumstances as personal financial situation, the offer of a rebate by a manufacturer, or low financing rates. The latter two are intended to stimulate a more immediate purchase and were initially offered on a seasonal basis or when the economic situation dictates such programs. Consumers are now so accustomed to looking for rebate offers they will actually postpone a purchase decision until one is available.

POST-PURCHASE EVALUATION

Purchases involve risk, and the higher the cost of the purchase, the greater the risk for the consumer. Once the decision to purchase has been made, the delivery order signed, and the bank loan secured, certain common questions arise. Did I make the right decision? Do I feel good, bad, or indifferent about the purchase?

The purchase of routine items is based on past experience and satisfaction; therefore, there is a positive, secure feeling after the purchase that says, "I trust this product." Conversely, other purchases may result in dissatisfaction leading to brand switching, a process involving more purchases and evaluations. Such dissatisfaction is the result of

cognitive dissonance, which is defined as the unsettled state of mind experienced by an individual after he or she has taken action. Its presence suggests that the consumer is not confident that he or she has made the right decision. The customer may begin to wish that another alternative had been chosen as the mind goes through numerous "what if" scenarios.

cognitive dissonance

The consumer can overcome cognitive dissonance by taking certain actions. In the example of the automobile purchase, a person could reread favourable consumer reports, get out the brochures again and review all the positive attributes, or perhaps talk to a friend about the purchase.

From a marketing perspective, the organization should initiate appropriate follow-up activities to put the consumer's mind at ease. In the automobile purchase decision, simply keeping in touch through service reminder notices may be all that is required. Progressive companies understand the importance of satisfaction and realize that the sale is simply the first step in what they hope will be a long-term relationship.

Influences on Consumer Behaviour

3. Describe the influences that affect consumer behaviour and lifestyle choices.

The purchase decisions of Canadian consumers are primarily influenced by psychological, personal, social, and cultural factors. Collectively, these variables represent a dynamic consumer situation that has a dramatic influence on if, how, and when consumers will buy. Understanding the customer is essential if an organization is to maximize the effectiveness of the marketing strategies it devises and implements. Variables such as product, price, availability, and various forms of marketing communication activities are manipulated in such a way that collectively and positively they have an influence on consumers. Refer to Figure 4.3 for a summary of influences on consumer behaviour.

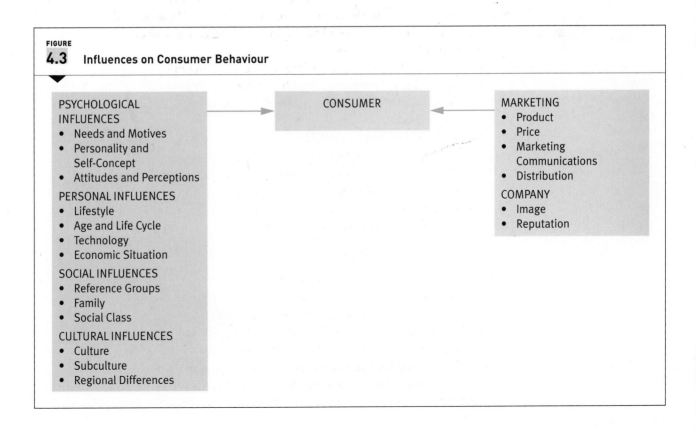

FIGURE 4.3   Influences on Consumer Behaviour

PSYCHOLOGICAL INFLUENCES
- Needs and Motives
- Personality and Self-Concept
- Attitudes and Perceptions

PERSONAL INFLUENCES
- Lifestyle
- Age and Life Cycle
- Technology
- Economic Situation

SOCIAL INFLUENCES
- Reference Groups
- Family
- Social Class

CULTURAL INFLUENCES
- Culture
- Subculture
- Regional Differences

CONSUMER

MARKETING
- Product
- Price
- Marketing Communications
- Distribution

COMPANY
- Image
- Reputation

PSYCHOLOGICAL INFLUENCES

The primary psychological characteristics that influence consumer behaviour and purchase decisions are needs and motives, personality and the self-concept, attitudes and perceptions, and lifestyles.

needs

motives

NEEDS AND MOTIVES   Let us clearly distinguish between needs and motives. The term **needs** suggests a state of deprivation or the absence of something useful, whereas **motives** are the conditions that prompt the action necessary to satisfy a need (the action stimulated by marketing activities). The relationship between needs and motives is direct in terms of marketing activities. Needs are developed or brought to the foreground of consumers' minds when products' benefits are presented to them in an interesting manner (e.g., in conjunction with a lifestyle that the targeted people associate themselves with) so that they are motivated to purchase the product or service.

hierarchy of needs

Needs are classified in an ascending order, from lower-level to higher-level (Figure 4.4). In this **hierarchy of needs**, an individual progresses through five levels:

1. *Physiological Needs*—Food, water, sex, and air (basic survival needs)
2. *Safety Needs*—Security, protection, and comfort
3. *Social Needs*—A sense of belonging; love from family and friends
4. *Esteem Needs*—Recognition, achievement, and status; the need to excel
5. *Self-Actualization Needs*—Fulfillment; realization of your potential (achieving what you believe you can do)

There are two principles at work in this hierarchy:

1. When lower-level needs are satisfied, a person moves up to higher-level needs.
2. Satisfied needs do not motivate. Instead, needs yet to be satisfied influence behaviour.

FIGURE
4.4

The Hierarchy of Needs

Source: Motivation and Personality 3rd edition by Maslow, © Adapted by permission of Pearson Education Inc., Upper Saddle River, NJ.

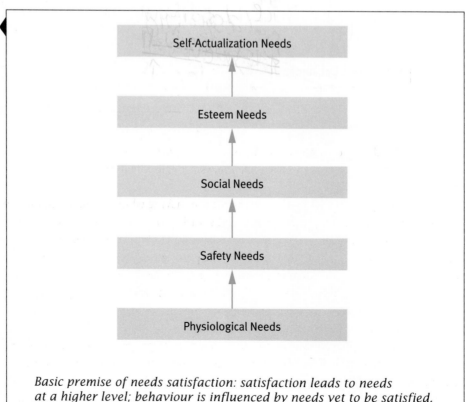

Basic premise of needs satisfaction: satisfaction leads to needs at a higher level; behaviour is influenced by needs yet to be satisfied.

* Trademark, used under license.

The biggest breakthrough in gum since bubbles.

(Now you can whiten your teeth & help keep them that way.)

Trident White PEPPERMINT WHITENS 2 WAYS

Wow. A gum clinically proven to get rid of stains — and help keep stains from coming back. And best of all, it tastes great.

Reprinted by permission of Cadbury Adams Canada Inc.

FIGURE 4.5

Trident White gum appeals to the social needs of consumers

Understanding consumers' needs is essential for a marketing organization. Consider the following example in which a marketer calls attention to the social needs of consumers.

In recent years, consumers have obsessed about having whiter teeth. In response to this need marketers of toothpaste introduced a variety of new products such as Crest Whitestrips and Crest Night Effects and Colgate Total Plus Whitening and Colgate Simply White. Wanting a piece of the action, the gum category launched new products as well. Trident White, for example, promises to get rid of stains and help prevent stains from coming back (see Figure 4.5 for an illustration). The desire to be accepted by peers (that is, the need for social satisfaction) is commonly appealed to in advertising for personal-care products and clothing.

Esteem needs are addressed in messages that portray people in successful business roles and occupations; a senior executive is shown travelling first-class on an airline or driving an automobile symbolic of success, such as a Mercedes-Benz, Porsche, or Jaguar. Messages that depict someone as being attractive to the opposite sex or having lots of friends target social and esteem needs.

personality

PERSONALITY AND SELF-CONCEPT **Personality** refers to a person's distinguishing psychological characteristics, those features that lead to relatively consistent and enduring responses to the environment in which that person lives. It is influenced by self-perceptions that, in turn, are influenced by physiological and psychological needs, family, culture, and reference groups. Why would someone pay $100 000 or more for a Porsche 911 Carrera when a less expensive automobile will perform the same task? Such a purchase is based on the image we desire to have of ourselves. To appreciate this principle, one must understand the self-concept theory.

self-concept theory

Self-concept theory states that the self has four components: real self, self-image, looking-glass self, and ideal self.[4]

1. *Real Self*—An objective evaluation of one's self. You as you really are. One's perception of the real self is often distorted by the influence of the other selves.
2. *Self-Image*—This is how you see yourself. It may not be the real self but rather a role that you play with yourself.
3. *Looking-Glass Self*—How you think others see you. Your view of how others see you can be very different from how they actually see you.
4. *Ideal Self*—This is how you would like to be. It is what you aspire to be.

Marketers use this self-concept theory to their advantage. They know that, human nature being what it is, many important decisions are based on the looking-glass self and the ideal self. Goods and services that help to fulfill the ideal self are appealing to the consumer.

The men's grooming market presents a good illustration of the self-concept. Today's men are falling prey (as women have in the past) to feeling insecure about aging. They are now getting manicures and skin treatments and many are pursuing cosmetic surgery. Males, no doubt, are being influenced by the body images presented in magazines such as *Maxim* and *Men's Health* and by popular makeover shows such as *Queer Eye for the Straight Guy*. It seems that physical imperfection, age, and an undeveloped fashion sense can be crippling disabilities to contemporary males. Marketers have responded by launching face scrubs, moisturizers, and cleansing products for men. See Figure 4.6 for an illustration. Brands such as Biotherm Homme, L'Oréal VIVE, and Nivea for Men are capitalizing on men's insecurities and how they feel about themselves. Gillette has signed the British-based but international soccer star David Beckham to be its face of the future.

Marketers must stay abreast of such changes among consumers. A shift in emphasis with regard to the various elements of the self should result in new or different marketing strategies. Based on the grooming example above, many experts are forecasting that the male skin-care category could grow as large as the women's category—what an opportunity for companies that market personal-care products!

attitudes

ATTITUDES AND PERCEPTIONS **Attitudes** are an individual's feelings, favourable or unfavourable, toward an idea or object (the product or service). Generally, marketing organizations present their products to consumers in a way that agrees with prevailing attitudes. Marketers have found that it is expensive to try to change attitudes.

Considering how difficult it is for parents to understand their teenagers, do marketers have a chance of understanding them? The answer is yes, if they consider some basics about teen attitudes. For example, a teen that fancies him- or herself on the very edge of what the rest of the world considers normal will be attracted to products where the advertising message pushes the boundaries. PepsiCo's Mountain Dew brand was one of the first brands to discover this notion. The "Do the Dew" campaign, which was

Mountain Dew
www.mountaindew.com

FIGURE 4.6

Is it male insecurity or simply a male desire to look and feel better that marketers are appealing to?

closely aligned to extreme sports and exhilarating situations, was an instant hit with teens. In fact, marketers only recently realized the power of the word "extreme" with this age group. An attitudinal shift by marketers of Right Guard deodorant resulted in a complete brand facelift including new scents and a new brand name—Right Guard Extreme Sport. Right Guard Extreme Sport advertising features over-the-top comedian Rick Green, another good fit for the teen audience.

While it is difficult for a marketing organization to change attitudes, it must be prepared to act when consumers' attitudes do change. Marketers of beer and food products have reacted to changing attitudes among Canadians. A poll conducted by Ipsos-Reid indicated that 93 percent of Canadians try to make healthier eating decisions, and 35 percent of Canadians would try low-carbohydrate beer. Consequently, Sleeman Brewing launched Sleeman Clear (4 percent alcohol and 2.5 grams of carbs) and Molson launched Molson Ultra (4.5 percent alcohol and 2.5 grams of carbs).[5] If these brands deliver on taste they could carve out a niche in the very competitive beer market. After all, the product does reflect the attitude—in theory at least!

The moral in these illustrations is simple: products must first be aligned with the psyche of the consumers before they will consider buying a particular product. Further, if a company decides to launch a new product, it must consider consumers' attitudes before proceeding too far with a project.

perception

Perception refers to how individuals receive and interpret messages. Marketers know that different individuals perceive the same product differently and they accept only those messages that fall in line with their needs, attitudes, and self-concept. They tend to ignore other messages. A variety of marketing actions influence consumer perceptions—advertising, pricing, packaging, and place of purchase—but perceptions differ because consumers are quite selective about the messages they receive. Selectivity is based on their level of interest and their needs. There are three levels of selectivity:

1. *Selective Exposure*—Our eyes and minds notice only information that is of interest.
2. *Selective Perception*—We screen out messages and information that are in conflict with previously learned attitudes and beliefs.
3. *Selective Retention*—We remember only what we want to remember.

To understand how perception works, consider a situation in the automobile market. The design and styling of a car typically leads to a "love it" or "hate it" attitude among consumers for any particular car. Chrysler's PT Cruiser, for example, is perceived by many consumers to be too toy-like, and they hate it—others simply adore the retro look and sleek lines, and they love it.

Styling is not the only reason why consumers either like or hate an automobile. A key reason for a dramatic shift in market share toward Japanese and European models and away from domestic models produced by General Motors and Ford is the consumer perception that foreign models are more reliable. Despite the implementation of marketing strategies that have improved perceptions of quality and reliability, domestic manufacturers still suffer from poor reputations.[6] It seems that no amount of advertising can overcome that negative perception. A common phrase applies here: "Perception is reality." And it is perceptions held by consumers that marketers must deal with.

On a more positive note, consumers will quickly tune in to messages for items they are contemplating purchasing. A pending purchase of a digital camera or a laptop computer represents a situation where consumers will want lots of product information: ads for cameras and laptops suddenly become relevant—they notice them! This selective nature of perception helps explain why only some people respond to marketing activities; others quite simply do not. The challenge for marketers is to penetrate the perceptual barriers—they must design messages and strategies that will command attention and compel the reader, listener, or viewer to take action.

> 4. Outline the various behavioural influences that affect consumer purchase decisions.

PERSONAL INFLUENCES

lifestyle

LIFESTYLE   **Lifestyle** is a "person's pattern of living as expressed in his or her activities, interests, opinions, and values."[7] Marketing organizations try to determine who buys their product on the basis of demographic variables, such as age, income, gender, and education. Nevertheless, individuals with these variables in common, even who look alike and live side by side, can be entirely different in their lifestyle. It is the psychographic profile, obtained through research, that indicates differences between people and why different people buy the products they do. Psychographic research determines the activities (work, sports, and hobbies), interests (family, friends, social situations), and opinions (social issues, business, or politics) of consumers (commonly referred to as their AIOs). When a person's lifestyle is combined with demographic data, a more complete picture of an individual emerges—a picture that allows marketers to understand how someone interacts with others and their surroundings.

The compilation of data places people in *descriptive classifications* (descriptions of people with similar tendencies). In Canada, Millward Brown Goldfarb, a prominent research company that conducts lifestyle research, has divided the Canadian population into nine distinct classifications: protective providers, up and comers, les petite vie, mavericks, contented traditionalists, joiner activists, passive malcontents, disinterested outsiders, and tie-dyed greys. For a summary of these classifications, see Figure 4.7.

Psychographic information shows how an individual's interest in a particular product depends on his or her lifestyle. Automakers produce and market a range of vehicles to satisfy the requirements of various lifestyle groups. Trendy sports cars with European

FIGURE
4.7

Lifestyle Segments in Canada

Source: Millward Brown Goldfarb, Trendz 2003.

Millward Brown Goldfarb has identified nine different consumer segments in Canada. Each segment is motivated by a unique set of attitudes and beliefs.

Protective Providers
- Hardworking; value personal initiative and commitment to family
- Financially strained
- Unlikely to be involved in politics or social activist groups
- Price conscious and less brand loyal

Up and Comers
- Outgoing but like time alone for solitary pursuits
- Materialistic and seek instant gratification
- Enjoy the latest gadgets (anything new)
- Optimistic outlook and ambitions for wealth and power
- Traditional values and friendships are important

Les "Petite Vie"
- Uncomfortable with pace of modern life
- Friends and family very important
- Respect business leaders
- Favour government involvement in economic and social programs
- Open-minded on sexual matters
- Overwhelmingly French-speaking and Roman Catholic

Mavericks
- Individual's rights important
- Dislike government intervention
- Confident and self-reliant
- More likely to engage in risky activities and adventures
- Tend to be leaders and enjoy challenges
- Seek wealth and power

Contented Traditionalists
- Well-adjusted, happy individuals
- Family more important than personal goals
- Loyal and trustworthy

- Active in community
- Religious focus and conservative values
- Brand loyal

Joiner Activists
- Value education and personal growth
- Satisfied with career and life's challenges
- Liberal social attitudes
- Active in community
- Optimistic outlook and non-religious approach to life
- Concerned about health, environment, and cultural issues

Passive Malcontents
- Unhappy and dissatisfied with job, family, and social life
- Strong belief in law and order
- Live day-to-day; do not strive to get ahead
- Patriotic and trusting of government
- Not health conscious

Disinterested Outsiders
- Casual indifference to problems facing society
- Not very interested in anything beyond daily lives
- Willing to bend rules and lack respect for authority
- Dislike change
- Not health conscious and watch a lot of television

Tie-Dyed Greys
- Progressive attitudes about social issues
- Less materialistic and more independent than peers
- Open-minded on moral issues
- Suspicious of big business ethics
- Environmentally conscious and slightly uncomfortable with technology

FIGURE 4.8

A lifestyle advertising message directed at consumers wanting to satisfy status and prestige needs

or Japanese styling appeal to *up and comers* (outgoing, ambitious individuals with materialistic values and instant gratification needs); refer to Figure 4.8 for an illustration. In contrast, a family minivan made by Ford or Chrysler appeals to a *contented traditionalist* (someone motivated by family and friends, conservative values, loyalty, and security). Psychographic jargon embraces an array of terms to describe people. Those just mentioned are only a few of them.

Psychographics allow the marketing organization to position its products effectively in the marketplace and to communicate better with its target markets. To illustrate, consider the lifestyle of the 13- to 24-year-old age group in Canada, a group referred to as Generation Y. The youth market is a fickle market, and one that has been traditionally difficult to reach. But Generation Y is the Internet generation and they are very different from previous generations in how they consume the media. Not only do they spend more time with the Internet than television, the Internet is a medium from which all other media decisions get made.

Such knowledge about an age group is valuable to marketers responsible for devising advertising strategies. If marketers like the Gap, Old Navy, Nike, and Coca-Cola aren't communicating online they won't be on this group's radar screen. Further, viral marketing is an invaluable tool for reaching Generation Y. **Viral marketing** is a situation where the receiver of an online message is encouraged to pass it on to friends. For new product launches, Generation Y can effectively create a buzz by "word of mouse."[8] Different lifestyles necessitate different marketing and marketing communications strategies.

For more insight into how lifestyle changes are affecting marketing practice, read the Marketing in Action vignette **Hectic and Healthier Lifestyles Are Driving Change**.

viral marketing

MARKETING IN ACTION

Hectic and Healthier Lifestyles Are Driving Change

Restaurants and bars are wondering where their customers have gone. It seems that Canadian homes are the new competition for restaurants. Busy families, nutritional concerns, and takeout-savvy baby boomers are factors contributing to less eating in restaurants such as McDonald's, East Side Mario's, and all of their competitors.

In today's health-conscious, time-strapped culture, the days of heavy drinking and long hours at the pub with colleagues are declining. Now, people are more interested in beating the traffic and just getting home. And they have good reason to do so. Right now, a third of middle-aged Canadians consider themselves workaholics and claim they don't have enough time to spend with their family and friends. Moreover, a growing number of Canadians claim severe "time stress." To alleviate the stress, many Canadians are exercising at the gym rather than drinking at the pub.

Many Canadians, especially baby boomers, are also increasingly concerned about healthy food options. And while restaurants are responding with the introduction of healthy and low-carbohydrate menu choices, customers still seem to want to cook at home—or at least want to eat at home. Stopping at a Swiss Chalet pickup station has always been a popular meal option!

These trends are good news to food marketers, especially those that offer convenience foods. However, in today's culture, convenience also means consumers are looking for quick, tasty, and healthy food alternatives that fit their lifestyle. Nutritional concerns also have time-strapped parents taking back control of their children's diets. Their concern for obesity now takes precedence over the convenience of fast food.

If people are eating less in restaurants where is the business going? You guessed it: supermarkets are benefiting from the trend.

Adapted from Lesley Young, "Will that be to go?" *Marketing*, March 29, 2004, p. 3.; Tavia Grant, "Hearth & home replaces bars and booze," *Globe and Mail*, January 25, 2002, p. C1; and "A grocery gold mine," *Marketing*, July 16, 2001, p. 22.

Photo courtesy of Sobey's Inc.

AGE AND LIFE CYCLE   Individuals and families progress through a series of stages, starting with being a young single adult, progressing to marriage and parenthood, and ending as an older single individual. Understanding the stages in the life cycle offers insight into household purchase decisions. Life cycle theory is based on the changing needs of a family as it progresses through the various stages. For example, as one grows older tastes in such things as food, clothing, travel, and sports activities change. An individual who is a sports enthusiast may shift from a competitive mode to a recreational mode, or one's travel desires may shift from being adventurous to being more relaxed.

Marketers tend to define their target markets on the basis of age and life cycle and devise appropriate marketing strategies suited to particular stages. Certainly the needs of a young working family with children will be quite different from those of an older married couple with no children living at home. Different types of buying occur in each stage. But this reflects the traditional family formation. Today, marketers must consider the nontraditional family formations since the needs and buying motivations of unmarried couples, childless married couples, same-sex couples, and older married couples are quite different. Making any product appeal to such a cross-section of families is a challenge for marketers.

The key groups in the first two decades of the new millennium are the baby boomers and Generation Y. Companies will launch new products geared specifically to mature targets, and reposition existing products to make them appeal to older people. At the same time they must also attract new, younger customers—a real marketing dilemma. Toyota, for example, faces a situation where their primary buyer is aging—the average age is around 45, one of the highest in the automotive industry. Toyota is currently a very successful company, but it must address the long term by attracting new, young car buyers. In response, Toyota launched the Echo and the Scion to appeal directly to younger buyers with modest budgets, and the MR2 Spyder sports car for young adults with more money to spend.

Toyota Scion
www.scion.com

TECHNOLOGY   Several factors are combining to make dramatic changes in the way in which consumers buy goods and services. These factors include the growing numbers of time-pressed consumers, the availability of information through the Internet, and transaction convenience offered by retailers and banks. Canadians are a "connected" society; 61 percent of the population now uses the Internet. We are information seekers with a "need for speed." The latest social survey conducted by Millward Brown Goldfarb shows that 34 percent of Canadians now do their banking online.[9]

Consider the role of plastic cards in the purchasing process. According to a recent study, 67 percent of people prefer to use debit or credit cards to make purchases rather than cash or cheques. The Interac network has had a profound and positive impact on the daily lives of Canadians. People can leave home with their keys and their bank card, and know that they don't have to worry about anything else. It was only a short while ago that a consumer would go to a bank and withdraw $500 to spend over two weeks. When ABMs were introduced, the $500 transaction was replaced by five $100 withdrawals. Today, consumers will make several debit card purchases rather than going to the ABM. It is technology that is changing our purchasing behaviour.

The preference for using plastic is expected to continue in the next decade as the availability of automatic banking machines expands—they are available at convenience stores, gas stations, hockey rinks, and restaurants. Consumers' excessive use of debit cards is somewhat bewildering as they work to the advantage of the banks. With credit cards at least there is a grace period before interest rates kick in. We are embracing smart cards slowly—plastic cards with an embedded microchip that can be programmed to carry electronic cash. Wal-Mart and Starbucks offer cash cards to patrons that can be reloaded at point-of-purchase when the need arises. A card in the consumer's hand often leads to impulse purchasing, a phenomenon that marketers are well aware of.

ECONOMIC SITUATION   The economy directly or indirectly influences the attitudes, values, and lifestyles of Canadian society. There is little doubt that the cyclical nature of the economy shapes the purchase decisions of consumers. When the economy is in recession, for example—a situation where inflation, unemployment, and interest rates may be on the rise—the discretionary income of consumers may be low. Consequently, major purchases will be delayed, and consumers will make products they do have last longer; new purchases of items such as a larger house, a renovation, a car, or a major appliance may be placed on hold. Marketing organizations must be prepared to adjust their marketing strategies as the economy enters various cyclical stages (refer to Chapter 2) and as consumers' attitudes and perceptions change.

Conversely, if the economy is booming, consumers are more likely to purchase more goods and services. The construction and housing industries are good examples of markets that accommodate Canada's economic shifts. When mortgage rates decline, the cost of carrying a mortgage drops; therefore, there is a frenzy as first-time buyers enter the market and current homeowners consider trading up to larger accommodations even though the steady demand forces the price of housing up. Generally, business organizations remain conservative in hard times and are aggressive in good times.

SOCIAL INFLUENCES

The social factors that influence the purchase decision process include reference groups, the family, and social class.

REFERENCE GROUPS   A **reference group** is a group of people with a common interest that influences its members' attitudes and behaviour. Reference groups that people are commonly associated with include fellow students in a class, co-workers, sports teams, hobby clubs, civic and recreational associations, and fraternal organizations. It can also be your immediate *peer group*—the friends you hang with. A member of a group experiences considerable pressure to conform to the standards of the group, to "fit in." The desire to fit in influences the type of products a member will purchase.

The influence of reference groups is quite strong among younger people. For example, adolescents and teens share a desire to wear the latest fashions, to shop at the trendiest stores, or to have parts of their body pierced. It's all part of their social scene and their desire to satisfy social needs. Many young people see themselves as part of the hip-hop generation. They wear baggy clothing and caps tipped to the side, listen to rap music, and idolize rap artists and sports stars who portray the rap image. By wearing the rap uniform, there is a sense of belonging.

From a marketing perspective, rap artists are known to include product mentions in their lyrics. Initially such unplanned brand exposure was free, but now some marketers pay dearly for the privilege. Going a step further, many brands have struck endorsement deals to maximize the potential influence of rap artists. Hip-hop icons who have struck endorsement deals include Jay-Z (Reebok), Usher (Twix), Beyoncé Knowles (Pepsi, L'Oreal), Busta Rhymes (Mountain Dew), and LL Cool J (Dr. Pepper). These brands recognize the marketing strength of black music and its artists.[10]

Reebok was quick off the mark identifying the hip-hop influence and went directly at hip-hop youth with a new brand called RBK. RBK is the moniker for a street-inspired collection of young men's fashions that include long shorts, T-shirts, athletic-style

reference group

jerseys, tank tops, and shoes. The brand is associating itself with a hip, urban basketball scene and includes an endorsement from NBA star Allen Iverson.[11] Once a few kids buy in, the wave of acceptance is sure to follow—at least that's the thinking at Reebok.

Because of young people's fickle nature, it is difficult to develop an effective marketing strategy that will have an influence on them. But by pinpointing the reference groups that affect young people, or any other group for that matter, a marketing organization can develop appropriate strategies for reaching them.

FAMILY   Various members of a family think and act as individuals, and the decisions they make can influence household purchases. The actual impact each member has on the decision depends on the type of product or service under consideration. In the past, the impact each person had on the purchase decision was related to the traditional roles of household members. For example, fathers were in charge of cars and household repairs and mothers in charge of groceries and other household products. Traditionally, purchase decisions were classified as husband-dominant, wife-dominant, or shared equally.

Today, the lines are blurring between the sexes, and the decision-makers are not who they once were. Companies must be aware that women today purchase 50 percent of all automobiles, own 54 percent of all mutual funds, buy 50 percent of all personal computers, and influence 40 percent of all home-improvement projects.[12] Marketers must be aware of these changes and adjust their marketing strategies appropriately.

In dual-income households, much of the decision making is shared between partners. No longer can marketers of food and other household products assume the woman is the primary buyer, just as a financial adviser cannot assume a man makes all of the investment decisions. Similar thinking applies to liquor and wine. In Ontario, the LCBO (Liquor Control Board of Ontario) discovered that women make up 56 percent of its customers and account for 60 percent of all wine purchases. This information led to a shift in marketing direction—everything from store designs to ad campaigns are now female-friendly.

Changing roles and responsibilities among male and female heads of households are changing how marketers view target marketing. Consequently, some marketers are double targeting. **Double targeting** involves devising a single marketing strategy for both sexes or devising separate strategies to appeal to the different sexes. In its simplest form, a product would have one strategy for females and another for males. The risk of such an undertaking is in the confusion it may cause among females and males. They may ask: for whom is this product intended?

Mark's Work Wearhouse employs a dual targeting strategy. Traditionally, Mark's focused on men's work, outdoor, and casual clothing, but through marketing research the company discovered that 50 percent of shoppers were female—women buying for men. The company realized it was missing an important market. Mark's added female clothing and started targeting women 25 to 54 years old. Mark's now advertises in magazines such as *Canadian Living* and *Chatelaine* and prominently displays women's wear in sale flyers. Mark's goal is to have a product sales mix of 20-percent traditional work wear, 40-percent men's casual, and 40-percent women's casual within five years.[13] See the illustration in Figure 4.9.

The *role of children* also has to be considered by the marketer. Children often influence purchase decisions in three areas: items for themselves, items for the home, and family vacations. In Canada, 2.5 million 9- to 14-year-olds spend $1.7 billion of their own money each year and influence $20 billion in family spending. They use their own money to buy clothes, shoes, and snacks. It is estimated that by age 10 they have memorized between 300 and 400 brand names. Research also shows that time-pressed and guilt-ridden parents respond favourably to 75 percent of kids' requests—a bonanza for sharp marketers![14]

double targeting

Mark's Work Wearhouse
www.marks.com

*New season,
different pace,
a time to show you
mean business.*

The great look of
Business Casual
has arrived.

Mark's Work
Wearhouse
Clothes That Work.
Visit us at marks.com

Courtesy of Mark's Work Wearhouse

FIGURE
4.9

**Mark's Work Wearhouse
adopted a double targeting
strategy when it discovered
50 percent of shoppers were
female**

Speaking personally, I can't imagine my parents coming to me and saying, "What kind of TV should we buy?" That would never have happened. But the times are changing fast, as tweens and teens influence purchase decisions on furniture, computers, stereos, and televisions. Marketers are realizing that activity directed at children now will help form impressions and habits that will influence their buying patterns as adults. Further, the tweens and teens of today are the generation that will kick Internet buying into high gear.

From a marketing viewpoint, it is essential to determine who has the most influence within a family situation. Once this is known, strategies containing an appropriate message and using suitable media can be directed at the decision maker and the influencer. In spite of these changes, it is still generally safe to say that in households headed by an adult male and an adult female—or a same-sex household, for that matter—the more expensive a product or service the greater the likelihood of a shared decision in order to make the right decision.

social class

SOCIAL CLASS A person's social class derives from a system that ranks or classifies people within a society. **Social class** is the division of people into ordered groups based on similar values, lifestyles, and behaviours. This division into groups is based on such variables as income, occupation, education, and inherited wealth. In Western society, class groups are divided as follows: upper-upper, lower-upper, upper-middle, lower-middle, upper-lower, and lower-lower. Individuals can move in and out of the various social classes as they go through life. As an example, the young business executive on the rise in the corporate world could move rapidly from, say, a lower-middle class background to a lower-upper class level as he or she gains more power, responsibility, and salary in an organization. Conversely, a senior executive accustomed to a certain style of living and a certain social circle could suffer socially if he or she suffered a job loss. The fallout would affect the social position of the entire family.

A person's place in the class structure influences his or her purchases of housing, automobiles, clothing, travel, and entertainment. The lower-upper class executive, if single, is likely to live downtown, drive a trendy automobile that reflects achievement, and wear custom-designed suits. Such purchases help create or maintain the image that goes with the corporate position.

CULTURAL INFLUENCES

culture

CULTURE **Culture** refers to behaviour learned from external sources—such as the family, the workplace, and education—that help form the value systems that hold strong sway over every individual. Over time, people's values can change. North America's value system is largely shaped by a demographic phenomenon—the baby boom generation.

An irony about Canadian culture is how we define ourselves. There is a tendency for Canadians to define ourselves not by who we are but by how we differ from Americans. For example, Canadians often self-identify as less patriotic than Americans, less proud of their achievements, and more modest about their accomplishments. A vast majority of Canadians (81 percent), however, agree strongly that they are proud to be Canadian. Fewer than half of the French-speaking population in Canada agree strongly that they are proud to be Canadian.[15]

In terms of values, goals, and aspirations, Canadians continue to place love and marriage at or near the top of the list of personal goals. Trends such as women's rights, common-law relationships, and higher divorce rates have had little impact on our desire to marry and raise a family. Non-urban Canadians place a greater emphasis on family goals, while urban dwellers tend to have goals that are more individually focused.

Values that Canadians consider most important include not letting down family, respecting human rights, maintaining high ethical conduct, exercising the right to vote, and respecting law and order. Non-urban Canadians place greater emphasis on family life, and they are more conservative about issues of morality such as violence, homosexuality, and nudity. Research indicates that half of Canada's non-urban dwellers believe that abortion and homosexual relationships are morally wrong, compared to a much smaller percentage of urban dwellers.[16] These descriptions of various values are but a snapshot of the present Canadian situation.

Values change over time. People grow older and acquire different needs, responsibilities, and attitudes, all of which influence buying behaviour. In the 1980s materialism prevailed, and individuals constantly strived to possess—a larger house in comparison with those owned by their parents and grandparents or a prestigious automobile that suggested success. By contrast, the 1990s saw boomers looking for relaxation; they wanted to work less and were willing to accept less financial reward. A sense of equilibrium and simplicity had set in. In purchasing goods, strategic consumption had replaced conspicuous consumption.

More recently, many Canadians are working both ends of the consumption spectrum. Middle-class Canadians are trading up to more expensive products, forcing marketers to rethink just who the luxury consumer is. An emerging category of consumers referred to as "new luxury" willingly pay more—in some cases thousands of dollars more—for what they view as premium products and services.

The trading up phenomenon by middle-class Canadians is the result of families having higher disposable incomes at a time when family size has shrunk. The average household income in 2000 was $55 000, compared to $41 000 in 1971 (amounts in 2001 dollars), and the number of persons per household in the same period has dropped from 3.5 to 2.5. Middle-class families also show a tendency to trade down on everyday household items (they spend high on specific and gratifying purchases and low on everyday necessities). See Figure 4.10 for an illustration. Caught in the middle are mid-

The television is going to miss you.

In a Viking kitchen, dinnertime becomes prime time. 1-888-845-4641 or vikingrange.com

Quebec 800-361-0799 Ontario 888-565-0801 Western Canada 800-663-8686
Viking Professional and Viking Designer products were previously marketed in Canada under the Ultraline brand name.

Courtesy of Viking Range Corporation

FIGURE
4.10

Consumers' willingness to trade up on important purchases presents opportunity for companies marketing more expensive goods

priced products and retailers who see a good portion of their customers departing—going upscale in some categories (e.g., automobiles and electronic equipment) and downscale in others (e.g., private-label products available in supermarkets and drugstores).[17]

These examples show how the values of the Canadian society can change. Marketers monitor the changing values of society and of subgroups in society in order to identify the new needs that the change produces. A firm's ability to adapt marketing strategies to the changing personality of the Canadian marketplace ultimately determines success or failure.

For more insight into cultural and lifestyle factors that influence Canadian buying decisions, read the Marketing in Action vignette **The Hearts and Minds of Canadians**.

subculture

SUBCULTURE   Many diverse subcultures exist within the Canadian culture. A **subculture** is a subgroup of a culture, which has distinctive attitudes and values that set it apart from the national culture. Canada's subcultures are evident in cities, where parts of urban and suburban neighbourhoods contain large populations of one ethnic group. Canada has long prided itself on this difference in ethnic composition. Very often, these ethnic groups are served by their own media, which provide marketers with an effective means of reaching them.

Prudent marketers are recognizing the opportunities that these markets represent. By 2011 it is estimated that 45 percent of Toronto's population will consist of members of ethnic minorities.[18] Such a number suggests the full marketing implications for mainstream marketers that are currently ignoring the language markets. To reach Toronto, a company will have to turn to ethnic marketing sooner or later. Vancouver is another major urban market with a high ethnic concentration. In both markets, Chinese-Canadians and South Asians are the largest visible minorities.

Because of their unique characteristics and attitudes, *adolescents* can generally be said to belong to a subculture. Some adolescent groups differentiate themselves from the main culture more obviously than other groups do. The "punks" of the 1980s, the "skin-heads" of the 1990s, and the "Goths" of the early 2000s differentiated themselves from the more traditional teenage groups through their taste in music, the style of their clothing and accessories, and their physical appearance. The products they purchased and the activities they participated in were different from those of mainstream teenagers.

Generally speaking, the adolescent market is status-conscious and brand name–oriented. They buy what is "in," what is "right," and what is needed to be "cool." As indicated earlier in the chapter, they are subject to a high degree of peer pressure. Teens—by their significant numbers and substantial buying power—are among marketers' most coveted demographic groups. They are volatile and switch allegiances fast, so marketers have to be ready to react to rapid changes in tastes and preferences.

Marketers have to understand teens to be successful. A saturation campaign may generate brand awareness, but youth are going to recognize this as a massive effort to get money out of their wallets.[19] Real success today comes from nontraditional campaigns directed at different niches of the youth market. Marketers must be in synch with the mindset of teens while not being too blatant with their marketing efforts. For example, friends, online communications, celebrity endorsements by sports stars, and product samples hold more sway with teens than traditional forms of media advertising. Youth today are advertising-savvy and hard to influence—they want to discover brands through underground channels and not classic ads.[20]

Brands such as Nike and Hilfiger are successful because they appeal to a variety of different youth targets. These brands target different youth with different messages and

MARKETING IN ACTION

The Hearts and Minds of Canadians

Wow! Automakers have finally figured out that there is something unique about the hearts and minds of Canadians that make us prefer different kinds of cars, and finally they are tailoring their product mix accordingly.

Kidding aside, a majority of product decisions are made in the United States, and many decisions are predicated on the assumption that whatever was good for the American market was good enough for Canada. But what was easy for them to sell us wasn't necessarily what we wanted to buy. That sounds like production-era marketing mentality, and that's not good enough today!

One thing the decision-makers do know is that lower Canadian incomes, higher taxes, and higher gas prices drive us to buy smaller, economical vehicles. But, do we actually prefer these cars?

Apparently Canadians buy twice as many minivans and two-thirds as many sport utility vehicles as Americans. Why is this so? Research evidence on social values provided by Environics Research Group and General Motors explains the differences. SUV owners in Canada and the United States tend to be confident, adaptable, and not at all afraid of the future. They believe in personal responsibility and work hard to achieve their goals. In contrast, the minivan owner is more likely to be family-focused, time-stressed, risk-averse, and anxious about violence and technology. They are practical and pragmatic shoppers.

Canadians have a different set of social values that marketers must deal with. Americans are outer-directed risk takers who are more concerned with maintaining social order and tradition. Canadians are more inner-directed and security-seeking, and yet are more socially liberal and tolerant of individual diversity.

Americans celebrate those who live the American Dream—working hard and reaping the rewards—expensive car, home, and vacations. Canadians want to achieve equitable balance and have a fair distribution of wealth—the Canadian Dream includes a strong social safety net. Therefore, our values reflect more understated consumption. We buy not on what products and brands say about us but more on what products do for us. For these reasons we do prefer affordable and practical cars. Marketers, therefore, must distinguish between American consumers and Canadian consumers, eh?

BMW acknowledged this Canadian uniqueness by subtly changing its advertising tagline. Everywhere else BMW uses the phrase "The Ultimate Driving Machine" to summarize its message to consumers— but in Canada, it's "The Ultimate Driving Experience."

Adapted from David MacDonald and Michael Adams, "We are what we drive," *Marketing*, March 15, 2004, p. 42.

Antonio Mo/Taxi/Getty Images

advertise in special-interest publications that reach unique youth target audiences. They also have a strong online presence. Nike goes the distance when reaching its various target markets, but in terms of getting today's youth to buy its sneakers what it does on the street is a huge influence. The message and the manner in which it is delivered must be relevant to the teen segment.

In assessing cultures and subcultures, marketers must decide if a national marketing strategy is suited to everyone or if subcultures should be isolated and appropriate strategies developed for them. A prudent manager may conclude that consumers across the country need the same products, but the way in which products are presented will vary. This concept is discussed in greater detail in the next section.

REGIONAL DIFFERENCES   Are regional cultural differences in Canada significant enough to warrant unique marketing strategies? The most obvious differences are the ones between English-speaking Canada and French-speaking Canada. A common strategy in the past was to adapt English advertising for the French Canadian market, but such strategies produced only limited success and, often, failure. French Canadians do not respond to the same cues and triggers as do English-speaking Canadians, nor do they watch the average Canadian television programming. As consumers, francophone Quebecers as a whole tend to be characterized by: (1) their positive cultural values of family loyalty and pride; (2) their emotional rather than rational decision-making behaviour; and (3) their unique social- and community-driven leisure behaviour.[21] Marketers must recognize such differences and develop marketing programs that lend themselves to the Quebecers' value structure. For additional information about the uniqueness of the French Quebec market refer to Figure 4.11.

In the context of marketing, francophone Quebecers, by and large, tend to be more emotional than English Canadians and to respond to different stimuli. Brand, service, and selection are decided on an emotional basis more than on a purely rational one. Marketers who understand that the values of Quebecers are different recognize that these consumers seek different benefits from a product. Therefore, a solid advantage must be established first, and then, to maintain loyalty, the advantage must be communicated in a manner that will have an impact on the francophone Quebec consumer. Quebecers want products that are like them and that respect the fact that they are different.

A dilemma faced by Dunkin' Donuts franchisees in Quebec offers a good illustration. The once unrivalled champion of the Quebec doughnut market has been rapidly losing ground to Tim Hortons and is being undermined by the questionable product decisions of Allied Domecq, its American owner. The American head office ordered the removal of *fèves au lard et cretons* (a customer favourite) from the breakfast menu. Baked beans and toast smeared in pork fat may be expendable to an American decision maker, but Quebec customers were not pleased. In place of the beans, the restaurants were ordered to bake muffins twice their current size and serve them for breakfast.

For more than 40 years, Dunkin' Donuts has been one of the less-publicized elements of Quebec's distinctiveness. An ill-suited American-style menu will not work in Quebec. Further complicating matters was a new advertising campaign that failed to consider Quebecers' unique tastes.[22] The future does not look bright for Dunkin' Donuts in Quebec.

PepsiCo has succeeded in Quebec by recognizing and capitalizing on its distinctiveness. Knowing that humour is important to Quebecers, PepsiCo has employed French comedian Claude Meunier in a long-running advertising campaign that sends Quebecers laughing all the way to the Pepsi cooler. The Meunier campaign is unique in the Pepsi system, and it is the longest-standing campaign and longest-standing celebrity endorsement in the history of the brand. As a result of the campaign, Pepsi has become the market leader in Quebec.

Quebec, it seems, is a society that thrives on local heroes, whether they are from the world of sports, arts, business, or even politics. Quebecers will elevate to hero status anyone who is seen as contributing in a big way to their uniqueness. Therefore, marketing managers who, from the outset, plan strategies with Quebec in mind and who implement programs that are culturally relevant will garner success.

A decision that many marketing executives must make is whether or not to develop unique marketing strategies for the Quebec market. Are the language and cultural differences significant enough to justify such an investment? Here are just a few of the unique characteristics of the French Quebec market.

Attitudes and Opinions

	French Quebec %	Rest of Canada %
I enjoy keeping fit	59	48
I prefer low-fat or light foods	43	33
I consider myself to be a risk-averse investor	42	18
I like to dine at fine restaurants as often as possible	41	26
I seldom make a financial move without expert advice	31	22
I am more of a spender than a saver	22	32
A career should be an individual's first priority	20	34
Health-related issues are given too much attention these days	39	27

Personal Consumption

	French Quebec %	Rest of Canada %
Buy lottery tickets	68	56
Drink wine	60	47
Own personal life insurance	49	27
Shop at specialty stores for fruit and vegetables	45	23
Ride a bike	44	28
Use a cell phone	11	23
Own a swimming pool	13	4
Eat snack cakes	55	20

Based only on the above statistics, it can be observed that French Quebecers probably enjoy a higher level of fitness than the rest of Canada, are conservative investors, like to save rather than spend, place family ahead of career, like to indulge in fine foods, wines, and snacks, and are less likely to use a cell phone. You be the judge. Should unique marketing strategies be devised for this market?

FIGURE 4.11

The Uniqueness of the French Quebec Market

Source: Adapted from Andrea Haman, "Quebecers snub diets and compacts for port and luxury cars," *Strategy*, April 9, 2001, figures cited from PMB 2000 (two-year database).

What about the rest of Canada? Is Western Canada different from Central Canada and Eastern Canada? There are differences, but it's the significance of the differences that dictates the need for unique regional marketing strategies. From an annual survey conducted by the Print Measurement Bureau it appears that Westerners are closer to

Torontonians than either group would like to admit, but what distinctions there are seem to hark back to pioneer stereotypes.

To illustrate, consider the nature of alcohol and beer consumption. In Western Canada more rye whiskey (21 percent of population) is consumed compared to in Toronto (16 percent of population). Slightly more Westerners partake of beer, but what they drink beer *from* is revealing. In the West the sheer practicality of canned beer is embraced by 30 percent of the population compared to only 12 percent in Toronto. Such knowledge could play a role in the development of new advertising campaigns for beer brands, at least in terms of the type of container displayed in the ads.

The spending habits of the two regions tend to mirror consumer behaviour. Toronto households spend more on food, clothing, and personal-care products than those in Calgary or Vancouver. Westerners make up for the shortfall by spending more on recreation, alcohol, and tobacco.[23]

SUMMARY

Consumers, through their decision to purchase a product or service, determine an organization's success. Since organizations cannot control consumers, it is essential that they understand them so that they can adapt their strategies to consumers' thinking and behaviour.

The consumer decision-making process involves five distinct stages. These stages include problem recognition, information search, evaluating alternatives, the purchase decision, and post-purchase behaviour.

This chapter discussed the dynamics of consumer behaviour and illustrated how marketing organizations can use behavioural information to advantage when developing marketing strategies. The study of consumer behaviour deals with why people buy the products and services they do and explains why two or more people behave differently or similarly. It has shown that purchase decisions are primarily based on four major influences: psychological, personal, social, and cultural. Collectively, these factors present a dynamic situation that marketers must understand.

Psychological influences include needs and motives, personality and self-concept, and attitudes and perceptions. Personal influences include lifestyle considerations, age and life cycle, how consumers adapt to technology, and economic circumstances faced by individuals. Social factors embrace reference groups, family, and social class circumstances. Cultural influences embrace Canadian culture as a whole while considering various subcultures such as ethnic groups and youth groups and regional differences.

Marketing organizations possessing knowledge of the influences on behaviour are adept at developing target-market profiles and at using these profiles to prepare marketing strategies that trigger a response from the target markets.

KEY TERMS

attitudes   90

cognitive dissonance   87

consumer behaviour   83

culture   100

double targeting   98

evaluation   85

evoked set   85

hierarchy of needs   88

information search   84

lifestyle   93

motives   89

needs   88

perception   92

personality   90

problem recognition   84

purchase decision   86

reference group   97

self-concept theory   90

social class   100

subculture   102

viral marketing   95

REVIEW QUESTIONS

1. Briefly explain the steps in the consumer purchase decision process.
2. What is the difference between a routine purchase and a complex purchase?
3. Briefly explain what cognitive dissonance is.
4. Identify the five levels of the hierarchy of needs. Provide two new examples that demonstrate the application of needs and motivation theory.
5. Briefly explain the four components of the self-concept theory and illustrate how they have an influence on marketing strategy. Provide two new examples that demonstrate the application of this theory.
6. Briefly explain how perceptions held by consumers influence buying decisions.
7. Explain the difference between selective exposure, selective perception, and selective retention.
8. Explain how an understanding of consumer attitudes is essential before developing a marketing strategy. Provide an example that has considered the importance of understanding consumer attitudes.
9. What role does one's age and life cycle status play in the development of a marketing strategy?
10. What is double targeting? Provide a new example of a brand or company that practises double targeting.
11. What is the difference between culture and subculture? What are the implications of culture and subculture on marketing activity?

DISCUSSION AND APPLICATION QUESTIONS

1. Compare and contrast your own behaviour when making the following purchase decisions:

   a) A new business suit for an important job interview
   b) An audio component set or computer system
   c) A case of beer

2. "Marketing strategies that appeal to our desires are more effective than those appealing to current needs." Discuss. Provide some examples to justify your viewpoint.

3. Examine the role of reference groups in the purchase of the following products:

   a) Blue jeans
   b) Personal computers
   c) Chocolate bars
   d) Cosmetics

4. On the basis of your knowledge of the hierarchy of needs and the theory of motivation, what level of needs do the following products appeal to? (Consider the slogan and anything you may know about the product's advertising.)

   a) Labatt Blue "Cheers. To Friends"
   b) Jaguar "Born to Perform"
   c) Gillette "The Best a Man Can Get"
   d) Harley-Davidson "Things Are Different on a Harley"
   e) Lexus "The Relentless Pursuit of Perfection"
   f) Gatorade "Is It In You?"

5. Assess some of the points raised in the chapter regarding regional Canadian markets. Conduct some secondary research on this issue and determine the practicality of implementing regional marketing strategies in Canada. Is it worthwhile or not?

6. How important will it be to market directly to subcultures in the future? Are Canadian marketing organizations adequately addressing this issue with their marketing strategies? Discuss, and provide relevant examples to substantiate your position.

7. Can a brand survive by simply associating with the lifestyle of a prospective target market? Do lifestyle appeals influence consumers to buy? Examine the issues surrounding lifestyle marketing and provide relevant examples to substantiate your position on its effectiveness or ineffectiveness.

E-ASSIGNMENTS

1. Assume you have made a decision to purchase a laptop computer. Gathering information about the various brands will be an important first step before you decide what make and model to buy. Using only the Internet (e.g., search engines, company websites and online publications), compare and contrast three different brands. Once you have completed your investigation, identify the advantages and disadvantages of using the Internet for information-gathering purposes.

2. The Environics Research Group has developed a list of consumer psychographic segments. Visit the Environics website (http://erg.environics.net/ surveys) and complete the survey on the interactive page. Your results will be instantly tabulated to determine which category you belong to so you can read about your psychographic profile. Compare your results with those of other students. What observations can you make about the survey results?

ENDNOTES

1. James F. Engel, David T. Kollatt, and Roger D. Blackwell, *Consumer Behaviour*, 2nd Edition (New York: Holt Rinehart and Winston, 1973), p. 5.

2. "General Social Survey: Internet Use," *The Daily*, Statistics Canada, March 26, 2001.

3. "E-tire kickers," *Marketing*, March 27, 2000, p. 30.

4. John Douglas, George Field, and Lawrence Tarpey, *Human Behaviour in Marketing* (Columbus, OH: Charles E. Merrill Publishing, 1987), p. 5.

5. Sara Minogue, "The war on fat," *Strategy*, October 20, 2003, p. 15.

6. Greg Keenan, "It's okay for people to loathe your car; just don't bore them," *Globe and Mail*, October 10, 2003, pp. B1, B6.

7. Philip Kotler, Gordon McDougall, and Gary Armstrong, *Marketing*, Canadian Edition (Scarborough, ON: Prentice-Hall Inc., 1988), p. 142.

8. Jim Meskauskas, "Millennials surfing: Generation Y online," *Imedia Connection*, October 15, 2003, www.imediaconnection.com.

9. "The state of affairs in the nation today," *Consumer TrendZ 2003*, Millward Brown Goldfarb.

10. Gail Mitchell, "Anyone doubting hip-hop's marketing clout need look no further than Jay-Z's feet," *Rolling Out*, May 23, 2003, www.mobe.com/next/hiphop.htm.

11. Richard Linnett, "Reebok re-brands for hip-hop crowd," *Advertising Age*, January 28, 2002, pp. 3, 27.

12. Paul-Mark Rendon, "The power of women," *Marketing*, August 19/26, 2004, p. 4.

13. Norma Ramage, "Mark's keeps an eye on the ladies," *Marketing*, February 10, 2003, p. 2.

14. Michelle Halpern, "Cute, but scary," *Marketing*, August 9/16, 2004, p. 13.

15. "The state of affairs in the nation today," *Consumer TrendZ 2003*, Millward Brown Goldfarb.

16. Ibid.

17. Chris Daniels, "Almost rich," *Marketing*, April 26, 2004, pp. 9–12.

18. Malcolm Dunlop and Christine Comi, "Multicultural explosion," *Strategy*, February 11, 2002, p. 25.

19. David Showcroft and Mike Farrell, "Peer pressure is huge factor in success of brands," *Strategy*, January 3, 1998, p. 34.

20. Karl Moore, "Gotta get that buzz," *Marketing*, June 28/July 5, 2004, p. 9.

21. "What Quebec Wants," *Sales and Marketing Management in Canada*, July 1991, p. 16.

22. Graeme Hamilton, "Quebecers want distinct menu," *National Post*, May 24, 2003, p. A3.

23. "Getting to know Western Canada," *Strategy*, October 8, 2001, p. 21.

© Steve Craft/Masterfile

Business-to-Business Marketing and Organizational Buying Behaviour

In business-to-business marketing, organizations market goods and services to other organizations. Marketing strategies used in the business-to-business market are quite different from strategies used in the consumer market. Firms succeed in the business-to-business market when they fully understand the complex buying process that is involved and the criteria that are used to evaluate purchase decisions. Today, suppliers in business-to-business marketing must also embrace the e-commerce model as more and more buying organizations continue to adopt automated and collaborative purchasing models. By doing so, they are able to reduce costs and improve customer service.

The business-to-business market comprises business as well as industrial, government, institutional, and professional segments. In serving these diverse markets, organizations must identify the unique demands and needs of each, and then develop responsive marketing strategies showing how their products or services will resolve a special problem or satisfy a particular need.

This chapter illustrates the characteristics that influence organizational buying behaviour.

The Business-to-Business Market

business-to-business market

1. Identify the types of customers comprising the business-to-business marketplace.

The **business-to-business market** comprises individuals in an organization who are responsible for purchasing goods and services that the organization needs to produce a product or service, promote an idea, or produce an income. The business-to-business (or B2B) market can be divided into five distinct buying groups: business and industry, governments, institutions, wholesalers and retailers, and professions.

BUSINESS AND INDUSTRY

Much of Canada's economic progress in the 20th century was due to growth in manufacturing. However, since the 1960s services have contributed an increasing share of total output and employment. Currently, service-producing industries represent about 68 percent of economic production and goods-producing industries the remaining 32 percent. Among service industries the largest in terms of size are financial services (finance, insurance, and real estate), wholesale and retail trade, healthcare and social assistance, and public administration. Manufacturing makes up more than half the goods-producing sector. Other goods producers include agriculture, mining and oil extraction, utilities, and construction industries.[1]

Growth in service-related jobs is a reflection of a strong investment in technology in industries such as trade, finance, and business services (e.g., computer services, communications services, and engineering and scientific services). Also, a shift among manufacturers toward outsourcing has created growth in services. **Outsourcing** is defined as the contracting of services or functions previously done in-house. For example, most companies at one time purchased photocopying machines. Employees would do their own copying or, if large quantities were required on a continuous basis, a separate department would be responsible for printing needs. This is a service that a specialist like Xerox Canada Ltd. provides, for a fee. Xerox has positioned itself as a document services specialist (Figure 5.1). Other services that are now commonly outsourced include information processing, payroll, advertising, logistics and distribution planning, legal services, and e-business transaction services. The demand for specialists in these and other service areas has grown immensely.

Business and industrial organizations are grouped under the categories of users, original equipment manufacturers, wholesalers and retailers, and service businesses. For a brief description of these categories, see Figure 5.2.

outsourcing

Xerox Canada
www.xerox.ca

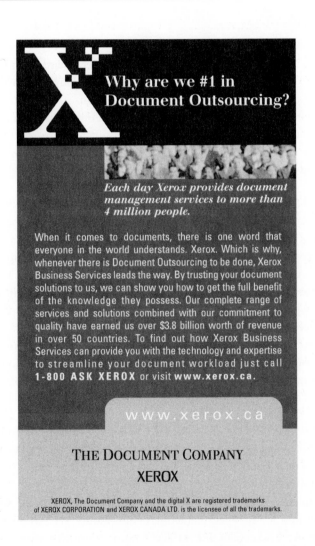

FIGURE
5.1

Xerox communicates its document services to companies interested in outsourcing

Courtesy of Xerox Canada

FIGURE
5.2

Categories of Business and Industry Organizations

Users

Organizations that purchase products to produce other products (e.g., a firm purchases capital equipment, such as machinery, in order to manufacture products on an assembly line).

Original Equipment Manufacturers (OEMs)

Companies purchasing industrial products that are incorporated directly into other products (e.g., General Motors is an OEM because it purchases finished radios, spark plugs, tires, and other products to install in its automobiles).

Wholesalers and Retailers

Intermediaries that purchase products to sell to other intermediaries or to final users (Safeway, The Bay, Canadian Tire).

Service Businesses

A variety of businesses including leisure and personal services, food and beverage services, accommodation services, and business services (e.g., Royal Bank, London Life, McDonald's, Sheraton Hotels, Air Canada). Collectively, these organizations need a variety of goods and services in order to conduct their business operations.

GOVERNMENTS

Collectively, the federal, provincial, and municipal governments form Canada's largest buying group. Governments tend to have a specialized buying procedure involving detailed order specifications and tender submissions from potential suppliers. Government contracting opportunities are advertised online through the Government Electronic Tendering Service (GETS). GETS is an outsourced operation provided by Mediagrif Interactive Technologies Inc. (MERX). About $5 billion in government contracts are advertised annually on this system.[2]

MERX
www.merx.com

INSTITUTIONS

The third major buying group is the institutional market, which includes hospitals, restaurants, and educational establishments. These customers require a variety of products and services from potential suppliers. The government funds hospitals and educational establishments, so operating objectives are not based on profit. Their motivation for buying is based on improving health care or quality of life. That said, budgets in this sector are not what they used to be so buyers actively search for lower-cost alternatives. In health services, for example, many hospitals now purchase through online electronic exchanges. Two Toronto hospitals currently buy through an exchange operated by Global Healthcare Exchange LLC and have saved more than $2 million in purchasing costs.[3] Online exchanges are discussed in more detail later in the chapter.

WHOLESALERS AND RETAILERS

Business organizations use wholesalers and retailers to resell their goods and services. Typically, a wholesaler purchases finished products (e.g., a grocery wholesaler, such as Loblaws or Sobeys, will purchase goods from suppliers, such as Kraft, General Mills, and Procter & Gamble), holds those goods in inventory in its warehouse, and then ships them to retailers (Loblaws, Zehrs, Valu-Mart, etc.) as demand dictates. In the grocery industry, it is quite common for national marketing organizations, such as Kraft or Procter & Gamble, to present a sales plan to their key account customers (e.g., Loblaws, Safeway, Sobeys) at the start of a year. At that time, marketing support from the selling organization and volume commitments from the customers are negotiated and agreed to.

PROFESSIONS

The professional market consists of doctors, lawyers, accountants, architects, engineers, and so on. The products that professionals buy usually improve the efficiency of their practice; for example, the purchase of computers and other communications equipment enhances productivity in an accounting office or law office.

It should be recognized that these four buying groups (business and industry, governments, institutions, and professionals) may require the same or similar products and services, but their needs and the reasons why they buy are quite different. For this reason, marketing organizations must develop precise marketing strategies for each segment of the market.

The Characteristics of Organizational Buying Behaviour

When a marketing firm develops a marketing mix that it can use to approach business customers, it should understand the elements that influence the decision-making process in organizations. **Organizational buying** may be defined as the decision-making process by which firms establish what products they need to purchase and then identify, evaluate, and select a brand and a supplier for those products.

Business markets are quite different from consumer markets (Figure 5.3). Their principal distinctions are that they have fewer buyers than consumer markets; the buyers

2. Describe the unique characteristics of organizational buying behaviour.

organizational buying

Consumer Marketing	Business-to-Business Marketing
Product Products are standardized, purchased frequently, and marketed by brand name.	Products are complex and marketed on the basis of a combination of price, quality, and service. Products are purchased less frequently.
Price Distributors are offered a list price and a series of discounts. Savings are passed on to consumers.	The same as consumer marketing, plus extensive price negotiation or contract bidding.
Marketing Communications Mainly advertising, with support from sales promotion and direct marketing techniques. Personal selling used in the channel of distribution.	Mainly personal selling, with support from sales promotion, direct marketing, and Internet communications. Mass advertising is now more common than in previous times.
Distribution Mainly traditional channels— manufacturer to wholesaler to retailer to consumer.	Short, direct channels due to need for personal selling and high dollar value of transaction.
Purchase Decision Made by an individual or household members.	Made by influence centres (users and non-users) and buying committees.
Buying Behaviour Consumers more subject to emotional appeals that play on concerns about image, status, prestige.	Organizational buyers are more rational due to the formality of the purchase decision process.

FIGURE
5.3

Some Differences between Consumer and Business-to-Business Marketing

tend to be concentrated near each other; the market presents different kinds of demand; the buying criteria are practical; and a formal buying process is used. Organizations involved in business-to-business marketing have accepted the concept of relationship marketing more quickly than have consumer goods companies and have formed supply chain management systems that link the information systems of the various participants. Efficient operations of these systems provide cost savings for all. The concept of *e-procurement* (discussed later in this chapter) is growing rapidly. Let us examine the characteristics of organizational buying behaviour in detail.

NUMBER OF BUYERS

There are fewer buyers or customers in the business-to-business market than there are in consumer markets, but the few buyers have immense buying power. To illustrate, the "Big Three" domestic automobile manufacturers (General Motors, Ford, and DaimlerChrysler) dominate their industry. Firms like these are few in number but purchase incredible quantities of products (e.g., tires, windshields, engine parts, and so on). In the business market procurement officers buy in large quantities, so the dollar value of individual purchases is much larger than it is in the consumer market. It is important for suppliers to invest in marketing communications to create awareness for the company and its products. Both personal selling and online communications are vital. Today more than 90 percent of procurement officers use the Internet to identify and communicate with potential suppliers.[4]

LOCATION OF BUYERS

Business markets tend to concentrate by area; the Quebec City to Windsor corridor is a popular location for manufacturers. Ontario and Quebec account for 68 percent of the nation's manufacturing establishments, 76 percent of the value of goods manufactured, and 76 percent of people employed in manufacturing industries.[5] This area is also the centre of banking and financial services in Canada. Resource-based industries, such as agriculture, forestry, and fishing, dominate other regions.

To identify and locate potential target markets, marketing firms utilize the North American Industry Classification System (NAICS). This is a numbering system established jointly by the United States, Canada, and Mexico (post North American Free Trade Agreement) that provides statistical information about business activity across North America.

The classification system subdivides the main classifications into major industry segments; for example, a major classification may be retail trade. The system then subdivides retail trade into categories such as general merchandise stores, department stores, variety stores, and miscellaneous general merchandise stores. Further subdivision will identify firms by sales volume and number of employees. NAICS is useful for tracking down prospective customers and obtaining basic information about them so that better marketing strategies can be developed.

The combination of fewer buyers with higher dollar value and more geographic concentration makes personal selling an attractive and practical way to market goods and services to these markets despite the high costs of such an activity. However, other promotional techniques, such as direct mail, telemarketing, and online communications, now play an expanding role in helping firms penetrate the business-to-business marketplace. The growth of e-commerce and its impact on supply chain management is an opportunity for many companies. While online procurement was only 5 percent of all procurement in 2002, it is expected to be as high as 35 percent by 2005.[6] Marketing organizations must prepare for such a dramatic shift in buying procedure.

DEMAND CHARACTERISTICS

There are two types of demand in the business-to-business market: derived demand and joint (shared) demand. **Derived demand** is a concept that states that the demand for products sold in the business-to-business market is actually derived from consumer demand, or demand ultimately created by the final user. To illustrate this relationship, consider what happens when soft drink manufacturers switched from steel cans to aluminum cans. As beverage manufacturers such as Coca-Cola, PepsiCo, and Molson moved to widespread use of the aluminum can, which consumers wanted, the manufacturer's demand for products produced by aluminum manufacturers increased dramatically. At the same time, demand fell for glass and steel containers so manufacturers of these products were affected negatively.

Joint or shared demand occurs when industrial products can be used only in conjunction with others—when the production and marketing of one product is dependent on another. This happens when the various parts needed for a finished product may arrive from various sources to be assembled at one central location. To manufacture Maxwell House coffee, for example, Kraft Canada would need coffee beans (probably imported from South America), plastic lids (from a plastics manufacturer who produces the lids to Kraft's specifications), glass or plastic jars (from a glass manufacturer or plastics manufacturer), paper labels (from a printing shop), and a cardboard shipping case (from another paper products supplier).

If any of these components is unavailable, demand for the other components will decrease, and the production and marketing of Maxwell House coffee will be adversely affected. Phenomena such as strikes and natural disasters that make certain items scarce can also lessen demand for other items. For this reason, business marketers often have alternative sources of supply available. The use of electronic ordering systems (customer relationship management programs) also helps ensure a steady flow of inventory through the channel of distribution.

THE BUYING CRITERIA ARE PRACTICAL

In business and industry, the buying criteria tend to be practical and rationally pursued. Although impractical or irrational motives may sometimes be present, they generally play a small role. Quality, price, and service form the basis for buying decisions in business and industry.

Central to the buying procedures of organizations is a vendor analysis. A **vendor analysis** entails an evaluation of potential suppliers. They are assessed based on their technological ability, consistency in meeting product specifications, overall quality, on-time delivery, their ability to provide needed quantity, and their reputation in their industry. How well a supplier rates in these areas affects its chances of selection, but price also plays a key role in the decision. Before signing a deal, the buyer may request bids based on predetermined specifications or negotiate an acceptable price from a supplier that the vendor analysis indicates is acceptable.

Let us examine these criteria in more detail:

1. *Price*—Price is usually evaluated in conjunction with other buying goals. The lowest price is not always accepted. A company will consider the differential advantages offered by vendors and evaluate price in the context of other purchase criteria. Where the cash outlay is significant, cost is viewed from a long-term perspective. Potential long-term savings as a result of the purchase are weighed against the high purchase cost in the short term.

derived demand

joint or shared demand

vendor analysis

2. *Quality*—Business customers look for sources of supply that can provide the same unvarying quality with each order. Since a supplier's product becomes part of a new product during manufacturing, it could affect the quality of the final product if the supplier's product were inconsistent in quality. Generally, when business customers assess price–quality relationships, they do not sacrifice quality for price.

3. *Service and Services Offered*—Customers frequently review a supplier's reputation for keeping its current customers satisfied. They do so by contacting other customers to see how well the supplier performs the service function. The primary concern of the buying organization is that repair and replacement services be readily available when needed. The sales representative will play a key role in managing the customer relationship.

4. *Continuity of Supply*—Customers are concerned about the long-term availability of a product or service. They want to know how reliable the supplier is in meeting customer demand. To maintain a steady source of supply, customers often deal with numerous suppliers, knowing that such factors as strikes could halt the flow of a product from any one supplier. Further, the location of potential suppliers is now less important in the decision-making process. Companies now search the world for suppliers who can best combine the features of price, quality, and delivery. In the automobile industry, North American suppliers must compete for contracts with suppliers from the Far East and Europe. The presence and use of the Internet has facilitated the ongoing search for new, better, and less costly suppliers. For more details, refer to the section on e-procurement and the Marketing in Action vignette **Dell Leads the Way**, which appear later in this chapter.

A FORMAL BUYING PROCESS IS FOLLOWED

In many business organizations, one individual has the authority to sign the purchase order, but many other individuals may influence the purchase decision. There are two primary causes of this situation in modern business. First, businesses today often utilize **buying committees**, which bring individuals together to share the responsibility of making the purchase decision. Second, businesses may hold meetings of various informed groups of people in order to arrive at a purchase decision. This informal approach, involving several people in the organization, is called a **buying centre**.

buying committees

buying centre

1. *Buying Committees*—To illustrate the concept of a buying committee, we will assume that a firm is considering the purchase of a million-dollar piece of production-line equipment. Since the financial ramifications are significant, it is imperative that the best possible decision is made. Consequently, the firm appoints a committee consisting of key personnel from various disciplines—production, engineering, finance, marketing, and purchasing—so that the decision can be evaluated from a variety of angles. Theoretically, such a decision-making process is very rational, and the participants are comforted to know that a costly purchase decision is a shared one.

2. *Buying Centres*—In buying centres, which are more informal than buying committees, the individuals involved have certain roles. Researchers have identified five specific roles:

   Users: those who use the product (e.g., laptop computers or cell phones used by travelling businesspeople)

   Influencers: those who assist in defining specifications for what is needed (e.g., an engineer designs a production line)

   Buyers: those with the authority and responsibility to select suppliers and negotiate with them (e.g., a purchasing agent)

Deciders: those with formal or informal power to select the actual supplier (e.g., a high-dollar-value purchase of technical equipment may ultimately be the responsibility of a vice-president of manufacturing)

Gatekeepers: those who control the flow of information to others in the centre (e.g., a purchasing agent may block certain information from reaching influencers and deciders).

From a marketing perspective, it must be determined who on the committee or within the buying centre has the most influence. Once that is known, the best means of communicating with the influence centre must be determined. What role should personal selling, sales promotion, advertising, and direct marketing have in the overall strategy, and what priority should each have?

CENTRALIZED PURCHASING

In today's economic environment, buying organizations are looking for the best possible prices and value for dollars spent. Consequently, many firms have developed centralized purchasing systems in order to secure better price discounts based on volume purchases. For example, the Bay, Zellers, and Home Outfitters, all owned by Hudson's Bay Company, have formed one large buying division that purchases for each retail division. In these situations, marketers must deal with just a few buyers, all at a high level of management. Hudson's Bay also links hundreds of Bay, Zellers, and Home Outfitters vendors to buying groups for the interchange of electronic procurement documents.

Retailers are concerned with offering consumers a balanced assortment of merchandise. **Assortment** refers to the variety of products—the types, models, and styles of product that meet a retailer's target-market needs. Assortment decisions are based on how well the supplier's product "fits in" with the merchandise mix. Decisions on what product lines to carry and how much inventory to stock are made easier by sophisticated computer-controlled systems. Working from the electronic cash register at the point of sale, a retail buyer can track the movement of goods in all retail outlets on a daily basis. Automatic computer ordering is now the standard practice. Such systems consider product movement, desired inventory levels, and delivery time. Where relationship management models exist, an order request from a buyer will automatically trigger delivery from a supplier.

assortment

PERSONAL CHARACTERISTICS

Business buyers are just as human as other consumers; thus, the more knowledge a marketer has about the specific buyer, the more impact the marketing message can have. To address the needs of certain personalities, emotional appeals centred on status and prestige may be included in overall marketing strategies, along with ordinary rational appeals. Marketers also recognize that many business decisions are influenced or made in social settings such as on the golf course, over a drink after a squash match, or at a sports or theatre event of some kind. Entertaining customers is an essential aspect of business-to-business marketing.

Many experts believe personal lifestyle considerations will impact future B2B buying decisions. As the children of baby boomers (a generation referred to as Generation X) take over management positions, they will bring a new mindset to the corporation. For more insight into this way of thinking, read the Marketing in Action vignette **A New Generation of Buyers**.

RELATIONSHIPS ARE SOUGHT

In today's marketplace, organizations that deal directly with one another (suppliers, manufacturers, and distributors) are doing so in a more cooperative, less competitive way. Programs are being established to evaluate the flow and use of goods and services through the channel of distribution. The aim of a partnership is to devise and implement strategies that will produce mutual benefits for all participants. The concept of building relationships is discussed in detail in the next section.

MARKETING IN ACTION

A New Generation of Buyers

Canada's population is aging, and baby boomers are a key target for consumer marketing strategies. But what's happening in B2B marketing? As baby boomers retire and are replaced by people their children's age (Generation X—people in their mid-20s to mid-30s), a new breed of manager will be making key buying decisions. This new group of managers will bring different attitudes and behaviours and pose new challenges for marketers.

"If you speak to them as a business and don't consider the generational factors at play, you may end up alienating them," says Stephen Munden, director of research at Warrillow & Co., a Toronto-based marketing firm. His research shows that Generation Xers do not respond to the same strategies as baby boomers, for they have been left a legacy that they have to clean up in terms of moral values and corporate values.

Not only is this age group moving into management, they are also starting up new businesses at alarming rates—10 percent of people under 30 are actively trying to establish their own business. Many have experienced the corporate world and have decided to branch out on their own.

Traditional B2B marketers segment the market demographically—by industry type, size, location, and so on, but Munden suggests that psychographics be included—the owners' or managers' orientation must be added to the economic orientation of the buying company since the company's corporate culture is influenced by their personality.

Some differences that have been identified between boomers and Generation X that will impact B2B marketing strategies are that:

- Generation Xers value access to information and assimilate data more quickly than baby boomers.
- Branding is important to Generation Xers. Branding is their code for quality; they respect brands that are successful and show leadership in their industries.
- Generation Xers are comfortable carrying high debt to start their own business, yet they are more economically conservative than boomers.

If the tendencies of buyers are changing, the tendencies of marketers also must change. The personal characteristics of this new generation of managers confirm the influential role that online communications and online buying and selling will play in the future. Any marketing organization that doesn't adjust its marketing strategies accordingly will suffer the inevitable consequences.

Adapted from Bruce Gillespie, "Get ready for new wave," *Financial Post Edge*, November 24, 2003, pp. FE1, FE3.

Andrew Errington/Stone/Getty Images

Integration and Partnering in Business-to-Business Marketing

The manner in which business-to-business organizations do business with each other is changing. What is becoming increasingly common is the trend toward buyer–seller cooperation and the formation of partnerships. Earlier in the text, this partnering was referred to as **customer relationship management (CRM)**. There are numerous other expressions used to describe CRM—*relationship marketing, strategic alliances, partnerships,* and *value-added marketing*. Movement toward the formation of partnerships is due, in part, to the rationalizing and restructuring of operations that firms have gone through in recent times. In the process of evaluating business practices, firms have discovered newer and more efficient methods. As well, the increasing level of competition between similar products has contributed to the partnership concept, since it can give an otherwise undistinguished product an edge in the marketplace.

customer relationship management (CRM)

Acceptance of this concept has created a fundamental change in the seller–buyer relationship. The essential ingredient is an integrated tie between customers and their suppliers. This means that members of a channel of distribution create closer links among themselves (Figure 5.4). When partnering is applied to marketing a business or industrial product, the marketer must acquire more detailed information about its customers and their operations. The marketer must be more familiar with the role its product plays in the customer's operation. Therefore, collecting information about the customer and their operations is an essential element in the marketing process.

Partnering is also changing the nature of communications with customers. Salespeople still play a key role, but rather than calling on customers individually,

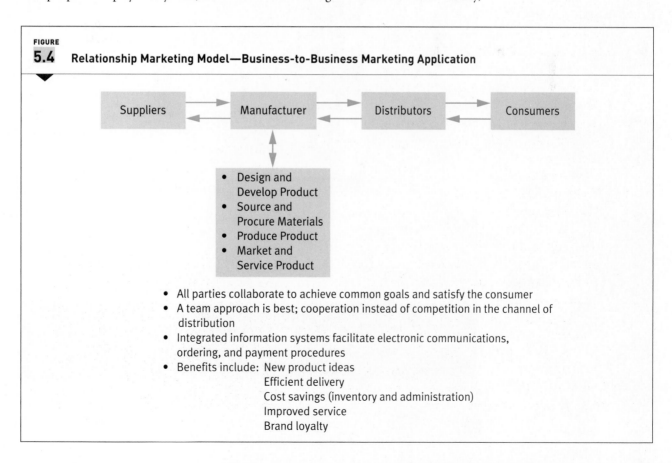

FIGURE 5.4 Relationship Marketing Model—Business-to-Business Marketing Application

Suppliers ⟷ Manufacturer ⟷ Distributors ⟷ Consumers

- Design and Develop Product
- Source and Procure Materials
- Produce Product
- Market and Service Product

- All parties collaborate to achieve common goals and satisfy the consumer
- A team approach is best; cooperation instead of competition in the channel of distribution
- Integrated information systems facilitate electronic communications, ordering, and payment procedures
- Benefits include: New product ideas
  Efficient delivery
  Cost savings (inventory and administration)
  Improved service
  Brand loyalty

project teams

project teams are being formed to deal with customers' needs more effectively. Under the leadership of an account manager (sales representative), the team may include customer service people, engineers, traffic specialists, information systems specialists, and so on. Essentially, a team from the marketing organization is dealing with a team (buying committee) representing the customer. The two teams work together to achieve common goals. They devise programs that are compatible so that all parties benefit. As an example, consider that the core business at FedEx is the delivery of packages for many companies. This is the concept of *outsourcing*, discussed earlier. See the advertisement in Figure 5.5.

In the partnership process, companies seek partners anywhere in the world. General Motors was the first automobile manufacturer to adopt a global supply sourcing policy to strengthen its worldwide buying power. GM's goal is to obtain components at the best possible price from suppliers. Such a relationship calls for long-term contracts—some for the life of the model—so that suppliers are guaranteed the necessary volume to

FIGURE
5.5

Many companies outsource delivery and shipping functions to experts such as FedEx.

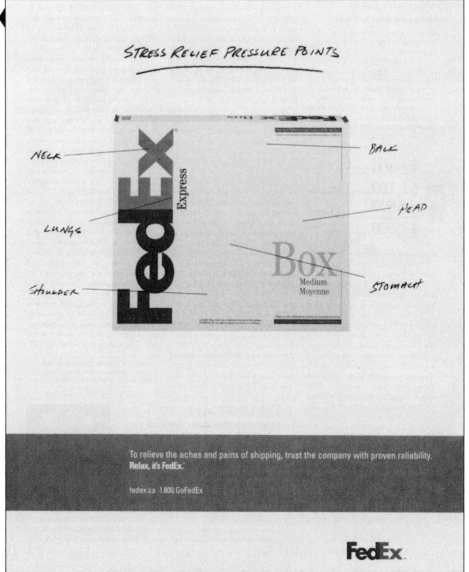

support their capital investments that will reduce costs and improve quality. For General Motors and its suppliers, the goal is to design, produce, and market a better-quality car in a shorter space of time. If the goal is achieved, the partners prosper financially.

In any partnership, however, one member of the channel usually has more control than other members. From the example above, General Motors pressures suppliers for the lowest possible prices for parts. If GM is suffering financially, some of the burden is passed on to suppliers. The Ford Motor Company recently announced that its present domestic parts suppliers must eventually match the prices of lower-cost rivals, including those based in low-wage countries such as China. Such a move is necessary because Ford and other domestic manufacturers are losing market share to Japanese and European rivals. The impact on suppliers is clear: they must consider moving their production out of North America to lower-cost countries.[7]

Another form of partnering is frequently referred to as reverse marketing. **Reverse marketing** is an effort by organizational buyers to build relationships that shape suppliers' goods and services to fit the buyer's needs and those of its customers. In other words, the buyer sets the product specifications and the seller produces the goods to those specifications. Private-label products, such as President's Choice (or PC), sold at various Loblaws, Zehrs, and Value-Mart outlets, and Mastercraft products, sold at Canadian Tire, are examples.

reverse marketing

Private-label products meet the quality standards established by the distributor (Loblaws and Canadian Tire). To retain the business, source manufacturers must maintain standards at all times and produce the goods within price constraints established by the distributor. Suppliers who fail to maintain the desired standards set by manufacturers or fail to stay within price guidelines could lose the supply contract. Therefore, a supplier cannot have too much of its business tied up with any single distributor. If they lose the contract they usually face significant financial hardship. An example of this type of relationship is Wal-Mart's recently formed partnership with Levi Strauss & Company: Wal-Mart will market an exclusive line of Levi's Signature jeans at a price of $39 or less, well below Levi's price in other retail outlets.[8]

E-PROCUREMENT

The Internet has spawned e-procurement buying opportunities. **E-procurement** is an Internet-based business-to-business marketplace through which participants are able to purchase supplies and services from each other. With improved efficiency, businesses can access procurement sites and services to get multiple bids, issue purchase orders, and make payments. E-procurement has been growing as major companies, often in the same industry, seek to slash purchasing costs.

e-procurement

4. Describe the influence of e-procurement practices on business-to-business markets.

In 2003, combined B2B sales in the private and public sectors totalled $19.1 billion, a 40-percent increase over the previous year's levels.[9] Such a significant rate of growth reconfirms the importance of online marketing activities for suppliers in the future. The concept of e-procurement is the future for business-to-business marketing organizations. As Robert Lent, senior vice-president and co-founder of Ariba Inc., suggests, "You will either buy on a B2B market, sell on a B2B market, create a B2B market or be killed by a B2B market."[10]

Combining customer relationship management practices with e-procurement models fosters long-term relationships with buyers and sellers and presents a situation where participants are directly influenced by the decisions and actions of other participants. Dell Computers Inc. is a leader in practising electronic supply chain management and using e-procurement systems. For insight into its sophisticated planning systems, read the Marketing in Action vignette **Dell Leads the Way**.

MARKETING IN ACTION

Dell Leads the Way

In procurement circles, Dell is recognized as a true innovator. Stop and consider that Dell never assembles a computer system until it has received an order for it; every system it makes has a customer waiting for it—and they don't wait very long!

When we think of marketing we typically view results in terms of sales and profits, but a company such as Dell—which is so efficient on the cost side of the equation—can worry less about sales revenue and still meet profit goals.

Like most companies, Dell's supply chain management process used to rely on manual procedures and paperwork that limited its ability to maintain optimal balance between supply and demand and to react to changes in the marketplace.

Accenture, a management consulting company, designed and implemented an automated system that changed things dramatically at Dell. Dell can now take thousands of orders that are received by telephone or online, translate them into millions of component requirements, and work directly with its suppliers to build and deliver products to meet customer demand. Suppliers use an Internet portal to view Dell's requirements as well as changes to forecasts based on marketplace demands and their ability to meet Dell's delivery needs. Only the parts required by Dell get delivered to manufacturing facilities in various parts of the world.

Amazing as this may sound, Dell schedules every manufacturing line in every facility around the world every two hours and they bring into the facility only two hours' worth of materials. Each facility maintains only about six hours' worth of inventory. At any given time Dell holds only four days of inventory in its entire system, whereas most competitors carry 30 days or more. An order received from a customer triggers the entire system.

Any marketing organization doing business with Dell must be online and have the ability to respond quickly to changing conditions. Reliable order fulfillment is absolutely crucial, or you'll quickly become a former supplier. For Dell, the electronic supply management system has decreased cycle times in factories and reduced the need for warehouse space. For suppliers, there is less product obsolescence and lower transaction costs.

Dell suppliers are involved in an online community that does $25 billion worth of business annually. To make it work efficiently all parties have a keen eye on the future!

Adapted from "Dell: Build-to-Order Manufacturing, A Case Study," www.accenture.com.

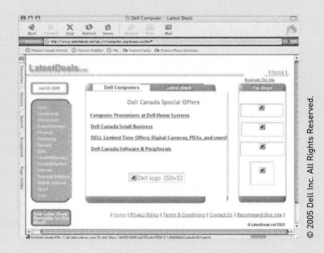

Types of Buying Decisions

5. Identify the various types of organizational buying decisions.

The types of buying decisions that business and industrial organizations face are classified according to the *time* needed to make the decision, the *cost* (and risk associated with high-cost decisions), and the *complexity* of the product. There are basically three types of buying situations: new task, modified rebuy, and straight or full rebuy.

FIGURE
5.6

Types of Buying Decisions in Business-to-Business Markets

Type	Price	Risk	Knowledge	Involvement
New Task	High	High	Limited. Must seek information on best alternatives	Buying committee
Modified Rebuy	Medium	Some	Good. Seek out new information for better products	Buying committee, buying centre influence, or purchasing agent
Straight Rebuy	Low	Minimal	Good. Product considered acceptable	Low. Routine order by purchasing manager

NEW-TASK PURCHASE

What is called a **new-task purchase** occurs when a business buys a product, usually an expensive one, for the first time. The organization lacks familiarity with the item, so it seeks information that will assist it in making the best decision. Since the product represents a high risk because of its great costs, numerous individuals often participate in the evaluation and decision—sometimes, for example, through a buying committee. Capital equipment such as new buildings, custom-designed production equipment, and communications equipment are examples of new-task purchases.

new-task purchase

MODIFIED REBUY

In a **modified rebuy**, an organization purchases a product, usually of medium price, that it purchases infrequently. Typically, the organization is less than satisfied with the product it currently uses and so searches the marketplace for a substitute that will perform better—one that will, for example, operate more efficiently and save the firm money. Savings in the long term can be measured against any short-term cost increases. Possible modified rebuys may include, for example, replacing power tools, telecommunications equipment, or automobile parts. The buyer often switches allegiance to another supplier based on current needs and situation.

modified rebuy

STRAIGHT (OR FULL) REBUY

Straight or full rebuys are used for inexpensive items bought on a regular basis. Essentially, they are routine reorders requiring no modification, since the needs they fulfill remain relatively constant. Because the risks are low, the decision is a simple one, much like the routine purchase made by a consumer. The ongoing purchase of office supplies and paper products qualifies as a straight rebuy.

straight or full rebuys

As discussed earlier in the chapter, electronic ordering and reordering systems can be used in each of these buying situations. A summary of the key differences among the types of buying decisions is included in Figure 5.6.

Steps in the Buying-Decision Process

6. Identify the steps involved in the organizational decision process.

Since business organizations and similar groups generally exhibit rational buying behaviour, the decision-making process tends to be clearly defined. The typical buying model has eight stages (see Figure 5.7). Let us examine each of these stages.

FIGURE
5.7

A Typical Buying Decision Model in Business Organizations

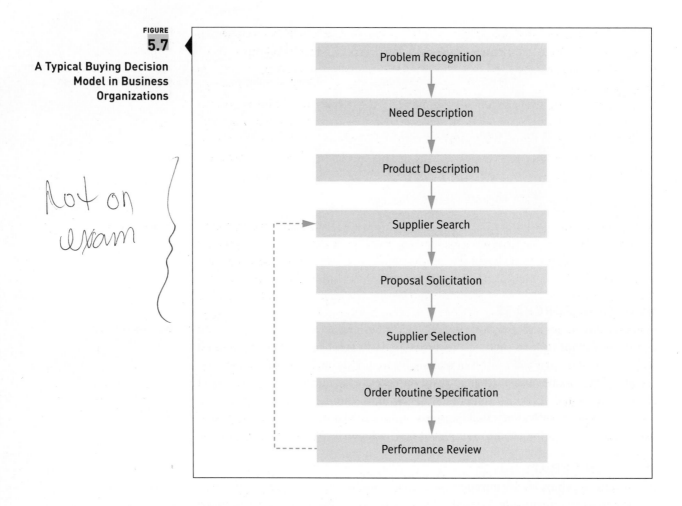

Not on exam

Problem Recognition

Need Description

Product Description

Supplier Search

Proposal Solicitation

Supplier Selection

Order Routine Specification

Performance Review

PROBLEM RECOGNITION

problem recognition

As the initial stage, **problem recognition** describes the fact that a change has occurred in the organizational environment, which reveals a problem or a new need that must be resolved. For example, a computerized inventory system signals that it is time to reorder; plant personnel become dissatisfied with production capacity; purchasing is not satisfied with some of the current suppliers because of their slow, unreliable delivery and lack of sufficient supplies; or marketing determines that an internal information and communications system more efficient than the present one is needed.

NEED DESCRIPTION

need description

For the **need description**, the buying organization identifies the general characteristics and qualities of the needed item or service. In effect, it starts to look at potential solutions by reviewing alternatives that have been successful in the past.

PRODUCT DESCRIPTION

product descriptions or specifications

With a general solution in mind, the buying organization now establishes precise **product descriptions** or **specifications** of the item needed. The process of formally describing the characteristics of the product ensures that needs are clearly communicated both within the organization and to potential suppliers. It is now common for this information to be posted online for members of the present supply chain management system to consider, or it can be posted separately to attract new vendors.

The quantity required is usually stipulated at this time, which assists suppliers in submitting bids. Specifications may consist of blueprints for a new production line, documented copy quality and maximum run length for a photocopier, or stipulations on temperature tolerances for a machine tool. The specifications are key criteria against which a potential supplier's products are evaluated. At this stage, too, the buying organization usually determines who will be responsible for deciding on the purchase. Will the responsibility remain with the purchasing manager, or will a buying committee be formed? The marketing organization must be ready to identify those with the most influence and direct its communications appropriately.

SUPPLIER SEARCH

During the **supplier search** stage, the buying organization looks for potential suppliers. Usually, two key decisions need to be made in the purchase process: first, which product or service the organization should buy, and second, from what particular supplier it should buy. Buying organizations, at this point, search for and qualify acceptable suppliers, using the *vendor analysis* discussed earlier in this chapter. To qualify a supplier means that the buying organization determines that the supplier can provide the product in a steady, reliable manner.

At the same time, marketing organizations evaluate the prospective buyers. Potential sources of information for both organizations include trade indexes, internal records of any past dealings with the other organization, trade advertising journals, and sales representatives. Trade indexes referred to frequently in Canada include *The Canadian Trade Index, Scott's Industrial Index, Canadian Key Business Directory, Frasers Trade Index*, and the North American Industry Classification System (discussed earlier in the chapter).

To ensure that they are seriously considered, potential suppliers must make themselves known to buyers. They must be listed in trade indexes for the products and services they provide, and they must actively communicate with potential customers through some combination of promotional programs. The must also have an easy-to-navigate yet information-laden website from which potential buyers can evaluate products and services. A company's reputation (as communicated across an industry by positive word of mouth) also plays a role in the supplier selection process.

PROPOSAL SOLICITATION

In **proposal solicitation**, the buying organization seeks and evaluates detailed written proposals from acceptable suppliers. Depending on the complexity of the purchase, the proposal could consist of a formal bid, a written quotation, or a price catalogue reference.

1. *Formal Bid*—A **bid** is a written tender submitted in a sealed envelope by a specified deadline. There are two forms of bids:

    - A **closed bid** is a written, sealed bid submitted by a supplier for review and evaluation by the purchaser on a particular date. The bid is based on specifications, or precise descriptions of what are required, published by the purchaser. Usually, the bid from the lowest "responsible" supplier is accepted; that is, one who is reputed to be dependable and stable. For the bidding process the submission of electronic bids is now an acceptable and convenient practice.

    - An **open bid** is less formal and may involve only a written or oral price quotation from a potential supplier. The quotation usually specifies how long the price is in effect. Typically, during an open bidding process buyers and sellers negotiate a price.

supplier search

proposal solicitation

bid

closed bid

open bid

quotation

2. *Quotation*—A **quotation** consists of a written document, usually from a sales representative, that states the terms of the price quoted.
3. *Price Catalogue Reference*—In this situation, the price is obtained by referring to a catalogue where all prices are listed. Buyers usually maintain current supplier catalogues on file. This procedure is common for routine orders of standardized products and supplies.

SUPPLIER SELECTION

supplier selection

At the **supplier selection** stage, the buying organization evaluates the proposals of qualified suppliers and selects the one that matches its needs. Each proposal is assessed with reference to the purchase criteria. In a complex buying situation, the supplier's proposal might be judged on such factors as price, quality, delivery, technical support service, warranties, and trade-in policies.

While weighing these many variables, buyers usually attempt to negotiate a better price with the short-listed suppliers. The bargaining process between buyers and sellers is now at its peak and there may be pressure on suppliers to drop their price. As mentioned earlier in the chapter, prominent retail chains place significant price pressure on potential suppliers, to the point where the supplier must evaluate if the sale is financially viable.

The influence of buying centres (informal) or buying committees (formal) must be considered and their members addressed by the marketing organization during this phase. Another option for the buying organization is to select several sources of supply for its own protection, assuming there are equal alternatives to choose from.

For routine purchases, there is not much distinction between the solicitation and the selection stages. Where costs and risks are low, solicitation and selection can occur simultaneously.

ORDER ROUTINE SPECIFICATION

order and reorder routine

After the supplier has been selected, the buying organization and marketing organization (the successful supplier or suppliers) agree on an **order and reorder routine** stipulating such matters as the procedure for accepting orders, delivery times, return policies, quantities to be ordered, repair and service policies, and any other factors judged important by the buyer. However, now that so much ordering is done electronically, automatically, and without any human input, much of the administrative tasks and paperwork associated with traditional ordering procedures have been eliminated.

PERFORMANCE REVIEW

Since businesses are constantly looking for products and services to improve the efficiency of their operations, there is no guarantee that the relationship between a buyer and seller will be a lasting one. In fact, the relationship may last only as long as the last price quotation. Once the purchaser receives a lower quotation, a new supplier may replace the existing one even if the current supplier has been satisfactory. General Motors, for example, implements price reviews on automobile parts every 30 days. It does not wait for a contract to expire. Current suppliers must offer prices that are very close to the lowest prices GM finds at that time, or risk losing the business.[11]

performance reviews

To ensure that their operations remain as efficient as possible, businesses implement **performance reviews**. As the final step in the buying process, the buying organization establishes a system of obtaining and evaluating feedback on the performance of the supplier's products. The purchasing manager will design an internal system for securing responses from user groups. Depending on whether the feedback is positive or negative, a decision to continue with or to drop a supplier is made. New price negotiations could also occur at this stage.

To marketers, this procedure demonstrates that the sale is never over. To avoid being dropped as a supplier, marketing organizations must accept criticisms and adapt their strategies, when necessary, to ensure that customers' needs are continuously satisfied. It has been shown that strong personal and business relationships develop when marketing organizations take fast, corrective action to resolve customer problems.

The steps involved in buying business and industrial goods are complex and require considerable attention on both the buying and selling sides as companies today are constantly searching for better value. As discussed in the previous section, e-procurement practices are now more common and partnerships are forming between members of the supply chain.

SUMMARY

The business-to-business market comprises four primary buying groups: business and industry, governments, institutions, and the professions, all of which require a vast array of products and services. This market has fewer buyers but larger buyers than the consumer market and is concentrated in certain geographic areas.

Business markets are quite different from consumer markets. The principal distinctions are that they have fewer buyers than consumer markets; the buyers tend to be concentrated near each other; the market presents different types of demand; the buying criteria are practical; and a formal buying process is used. Rational buying criteria include price, quality, service and services offered, and consistency of supply. Further, a buying committee (a formal group within the organization) or a buying centre (an informal group in an organization) will influence buying decisions.

Personal or lifestyle influences must now be considered in the business-to-business seller–buyer relationship. Including lifestyles in the marketing equation is based on the notion that new, younger managers with different attitudes are taking over management positions from older, more traditional-style managers.

Relationship marketing practices are also more prevalent in business marketing than in consumer marketing. The business-to-business economy has embraced the Internet, and many companies are forming cooperative ventures to achieve more cost efficiency in their respective operations. For many industries, the entire supply chain is automated, using buyer–seller customer relationship management programs and the introduction of e-procurement purchasing models.

The types of buying decisions that business organizations face are classified according to time needed to make the decision, the cost, and the complexity of the product. New-task, modified rebuy, and straight (full) rebuy are the different types of purchases made by organizational customers.

The basic buying process is a series of eight steps: problem recognition, need description, product description, supplier search, proposal solicitation, supplier selection, routine order specification, and performance review.

The challenge for marketers in approaching the business market is to consider the different buying behaviours in each of the major segments and then develop effective and efficient marketing mixes that will satisfy them. The approaches taken will vary from one segment to another. As well, they may have to tailor their strategies to specific companies because the unique needs and problems of one company will vary from another. Based on the rapid adoption of electronic buying and selling, a marketing organization must have an online presence or risk being shut out by buyers looking at the convenience and efficiency that e-commerce presents.

KEY TERMS

REVIEW QUESTIONS

1. What are the four major buying groups comprising the business-to-business market?

2. How is buying behaviour different in the business market from that in the consumer market?

3. Explain the influence the following characteristics have on organizational buying behaviour:
   a) Number of buyers
   b) Location of buyers
   c) Derived demand and joint demand
   d) Centralized purchasing

4. Briefly describe the primary buying criteria in business-to-business buying situations.

5. Distinguish between a buying committee and a buying centre.

6. Explain the concept of e-procurement. What benefits does the e-procurement model offer a participating company?

7. What is the difference between a new-task purchase and a modified rebuy?

8. Briefly describe the steps in the decision-making process that organizations follow to make purchases.

DISCUSSION AND APPLICATION QUESTIONS

1. If interest rates and inflation were to rise and consumer demand for colour television sets declined, how would demand be affected in industries other than television production? Provide examples to illustrate your viewpoint.

2. "Developing partnerships with suppliers and customers is crucial to the success of business-to-business marketing organizations." Do you agree or disagree with this statement? Justify your position.

3. Should lifestyle considerations be factored in to the marketing of business-to-business goods and services? Are today's new and younger managers any different from their predecessors? Conduct some research on this topic and develop a position on it. Provide relevant examples or illustrations to substantiate your position. Refer to the appropriate section of the chapter for initial discussion on the issue.

E-ASSIGNMENT

Visit the purchasing manager of a local manufacturing company or service-based organization (e.g., a hotel, hospital, or college). Discuss with him or her the procedures that the organization uses for a modified rebuy or new-task purchase (perhaps examine a recent purchase in detail). What factors were most important in arriving at the purchase decision? How has this company integrated the Internet (online buying) into its buying operations? How extensive is its e-commerce activity? What advantages has the Internet provided? Report your findings to the class.

ENDNOTES

1. "Gross Domestic Product by Industry," *The Daily*, July 29, 2004, Statistics Canada, www.statcan.ca/Daily.

2. http://contractsCanada.gc.ca/en/tender.

3. Grant Buckler, "Online exchange yields healthy hospital savings," *Globe and Mail*, March 21, 2002, p. B20.

4. Online Procurement Trends, Advertising Supplement, *Canadian Business* 2004.

5. *Marketing Research Handbook*, 2002, pp. 181–182.

6. Online Procurement Trends, Advertising Supplement, *Canadian Business*, 2004.

7. Norihiko Shirouzu, "Ford, GM push suppliers for aggressive price cuts," *Globe and Mail*, November 18, 2003, p. B16.

8. Dana Flavelle, "Wal-Mart, Levi form marketing agreement," *Toronto Star*, November 5, 2003, pp. E1, E11.

9. Terry Webber, "Online sales up 40% in 2003," *Globe and Mail*, April 16, 2004, www.globeandmail.com.

10. John Partridge, "Two banks, Bell part of big e-commerce venture," *Globe and Mail*, September 7, 2000, pp. B1, B11.

11. Norihiko Shirouzu, "Ford, GM push suppliers for aggressive price cuts," *Globe and Mail*, November 18, 2003, p. B16.

Marketing Planning

This section concentrates on two essential elements of strategic marketing planning. First it discusses the concept of market segmentation and the identification of target markets. The focus then shifts to the strategic planning process, where links are drawn between various types of plans in an organization.

Chapter 6 illustrates how organizations use information about consumers to identify market segments and pursue target markets where profitable opportunities exist. The concept of product positioning is introduced.

Chapter 7 draws relationships between planning at the corporate level and planning at the operational or marketing levels of an organization.

PART

3

© Jerzyworks/Masterfile

Market Segmentation and Target Marketing

Learning Objectives

After studying this chapter, you will be able to

1. Describe the various levels of market segmentation.

2. Describe the process used and information needed to identify and select target markets.

3. Describe the various types of segmentation strategies commonly used in contemporary marketing practice.

4. Explain the concept of positioning and its role in contemporary marketing practice.

What Is a Market?

market

market segmentation

Before discussing market segmentation, let us review what a market is. A **market** is a group of people who have a similar need for a product or service, the resources to purchase the product or service, and the willingness and ability to buy it. The reality of this explanation is that most products and services are marketed to smaller groups (called segments) that fall within the larger mass market. This practice is referred to as **market segmentation**.

Essentially, a firm adopts a market segmentation strategy that is best suited to achieve its goals and objectives while staying within the financial resources that are available. Organizations now have the ability to reach individual consumers with unique marketing strategies. This is the ultimate form of market segmentation, a concept that will be discussed in detail in this chapter.

The Levels of Market Segmentation

1. Describe the various levels of market segmentation.

Marketers choose among four basic segmentation alternatives: mass marketing, market segmentation, niche marketing, and direct (one-to-one or individual) marketing. Depending on the size of an organization and the resources available, an organization may employ several of these alternatives at one time. By no means are these strategies exclusive.

MASS MARKETING

mass marketing

An organization practising **mass marketing** implements one basic marketing strategy to appeal to a broad range of consumers. It does not address any distinct characteristics among the consumers. In effect, the nature of the product or service is such that it enjoys widespread acceptance. In contemporary practice, this type of marketing is the exception rather than the rule, but certain products and services are suited to this approach.

Perhaps the best example of mass marketing today is Wal-Mart. While positioned as a discount department store, Wal-Mart offers everyday prices and product selection that attracts a wide cross-section of the North American population. It seems that people of all income brackets like a bargain! Wal-Mart has been so successful (it is now the leading department store in Canada and the United States) that it has forced financial hardship on competitors who were once classified as mass marketers. Eaton's, for example, a Canadian retailing institution, could not fend off Wal-Mart and eventually went out of business. Zellers, once Canada's leading discount department store, has lost significant ground to Wal-Mart and this lack of success indicates how difficult it is to implement a mass marketing strategy today.

In the retailing sector consumers are either trading up or trading down in terms of the quality of goods they are buying and the quality of stores they are shopping in. Consumers shopping for fashion goods, for example, will not shop at Wal-Mart, Sears, or The Bay. Instead they will migrate to upscale boutiques where there is a better selection of goods and better service. Stores such as Harry Rosen or Holt Renfrew are more to their liking. Such a distinction refers to the concept of market segmentation and a firm's ability to distinguish itself from its rivals. In today's very competitive and differentiated marketplace, stores like The Bay, Sears, and Zellers are not connecting with consumers.

MARKET SEGMENTATION

Market segmentation is the division of a large market (mass market) into smaller homogeneous markets (segments or targets) on the basis of common needs and/or similar lifestyles. Segmentation strategies are based on the premise that it is preferable to tailor marketing strategies to distinct user groups, where the degree of competition may be less and the opportunities greater. For example, the automobile market is divided into many different segments: economy, mid-size, luxury, sport utility, and so on, based on the needs and lifestyles of different groups of people.

With market segmentation, a company specializes by concentrating on segments of the population. For example, Campbell's Soup has traditionally marketed to moms but recently decided to switch its emphasis and target kids directly with advertising messages. Campbell's rationale is simple: parents and kids are collaborating on purchase decisions these days, and soup as a food is wet and ideal for slurping, making it an interesting category for kids. Kids said they would embrace the Campbell's brand if they were communicated with directly—good news for a mature brand in a flat market, as it represents a new opportunity.[1]

The Campbell's example demonstrates market segmentation based on age and gender, but there are many other ways to segment a market. Staying abreast of external trends is another factor influencing segmentation decisions. For example, Canada's growing obesity rate and the resulting junk food backlash are well known, but as sizes have increased another transformation is quietly underway—appealing to the plus-sized woman.

In fashion, where a ridiculously small size is the holy grail, plus sizes were being neglected. Roughly 30 percent of Canadian women wear size 14 and up, and at least two-thirds of American women are overweight. Knowledge of such data represents opportunity. Cotton Ginny, a retailer that has served the plus-size market for years, is placing greater emphasis on its larger line, Cotton Ginny Plus. As well, visual displays of larger-sized clothing are now much more prominent in their stores. Based on the premise that larger-than-average women feel unwelcome and uncomfortable working out in regular gyms, a health club called Curves (started in 1992) has been expanding rapidly in recent years. It too has responded to the obesity trend and self-image concerns raised by women.[2]

To maximize profits, a firm commonly has to operate in many different segments. A successful segmentation strategy enables a firm to control marketing costs, allowing it to make profits. As well, the organization may be able to develop a distinct niche for itself or for a product line or brand that it markets. For example, Gatorade established the sports drink segment of the beverage market, and to this day dominates the category in terms of market share. As described above, the Curves fitness chain hopes to achieve similar success.

On the downside, organizations employing market segmentation must be alert to shifting consumer trends and the cyclical patterns of the economy or suffer the consequences. For example, the sale of regular Campbell's soups fell in the midst of the

Cotton Ginny
www.cottonginny.ca

low-carbohydrate phenomenon. Consumers were looking for lower-calorie, lower-carbohydrate products. Campbell's responded with several new product lines that compensated for lower sales on regular lines. There could have been drastic financial consequences had Campbell's not responded. Similarly, growth prospects for Curves could dwindle quickly once the concern for obesity subsides and the demand for a place where plus-sized women can feel comfortable exercising passes.

The combination of demographic, psychographic, and geographic information is commonly used to segment a market. These concepts are discussed in detail in the next section of the chapter—"Identifying and Selecting Target Markets." Refer to Figure 6.1 for a visual illustration of the levels of market segmentation and a brief explanation of each level.

NICHE MARKETING (SUB-SEGMENTATION)

Niche marketing takes market segmentation a step further. Here, the marketer focuses on subgroups within a market segment. The subgroup has unique and identifiable characteristics, and even though the segment is small it presents sufficient opportunity and profit potential. Small segments tend to have fewer competitors than do larger market segments.

The Canadian beer market can be divided into segments: regular beer, premium beer, and value beer. Most of the competition is in the regular beer segment as it represents about 90 percent of all beer sold in Canada. An endless variety of well-known brands marketed by Molson and Labatt compete for market share in this segment: Blue, Blue Light, Canadian, Canadian Light, Coors, Coors Light, Budweiser, Bud Light, and so on.

FIGURE
6.1

The Levels of Market Segmentation

Mass Marketing
One marketing strategy appeals to a broad range of consumers. Distinct characteristics of consumers are not considered when devising strategies.

Market Segmentation
Unique marketing strategies are devised based on the unique characteristics of specified customer groups. The customer groups are identified based on similarities in demographics, psychographics, geographics, and behaviour responses.

Niche Marketing
Unique strategies are devised for a particular segment of a bigger market. All marketing strategies are dedicated to this one particular segment.

Direct or One-to-One Segmentation
Unique marketing strategies are devised for the unique needs and preferences of individual customers.

The premium and value segments are described as niches, and competitors here are much smaller companies. In the premium niche Sleeman Brewing is the largest. Sleeman has quietly gained ground by directing its resources solely at the premium niche and premium beer drinker. Sleeman markets its beers at premium prices in distinctively clear bottles and has built a solid reputation based on its heritage as a family-owned craft brewery battling the giants.[3] More recently, Sleeman has benefited from consumers' natural migration away from mainstream beers and toward craft beers. The niche is now a little bigger than it used to be.

Sleeman Brewing
www.sleeman.com

The value segment is characterized by lower prices, so it is of little interest to Molson and Labatt in the long term. Low prices have a negative impact on profit margins. The Lakeport Brewing Corp. has cornered the value niche with "buck-a-beer" pricing on several brands. Such a low price has lifted Lakeport's market share in the Ontario at-home market to 5 percent from 1.8 percent. President and CEO Theresa Cascioli says, "We have shown customers that you don't have to spend $34 a case to get great tasting beer." Lakeport focuses on older but heavy beer drinkers who don't want to pay too much. Lakeport is happy to let Molson and Labatt squabble over the younger beer drinkers.[4]

DIRECT (ONE-TO-ONE OR INDIVIDUAL) MARKETING

In the context of market segmentation, **direct marketing** (or **one-to-one marketing** or **individual marketing**) refers to a situation where unique marketing programs are designed specifically to meet the needs and preferences of individual customers. The ability to implement such precise strategies is based on the concept of relationship marketing and the database marketing techniques that were presented in Chapters 1 and 3.

direct marketing (one-to-one marketing; individual marketing)

Today, organizations have access to advanced information technology that involves the development and management of sophisticated computer and communication systems. Such systems collect information internally and externally and meet the companies' new requirements for information processing. A company collects demographic, psychographic, media, and consumption information on customers in order to target them more effectively. Such information is available from the home (electronic meters that detect television viewing), businesses (scanners at retail checkout counters), online/CD-ROM databases (indexes to business publications and statistical data on firms and households), and interactive online communications with customers.

With so much useful information available, companies are adopting a new concept called mass customization. **Mass customization** refers to a marketing system that can produce products and personalize messages to a target audience of one. This concept is not new to marketing, but its potential use by so many is a dramatic change from the past. Tailor shops, for example, have always offered ready-made suits while also providing made-to-measure suits for customers seeking the perfect fit and better quality. Mass customization is an extension of this way of doing business.

mass customization

When communicating with customers, marketers are shifting from the traditional media (television, radio, newspaper, magazines, and outdoor) that reach the masses toward a direct approach (telemarketing, direct mail, direct response television, online communications, and text messaging through cell phones). Technology is like a steam roller, and a marketing organization is either on top of it or under it. For many organizations the leap into true database marketing and one-to-one dealings with customers is a difficult one. Lack of corporate commitment, limited internal expertise, and a lack of proper assessment of marketing needs have delayed movement.

Kraft Foods is an example of a company that has taken to relationship marketing with a vengeance. Kraft saw all kinds of inefficiencies in its mass advertising programs (the costs were outweighing the benefits), so it carefully examined the merits of relationship marketing practices in order to correct things. Kraft experimented with a

FIGURE 6.2

Customers can build their own cars and determine the price at Ford's website

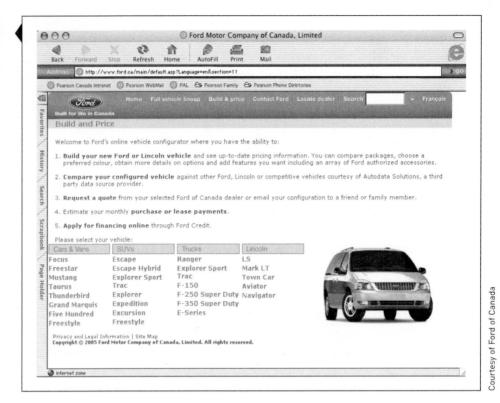

flurry of Web promotions, direct-mail and database marketing programs, custom publishing, and television sponsorships. The company and most of its brands have Internet sites, and the sites are a means of collecting information about customers. Simply put, the Web provides an excellent opportunity to add "stickiness" to an existing relationship between Kraft and its customers.

It is imperative that Canadian companies integrate e-marketing strategies with traditional marketing strategies. A U.S.–based study reveals that Web-savvy consumers are younger and more affluent—a desirable market to reach. They lead more active lives and because they have integrated the Internet into their lives it has changed the way they live, work, and buy. They are active buyers online and they are more active buyers at retail stores.[5] Online consumers are powerful, a growing consumer force that is dramatically reshaping the marketing landscape. Canadian statistics reveal that 7.9 million of 12.3 million Canadian households had at least one member using the Internet regularly in 2003. A little more than 30 percent of these households have purchased goods online.[6]

Progressive-minded companies are discovering new, cost-efficient ways to reach their customers. Through traditional forms of advertising, the Ford Motor Company encourages potential customers to visit its website for information about Ford's products. The customer can actually build and price a new car while at the site. See the illustration in Figure 6.2.

Involvement in database marketing shows the direction that marketing is heading in. Access to more precise information has shifted the focus of marketing from conquest (attracting a new customer) to retention (keeping a current customer). The benefit of database marketing is in building a lifetime relationship with a customer. The database is the vehicle for forming that relationship.

Additional discussions of database marketing applications are included in Chapter 3 (marketing research), Chapter 14 (advertising), Chapter 15 (direct response and interactive communications), and Chapter 17 (e-marketing).

Courtesy of Ford of Canada

FIGURE 6.2 continued

Identifying and Selecting Target Markets

2. Describe the process used and information needed to identify and select target markets.

Segmentation involves three steps: (1) identifying market segments, (2) selecting the market segments that offer the most potential (e.g., profit or future competitive position), and (3) positioning the product so that it appeals to the target market. Once these steps have been taken, an organization shifts its attention to developing a marketing mix strategy. Typically, a company pursues those target markets that offer the greatest profit potential.

When identifying target markets, an organization will use marketing research to learn the demographic, geographic, psychographic, and behaviour-response characteristics of the market (Figure 6.3). What emerges from these characteristics is a target-market profile—a portrait of the ideal customer around which the marketing strategy will be devised and delivered. Let us examine each one of these segmentation variables.

DEMOGRAPHIC SEGMENTATION

Demographic segmentation is defined as the division of a large market into smaller segments on the basis of combinations of *age, gender, income, occupation, education, marital status, household formation,* and *ethnic background.* Marketers monitor trends among these demographic characteristics and adjust their marketing strategies accordingly. As discussed in Chapters 2 and 4, several demographic trends will influence the direction of marketing activities in the future: the aging population (age and life cycle), the changing composition of households and the roles of key members (gender), and the evolving ethnic mix (ethnic background). Refer to Figure 6.4 for a look at the state of Canada's population by age in 2004.

demographic segmentation

AGE AND LIFE CYCLE   Looking specifically at *age,* the Canadian market is classified and described according to age ranges: *millennials* describe those born after 1982; *Generation Y* describes young adults born between 1976 and 1981; *Generation* X

FIGURE
6.3

Variables for Identifying Target Markets

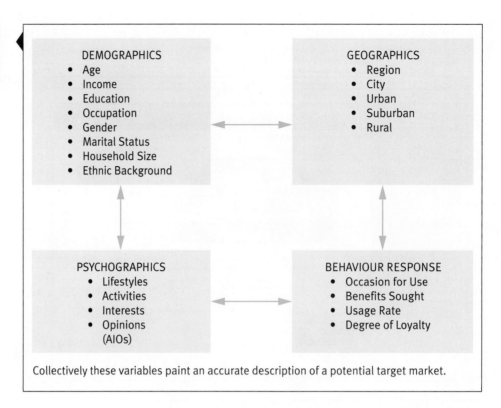

DEMOGRAPHICS
- Age
- Income
- Education
- Occupation
- Gender
- Marital Status
- Household Size
- Ethnic Background

GEOGRAPHICS
- Region
- City
- Urban
- Suburban
- Rural

PSYCHOGRAPHICS
- Lifestyles
- Activities
- Interests
- Opinions
  (AIOs)

BEHAVIOUR RESPONSE
- Occasion for Use
- Benefits Sought
- Usage Rate
- Degree of Loyalty

Collectively these variables paint an accurate description of a potential target market.

FIGURE
6.4

Canada's Estimated Population Structure in 2004

"Canada's Estimated Population Structure in 2004," adapted from the Statistics Canada publication Annual demographic statistics, 2000, Catalogue 91-213, April 5, 2001.

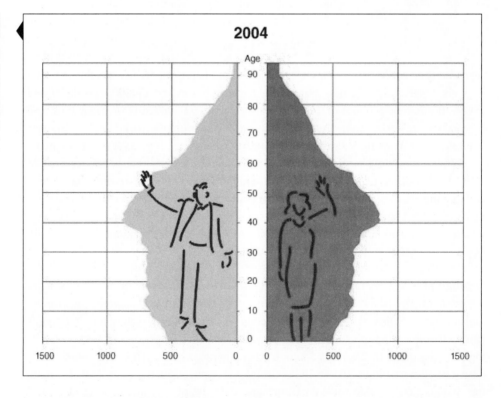

2004

describes people born between 1961 and 1981; *baby boomers* are the largest group of consumers and were born between 1946 and 1964; and the *greys* are the oldest group, born prior to 1946.

In terms of market segmentation each of these groups share common characteristics, but marketers must be careful not to stereotype all consumers within the various segments as being universally alike. For example, simply because someone is old doesn't mean they are not leading an active life or are not trying new products. Many organizations dwell on attracting new, younger consumers while neglecting the potential of older consumers because of stereotypes.

Canadians older than 50 years are free of financial obligations such as children and mortgages and many have developed a taste for the finer things in life. The sales of luxury automobiles and premium beers, for example, exceed the growth of mainstream retail goods in the same categories. The sale of BMW cars has risen 18 percent in the past five years while mid-range domestic automobiles have grown by only 4 percent.[7] Trends like this represent opportunities for brands like BMW and Mercedes but pose problems for Ford and General Motors.

Each generation has a different outlook, different values, and different needs, so the challenge facing many products is how to retain older customers while trying to attract new customers. Let's examine some of the more common tendencies within each age group.

Youth Market (Millennials) The **youth market** is very important to companies because brand loyalties are just in their formative stages. The youth market can be segmented further: children 1–9 years, tweens 9–13 years, and teens 13–19 years. The Canadian tween market alone numbers 2.5 million and spends $1.8 billion annually on items such as candy, shoes, clothes, and music.[8] There are 3.3 million Canadian teenagers who are heavily influenced by the music scene, so that's where marketing organizations want to be.

youth market

The youth market is a hard market to reach and it is influenced less by traditional mass media advertising. Currently, 34 percent of Canadian teens own a cell phone and 84 percent of them use the Internet regularly. Statistics like these strongly suggest that text messaging and online communications will be more important to marketers in the future. As well, teens seem to be influenced more by grassroots promotions and experiential marketing efforts and less by mainstream advertising campaigns on television and radio. Essentially, the youth market is in a transition stage, shifting away from the mass media and toward the electronic media. How to effectively reach them poses a real challenge for marketers. See Figure 6.5 for an illustration

The sale of lifestyle is an important aspect of youth marketing strategy. Bluenotes is a Canadian, youth-focused retailer that targets 12- to 22-year-olds. According to Charla Caponi, director of public relations, "Tweens like to see that there's an image behind something. There has to be some credibility." As a result, Bluenotes' promotions are always tied to a band, celebrity, or image that youth look up to. The promotions also include an in-store component; music and ticket draws for concerts and online communications usually play a key role. Says Caponi: "The Internet is their social hub. It's where they go to connect with friends and make new ones; it's their surefire source of entertainment, and it's their immediate access to anything they need to know."[9]

Generation X and Generation Y   *Generation X*, or the *Nexus generation* as some refer to them, were born in the sixties and seventies and are between the ages of 26 and 44. Some general characteristics of this generation include the following: they live in the present, like to experiment, and look for immediate results. They are selfish, cynical, quick to blame others for their mistakes, and dependent upon their parents. More than 40 percent of them still live with their parents or have left home only to return to their parents.[10] Generation X has learned from their parents' mistakes. They are marrying later, having kids later, and want to spend more time with their family.

A subset of Generation X is *Generation Y*. This is a group of 18- to 25-year-olds whose attitudes are very different from Generation X. Members of Generation Y are

FIGURE
6.5

Text messaging and online communications will become more important to marketers as the use of cell phones and the Internet grows among Canadian youth

© Scott Tysick/Masterfile

generally optimistic and have a great deal of confidence in themselves. They believe a bright future and good times are ahead for them.[11] Toyota is actively chasing Generation Y with brands like Scion: priced sensibly for entry-level buyers, the Scion will be attractive to this group. Advertising and promotional activities for the Scion present a young, hip image in keeping with the expectations of the young target audience. Refer to Figure 6.6 for an illustration.

Baby Boomers   *Boomers* are entering middle age or are beyond middle age, falling into the 40- to 60-year-old category. They are by far the largest age segment (see Figure 6.4). They will be the major buying influence over the next 20 years.

When marketing to the various generations, however, an irony exists. There is a tendency for marketers to focus on younger generations in order to bring new customers into the fold when perhaps they should be concentrating on older customers. For example, 18- to 24-year-olds represent 13 percent of adults but account for only 6 percent of new car sales, whereas 35- to 54-year-olds represent 40 percent of adult buyers and 48 percent of new car sales.[12]

Keith Hilmer, president and creative director at BOOM Communications, says: "When you look at the huge numbers the boomers represent—and their buying power— it's almost like marketers haven't been looking at the facts for the last 10 years." Marketers have operated on the assumption that brand preferences are solidified by age 25 so boomers' preferences were locked in. Current research debunks this notion and shows that fully 70 percent of them are likely to purchase packaged-goods brands other than those they usually buy. Marketers stand to lose if they don't stay relevant to boomers.[13]

Greys   The *grey market* is expected to be quite different from past generations. The current emphasis on health and physical well-being suggests that they will not be "old," either physically or in outlook. They are also expected to retain the spending patterns of

6.6   The Toyota Scion presents a youthful image to attract first-time buyers

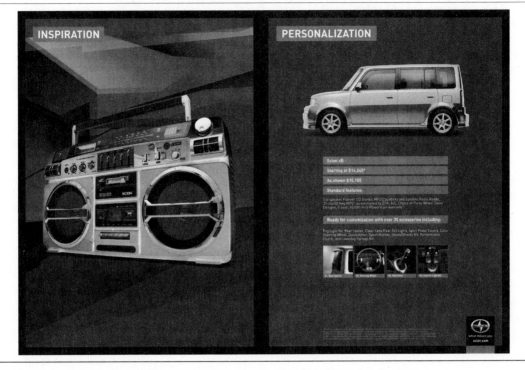

their younger days. Consequently, marketers' perceptions of older consumers will have to change. Many organizations perceive older consumers to be duds. They don't buy anything, they're too brand-loyal, cheap, focused on keeping what they have, old—they're no fun.

Prudent marketers have a different perspective. They realize that our oldest consumers are our wealthiest consumers and that many of them have no plans to slow down their spending in preparation for or during their retirement years. Quite the opposite is occurring. The next generation of senior citizens is snapping up luxury cars, dream vacations, and restaurant meals. Some well-to-do seniors say there's no plan to save money for future generations—once their kids' education is paid for they should be able to take care of themselves.[14]

Recently there has been pressure on governments to abolish existing retirement laws. An increasing number of Canadians are choosing a retirement lifestyle that includes some form of employment, such as part-time work or consulting. Their goal is to retain the lifestyle they have grown accustomed to. These trends clearly indicate the need for marketing organizations to pay much closer attention to seniors. Growth opportunities exist in markets such as travel, entertainment, automobiles, housing, health care, and financial planning services. New products will have to be positioned to appeal to the needs of older targets, and existing products will have to be repositioned in order to survive.

Demographic trends pose a conundrum to marketers. For example, how does a brand become attractive to young people without alienating its older core users? They know that if they do not attract new customers while they are young, chances are they may never get them at all. When managers see the average age of their core user progressively rising, they know they have a problem on their hands.

For more insight into the challenges of marketing to the various generations of consumers, read the Marketing in Action vignette **Target the Attitude**, **Not the Age**.

Target the Attitude, Not the Age

Is it possible to market the same product to teenagers and their parents? Most people would say it's not possible, but it seems that we are now living in an era where parents are acting younger and their children are acting older. Simply put, baby boomers refuse to act their age. At the same time the children of boomers (Generation X and Generation Y) are acting more responsibly. They demonstrate maturity well beyond their age.

If this is the case, then double targeting will become more of a reality for marketers. Many experts hold the notion that consumers no longer act their age. If they are correct, then segmenting markets based on age will be meaningless. They will have greater success if they focus on psychographics and by breaking away from old stereotypes about people.

Three factors are fuelling this trend: life expectancy has increased; boomers now represent the majority of consumers, making their traits more mainstream; and there is more cross-over between generations due to increased access to information. Age, it seems, no longer defines who we are. Today's youth not only have positive relationships with their parents, but also share things in common—they listen to the same music, watch the same TV shows, and even wear the same clothes.

The implications of these trends are clear. Marketers will have to look at the various life stages and adapt their marketing strategies accordingly. Suzuki Canada recognized this trend and developed a unique TV commercial for the Suzuki Swift Plus. In the commercial there is a "yummy mummy" behind the wheel with her teenage son as a passenger. She's pointing out landmarks—where she had her first kiss, where she met her husband. The son seems impatient listening to the mother. The commercial ends with a surprise twist: the car belongs to the son.

Toyota Camry is also targeting a young and old audience at the same time. A television commercial shows a father turning up the volume on his teenage daughter's CD, much to her surprise. As the car passes by, young onlookers can hear the music playing.

Mitsubishi went full throttle with an advertising campaign and discount financing package that was targeted at the twentysomething age group. The young people bought the car, but weren't able to keep up with the payments once they kicked in; Mitsubishi lost $683 million on the venture. The company now admits it was a mistake to target young consumers exclusively. A new positioning strategy with the theme "Spirited cars for spirited people" has done much better. It speaks to any age group because it reflects an attitude that people share regardless of their age.

Now what is the moral to the story? The key to success is finding common values and attitudes across age groups. That can be done only by monitoring life stages and reflecting common tendencies of the stages in marketing communications. If it works, a company will save money in the short term and the long term while producing better sales results. Just ask Mitsubishi!

Adapted from Lisa D'Innocenzo, "The Ageless Consumer," *Strategy*, March 8, 2004, pp. 1, 4.

© Tim Mantoani/Masterfile

GENDER   *Gender* has always been a primary means of distinguishing product categories: personal-care products, magazines, athletic equipment, and fashion goods are categorized according to the gender of the buyer. With more and more women in the workforce outside the home each year (a significant change from earlier generations) and the changing roles of men and women in Canadian households, the marketing orientation will become increasingly "unisex" as both sexes buy and use similar products.

Marketers have been missing the mark for too long with advertising campaigns that portray males as dolts or illustrate who women are not, as opposed to who they are. Women have gained ground as influencers and buyers in traditionally male-skewed markets. They own 54 percent of all mutual funds, buy 50 percent of all new computers and 50 percent of all new sports equipment, and are even buying 40 percent of all condoms sold.[15] Statistics such as these justify a unisex targeting notion in numerous product categories.

When communicating with such an empowered woman, an organization must be very careful not to portray women in stereotypical situations—and should be ready to suffer the consequences if it does. A message will have impact if it communicates to a woman based on how she sees herself or wants to see herself. It understands that women are different from men. Nike Inc. is often cited as a brand that does it right with women. Nike communicates intelligently with women while recognizing they lead multidimensional lives. Advertising messages focus on women's inner confidence and self-esteem. Rather than competing against men or measuring up in the eyes of others, Nike's message is one of personal satisfaction. The strategy is right on the mark![16]

Recognizing opportunity, investment firms such as Desjardins Financial are targeting women. As shown in Figure 6.7, Desjardins markets a financial product to young working women who want to save for their children's education. By portraying women in contemporary roles, Desjardins is demonstrating a progressive approach to implementing marketing strategy.

What about the male side of the gender equation? Men tend to be very sensitive about how they are portrayed in advertisements. Some go as far as to say that men are the new women, meaning they are stereotyped as hopeless cooks, sports addicts, and unromantic husbands. While marketers believe such stereotypes are nothing more than good-natured ribbing, they must tread carefully. Salon Selectives, a shampoo brand, recently ran an ad called "Customized Boyfriend." In the ad a young women imagined her guy turning into a hunk with washboard abs. Interrupting her fantasy, her boyfriend belches and suddenly reverts to his dumpy, out-of-shape self.[17] You judge the situation: is this the way to sell shampoo?

How and why women and men buy must be factored into marketing strategies. To illustrate, both females and males buy automobiles, but they do so for very different reasons. Women exhibit more rational behaviour—they study auto safety, maintenance and repair reliability, as well as comfort and environmental features. They want safe, go-anywhere and do-anything vehicles to accommodate their diverse goals. In contrast, men exhibit more emotional behaviour—it is the look, the style, and the feel of the car that piques their interest. They want to know the engine specifications and how long it takes to go from zero to 60. Women want function; men want flash! No single marketing strategy will work on customers with such different needs.

ETHNIC BACKGROUND   Canada's *ethnic diversity* will present new opportunities for Canadian marketers. As discussed in Chapter 2, people within the Canadian culture represent many diverse subcultures (subgroups of a larger population) that have distinctive lifestyles based on religious, racial, and geographic differences. The latest Census data

FIGURE
6.7

Gender segmentation: An advertisement directed at working female adults

(2001) show that Canada's visible minorities represent about 13.4 percent of the population. More-recent immigrants (those arriving during the 1990s) have a tendency to migrate to large urban areas. Nearly 73 percent of immigrants who came in the 1990s lived in just three metropolitan areas: Toronto, Vancouver, and Montreal. In Toronto alone, visible minorities now comprise 43.7 percent of the population.[18]

Since ethnic communities are concentrated by location, they are accessible market niches for marketing organizations to pursue. Wal-Mart was among the first to see this trend developing and took appropriate action to capitalize on it. Since 1997, Wal-Mart has mounted television commercials using real people of ethnic origin, telling their own stories, in their own languages, about their relationships with Wal-Mart. Wal-Mart serves more ethnic markets than any other retailer in Canada. Initially, it focused on Italian, Portuguese, South Asian, and Cantonese. More recently, it has added Spanish, Mandarin, and Southeast Asian languages. Wal-Mart makes language decisions on a market-by-market basis. It is not surprising that Wal-Mart is dominating the department store market in Canada.[19]

Swedish retailer Ikea has noticed a sharp increase in demand for ethnic-inspired prints, carpets, and household furnishings. Traditionally, these products were marketed alongside mainstream goods under Ikea's advertising slogan "Be unboring." Ikea now has an ethnic marketing team in place to devise strategies to promote ethnic household furnishings and household products. "People are looking for ethnic products to express themselves and to create a unique home," says Nandini Venkatesh, communications manager for Ikea.[20] A classic example of seeing a need and filling a need, Ikea is a step ahead of its competitors.

GEOGRAPHIC SEGMENTATION

Geographic segmentation refers to the division of a large geographic market into smaller geographic or regional units. The Canadian market can be divided into five distinct areas: the Maritimes, Quebec, Ontario, the Prairies, and British Columbia. Geographic considerations used in conjunction with demographics provide the marketer with a clear description of the target market, and from this description marketing strategies can be developed. As discussed in Chapter 4, different strategies may be required for different regions, providing those differences are significant and the potential returns profitable. The most obvious difference is in Quebec, where the language and cultural characteristics require the use of original marketing strategies. Many companies simply adapt their English market campaigns into French and expect them to work. This is far from reality. The uniqueness of the French Quebec market almost demands unique marketing strategies. As many would say, "You get what you pay for!"

geographic segmentation

The political environment may also influence geographic marketing decisions. In Quebec, Molson spends most of its money on its Molson Dry brand, instead of Canadian, which is the main brand in all other regions. E. D. Smith & Sons displays a maple leaf on all of its packages but not on its Habitant brand of soup, which is sold only in Quebec. Kraft sells its P'tit-Quebec brand of cheeses only in Quebec. The product was designed specifically to meet the taste preferences of Quebecers, who apparently like softer-tasting cheeses.[21]

Geographic regions are subdivided into *urban* and *rural* areas. Within urban metropolitan areas, the market can be divided further on the basis of location: urban downtown, suburban, and regional municipalities that surround large cities. More Canadians than ever before are living in urban metropolitan areas. In fact, close to 80 percent of Canadians live in urban areas. There is also a concentration of population in four broad urban regions: the extended Golden Horseshoe area of southern Ontario; Montreal and environs; British Columbia's lower mainland and southern Vancouver Island; and the Calgary–Edmonton corridor. Fifty-one percent of Canada's population lives in these areas.[22] Considering the distribution of Canada's regional and urban populations, it is not surprising that successful marketing strategies have an urban orientation.

The combination of geographic and demographic segmentation has spawned the use of the term "geodemographics." **Geodemographic segmentation** is the isolating of dwelling areas (e.g., areas within a city) according to geography and demographics, on the basis of the assumption that people seek out residential neighbourhoods in which to cluster with their lifestyle peers. For example, younger, higher-income households may choose to cluster in redeveloped downtown areas, and dual-income, traditional families may concentrate in suburbia. Applying the same principle on a regional basis, practitioners refer to regional marketing strategies as micro-marketing. **Micro-marketing** involves the development of marketing strategies on a regional basis, giving consideration to the unique needs and geodemographics of different regions. Many Canadian marketing organizations are moving away from "broadstroke" national marketing strategies toward strategies based on regional considerations and opportunities.

geodemographic segmentation

micro-marketing

psychographic segmentation

PSYCHOGRAPHIC SEGMENTATION

Psychographic segmentation is market segmentation on the basis of the activities, interests, and opinions (the lifestyles) of consumers. Psychographic segmentation is multidimensional: it considers a variety of factors that affect a person's purchase decision. Such information is advantageous to marketers because it tells them not only who buys, but also *why* they buy. This combined with demographic and geographic information provides a more complete portrait of a target market.

Many of the variables that comprise psychographic segmentation were discussed in Chapter 4, "Consumer Buying Behaviour." Variables such as needs and motivation, attitudes and perception, personality and the self-concept, and reference groups combine to influence one's lifestyle. When organizations target psychographically, they present products in line with the lifestyle of the target market so that the personality of the product matches the personality of the target.

Axe
www.theaxeeffect.com

The marketing strategy that launched Axe deodorant was based on psychographic profiling. The primary target market was males 18 to 25 years old. Referred to as the "Axe Man," he is a cheeky devil who has lots of sex—generally weekly, often more frequently. He rarely dates and often goes with a group of guys to parties. At age 21 he goes to bars to hook up, and won't admit he's in a relationship even if he is. Words like *boyfriend* and *girlfriend* are rarely spoken by the Axe Man. Men in the target group fall into classifications such as "pimp daddy," "player," and "sweetheart." This kind of information is what Unilever marketers call "brain food." It may seem like more information than is needed to sell men's deodorant, but it is very relevant for a brand dedicated to helping men "compete in the mating game."[23] The initial ads for Axe showed women literally flinging themselves at guys wearing Axe. Every man's dream!

In Canada, numerous psychographic research studies have been conducted, resulting in a variety of descriptive classifications of the Canadian population. One such company, Millward Brown Goldfarb of Toronto, has classified Canadians into nine psychographic cells (these were presented in Chapter 4). Automakers produce and market a range of vehicles to satisfy the requirements of the Canadian lifestyle groups. Trendy sports cars with European styling appeal to "up and comers" and "bold achievers," while a family station wagon or a minivan appeals to "contented traditionalists" or "joiner activists." Refer to Figure 6.8 for an illustration.

Knowledge of the target market is essential for designing effective marketing strategies. Best Buy has recently adopted a unique marketing strategy based on the different needs and preferences of its best customers. For insight into Best Buy's marketing and merchandising strategies, read the Marketing in Action vignette **Best Buy Tailors Strategies to Best Customers**.

BEHAVIOUR RESPONSE SEGMENTATION

behaviour response
segmentation

Behaviour response segmentation involves dividing buyers into groups according to their occasions for using a product, the benefits they require in a product, the frequency with which they use it, and their degree of brand loyalty. It is used in conjunction with other segmentation variables.

OCCASIONS FOR USE
In order to increase the consumption of the product, marketers using the occasion-for-use segmentation strategy show how the product can be used on various occasions. For example, advertisers show such products as eggs, breakfast cereals, and orange juice being consumed at times other than their traditional mealtimes. Other products are associated with special occasions and are promoted heavily at these times. Flowers and chocolates, for example, are associated with Valentine's Day,

First, your career took off.

The 2004 TSX. The promotion. The raise. The power suit. And now, the automobile that can match your pace. The TSX features a responsive i-VTEC engine, Drive-By-Wire Throttle System, and lavish leather interior. Success is ever so sweet.

ACURA

Courtesy of Honda Canada Inc.

**FIGURE
6.8**

A lifestyle message directed at the "up-and-comer" psychographic segment

Mother's Day, Easter, and Christmas. Branded advertising campaigns are more visible during these special time periods.

BENEFITS SOUGHT   Benefit segmentation is based on the premise that different consumers try to gratify different needs when they purchase a product. For example, a car buyer may place greater emphasis on style and road-handling ability; a shampoo buyer may want conditioning or dandruff control. If the target market is rational in nature, marketers will focus on quality, price, efficiency, and dependability. If the target is influenced by emotions, different forms of presentation that play on feelings (sex, fear, love, status, etc.) can be used. To see the difference, consider a product such as blue jeans. An inexpensive, private-label brand purchased at a discount department store will perform the same function as a high-priced, designer-label brand purchased at a high-end fashion retailer. The reason people buy one brand of jeans instead of another derives from a combination of demographic (age, income, education, and occupation) and psychographic (activities, interests, and opinions) variables.

MARKETING IN ACTION

Best Buy Tailors Strategies to Best Customers

If marketing today is about managing relationships, then finding ways to get more business out of your best customers must be a marketing priority. Best Buy is moving full steam ahead with a marketing program that involves tailoring marketing strategies by store location to its most profitable customers. The target may be a young male looking for the latest technology or it could be a busy soccer mom looking for ways to entertain the kids.

Most retailers—including many of Best Buy's competitors—tend to establish one store format and use it for all locations. Best Buy sees things differently. Granted, there will be the same merchandise available in all stores, but greater emphasis will be placed on products that are selling well in each location. The objective is to sell *more*! The customer-centric concept has been tested in the United States and has generated 7 percent more business when compared to traditional stores.

According to Kevin Layden, CEO of Best Buy Canada, "the aim is to clearly differentiate Best Buy. We want to reorganize ourselves around our customers." Best Buy is an American-based company that acquired Future Shop (a Canadian electronics retailer) a few years ago. The combined company now controls about 29 percent of Canada's $16-billion computer and consumer electronics market. It is the market leader and it wants to stay the leader!

To distinguish itself from competitors, Best Buy has introduced three new services:

- The Geek Squad—a 24-hour computer support team that is dispatched to customers' homes when called
- Best Buy for Business—computer assistance and other help for small business customers (one to nine employees)
- Best Buy for Home—shows people how the latest home theatres and office products work and connect with the home.

Best Buy plans to target its best customers with new programs tailored to their specific needs. The key targets include:

- Affluent professionals who want the best technology and entertainment experience
- Focused, active younger males who want the latest technology and entertainment
- The family man who wants technology that improves his life; a practical adopter of technology
- The busy suburban mother who wants to enrich her children's lives with technology and entertainment
- Small business customers who require the latest technology at a reasonable price

The sales history of a particular store will help determine which target or targets will be given priority. The amount of space allocated to various product lines and the nature of merchandising strategies will vary by location.

Adapted from Marina Strauss, "Best Buy courting its best customers," *The Globe and Mail*, August 13, 2004, p. B3.

Dick Hemingway

FIGURE

6.9   An Illustration of a Target-Market Profile

Demographic Profile
Predominantly male (ratio is 85% male and 15% female), 40 to 55 years old, post-secondary education, managers and professionals, $75,000 plus annual income, and residing in major urban markets.

Psychographic Profile
The primary customer likes to travel frequently (numerous short-trips during a year with at least one extended vacation). They have an adventurous orientation, like to break away from the daily routine on weekends, seek stress-busting activities, and truly enjoy the freedom of the open road. A sense of balance between work and play is important. This group has been labeled "weekend warrior."

Geographic Profile
The core customer is an urban dweller (downtown or suburban location). Rural customers exist but are more difficult to reach than urban customers and share a different psychographic profile.

Behaviour Response
Present users are extremely brand loyal and were attracted to the brand based on its heritage, image, and reputation. Potential users will be attracted to the brand based similar intangible characteristics—image is very important.

The above profile describes the primary customer of Harley-Davidson motorcycles. Harley-Davidson distinguishes itself from other motorcycle brands based on its heritage, image and reputation—a reputation that the company really doesn't have much control over. The company is very successful and many buyers like the ones described above enjoy the motorcycle and its image. These buyers are often referred to as HOGs which stands for Harley Owners Group.

Adapted from "Money Hog," an advertorial appearing in the National Post, Driver's Edge Section, January 3, 2002, p. DE11.

USAGE RATE   Frequency of use is an important segmentation variable. Marketers will conduct research to distinguish the characteristics of a heavy user from those of a medium or light user. Very often, an 80/20 rule applies; that is, 80 percent of a product's sales volume and profits comes from 20 percent of its users (heavy users). The trick is to identify the profile of the heavy users and then attract more of them. For example, Campo-Phenique is a topical antiseptic product that offers relief from insect bites, cold sores, blisters, and cuts, and consequently has many potential users. After mining all kinds of research data, Campo-Phenique narrowed its target list down to a limited number of target user groups: inline skaters, heavy make-up users, horseback riders, campers, hunters, photographers, outdoor gardeners, and fisherman. The brand usage of these groups was about 50 percent above average.[24] The benefits of the product are communicated in a manner that will attract those potential users.

LOYALTY RESPONSE   The degree of brand loyalty a customer has also influences segmentation strategy. As with usage-rate segmentation, the marketing organization should conduct research to determine the characteristics of brand-loyal users and what motivates them to buy a particular brand. Strategies would then be developed to attract users with similar profiles and behaviour tendencies. Consideration must be given to users with varying degrees of loyalty. For example, defensive activities (for defending or retaining market share) are directed at medium and heavy users to maintain their loyalty. Distributing coupons on the package for use on the next purchase is an example of a defensive activity. Offensive tactics, such as trial coupons delivered by the media, are employed to attract new users and users of competitive brands. Because brand switching does occur, marketers must be conscious of customers at both ends of the loyalty spectrum.

Acumen Research Group Inc. divides consumers into four loyalty categories: *truly loyal, emotionally loyal, circumstantially loyal*, and *not loyal*. Truly loyal customers offer high value to a brand since they resist competitive offerings. Emotionally loyal customers show a high level of satisfaction but are vulnerable to competitive offerings. They will take a look around and may switch if they perceive another brand to be better. Circumstantially loyal customers like the product but they have not formed a relationship with it. They are very vulnerable to competitive offers. Customers who are not loyal show their loyalty elsewhere and they are difficult to convert to loyalty. Generally speaking, truly loyal and emotionally loyal customers have a strong relationship with a brand.[25] These customers show their allegiance by consistently choosing one brand over all others. Perhaps that explains why market leaders like Coca-Cola, iPod, and Nike enjoy so much success and why their competitors have to strive so hard to attract new customers to build their brands.

For an illustration of a target-market profile based on demographic, psychographic, and geographic variables, refer to Figure 6.9 on the previous page.

3. Describe the various types of segmentation strategies commonly used in contemporary marketing practice.

Market Segmentation Strategies

Assuming that the marketing organization has identified and selected the target markets it wishes to pursue, the next decision deals with the degree of coverage and activity in the various segments. This section will focus on specific segmentation strategies: market differentiation, niche marketing or market concentration, and market integration.

MARKET DIFFERENTIATION

market differentiation

Market differentiation involves targeting several market segments with several different products and marketing plans (different marketing strategies for each product and segment).

To illustrate the use of market differentiation, consider the marketing situation at QTG Canada Inc. QTG is a company name (in this case an acronym) that represents the merged entities of Quaker Oats, Tropicana, and Gatorade. Quaker makes a variety of cereal and snack food products under brand names such as Harvest Crunch, Life, Cap'n Crunch, and Quaker Chewy Granola. QTG also markets a variety of fruit juices under the Tropicana name, and Gatorade is a firmly established energy drink and is by far the dominant brand in that segment of the beverage industry.

QTG is not dependent on one type of market or one type of customer to build its business. It differentiates itself by participating in several different markets. The target-market profile of consumers buying Life Cereal is very different from the one for consumers buying Chewy Granola Bars or Gatorade. Gatorade has a strong appeal to individuals actively involved in fitness programs. In fact, the bottle has become part of one's wardrobe at the fitness centre. Decisions about product, price, advertising, and promotion and where the product should be available are different for each product line marketed by QTG.

Differentiation offers QTG and other multiproduct companies significant benefits. Essentially, they are not putting all of their eggs in one basket, a situation that can be financially ruinous if things suddenly turn sour in a market. With differentiation, if one segment of the business should happen to go a little soft (e.g., sales of cereal start to slump), the situation could be offset by stronger sales performance in other segments. In QTG's case, the sales of Tropicana fruit juices have soared in recent years because consumers have demanded new beverage alternatives suited to their healthier lifestyles; Tropicana responded by launching many new combinations of flavours. At the same time, the sales of cereal products have been languishing. The company has balance.

On the risk side, the costs of differentiation can be high since the company offers a number of product variations, operates in new or different distribution channels, and promotes a multitude of brands. Since financial resources for marketing are usually scarce, companies generally evaluate potential revenues carefully against the costs of obtaining them to ensure that adequate profits will be achieved.

NICHE MARKETING (MARKET CONCENTRATION)

Niche marketing, or **market concentration,** is defined as targeting a product line to one particular segment and committing all marketing resources to the satisfaction of that segment. Niche marketing is a good strategy for small companies that have limited resources and for large companies wanting to target specific segments with specialized products. Often the segments pursued are quite small, so the key to success is in finding opportunities that do not require large economies of scale in production and distribution. Attractive niches have the following characteristics:

1. The niche is sufficiently large and has enough purchasing power to be profitable.
2. It is of negligible interest to major competitors so that there is little threat from these firms.
3. The firm has the required skills and resources to serve the segment effectively.
4. The firm can defend itself from an attacking competitor.

To understand the importance of these four characteristics, consider that sports television stations are a niche segment of the television market. There was a time in Canada when TSN (RDS in Quebec) was the only sports channel broadcasting on cable television. Both TSN and RDS identified a niche and developed it—they literally owned the market. TSN and RDS are now part of Bell Globemedia, a huge media corporation that includes a host of conventional networks and cable channels.

TSN's growth didn't go unnoticed. Rogers Communications launched Sportsnet, and the Headline Media Group launched a channel called The Score. The sports market was then fragmented further with the introduction of several digital channels, such as Leafs TV and Raptors NBA TV, both owned by Maple Leaf Sports and Entertainment.

In the context of niche marketing, one question remains. Is there enough audience for so many sports channels? These sports channels also compete with major commercial networks such as CTV and CBC for the broadcast rights to various sports properties. Audience statistics reveal that the digital channels are being dwarfed by the cable channels. TSN audiences are twice the size of Sportsnet and five times the size of The Score.[26] Digital channels such as Maple Leafs TV and Raptors TV are barely on the radar screen. Nonetheless, TSN had all of the audience at one time. The niche has expanded and the competition for audience is much stronger today. Despite the new competition, TSN has defended its leadership position effectively and remains profitable. Other stations are finding the situation more difficult to deal with—a good lesson for niche marketers.

MARKET INTEGRATION

Market integration is an expansion from a single segment into other similar segments. Market integration is followed for several reasons. First, the needs of consumers change; as consumers mature, their needs, attitudes, and outlook are altered. Second, new competition enters a particular segment, posing a threat to firms already there; in other words, the segment becomes more fragmented. Third, products and markets reach the maturity stage of the product life cycle and are threatened by new technology, which results in new, innovative products. To survive, a company must alter its marketing mix to stay in tune with current customer demands.

Consider the battle that is going on in the supermarket, department store, and pharmacy markets in Canada. There was a time when these three markets were unique and the competition within each was very direct. Shoppers Drug Mart competed with London Drugs and Guardian Drugs. Loblaws competed with Sobeys, A&P, and Safeway. Wal-Mart competed with Sears, The Bay, and Zellers. Wal-Mart changed the playing field for all of these markets and competitors when it added full-service pharmacies and food sections to its stores. Wal-Mart is now opening superstores with equal space devoted to food items. Loblaws responded by adding a pharmacy, clothing lines, and more household goods. Shoppers Drug Mart added more food lines and started building super-sized stores to compete with the others.

McDonald's has managed to stay well in front of its key competitors by consistently taking action first. Innovations such as expanded menus (beyond hamburgers), drive-throughs, 24-hour service, seasonal restaurants, strategic alliances with Wal-Mart (having outlets right in Wal-Mart stores), opening smaller restaurants in smaller markets, and "lighter choices" menus for calorie- and carbohydrate-conscious consumers give McDonald's an edge on its rivals. One of its latest innovations is the two-window and two-lane drive-through. There's no more waiting in line behind someone with a really big order!

These examples suggest that the battle for customers today is more intense. Each company described above has changed or expanded its operations in response to competitive threat and the consumers' need for convenience. Companies employing an integration strategy do not stand still—they evolve with the marketplace, hoping to expand faster and more effectively than their competitors. To stand still could mean the demise of the company.

Market integration is based on the premise that one way to expand volume and market share is to appeal to users of similar products in other market segments. That's exactly what Wal-Mart did. Appealing to new-user segments usually involves a marketing strategy that is different from the original strategy. When a company departs from its original concept, one that was successful and profitable, uncertainty and risk prevail.

4. Explain the concept of positioning and its role in contemporary marketing practice.

Market Positioning Concepts

positioning

Once a target market has been identified and a product developed to meet the needs of the target, the next step is to position the product. **Positioning** refers to the place a product occupies in the customer's mind in relation to competing products. It involves (1) designing and marketing a product to meet the needs of a target market, and (2) creating the appropriate appeals to make the product stand out from the competition in the minds of the target market (through marketing mix activities). How a consumer perceives a product is influenced by image initially (pre-purchase stage) and actual experience with a product (post-purchase stage).

Harvey's provides an excellent example of positioning. It occupies an underdog position in the fast-food market, so to be like its competitors and to deliver a me-too message about the food it sells won't cut it with customers. McDonald's, Burger King, and Wendy's have all discovered health and have added new product lines. While these three restaurants seem to be chasing rabbits with a variety of salads, Harvey's aims its marketing squarely at guys and offers a menu and message that extols the glory of the grease.[27] They have introduced the Big Harv and use the advertising slogan "Long live the grill." Harvey's knows what its customers want and gives it to them! Refer to Figure 6.10 for an illustration.

FIGURE
6.10 Harvey's positions itself differently than other fast-food restaurants

The positioning that a company desires and the perceived positioning of a product by consumers are often quite different. In positioning a product, organizations collect information about a brand's attributes and about the attributes of competing brands. From the data collected, marketers can plot all brands on a perceptual map. Once plotted, a marketer can see where changes in marketing strategy are necessary if a brand is to improve or alter its image with consumers. As well, gaps on the map (places not occupied by any existing brands) may show where new marketing opportunities exist.

To illustrate the concept of positioning and perceptual mapping, consider the Canadian retailing market, with a focus on fashion retailers. In this market, department stores compete with specialty stores. For the sake of the illustration, let us assume that stores can be classified into three broad categories: top-end (high price and quality), middle-of-the-road (average price and quality), and low-end (lower price and quality).

Competitors are plotted on a two-dimensional axis that considers the attributes of price and quality. With reference to Figure 6.11, the map shows that discounters, such as Wal-Mart and Zellers, are positioned in the lower-price and lower-quality quadrant, while stores such as Holt Renfrew and Harry Rosen are in the higher-price and higher-quality quadrant. Department stores such as Sears and The Bay are in the middle along with a battery of specialty retailers selling clothing, electronics goods and appliances, and home furnishings. As indicated in an earlier discussion of department stores, the stores in the middle are suffering. Customers' shopping patterns are shifting to stores at the higher and lower ends of the spectrum and those in the middle are being squeezed. Such a trend is the result of economic and income circumstances along with miscues in marketing strategy. It is rumored that HBC (Hudson's Bay and Zellers) is for sale to an American corporation—Target stores—the number-two U.S. discount department store. The combination of Wal-Mart's pricing strategies, consumers' preference for convenience and

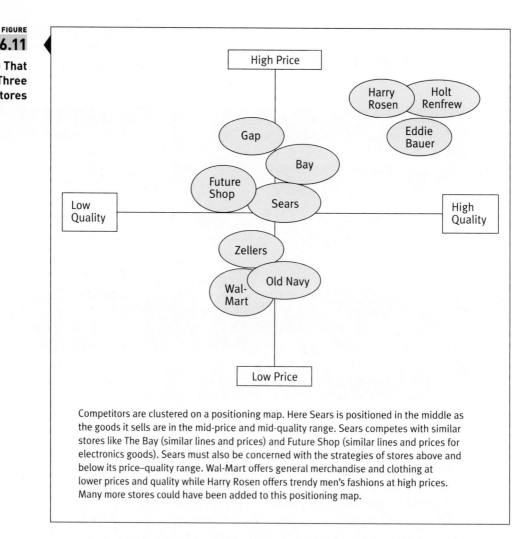

Competitors are clustered on a positioning map. Here Sears is positioned in the middle as the goods it sells are in the mid-price and mid-quality range. Sears competes with similar stores like The Bay (similar lines and prices) and Future Shop (similar lines and prices for electronics goods). Sears must also be concerned with the strategies of stores above and below its price–quality range. Wal-Mart offers general merchandise and clothing at lower prices and quality while Harry Rosen offers trendy men's fashions at high prices. Many more stores could have been added to this positioning map.

value, and The Bay and Zellers' inability to find the right formula to compete have contributed to HBC's situation.

When developing a marketing strategy, positioning strategy is really the foundation. All marketing activities revolve around what a company or brand wants the customer to understand about itself.

TYPES OF POSITIONING   The impression or perception a consumer holds about a product is directly influenced by the impact of the marketing strategy. Tangible factors such as price, quality, where a product is available, and the style of advertising influence consumers' perceptions positively or negatively. In the implementation stage, there are several common strategies used to position a product. Here are a few of them.

head-on positioning

Head-On Positioning   In **head-on positioning**, one brand is presented as an alternative equal to or better than another brand. This strategy is usually initiated by a brand challenger, typically the number-two brand in the market. The strategy is to show people who declare they regularly use one brand actually choosing another product. The "Pepsi Challenge" is now a classic example of such head-on positioning. In the television commercials for this campaign, non-believers were challenged in a taste test. Once they experienced the taste of Pepsi, their conclusion was rather obvious. In one famous television commercial, the driver of a Coke truck is seen secretly taking out a Pepsi from a store cooler. The remaining cans tumble out of the cooler, drawing attention to the driver.

Other examples of head-on positioning include the battle between Energizer and Duracell (the battery wars). Energizer, the challenger, built an extensive marketing campaign around the Energizer Bunny. The strategy was memorable and effective. So effective in fact that Energizer took over the lead in the market.[28] As Energizer says, "It keeps going and going."

Head-on positioning requires financial commitment, since the brand leader is likely to react with increased marketing spending. In the past, a direct counterattack by the brand leader was unlikely. A brand leader preferred to let its number-one position and product benefits speak for it. In many markets today, the level of competition is so intense even brand leaders resort to using head-on strategies.

Brand Leadership Positioning   Brands that are market leaders can use their large market share to help position themselves in the minds of consumers. Their marketing communications are designed to state clearly that the product is successful, a market leader, and highly acceptable to a majority of users. Coca-Cola has successfully used this approach to build the world's most recognized brand. "Coke is it," "Can't beat the real thing," "Always Coca-Cola," and more recently "Real" are examples of universally recognizable signatures. The brand name, unique bottle, and popular slogan are a deadly combination for Coca-Cola—they are instantly recognizable by consumers everywhere.

Visa portrays its leadership positioning strategy by focusing on transactions and acceptance virtually everywhere in the world. The Visa advertising slogan "All you need" confirms its leadership position in the customer's mind (Figure 6.12).

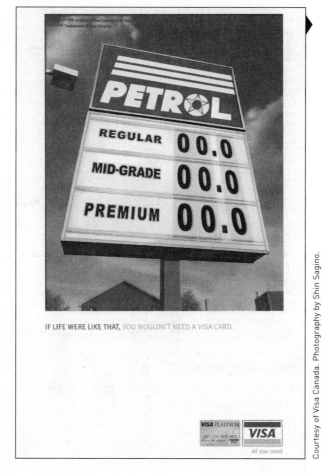

FIGURE
6.12

An Illustration of Brand Leadership Positioning

Courtesy of Visa Canada. Photography by Shin Sagino.

Product Differentiation Positioning   Product differentiation is a strategy that focuses on the unique attributes or benefits of a product—those features that distinguish one brand from another. Gillette's Right Guard Sport Power Caps deodorant is a good example of differentiation. With so many deodorants to choose from why should someone buy Right Guard Power Caps? Because Gillette emphatically states it is the "strongest, toughest gel on the market. It provides the right kind of protection by stopping odours before they start." With words like these, Gillette presents a compelling argument—it makes claims that other brands perhaps cannot make. For an illustration, see Figure 6.13.

In the tea market, Tetley is the market leader and its positioning strategy has always been based on product differentiation. Tetley's round tea bags—each with 2000 perforations—ensure free-flowing flavour, a significant point of difference over its competitors.

Technical Innovation Positioning   Technical innovation is often more important for a company as a whole than for individual products. Companies seeking to project an image of continued technical leadership will use this strategy to position themselves as

FIGURE 6.13

Gillette differentiates itself from other brands by focusing on qualities such as strength and toughness

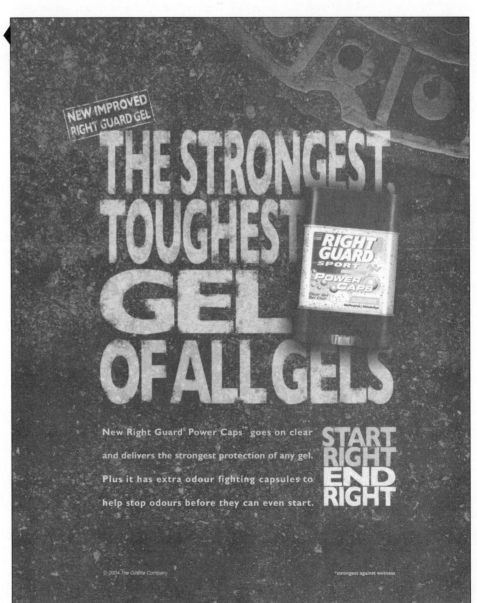

representing the leading edge of technology. Such a position if firmly established in the minds of customers will benefit new products when they are introduced to the market. At the product level, technology can create an advantage that will set one product apart from the others and make it more appealing to the customer. A company such as 3M sets the standard for innovation—Scotch tape, Post-it Notes, and Thinsulate are some of its new-product innovations. 3M invests heavily in research and development and constantly brings new products to market. Regardless of the product, 3M ties all of its communications together with the slogan "From need to . . . 3M innovation."

Innovation can turn an existing market upside down. It was only a few years ago that wooden hockey sticks ruled the market. Now, one-piece composite metal sticks such as the CCM Vector 110 and Easton Synergy dominate the market.

Lifestyle Positioning   In crowded markets where product attributes are perceived as similar by the target market, firms must look for alternative ways of positioning their products. The addition of psychographic information has allowed marketers to develop marketing communications on the basis of the lifestyle of the target market. Essentially, the product is positioned to "fit in" or match the lifestyle of the user or to appeal to potential users on the basis of satisfying esteem needs. Products in categories such as beer, alcohol, perfume, automobiles, and travel frequently use this strategy, as do brands that want to attract a youthful customer.

Lifestyle positioning uses emotional appeals, such as love, fear, sex, status, and adventure, in order to elicit a response from the target. The Mercedes illustration in Figure 6.14 has a lifestyle orientation and appeals to the esteem needs of potential customers.

A brand like Mountain Dew presents a completely different lifestyle. Mountain Dew's image—as projected in wild and crazy advertising through the "Do the Dew" campaign—has created a tight link with thirst-quenching teens. These teens enjoy having an outrageous time with the brand outdoors and like the extreme sports that Mountain Dew is associated with. Among teens, the brand is seen as energetic, upscale, and youthful, exactly the image that PepsiCo wants it to have (Mountain Dew is a PepsiCo brand).

Refer to Figure 6.15 on page 159 for a summary of the steps involved in market segmentation and positioning. Once the target market has been identified and the positioning strategy established, attention is shifted to the development of a marketing strategy using the elements of the marketing mix.

REPOSITIONING   In a competitive marketplace, marketing organizations must be ready to alter their positioning strategies. It is unrealistic to assume that the positioning strategy that is adopted initially will be appropriate throughout the life cycle of a product. Therefore, products will be repositioned on the basis of the prevailing environment in the marketplace. **Repositioning** is defined as changing the place that a product occu-   *repositioning*
pies in the consumer's mind in relation to competitive products. There are two primary reasons for repositioning or adapting a product. One, the marketing activities of a direct competitor may change, and, two, the preferences of the target market may change.

The process of repositioning is based on a brand's continuous monitoring of such changes. Companies that do not monitor change often lose touch with their customer and suffer in terms of lower sales and declining market share. Nowhere has this been more evident than with an aging brand like Cadillac. With the average age of a Cadillac buyer over 60, changes were essential in order to attract a younger audience. The transformation of Cadillac began in 2002 when Cadillac launched a new model—the Escalade—with an aggressive, angular look and completely new image. The new Escalade and the sportier XLR model attracted new customers in the 45-year-old age

FIGURE
6.14

Mercedes-Benz is positioned to match the lifestyle of potential customers

There comes a point in your life when you make a point.

2005 C55 AMG. 360 hp. 0-100 in 5.1 sec. Seriously, adjust your headrest. Mercedes-Benz. You're Ready.

Courtesy of Lowe Roche. David Glen—Art Director, Allen Oke—Writer.

range. The image change was reinforced with an advertising campaign built around the Led Zeppelin classic "Rock and Roll."

An unintentional result of Cadillac's renovation was the brand's appeal among celebrity athletes and musicians, most notably rappers. Reference to Escalade appeared in dozens of popular hip-hop songs, and since many artists drive the vehicle, the impact on sales was significant. General Motors admits, "It's the type of recognition you simply cannot buy."[29] Nonetheless, the publicity generated was an added bonus to the repositioning strategy.

The concepts of positioning and repositioning are important to understand. Potential marketers must realize that marketers do not position brands, consumers do. Once a brand's basic positioning has become set in the customer's mind, there is little marketers can do to influence it, and any change that can be effected tends to happen extremely slowly. Therefore, if a positioning strategy is working, a company should avoid the temptation to change things. With regard to positioning strategy perhaps the old expression should apply: "If it ain't broke, don't fix it."

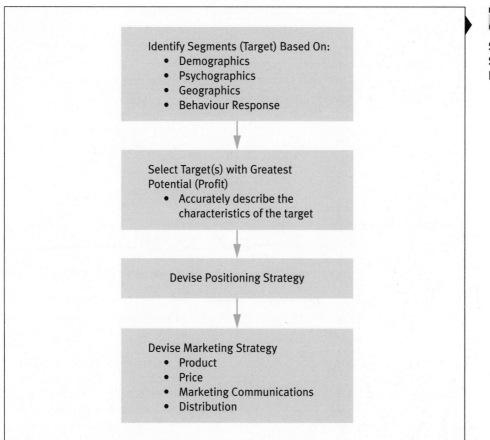

FIGURE
6.15

Steps Involved in Marketing Segmentation and Positioning

SUMMARY

This chapter discussed the key concepts associated with marketing strategy and market segmentation. A market was defined as a group of people having a similar need for a product or service, the resources to purchase the product or service, and the willingness and ability to buy it.

Marketers choose among four basic segmentation alternatives: mass marketing, market segmentation, niche marketing, and direct or individual marketing. Mass marketing involves marketing one product for a broad range of customers. Market segmentation tailors marketing strategies toward unique customer groups based on common needs and similar lifestyles. Niche marketing segments a market even further by concentrating all marketing activities on one small segment of a market. Direct or individual marketing involves creating unique marketing strategies for individual customers. The most common approach to segmentation for an organization is to identify their target markets as precisely as possible. They do so

by making good use of information provided by demographics (age, gender, income, education, occupation, and so on), geographics (regional location and location within a region), and psychographics (activities, interests, and opinions). The organization will constantly monitor trends in these areas so that it can adapt its marketing strategies accordingly.

Behaviour response segmentation is another variable that can be used to develop more effective marketing strategies. This type of segmentation deals with the occasion for using a product, the benefits sought by consumers, the frequency of use, and the degree of brand loyalty. Once the organization has identified and selected the target markets to pursue, the next decision deals with the degree of coverage and activity in each segment. There are three basic alternatives: market differentiation, niche marketing, and market integration. Any combination of strategies could be used, and such combinations are common in larger organizations operating in many different types of markets.

Positioning involves designing a product or service to meet the needs of a target market and then creating the appropriate marketing appeals so that the product stands out in the minds of consumers. Some common positioning strategies include head-on comparisons with competitors, product differentiation, technical innovation, brand dominance, and lifestyle approaches. As a product matures, such factors as competitive activity and changing consumer preferences will force the re-evaluation of positioning strategies.

KEY TERMS

behaviour response segmentation   146

demographic segmentation   137

direct marketing (one-to-one marketing; individual marketing)   135

geodemographic segmentation   145

geographic segmentation   145

head-on positioning   154

market   132

market differentiation   150

market integration   151

market segmentation   132

mass customization   135

mass marketing   132

micro-marketing   145

niche marketing (market concentration)   151

positioning   152

psychographic segmentation   146

repositioning   157

youth market   139

REVIEW QUESTIONS

1. Identify the four conditions that must be present for a market to exist.
2. Explain the difference between mass marketing and market segmentation.
3. Explain the concept of niche marketing. What are the risks associated with being a niche marketer?
4. Explain the concept of direct segmentation (individual segmentation). What are the costs and benefits of this form of segmentation?
5. What is the difference between demographic segmentation, geographic segmentation, and psychographic segmentation?
6. Explain why it is important for marketing organizations to monitor demographic trends in Canada.
7. What is the relationship between geodemographic segmentation and micro-marketing strategies?
8. Briefly describe the four types of behaviour response segmentation and provide an example of each.
9. Explain the difference between a market differentiation strategy and a market integration strategy.
10. Explain the relevance of positioning and repositioning in marketing practice.

DISCUSSION AND APPLICATION QUESTIONS

1. Cite some examples of niche marketing in your community. Briefly explain the strategies used by these companies.

2. Can one product be successfully positioned to be attractive to several different target markets (e.g., twentysomethings and baby boomers) at the same time? Discuss and provide examples to verify your position.

3. Divide the following markets into segments on the basis of categories of products within the market. Identify three major brands in each subcategory and the differential advantage of each.

a) Coffee
b) Deodorant
c) Laundry detergent
d) Soft drinks
e) Cereal

4. Provide two new examples of companies or products (goods or services) that segment their market according to the following:

a) Age
b) Ethnic mix
c) Income
d) Marital status
e) Lifestyle

5. Provide two new examples of companies that are applying a market differentiation strategy and two new examples of a company applying a market integration strategy. Briefly explain each example to show how the strategy is being implemented.

E-ASSIGNMENTS

1. Assume that you are the brand manager for an existing chocolate bar (pick one). You would like to reposition the bar so that it is attractive to the tween market in Canada. You lack information on this market segment. Conduct an Internet search to uncover relevant demographic and psychographic information about tweens. On the basis of this information, how will you reposition the chocolate bar? What strategies will you recommend?

2. Assume you are the director of marketing for Mazda Canada. Your immediate objective is to develop a positioning strategy for the Mazda Miata so that it is more appealing to the twentysomething crowd. Currently, the Miata is popular with the 35-plus age group, who like to buy older models of the car rather than new models. Mazda's business goal is to sell more new models. What will the positioning strategy be and how will you implement it?

ENDNOTES

1. Stephanie Thompson, "Campbell aims squarely at kids with push for pastas and soups," *Advertising Age*, May 31, 2004, p. 62.

2. Terry Poulton, "Canada's new fashion leader: the plus-sized woman," *Strategy*, April 5, 2004, pp. 1, 7.

3. Oliver Bertin, "Sleeman brews balance of risk and caution," *Globe and Mail*, June 20, 2001, p. M1.

4. Keith McArthur, "In Hamilton, they like beer cold . . . and cheap," *Globe and Mail*, July 10, 2004, p. B4.

5. "Study finds Web-savvy are young, affluent consumers," *Toronto Star*, March 27, 2001, p. D5.

6. "By the numbers," *Toronto Star*, September 5, 2004, p. C3.

7. Hollie Shaw, "Skip the Chevy—Buy yourself a Beemer," *Financial Post*, July 10, 2003, p. 19.

8. Michelle Halpern, "Cute, but scary," *Marketing*, August 9/16, 2004, p. 13.

9. Ibid., p. 14.

10. www.cc.colorado.edu/Dept/EC/generationx96/genx/genx3.html.

11. Masha Geller, "Study: Gen Y spends $172 billion," *Media Post*, September 4, 2003, www.mediapost.com.

12. Hillary Chura, "Ripe old age," *Advertising Age*, May 13, 2002, p. 16.

13. Patti Summerfield, "Rediscovering boomers," *Strategy*, May 5, 2003, pp. 1, 4.

14. Sandra Martin, "Boomers feathering empty nests," *FP Money*, March 27, 2004, p. IN1.

15. Paul-Mark Rendon, "The power of women," *Marketing*, August 9/16, 2004, p. 4.

16. Guy Dixon, "What women want, and don't want, in ads," *Globe and Mail*, April 18, 2003, p. B8.

17. John Heinzl, "Men: Ad industry's new target," *Globe and Mail*, April 6, 2001, p. M1.

18. "Proportion of Foreign-Born Population, Census Metropolitan Areas," Statistics Canada, www.statcan.ca.

19. Judy Waytiuk, "Discounter diversity, *Marketing*, May 19, 2003, p. 8.

20. Lucy Saddleton, "Mainstream retail spices it up," *Strategy*, April 19, 2004, pp. 4, 10.

21. Keith McArthur, "Oh? Canada? Ads beg to differ," *Globe and Mail*, July 1, 2004, pp. B1, B18.

22. Statistics Canada, *The Daily*, March 12, 2002, www.statcan.ca/english/dai-quo.

23. Jack Neff, "Analyzing 'Axe man,' " *Advertising Age*, June 24, 2004, pp. 4, 32.

24. www.businessgenetics.com.

25. Acumen Research Group Inc., www.acumenresearch.com.

26. Geoff Dennis, "Too many men on the ice," *Strategy*, August 12, 2002, p. 15.

27. John Burghardt, "Look at me, I'm innovative," *Strategy*, June 14, 2004, p. 11.

28. Jack Neff, "Razor duel a feint in battery battle," *Advertising Age*, August 23, 2004, pp. 4, 37.

29. John Intini, "A Brand Reborn," *Maclean's*, February 23, 2004, pp. 36, 37.

© Steve Chenn/CORBIS

Strategic Marketing Planning

After studying this chapter, you will be able to

1. Distinguish between strategic planning and tactical planning.

2. Identify the distinctions and relationships between corporate planning and marketing planning.

3. Describe the relationships between the various stages of the planning process.

4. Identify the role and influence of corporate plans and their influence on marketing plans.

5. Explain the control procedures used in marketing planning.

6. Describe the various types of strategies used by the company as a whole, and by the marketing departments, for marketing goods and services.

Before developing a **marketing plan**—a document that outlines the direction and activities of an organization, product, or service—a marketer must consider the plan for the rest of the organization. Marketing strategies are directly influenced by the overall business plan or corporate plan. A corporate plan provides direction to all the operational areas of a business, from marketing and production to human resources and information systems. To understand marketing planning, therefore, it is imperative that we know the planning process of an organization and appreciate the interaction of plans at different levels of the organization.

marketing plan

The Business Planning Process

Strategic business planning involves making decisions about three variables: objectives, strategies, and execution or tactics. Let us first define these planning variables:

1. Distinguish between strategic planning and tactical planning.

1. **Objectives** are statements that outline what is to be accomplished in the corporate plan or marketing plan. For instance, they outline how much profit or market share is to be achieved over a one-year period. Objectives are specific, measurable, and time-based.

objectives

2. **Strategies** are statements that outline how the objectives will be achieved. Strategies usually identify the resources necessary to achieve objectives, such as money, time, people, and type of activity.

strategies

3. **Execution**, or **tactics**, refers to the plan of action that outlines in specific detail how the strategies are to be implemented. Tactical plans usually provide details of an activity's cost and timing.

execution (tactics)

A diagram of the business planning process as it applies to marketing is provided in Figure 7.1.

STRATEGIC PLANNING

When a company embarks on a plan, it anticipates the future business environment and determines the courses of action it will take in that environment. For example, a firm will look at trends in the areas of the economy, competition, demography, culture, and technology and then develop a plan that will provide for growth in such changing times. A typical plan considers the long-term (three to five years) and the short-term (one year) situations. For example, a firm devises a five-year plan that sets the guidelines and the direction the company will take. This is the long-term plan. Each year, the plan will

FIGURE 7.1   Business Planning Process—Marketing and Marketing Communications Orientation

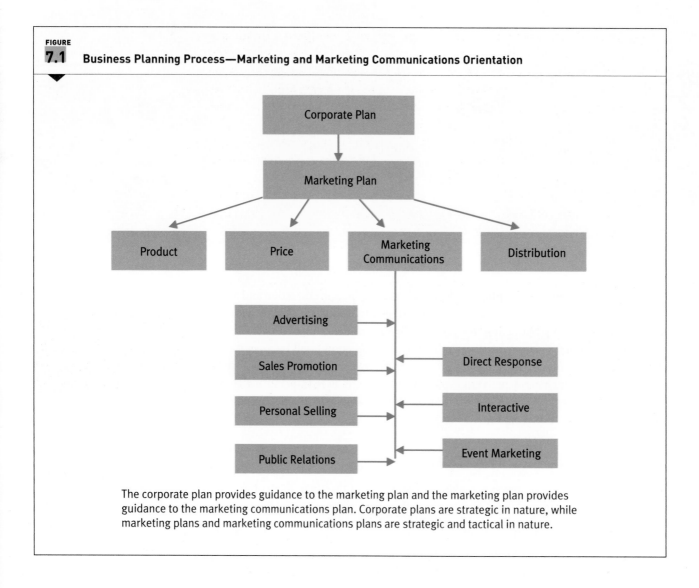

The corporate plan provides guidance to the marketing plan and the marketing plan provides guidance to the marketing communications plan. Corporate plans are strategic in nature, while marketing plans and marketing communications plans are strategic and tactical in nature.

be evaluated and, where necessary, revisions made on the basis of economic and competitive circumstances. This is the short-term plan.

strategic planning

Strategic planning is the process of determining objectives (stating goals) and identifying strategies (ways to achieve the goals) and tactics (specific action plans) that will help achieve the objectives. It is a comprehensive process done at most levels of an organization. A **corporate plan** originates at the top of the organization and is largely based on input from senior executives, such as the president and the vice-presidents.

corporate plan

Such plans are usually not elaborate documents, since their purpose is to identify the corporate objectives to be achieved over a specified period. The corporate plan acts as a guideline for planning in the various operational areas of the company.

Business planning throughout the organization begins and ends at the corporate or senior management level. The senior management formulates the overall strategic direction for the organization and establishes the financial objectives the company should aspire to (sales, profits, return on investment). Then, in accordance with the objectives and directions passed down from the senior management level, the marketing department develops marketing plans that embrace objectives, strategies, and tactics for individual products, divisions, or target markets.

Marketing plans consider such matters as the marketing mix (product, price, distribution, and marketing communications), target market characteristics, and control and evaluation mechanisms that determine the effectiveness of the strategies that are implemented. Essentially, the plan outlines how the various components of the marketing mix will be utilized to achieve marketing objectives. The content of a marketing plan is presented in more detail later in this chapter.

The phrase "a chain is only as strong as its weakest link" is an appropriate description of the relationships between various elements of a plan. Strategic planning attempts to coordinate all the activities so that the various elements work harmoniously. In the case of marketing and advertising, all the activities must present a consistent message for the company about its products in order to create a favourable impression in the minds of consumers. One weak link in the chain can create conflict or confuse the target market. For example, a product's selling price could be set too high in relation to the customer's perception of quality. Or, the product fails to live up to the promises made in advertising. Inconsistent activities spread over numerous company products could seriously disrupt attempts to achieve marketing and corporate objectives.

Corporate Planning

In Figure 7.1, business planning is divided into two distinct categories: (1) corporate planning, and (2) operational planning, which includes marketing planning. Corporate planning is the planning done by the top management and usually includes three variables: a vision statement or mission statement, a statement of corporate objectives, and a statement of corporate strategies.

Since the corporate plans provide direction for all the functional areas of the company, including marketing, they tend to be long-term in nature and broad in scope, and consider the overall well-being of the organization.

VISION STATEMENT OR MISSION STATEMENT

A **vision statement** or **mission statement** is the foundation of the corporate plan; it is a statement of the organization's purpose. It reflects the operating philosophy of the organization and the direction the organization is to take. Such statements are related to the opportunities the company seeks in the marketplace. They may be quite detailed or very brief in their content. Refer to Figure 7.2 for an illustration.

CORPORATE OBJECTIVES

Corporate objectives are statements of a company's overall goals and take their direction from the mission statement. They may state how much return on investment or what level of sales or market share is desired of a particular market segment. Objectives may also include statements about where the company might diversify, what businesses to acquire, and other goals. Good objective statements are written in quantifiable terms so that they can be measured for attainment. Consider the following examples:

- To increase total company sales revenue from $500 million to $550 million (in a specified period)

- To increase market share from 25 percent to 30 percent (in a specified period)

- To demonstrate leadership in the areas of social responsibility and corporate citizenship

Objectives like these provide the framework for the development of detailed plans in the operational areas of the organization, with marketing being one of those areas. Typically, the marketing plans for various divisions of a company or the various brands

2. Identify the distinctions and relationships between corporate planning and marketing planning.

vision statement (mission statement)

corporate objectives

FIGURE

7.2

**A Vision Statement and
Supporting Statements**

Kraft Foods

Kraft Foods is a global leader in branded foods and beverages with 2003 net revenues of more than $31 billion. Kraft is the largest food and beverage company in North America and the second largest in the world.

Our Vision
Helping people around the world eat and live better.

Our Values

- *Innovation—Satisfying real-life needs with unique ideas*
- *Quality—Fulfilling a promise to deliver the best*
- *Safety—Ensuring high standards in everything we make*
- *Respect—Caring for people, communities, and the environment*
- *Integrity—Doing the right thing*
- *Openness—Listening to the ideas of others and encouraging an open dialogue*

PepsiCo

PepsiCo is a world leader in convenient foods and beverages with revenues of almost $27 billion. The company consists of a snack business (Frito Lay), beverage business (Pepsi-Cola products and Tropicana juices and Gatorade), and a packaged food business (Quaker Oats)

Mission Statement
Our mission *is to be the world's premier consumer products company focused on convenient foods and beverages. We seek to produce healthy financial rewards for investors as we provide opportunities for growth and enrichment to our employees, our business partners and the communities in which we operate. And in everything we do, we strive for honesty, fairness, and integrity.*

Sources: www.kraft.com and www.pepsico.com.

set financial and market-share objectives. The success or failure of individual products has an impact on whether or not overall corporate objectives are achieved.

CORPORATE STRATEGIES

corporate strategies

The next step is to identify corporate strategies. **Corporate strategies** are plans outlining how the objectives are to be achieved. When devising strategies an organization considers several factors: marketing strength; degree of competition in markets the company operates in; financial resources (e.g., the availability of investment capital or the ability to borrow required funds); research and development capabilities; and commitment (i.e., the priority the company has placed on a particular goal). Kraft Foods, for example, is a global leader in food manufacturing and marketing. To retain its position, Kraft's strategy is to market superior products that meet the ever-changing needs of modern consumers and to ensure it is operating in product segments that offer the greatest return on investment. Kraft also places a priority on its commitment to social responsibility.[1] Refer to Figure 7.3 for details.

A company can achieve growth through any one, or combinations, of the following corporate strategies.

penetration strategy

PENETRATION STRATEGY A **penetration strategy** calls for aggressive and progressive action on the part of an organization. Growth is achieved by building existing businesses (either company divisions or product lines). As described above, Kraft

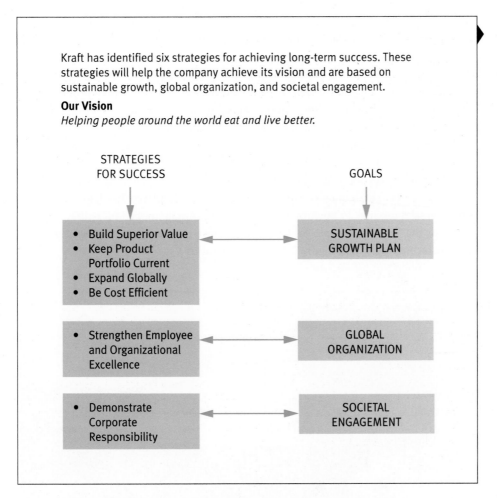

FIGURE

7.3

Kraft Has Identified Six Company Strategies for Long-Term Success

Source: Adapted from www.kraft.com/ profile/company_strategies.html.

follows a penetration strategy. Kraft markets products under several familiar brand names, such as Kraft (cheeses, salad dressings, sauces, and packaged dinners), Nabisco (cookies and crackers), Maxwell House (one of the world's leading brands of coffee), and Philadelphia (cream cheeses). Kraft devises annual marketing plans that are designed to improve the business performance of each of it brands, to penetrate the market further by expanding sales and increasing market share. Kraft wants to stay a step ahead of its competitors and maintain a strong presence among consumers.

ACQUISITION STRATEGY   An **acquisition strategy** involves the purchase of another company or parts of a company. A strategy based on acquisition allows a company to enter an attractive market quickly and it may be less costly in the long term. In contrast, the time required to develop new products can be extensive and the financial commitment considerable. Reebok International recently acquired Montreal-based Hockey Co. Holdings Inc., the makers of CCM, Koho, and Jofa hockey equipment and apparel. What would the motive be for such an acquisition? Nike owns Bauer, another top line of hockey equipment, but Bauer is not as prominent as the various Hockey Co. brands. This will be one of the few cases where Reebok will have a bigger market share than Nike in a sports category. It sets the stage for some intense competition for sales and market share growth.[2]

acquisition strategy

NEW-PRODUCTS STRATEGY   A **new-products strategy** requires considerable investment in research and development. Such a strategy also requires financial commitment

new-products strategy

over an extended period, as it takes considerable time to develop a new product. And the odds of successfully marketing a new product remain low.

Whirlpool is a strong and trusted brand name in the appliance business, but the company is no longer content to be the largest maker of appliances. Its new attitude is expressed as "Thinking outside the box, inside the home." Among the new-product ideas Whirlpool is considering are a line of modular garage accessories, all-in-one picnic units that slide into the back of the family minivan, and a line of jetted baths—the first actual whirlpools in Whirlpool's 91-year history. None of these new ideas are related to its existing range of products—refrigerators, ranges, washers, and dryers.

Apple made a corporate decision to pursue new-product opportunities in the entertainment market. The launch of the iPod, a digital music player, has had a dramatic impact on sales revenue. In the fourth quarter of 2004 Apple shipped more than 800 000 iPods. For the first time, Apple sold more iPods in a quarter than it did its signature Macintosh computers.[3] See Figure 7.4 for an illustration.

FIGURE
7.4

New products like Apple's iPod bring new revenue to a company

Mario Jose Sanchez/CP Photo Archive

VERTICAL AND HORIZONTAL INTEGRATION STRATEGIES   In a **vertical integration strategy**, one organization in the channel of distribution owns and operates organizations in other levels of the channel. For example, Apple Computer has traditionally marketed its range of computer products and accessories through an independent dealer network and various catalogue merchants, but in an attempt to get closer to its customers decided to open its own retail network. Owning and operating retail stores is not Apple's area of expertise, the venture is costly, and there is a risk of alienating existing retailers who have been loyal to the brand. Nonetheless, Apple sees benefit in getting closer to its customers.

vertical integration strategy

In a **horizontal integration strategy**, one organization owns and operates several companies at the same level in the channel of distribution. The objective of horizontal integration is to control greater market share within a certain segment of a market. For example, Cara Operations, a Canadian restaurant chain, owns and operates seven different restaurants: Swiss Chalet, Harvey's, Second Cup, Kelsey's, Montana's, Outback Steakhouse, and Milestone's. Collectively, systemwide sales for these restaurants amount to $1.3 billion annually. Cara's strategy as expressed by Gabriel Tsampalieros, president and CEO, is clear: "When you play in a market like Canada with its limited population, you recognize that to grow to a certain size, you've got to have flexibility to play in different price points."[4]

horizontal integration strategy

Cara Operations
www.cara.com

STRATEGIC ALLIANCE STRATEGY   Strategic alliances are now very popular among companies wanting to find ways of reducing costs or improving operating efficiencies. A **strategic alliance** is a relationship between two or more companies who decide to work cooperatively to achieve common goals. Imperial Oil Limited and Tim Hortons formed a strategic alliance that calls for Tim Hortons food kiosks in 300 Esso stations across Canada. Both firms are trying to transform the neighbourhood gas station into a lunch destination and have dubbed the concept "dashboard dining." With the alliance Imperial Oil hopes to wean itself from its dependence on the slim profit margins of retail gas sales, and Tim Hortons will be able to expand at an unprecedented rate and at much lower cost. Once completed, the kiosks will account for 1 in 10 of all Tim Hortons locations.[5]

strategic alliance

Couche-Tard, the owners of Mac's (milk stores), formed alliances with a variety of food-service providers in an effort to stay ahead of competitors. The alliance involves food-service counters for Subway, A&W, and Timothy's Old World Coffee. In fact, some of the new and larger stores will have all three partners in one Mac's location. Alliances like this one offer benefits to all partners. Timothy's, for example, could not expand at the same rate if it were doing things on its own; the company sees the partnership as a great opportunity.[6]

Couche-Tard
www.couchetard.com

DIVESTMENT STRATEGY   Bigger is not always better! Rather than expanding, some companies are consolidating their operations by **divesting** themselves of operations that are not profitable. Divestment alternatives include downsizing, closing, or selling parts of a company. Levi Strauss & Co. is contemplating selling its successful line of Dockers casual clothing because the company overall is struggling to reverse years of declining sales. The company—which got its start by selling mining supplies and jeans to California prospectors in the Gold Rush era—has cut jobs, closed factories, seen its credit rating slashed, and resorted to selling a profitable unit of the company in order to right the ship.[7]

divesting

Molson Inc. is another company examining a divestment strategy. It is contemplating the sale of some or all of its sports and entertainment division, which includes partial ownership of the Montreal Canadiens (Molson used to own the entire team but sold its majority stake several years ago), concert producer House of Blues, and the Molson Indy races that run in Toronto and Montreal. Molson's overall strategy is to focus on its core business—brewing and marketing beer.[8]

strategic business unit (SBU)

The examples cited throughout the corporate strategy section illustrate the concept of strategic business units. A **strategic business unit (SBU)** is a unit of a company that has a separate mission and objectives and can be planned independently of the other businesses of the company. The growth potential of each business unit determines the level of marketing support (time, money, and human resources) it receives. The parent company is responsible for establishing strategic business unit priorities. In the case of Molson, the sports and entertainment division is not as important as it once was. At Whirlpool there is a strong desire to build new products for new markets. It can be observed, then, that companies face different circumstances and make unique decisions based on situation.

portfolio analysis

When a company analyzes its business units, it assesses the strengths and weaknesses of each unit, recommends additions and deletions when necessary, and allocates resources according to growth-potential opportunities. In marketing terms, the company is conducting a **portfolio analysis**.

For more insight into corporate strategies and their relationship to marketing strategies, read the Marketing in Action vignette **Research and Targeting: Cara's Key to Success**.

Marketing Planning

> 3. Describe the relationships between the various stages of the planning process.

The marketing department operates under the direction of a chief marketing officer (or similar title) within the guidelines established by the senior management or executive branch of the organization. The objectives, strategies, and action plans developed by marketing are designed to help achieve the overall company objectives. Where planning is concerned, the major areas of marketing responsibility include:

1. Identifying and selecting target markets
2. Establishing marketing objectives, strategies, and tactics
3. Evaluating and controlling marketing activities

marketing planning

Marketing planning is the analysis, planning, implementation, evaluation, and control of marketing initiatives in order to satisfy target market needs and achieve organizational objectives. It involves the analysis of relevant background information and historical trend data and the development of marketing objectives and strategies for all products and services within the company. The integration of the various elements of the marketing mix is outlined in the marketing plan of each product. Other elements of marketing planning include target-market identification, budgeting, and control mechanisms.

Marketing plans are short-term in nature (one year), specific in scope (they deal with one product and outline precise actions), and combine both strategy and tactics (they are action-oriented). They are also subject to change on short notice, as a result of economic shifts or competitive activity. Figure 7.5 (p. 172) summarizes the stages of marketing planning.

The Marketing Plan

While there is no typical format for a marketing plan (i.e., the content and structure varies from company to company), it is usually subdivided into two major sections: background information and plan. In terms of background the company conducts a

MARKETING IN ACTION

Research and Targeting: Cara's Key to Success

Cara Operations has successfully embarked upon a horizontal integration strategy to build an enviable position in Canada's restaurant industry. In fact, its business model is the envy of many competitors and other restaurants throughout North America. Cara's marketing strategies have contributed to the company's overall success.

Cara comprises seven unique restaurants—Swiss Chalet, Harvey's, Second Cup, Kelsey's, Montana's Cookhouse, Outback Steakhouse, and Milestone's. Each restaurant appeals to a slightly different target market, with unique food offerings, different price points, and different atmosphere. Cara's success—$1.5 billion in annual sales—is attributed to intensive research into consumer preferences, increased marketing activity, and updated positioning strategy. Cara clearly defines each brand so that one brand does not encroach on the other.

To stay abreast of trends, Cara invests heavily in consumer research. The company collects data from 21 different sources, including Fasttrack, PMB, individual surveys, focus groups, and approximately 7000 interviews with customers each year. Just disseminating the information to the different brands costs $1 million a year. To say the least, Cara is into database marketing! Gabriel Tsampalieros, president and CEO of Cara, says, "We are not slaves to data but we have to intrinsically understand consumer trends and be able to identify them three years before they become a trend."

The most successful of Cara's restaurants is Swiss Chalet. Swiss Chalet has always been popular with an older target audience, but recently steps have been taken to attract younger customers. Swiss Chalet has been upgrading its restaurants. There are more promotions, new menu offerings, a focus on takeout and delivery, and a new interactive website. Trends such as health and wellness (concern for obesity), time-pressed consumers (the need for convenience), and changing media consumption habits (more time spent online and less time with television) have spawned the changes. Young families that used to frequent McDonald's and other fast-food restaurants now flock to Swiss Chalet.

Swiss Chalet is ideally positioned in the marketplace. According to Tsampalieros, "It plays to the home-meal replacement market through takeout, delivery and drive-through, while the restaurant offers full-service dining at a very affordable price. The combination offers phenomenal value."

What about the other restaurants? Harvey's is focusing on males and hamburgers, and the "Long live the grill" advertising campaign has clearly differentiated the brand from competitors. It's working, so Harvey's is resisting the temptation of entering unfamiliar territory by adding diet-conscious menu items. Leave that to the competitors.

Second Cup is in a battle with Starbucks for coffee supremacy. Second Cup is attempting to retain loyal customers and attract new ones in a very competitive market. To achieve this objective there has been a bigger investment in marketing in the form of sponsorships, a new website, tongue-in-cheek billboards, and remodelled stores.

The other restaurants are taking more of a local approach to marketing. Kelsey's promotes itself as your local neighborhood bar and grill. Its marketing strategy focuses on local events and sponsorships. Generous portions of food at reasonable prices are also good for business! Montana's Cookhouse adopts a similar marketing strategy.

Cara is managing a restaurant empire with each brand at a different stage of its life cycle—a complex challenge to say the least. The company's strength is in branding. Cara understands competitive intelligence, brand health, core competencies, best practices, and what's working at each chain. Cara believes in continuous fine-tuning of operations and the need for clear differentiation among its brands both internally and externally.

Adapted from Sarah Dobson, "Cara's Winning Combination," *Marketing*, October 28, 2002, pp. 10–14.

Dick Hemingway

FIGURE
7.5   The Marketing Planning Process

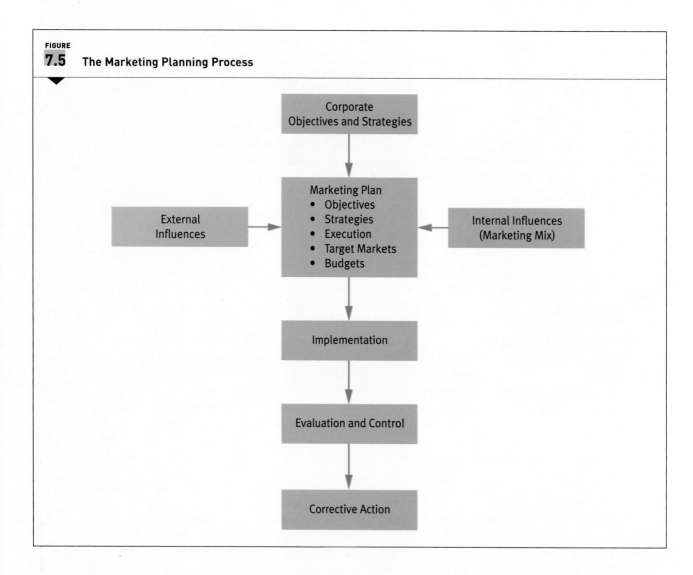

situation analysis (environmental analysis)

SWOT analysis

situation analysis (sometimes called **environmental analysis**) in which data and information about external and internal influences are compiled. External considerations include economic trends, social and demographic trends, and technology trends. As well, information is compiled about the market, competition, and customers.

Using this information, a **SWOT analysis** (an evaluation of a brand's strengths, weaknesses, opportunities, and threats) is undertaken. The SWOT helps to crystallize the present situation and provides guidance for developing marketing strategies. In the marketing plan, the objectives, strategies, and tactics for the brand or company are clearly delineated. The following is a description of the various elements of a marketing plan.

MARKETING PLAN BACKGROUND—SITUATION ANALYSIS

As a preliminary step to marketing planning, a variety of information is compiled and analyzed.

EXTERNAL INFLUENCES

4. Identify the role and influence of corporate plans and their influence on marketing plans.

1. *Economic Trends*—Basic economic trends dictate the nature of marketing activity (e.g., if the economy is healthy and growing, more resources are allocated to marketing activity; if the economy is in a recession, a more conservative approach is often adopted).

2. ***Social and Demographic Trends***—Basic trends in age, income, immigration, and lifestyle influence decisions on what target markets to pursue. For example, the Canadian population is aging and there is a steady migration of the population to urban areas. Health and wellness trends (e.g., the low-carbohydrate phenomenon) must also be considered. These factors necessitate a change in marketing strategy.

3. ***Technology Trends***—The rapid pace of change (e.g., in telecommunications equipment) influences the development of new products, shortens product life cycles, and influences the communications strategies used to reach customers.

4. ***Market Size and Growth***—A review is made of trends in the marketplace over a period. Is the market growing, remaining stable, or declining?

5. ***Regional Market Importance***—Market trends and sales volume trends are analyzed by region to determine areas of strength or weakness, and areas to concentrate on in the future.

6. ***Market Segment Analysis***—The sales volume for a total market and for segments within a market are reviewed. For example, the coffee market is analyzed in terms of regular ground coffee, instant coffee, decaffeinated coffee, and flavoured coffee.

7. ***Seasonal Analysis***—An examination is conducted of seasonal or cyclical trends during the course of a year. For example, special holidays, such as Christmas, Thanksgiving, Hallowe'en, and others, often have an impact on sales volume.

8. ***Consumer Data***—Current users of a product are profiled according to such factors as age, income, gender, lifestyle, and location.

9. ***Consumer Behaviour***—A review is made of the degree of loyalty customers exhibit towards a product or brand. Are customers loyal, or do they switch brands often? Other factors considered are benefits consumers seek in the product and how frequent their purchases are.

10. ***Other Factors***—Factors such as pack size trends (regular size, single size, family size, etc.), colours, scents or flavour; analysis of products sold; or other relevant areas play a role in the planning process.

11. ***Media***—Trends in competitive spending on media advertising will influence marketing communications decisions and budgeting.

PRODUCT (BRAND) ANALYSIS   An assessment of a brand's marketing mix strategy is reviewed at this stage. An attempt is made to link marketing activities undertaken in the past year with the sales volume and market share that was achieved—did the plan work? Is the brand meeting consumers' expectations?

1. ***Sales Volume***—Historical sales tends are plotted to forecast future growth.

2. ***Market Share***—Market share success is the clearest indicator of how well a brand is performing. Market share is examined nationally and regionally in order to identify areas of strength and weakness.

3. ***New-Product Activity***—The success or failure of new product lines introduced in recent years is highlighted (e.g., new pack sizes, flavours, product formats, and so on).

4. ***Distribution***—The availability of a product nationally or regionally is reviewed. Distribution is also assessed based on type of customer (e.g., chains versus independents, and the successes or failures of online distribution initiatives).

5. ***Marketing Communications***—An assessment of current activities will determine if strategies are to be maintained or if new strategies are needed. A review of media spending and utilization (e.g., television, newspaper, magazines, outdoor, online communications, events and promotions, and so on) is used to assess their impact on brand performance, nationally and regionally.

COMPETITIVE ANALYSIS   Major competitors are identified and their performance is analyzed. Essentially, a competitive product is reviewed much like a company's own brand. A manager will want to know a competitor's sales volume trends and market share trends and what marketing activities they have undertaken to produce those trends. This calls for a review of the competitor's marketing mix activities.

SWOT ANALYSIS   Once the market, product, and competitor information is assembled, the next step is an appraisal of it. Such an appraisal is referred to as a SWOT analysis. The acronym SWOT stands for strengths, weaknesses, opportunities, and threats. A SWOT analysis examines critical factors that have an impact on the nature and direction of a marketing strategy. Strengths and weaknesses are internal factors (e.g., resources available, research and development capability, production capability, and management expertise), while opportunities and threats are external factors (e.g., economic trends, competitive activity, and social and demographic trends).

The end result of a SWOT analysis should be the matching of potential opportunities with resource capabilities. The goal is to capitalize on strengths while overcoming weaknesses. A SWOT analysis can be conducted at any level of an organization— product, division, or company.

To understand the importance of analyzing market situations, consider Sleeman Brewery's position in the Canadian beer market. Sleeman is the largest of the microbrewery operations, but its recent success is more the result of misfortune by competitors rather than good marketing strategy of its own. Mainstream brands produced by Molson (Canadian and Export) and Labatt (Blue) are in decline because young drinkers are showing preference for premium brands. As well, steady price increases by Molson and Labatt over the past few years have caused the discount segment to expand. Sleeman finds itself in the sweet spot of the beer market because half of it sales come from discount beers and the other half from premium beers.[9]

For a summary model of the background section of a marketing plan refer to Figure 7.6.

FIGURE
7.6

Content of a Marketing Plan—Background Section

Background Information

External Influences
- Economic trends
- Social and demographic trends
- Technology trends

Market Analysis
- Market size and growth rates
- Regional market importance
- Market segment analysis
- Seasonal analysis
- Consumer data (target user)
- Consumer behaviour (category and brand loyalty)
- Product trends
- Media expenditure trends

Product Analysis
- Sales volume trends
- Market share trends
- Distribution trends
- New product activity
- Marketing communications activity

Competitive Analysis
- Market share trends
- Marketing activity assessment
- Competitive innovations

SWOT Analysis
- Strengths
- Weaknesses
- Opportunities
- Threats

MARKETING PLAN—PLAN SECTION

POSITIONING STRATEGY STATEMENT   The concept of positioning strategy was discussed in Chapter 6. There, it was stated that positioning attempts to place a desirable image about a product, service, or company in the minds of customers. In the context of the marketing plan, a positioning strategy statement acts as a focal point for the development of marketing strategies and the utilization of the marketing mix.

Effective positioning strategy statements are realistic, specific, uncomplicated, and they clearly distinguish what the brand has to offer. To illustrate, consider the positioning statement for Visa Canada:

VISA gives you the confidence that you are able to do anything.

The benefits of having and using a Visa card are successfully portrayed in an advertising campaign that says your Visa card is "All you need." The present execution of this positioning strategy shows unrealistic situations in which a Visa credit card would not be needed (e.g., a golfer on a tee addressing the ball with a super-sized club-head, or a sign at a gasoline station showing the cost of gas as $0.00). Unfortunately, such situations do not exist; hence the need for Visa. Refer to Figure 7.7 for an illustration of Visa Canada's positioning strategy.

FIGURE
7.7

A print execution demonstrating Visa Canada's leadership positioning strategy

Courtesy of Visa Canada. Photography by Mark Zibert

marketing objectives

MARKETING OBJECTIVES   **Marketing objectives** are statements identifying what a product or service will accomplish over a one-year period. Typically, marketing objectives concentrate on sales volume, market share, and profit (net profit or return on investment), all of which are quantitative (as opposed to qualitative) in nature and measurable at the end of the plan cycle. Objectives that are qualitative in nature could include new-product introductions, new additions to current product lines, product improvements, and packaging innovations. To illustrate the concept of marketing objectives, consider the following sample statements:

1. *Sales Volume:* To achieve a unit volume of 200 000 units by the end of the year, an increase of 10 percent over the current year sales.

2. *Market Share:* To achieve a market share of 30 percent in 12 months, an increase of four share points over the current position.

3. *Profit:* To generate an after-budget profit of $600 000 in the next 12 months.

4. *Product:* To launch a new package design in the fourth quarter of this year.

Objectives should be written in a manner that allows for measurement at the end of the year. Were a particular set of objectives achieved or not?

marketing strategies

MARKETING STRATEGIES   **Marketing strategies** are the "master plans" for achieving marketing objectives. Marketing strategies usually include three main elements: a description of the target market, discussion about how the various elements of the marketing mix will be used, and a budget. All marketing strategies must fit with the positioning strategy described in the previous section.

target market

Target Market   When developing a marketing plan, the planner identifies, or targets, markets that represent the greatest profit potential for the firm. A **target market** is a group of customers who have certain characteristics in common: similar needs, habits, and lifestyles. The planner must ask what these are and determine if there is one primary user group or several user segments that have a need for the product or service. After gathering this information, the manager defines the target market in terms of demographic (age, income, gender, education, and occupation), psychographic (lifestyle), and geographic (location) characteristics. To demonstrate, the following profile might represent the *primary target market* for an upscale automobile, or someone interested in the services of a financial planning company:

Age: 25 to 49 years old
Gender: male or female
Income: $75 000 plus annually
Occupation: Managers, owners, professionals, executives (referred to as MOPEs)
Education: College or university
Location: Cities of 200 000 plus population
Lifestyle: Progressive thinkers and risk takers who like to experiment with new
    products and who are interested in the arts, entertainment, and vacation travel.

Additional targets—or *secondary targets,* as they are referred to—will have a different profile. Pursuing secondary targets offers potential for incremental sales and profit. Consider the situation Avon faces. Avon is the world's largest direct seller of cosmetics to women, but it is targeting men with a new line of skincare products under the brand name "M." The launch of "M" comes as the market for men's grooming products is taking off. The line includes face wash, after-shave balm, moisturizer, and anti-aging wrinkle cream. Apparently the line between masculinity and vanity is blurring, particularly among younger males.[10]

Marketing Mix   At this stage of the planning process, the role and importance of each element in the marketing mix and those activities that comprise each element of the mix are identified. The task is to develop a plan of attack so that all the elements combine to achieve the marketing objectives. For example, in the soft drink business, both Coca-Cola and PepsiCo offer products of comparable quality and price. Therefore, it is the strength of their advertising (a marketing communications strategy) and their availability (distribution strategy) that determines competitive advantage. Both brands will invest heavily in these two areas. Different brands facing different situations may utilize the various elements of the marketing mix a different way.

Budget   The corporate plan has already identified a total marketing budget for the company, giving consideration to the overall profit concerns for the forthcoming year. The budget must be allocated across all company products on the basis of the firm's analysis of current priorities or profit potential. Managers responsible for product planning must develop and justify a budget that allows enough funds to implement the strategies identified in their marketing plan and to achieve the financial objectives identified for the product. The final stage of the budgeting process is the allocation of funds among the activity areas in the plan (product development, marketing research, advertising, sales promotion, personal selling, event marketing, and direct marketing). It should be recognized that there is much competition internally among brand managers for budget resources.

MARKETING EXECUTION   **Marketing execution**—or **marketing tactics**, as they are often called—focus on specific details of activities that were identified in the strategy section of the plan. In general terms, a tactical plan outlines the activity, how much it will cost, what the timing will be, and who will be responsible for implementation. Detailed tactical plans for all components of the plan—product improvement, advertising, sales promotion and marketing research, and so on, are included here.

marketing execution (marketing tactics)

A summary of the information that is usually included in the plan section of a marketing plan appears in Figure 7.8.

FIGURE
7.8

Content of a Marketing Plan—Plan Section

Marketing Plan

Positioning Statement

Marketing Objectives
- Sales volume
- Market share
- Profit
- Other

Marketing Strategies (strategic priorities)
- Target market description
- Marketing mix strategies
  - Product
  - Price
  - Marketing communications
  - Distribution
  - Marketing research
  - Budget

Marketing Execution (specific action plans)
- Product
- Price
- Marketing communications
- Distribution
- Marketing research
- Profit improvement

Financial Summary
- Brand profit & loss statement

Marketing Budget
- Allocation by activity
- Allocation by time (month, quarter, etc.)

Marketing Calendar

Activity schedule by month

5. Explain the control procedures used in marketing planning.

marketing control

MARKETING CONTROL AND EVALUATION   Since clearly defined and measurable objectives have been established by the organization and by the marketing department, it is important that results be evaluated against the plans and against past performance. This evaluation indicates whether current strategies need to be modified or whether new strategies should be considered. **Marketing control** is the process of measuring and evaluating the results of marketing strategies and plans and taking corrective action to ensure that the marketing objectives are attained. Marketing control involves three basic elements:

1. Establishing standards of marketing performance expressed in the form of marketing objectives
2. Periodically measuring actual performance (of the company, division, or product) and comparing it with the established objectives
3. Taking corrective action (e.g., developing new strategies) in those areas where performance does not meet the objectives

Refer to Figure 7.9 for a diagram of the control process. The nature of an organization's control process can vary and the frequency of evaluation is left to the discretion of the management. For evaluating the effectiveness of marketing strategies, there are three primary measures or indicators: *marketing activity reviews*, *financial reviews*, and *strategic control reviews*.

MARKETING ACTIVITY REVIEWS   The effectiveness of a marketing plan is measured against a few key indicators: *sales volume*, *market share*, and *profit*. Activity reviews

FIGURE
7.9

Marketing Control Process

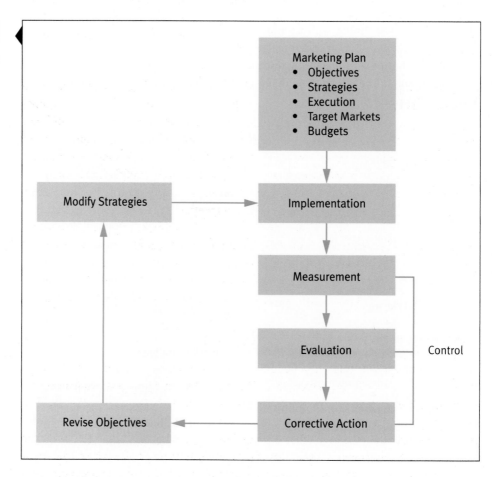

typically occur on a quarterly basis and often involve a gathering of brand managers, sales managers, and some senior marketing executives. Planning cycles that have activity reviews built in give an organization the opportunity to make strategic adjustments during the course of a year.

For any of the three indicators (sales, market share, and profit) the managers will compare *actual results* versus *planned results* and *actual results* versus *results for the same period a year ago*. Understanding why sales are up or down is the responsibility of the sales managers and brand managers, so naturally there is much discussion among these managers to figure out the results and agree on how to proceed. By reviewing performance and customer feedback together they can mutually agree on revised figures and marketing activities for the balance of the year.

Part of the marketing activity review should also include a review of competitor activity. What are the competitors doing? Are they gaining or losing market share? Such analysis attempts to link marketing activities to share performance in an effort to determine which activities are effective and which are ineffective.

FINANCIAL REVIEWS   As part of the organization's marketing control process, periodic profit reviews are conducted for all product lines and divisions. Key variables in a profit review are up-to-date *sales forecasts*, *costs*, and *marketing budgets*.

Since senior executives are largely evaluated on profit the organization generates and the value of a company's stock, the financial review process can be challenging for the marketing department. For example, if it is forecast that profit will fall short of expectations by the end of the fiscal year, marketing budgets will have to be trimmed. Such reductions could occur by product, by division, or by region. For example, the advertising budget could be slashed in order to protect other marketing activities. A financial review forces managers to establish priorities and withdraw funds from those activities that will feel the effects the least.

STRATEGIC CONTROL REVIEWS   Strategic control is more long-term in nature than marketing control. Since conditions in the marketplace (economy, technology, competition, and governments) change rapidly, marketing strategies soon become outdated. An organization must be ready for change! Therefore, strategic reviews are intensive and are conducted every three to five years. Within this framework, marketers reassess marketing strategies for all products annually, during the preparation of the marketing plan.

The primary instrument for evaluating strategic direction and overall effectiveness of marketing activities is a marketing audit. A **marketing audit** is a systematic, critical, and unbiased review and appraisal of the marketing department's basic objectives and policies, and of the organization, methods, procedures, and people employed to implement the policies.[11] An external consultant often conducts the marketing audit in order to eliminate any political bias that may exist in an organization. The task of the auditor is to evaluate plans and the quality of the marketing effort as objectively as possible.

marketing audit

Keeping Pace with Change

In contemporary marketing, an organization must be flexible in order to take advantage of new developments in the marketplace. Throughout the planning cycle, a firm is presented with new threats and opportunities that can make a plan obsolete rather quickly. Consequently, the wise marketing manager builds a contingency plan into a master plan. A contingency is the possibility of something happening that poses a threat to the organization. A **contingency plan** involves the identification of alternative courses of action that can be used to modify an original plan if and when new circumstances arise.

contingency plan

A contingency plan is based on "what if" or "worst-case" situations. If these situations develop, the organization is ready to implement alternative strategies. Some events that would require alternative action would be:

1. The competition unexpectedly increases its level of media advertising.
2. The competition reduces its price to build market share.
3. A new competitor enters the market.
4. A strike in your own plant halts production of your product.
5. A new trend emerges that changes market conditions.

Such situations add a dimension of foresight to strategic marketing planning and force the manager to plan for the unexpected at all times. For example, the National Hockey League player lockout during the in 2004–05 season had a direct impact on brands that advertise during hockey games and on businesses that relied on pedestrian traffic to and from games. Alternate strategies had to be employed. Brand advertisers shifted their television budgets to other sports or regular programming. Restaurants and bars located on the Red Mile (a route to and from the Pengrowth Saddledome in Calgary—the arena where the Calgary Flames play) had to quickly develop alternative promotions linked to other sports events to attract customers.

Some Fundamental Marketing Strategies

As discussed earlier in the chapter, corporate strategies plot the basic direction an organization will take for an extended period—it may follow an acquisition strategy, a penetration strategy, a new-product development strategy, or a vertical or horizontal integration strategy, among many potential alternatives.

Once the basic direction is established, individual products must develop their own marketing strategies that will be implemented over a one-year period. The collective success or failure of the products influences the overall health of the organization and whether or not corporate objectives are achieved. Some of the more fundamental marketing strategies have labels similar to the corporate strategies discussed earlier. Refer to Figure 7.10 for a visual illustration of these strategies.

MARKET PENETRATION

market penetration

Strategies that focus on **market penetration** are aimed at improving the market position of an existing product in existing markets. Essentially, these strategies attempt to increase sales to current users while stealing market share from competitors. In this

6. Describe the various types of strategies used by the company as a whole, and by the marketing departments, for marketing goods and services.

FIGURE 7.10

Fundamental Marketing Strategies

	EXISTING PRODUCT	**NEW PRODUCT**
EXISTING MARKET	Market Penetration	Product Development
NEW MARKET	Market Development	Diversification

respect, the marketing mix elements are modified to develop a better formula for getting current and new customers to buy. Among the options are improving the product, lowering the price, changing the style of advertising, or any combination of these.

In the soft drink market, Pepsi-Cola employs a penetration strategy. The brand aggressively targets Coca-Cola drinkers and presents them with information that tempts them to switch brands. Some ads go as far as to show Coke drinkers enjoying the refreshing taste of a Pepsi. A television commercial for Pespi Edge (a low-carbohydrate cola beverage) shows a former Coke drinker selling off all of his Coca-Cola branded merchandise in a yard sale.

In the United States, the battle for the multi-billion-dollar erectile dysfunction market is a war between Viagra, Levitra, and Cialis. There's aggressive marketing all around to steal market share. Cialis, the newest of the three brands, makes claims that it works for 36 hours and offers new users trial samples to get them hooked. If users are not satisfied, the manufacturer (Eli Lilly & Co.) will provide the user with samples of Viagra or Levitra at their expense. Such an offer shows confidence in the performance of the product. In Europe Cialis has earned itself a nickname—"le weekend."[12]

MARKET DEVELOPMENT

A company pursuing a strategy based on **market development** attempts to market existing products to new target markets. Such strategies attempt to attract consumers of different demographic categories, different lifestyles, or different geographic areas. To illustrate, retailer Home Depot plans to open smaller neighbourhood stores to its slate of big-box stores. Referred to internally as community stores, they will be about half the size of the big-box outlets and be targeted at smaller communities with populations of 20 000 to 40 000. Home Depot's market share is stuck in the 12-percent range and it has reached a mature stage of development. Geographic expansion to smaller centres represents a growth opportunity.[13]

market development

Home Depot is also launching "urban stores" that will focus on upscale items such as lamps, kitchen tiles, home decoration, towels and pillows, among many other lines. The goal is to offer shoppers a boutique-style shopping experience. These stores will continue to offer traditional hard goods such as tools and appliances but the focus is on design-oriented items. Home Depot has determined the same store formula doesn't work everywhere. The company believes this new concept will appeal to urban consumers who do not have the time to trek out to the suburbs. Thus far, the only urban store is located in West Vancouver, but there are plans for more to follow.[14]

Toyota used a market development strategy when it redesigned the Matrix model to entice a younger target audience. The more stylish and sporty look is illustrated in Figure 7.11 For additional insight into market development strategies and product development strategies, read the Marketing in Action vignette **Toyota Pursues Younger Customers** on page 183.

PRODUCT DEVELOPMENT

In the case of a strategy involving **product development**, new products are offered to current target markets, or existing products are modified and marketed to current users. Such initiatives may include the introduction of new sizes, colours, and flavours. Expansion of a product line by extending the line is quite common. This involves the use of the same brand name on new products or related products (a family of products).

product development

Oral-B is a well-known brand that makes dental-care products. The entire dental-care market has been expanding rapidly in recent years based on consumers' obsession with having white teeth. The trend has spawned many new products. Oral-B recently

FIGURE
7.11 **Toyota Matrix appeals to a youthful target market**

05 // matrix xr   So versatile, add a roll of duct tape and you can take on the world.

Courtesy Toyota Canada. Photo by Michael Moore Photography

launched Oral-B Brush-Ups, a "textured teeth wipe that gives you that just-brushed feeling, anytime, anywhere." Placing the cloth on a finger, you simply wipe your teeth and gums clean. A competitor like Crest also gains market advantage by launching new products. The Crest name helped develop a new category of products—tooth whiteners—and appears on products such as Crest Whitestrips and Crest Night Effects.

In the soft drink market both Coca-Cola and PepsiCo have launched new products to build sales and market share. Recent new lines from Coca-Cola include Vanilla Coke and a lime-flavoured version of Diet Coke. Keeping pace, PepsiCo launched Vanilla Pepsi and lemon-flavoured Pepsi. More recently, Coca-Cola lunched Coke C2, a low-calorie, low-carbohydrate beverage, and PepsiCo launched Pepsi Edge, a similar type of product. The competitive nature of this market dictates that key brands stay competitive with each other. To fall behind is a formula for failure.

MARKETING **IN ACTION**

Toyota Pursues Younger Customers

Toyota is a successful automobile company. In fact, it is on the verge of surpassing Chrysler to become the third-largest seller of cars in North America. General Motors and Ford lead the pack. Sometimes you become a victim of your own success, however, and that's exactly the dilemma that Toyota finds itself in.

The average age of a Toyota customer is 50. Toyota's older average age is due to its success at getting loyal younger buyers from the past to trade up to more expensive Toyota models as they get older. The Corolla, for example, is their number-one selling car in Canada, while Camry is one of the leaders in overall car sales in North America.

Toyota's corporate objective is to attract a younger buyer and to do so will require a combination of new product lines and the restyling and reimaging of some existing car lines. Demographic trends strongly suggest that Toyota make the move toward a younger customer. The population group referred to as Generation Y, echo boomer, or millennial (late teens and early twenties right now) is going to be huge and they are just entering their car-buying years. Toyota estimates there will be 4 million of them a year until 2010. That's a market worth pursuing!

Some initial steps taken by Toyota include the restyling of the Celica model. The sportier look of the Celica has dropped the average age of the Celica owner to 36 years from 44 years. The Echo was launched in 2000 to attract young first-time buyers, but it also had widespread appeal among older customers looking for economy. The Echo has been an overwhelming success.

Toyota also launched the Matrix, a 5-door wagon aimed at the 20-something target market. The Matrix is a hybrid of a sports car and an SUV, with compact-car pricing. It is ideally positioned to meet the needs of new, young buyers.

The marketing strategy for the Matrix included media advertising, events and promotions. The goal was to associate Matrix with the target's lifestyle, which includes entertainment, socializing, fitness, and recreation. Media opportunities were chosen that would reach the target while they were enjoying those activities. The ad campaign included full-motion cinema ads, health club posters, and bar posters. A contest, "The Toyota Matrix—Drive It, Win It," called for entries online. Close to 11 000 entries were submitted.

Adapted from information provided by Toyota Canada; Kae Inoue, "Toyota covets young buyers," *Financial Post*, January 9, 2002, p. FP6; Tobi Elkin and Jean Halliday, "Toyota launches Corolla campaign," *Advertising Age*, February 25, 2002, pp. 4, 29; and News Line, *Marketing*, February 25, 2002, p. 3.

Comstock

DIVERSIFICATION

diversification

Diversification, as it applies to products, refers to the introduction of a new product to a completely new market. In effect, the company is entering unfamiliar territory when it uses this strategy. Such a strategy requires substantial resources for research and development, initially high marketing expenses, and a strong commitment to building market share. To illustrate, consider Apple Computer's recent marketing adventures.

Apple Computer—always a niche player in the computer market, and always a company that does things differently—opted for diversification when it decided to open up its own retail stores. There was irony in the decision, because competitors like IBM and Gateway were in the process of closing their retail operations. The market was soft and customers preferred to buy directly. Apple's main selling points are that its products are cool and sexy—not the same kind of bland, generic-looking PCs that everyone else has. Apple believes its loyal customers will be more than willing to visit the company's retail locations. Some analysts believe this is misguided, and that it will prove to be simply a time-consuming way to lose a lot of money.[15]

iTunes
www.apple.com/itunes

More recently, Apple has ventured into the music business with its iTunes music stores. iTunes software creates a new model for making money from downloadable songs. The cost to the consumer is 99 cents a song. Apple sees iTunes as a drop in the kitty, almost a loss leader intended to build a new generation of Apple enthusiasts and to induce sales of its more profitable iPod. The iPod (a relatively new product) holds the largest share in the fragmented but growing portable digital music player market. In terms of diversification, Apple has moved from the computer business into the entertainment business.[16]

SUMMARY

The quality of marketing planning in an organization is influenced by the business planning process itself. In terms of marketing, two different but related plans are important: the corporate plan and the marketing plan. Each plan is based on the development of objectives, strategies, and tactics. A corporate plan provides direction to a marketing plan; a marketing plan provides direction to the various components of marketing, such as product strategy and marketing communications strategy.

Business planning is a problem-solving and decision-making effort that forces management to look at the future and to set clear objectives and strategies.

Business planning is divided into two broad areas: corporate planning and operational planning, which marketing is a part of. Corporate planning starts with the development of a vision or mission statement, followed by corporate objectives and strategies. These plans consider both the short term and the long term. Some of the more common corporate strategic alternatives include penetration strategies that focus on more aggressive marketing, acquisition strategies, entering and developing new markets, new-product development programs, forming strategic alliances, vertical and horizontal integration strategies, and divestment strategies.

Strategic marketing planning involves reviewing and analyzing relevant background information and conducting a SWOT analysis, establishing appropriate marketing objectives, devising a positioning strategy, identifying target markets, devising marketing strategies (utilization of the marketing mix) and marketing executions (specific action plans to implement the strategies), accessing budget support, and implementing control procedures.

The more commonly used marketing strategies include market penetration, market development, product development, and diversification. Once the strategies are implemented they are subject to evaluation. The evaluation and control process attempts to draw relationships between strategic activities and results. The organization determines which activities are effective or ineffective and then alters its strategy as needed. Due to uncertainty in the marketplace, wise marketing planners build in contingency plans to the overall marketing plan. Such plans force planners to consider in detail the environments that influence marketing activities.

KEY TERMS

REVIEW QUESTIONS

1. In planning, what are the basic differences among objectives, strategies, and tactics?

2. What is a mission statement and what role does it play in terms of corporate and operational planning?

3. What is the relationship between a corporate plan and a marketing plan?

4. At the corporate planning level, what is the difference between an acquisition strategy and a strategic alliance strategy?

5. What is the difference between a vertical integration strategy and a horizontal integration strategy?

6. What is a SWOT analysis?

7. What is the relationship between a positioning strategy statement and the marketing strategies and executions of a brand or company?

8. In this chapter, marketing strategies are described as the "master plans" for achieving marketing objectives. What does this mean?

9. What is the difference between a marketing activity review and a financial review?

10. What is a contingency plan, and why is such a plan necessary?

11. At the product planning level what is the difference between a market development strategy and a new-product development strategy?

DISCUSSION AND APPLICATION QUESTIONS

1. Has the concept of relationship marketing (Chapter 1) had an influence on strategic planning? What is your opinion?

2. Provide additional examples of the following corporate strategies:

    a) Strategic alliance
    b) Acquisition
    c) Divestment
    d) Vertical integration
    e) Horizontal integration
    f) Penetration

3. Identify a product (a good or a service) that uses the following marketing strategy. Provide an explanation of each strategy as it applies to the brand and company.

    a) Market penetration
    b) Market development
    c) Product development
    d) Diversification (product)

4. Marketing evaluation and control procedures tend to be quantitative in nature. Is this the best approach for measuring the effectiveness of marketing strategies? Can you suggest any alternatives?

5. The chapter discusses the importance of identifying primary and secondary target markets. Provide some additional examples of products and services that have expanded their sales and market shares by pursuing secondary targets. How did they target these markets (e.g., new product lines, new advertising messages, and so on)?

6. Refer to the vignette "Toyota Pursues Younger Customers." Conduct some secondary research to see what other companies are doing. Are they after the same target audience? Have they introduced new models and new advertising strategies to entice a younger customer into the fold? Provide examples to illustrate what is going on.

E-ASSIGNMENT

The purpose of this assignment is to determine how and why companies use different corporate strategies to achieve growth. Conduct some secondary research on the Internet to determine the type of corporate strategy being implemented by the following firms. What conditions are prompting the use of these strategies?

a)   London Drugs

b)   Colgate-Palmolive

c)   Bombardier Inc.

d)   Four Seasons Hotels

e)   Jean Coutu

You may find that these companies use several different strategies at the same time. Provide examples of their activities to verify the strategies they employ.

ENDNOTES

1. www.kraft.com/profile/company_stategies.html.

2. Wojtek Dabrowski, "Reebok hones its power play," *Financial Post*, April 10, 2004, p. FP6.

3. http://thescotsman.scotsman.com/index.cfm?id=428152004.

4. Sarah Dobson, "Winning combo," *Marketing*, October 28, 2002, p. 10.

5. "Esso to serve up Tim Hortons," *Globe and Mail*, March 27, 2002, p. B8.

6. Sean Silcoff, "Couche-Tard to Take on Hortons," *Financial Post*, August 11, 2004, pp. FP1, FP6.

7. Michael Kahn, "Levi Strauss explores sale of Dockers brand," *Financial Post*, May 12, 2004, p. FP16.

8. Bertrand Marotte, "Molson considering selling some sports and entertainment assets," *Globe and Mail*, July 13, 2004, p. B6.

9. Paul Brent, "Sleeman feasts on Molson Misfortunes," *Financial Post*, August 6, 2004, pp. FP1, FP4.

10. Lauren Foster, "Avon calling – this time for men," *Financial Post*, August 11, 2004, p. FP4.

11. *Dictionary of Marketing Terms*, Barron's Educational Series Inc., 1994, p. 327.

12. "Cialis offers free samples of rival drugs," *Financial Post*, July 13, 2004, p. FP4.

13. Hollie Shaw, "Big-box giant Home Depot thinks small," *Financial Post*, August 20, 2004, pp. FP1, FP6.

14. John Greenwood, "Home Depot tries new format," *Financial Post*, September 21, 2004, p. FP6.

15. Mathew Ingram, "Apple Computer takes the road less traveled," *Globe and Mail*, October 27, 2001, p. B7.

16. Alice Cuneo, "Apple transcends a lifestyle brand," *Advertising Age*, December 15, 2003, p. S-2.

Product

This section discusses the first element of the marketing mix: the product.

Chapter 8 examines product strategy and includes such topics as branding and brand name strategies, packaging and labelling strategies, and the concept of customer satisfaction programs.

Chapter 9 takes a management viewpoint and discusses how products are managed throughout their life cycle.

PART

4

CHAPTER

8

Product Strategy

Learning Objectives

After studying this chapter, you will be able to

1. Define the total product concept and explain the concept of the product mix.

2. Outline the classifications and sub-classifications of consumer goods and industrial (business) goods.

3. Explain the role and importance of branding and brand names in the development of product strategy.

4. Characterize the various stages of brand loyalty.

5. Explain the role of packaging decisions in the development of product strategy.

Product strategy is but one element of the marketing mix. This chapter presents the key decision-making areas for marketers when they are developing a product strategy. The key elements discussed in this chapter include the product mix, product classifications, brand name and packaging considerations, and brand loyalty.

1. Define the total product concept and explain the concept of the product mix.

The Total Product Concept

A **product** is "a bundle of tangible and intangible benefits that a buyer receives in exchange for money and other considerations."[1] In effect, the consumer purchases much more than the actual object. To demonstrate, consider the purchase of a luxury automobile like a Porsche. The decision to purchase is not based on transportation needs. This is a car you do not really need; you buy it in order to display your achievements and success. Such a purchase is bound up with the intangibles of prestige, status, and image.

product

This example illustrates that a product is more than the actual physical object. There are several elements that a marketer can emphasize when attempting to attract consumers; those elements comprise the benefits that a buyer receives. This package of benefits is referred to as the **total product concept**. It includes the physical item as well as the package, brand name, label, service guarantee, warranty, and image presented by the product.

total product concept

THE PRODUCT MIX

The **product mix** is the total range of products offered for sale by a company. It is the collection of product items and product lines that a firm tries to market. Each of the products or product items in the mix appeals to a particular segment, and in a way that makes it distinct from the offerings of the competition. Most, if not all, large consumer packaged-goods companies have a complete product mix; that is, they offer for sale a variety of different products that appeal to different user segments. Kraft Foods, for example, markets products in a variety of categories that include beverages, convenient meals, cheese, grocery products, and snacks.

product mix

A **product item** is defined as a unique product offered for sale by an organization. The key word in this definition is unique. Marketers refer to the distinguishing product characteristic or primary benefit of a product or service, the one feature that distinguishes a product from competing products, as the **unique selling point (USP)**. These features may include the format of the product, the sizes and variety available, or the ingredients contained in the product. To illustrate, consider the following examples.

product item

unique selling point (USP)

With so many cereals available to choose from, how does a consumer distinguish one product (brand) from another? Capitalizing on trends toward health and wellness,

Post Selects
**www.kraftfoods.
com/postcereals**

a host of multigrain cereals have been launched in recent years. In fact, a relatively new category of cereals, referred to as the multi-mix category, is growing faster than any other segment. Kraft Foods recently launched a line of multi-mix cereals called Post Selects, a product that combines the benefits of whole gains with fruit. "Consumers want it all in their cereal—they want something made with wholesome ingredients that tastes great at the same time."[2] Post Selects is a balance of those things—that combination is their USP. Post Selects is available in three flavours: Wild Blueberry Almond Crunch, Cranberry Almond Crunch, and Banana Nut Crunch.

Dove soap (a Unilever brand) has built its success around one fundamental unique selling point—gentleness. Dove's gentle cleansers and moisturizers leave a person's skin soft, smooth, and healthy looking. That selling concept has recently been extended to new Dove product lines: Dove Essential Nutrients (a line of skin creams and lotions), and Dove Moisturizing Body Wash. In the dish detergent market, Dawn (a Proctor & Gamble brand) distinguishes itself from other brands by emphasizing its grease-cutting ability, using slogans like "a drop of Dawn and grease is gone" and "lift grease fast." A strong visual image of the package reinforces the unique selling point. See the illustration in Figure 8.1.

**FIGURE
8.1**

**Dawn dish detergent offers
a unique selling point**

Lift grease fast.

GET DAWN AND GET DONE.

Courtesy of Proctor & Gamble

Men's Deodorant and Antiperspirant	Women's Antiperspirant	Bar Soap
Speed Stick 24/7	Lady Speed Stick Clean Glide Antiperspirant Stick	Irish Spring Vitamins
Speed Stick Lightning	Lady Speed Stick Antiperspirant Invisible Stick	Irish Spring Aloe
Speed Stick Avalanche	Lady Speed Stick Aloe Antiperspirant Invisible Stick	Irish Spring Original
Speed Stick Cyclone	Lady Speed Stick Antiperspirant Gel	Irish Spring Sport
Speed Stick Ultimate Antiperspirant	Lady Speed Stick Antiperspirant Stick	Irish Spring Icy Blast
Speed Stick Deodorant		Palmolive Naturals
Speed Stick Clear Deodorant		Softsoap Glycerine Bar
Speed Stick Plus Antiperspirant		

This is a sample of the product lines in Colgate's Personal Care category. Other lines in the same category include liquid hand soaps and body washes.

Source: Adapted from www.colgate.ca/english/ourproducts/personalcare/.

FIGURE
8.2

An Illustration of Product Line Width and Product Line Depth

A **product line** is a grouping of product items that share major attributes but may differ in terms of things like size, form, or flavour. For example, a popular brand of cereal such as Cheerios was once a standalone product in a few different package sizes. Now Cheerios offers several varieties, including Frosted Cheerios, Honey Nut Cheerios, Multi Grain Cheerios, Apple Cinnamon Cheerios, and a new line of Berry Burst cereals. The Berry Burst product undoes the morning ritual of adding fruit to the cereal. The fruit, which reconstitutes itself, is already available in the box. By offering an expanded range of products Cheerios appeals to the taste needs of all family members regardless of age.

A firm's product line is described in terms of width and depth. **Product line width** is the number of lines in the mix. **Product line depth** refers to the number of items in the line. All items and lines collectively form a firm's product mix. Colgate-Palmolive markets products in many categories—oral care, personal care, household care, fabric care, and pet nutrition. Within each category there is product line width and depth. For example, in the personal-care category width is described by the various brands: Irish Spring, Palmolive, and Softsoap. Within the Irish Spring line depth is described by scent: Irish Spring Original, Irish Spring Vitamins, Irish Spring Aloe, and Irish Spring Sport. For a more complete illustration of this concept see Figure 8.2.

The width and depth of a product mix depend on the firm's overall marketing strategy. Packaged-goods firms such as Unilever and Colgate-Palmolive have large product mixes that are both wide and deep. They want to balance risks, offset seasonal sales fluctuations, and address the various needs of customers.

product line

product line width
product line depth

Product Classifications

Products are divided in two basic ways. First and most important, a product is classified according to the target market it is intended for. Second, it is classified according to the durability and tangibility it offers.

2. Outline the classifications and sub-classifications of consumer goods and industrial (business) goods.

Products are also broadly classified into two groups on the basis of who buys them and why; these groups are called consumer goods and industrial (business) goods. **Consumer goods** are products and services purchased by consumers for their own personal use or benefit. **Industrial (business) goods** are those products and services purchased by businesses, industries, institutions, and governments that are used directly or indirectly in the production of another good or service that is resold, in turn, to another user (possibly a consumer).

A **nondurable good** is a tangible good normally consumed after one or a few uses. Examples include everyday products such as toothpaste, beer, coffee, milk, and detergent. These products are replenished frequently. A **durable good** is a tangible good that survives many uses. Examples include automobiles, appliances, personal computers, and athletic equipment. These items are purchased infrequently. **Services** are intangible; they are activities and benefits we take advantage of but do not take possession of. Examples include banking and financial services, hotels, household-care services (lawn and garden maintenance or painting and decorating), and repair services. Service industry marketing strategies are discussed in Chapter 18.

consumer goods

industrial (business) goods

nondurable good

durable good

services

CONSUMER GOODS

Consumer goods are commonly classified into four categories: convenience goods, shopping goods, specialty goods, and unsought goods (Figure 8.3). This classification is based on consumer buying behaviour.

convenience goods

CONVENIENCE GOODS **Convenience goods** are those goods purchased frequently, with a minimum of effort and evaluation. Typical examples include food items like bread, milk, cookies, and chocolate bars, and personal-care products such as soap, deodorant, and shampoo. Convenience goods fall into the "routine" decision-making process discussed in Chapter 4.

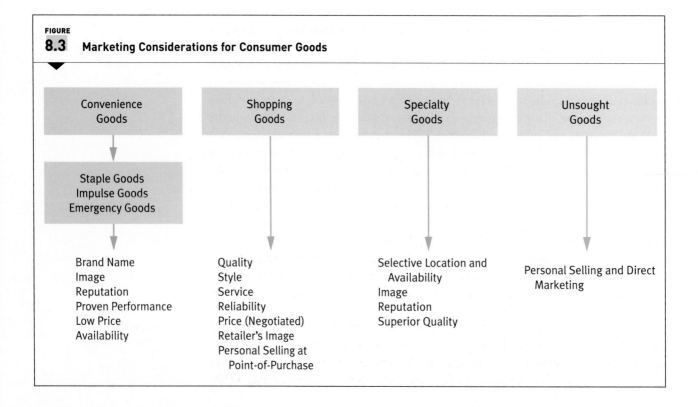

FIGURE 8.3 Marketing Considerations for Consumer Goods

Convenience goods are subdivided into three categories: staples, impulse goods, and emergency goods. A **staple good** is one that is regularly needed or used, such as orange juice, bread, deodorant, and headache medicine. People buy many of these items by brand, remaining loyal to such names as Tropicana, Gillette, Secret, Tylenol, and Advil. An **impulse good** is a good purchased on the spur of the moment: certain items purchased in a supermarket, such as candy bars, chewing gum, and magazines, are examples of impulse goods. Availability is a key issue; thus, impulse items are often found at checkout counters. An **emergency good** is purchased suddenly when a crisis or urgency arises; a snow shovel purchased at the first snowstorm of the season or a tensor bandage purchased when a muscle becomes strained are examples of emergency goods.

Generally, consumers do not spend much time purchasing convenience goods (e.g., price comparisons from store to store are unlikely). Therefore, it is in the best interests of the marketing organization to inform the consumer of the merits of the product through advertising and promotion and to make sure that the product has an attractive, eye-catching package and is readily available when consumers need it.

SHOPPING GOODS   **Shopping goods** are goods that the consumer compares on such bases as suitability, quality, price, and style before making a selection. Other factors of concern to the shopper include dependability, service, functionality, guarantees, and warranties. Examples of shopping goods include automobiles, clothing, major appliances, household furnishings, decoration services, and major repairs around the house. The price of shopping goods tends to be higher. Therefore, buying behaviour tends to be more rational in nature.

Marketing considerations deemed important for shopping goods include being located near competitors where comparisons can be easily made; having a consistent and attractive image (proven performance has advantage over little-known brands); and having effective communications so that awareness among consumers is high when their need for the product arises.

To illustrate these principles, consider how the "idle repairman" gives Maytag a competitive advantage in the appliance market. Maytag's marketing strategy emphasizes quality, and all of its advertisements are variations of the same theme: a bored repairman, dressed and ready to go to his job, but no opportunity to do so. Such a consistent message over time has given Maytag an excellent reputation and customers a basis for comparison with other brands.

SPECIALTY GOODS   **Specialty goods** are goods that consumers make an effort to find and purchase because the goods possess some unique or important characteristic. In effect, the consumer has already decided what item to buy. It is simply a matter of making the shopping excursion to buy it. Generally speaking, the marketing considerations that are important for specialty goods include the image and reputation resulting from communications, product quality, and the availability of goods in the appropriate stores (e.g., selective locations that make the product special). The price, usually a high one in keeping with the product quality and the prestigious image created by other marketing activities, is also a consideration in marketing specialty goods. A Cartier watch, for example, could be classified as a specialty good on the basis of these criteria.

UNSOUGHT GOODS   **Unsought goods** are goods that consumers are unaware they need or that they lack knowledge about. Essentially, an unsought good is an item that, although useful or valuable, is of such a nature that the consumer lacks interest in purchasing it. Encyclopedias are the most widely cited example of unsought goods. While

staple good

impulse good

emergency good

shopping goods

specialty goods

unsought goods

the product has a clear educational value, its availability in a library or online via the Internet means that there is little incentive to purchase it. Life insurance is another example, as it is a product many consumers are uncomfortable discussing. It is a product many people postpone considering and purchasing.

Given the nature of unsought goods, the primary influence on decisions to purchase is personal selling. Advertising will create awareness, but it is a consistent and persistent sales message that precipitates action by consumers.

INDUSTRIAL (BUSINESS) GOODS

By definition, industrial (or business) goods are products and services that have a direct or indirect role in the manufacture of other products and services. These goods are classified not on the basis of consumer behaviour but by the function the good has in the production of another good. The major marketing considerations for industrial goods are price (low price based on price negotiation and bidding), personal selling, ability to meet customer specifications, and the reliability of supply when direct channels of distribution are used.

Typically, industrial (business) goods are subdivided into three categories: capital items, parts and materials, and supplies and services (Figure 8.4).

capital items

CAPITAL ITEMS   **Capital items** are expensive goods with a long life span that are used directly in the production of another good or service. Whether an item has a direct or indirect role in the production process determines which of the two types of capital item it is.

installations

Installations are major capital items used directly in the production of another product. Examples of installations include buildings, production line equipment (e.g., robots in assembly plants), and computer systems. These goods are characterized by their high price, long life, reliance on strong personal selling programs to gain customer acceptance, technical sales and support service, and direct channels of distribution. A lengthy and complex decision-making process confronts the marketer of installations.

accessory equipment

Accessory equipment refers to items that are usually not part of a finished product but that do facilitate a firm's overall operations. Their role is indirect. Typically, these goods are much less expensive than installations and include such products as microcomputers, photocopier machines, power tools, and office furnishings. These goods are characterized by their reasonably long life, the significance of price negotiation in the marketing process, and the unique features of the product that appeal to rational buying motives.

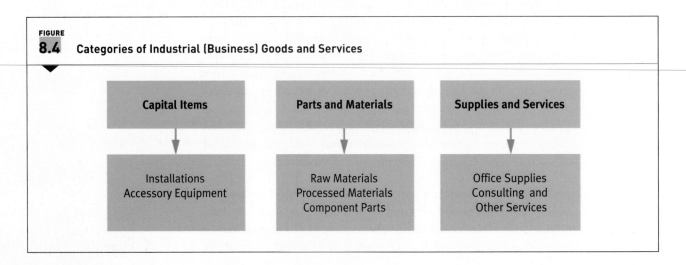

FIGURE 8.4   **Categories of Industrial (Business) Goods and Services**

PARTS AND MATERIALS   **Parts and materials** are less expensive goods that directly enter another manufacturer's production process. These goods are an integral part of the customer's product and affect its quality. Parts and materials are subdivided into three categories: raw materials, processed materials, and component parts.

parts and materials

Farm goods and other materials derived directly from natural resources are **raw materials**. Raw materials from natural resources include crude oil, lumber, and iron ore. Farm goods include wheat, livestock, fruits, vegetables, and milk, all of which are used by food processors in the manufacture of packaged consumer food products, such as bread, cheese, and jams.

raw materials

Processed materials are materials used in the production of another product, but which are not readily identifiable with the product. Examples include DuPont Nylon, a synthetic fibre used in clothing and other fabrics, and other yarns that become part of cloth fabrics. In each example, the original material is further processed or fabricated in the manufacturing process of another good so that it changes form.

processed materials

Component parts are goods that are used in the production of another product but do not change form as a result of the manufacturing process. Typically, these items are part of an assembly-line process. In the assembly of an automobile various components of the car are fitted together in sequence as the product automatically moves along a line. The tires, steel frame, seats, dashboards, engines, steering columns, doors, glass windows, radios, and other parts are classified as components to an automobile manufacturer. They arrive at a manufacturing facility ready for assembly. Price negotiation and continuity of supply are important considerations in the purchase of component parts.

component parts

SUPPLIES AND SERVICES   Supplies and services are those goods purchased by businesses and industries that do not enter the production process but facilitate other operations of the organization.

Supplies are standardized products that are routinely purchased with a minimum of effort. Typically, they are divided into three categories: maintenance, repair, and operating supplies. Paint is an example of a maintenance supply; bearings and gears are examples of repair supplies; writing instruments, paper and stationery, toner cartridges, and fastening devices are examples of operating supplies. Customers of such items look for quality at a good price. Purchasing agents also perceive service by the supplier's sales representatives to be important.

supplies

Services are the intangible offerings required to operate a business efficiently. Services are diverse, both in nature and in cost. For example, repair services or ongoing maintenance contracts such as groundskeeping or janitorial services may be relatively inexpensive. By contrast, a management consulting service employed to analyze the management practices of a firm is expensive, as are specialized services such as advertising or information processing. In the case of ongoing services, such variables as price and service reliability are important to the buyer; for specialized, complex services, the reputation and quality of the people performing the service are important. For example, companies that lack expertise in technology are actively pursuing software-development specialists and Internet marketing specialists to assist them in establishing an online marketing presence.

Branding and Brand Names

3. Explain the role and importance of branding and brand names in the development of product strategy.

Just what is a brand? This very question was asked of several marketing professionals and the responses varied considerably:[3]

"A promise that is publicly conveyed by everything a customer can observe: the brand name, logo, advertising, signage, storefront, billing statements, displays, and shopping environment." [This explanation considers retailers to be brands.]

"A name, logo, and/or symbol that evokes in customers a perception of 'added value' for which they will pay a premium price."

"A product with a personality."

It seems that a brand is more than the tangible product. How a consumer perceives a product largely depends on the brand name and what it stands for; that is, on the image that marketing has developed for it over an extended period. For example, such names as BMW and Mercedes suggest quality and status, whereas Volvo has developed an image and reputation for safety. Nike sells shoes, but it is known for bringing out the power within people—the power to do better! Apple is a user-friendly, different type of computer when compared to all other brands of computers.

The *Dictionary of Marketing Terms* defines a **brand** as an identifying mark, symbol, word(s), or combination of same that separates one company's product from another company's product.

The key components of a brand are:

- *Brand Name*—The **brand name** is that part of a brand that can be spoken. It may consist of a word, a letter, or group of words and letters. Examples include such names as Nike, Mr. Clean, Gatorade, Pepsi-Cola, Mennen Speed Stick, WD40, Dove Sensitive Skin, Lexus, Listerine, and Yahoo!

- *Brandmark or Logo*—The unique design, symbol, or other special representation of a company name or brand name is referred to as a **brandmark** or **logo**. Examples include the blue Ford oval that appears on the front or back of the cars, on dealer signs, and in advertising and promotional literature; Nike's famous swoosh that appears on all its shoes; or Apple Computer's famous apple with a bite taken out of it. Figure 8.5 includes a selection of brandmarks.

- *Trademark*—That part of a brand which is granted legal protection so that only the owner can use it. The symbol ® is the designation of a registered trademark. Trademarks include the brand names and symbols described above. Coke® and Coca-Cola® are registered trademarks of the Coca-Cola Company. The Nike swoosh is a trademark of Nike. The swoosh is so well known that it can stand alone in advertisements and communicate a message about the brand. In some cases, trademarks become so well known that they become household words. When this

brand

brand name

brandmark or logo

Courtesy Petro-Canada Inc., Nissan Automobile Company (Canada) Ltd., Honda Canada, Infiniti

FIGURE 8.5

A Selection of Brandmarks

happens the trademark holder is a victim of its own success, because the trademark loses its distinct nature. Such is the case of famous trademarks like Xerox, Kleenex, Band-Aid, and Fibreglass.

- *Patent*—A **patent** protects a manufacturing process or product design from being copied by competitors. It gives a manufacturer the sole right to develop and market a new product, process, or material as it sees fit. An industrial design registration protects appearance, while a true patent protects function. Under Canada's Patent Act, the maximum life of a Canadian patent is 20 years from the date on which the application is filed. Holding a patent on a particular design or process protects the inventing company from copycat products.

patent

BRANDING STRATEGY

Many types of brands exist and they can be distinguished according to who names them. Most of the brands mentioned in this section so far are manufacturer's brands or national brands. These brands are usually supported with their own marketing strategies to make them competitive and distinctive in the marketplace.

NATIONAL BRANDS   A national brand organization has two brand name options: an individual brand strategy or a family brand strategy, both of which offer advantages and disadvantages.

Individual Brand Strategy   An **individual brand** is a means of identifying each product in a company's product mix with its own name. This brand name strategy is common among large grocery products manufacturers, such as Procter & Gamble and Kraft Canada. Some Procter & Gamble names include Scope (mouthwash), Secret (deodorant), and Crest (toothpaste). Kraft names include Minute Rice (instant rice), Dream Whip (dessert topping), Shake 'n Bake (coating mix), and Jell-O (gelatin).

individual brand

Very often, a marketing organization operates in several market segments of a product category. In this case, a multibrand strategy is used. The term **multibrand strategy** refers to the use of a different brand name for each item a company offers in the same product category. To illustrate, Unilever Canada makes and markets tea under a variety of brands—Red Rose, Salada, PG Tips, and Lipton Tea. Through advertising, each brand has acquired a different image among consumers. In effect, the brands compete against one another, but the revenues they generate all return to the same source.

multibrand strategy

An individual brand name is sometimes extended to an innovation in the market. For example, when Pfizer Healthcare launched a new mouthwash in a dry format the product was called Listerine PocketPaks. Listerine is the market leader in the liquid mouthwash category. When Procter & Gamble launched Whitestrips, a gel-coated strip that whitens teeth, the Crest name was added. The product is known as Crest Whitestrips. Such marketing decisions give a brand instant credibility among distributors and consumers.

Family Brand Strategy   A **family brand** exists when the same brand name is used for a group of related products. Family brand names are usually steeped in tradition and quickly come to mind because they have been on the market for a long time. Examples include such names as Heinz, Campbell's, Quaker, Jell-O, Christie, and Del Monte. These brand families take three different forms:

family brand

1. *Product Family*—In this case, a group of products holds its own family name. Jell-O dessert products, Post cereals, Aunt Jemima pancake and syrup mixes, and Tylenol cough and cold remedies are a few examples.

2. ***Company Family***—Here, the brand name is also the company name. Heinz (ketchup, juices, sauces, baby food, and other food products) and Nike (footwear, hockey equipment, golf equipment, and sportswear) are two examples. Other popular company brand names include Kodak, Sony, and E. D. Smith.

3. ***Company and Product Family***—In this case, the marketing organization combines both variables. The company name makes up part of the brand name, with another brand name making up the other part. Examples include:

Company	Product
Campbell's	Healthy Request Soup, Kitchen Classics, Select Soups, Chunky Soups
Gillette	Right Guard, Foamy, Silkience, Sensor, M3 Power
Volkswagen	Golf, Beetle, Jetta, Passat, Toureg, Phaeton

A family brand strategy offers two *advantages* to a marketing organization. First, promotional expenditures for one product will benefit the rest of the family by creating an awareness of the brand name, and second, new products become accepted readily, since they capitalize on the success and reputation of the existing family products. Capitalizing on the strength of a popular brand name gives instant credibility to a new product among consumers and distributors. There is a carryover of reputation. For example, a tooth whitener called Night Effects has no image or reputation to call upon. But the name Crest Night Effects has instant impact.

A family brand strategy has a *disadvantage* as well. The failure or poor quality of a new product could tarnish the image of a family of products; for that reason, such products are usually removed from the market quickly by the marketing organization.

In deciding what brand strategy to use, a company analyzes its own situation in relation to its corporate and marketing strategies. Unilever is now placing its corporate brand name more prominently across all product line packages, a departure from its previous strategy when the corporate name simply lurked in the background. Unilever has decided that corporate branding is more cost-efficient. Sony also uses the company name as the primary brand name, and for good reason. Sony is highly recognized for its quality products and excellent reputation. Product innovations such as the VCR, the Walkman, and the flat-screen television (Sony Wega) enhance its reputation. Sony was the first electronics company to build high-quality products that looked attractive. The combination of brand name, quality, and styling comprise Sony's brand strategy.

CO-BRANDING   A brand strategy now gaining popularity among national brand manufacturers is co-branding. **Co-branding** occurs when a company uses the equity in another brand name to help market its own brand-name product or service. The marketer feels that using multiple brand names in conjunction with a single product or service offering provides greater value to demanding customers.

Co-branding strategies come in many different forms. For example, Wendy's, the owner of Tim Hortons since 1995, will put both brands in the same building. Marketing both brands together produces cost efficiencies on the operations side of the business. The two restaurants have similar customers and are equally adept at attracting customers. Nestlé, a prominent brand name on its own, opted to co-brand with prominent chocolate bar names when launching new ice cream products: Nestlé Rolo, Nestlé Coffee Crisp, and Nestlé Mackintosh. Nestlé owns the chocolate bar brand names. Breyers, a Nestlé competitor, uses the same strategy. It markets Breyers M&M's Mint, Breyers Snickers, and Breyers Twix.[4] See Figure 8.6 for an illustration.

co-branding

Nestlé Ice Cream
www.nestle-icecream.com

Dick Hemingway

FIGURE
8.6

An example of a co-branding strategy

When using a co-branding strategy, a key issue to consider is "fit." It is essential for both brands to complement each other. As described above, the transfer of chocolate bar brand names into the ice cream category is a good fit.

PRIVATE-LABEL BRANDS   A **private-label brand** is a brand produced to the specifications of the distributor (wholesaler or retailer), usually by national brand manufacturers that make similar products under their own brand names. Some examples of these brands are:

private-label brand

Company	Brand Name
Canadian Tire	Mastercraft, Motomaster, Persona
Sears	Kenmore, DieHard, Craftsman
Zellers	Cherokee, Truly
Loblaws	President's Choice
Sobeys	Compliments (replaced Smart Choice and Our Compliments)

President's Choice
www.presidentschoice.ca

The private-label brand was originally conceived as a means by which a retailer could provide the price-conscious consumer with a product of reasonable quality as an alternative to national brands. Loblaws is a leader in private-label branding with its President's Choice (PC) brand, which is marketed in all Loblaws-owned outlets (Loblaws, Provigo, Zehrs, Super Value, and others). In the supermarket business, private-label brands are extremely popular. According to Nielsen Media Research, an estimated one in five items sold in North American grocery stores is a private-label product. Some of the largest private-label categories are in traditional commodities such as paper products, plastic bags, and wraps. For instance, nearly half (46 percent) of aluminum foil sales are private-label products, and one-third (32 percent) of paper towel sales are private-label products.[5]

Private-label brands have taken business away from national brands. Consequently, many manufacturers have adopted a "three-and-out" approach: either you are among the top three brands in a given category, or you're out. Many manufacturers once marketed second-tier brands, but many of them have been withdrawn from the market. Unilever, for example, has pared its brands from 1600 in the 1990s to just 200 today—a sure sign of the popularity of private-label brands![6]

generic brand

GENERIC BRANDS   A **generic brand** is a product without a brand name or identifying features. The packaging is kept simple; a minimum of colour is used, and words simply identify the contents—for example "Corn Flakes," or "Chocolate Chip Cookies." Generic brands are common in such product categories as cereals, paper products, canned goods (fruits, vegetables, and juices), and pet foods, among others. Consumers who purchase generic brands may sacrifice a little in quality but appreciate the savings they offer. In Canada, it was Loblaws and its related supermarkets (Super Value and Zehrs, to name two) that popularized the use of generic brands. They encouraged shoppers to look for "yellow label" products to save money. Competitors quickly followed suit.

Private-label and generic brands intensify competition. Shelf space is limited, so it is more difficult for national brands to compete for space. As well, computer technology allows retailers to eliminate quickly any national brand product lines that are not moving at a desired rate. As indicated in the private-label section, some manufacturers have voluntarily withdrawn products that can no longer compete. Others have chosen to fight the battle by introducing new brands in different price segments of a product category. To protect its position in the cookie market, Dare Foods now markets Dare Premium cookies (high price and quality), Dare Classic cookies (medium price), and Dare cookies (lower price).

licensed brand

LICENSED BRANDS   Brand image is a powerful marketing tool and a valuable asset to marketing organizations. The use of one firm's established brand name or symbol on another firm's products can benefit both firms financially. To make such an arrangement, the owner of the brand name or symbol enters into a licensing agreement with a second party. Licensing is a way of legally allowing another firm to use a brand name or trademark for a certain period (the duration of the contractual agreement). The licensee usually pays a royalty to the company owning the trademark. When a brand name or trademark is used in this manner, it is called a **licensed brand**. Clothing lines often adopt well-known brand names. Brand names such as Molson, Coca-Cola, Nike, and Adidas appear on T-shirts and sweatshirts. Sports leagues, such as the NHL, NBA, and Major League Baseball, also market the rights to their team logos and trademarks to clothing manufacturers. Putting brand names on clothing provides moving advertisements for the owners of the brand name or trademark and ready-made promotion for the owners of the licensed product.

limited-edition brand

LIMITED-EDITION BRANDS   As the name suggests, a **limited-edition brand** is a brand intended to be on the market for only a short period of time, as it capitalizes on the popularity of an event or individual. Perhaps the best example of a limited-edition brand was the phenomenal success of Flutie Flakes in northeastern United States and Southern Ontario. The Flutie Flakes cereal was named to take advantage of the popularity of Doug Flutie, the former star quarterback of the Buffalo Bills. Capitalizing on the success of Flutie and the rise of the Buffalo Bills from the football cellar to playoff contender, PLB Sports, the manufacturer of the cereal, could not keep up with demand for the product. Wegmans, a New York supermarket chain, was selling 14 500 boxes a week, more than four times the amount of its previous top-selling cereal.[7] Companies possessing the foresight to market limited-edition brands must do so effectively in the short term if profits are to be made. Should the popularity of the star fade, the brand could face a quick exit from the market. Doug Flutie is long gone from Buffalo!

cult brand

CULT BRANDS   Unique in the world of branding is the cult brand. A **cult brand** is a brand that captures the imagination of a small group of devotees who then spread the word, make converts, and help turn a fringe product into a mainstream name. Cult brands are not fads; instead, they start out small and build a steady following, sometimes over many years. Many cult brands decide to stay small, for that is the key to their success; they are hard to get. In contrast, other cult brands opt for growth and eventually become leading national brands.

Brands such as Apple, Krispy Kreme, Mazda Miata, and Harley-Davidson qualify as cult brands based on how they approach customers. According to Matt Ragas, author of *The Power of Cult Branding,* "Cult brands dare to be different. Cult brands sell lifestyles. In cult branding, the management and marketers behind it are willing to take big risks and they understand the potential pay-off."[8] Apple, for example, launched a digital music recording device called iPod. Its unique design was an instant hit with youth—iPod itself gained cult status among its followers. The iPod has had a dramatic and positive impact on Apple's financial situation.[9]

For more insight into the nature of branding, the naming of brands, and how brands influence consumers, read the Marketing in Action vignette **Brand Crafting**.

Lexicon Branding
www.lexicon-branding.com

THE BENEFITS OF BRANDS

Branding offers consumers and marketing organizations several benefits. Some of the benefits for the consumer are as follows:

1. Over time, the brand name suggests a certain level of quality. Consumers know what to expect; they trust and have confidence in a brand.
2. There can be psychological rewards for possessing certain brands. For example, purchasing a BMW automobile might suggest achievement for the owner, while wearing a suit with a designer label may make one feel stylish.
3. Brands distinguish competitive offerings, allowing consumers to make informed decisions. Such names as Minute Rice, Lipton Cup-A-Soup, and Dove Sensitive Skin (soap) suggest clear messages or benefits about the product.

The marketing organization also enjoys benefits:

1. Branding enables the marketer to create and develop an image for a product or service. Through effective marketing communications Volvo is known for "safety," Nike is known for "empowerment," and tea drinkers know that Tetley's perforated tea bag offers the "best tasting" tea. In most advertising, a close relationship exists between a brand and its slogan. In the case of Gillette, the slogan is "The best a man

MARKETING IN ACTION

Brand Crafting

Have you ever wondered where brand names such as BlackBerry, Viagra, and Porsche Cayenne came from? What were these companies thinking when they selected these brand names? Brand names play a significant role in branding strategy for everything the company does in terms of communications and image creation revolves around the name.

When Research In Motion (or RIM, as it's commonly called) was looking for a name for its wireless email device, a company called Lexicon Branding recommended BlackBerry. From Lexicon's perspective the word blackberry indicated speed. It is a symmetrical word, with *black* and *berry* each having five letters. It's playful, friendly, seems like something that can be held in the hand, and ends in a "y," which makes it seem approachable. Capitalize both Bs, and the unusual name becomes a true success in the market.

Lexicon Branding also came up with Pentium and PowerBook, both extremely powerful brands in the computer market. Lexicon divides brand names into a few basic categories:

- Words created from other words—PowerBook and InDesign
- Nouns—Outback and Embassy Suites, which are real names
- Words that are simply created—Celeron and Dasani
- Compressed names—Optima, which is the word optimal without the final "l."

Cadillac went in an entirely new direction when it relaunched the Cadillac brand a few years ago. At the time, Cadillac buyers were older and accustomed to names such as DeVille and Eldorado. The car was completely redesigned to present a contemporary image that was hoped to attract a much younger audience. The target audience Cadillac wanted to reach was buying the Lexus LS 430, the Mercedes-Benz S500, or the BMW 33i. What did these brands have in common? The names had letters and numbers.

The name chosen for Cadillac was the CTS. Cadillac dealers didn't know what to make of the name initially, but the car was a C-class Touring Sedan, so it became CTS. Additional brands followed: the SRX was the S-Class Reconfigurable Crossover, and the XLR was the Exclusive Luxury Roadster.

Most dealers now think the three-letter names are great. They are modern and give Cadillac a better opportunity to compete with Mercedes and BMW. People who buy those kinds of cars are used to that sort of naming system. The focus is squarely on the name Cadillac and the three-letter model. Cadillac wants to be recognized among younger luxury-car buyers. When they think of BMW or Mercedes, General Motors now thinks they will think of Cadillac as well.

Adapted from Harvey Schacter, "What's in a name? Plenty, *Globe and Mail*, May 5, 2004, p. C4; and "Alphabet soup: Cadillac sticks to ABCs," *The Sunday Sun*, October 26, 2003, p. DS9.

Courtesy General Motors of Canada Limited

can get." Gillette backs up this promise by consistently bringing innovative grooming products to the market. See Figure 8.7 for an illustration. Nike's famous "Just do it" campaign aptly summarizes its empowerment mission. Here are a few other examples:

- VISA—"All you need."
- 3M—"From need . . . to 3M Innovation."
- FedEx—"Relax, it's FedEx."
- Avis—"We try harder."

2. Satisfied customers will make repeat purchases and hopefully remain loyal to a brand. This loyalty stabilizes market share and provides for certain efficiencies in production and marketing.
3. A good brand name will communicate the point of difference (USP) and highlight the distinctive value added. For example, the name Lean Cuisine addresses two strategic issues: *lean* communicates the low-calorie benefit, and *cuisine* implies that

FIGURE
8.7

Gillette's slogan reinforces the promise made by all of its products in the male grooming category

it tastes good. The name is meaningful and pleasant sounding. Household goods tend to have names that communicate what they do (e.g., Ziploc, Spray 'n Wash, S.O.S., and Mr. Clean).

Creating and using brand names is a crucial aspect of product strategy, since the attributes of a brand—its package and logo and its image—influence other marketing activities, specifically pricing and promotion. Given the cost of marketing activities, a brand (name and trademark) must be more than just a tool for distinguishing one brand from another. It must communicate the key point of difference and highlight the distinctive value added.

BRAND LOYALTY

Brand loyalty is defined as the degree of consumer attachment to a particular brand of product or service. This degree of attachment can be weak or strong and varies from one product category to another. Brand loyalty is measured in three stages: brand recognition, brand preference, and brand insistence.[10] Refer to Figure 8.8 for a visual illustration.

In the early stages of a product's life, the marketing objective is to create **brand recognition**, which is customer awareness of the brand name and package. Once awareness is achieved, a brand may offer customers free samples or coupons to tempt them to make the first (trial) purchase.

In the **brand preference** stage of a product's life, the brand is in the ballpark—that is, it is an acceptable alternative and will be purchased if it is available when needed. If it is unavailable, the consumer will switch to an equal, competitive alternative. For example, if Pepsi-Cola is requested at McDonald's and the order cannot be filled because the product is unavailable there, the consumer will usually accept the substitute, in this case Coca-Cola.

At the **brand insistence** stage, a consumer will search the market extensively for the brand he or she wants. No alternatives are acceptable, and if the brand is unavailable, the consumer is likely to postpone purchase until it is. Such a situation is a marketer's dream, a dream rarely achieved. Some critics insist that the original Coca-Cola product (now called Coke Classic) reached a level beyond brand insistence. So strong was the attachment that the product could not be changed. When it was, the backlash from the

4. Characterize the various stages of brand loyalty.

brand loyalty

brand recognition

brand preference

brand insistence

FIGURE
8.8

The Stages of Brand Loyalty

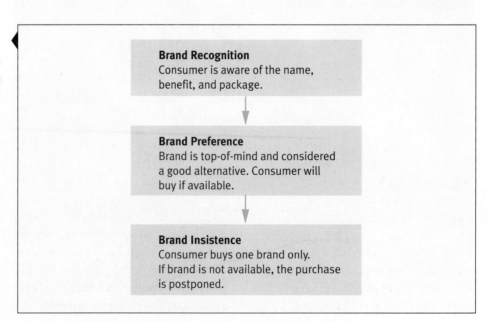

Brand Recognition
Consumer is aware of the name, benefit, and package.

Brand Preference
Brand is top-of-mind and considered a good alternative. Consumer will buy if available.

Brand Insistence
Consumer buys one brand only. If brand is not available, the purchase is postponed.

consumer franchise was so strong that the company had no alternative but to bring the original product back under the name Coca-Cola Classic.

The task of the marketer is to keep customers loyal. Study after study has shown that it is many times more difficult and expensive to convert a new customer than it is to retain a current customer. In preserving loyalty, companies cannot take their customers for granted. Many brands are instituting customer relationship management (CRM) programs that are specifically designed to keep a customer a customer. The concept of CRM was discussed earlier in the textbook.

The benefits of brands and the various levels of brand loyalty are what marketers refer to as brand equity. **Brand equity** is defined as the value a consumer derives from a product over and above the value derived from the physical attributes, those characteristics and associations that are linked to a brand that can add value to it. Equity is the result of good marketing and it is measured in terms of four variables: name awareness, a loyal customer base, perceived quality, and the brand's association with a certain attribute.

brand equity

Another explanation of brand equity is related directly to monetary value. Brand equity is defined as the value of a brand to its owners as a corporate asset.[11] For example, consumers' attitudes and feelings about a product, as in the above-mentioned case of Coca-Cola, help establish brand value. It is not ironic that Coca-Cola consistently ranks as the leading global brand in terms of value—a staggering value of $67.39 billion. Other top-five global brands include Microsoft, IBM, GE, and Intel. Toyota has just moved into the top-10 global brand group based on its solid reputation for quality and its competitive edge in hybrid cars.[12]

For more information on the importance of brand names and the impact that they have on consumers, refer to the Marketing in Action vignette **Brand Power: What Makes a Great Brand?**

Packaging and Labelling Strategies

5. Explain the role of packaging decisions in the development of product strategy.

How important is a package? Very important! Packaging has become an essential element in building a brand's image. Packages have to change with the times, but they must not lose touch with the identity that gave them their special appeal. Coca-Cola, for example, has kept its signature alive by using the original handwriting of a company accountant from nearly a century ago. Today's white-on-red logo is recognizable even in other alphabets. Coke has not had to change. But, then, other brands do not have the same stature as Coca-Cola.

Package designers understand that 40 percent of communications is visual, and 80 percent of visual communications is conveyed through colours and shapes. Coca-Cola, for example, is associated with the colour red, Pepsi-Cola is blue, and Tide detergent is orange. Further, a package must capture the attention of consumers in the blink of an eye. The goal is to stand out among the clutter of other packages on store shelves.

The launch of L'Oreal Kids shampoo by L'Oreal Canada demonstrates how a package can contribute to the success of a product. The package has a fish eye as its main graphic element and the brightly coloured bottle is shaped like a fish, with the eye and a mouth formed to dispense product (see Figure 8.9). The squeezable bottle floats in water, so the package is a toy as well as a hair-cleaning product. A less obvious but differentiating marketing element is that the bottle is made of low-density polyethylene that lets the product's fragrance actually come through the packaging. When customers are in the aisle, they can actually smell the fragrances. L'Oreal Kids captured 49.5 percent of the children's hair care market within three months of its launch.[13] Sales results like this verify the importance of an attention-getting package in a cluttered retail shelf environment.

Brand Power: What Makes a Great Brand?

Brand names, trademarks, logos, and advertising slogans all play a major role in creating an image with consumers. Whether it applies to a product or service or to a company itself, the right name can produce customer loyalty, recognition in the marketplace, and money at the bottom line. The opposite is also true. A bad brand name can bury a company in obscurity or sink a new product faster than you can say Edsel.

To illustrate, consider the case of Nike. Scott Bedbury, the man who gave the world "Just do it," started working for Nike in 1987, when it was a $750-million company. Seven years later, Nike was a $4-billion business. In between, Bedbury directed Nike's worldwide advertising efforts and broke the "Just do it" branding campaign. According to Bedbury, building a great brand depends on knowing the right principles. Among these principles are the following:

1. **A great brand is in it for the long haul**—Think long term: a great brand can travel worldwide, transcend cultural barriers, speak to multiple audiences, and let you operate at the higher end of the positioning spectrum—where you can earn solid margins over the long term.

2. **A great brand can be anything**—Anything is brandable. Nike, for example, leverages the deep emotional connection that people have with sports and fitness. In computers, most people do not know how processors work or why they are superior to the competition. But what they want is a computer with "Intel inside." Intel is a classic case in branding strategy.

3. **A great brand knows itself**—The real starting point is to go out to customers and find out what they like or dislike about the brand and what they associate as the very core of the brand concept. The customer's view of a brand can be very different from that of company executives.

4. **A great brand invents or re-invents an entire category**—Such brands as Apple, Nike, and Starbucks made it an explicit goal to be protagonists for each of their product categories. Apple was a protagonist for an individual: anyone wanting to be more productive, informed, and contemporary. At Nike, Phil Knight (company founder and CEO) is the consummate protagonist for sports and athletes.

5. **A great brand taps into emotions**—The common ground for great brands is not performance. They recognize that consumers live in an emotional world. Emotions drive most, if not all, of our decisions.

6. **A great brand has design consistency**—They have a consistent look and feel and a high level of design integrity. Consider such brands as McDonald's, Coca-Cola, and Disney. They refuse to follow any fashion trend that does not fit their vision.

7. **A great brand is relevant**—Many brands try to position themselves as "cool." More often than not, brands that try to be cool fail. Being cool is not enough to sustain a brand. A brand has to be relevant—it provides what people want, and it performs the way people want it to. Consumers are looking for something that has lasting value.

Sony is an example of a brand that embraces a good many of these characteristics and as a result stands out in the customer's mind. Sony makes and markets top-quality products and by being so consistent in its approach to manufacturing and marketing

Dick Hemingway

has developed an enviable reputation in the electronics industry. The key to Sony's success can be traced to two key areas: it was the first electronics company to build products of high quality that also looked attractive. At Sony, style is an important aspect of the brand equation. According to *Forbes* magazine, "Sony consistently introduces products that delight people, capturing their imaginations. Sony's products stop you in your tracks. The brand acquires almost mythical quality."

Perhaps it can be concluded that really popular and firmly established brands share certain branding characteristics. But brands like Coca-Cola, Nike, Harley-Davidson, and Sony go a step beyond. These brands express an attitude toward life that can be extended into a variety of different areas. Therefore, a true brand transcends product format. The relationship with the consumer has just as much or more to do with the beliefs the brand expresses than the product itself. As markets change, the brand has to use the power of that relationship to expand and evolve into new formats and markets. Those that do not are destined to fail.

Adapted from Bill Robinson, "Five Best Companies," *Forbes*, www.forbes.com/2002/08/01/; and Scott Bedbury, "What great brands do," www.fastcompany.com/10.bedbury.html.

THE ROLE AND INFLUENCE OF PACKAGING

Packaging is defined as those activities related to the design and production of a product's container or wrapper. But more than that, it is the combination of the package (which attracts the consumer's attention), the product (the quality inside the package), and the brand name that contributes to the image held by consumers. It is an integral part of product strategy.

packaging

Some recent statistics reveal how important packaging is in the marketing of a product. More than 80 percent of purchase decisions at a supermarket are made within the store, and 60 percent of those are made on impulse. In the average 22-minute shopping trip, a consumer spends only 12 seconds in front of any product category and views an average of 20 products.[14] A product's marketing life is thus reduced to seconds. The package must work hard to make the product appeal to the senses in a convincing way.

Marketers now see packages having a growing influence on purchase decisions amid ongoing media fragmentation. Changes in media and consumer lifestyles are now

FIGURE 8.9

A unique package design that attracts attention

Compliments of L'Oréal Canada

forcing a dramatic shift, making the package itself an increasingly important selling medium. Therefore, it is important for a brand to create and maintain a consistent brand identity. For example, a brand may be available in a variety of package formats based on product composition, sizes, scents, shapes, and so on. From one container to another, the design of the package must have a consistent look and colour scheme (see Figure 8.10).

As suggested earlier, the power of colour cannot be underestimated. The yellow colour of the Kodak film box is so well known it is often called "Kodak yellow." Because they are emotional triggers—and, consequently, powerful marketing tools—colours are carefully selected. For example, the colour red demands attention and is a sign of power—Coca-Cola owns the colour red and is the market leader in the soft drink business. Dark colours project richness, while white denotes purity and freshness. For this reason dark colours are dominant in the coffee section of a supermarket. In contrast, paper products are often packed in clear-wrapped packages to accent the purity of the product itself.

In devising packaging strategies, package shapes and textures, colours, brandmarks, symbols, personalities, illustrations, photography, and type styles are all considered. Used correctly, they can trigger instant recognition of a brand—think of Tide's swirl of orange and yellow; Campbell's Soup's red-and-white can; and Quaker Oats' kindly-looking Quaker man. All of these cues combine to form a connection with customers. The strength of that connection plays a key role in building and maintaining brand loyalty.

COMPONENTS OF A PACKAGE

The package is what consumers look for when they are thinking of a purchase; marketers, therefore, spend considerable time and money developing effective, functional, and eye-catching designs. There are four basic components to a package. The **primary package** contains the actual product (e.g., the jar containing the jam, the tube of toothpaste, and the plastic bottle holding shampoo or liquid soap).

The **secondary package** is the outer wrapper that protects the product, often discarded once the product is used the first time. The box that tubes of toothpaste are

primary package

secondary package

FIGURE
8.10

Strong brand identification across all package formats presents a consistent image to customers

packed in is an example. Even though these outer packages are discarded, they are important to the marketer as it is their design that attracts the customer's eye to the product.

Labels are printed sheets of information affixed to a package container. A label can be wrapped around a jar of coffee, a can, or a cardboard canister, or glued to a flat surface at the front or back of a rigid surface. Labelling is discussed in detail in a following section.

Packages are packed in cartons, usually corrugated cardboard cartons, to facilitate movement from one destination to another. The **shipping carton** is marked with product codes to facilitate storage and transportation of merchandise. Today, more products are being shrink-wrapped, a process of putting a plastic wrap on the product packed on cardboard trays (e.g., fruit juices and soft drinks).

labels

shipping carton

FUNCTIONS OF A PACKAGE

Essentially, a package has three basic functions. It must protect the product, market the product, and offer convenience to the consumer.

PROTECT THE PRODUCT   Since a product may pass through many warehouses on its way to the consumer, even those products that are not fragile require protection. The degree of protection needed depends on how long the products will be in storage, how they will be transported, what kind of handling they will experience, and how much protection from heat, light, and moisture they will need.

MARKET THE PRODUCT   A retailer is concerned about the size and shape of the package, since shelf space is limited, and whether or not enough information is on the package to resell the product. For example, will it provide adequate information for consumers who examine products in a self-serve store environment?

In its communications function, the package does everything a medium such as television or a magazine should do. For this reason, a package design should be researched with consumers because the package is loaded with psychological implications. It is the "look" of the package that helps the consumer form opinions about quality, value, and performance.

Packages are also useful for communicating the details of a promotion. Package *flashes*, temporary design elements that appear on the front of the package, announce promotional offers. Coupons, cash rebates, and contests are commonly flashed on package face panels. Details of the promotion can be found elsewhere on the package or through point-of-purchase display material close by. An illustration of promotional packaging appears in Figure 8.11.

PROVIDE CONVENIENCE TO CONSUMERS   A package should be easy to carry, open, handle, and reseal. For example, if the product is a liquid, it should pour without spills or drips (e.g., squirt tops on dish detergent containers and no-drip spouts on liquid laundry detergent containers). If the product is heavy or bulky, handles often become an important aspect of the package design. Examples of convenience in packaging include resealable plastic lids for jars and cans, twist-off caps, straws on fruit juice cartons, canned goods with moulded metal bottoms that allow stacking, and portable-sized prepared food packages that are ideal for lunch boxes.

Coca-Cola was thinking convenience with its recent launch of "Fridge Mate" packaging. The packaging was designed to resolve an age-old problem—how to place a case of pop in the fridge without taking up too much space. The new longer and leaner 12-pack carton automatically dispenses a can of Coca-Cola. Ironically, the idea for the new

FIGURE 8.11

Packages are a useful medium for communicating sales promotion offers

container came from Alcoa, the aluminum can supplier. Alcoa developed the design after studying what consumers did with the traditional 12-pack. Coca-Cola announced that all of its soft drinks would eventually be available in the new cartons. An illustration of the new carton appears in Figure 8.12.

PACKAGING AND THE ENVIRONMENT

With regard to packaging, social and environmental issues have forced manufacturers to think more creatively. Product safety is a major concern of consumer groups and governments. Unforeseen scares, such as the notorious Tylenol incident in the mid-1980s, in which deaths were temporarily linked to packages of Tylenol, must be avoided at all costs. As a result of such scares, the pharmaceutical industry brought to market the concept of tamper-proof packaging. Most drug products now have extra seals on the inner

FIGURE 8.12

The new Coca-Cola carton provides convenience to consumers and solves a space problem in the refrigerator

and outer packages, and consumers are advised by manufacturers not to purchase a product if either of those seals is broken.

Consumers are also concerned about unnecessary and extravagant packaging that adds to the cost of the product and waste at landfill sites. As well, the excessive use of raw materials is depleting Canada's natural resources. A company must respond to these concerns, but sometimes the objectives of a company are in conflict with environmental issues. The Brick Brewing Company, for example, launched the first plastic beer bottle in Canada in 2002. The plastic bottles keep beer colder for a longer period and the beer is just as fresh as beer in glass bottles, plus they are unbreakable and resealable. Barrier layers help keep the beer carbonated. Compared to glass, fewer materials are used in the production of the plastic bottle (good for the environment), but while glass bottles can be washed and reused 15 to 20 times, the plastic bottles can't be reused and are proving a challenge to recycle (bad for the environment).[15] Do the benefits of the plastic package to the company outweigh the environmental costs?

LABELLING

Labels are those parts of a package that contain information. A label serves three functions: it identifies the brand name and the owner of the brand; it provides essential information to the buyer; and it satisfies legal requirements where applicable. In the case of food products, labels may also communicate nutritional information. The typical components of a label include the brand name, usually in a distinctive font, an illustration that represents the product (e.g., a cup of steaming coffee on a coffee jar), directions for use, a universal product code, and information that is mandated by law. The universal product code, or the UPC as it is commonly called, is a series of black lines that appear on virtually all consumer packaged goods. These bars identify the manufacturer and product item (brand, size, variety, and so on). Electronic scanners at the point of sale read these codes. For retailers, the UPC symbol offers several benefits, namely reduced labour costs, better records on product turnover (allowing quicker and better informed decisions on what items to carry), and greater inventory control (automatic reorder points are established).

The mandatory information includes the volume or weight of the product and the company name and address. With new legislation coming into effect for food products, Canadian marketers will soon be able to trumpet health benefits of their products in three areas: nutrition labelling, nutrient content claims, and health claims. The legislation makes nutrition labelling mandatory on most pre-packaged foods. The information will be included in a Nutrition Facts box on the package.[16]

SUMMARY

A product is a combination of tangible and intangible benefits offered to consumers. Marketing organizations develop and market a total product concept. This concept includes the physical item, the image, the brand name, the level of sales support, and other activities.

The total range of products offered for sale is referred to as the product mix. Products are classified according to characteristics such as durability and tangibility. Products are also classified either as consumer goods or industrial (business) goods. Consumer goods are intended for the personal use of the customer, while industrial goods are generally used in the production of other goods and services. It is the use by the customer that distinguishes consumer goods from industrial goods.

Consumer goods are further subdivided into convenience goods, shopping goods, and specialty goods. These types are generally distinguished by price and by the time taken to purchase the item. Industrial goods are subdivided into three categories: capital items, parts and materials, and supplies and services.

How a customer perceives a product largely depends on the brand. Marketing organizations use branding as a means of identifying products and developing an image. Branding involves a number of decisions in the areas of brand name, brandmark (logo), and trademarks. Broadly speaking, an organization has two branding options: individual brands or family brands.

Recently, some packaged-goods manufacturers have introduced a co-branding concept, in which two brand names share equal billing on one product. Private-label brands and generic brands are other strategies used by distributors of consumer goods. Their presence and popularity with consumers has negatively impacted the sale of national brands. Consumers come to trust what the brand name stands for and, if they derive satisfaction from the brand, to develop certain levels of brand loyalty. Loyalty is expressed in terms of recognition, preference, and insistence.

Packaging plays an integral part in the product mix. Decisions that must be made about packaging concern the type and nature of package to use, when to alter the package design, and the labelling and shipping requirements. Packages selected must fulfill four basic functions. A good package protects the product, markets the product, provides the consumer with convenience in handling and using the product, and is environmentally safe.

KEY TERMS

accessory equipment   194
brand   196
brand equity   205
brand insistence   204
brand loyalty   204
brand name   196
brand preference   204
brand recognition   204
brandmark or logo   196
capital items   194
co-branding   198
component parts   195
consumer goods   192
convenience goods   192
cult brand   201
durable good   192
emergency good   193
family brand   197

generic brand   200
impulse good   193
individual brand   197
industrial (business) goods   192
installations   194
labels   209
licensed brand   200
limited-edition brand   201
multibrand strategy   197
nondurable good   192
packaging   207
parts and materials   195
patent   197
primary package   208
private-label brand   199
processed materials   195
product   189
product item   189

product line   191
product line depth   191
product line width   191
product mix   189
raw materials   195
secondary package   208
services   192
shipping carton   209
shopping goods   193
specialty goods   193
staple good   193
supplies   195
total product concept   189
unique selling point (USP)   189
unsought goods   193

REVIEW QUESTIONS

1. Explain what is meant by the "total product concept."
2. What is the difference between product line depth and product line width? Provide some examples other than those in the text to illustrate the difference.
3. What is the difference between a durable good and a nondurable good?
4. Describe the characteristics of the following goods:
   a) Convenience goods
   b) Shopping goods
   c) Specialty goods
   d) Unsought goods
5. There are three categories of convenience goods. Identify and briefly explain each category.
6. What are the three classifications of industrial (business) goods?

7. What is the difference between a brandmark and a trademark?
8. What is the difference between an individual brand strategy and a family brand strategy?
9. Explain the concept of co-branding. Can you identify any benefits in using such a strategy? Provide some new examples of co-branding to dramatize the benefits the strategy offers.
10. What is the difference between a private-label brand and a generic brand?
11. Distinguish between brand recognition, brand preference, and brand insistence.
12. What is brand equity? How is it determined?
13. Briefly describe the basic functions of a package.

DISCUSSION AND APPLICATION QUESTIONS

1. Provide two examples of each of the following types of industrial (business) goods:

   a) Installation

   b) Accessory equipment

   c) Component part

   d) Processed material

2. Provide examples of five different private-label brands other than those mentioned in the chapter. Conduct some secondary research on a few of these brands to determine how popular they are.

3. Review the vignette "Brand Crafting." Cadillac has decided to use brand names containing a sequence of letters. Other brands use combinations of letters and numbers. Are brands moving away from traditional sub-brands (e.g., Chevrolet Impala or Mazda Protégé) and toward the use of letters and numbers? Are there advantages and disadvantages to such a switch? How will it affect brand image? Evaluate the situation and present a position on it.

4. Examine the vignette "Brand Power: What Makes a Great Brand?" Using the criteria identified in the vignette, select a great brand name (in your opinion) and provide an explanation as to why it enjoys such status.

5. Select any two packages on the market. Choose one you think is good and one you believe is not so good. Discuss the marketability of each package.

E-ASSIGNMENT

Evaluate the following brand names in terms of the desirable characteristics a good name should possess (refer to the Marketing in Action vignette "Brand Power: What Makes a Great Brand Name"). Visit the website for each name and explore a few pages at each site. Does the website project a good image for the brand? Examine how colour is used at each website. Does colour influence your perception of the brand (positively or negatively)? Explain. Use other brand names and websites, if you wish. The brands:

Coca-Cola **www.coca-cola.com**

Nike **www.nike.com**

Starbucks **www.starbucks.com**

Apple **www.apple.com**

McDonald's **www.mcdonalds.com**

ENDNOTES

1. Lawrence Reny et al., *Decisions in Marketing* (Plano, TX: Business Publications Inc., 1984), p. 20.

2. Lisa D'Innocenzo, "Fruit is hero in new Post cereal spot," *Strategy*, July 28, 2003, p. 3.

3. John Heinzl, "The attack of the brand flakes," *Globe and Mail*, November 24, 2000, p. E1.

4. www.icecreamusa.com.

5. "Europe, U.S. Still the Largest Private Label Markets but Other Regions Seeing Huge Growth," news release, AC Nielsen, www.acnielsen. com.ca/News/PrivatelabelGlobalStudy.html., September 16, 2003.

6. "Store-brand makes a name for itself," *Marketing*, August 11/18, 2003, p. 30.

7. Lawrence Carrell, "Bills are out but Flutie's still scoring with flakes," *Globe and Mail*, January 7, 1999, p. B7.

8. Martha Iagace, "Cult Brands: Lessons Learned at Apple, ESPN, and PepsiCo.," *HBS Working Knowledge*, December 23, 2002, www.hbsworkingknowedge.hbs.edu/pubitem.html.

9. "Cult Brands," *Business Week Online*, August 24, 2004, www. businessweek.com/magazine/content/04_31.

10. Dale Beckman, David Kurtz, and Louis Boone," *Foundations of Marketing* (Toronto: Holt, Rinehart and Winston, 1988), pp. 316–317.

11. "A dictionary of Branding Terms," www.landor.com/index. cfm?fuseaction=cBranding.getLexixon, November 2003.

12. "The 100 Top Brands," *Business Week*, August 2, 2004, p. 68.

13. Astrid Van Den Broek, "Message in a bottle," *Marketing*, May 11, 1998, pp. 16–17.

14. Jo Marney, "More than a pretty face," *Marketing*, April 10, 1995, p. 25.

15. Susan Pigg, "Brick hopes plastic bottle hits spot," *Toronto Star*, October 2, 2002, pp. E1, E10.

16. Leslie Young, "New health claims rules applauded," *Marketing*, June 25, 2001, p. 3.

© Jean-Yves Bruel/Masterfile

9

Product Management

After studying this chapter, you will be able to

1. Describe the organizational systems for developing and managing products.

2. Describe the nature of product-related decisions.

3. Explain the impact the product life cycle has on the development of marketing strategies at each stage of the cycle.

4. Describe the alternatives available to an organization for developing new products.

5. Identify and explain the steps in the new product development process.

Product management concerns three key areas: (1) the internal organization structure for managing current products; (2) the allocation of resources for the development of new products; and (3) dealing with changing market needs, especially as products progress through their life cycles. In this third area, the firm must be aware of the need to change marketing strategies during the various stages of the product's life cycle. Organizations realize that demand for the products they offer for sale now will not last forever.

The influence of technology is changing the way a company thinks about new-product development and how it manages existing products. In a nutshell, every decision has to be made more quickly. Standing still means a company could lose a step to a competitor—the financial impact could be costly. Difficult decisions must be made about what new products to introduce and when, and what existing products should be dropped and when. This chapter will look at the key areas involved in product management.

Organization Systems for Managing Products

1. Describe the organizational systems for developing and managing products.

The trend in contemporary marketing practice is to combine various organizational structures so that products may be developed and marketed more efficiently than before. In packaged-goods companies, an organizational structure called the *brand management system* has traditionally been the norm, but, more recently, it has given way to *category management* and *geographical management systems*. Companies in business-to-business marketing are moving toward target-market management systems. For example, business-to-business organizations develop new products and manage existing products to meet the needs of particular market segments (e.g., communications, health, transportation, and so on) or particular industries (e.g., chemicals, banking, and so on). The type of management system used often depends on three factors: an organization's size, growth objectives, and resources.

BRAND MANAGEMENT

A **brand manager** (product manager) is an individual who is assigned the responsibility for the development and implementation of marketing programs for a specific product or group of products. For example, at Colgate-Palmolive Canada, a multi-product, multi-category company, the oral care category may have several brand managers: one for Colgate toothpastes (there are many varieties), another for Colgate tooth-whitening products, and another for Colgate toothbrushes.

brand manager

215

In a brand-management system, all company brands are divided up so that managers are responsible for the marketing activity of one brand or group of brands. The brand manager works closely with others in the organization and with external suppliers in such areas as advertising and promotion, package design, and marketing research. For multi-product companies, this system ensures that all products receive equal attention in planning, even though some products may have a higher marketing profile when plans are implemented. A diagram of the brand management system is presented in Figure 9.1. In this system, it is assumed that the manager is ultimately responsible for all marketing mix elements. In many organizations, the manager may also be responsible for the profitability of the brand.

CATEGORY MANAGEMENT

category manager

A **category manager** is an individual who is assigned the responsibility for developing and implementing the marketing activity for all products grouped in the category. The category management system is a management structure that groups products according to their similarity to one another. Naturally, products in the same category are closely related. Colgate-Palmolive markets products in several categories: oral care (Colgate toothpaste, whitening products, dental gum, and toothbrushes), personal care (Mennen Speed Stick deodorant products, Irish Spring soap, and SoftSoap hand soap), household care (Palmolive dishwashing liquid, Murphy's cleaners, Ajax and Javex bleach), and fabric care (Arctic Power detergent and Fleecy fabric softener). A category manager would be responsible for each of these marketing units.

In this system, the category manager adopts a more generalized view of the business than would an individual brand manager in the brand management system (Figure 9.1). In Canada, the system has become popular as manufacturers realize they must work more closely and cooperatively with retailers (relationship marketing), who have significant buying power and who organize their shelves according to the sales volume of brands within each product category.

Leading supermarkets such as Loblaws, Zehrs, Sobeys, and Safeway work with suppliers cooperatively and manage categories of products instead of individual brands. Buyers at these and other chain stores deal with all suppliers within a category (e.g., pet food, snack food, soft drinks, juice beverages, and so on). Electronic scanning determines which products are moving well. This information determines which products to carry, and which ones to delete as new products come along. The goal of space-management programs is to improve sales in each category.

Supermarkets are always experimenting with their merchandising strategies in order to sell more product. One concept that has become popular is the "power aisle." In a power aisle complementary products are merchandised together. For example, soft drinks may be on one side of the aisle and salty snack foods on the other. Such a strategy is ideal for PepsiCo since its beverage products (Pepsi-Cola, Mountain Dew, and others) will be in close proximity to its snack foods (Frito-Lay and Doritos). While the aisle would include competitors' products as well, Pepsi has an advantage because they operate in both categories. Coca-Cola does not have a snack food division. Initial research on this merchandising strategy showed an increase in sales of Frito-Lay products by 21 percent and sales of all soft drinks, not just Pepsi, increased modestly.[1]

REGIONAL MANAGEMENT

regional marketing management

Geography plays a key role in a **regional marketing management** system. In this management structure, decision making is decentralized. Instead of an organization being divided up into production, marketing, finance, and by division of products, a country

9.1   **Alternative Product-Management Systems**

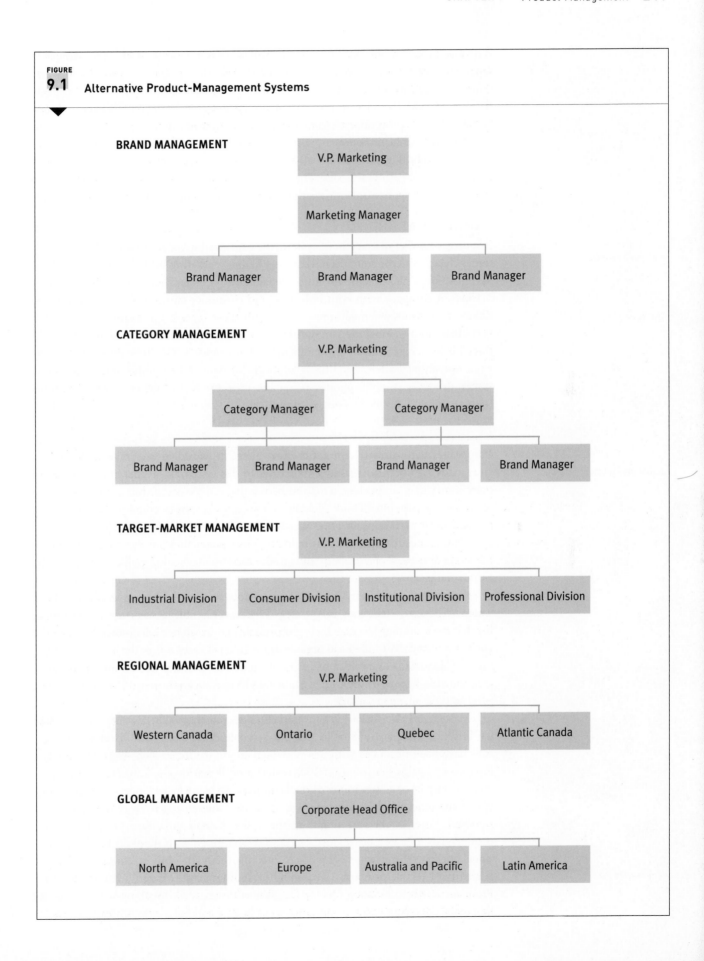

is divided up geographically into regions. Molson Breweries, for example, has established separate companies to manage three regions: Western Canada, Ontario/Atlantic, and Quebec. A national marketing team manages a group of brands referred to as "strategic national brands." Canadian and Export are in this group. Each region has a staff of marketing, sales, and promotion personnel who develop marketing strategies and implement programs for "strategic regional brands." As well, regional teams execute national brand strategies. According to Molson, such a system allows a company to build on its strengths and chip away at its weaknesses. The closer the decision makers are to the action, the quicker is the response time for planning and implementing new marketing strategies.[2]

TARGET-MARKET MANAGEMENT

target-market management system

In a **target-market management system**, the organization recognizes that different customer classes with different needs require different marketing strategies (see Figure 9.1). Such a strategy makes sense for multi-divisional companies dealing with diverse target markets. A company with both industrial and consumer customer bases would utilize different strategies when communicating with those targets. For example, Ericsson, a participant in the global telecom industry, recently divided its management system into three business segments on customers instead of products. The three divisions are network operations (wireless and fixed solutions for data and telecommunications), consumer products (mobile phones being the core product), and enterprise solutions (permanent and mobile business communications systems).

GLOBAL MANAGEMENT

global management structure

Companies with growth aspirations now view the world as one market. What has emerged is a **global management structure**. In this system, ideas that are developed in one country may be considered for another, so that economies of scale are achieved. The often-used expression "Think globally, act locally" is now a common salute among multinational marketers. In other words, while brand managers and marketing managers in Canada are responsible for marketing in Canada, they are also influenced by the decisions of managers elsewhere. In extreme cases managers in small countries can be eliminated entirely.

Procter & Gamble's management philosophy is global where possible and local where necessary. In following this strategy Procter & Gamble faces a common dilemma: in what areas do they leverage their global scale and in what areas do they leverage the talent and creativity of the local organization? In most cases it is in the area of advertising. In Canada, for example, a majority of the television commercials for P&G brands are created in Europe or the United States. Slight modifications may be made to the ads prior to their airing in Canada.[3]

MasterCard also makes certain marketing decisions globally. MasterCard launched its "Priceless" campaign theme in 1997, and to date, 372 MasterCard Priceless commercials have been produced with ads now seen in 106 countries and 49 languages. The Priceless campaign has won over 100 creative awards worldwide. Canada is a lean operation that's part of a huge multinational company, so being locked into a set brand strategy often comes with the territory. The "priceless" advertising strategy was adapted to Canadian tastes by showing situations that reflect Canadian culture. One of the latest commercials follows a boy named Drew who isn't gifted with the skills to play professional hockey, yet still achieves his goal of making the NHL—but in a unique and unexpected twist (think Zamboni). According to Tammy Scott, MasterCard Canada's Vice President of Brand Building, "MasterCard's new Priceless ads touch on several qualities that make Canadians unique—like our love of hockey and our quirky sense of humour."*

*"MasterCard breaks new Priceless ads," *Adnews*, December 13, 2005.

Other Canadian settings and famous people in past Priceless campaigns include cottage country and its recreational pleasures, former hockey legend Bobby Orr, and Cassie Campbell of the Canadian women's national hockey team. The word "Priceless" also appears in all other forms of marketing communications.[4] Refer to the illustration in Figure 9.2

A Closer Look at Product Decisions

A brand manager (product manager or category manager) is responsible for all areas of the marketing mix. A brand manager must establish profitable and fair prices; decide on the use of promotional elements, such as advertising, sales promotion, and event marketing; and decide on where the product should be available to customers.

Being more specific about the product, decisions occur in several key areas: modifying the product, altering the product mix, introducing a new package design, and maintaining and withdrawing a product from the market.

PRODUCT MODIFICATIONS

Products are modified in many ways and for many reasons. Changes in style are often implemented to give a product a contemporary look; automobiles are redesigned to appeal to changing consumer tastes and preferences. The home appliance industry recently introduced brighter, technologically innovative products (refrigerators, stoves, washers, and dryers) in stainless steel or vibrant colours such as blues, yellows, and reds, and commercial sizes. The addition of a fashion aspect to appliances (something that may seem odd) added some enthusiasm to a stagnant industry and gave manufacturers

2. Describe the nature of product-related decisions.

a niche in which to position their products uniquely. In the consumer electronics industry look at what has happened to televisions. Owning a flat-screen television or a wall-mounted plasma screen makes a fashion statement and shows how televisions have changed over the years. The old black-box and contoured screen is becoming a dinosaur.

Functional modifications make a package easier or safer to use. A no-mess pour spout to a container for a liquid product is an example of a functional modification. Quality modifications include improvements such as making the product more durable (e.g., floor wax or furniture polish), improving the taste (a beverage or food product), and improving the speed (a personal computer). Golf is an industry that relies on subtle product improvements in club design or ball technology to sustain growth and differentiate products. Refer to Figure 9.3 for an illustration.

PRODUCT MIX

As discussed in the previous chapter, product mix decisions concern the *depth* and *width* of a product line. The addition of new products and the creation of extended versions

FIGURE
9.3

Modifications in design are crucial in order to continuously improve a product

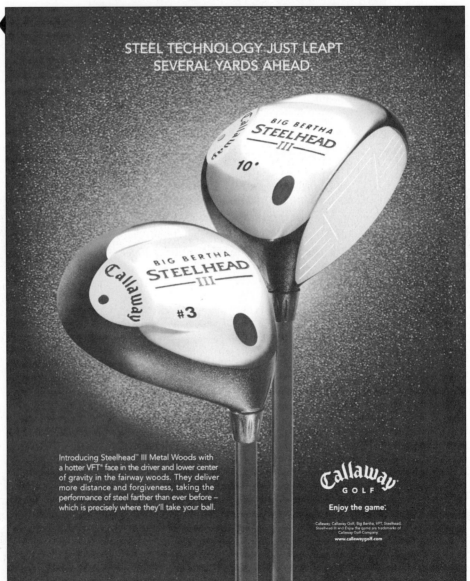

of existing products are the lifeline of growth-oriented marketing organizations. To foster growth, a manager looks for gaps in the marketplace (perceived opportunities) and recommends developing products for the opportunities with the highest potential.

This procedure is referred to as **product stretching** and is defined as the sequential addition of products to a product line so that its depth or width is increased. Stretching can occur in several ways. Colgate-Palmolive makes 19 types of Colgate toothpaste in various sizes (that's a lot of choice!), and does so for good reason. While meeting the unique needs of different customers, new items drive sales growth. At Unilever, Dove was once a bar of beauty soap well known for its gentle characteristics. Today, the brand name appears on antiperspirants, body washes, and shampoos. It is the flagship brand of Unilever's personal-care portfolio and the world's number-one cleansing brand.[5] Refer to the illustration in Figure 9.4.

product stretching

PACKAGING DECISIONS

Packaging is an integral part of product strategy. It is common for consumer goods to undergo several package-design changes throughout their lives. Similar to the periodic redesign of an automobile, package changes are intended to bolster the image of the product, provide a contemporary appearance, or fulfill some other product and marketing objective. The chocolate market, for example, is a crowded and competitive

FIGURE 9.4   Stretching a branded product line into new product categories

Dick Hemingway

market. How does a brand distinguish itself amid the clutter? After Eight (dinner mints) opted for new packaging to encourage more frequent consumption. Individually wrapped chocolates were introduced so that the indulgent treat can travel with the chocolate lover. Refer to Figure 9.5 for a visual presentation of the package.

MAINTENANCE OR WITHDRAWAL

One of the toughest decisions facing a manager is whether or not to cut the lifeline of a product. Such a decision should be based on profit or loss and strategic fit, but other factors, such as sentiment and emotion (attachment to long-established products), enter into the decision as well. It is unrealistic to think that products will remain profitable indefinitely, particularly in today's fast-paced marketplace. General Motors decided to end production of its oldest brand, Oldsmobile, just recently. The decision to pull the plug was difficult but was due in part to the brand's middle-aged reputation. The company tried to spruce up the line with models such as the Intrigue and the Aurora, which were designed to attract a younger buyer. But it never happened. Unable to find an approach that would work, the decision was made to scrap the brand.[6]

FIGURE 9.5

Nestlé introduces its After Eight mints in a new product shape and new package

Next on the chopping block at General Motors are the Chevy Cavalier and the Pontiac Grand Am. In 2005, the production of both brands will be halted despite their popularity in years past. "If a name carries baggage, GM is dumping it," according to vice-chairman Robert Lutz. "When you're making a big change you want to wipe the psychological slate clean, you change the name." Replacement cars have not been named yet.[7]

Sometimes decisions made about products are not the right decisions, or they are based on misdirected objectives that are in conflict with consumer expectations. Such decisions often backfire on the company. For insight into this phenomenon, read the Marketing in Action vignette **Profit Motives Rule Brand Decisions**.

3. Explain the impact the product life cycle has on the development of marketing strategies at each stage of the cycle.

The Product Life Cycle

Products go through a series of phases known as the **product life cycle**. The term refers to the stages a product goes through from its introduction to the market to its eventual withdrawal (Figure 9.6). According to the life cycle theory, a product starts with slow sales in the introduction stage; experiences rapid sales increases in the second (growth) stage; undergoes only marginal growth or even some decline when it reaches maturity; and then enters the decline stage, where sales drop off at a much faster rate each year. The variables of *time, sales,* and *profits* are the determinants of a product's stage in the life cycle. The life cycle concept is popular in strategic marketing planning. Since the conditions of each stage are quite different, the life cycle suggests that different strategies, or marketing mixes, should be used in each phase. This section of the chapter examines the four stages of the life cycle and discusses some of the marketing implications that each stage presents to the manager.

product life cycle

Although profit and time affect what stage an item is perceived to be in, sales is the primary indicator of what stage of the cycle a product has reached. Thus, the degree to which a market accepts and then rejects a product determines how long the life cycle of that product will be. All products do not have the same life cycles; some are quite long (Wrigley's Gum and Quaker Oatmeal), while others are quite short (Crystal Pepsi).

INTRODUCTION STAGE

As its name suggests, a product's introduction stage is the period after it has been introduced into the marketplace and before significant growth begins, during which the company tries to create demand for the product. It is a period of slow sales growth, since the product is new and not yet widely known. Losses are frequently incurred in this stage because research and development expenses must be recovered and a heavy investment in marketing is needed to establish an awareness of the brand. This marketing investment is a reflection of the company's commitment to building a viable market position.

The immediate objective during the introduction stage is to build demand and create brand name awareness. A sizable budget is allocated to marketing communications to create awareness of the item and to tempt people to try it. It is common for advertising to include incentives, such as coupons, that reduce the consumer's financial risk in making the first purchase. Widespread media coverage is also commonly used to communicate the product's benefits to the target market. Establishing an Internet presence is now very important for new products. By doing so, information about the product can be communicated well before the actual introduction of the product and create a pent-up demand for it. BMW Canada used an Internet strategy effectively when it introduced consumers to the new Mini, a sporty, retro-looking vehicle formerly known as the Mini Cooper. Demand was so high that there were waiting lists for the product when it was launched. Granted, the revival of the Mini garnered lots of unsolicited and positive publicity.

MARKETING IN ACTION

Profit Motives Rule Brand Decisions

Things are going along well and you are the number-one brand in the market. In this situation why would a brand risk changing its formula? Very simple: if the new formula costs less than the existing formula and if the customer cannot detect any tangible change in the product, the company makes more profit—"A penny saved is a penny earned."

Schlitz—"The beer that made Milwaukee famous"—was once the number-two brand in the United States. Management decided to reduce costs by shortening the brewing process and by using cheaper raw materials (corn syrup instead of barley malt). A new rushed process called "automated balanced fermentation" was implemented. The cost of brewing Schlitz plummeted—and so did market share. Consumers didn't like the taste and they couldn't find a head on their draft.

Coca-Cola, in reaction to market share gains by PepsiCo, changed the formula of Coke and launched New Coke with all kinds of marketing fanfare. Despite all of the research Coca-Cola conducted prior to the switch, the company never really told consumers it was going to take the existing Coca-Cola off the market. Coca-Cola instantly lost market share and found itself in the middle of a public relations nightmare. New Coke was withdrawn within 79 days of launch and replaced with the original flavour, now called Coca-Cola Classic.

Tim Hortons, Canada's leading food-service chain, shows steady increases in sales and profits from year to year. Yet to boost profit margins even further the company decided to have its restaurants reheat frozen doughnuts as opposed to baking them fresh on the premises. How much is Tim Hortons saving, and is it worth it? One thing's for sure: the new doughnuts don't taste as good as the old ones and they are a lot smaller. Is Tim Hortons being greedy? Will this change eventually backfire on Tim Hortons' management?

Adapted from David Menzies, "Watered-down brands," *Marketing*, April 19, 2004, p. 11.

Dick Hemingway

Setting prices high is common at the introduction stage, since it is easier to lower prices later on than to increase them should such a need arise. Such a strategy is designed to offset development costs as quickly as possible. Also at this stage, the firm attempts to secure as great a distribution as possible by offering distributors allowances and discounts. Obtaining widespread distribution is difficult for new, unproven products. For this reason, many new products are brought to market bearing established brand names. When P&G launches new oral care products, the Crest name is used. The name Crest provides instant credibility to the product with distributors and consumers.

The length of time a product stays in the introduction stage depends on how quickly or slowly consumers adopt the product or on the degree to which sales increase annually.

GROWTH STAGE

As indicated by the sales curve in Figure 9.6, the **growth stage** is a period of rapid consumer acceptance. Sales rise rapidly, as do profits. Several competitive brands generally enter the market at this stage, each seeking for itself a piece of the action; this means that aggressive marketing activity for the original product must continue in order to protect and build its market share.

growth stage

The emphasis of the activity in this stage shifts from merely generating awareness to include creating preference. Many of the activities implemented are designed to encourage consumers to prefer a particular product or brand. Depending on the degree of competition, the organization maintains or perhaps increases its marketing investment at this point. Advertising messages focus on product differentiation (unique selling points) and are intended to give consumers a sound reason why they should buy a particular product. Since more information about the target market is known at this point, messages and media selection become better suited to the target; therefore, the marketing activities tend to be more efficient at this stage. A greater variety of promotion incentives are also used, since it is important to get people to make both trial purchases (by continuing to generate awareness of the product) and repeat purchases (by encouraging preference and loyalty). In addition to coupons, refund offers and contests are commonly used, since they encourage multiple purchases by interested consumers.

Price strategies at this stage remain flexible; that is, they are often determined by competitive prices. If competitors have entered the market with lower prices, it is possible that price may be adjusted downward. How consumers perceive the product and the benefits it offers also influences pricing strategy. If one brand is perceived to offer better value, a higher price is possible. Since consumer demand is higher in the growth stage than it is during the introduction stage, distribution is now easier to obtain. In effect, the combination of consumer demand and trade incentives offered by the manufacturer makes the product attractive to new distributors and helps move the product through the channel of distribution.

FIGURE
9.6   **The Product Life Cycle**

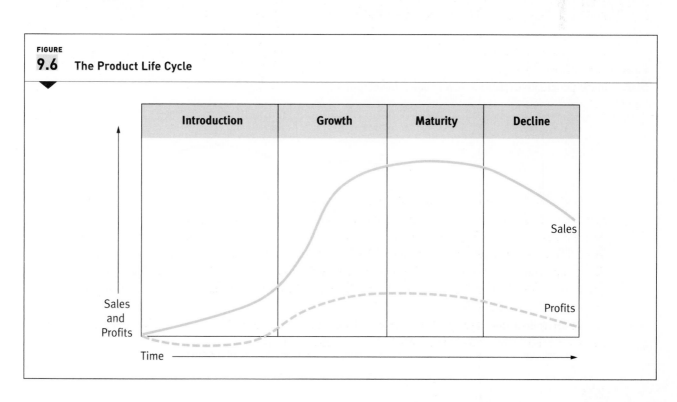

MATURE STAGE

mature stage

In the **mature stage** of a product's life cycle the product has been widely adopted by consumers; sales growth slows, becoming marginal; and eventually, a slight decline develops. Profits stabilize and begin to decline because of the expenses incurred in defending a brand's market-share position.

When a product is in the mature stage, advertising tends to give way to other forms of marketing communications—funds formerly allocated to advertising may be shifted into other areas such as sales promotion and price discounting. In the mature stage the objective is to conserve money rather than spend it. The goal is to generate profits from mature products that can be reinvested in the development of new products (Figure 9.7). There are exceptions to every rule, however, since this is a period where the only way to grow is to steal business from the competitor. In Canada's soft drink market, for example, sales are relatively flat from year to year. Both Coca-Cola and Pepsi-Cola are leading brands with similar spending patterns in marketing communications and trade promotions. If one company were to reduce its investment in advertising or trade promotions, what might happen to its market share? It is the nature of the competition that will determine how much is spent on marketing communications.

Generally, most products remain in the mature stage for a long period of time, so product managers are accustomed to implementing marketing strategies for mature brands. In maturity, a brand faces a choice. Does it adopt a defensive strategy and try to maintain market share, or does it adopt an offensive strategy and try to rejuvenate the brand? (See the section on extending the product life cycle for details about rejuvenation strategies.)

Should a defensive strategy be adopted, budgets are established at a level that will protect market share. Since maintenance of present customers (loyalty) is a priority, there is often greater spending on promotion activity than on media advertising. Promotions that encourage brand loyalty include cash refunds, contests, and giveaways with the purchase of a brand. Such offers are designed to encourage repeat purchase or multiple purchases at one time.

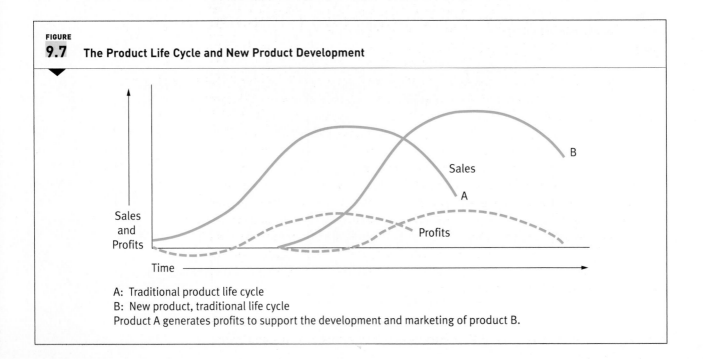

FIGURE 9.7   The Product Life Cycle and New Product Development

A: Traditional product life cycle
B: New product, traditional life cycle
Product A generates profits to support the development and marketing of product B.

The re-launch of the Volkswagen Beetle provides an example of a product that reached maturity rather quickly. Introduced in 1998, it was initially a "pay-anything-to-get-it, can't-keep-it-on-the-lot" success story. Nostalgic consumers willingly paid the sticker price and dealers drew up lengthy waiting lists. The Beetle was a success and it helped revive a stagnant brand (Volkswagen) in North America. Only a few years later, sales slumped by 23 percent and Beetles were in plentiful supply on dealers' lots in Canada and the United States. Now the emphasis is on price (low price), incentive packages, and cut-rate financing, much like any other vehicle on the market. An automotive star is suddenly an also-ran.[8]

Volkswagen Beetle
www.vw.com/newbeetle

The dilemma that the Beetle faces is much like any other mature product. What does the brand do once the initial euphoria fades? In the automobile market, most cars go through a style change, but with the Beetle its distinctive style is its defining characteristic, so style changes are not an option. Alternatives that involve other elements of the marketing mix will have to be explored.

To protect market share in the packaged-goods industry prices are often dropped, which reduces profits. Distribution will remain reasonably stable if the organization continues to offer trade discounts and allowances to wholesalers and retailers. However, as sales move from a slight growth to an actual decrease, distributors start to eliminate slower-moving products and replace them with exciting new product innovations. The concept of category management that was discussed earlier in this chapter comes into play. Since wholesalers and retailers want to carry only product lines that are moving at a desired pace, they often delete slow-moving items from their shelves. At the same time, manufacturers start to ponder the possible withdrawal of brands from the market some time in the future if they enjoy only second-tier status among distributors.

DECLINE STAGE

In the **decline stage** of the product life cycle sales begin to drop rapidly and profits are eroded. Products become obsolete as many consumers shift to innovative products entering the market. Price cuts are a common marketing strategy in a declining market, as competing brands attempt to protect market share.

decline stage

Because the costs of maintaining a product in decline are quite high, marketing objectives in the decline stage focus on planning and implementing the withdrawal of a product from the market. Marketers cut advertising and promotion expenditures to maximize profit or minimize potential losses, and to generate funds that can be invested in new products with greater profit potential. Since companies do not have the resources to support all products equally, the wise ones have products at various stages of the product life cycle so that the marketing strategies can be effectively managed within financial constraints (see Figure 9.7).

A summary of the key marketing influences on the product life cycle is included in Figure 9.8.

EXTENDING THE PRODUCT LIFE CYCLE

Many product managers attempt to rejuvenate their brands and extend their life cycles for as long as possible by employing a more offensive strategy in the mature stage. The three most commonly used strategies for extending the life cycle of a brand are to look for new markets, to alter the product in some way, and to experiment with new marketing mixes. The effect of life cycle extensions is illustrated in Figure 9.9. Let us examine each of these options in more detail.

TAP NEW MARKETS   Increasing the number of product users can be accomplished in three ways: by attracting competitors' customers, by entering new segments, and by converting non-users to users.

FIGURE 9.8 Product Life Cycle Characteristics and Strategic Marketing Focus

Stage	Characteristics	Strategy
Introduction	• Low sales • Negligible profits, even losses • No or few competitors • Innovative customers	• Large budget needed to create awareness for new product • Build distribution and expand market • Usually a high price is established • Promotion incentives for trial
Growth	• Rapid sales growth • Profits grow rapidly and peak • Mass-market customers • More competitors enter	• Market penetration • Brand preference encouraged through advertising and repeat-purchase incentives • Product differentiation • Large budget needed due to competition • Intensive distribution • Possibly lower price
Mature	• Marginal growth and then decline in sales • Profits start to decline • Mass market • Many competitors	• A sustained budget needed to protect current share position • Emphasis on promotion instead of on advertising • Repeat purchase incentives • Intensive distribution • Product improvements • Possible price decrease
Decline	• Rapid decline in sales • Product obsolete • Low profit; potential loss • Competition drops out • Laggards purchase	• Cut marketing support • Allocate profits to new products • Price cuts common • Eventual withdrawal

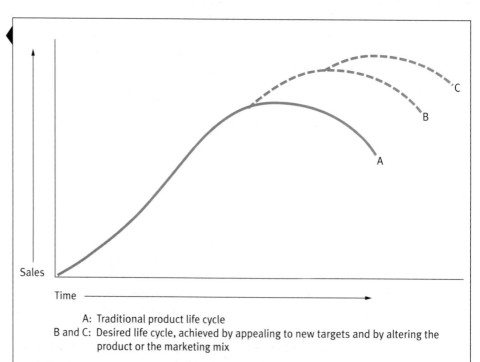

FIGURE 9.9 Life Cycle Extensions

A: Traditional product life cycle
B and C: Desired life cycle, achieved by appealing to new targets and by altering the product or the marketing mix

Attract Competitors' Customers   This strategy is common in packaged goods markets among brands following a market penetration strategy. Advertising and promotional incentives are designed to achieve trial purchases, tempting customers to switch brands at least temporarily. A brand like Pepsi-Cola, for example, aggressively pursues Coca-Cola through campaigns that incorporate the "taste test" challenge or that show Coca-Cola drinkers enjoying a Pepsi. One recent television commercial showed a Coca-Cola drinker selling all of his Coca-Cola merchandise (goods containing the Coke logo) in a yard sale. In the stagnant beer market, Blue, Budweiser, Coors, Canadian, and others battle head-to-head to get established and to get loyal drinkers to switch brands. The only way a brand can build share in a stagnant market is to attract users of other brands while keeping its current customers loyal.

Enter New Market Segments   This approach could involve geographic expansions (e.g., a regional brand expanding into other regions) or going after new demographic target markets (e.g., different age, income, or gender groups) with the same or different versions of a product. Mark's Work Wearhouse followed this approach. Mark's moved away from its construction roots in 1997 when it began offering men's casual "after work" clothes. Then, in 1999, it made sense to offer clothes for women—they comprised almost 70 percent of the store traffic because they bought for men. The strategy was successful. Overall sales increased and women's clothes now comprise 20 percent of overall sales.[9] Refer to Figure 9.10 for an illustration.

Big box-stores such as Future Shop, Costco, and Home Depot that are traditionally located in the suburbs are now opening smaller stores downtown. Unlike many U.S. cities, where the downtown core is stagnant, Canadian cities are perceived as happening places offering new sales potential. Since the shopping experience is different downtown (e.g., walk-in traffic instead of drive-in), these retailers are adjusting their merchandise and merchandising strategies to suit the needs of downtown shoppers.[10]

Convert Non-Users   It is not too late to attract new users at this point. Perhaps it is users of other products and services that provide the key to extended growth. For example, an individual may be persuaded to deal with more than one bank, in the search for the best interest rates for investments or loans. The business customer who has always relied on the postal service to deliver packages may be an attractive prospect for airfreight and overnight-courier-service companies. Many PC computer users purchased their first Apple computer when the iMac was launched. Perhaps their curiosity was piqued by all the marketing hype that supported the iMac. The iMac brought Apple back to life.

Alter the Product   In a product alteration strategy, the marketing organization changes certain characteristics of the product to attract new users. Some rejuvenation strategies include making improvements in quality, features, and style in order to encourage customers to purchase more of the product.

Quality Improvement   The marketing organization improves the primary benefit of a product and presents the product as "new and improved." For example, the product is made more durable than before, offers better colour than before, tastes better, or rides more smoothly along rough roads. A good example is Hostess Frito-Lay, a company that reformulated several of its popular brands including Doritos nacho-flavoured chips, Ruffles potato chips, and Lay's potato chips. Even though Frito-Lay controls about 40 percent of the snack-food market, it feared for its leadership position because of

Hostess Frito-Lay
www.fritolay.ca

Courtesy of Mark's Work Wearhouse

overcrowding (new product entries from current and new competitors). The new chips
were processed with cottonseed oil and were fried using new technologies. The result
was a better-tasting, crispier, and crunchier chip—benefits other competitors were not
offering. Lays chips were packed in bags that said, "New! Tastier and Crispier." Staying a
step ahead of the competition is the name of the game. Stand still and the competitor
will take business away from you!

Feature Improvements   The product is offered in new sizes, such as bonus packs,
which give more of the product for the same price (e.g., information such as "25 percent
more" appears on the package); or in new formats (e.g., laundry detergents are introduced in liquid formats under existing brand names, or bleach is added to the product
formula). See Figure 9.11. Another option is to modify the container to offer improvement or convenience in serving.

FIGURE
9.11 **Line extensions offering new features and benefits help extend the product life cycle**

Dick Hemingway

Binney & Smith, makers of Crayola products, followed a feature improvement strategy when it introduced washable crayons, which allow children to use their surroundings as a canvas without sending their parents to the cleaners. Masterpieces drawn on walls with the washable crayon are easily removed with mild soap and water from most surfaces. Research conducted by Binney & Smith revealed parents' concerns about how to remove unwanted marks on walls. Washable crayons meet that concern head-on.

Style Improvement   This strategy is appropriate for durable goods, such as major appliances, home entertainment products, and automobiles. In the automobile industry, familiar names—such as Cadillac, Lincoln, and Corvette—remain, but the style and appearance of these cars change from time to time. General Motors completely redesigned the Cadillac in 2002 to give it a younger, sportier appearance. The goal was to attract a younger customer—someone who would typically buy a BMW or Audi. The strategy worked! Cadillac sales have rebounded significantly, led by the Escalade (a luxury sport utility vehicle) and the CTS (a sporty looking sedan). Refer to the illustration in Figure 9.12.

FIGURE 9.12 A new, sportier styling attracted new customers to the Cadillac brand

320 horsepower. 315 pound-feet of torque.

One heated leather and wood-trimmed
steering wheel for you to hang on to.

INTRODUCING THE 2005 CADILLAC STS. Whether luxury is a great engine or a polished interior, here is something special to hold on to. Visit gmcanada.com   **CADILLAC STS** BREAK THROUGH

Add New Product Lines   In this situation the product is offered in different flavours or scents in order to entice a different user to try the product. The objective of the product line extension is to provide increased sales to the brand by meeting an unfulfilled need in the market. For example, Trident (a sugarless gum) recently launched Trident White as its response to the "tooth-whitening craze" that took hold in the market. The new line extends the basic healthy teeth positioning of the Trident brand, but while most whitening gums lack taste, Trident White delivers the whitening benefit along with fresh taste. Refer to the illustration in Figure 9.13.

The low-carbohydrate trend that prevailed in 2004 resulted in the launch of all kinds of new food products. Kellogg's, for example, was feeling some pressure in the presweetened cereal category and reacted by introducing Frosted Flakes and Froot Loops with one-third less sugar than regular varieties of the same brand. Coca-Cola introduced Coke C2 and Pepsi-Cola introduced Pepsi Edge. Both brands offered 50 percent less sugar and 50 percent fewer calories.

CHANGE OTHER MARKETING MIX ELEMENTS

Pricing   Since products usually enter the market with a high price, the mature stage is the time to reduce price. The practice of price discounting encourages consumers to try

Reprinted by permission of Cadbury Adams Canada Inc.

**FIGURE
9.13**

Trident gum attracts different users with a new product line that offers dual benefits

different products. Instead of having its price lowered permanently, a product might frequently be offered to distributors at a discount and with allowances so that they can, in turn, offer price specials to consumers on a temporary basis. For a variety of economic reasons the annual rate of growth in the automobile market is marginal at best. Therefore, most companies have resorted to using cash rebates and other financial incentives to motivate purchases of particular brands. Such incentives were originally designed to stimulate sales in the short-term, but now consumers are so accustomed to rebates they will actually postpone a purchase until one is offered.

Advertising   Since sales volume in the mature stage is stable, marketers are prudent about expenditures, particularly where advertising is concerned. Emphasis is placed on controlling product costs and spending only enough on advertising to maintain the current market position. Copy (message) changes are made in line with product improvements, new features, or style changes. There are exceptions to this fundamental principle (see the discussion about Coca-Cola and Pepsi-Cola that appeared in the product life cycle section of this chapter).

Sales Promotion   As stated earlier, the mature stage sees greater stress placed on sales promotion than on advertising. The use of promotions to get current customers to increase their purchases is crucial at this stage. Such promotions include cash refunds, contests, and premium offers (e.g., bonus items packed in a product, as when free toys are included in cereal boxes).

Distribution   The combination of product improvements and lower prices makes the product more attractive to distributors that have not yet carried the product. Because of this, the marketer seeks nontraditional channels of distribution. For example, marketers of food and snack food now sell some product lines through discount department stores, such as Wal-Mart and Zellers. Harvey's has established in-house restaurants in Home Depot stores. Tim Hortons has established a relationship with Imperial Oil and will be selling a full menu of products through Esso stations coast-to-coast in Canada. Strategies like these get customers into the retail outlets, and once they are there, they spend money on other items.

How a company manages mature products is a continuous challenge. For a look at how Mark's Work Wearhouse is planning for the future, read the Marketing in Action vignette **Brand Building at Mark's**.

CONSUMERS INFLUENCE THE PRODUCT LIFE CYCLE

The degree to which consumers accept or reject a product is the measure of its success or failure. Product acceptance is concerned with two areas: adoption or individual acceptance, and diffusion or market acceptance.

adoption

Adoption is defined as a series of stages a consumer passes through on the way to purchasing a product on a regular basis. The adoption process has up to five distinct steps: awareness, interest, evaluation, trial, and adoption (Figure 9.14). Not all consumers accept products at the same rate (e.g., the numbers buying in maturity are greater than growth). The gradual acceptance of a product from introduction to market saturation is referred to as the **diffusion of innovation**. Everett M. Rogers has conducted intensive research into the diffusion process, and he makes three conclusions. First, individuals require different amounts of time to decide to adopt a product; second, consumers can be classified on the basis of how quickly or how slowly they adopt a product; and, third, there are five categories of adopters.[11]

diffusion of innovation

Refer to Figure 9.15 for an illustration of the adopter categories and the proportion of the target-market population that each represents.

innovators

The **innovators** are the first group of consumers to accept a product. They are risk takers, ambitious, aggressive trendsetters who like to be apart from the mainstream. Eager to try new products, they represent only 2.5 percent of a target market.

early adopters

Early adopters are more discreet, but are a larger group of opinion leaders who like to try new products when they are new. They are strongly affected by the status and prestige of having a new item early. This group represents 13.5 percent of a target market.

early majority

The **early majority** represents the initial phase of mass-market acceptance. They follow the lead of early adopters and buy a proven commodity. This group represents 34 percent of a target market.

late majority

The **late majority** is the remainder of the mass market. This group is usually lower in social and economic status and tends to be older and willing to try only products that have been around for a while. They comprise 34 percent of a target market.

MARKETING IN ACTION

Brand Building at Mark's

Michael Strachan, the relatively new but highly experienced VP of marketing at Mark's Work Wearhouse, has some clear goals in mind. He was hired with the mandate to develop a marketing strategy to support the retailer's new profile. His goal is to expand Mark's well beyond its blue-collar roots to become known as a store that will satisfy all casual clothing needs. Mark's is a great brand in search of superbrand status!

Many new programs have been implemented to help achieve this goal. First there was the acquisition of Work World, a much smaller chain of work wear outlets. Work World locations that were retained were converted to the Mark's Work Wearhouse banner. With more clout, Mark's would be in better position to compete with big competitors like Costco and Wal-Mart.

In the late 1990s, Mark's began offering men's casual "after work" clothes and it made perfect sense to add women's clothes because women comprised 70 percent of the store traffic—women were buying clothes for their men. Ad campaigns comprised of outdoor boards and print ads were implemented to introduce the women's lines. That strategy has been successful: women's clothes now represent 20 percent of company sales revenue. (Refer to the advertising illustration in Figure 9.10.)

Strachan is a firm believer in marketing research. Focus groups in Vancouver, Edmonton, Calgary, and Toronto involving more than 1000 Canadians have had a say in what they think about Mark's. Two-thirds of the respondents felt the brand name reflected its blue-collar roots, but 95 percent of them were comfortable with the name. Any hint of changing the name (and it was up for review) was scrapped based on these research findings.

Strachan's research also told him growth would come from men's and women's casual clothing. As a result, an ad campaign revolving around a familiar tagline—"Clothes that work"—has been in place since the late 1990s. Under Strachan, the phrase has become the company's "major brand proposition" and a company mantra that appears on everything from the smallest indoor sign to the biggest outdoor bill-board. As well, stores have been redesigned to make them look sleeker, brighter, and more accessible—a better shopping experience overall.

In 2001, Canadian Tire acquired Mark's Work Wearhouse for $160 million. At the time, many observers felt the acquisition was a poor fit but sales results since then prove otherwise. Mark's now capitalizes on the strength of Canadian Tire's icon status. In five pilot stores Canadian Tire and Mark's are now sharing floor space. The combination offers benefits for both brands. Mark's can leverage Canadian Tire's customer demographic, which is wider than Mark's own demographic of 30- to 55-year-old men and women with active lifestyles and kids. This complements Canadian Tire's more heavily skewed male demographic.

Canadian Tire is also becoming more female-friendly. They are now showcasing items that female customers are interested in such as home décor and home organization. The cleaning-products section has been given additional space and new sections such as greeting cards and cut flowers have been added. Canadian Tire has plans to retrofit 280 locations across Canada so that they meet the expectations of female shoppers.

Both Mark's and Canadian Tire are performing well in the market, a sure sign of wise product decisions and sound marketing strategies being implemented by their marketing teams.

Adapted from Norma Ramage, "Mark's Super Brand Ambition," *Marketing*, March 29, 2004, pp. 8–11, and Lisa D'Innocenzo, "Luring women into the box," *Strategy*, December 7, 2003, p. 6.

Dick Hemingway

FIGURE
9.14

The Adoption Process

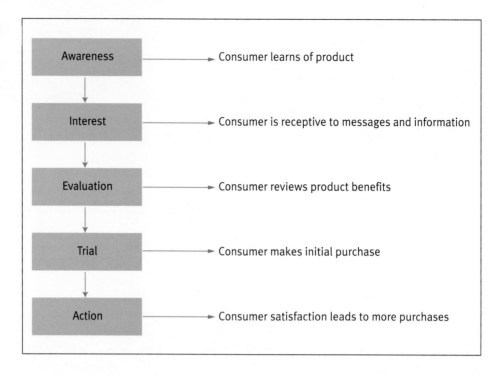

laggards

Laggards are the last to purchase and represent 16 percent of a market. Typically, they buy the same old things; that is, they do not like change. They are not influenced by advertising and brand image but are influenced by price and reference groups.

It should be noted that innovators and early adopters have moved on to new innovations by the time the mass market starts buying a product. For example, the price of flat-screen televisions has dropped and people in the early majority and late majority categories are starting to buy them. Innovators, however, have moved on to wall-mounted flat screens in order to be first on the block to own one. It's all part of their ambitious, trend-setting lifestyle.

THE LENGTH OF THE PRODUCT LIFE CYCLE

All products do not follow the same life cycle. So far, this chapter has presented what may be called the traditional product life cycle so that marketing strategies associated with each stage can be described. Let us examine some of the common variations in the length and shape of the product life. Refer to Figure 9.16 for a visual illustration.

FIGURE
9.15

Categories of Adopters

Source: Reprinted with the permission of The Free Press, a Division of Simon & Schuster, Inc., from *Diffusion of Innovations*, 4th edition by Everett M. Rogers. Copyright 1995 by Everett M. Rogers. Copyright 1962, 1971, 1983 by The Free Press.

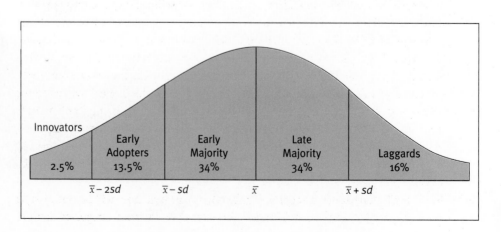

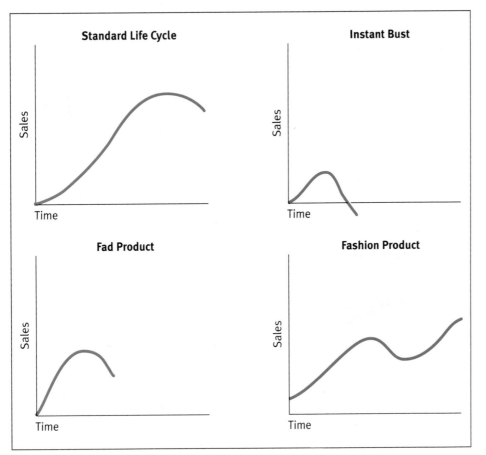

FIGURE
9.16

Variations of a Product Life Cycle

1. The term **instant bust** applies to a product that a firm had high expectations of and perhaps launched with a lot of marketing fanfare but that, for whatever reason, was rejected by consumers very quickly. A prime example is the Edsel, Ford's classic blunder of the 1950s. When New Coke was launched in 1985 to replace the old Coca-Cola, regular Coca-Cola customers went crazy. So strong was the public backlash the product was withdrawn after only 79 days on the market and replaced with the original flavour, now called Coca-Cola Classic. The *Washington Post* called the Coke fiasco "a marketing blunder of Edsel magnitude." Not to be outdone, Pepsi A.M., a breakfast cola that offered more caffeine and less carbonation, was a financial disaster for PepsiCo. **instant bust**

2. The cycle of the **fad** is reasonably short, perhaps one selling season or a few seasons, and usually financially successful for the organization. A fad could have something to do with clothing (leisure suits, mini-skirts, and tie-dye T-shirts), collectables (Cabbage Patch dolls, Hula Hoops, and mood rings), or lifestyle activities (fad diets and board games such as Trivial Pursuit). One may consider the low-carbohydrate phenomenon a fad. Many food and beverage manufacturers quickly reacted to the trend by marketing a flurry of products to meet consumer demand. The low-carb wave that roiled the light-beer segment is crashing, however. Once seen as a potential growth source, if brands such as Molson Ultra are retained they are destined to be nothing more than a very small niche that will eventually be withdrawn from the market. **fad**

3. The cycle of a **fashion** is a recurring one. What is in style now will be out of style later and, perhaps, back in style at an even later date. Product categories that are **fashion**

subject to fashion cycles include clothing (items such as business suits, skirts, and bathing suits), cosmetics, and automobiles. In the fashion industry, casual clothing (business casual) has been popular for quite a while but very recent trends indicate a strong return of the traditional business suit. The urban, business professional is sprucing up his or her wardrobe, and upscale haberdashers such as Harry Rosen and Holt Renfrew are reaping the benefits. Also making a comeback is the alligator-emblazoned polo shirt. The shirt, which epitomized preppy style in the 1980s and plunged in popularity almost as quickly as it peaked, is making a return in Canada, enjoying a stunning resurgence among teens and the golf and tennis set it was created for.[12] In the words of the old saying, "What goes around comes around."

These variations indicate that marketers must not be satisfied with passing through the various stages of the conventional product life cycle. Instead, strategies must be implemented that will initiate growth as the product matures. In this regard, many of the product and marketing mix decisions discussed in this chapter will come into play.

brand acceptance wall (BAW)

In the context of product acceptance by consumers, marketing experts now think that products face what is called the **brand acceptance wall** (**BAW**). The BAW is a barrier that stops most products from further consumer acceptance. The obstacle is caused by a combination of lack of consumer acceptance and an uncoordinated marketing communication strategy. Those brands that pass the wall become major market players. Gatorade, for example, started as a niche product, but its integrated and coordinated marketing strategy made it a major market brand. In contrast, Snapple, a product with broad market appeal, never generated sufficient brand acceptance to become a serious contender in the beverage market. Snapple has since retreated to regional markets, where it may not survive.

Leveraging a brand is another way of breaking through the BAW. Gatorade, for example, tapped into the aspirational element of the brand when it learned that the adult-sized drink was too large for kids to grip and contained too much liquid for kids to consume. Consequently, Gatorade introduced a 344-mL tetra-pak (a small carton-and-straw combination used in juice drinks) in three flavours: Fruit Punch, Cool Blue Raspberry, and Grape. Gatorade now appeals to a wider cross-section of the population.[13]

New Products vs. Rejuvenated Products

4. Describe the alternatives available to an organization for developing new products.

Some of the biggest decisions for a company deal with new product activity. Should a company invest considerable sums in developing a completely new product from scratch, or should it, at much lower cost, repackage and reposition existing products to extend their life cycle?

A brand name has built-in equity from the millions of dollars invested in it over time—there is an image tucked away in the consumer's brain, ready for recall. It is easy to take this image out and breathe new life into it. Reviving a tired image saves time, money, and the hassles associated with new product development. Considering the failure rate of new products—as many as 8 out of 10 new products fail—it is easy to see why many manufacturers now prefer to reposition or revive an image. To draw a comparison between the two approaches, consider the Frito-Lay examples cited earlier in this chapter. Reformulating Doritos nacho chips took six months from conception to store shelves, while development of Sun Chips, a totally new product line, took 10 years and millions of dollars.[14]

Finding out what the customer really wants reduces the product development cycle and helps reduce the risk of new product failures. Marketers are rejuvenating mature brands, giving them fresh starts by selling consumers on new uses for the product without substantially changing the product or its packaging, using brand extensions, or overhauling the brand's image.

Nestlé Canada followed a new product strategy by introducing beverage products that match current trends in drink consumption away from the home. For example, lattes are very popular in coffee shops year-round, and iced coffee beverages are popular in the warmer months of the year. Nescafé recently introduced home versions of these drinks—Nescafé Latte and Nescafé Ice Java. Refer to the advertisement in Figure 9.17. Truly new products like these create new revenue streams for marketers, especially if they are competing alone in a new category.

The key to successful **line extensions** is the brand name. A company must consider how far it can extend the name. A brand extension must fit in with the brand's parent, and it should reinforce the positive impression that potential consumers have of the brand. Simply tinkering with an existing brand name and trying to tie it in to another

line extensions

Courtesy of Nestlé Canada

FIGURE
9.17

New products produce new revenue streams for a company

Tide
www.tide.com/products

product does not guarantee success. Tide is a leading brand of detergent, and the brand has been extended considerably within the detergent category: Tide Powder, Tide Liquid, Tide with Bleach, Tide Stainbrush, Tide HE (High Efficiency), and Tide with a touch of Downy. Downy is another P&G brand in the fabric softener market. All of these are logical brand extensions.

Mentioned earlier in the chapter was Dove soap. Dove has become a multi-billion dollar brand over the past three years. Brand extensions from the original soap line include body wash, shampoo, and deodorant.[15] In contrast, Clorox is an established name and brand leader in the bleach business, but as a detergent it was a dismal failure. There is a peril associated with line extensions. If a brand extends itself too far, the customer gets confused about what the brand really stands for.

> **5.** Identify and explain the steps in the new product development process.

New Product Development

new product

In the truest sense of the word, a **new product** is a product that is truly unique and that meets needs that have previously been unsatisfied. Personal digital assistants (PDAs), such as the PalmPilot or BlackBerry, are truly new products. Advances in microcomputer technology, for example, are occurring so rapidly that the word "new" in this industry is relatively meaningless. Apple Computer Inc., for example, continues to invest heavily as it searches for breakthrough products in this rapidly growing market segment. Apple virtually reinvented itself when it launched the iMac computer, and now the iPod, Apple's venture into the music business, has rejuvenated the company again.

One may ask, for example, whether we need a gum that remedies erectile dysfunction when there are now several brands of pills available that perform this task. Wrigley—the maker of Juicy Fruit, Big Red, and several other popular brands of gum—thinks we do. Wrigley sees merit in the gum product. It would be easier on the stomach and it would act faster than Viagra's little blue pill. Wrigley has secured a patent for the new gum, and as part of the patent application stated that a man would have to chew the gum for about two minutes about a half-hour prior to having sex. Will consumers buy into the product concept, or will it be a huge waste of research and development money for Wrigley? That is the gamble associated with new product development. No doubt, Wrigley will be undertaking considerable marketing research.

Line extensions of existing brands are also classified as a form of new product. A well-known brand such as Crest toothpaste was originally marketed as a standalone product. Now there is Crest Complete, Crest Kids, Crest Sensitivity Protection, Crest Multicare, Crest Dual Action Whitening, and Crest Tartar Protection. The consumer's need for a nice smile has become very sophisticated.

In Canada, new innovations can be protected by patent if the innovation is registered in accordance with the Patent Act, administered by Consumer and Corporate Affairs Canada. Some organizations choose to ignore patent protection laws and produce and market copies of patented products, though doing so is illegal. These look-alike products are referred to as **knock-offs**. Technological products are especially prone to this practice, and it is a major concern. The presence of knock-offs shortens the innovation's life cycle. Consequently, there is less opportunity to recover development costs associated with the innovation.

knock-offs

THE NEW PRODUCT DEVELOPMENT PROCESS

The development of innovative products involves seven steps: idea generation, screening, concept development and testing, business analysis, product development, test marketing and marketing planning, and commercialization (Figure 9.18). In the 1960s, it

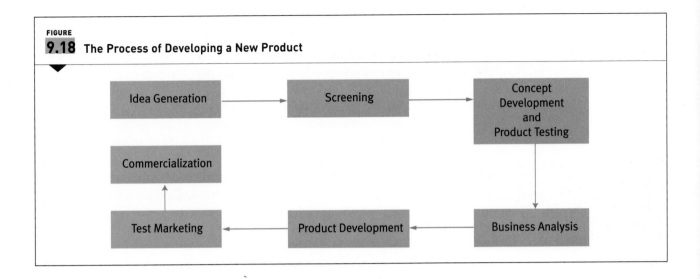

FIGURE
9.18 **The Process of Developing a New Product**

took about 60 product ideas to produce one successful new product. Today, however, the odds are much better. Companies are doing a better job of generating new ideas because they are catching more bad ideas earlier, they are using more formal and sophisticated development processes, and they are employing multi-functional teams to generate and develop concepts. Let us examine each step in the development process.

IDEA GENERATION All products stem from a good idea. Where do these ideas come from? Contemporary organizations are receptive to ideas from any source—customers, suppliers, employees, or marketing intelligence about competitors. Internally, a company may have a research and development department in place, with the sole responsibility for researching and developing ideas. Other companies may schedule regular meetings of executives and cross-sections of employees to brainstorm for potential opportunities.

Employees at Kellogg's work in cross-functional teams, with market researchers alongside food technologists and engineers. This organizational approach to new product development is paying dividends. One recent idea that met with success is Raisin Bran Crunch. The product offers thicker, coated flakes that do not get soggy in milk. Raisin Bran Crunch captured 1 percent of the cereal market without eroding the business of other Kellogg's bran cereals.[16]

Companies in the food and beverage business have had to react quickly to consumers' demand for low-carbohydrate products. Ideas came quickly at PepsiCo. The Pepsi-Cola division launched Pepsi Edge, the first full-flavoured cola with 50 percent less sugar, carbohydrates, and calories than regular colas. The Frito-Lay division launched Doritos Edge and Tostitos Edge, products that have fewer than half the carbohydrates of its top-selling tortilla chip brands. PepsiCo is committed to delivering the type of innovation that will grow its core brands and "better-for-you" snack brands. Pepsi Edge and Doritos Edge represent an opportunity for sustainable incremental growth.[17]

SCREENING The elimination of ideas begins with product **screening**. The purpose of screening is to quickly eliminate ideas that do not appear to offer financial promise for the company. Such a screening process is the responsibility of senior management, who must decide if the new idea is in line with the overall company strategy. For new ideas to be compared, a rating checklist or scale might be used in screening. Such a checklist would include criteria important to the company, such as patent protection, sales

screening

potential, threat of competition, compatibility with current products, marketing investment required, anticipated life cycle, degree of uniqueness, expertise in production, and capital investment required. An examination of these criteria allows a company to gauge the compatibility of each new product idea with the overall company strategy.

concept test

CONCEPT DEVELOPMENT AND TESTING   A **concept test** involves the presentation of a product idea in some visual form (usually a drawing or photograph) with a description of the basic product characteristics and benefits. The purpose of a concept test is to find out early how consumers react to the product idea. Typically, a consumer is provided with the product's picture, description, and price, and is then asked questions to determine his or her level of interest and the likelihood of the person purchasing the product. Such a step is a crucial one, since this feedback determines whether the firm invests in prototype product development, an expensive proposition. Companies proceed only with ideas consumers indicate to be of high interest. To gauge the level of acceptability, a firm may show different information about the same concept. It may, for example, test different prices in order to determine how price influences the level of interest in the concept and to see at what point the concept becomes uninteresting. Such information is important for the sales and profit projections in the next stage.

business analysis

BUSINESS ANALYSIS   A **business analysis** entails a formal review of some of the ideas accepted in the screening stage, the purpose of which is again to rank potential ideas and eliminate those judged to have low financial promise. By this time, the company is dealing only with product ideas that have been judged positively by potential customers. Consequently, the company must determine the market demand for the product and the costs of project production and marketing and estimate revenue and profit. Such a review includes a thorough evaluation of competitive offerings and their marketing strengths and weaknesses.

PRODUCT DEVELOPMENT   In this stage, the idea or concept is converted to a physical product. The purpose is to develop a prototype or several prototype models for evaluation by consumers. The **prototype** is a physical version of a potential product; that is, a product designed and developed to meet the needs of potential customers. The prototype is refined on the basis of feedback obtained in consumer research. In effect, the research and development department experiments with design and production capability to determine what type of product can be produced within the financial constraints established in the business analysis stage.

prototype

At Kellogg's R&D facilities, a pilot plant one-tenth the scale of an actual manufacturing facility runs test batches of cereals and snacks. Issues that must be resolved at this stage include the type and quality of materials available to use for manufacturing; the method of production and any additional capital requirements; the package configuration and its influence on production, shipping, and handling; and the time required for startup (the time needed to have all equipment and materials in place, ready for production).

At this stage, various functional areas of the firm must cooperate to ensure that the product is what the customer wants. What Engineering and Production can provide may not be what Marketing wants. Therefore, these departments work together to coordinate their plans.

Product development is a very expensive phase of the development process. In addition to pure research costs, the firm has to pay to have the prototypes constantly tested for consumer reaction. Marketers develop brand names, identify the key benefits, develop a price, and perhaps provide consumers with samples of the prototype for their perusal and use. The Pepsi Edge soft drink discussed earlier was thoroughly tested in qualitative and quantitative research studies over several months. The research indicated that respondents loved the taste of Pepsi Edge. Test scores suggested the product provided the perfect balance of taste and calories that no other soft drink offers. It would definitely be a project that would move forward … and fast! Many of the research techniques presented in Chapter 3 are used to collect this information.

TEST MARKETING AND MARKETING PLANNING   At this point, the company develops an introductory marketing plan to support test marketing. **Test marketing** is the first real acid test for the product. It is the stage at which consumers have the opportunity to actually purchase the product instead of simply indicating that they would purchase it. The test market allows the company to gain feedback in a relatively inexpensive way. Many marketers view the test market stage as mandatory; without it, a significant financial risk is faced. It tells the company whether a product should be launched regionally or whether it should be launched nationally, in which case the loss to the company would be great in the event the product fails. The test market evaluates the product and the marketing plan so that further modifications can be made to both, if necessary, prior to an expensive full-scale launch. Others feel the test market stage could be bypassed, since it tips off competitors about a firm's activity. It gives competitors time to react and develop imitations or plan defensive strategies for products already on the market.

test marketing

A firm may conduct several test markets in order to generate conclusive information to assist in the planning for market expansion. Even then, the results may mislead a company. Pepsi-Cola, for example, test marketed and then launched Crystal Pepsi (a clear version of Pepsi-Cola), but the product failed miserably. In contrast, Pepsi Edge, a product with one-half the calories and carbohydrates of regular Pepsi, has been a success.

COMMERCIALIZATION   **Commercialization** is the concluding step in the new product development process; the company puts together a full-scale production and marketing plan for launching a product on a regional or national scale. All the refining, adjusting, and tinkering with product design characteristics, production considerations, and marketing strategies is over at this point. The product should meet the needs and expectations of the target market. Marketing communications acquaint distributors and consumers with the product and what it offers. The product has now entered the introduction stage of the product life cycle described earlier in this chapter and is now subject to the costs and activities normally associated with that stage. The product will find future success only if the organization modifies its strategies as the product and market segment mature.

commercialization

SUMMARY

Product management concerns three key areas: the organization structure for managing products and services, the development of new products to stimulate growth in the organization, and the management of marketing strategies for products throughout their life cycles. The brand management system is most typical of packaged-goods companies and business-goods companies, although organizations are moving toward category management, marketing services management, target-market management, and global management organization structures. The key decisions in product management concern the development of new products and the rejuvenation of current products. Regarding current products, decisions revolve around product modifications, alterations to marketing mix strategies, and whether to keep a product in the market or withdraw it.

The product life cycle refers to the stages a product passes through from its introduction to its withdrawal from the market. The life cycle involves four stages: introduction, growth, maturity, and decline. The marketing strategies employed by the firm vary considerably from stage to stage. Generally, products remain in the mature stage for the longest period; the variables of time, sales, and profit are the indicators of what stage a product is in. The length of the life cycle varies from one product or product category to another. Some cycles are short (fads), while others are long (fashions). Regardless of the length of the cycle, the primary objective of the organization is to generate profits. Profits are maximized in the late growth and mature stages of the product life cycle; hence, organizations initiate strategies for extending these phases. These strategies include tapping into new markets by attracting new segments (competitors' users or non-users); altering the product by making quality, feature, or style improvements; or changing the marketing mix.

The degree to which consumers accept a new product determines its success or failure. Product adoption is concerned with a product's being accepted by individual consumers, whereas diffusion is concerned with acceptance by a market. People are categorized according to how quickly or how slowly they adopt a product. There are five categories of adopters: innovators, early adopters, early majority, late majority, and laggards.

There are seven steps in the research and development process for new products: idea generation, screening, concept development and testing, business analysis, product development, test marketing and marketing planning, and commercialization.

KEY TERMS

REVIEW QUESTIONS

1. Briefly describe the role and responsibility of the brand manager.
2. Briefly describe the following marketing management systems.
   a) Brand management
   b) Category management
   c) Regional management
   d) Target-market management
   e) Global management
3. Identify and briefly describe the four key areas of product decision making.
4. Briefly describe the characteristics and conditions that exist at each stage of the product life cycle. How do marketing objectives vary at each stage?
5. What factors determine the stage a product is at in the life cycle?
6. Briefly describe the marketing strategies an organization uses to extend the life cycles of its products.
7. What is the difference between adoption and diffusion of innovation?
8. What are the various stages in the consumer adoption process?
9. Identify and briefly describe the adopter categories.
10. Describe the differences between an instant bust, a fad, and a fashion.
11. What is a knock-off?
12. Briefly describe the seven steps in the new product development process.

DISCUSSION AND APPLICATION QUESTIONS

1. "The decision to withdraw a product from the market should be based on profitability only." Discuss the merits of this statement.

2. Provide examples of brands or companies that are using the following strategies to extend their life cycle: (a) entering new market segments, (b) altering the product, and (c) adding new lines. Explain the strategy in each case.

3. "The speed at which technology is advancing means that product life cycles will be much shorter." Is this statement true or false? If true, what are the implications for a company dealing with this situation? Provide some specific company or product examples.

4. In the global product management section of the chapter the concept of using strategies from other markets was discussed. Based on what you know about Canada and Canadian consumers (e.g., language and cultural backgrounds), is it practical to think that an advertising campaign devised elsewhere will work in Canada? What are the costs and benefits of utilizing such campaigns? Provide real examples to verify your position on the issue.

5. Review the vignette "Profit Motives Rule Brand Decisions." Will the product decisions made by Tim Hortons' management have a negative impact on business or will customers continue to support the business in spite of the changes? Some additional secondary research may shed some light on what has happened since the change. Evaluate the situation and formulate a position on the matter.

E-ASSIGNMENT

In this assignment, you will conduct a product life cycle analysis. Select one of the categories of products listed below and visit the website for each product or company. Then answer the questions. Use alternative product categories and two leading brands, if you wish.

Soft Drinks	Coca-Cola and Pepsi-Cola
Toothpaste	Colgate and Crest
Delivery Service	FedEx and UPS
Coffee Shops	Starbucks and Second Cup

1. What stage of the product life cycle is each product in? What conditions are these brands facing? Explain your position on the basis of information gathered from websites.

2. What strategies are these products using to build sales volume and increase market share? Are their marketing strategies similar to or different from what you have learned about strategies employed at the various stages of the product life cycle? Explain.

ENDNOTES

1. Constance Hays, "PepsiCo takes marketing to the aisles," *Globe and Mail*, August 3, 1999, p. B7.

2. Lara Mills, "Molson overhauls marketing team," *Marketing*, September 20, 1999, p. 3.

3. Susan Heinrich, "P&G still the best set up?" *Financial Post*, April 14, 2003, p. FP4.

4. Tracy Hanson, "Canadianizing a global campaign? Priceless," *Strategy*, March 8, 2004, p. 8

5. www.unilever.com/brands/hpc/dove.asp.

6. Chris Sorensen, "It's the end of the line for Oldsmobile," *Financial Post*, April 29, 2004, pp. FP1, FP8.

7. David Welch, "Headed for that showroom in the sky," *Business Week*, July 21, 2003, p. 52.

8. George Keenan, "Beetle-mania dies as car sales slow," *Globe and Mail*, December 6, 2000, p. B5.

9. Norma Ramage, "Mark's Super Brand Ambition," *Marketing*, March 29, 2004, p. 9.

10. Lisa D'Innocenzo, "Big box goes downtown," *Strategy*, December 1, 2003, p. 1.

11. Everett M. Rogers, *Diffusion of Innovations*, 3rd Edition (New York: Free Press, 1982), p. 246.

12. Hollie Shaw, "Alligator back in Great White North," *Financial Post*, www.financialpost.com, October 2004.

13. Lesley Young, "Gatorade targets pint-sized jocks," *Marketing*, August 19, 2002, p. 1.

14. Gary Strauss, "Companies freshen old product lines," *USA Today*, March 20, 2002, pp. B1, B2.

15. Andrea Zoe Aster, "News line," *Marketing*, February 3, 2003, p. 3.

16. "Kellogg puts the 'power of red' into breakfast," www.prnewsire.com, April 16, 2001.

17. "Pepsi North America to launch Pepsi Edge," and "Frito-lay launches new low carb Doritos," press releases, PepsiCo., www.pepsico.com.

Price

The role of price in the marketing mix is the focal point of this section.

Chapter 10 examines the factors that influence pricing decisions, the pricing objectives of an organization, and the methods used to determine price.

Chapter 11 dwells on management-related pricing decisions. Pricing policies are established, and then discussion centres on discounts and allowances, new-product pricing, and the role of leasing as a pricing option.

Richard Lam/CP Photo Archive

CHAPTER

10

Price Strategy and Determination

Learning Objectives

After studying this chapter, you will be able to

1. Explain the importance of price in marketing strategy.

2. Describe the various types of economic markets that Canadian firms operate in and their influence on pricing strategy.

3. Describe the influences that various external and internal forces have on pricing strategy.

4. Differentiate among profit, sales, and competitive pricing objectives.

5. Calculate basic prices, using a variety of pricing methodologies.

6. Describe a variety of legal issues that affect pricing strategy.

---

1. Explain the importance of price in marketing strategy.

price

This chapter introduces some of the basic pricing concepts used in marketing strategy. The discussion initially focuses on the variety of markets that Canadian firms operate in and the implications these different markets have for pricing strategy. The external and internal factors influencing pricing strategy are then discussed. Finally, the issues of how pricing strategy is used to achieve marketing objectives and what specific methods are available for determining prices are addressed.

The Definition and Role of Price

Price is defined as the exchange value of a good or service in the marketplace. The key word in this definition is "value." The value of a good or service is derived from its *tangible* and *intangible* benefits and from the perception a consumer has of it once he or she has been subjected to other marketing influences. Let us use an example to explain what tangible and intangible benefits are. A young male decides to buy a top-of-the-line model of Nike basketball shoes. They may be endorsed by a "star" basketball player such as Vince Carter. The shoe will have a very high price because it is made of the best materials and the finest technology that Nike is known for. Those are the tangibles the young buyer might look at. More than likely, however, the young male is more impressed with the style of the shoe and the aura that surrounds Vince Carter's endorsement of it. The shoe will impress his friends—and that's what he really wants. Those characteristics are the intangibles.

Prices take many forms and terms. Consider the following examples of price:

· Your college tuition fee
· A club membership
· The rate of interest on a loan
· Admission charged at a theatre
· A donation to a charity
· Rent charged for an apartment
· A fare charged on a bus or train
· A bid at an online auction site

From a marketing organization's perspective, price is the factor that contributes to revenues and profits. In planning price strategy, the firm must consider a multitude of variables in order to arrive at fair and competitive prices in the marketplace while providing reasonable revenues and profits internally.

Price is only one element of the marketing mix, but it can be the most important. For example, a prominent retailer like Wal-Mart relies on price to establish and maintain its image with consumers. Being a discount department store, Wal-Mart's objective is to offer customers good value at reasonable price levels. Wal-Mart uses the advertising slogan "Everyday low prices. Always" to make its point with consumers. At the opposite end of the scale are specialty retailers such as Harry Rosen, an upscale men's clothing emporium. Customers of Harry Rosen view price as an unimportant variable in the purchase decision. Instead, it is the image created by the high prices that attracts the upscale clientele.

In a relatively free market economy like Canada's, price is also a mechanism for ensuring adequate levels of competition. In a free and open market, where competition is strong, supply and demand factors influence price. Thus, when demand for a good increases, marketing organizations have the flexibility to increase price. When demand for a product drops, organizations tend to lower prices in order to entice consumers to continue to buy the product. To illustrate, consider what happens if the economy takes a bit of a downturn. People will hesitate to buy, or will postpone big purchases entirely. How does an automobile manufacturer react? It will offer price incentives such as cash rebates or low-interest financing packages to encourage immediate action. It is this freedom to set prices in response to the marketplace that ensures competition will occur.

Influences on Price

Several major influences are considered when establishing the price of a product: the nature of the market the product competes in, the nature of consumer demand for the product, production and marketing costs incurred by the firm, and the markups and profits expected by distributors. With the exception of production and marketing costs, all other influences are external to the firm.

NATURE OF THE MARKET

A firm's ability to establish price depends on the type of market it operates in. In the Canadian economy, there are several different types of markets: pure competition, monopolistic competition, oligopoly, and monopoly (Figure 10.1).

In a market environment of **pure competition**, there are many small firms marketing the same basic product; therefore, no single firm can dictate or offset the market. Commodities such as wheat, barley, and sugar fall into this category, as do financial securities such as mutual funds. The firm has no choice but to charge the going market price, because buyers can buy as much as they need at that price.

The market in this situation controls the selling price. The basic **law of supply and demand** applies: an abundant supply and low demand lead to a low price, while a high demand and limited supply lead to a high price. Often, it is simply expectations about supply or demand that have an impact on price. For example, if the supply of gasoline were expected to dwindle below normal demand, there would be a rush to buy the resource and its price would be driven up, at least temporarily. In other cases, it is the actual supply and demand that influences prices. The demand for stocks on the stock market influences the rate at which they are traded.

If a market is characterized as **monopolistic competition**, there are many competitors selling products that, though similar, are perceived to be different by consumers. Companies marketing packaged-goods items such as branded lines of coffee, cereal, toothpaste, and household cleaners operate in this kind of market. Marketing strategy is designed to distinguish one's own brand from the others. Such variables as product

2. Describe the various types of economic markets that Canadian firms operate in and their influence on pricing strategy.

pure competition

law of supply and demand

monopolistic competition

FIGURE
10.1   Canadian Markets and Their Price Implications

Factor	Pure Competition	Monopolistic Competition	Oligopoly	Monopoly
Competition and Product	Many sellers with same or similar product.	Many sellers with differentiated product.	Few large sellers with some product differentiation.	Single seller with unique product.
Price Decision Criteria	Price based on open market. How much should be produced?	Price based on competition and brand loyalty. How much should be produced and invested in marketing?	Price based on competition. Quick reaction to price changes. How much should be invested in marketing?	Price based on fair and reasonable profit for supplier.
Controls	None. Dictated by market dynamics.	Some.	Some (e.g., uniform beer pricing in retail outlets in some provinces).	By government or other regulatory body (e.g., CRTC).

quality, service, style, function, and packaging are used to convey a difference to the consumer. The use of such elements is referred to as non-price competition, and it is this that explains why leading brands, such as Crest and Colgate (toothpaste) and Sony (consumer electronics products), are perceived to be better than other brands. Because they are perceived as better they may be able to charge higher prices.

If the consumer thinks there are differences between the brands, brand loyalty can be created. Traditionally, consumers who are brand loyal are less likely to be influenced by price; that is, they are willing to pay a little more for the brand of their choice than for other brands. Consumers typically identify a few brands in a product category to which they remain loyal. At the point-of-purchase, they select the brand with the lowest price (e.g., if Colgate is priced lower than Crest, they purchase Colgate).

Generally, if a firm wishes to attract the users of its competitors' products on the basis of price savings, those savings must be more important than the other reasons why consumers buy products: reasons having to do with quality, image, and good service. In today's economy, disposable income is shrinking from year to year for a majority of people and as a result people are searching for better value in the goods they buy. Consequently, price has become a primary source of buying motivation.

oligopolistic market

In an **oligopolistic market**, there are a few large sellers of a particular good or service. Industries traditionally associated with oligopolies are the brewing industry, dominated in Canada by Molson and Labatt, and the gasoline industry, dominated by Petro-Canada, Imperial Oil, and Shell.

In an oligopoly, a competitor's actions are monitored closely. The competition is so intense that if one firm raises or drops its price, other firms will quickly do the same. For example, if the Royal Bank drops or raises its prime rate a quarter of a percent, within a day or two other national banks will follow suit. If Esso raises its prices, Petro-Canada and Shell are likely to follow quickly. In fact, in a matter of hours, usually overnight, the price at every gas station in a city will increase to exactly the same figure. This reaction is especially pronounced in markets where the products are basically the same.

To many consumers, this practice hints at collusion and price fixing, though independent investigations by Industry Canada (Bureau of Consumer Affairs) have never proven this to be so. Sometimes, price wars erupt between competitors and consumers temporarily enjoy bargain-basement prices. In a price war, the consumer is the only winner. Very often, the price war places financial hardship on the companies involved. Such is the case of Air Canada in its price battle with WestJet.

In a **monopoly**, a single seller of a good or service for which there are no close substitutes serves the market. With so much control, a company can manipulate supply and demand for the good or service and influence prices to the detriment of the public. In Canada, monopolies are not common, but they do exist in the service-industry sector as regulated monopolies. For example, utilities and power corporations such as SaskPower and Hydro-Quebec are provincially regulated monopolies. Cable television companies such as Shaw Cable and Rogers Cable that have protected market areas (e.g., the local communities that each serve) are also monopolies. A customer wanting cable television pays the going rate or looks at alternatives such as a satellite dish offered by Bell ExpressVu. In a regulated monopoly, the government allows the supplier to set prices to ensure a reasonable amount of profit is earned so that the company can maintain and expand its operations when needed. Price increases must go through an approval process before they are implemented. The CRTC, for example, approves all rates of cable television suppliers.

monopoly

CONSUMER DEMAND FOR THE PRODUCT

The number of consumers in a target market and the demand they have for a product has a bearing on price. Essentially, there are two common principles at work. First, consumers usually purchase greater quantities at lower prices. Second, the effects of a price change on volume demanded by consumers must be factored into the pricing strategy. To illustrate, if price is increased and demand drops significantly, the objective of the price increase (higher sales revenue or profit) will not be achieved. This principle is referred to as **price elasticity of demand**.

There are two types of demand: elastic demand and inelastic demand. **Elastic demand** describes a situation in which a small change in price results in a large change in volume (e.g., price increases by 5 percent and volume drops by 15 percent). If demand is elastic, the firm's total revenues go up as price goes down, and revenues go down when price goes up. **Inelastic demand** is a situation in which a price change does not have a significant impact on the quantity purchased. In this case, total revenues go up when prices are increased and go down when prices are reduced. For example, the Toronto Maple Leafs increase ticket prices every year. Every ticket for every game is always sold regardless of how well the team performs. These demand concepts are represented in Figure 10.2.

In Canada's two most common markets, monopolistic competition and oligopoly, demand is based on the need in the marketplace and the availability of substitute products. If demand for a product category is high, all competing firms can maintain high prices and reap the financial benefits. However, once a major competitor changes prices—say, lowers the price significantly—demand in the market can change. Such would be the case if a prominent brand like Dell Computer dropped its prices for an extended period. Being a leader in the PC market, such a move could put pressure on Compaq, Toshiba, Apple, and others to respond. Such an action could occur if an economy slows down and sales of all computer brands start to stagnate.

Consumer behaviour also has an impact on pricing strategy. A consumer may compare the price and quality of one product with other similar products; to other consumers, such matters as image, status, and prestige may be so important that the actual

3. Describe the influences that various external and internal forces have on pricing strategy.

price elasticity of demand

elastic demand

inelastic demand

**FIGURE
10.2**

**The Difference between
Elastic and Inelastic
Demand**

If demand is elastic, consumers are price sensitive. When price increases, demand goes down significantly.

In the illustration, when price increased from $500 to $750, revenue declined from $400 000 (800 units × $500) to $150 000 (200 units × $750).

If demand is inelastic, consumers are not price sensitive. A large increase in price has a limited effect on sales volume.

In the illustration, when price increased from $750 to $1500, revenue increased from $225 000 ($750 × 300 units) to $300 000 ($1500 × 200 units).

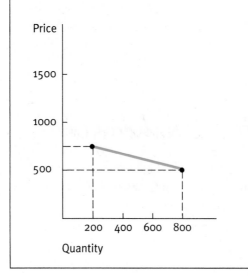

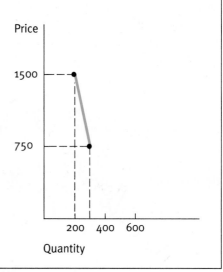

price of the product is ignored (a product such as a Rolex watch would be in this category). In the first case, the consumer behaves rationally, so the price of the product is important. In the second case, the consumer acts less rationally and is influenced by other factors, so price is less important. Thus, products aimed at status-seekers are apt to be priced high to convey prestige, while products targeted to the price-conscious would logically be priced low.

For more insight into how demand influences price, read the Marketing in Action vignette **Leaf Ticket Prices Soar But Still We Buy!**

PRODUCTION AND MARKETING COSTS

Costs that have a direct effect on price include the costs of labour, raw materials, processed materials, capital requirements, transportation, marketing, and administration. A common practice among manufacturing firms is to establish a total product cost, taking into consideration these elements as well as a desirable and fair gross profit margin. The addition of the profit margin to the cost becomes the selling price to distributors. Such a practice is based on the assumption that the resulting retail price will be acceptable to consumers. See Figure 10.3 for an illustration.

The pricing decisions of an organization become increasingly difficult as costs rise. If cost increases are gradual and the amounts are marginal, a firm can usually plan its strategy effectively; it can build prices around projected cost increases for a period of time, using, say, a one-year planning cycle. Unforeseen increases (those that happen quickly and unexpectedly) are a different matter. In such cases, a firm may choose to absorb the cost increases and accept lower profit margins, at least for the short term, in

MARKETING IN ACTION

Leaf Ticket Prices Soar But Still We Buy!

Go figure! The Toronto Maple Leafs haven't won a Stanley Cup since 1967, yet every game is a sellout. Further, among all National Hockey League teams the Leafs remain one of the richest. They don't have the highest payroll, but they are definitely in the top quarter. The money rolls in and the money rolls out and year after year the team makes a handsome profit. How does it do it?

In the old days, Maple Leaf Gardens, the former home of the team, was often referred to as the "Carlton Street Cashbox." Former owner Harold Ballard basically had a licence to print money. The teams were poor but the people kept coming—a marketing manager's dream. The Leafs now reside in the Air Canada Centre and the team is a much more efficient money-making machine because of extra seats, corporate boxes, lounge areas, and higher ticket prices. Every year ticket prices go up—and when the playoffs start, ticket prices increase again.

Most observers of the game will tell you that teams really make their money in the playoffs. The deeper the team goes into the playoffs the more money it makes. In 2002, for example, one industry insider pegged Maple Leafs profits at $2 million per home playoff game, and even more if they reached the finals. In two playoff series with the New York Islanders and the Ottawa Senators, a total of eight home games, it was estimated that the Leafs made $15 million in profit. "Playoff money is like money from heaven," says the insider.

That year the typical playoff game generated $4.1 million in revenue. That's double the gate for a regular-season game. Ticket prices virtually double for the playoffs! During the season there would be different prices for platinum and gold seats, but the Leafs charged $320 for both during the third-round playoff games. It seems that no opportunity is missed to maximize revenues and profits. The Leafs didn't make the fourth round that year, but had they the same tickets were going to increase to $420.

The Leafs' playoff prices are the highest in the league, and some team officials say privately they could charge even more because of the heavy demand. This is truly an example of charging what the market will bear. According to the fundamental laws of supply and demand, demand for Leaf tickets by far outstrips supply, at any price! Pity those poor Toronto Blue Jays. They compete in the same market, have won two World Series, and now they play before more empty seats than fans.

Adapted from Tony Van Alphen, "Leaf owners make killing," *Toronto Star*, March 8, 2002, pp. D1, D9.

Dick Hemingway

the hope that the situation will correct itself. If it does not, there is little choice but to pass the increase to channel members in order to ensure long-term profitability.

To illustrate, consider a situation currently faced by Kellogg's, General Mills, and other cereal manufacturers. In the past year (2004), wheat prices increased by 20 percent, rice and soy beans by 80 percent, and oil seed by 55 percent. The rising costs of making a box of Corn Flakes or Cheerios will start to eat into profits by as much as

FIGURE
10.3

**Cost Components of a
Packaged-Goods Product**

Cost Items		Actual Cost
	Ingredients	$15.75
	Packaging (inner/outer)	1.79
	Shipping Case	0.68
	Labour	1.48
	Manufacturing	0.20
	Warehousing	0.34
	Total Plant Cost	**20.24**
Add:	Freight Cost	1.36
	Total Product Cost	**21.60**
Add:	Gross Profit Margin (40%)	8.64
	List Price	**30.24**
Add:	Retail Profit Margin (25%)	7.56
	Retail Price (per case of 24)	37.80
	Selling Price at Retail	**1.57**

This example assumes a desired profit margin of 40% for the manufacturer of the product and a 25% markup at retail. The manufactured item is a case good that contains 24 packages in a shipping case. After all costs and profit margins are considered for the manufacturer and distributor, the price at retail is $1.57.

7 percent by the end of the year. Most grain-based packaged-food companies will begin the tricky process of raising prices. General Mills tried to raise prices on Cheerios in 2003 only to suffer nine straight months of declining sales as consumers switched to cheaper brands.[1]

cost reductions

Rather than increase prices, an option available to the organization is to search for and implement **cost reductions**, which are reductions of the costs involved in the production process. Examples of some cost-reduction measures include improving production efficiency (e.g., achieving lower long-term costs by adding automation), using less expensive materials (e.g., lower-priced ingredients and packaging materials), shrinking the size of a product (e.g., baking smaller cookies while maintaining the same pricing), and relocating manufacturing facilities to a region where production costs are lower (e.g., the migration of production from Canada to Mexico or the Far East).

Hostess Frito-Lay successfully implemented a cost-reduction program when it reduced the size of a bag of chips from 170 grams to 150 grams. Retail prices dropped accordingly. In the United States the weight of the package was reduced a further 7 percent with no corresponding drop in price. A small change in packaging can make a huge difference to a company's bottom line. Frito-Lay sells an estimated 1.18 billion kilograms of snack food each year. The 7-percent cut in package size will save the company US$154.7 million a year.[2]

Generally, a firm tries to combine cost reductions with reasonable price increases. It will remain competitive and move prices, when necessary, to protect the profitability of the firm. Should costs actually decline, the company has the option of lowering prices or taking advantage of higher profit margins. An example of an industry in which cost reduction has resulted in lower prices is the computer industry. The advancing technology of microcomputers and ancillary products has lowered prices within the industry. The lower prices, in turn, have resulted in expansion of the entire market so that all competitors have benefited.

CONSIDERATION OF CHANNEL MEMBERS

The ultimate price a consumer pays for a product is influenced by markups in the channel of distribution. Once the title to the product changes hands, pricing is determined at the discretion of the new owner. Like manufacturers, however, the distributors (wholesaler and retailer) who resell products usually have competition. They are concerned about moving the merchandise. Hence, their markup usually conforms to some standard in the industry that provides a reasonable profit margin.

To encourage channel members to charge prices that are in agreement with a manufacturer's overall marketing strategy, manufacturers consider several factors. They provide for an adequate profit margin (e.g., they consider the distributor's operating and marketing costs), they treat all customers fairly (e.g., all distributors are offered the same list price), and they offer discounts to encourage volume buying or marketing support (e.g., a portion of a discount offered by a manufacturer is passed on to the consumer by the distributor). In the latter case, the objective of the discount is to influence consumer demand during the discount period. Some examples of distributor markups are included in the "Pricing Methods" section of this chapter.

Pricing Objectives

4. Differentiate among profit, sales, and competitive pricing objectives.

In a pure business environment, the primary goal of the organization is to produce the highest possible rate of return to the owner (shareholder, partners, sole proprietor, and so on). Pricing strategies are part of a marketing strategy that must be in line with this overall company strategy.

A firm is not locked into one particular pricing strategy. In fact, each product or product line (market) will be assessed independently, and appropriate objectives will be established for the product in question. Organizations strive to achieve three basic objectives in pricing: profit maximization, sales volume maximization, and establishing a competitive position. Pricing objectives are often influenced by the stage of the product life cycle a product is in.

MAXIMIZING PROFIT

The goal of **profit maximization** is to achieve a high profit margin, a high return on investment, and a recovery of any capital invested. In this case, a company sets some type of measurable and attainable profit objective based on its situation in the market. Consider the following example:

profit maximization

> Objective: To achieve a net profit contribution of $2 000 000 and a return on investment (ROI) of 30 percent in fiscal year 200X.

While we cannot assess how conservative or how aggressive this objective is, it is certain that the organization will implement a marketing strategy to accomplish it. At the end of the year, the degree of success can be measured by comparing actual return to planned return. The profits obtained are redirected into new product development projects, which facilitate the organization's expansion into new markets. Historical trends pertaining to such ratios as a firm's return on investment or return on sales are also a factor in attracting potential new investors to the firm.

MAXIMIZING SALES VOLUME

The objective of **sales volume maximization** is to increase the volume of sales each year. A firm strives for a growth in sales that exceeds the growth in the size of the total market so that its market share increases. An example of a sales volume objective follows:

sales volume maximization

Objective: To increase sales volume from $15 000 000 to $16 500 000, an increase of 10 percent, in 200X.

To increase market share from 25 percent to 27.5 percent in 200X.

Sales levels, as we have seen, are affected by price; an increase in price can result in a decrease in demand and, therefore, a reduction in the quantity sold. In Figure 10.4, we see that when price goes down (P1 to P2), volume (quantity) goes up (Q1 to Q2); when prices go up, volume goes down.

An organization also develops the appropriate marketing strategies, including price strategy, for achieving sales objectives. In establishing these objectives, a firm considers the type of market it operates in and its elasticity of demand. Generally, brand leaders have the most flexibility in establishing sales and market-share objectives. Brands with a small share of the market tend to follow the trend established by the leader. To achieve market-share objectives a firm often sacrifices profit, at least temporarily.

ESTABLISHING A COMPETITIVE POSITION

The aim in this case is to minimize the effect of competitors' actions and provide channel members with reasonable profit margins. To attain such an objective, an organization assesses the competitive situation, including its own position in the market, and adopts a strategy termed *status quo pricing*—or, simply, **competitive pricing**—that puts its prices above, equal to, or below those of competitors. In effect, each competitor uses a pricing strategy to position itself in the consumer's mind.

competitive pricing

ABOVE COMPETITION   To set a price above a competitor, a product must be perceived as being of higher quality than the competitors' products or must offer customers an intangible benefit, such as prestige or status, or it will fail. Such a strategy provides a

FIGURE
10.4

Relationships between Price and Quantity

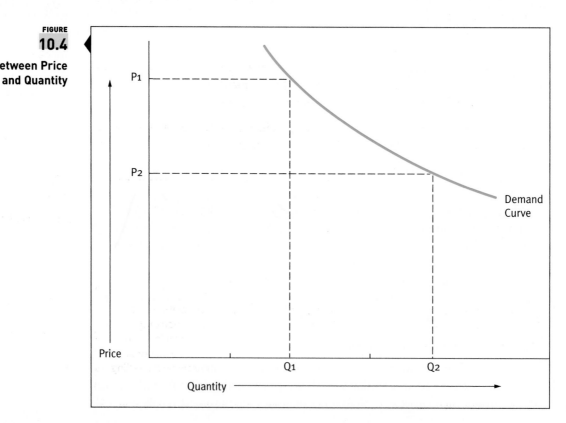

higher profit margin on each unit sold and is usually reserved for market leaders in a product category. Q-tips, for example, controls about 65 percent of the cotton swab market. Consumers perceive the brand with a high level of trust and confidence. As a result, Q-tips can charge more than its competing brands do.

EQUAL TO COMPETITION   A firm that uses this strategy adopts a conservative position because it does not want to be caught in price wars. In effect, the company is satisfied with its volume, market share, and profit margin and is content to follow the lead of others.

BELOW COMPETITION   Here, a firm uses price to secure and hold a certain position in the market. To accomplish this objective, the company must accept lower profit margins (unless it is producing so efficiently that profit margins are maintained despite the reduction in price). If the volume of sales rises significantly because of the low prices, production efficiency will increase, thus lowering costs further and improving profit margins.

Wal-Mart effectively demonstrates how a low-price strategy can work. Wal-Mart's combination of everyday low prices and good product selection has produced a leadership position in Canada's department store market. While other elements of their marketing mix have also played a role, the focus on price (low price) is what drives traffic to the stores. Zellers, an established Canadian retailer that once led the discount segment, has been forced to respond and is implementing strategies that emphasize marketing mix elements other than just price.

Pricing Methods

5. Calculate basic prices, using a variety of pricing methodologies.

A firm may use one or any combination of three basic methods in calculating prices for the products and services it markets: cost-based pricing, demand-based pricing, and competitive bidding (Figure 10.5).

COST-BASED PRICING

In the case of **cost-based pricing**, a company arrives at a list price for the product by calculating its total costs and then adding a desired profit margin.

cost-based pricing

The costs usually included in this calculation are as follows:

1. **Fixed costs** are those costs that do not vary with different quantities of output (e.g., equipment and other fixed assets, such as light, heat, and power).

fixed costs

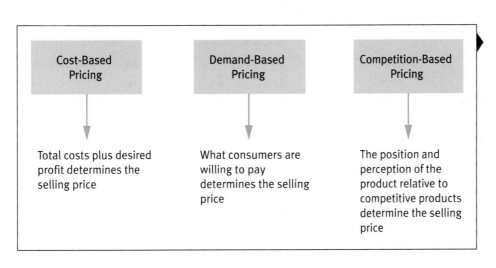

FIGURE
10.5
Pricing Methods

Cost-Based Pricing	Demand-Based Pricing	Competition-Based Pricing
Total costs plus desired profit determines the selling price	What consumers are willing to pay determines the selling price	The position and perception of the product relative to competitive products determine the selling price

variable costs

2. **Variable costs** are costs that do change according to the level of output (e.g., labour and raw materials). Variable costs rise and fall, depending on the production level—up to a point, per-unit variable costs frequently remain constant over a given range of volume. Generally, the more a firm is producing, the greater the quantities of raw materials and parts it buys, and this increased volume leads to lower unit costs; therefore, the variable costs should be lower.

For an illustration of these cost concepts refer to Figure 10.6, which shows how fixed, variable, and total costs vary with production output. In the long term, the firm must establish prices that recover total costs (i.e., fixed costs plus variable costs). To recover total costs the firm has a few options: *full-cost pricing, target pricing,* and *break-even pricing (break-even analysis).* All three consider the variables of costs, revenues, and profits. Refer to Figure 10.7 for the mathematical formulas and an example of each pricing method.

full-cost pricing

FULL-COST PRICING   In **full-cost pricing**, or cost-plus pricing, a desired profit margin is added to the full cost of producing a product. In such a system, profits are based on costs rather than on revenue or demand for the product. When a firm establishes a desired level of profit that must be adhered to, the profit goal could be interpreted as a fixed cost (see Figure 10.7).

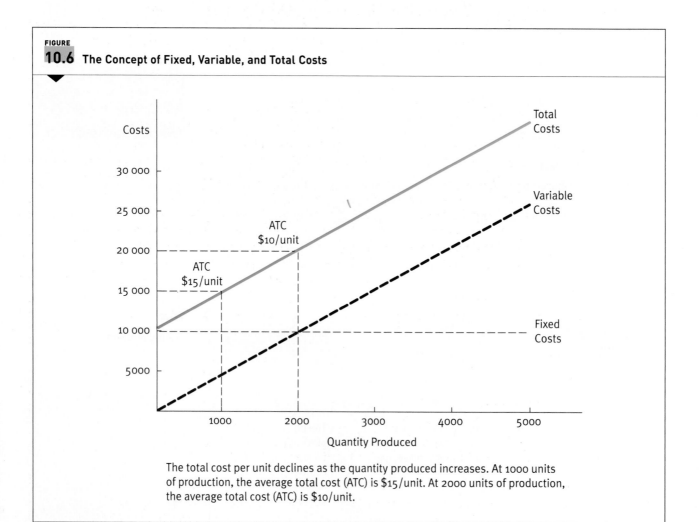

FIGURE
10.6 **The Concept of Fixed, Variable, and Total Costs**

The total cost per unit declines as the quantity produced increases. At 1000 units of production, the average total cost (ATC) is $15/unit. At 2000 units of production, the average total cost (ATC) is $10/unit.

FIGURE
10.7 Pricing Methods: Examples

1. Cost-Plus Pricing

A manufacturer of colour televisions has fixed costs of $100 000 and variable costs of $300 for every unit produced. The profit objective is to achieve $10 000 based on a production of 150 televisions. What is the selling price?

$$\text{Price} = \frac{\text{Total Fixed Costs} + \text{Total Variable Costs} + \text{Projected Profit}}{\text{Quantity Produced}}$$

$$= \frac{\$100\,000 + (\$300 \times 150) + \$10\,000}{150}$$

$$= \frac{\$155\,000}{150}$$

$$= \$1033.33$$

2. Target Pricing

A manufacturer has just built a new plant at a cost of $75 000 000. The target return on investment is 10 percent. The standard volume of production for the year is estimated at 15 000 units. The average total cost for each unit is $5000 based on the standard volume of 15 000 units. What is the selling price?

$$\text{Price} = \frac{\text{Investment Costs} \times \text{Target Return on Investment \%}}{\text{Standard Volume}}$$

$$+ \text{Average Total Costs (at Standard Volume/Unit)}$$

$$= \frac{\$75\,000\,000 \times .10}{15\,000} + \$5000$$

$$= \$5500$$

3. Break-Even Pricing

A manufacturer incurs total fixed costs of $180 000. Variable costs are $0.20 per unit. The product sells for $0.80. What is the break-even point in units? In dollars?

$$\text{Break-Even in Units} = \frac{\text{Total Fixed Costs}}{\text{Price} - \text{Variable Costs (per unit)}}$$

$$= \frac{\$210\,000}{\$0.80 - \$0.20}$$

$$= 350\,000$$

$$\text{Break-Even in Dollars} = \frac{\text{Total Fixed Costs}}{1 - \dfrac{\text{Variable Costs (per unit)}}{\text{Price}}}$$

$$= \frac{\$180\,000}{1 - \dfrac{\$0.20}{\$0.80}}$$

$$= \$240\,000$$

TARGET PRICING **Target pricing** is designed to generate a desirable rate of return on investment (ROI) and is based on the full costs of producing a product. For this method to be effective, the firm must have the ability to sell as much as it produces. The major drawback of this method is that demand is not considered. If the quantity produced is not sold at the target price, the objective of the strategy, to achieve a desired level of ROI, is defeated (see Figure 10.7).

BREAK-EVEN ANALYSIS **Break-even analysis** has a greater emphasis on sales than do the other methods, and it allows a firm to assess profit at alternative price levels. Break-even analysis determines the sales in units or dollars that are necessary for total revenue (price × quantity sold) to equal total costs (fixed plus variable costs) at a certain price. The concept is quite simple. If sales are greater than the *break-even point (BEP)*, the firm yields a profit; if the sales are below the BEP, a loss results (see Figures 10.7 and 10.8).

DEMAND-BASED PRICING

As the name suggests, the price that customers will pay influences demand-based pricing the most. In determining price, then, a company can proceed in two directions. One direction is to establish all costs and profit expectations at the point of manufacture, adding appropriate profit margins for various distributors, thus arriving at a retail selling price that hopefully is in line with consumer expectations. This approach is referred to as **chain markup pricing** or **forward pricing**.

The alternative is to work backward by first determining what the consumer will pay at retail. The profit margins for the various distributors are deducted in order to arrive at a total-cost price at the point of manufacture. Hopefully that price will be

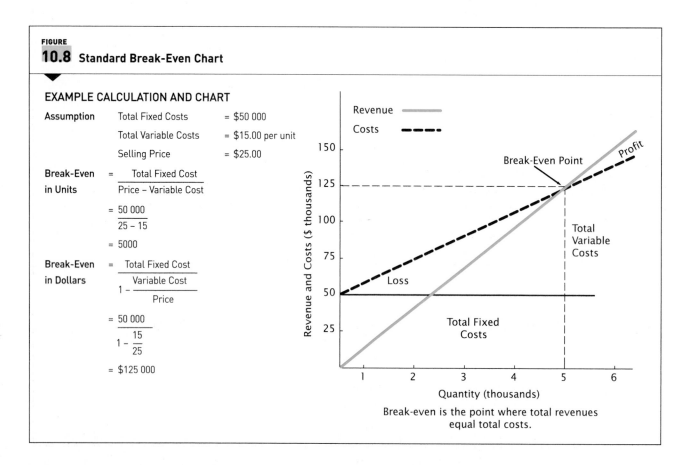

FIGURE 10.8 Standard Break-Even Chart

EXAMPLE CALCULATION AND CHART

Assumption	Total Fixed Costs	= $50 000
	Total Variable Costs	= $15.00 per unit
	Selling Price	= $25.00

$$\text{Break-Even in Units} = \frac{\text{Total Fixed Cost}}{\text{Price} - \text{Variable Cost}}$$

$$= \frac{50\ 000}{25 - 15}$$

$$= 5000$$

$$\text{Break-Even in Dollars} = \frac{\text{Total Fixed Cost}}{1 - \dfrac{\text{Variable Cost}}{\text{Price}}}$$

$$= \frac{50\ 000}{1 - \dfrac{15}{25}}$$

$$= \$125\ 000$$

Break-even is the point where total revenues equal total costs.

sufficient to cover the manufacturer's desired profit margin and costs. If there isn't enough profit the manufacturer will have to find ways of reducing costs or perhaps forgo producing and marketing the product. This approach is referred to as **demand-minus pricing** or **backward pricing**. Examples of these demand-based price calculations are included in Figure 10.9.

demand-minus pricing (backward pricing)

COMPETITIVE BIDDING

Competitive bidding involves two or more firms submitting to a purchaser written price quotations based on specifications established by the purchaser.

competitive bidding

Due to the dynamics of competitive bidding and the size, resources, and objectives of potential bidders, it is difficult to explain how costs and price quotations are arrived at. For example, let us assume that several firms are submitting bids for the opportunity to construct a new building. There could be great variation among price quotations if one firm considers all its costs and then adds a profit margin, while another firm sets its price at the break-even point. The objectives of firms submitting bids differ: some businesses simply want to win the contract, while others expect to earn a certain profit. Thus, if a firm builds a high profit margin into its bid, the likelihood of its being accepted by the purchaser diminishes.

FIGURE 10.9 Demand-Based Pricing Methods

1. Demand-Minus Pricing (Backward Pricing)

A CD and tape distributor has determined that people are willing to spend $30.00 for a three-CD/tape set of classic rock 'n' roll tunes. The company estimates that marketing expenses and profits will be 40 percent of the selling price. How much can the firm spend producing the CDs and tapes?

Product Cost
= Price × [(100 − Markup %)/100]
= $30.00 × [(100 − 40)/100]
= $30.00 × (60/100)
= $18.00

2. Chain Markup Pricing (Forward Pricing)

A manufacturer of blue jeans has determined that their total costs are $20.00 per pair of jeans. The company sells the jeans through wholesalers who in turn sell to retailers. The wholesaler requires a markup of 20 percent and the retailer requires 40 percent. The manufacturer needs a markup of 25 percent. What price will the wholesaler and retailer pay? What is the selling price at retail?

a) Manufacturer's Cost and Selling Price
= $20.00 + 25% Markup
= $20.00 + $5.00
= $25.00

b) Wholesaler's Cost and Selling Price
= Manufacturer's Selling Price + 20% Markup
= $25.00 + $5.00
= $30.00

c) Retailer's Cost and Selling Price
= Wholesaler's Selling Price + 40%
= $30.00 + $12.00
= $42.00

6. Describe a variety of legal issues that affect pricing strategy.

Competition Act
http://laws.justice.gc.ca/en/C-34

Pricing and the Law

The federal government oversees price activity in Canada through the Competition Act. The act covers many important areas that organizations must be aware of. Ignorance of the law is not a defence in a court of law should a firm find itself violating any rules and regulations. Some of the key legal issues are discussed in this section.

ORDINARY PRICE CLAIMS

A common practice among retailers is to quote sale prices using comparisons with the ordinary selling price of an article. For example, "Save up to 50 percent off the regular price." For the purposes of the law, no person or business shall

> make a materially misleading representation to the public concerning the price at which a product or like products have been, are, or will be ordinarily sold.[3]

The following general test can be used to determine whether an expression is in violation of the law:

> Would the use of the expression lead a reasonable shopper to conclude that the comparison price quoted is that at which the product has been ordinarily sold?[4]

When a comparison price is used to communicate the offer, it should be a recent and relevant price; that is, the price at which the product has normally been sold over an extended period of time. To comply with the law the definition of regular price means that an item must be sold at that price 50 percent of the time in the six months before running a sale advertisement, with 50 percent of the sales volume occurring at the regular price. In 2003, Suzy Shier Inc. agreed to pay a $1 million fine for violating this law. Suzy Shier was deficient in offering (a product) for a sufficient period of time, or having achieved sales in a sufficient volume at regular price, in order to make a claim that (the advertised price) was a sale price.[5]

Retail Council of Canada
www.retailcouncil.org

The Retail Council of Canada is lobbying to have this law changed. It would like to see a law based on time limits rather than sales volume. Their argument is based on the hyper-competitive nature of the current retail market (e.g., the law was written in much less competitive times). As well, consumers are now more accustomed to looking at sale prices than regular prices. The regular price is largely irrelevant to consumers.

For further details about problems associated with retail price strategies, read the Marketing in Action vignette **New Software Pushes New Price Strategy**.

MANUFACTURER'S SUGGESTED LIST PRICE

manufacturer's suggested list price (MSLP)

It is common for manufacturers to suggest that retailers charge a certain price for their products; this amount is called the **manufacturer's suggested list price** (MSLP). Such prices usually allow retailers adequate profit margins, but retailers can charge more or less if they want to. The laws on MSLP are somewhat vague. However, if a retailer has never charged the MSLP but uses it to suggest that a sale price offers a greater saving than it actually does, that retailer has broken the law. In this case, the message is misleading because the retailer has customarily sold the product at another price, a lower price. If both the regular selling price and the MSLP are quoted in a sales message, the intent to mislead is less pronounced.

Manufacturers cannot force distributors to sell goods at the prices they suggest. In 2003 John Deere Limited was ordered to pay via cash rebates totalling $1.1 million to consumers who bought a John Deere 100-series lawn tractor. John Deere was attempting to keep prices for the tractor high even though dealers wanted to sell the tractor for less. No manufacturer can refuse to supply or discriminate against a person (or business) because of its low pricing policy.[6]

MARKETING IN ACTION

New Software Pushes New Price Strategy

Consumers are so accustomed to sale pricing that they don't want to buy an item at regular price. Why do consumers have such an attitude? It has a lot to do with the amount and frequency of sale prices offered by department stores such as Sears, the Bay, and Zellers. To please customers and make a profit, department stores must find a better way of managing markdowns. Otherwise, they will suffer the financial consequences.

Some major retailers are experimenting with sophisticated new software programs to test principles similar to "yield management" pricing, a price strategy that airlines have mastered. For the record, yield management involves charging different prices in order to maximize revenue for a set amount of capacity at any given time. Capacity could mean the number of seats in an airline, theatre, or sports arena. Not everyone pays the same price to attend a hockey game—the trick is to optimize price for each level of seating based on proximity to the ice surface. In the case of an airline, the next time you are on a flight ask the person next to you what they paid for their seat. You'll be amazed at what the difference might be. One of you received a bargain!

With the new software programs, retailers are trying to do the same thing. An item such as a bikini is in demand for only a limited time; as the end of the season approaches, its value to customers plummets. The challenge for the retailer is how to outfox customers who have been willing to wait and wait for a bargain.

Technology is fuelling a new price revolution and it is producing a system that involves highly flexible prices—for everything from mortgages to eBay merchandise. Instead of taking a one-price-fits-all approach, buyers and sellers are meeting in customized marketplaces transformed by technology. Bricks and mortar stores are finding they have to drop prices to match what's available to customers online.

With exploding competition from discounters, specialty stores, and the Internet, department-store markdowns are soaring. Twenty years ago, marked-down goods accounted for about 8 percent of department store sales. Today that figure is closer to 40 percent.

Truthfully, retailers hate markdowns. Discount an item too late, and stores are stuck with truckloads of inventory. Too early, and they lose profits as people snap up bargains prematurely.

The technology, still fairly new and untested, requires detailed and accurate sales data to work well. It involves a highly sophisticated look at historical sales data in order to pinpoint just how long to hold out before a retailer needs to cut a price—and by just how much.

Retailers certainly hope the software programs will solve the markdown problem, but they must realize that it can't solve other retailing problems that are affecting profitability, such as poorly chosen merchandise, intense competition, or a weak economy. It is not the saviour but simply another tool in the war chest.

Adapted from Amy Merrick, "Retailers add markdowns to flexible pricing trend," *Globe and Mail*, August 7, 2001, p. B11.

Elena Rooraid/PhotoEdit Inc.

DOUBLE TICKETING AND BAR CODE PRICE VARIANCES

double ticketing

Double ticketing occurs when more than one price tag appears on an item. When this situation occurs, the product must be sold at the lower price. This provision of the law does not prohibit the practice but requires that the lower of the two prices be collected from consumers.

Double ticketing is now less of a problem as retailers in many industries have moved to bar code pricing and price scanning at the point of sale. Electronic price scanning is efficient, since the labour costs associated with tagging items are eliminated. Incorrect price scanning is now a complaint from customers. A study by the Quebec Office of Consumer Protection, an arm of the provincial government, found that 15.5 percent of items purchased were scanned incorrectly, and virtually all errors were made in favour of retailers. Stores in the study included Canadian Tire, Eaton's, The Bay, Sears, Wal-Mart, and Zellers.[7]

BAIT AND SWITCH

bait and switch

Bait and switch selling is the practice of advertising a bargain price for a product that is not available in reasonable quantity. A customer arrives at a store expecting to buy one product but is directed to another, often at a higher price. If the lack of supplies is beyond the control of the store or agent and this can be proven if challenged, the firm running this advertisement is not liable for penalty. Offering rain cheques is a way to avoid liability. A **rain cheque** guarantees the supply of the original product or a product of comparable quality within a reasonable time to those consumers requesting the product. Bait and switch selling tactics are illegal and any retailer using the practice is subject to heavy fines by the Competition Bureau.

rain cheque

PREDATORY PRICING

predatory pricing

Periodically, an organization employs a pricing strategy that is judged to be unfair because it violates the spirit of competition. One such negative practice is **predatory pricing**, which occurs when a large firm sets an artificially low price in an attempt to undercut all other competitors and place them in a difficult financial position and even drive them out of business.

Wal-Mart is often accused of predatory pricing because of the success of its "everyday low price" policies. In Canada, for example, retailers such as Consumer's Distributing, K-Mart, and Eaton's have all disappeared claiming they could not compete with Wal-Mart. But their failure to compete could be blamed on marketing strategies that go well beyond price competition. In Wal-Mart's defence, the company is simply giving consumers what they want—good value for the money they spend. It's nothing more than a competitive price situation.

Wal-Mart also faces some predatory price allegations in the Unites States. Wal-Mart currently accounts for one in every four dollars spent on toys, and this is placing financial hardship on all kinds of independent toy retailers as well as Toys "R" Us, a huge national toy retailer. Toys "R" Us is struggling to compete with Wal-Mart and has stated it might sell its 1200 toy stores worldwide before financial disaster sets in. It is speculated that potential buyers may be non–toy retailers, including Wal-Mart.[8] Could this be a case of predatory pricing?

Regardless of the situation, even though predatory pricing is against the law it is very difficult to prove legally and would be a very expensive undertaking for any company to pursue. Statistics from the Federal Bureau of Competition Policy show that from 550 complaints lodged by Canadian businesses, there were only 23 formal investigations, 3 cases going to court, and 1 conviction. To get a conviction, the Competition

Bureau must establish that prices are unreasonably low, as well as prove that the company had an explicit policy of using predatory pricing to eliminate competition. While the law acts as a deterrent, it does not shield companies from competitors able to set lower prices because they are genuinely more efficient.[9]

Companies that fail to compete soon fall by the wayside. Price, like quality, is simply one of the levels on which businesses compete. Canada is a free market. Shouldn't companies be able to price their products wherever they want?

PRICE FIXING

Price fixing refers to competitors banding together (conspiring) to raise, lower, or stabilize prices. While such a practice is common and relatively easy to implement, it is illegal under the Competition Act. Price fixing usually occurs in markets where price is the most important variable in the marketing mix. When implemented, there is an agreement between the participants that, if followed, will result in benefit for them all. As mentioned earlier in the chapter, oil and gasoline companies are often accused of price fixing as prices at the pump are perceived to increase by all firms simultaneously. Despite the perception, such charges have not been found to be true.

To discourage price fixing, the anti-conspiracy provisions of the Competition Act are clear—companies and their executives are accountable for illegal actions and could face stiff fines and jail terms if charged and found guilty. To illustrate, Toyota Canada Inc. has agreed to give $2.3 million to charity as part of a Competition Bureau investigation of its Access Toyota one-price selling system. Toyota did not admit it was guilty and the Competition Bureau did not find the company guilty. However, aspects of the one-price selling program would have been illegal had the program continued. In the Access pricing system dealers in a region would gather to set a price based on transactions and market knowledge. This led to significant price variations for the same model in various cities and regions of Canada and prices that were higher than in areas where customers could still negotiate a price.[10]

Alternative Pricing Strategies

BARTERING

A growing practice among many companies is the use of bartering. While bartering has been around for a long time, companies are beginning to realize that there are other ways of exchanging goods and services. Bartering is the practice of exchanging goods and services for other goods and services rather than for money. **Bartering** involves reciprocal agreements between two or more companies in the exchange of goods and services they provide each other. Companies prominent in the bartering business include Barter Business Exchange, Barter Connection Inc., and Nationwide Barter Corp. These companies act as commissioned brokers for thousands of companies that want to exchange goods by bartering.

Companies involved in bartering see numerous advantages: it conserves cash flow, increases market exposure, and offers an opportunity to enhance sales with clients who would not otherwise purchase products. For small businesses, where cash flow is a concern, bartering represents great opportunity. Essentially, there are two types of bartering systems: retail barter exchanges and corporate barter companies. In a **retail barter exchange**, small companies trade products and services among themselves, with each company paying the barter exchange a transaction fee. In contrast, a **corporate barter company** takes possession of the goods and attempts to redistribute them among exchange members. The barter exchange takes a commission between 3 and 5 percent, generally from both the buyer and the seller.

price fixing

bartering

retail barter exchange

corporate barter company

In a bartering environment, companies pay an initiation fee to sign on with an exchange, at which point they are granted access to the range of offerings being tendered by other members. Participants receive credits for the goods and services they offer, which they use to purchase what they want from other participants. Traditionally, brokers employed by the barter exchange helped arrange deals. The bulk of commercial barter still goes through brokers, but a growing number of items are listed online, and a small but growing share of all barter is done entirely online. A Canadian entrant in this field is Unibax (Unibax.com), operated by GWC Online Systems Inc. Unibax has developed an international, multilingual, online barter exchange that allows someone to trade with companies throughout the world.[11]

ONLINE AUCTIONS

auction

The Internet is the new arena for auctions. An **auction** is a method of sale whereby an object for sale is secured by the highest bidder. On the Internet, the online auction operates on the same principle. Online auctions are operated in several environments: business-to-business, business-to-consumer, and consumer-to-consumer.

In business-to-business situations, online bidding has the effect of widening the supplier pool for a good or service. In bidding for contracts, the lowest price is often the winning price. So, in theory, if there is lots of bidding prices should be lower. In business-to-consumer markets and consumer-to-consumer markets, consumers compete against one another to drive up the price for the auctioned item—in some cases, above the fair market value. Consumers should be aware of regular retail pricing before getting involved with online bidding. eBay.ca is an example of an online auction company (see Figure 10.10).

More details about online pricing are included in Chapter 17.

FIGURE
10.10

An online auction website

These materials have been reproduced with the permission of eBay Inc. COPYRIGHT © EBAY INC. ALL RIGHTS RESERVED.

SUMMARY

Price refers to the exchange value of a good or service in the marketplace. Prices are offered in many different forms, including fares, commissions, interest rates, and fees. In the Canadian economy, an organization's control over price is influenced by the nature of the market it operates in. The four basic markets are pure competition (where no control exists, since prices are controlled by the market), monopolistic competition (where firms have some control, but are mainly directed by the competition), oligopoly (where organizations also have some control but where pricing is directed even more by competition—a sort of follow-the-leader type of approach), and monopoly (where pricing is controlled by governments or some government-designated body).

Three major variables affect a firm's pricing activities: consumer demand for a product; channel members, whose profit margins are considered in a firm's estimation of the final price; and, finally, costs, which affect the ability of a company to produce and market a product that will yield an adequate and reasonable profit margin for the firm and fair prices for customers.

The prices established by an organization are part of an overall marketing strategy that is designed to achieve specific objectives. The three basic pricing objectives are maximizing profit (improving owners' return on investment), maximizing sales volume (improving growth rates and market share), and establishing competitive position (maintaining adequate profit margins so that all companies that sell the product remain satisfied).

Specific methods for calculating price include cost-based pricing, demand-based pricing, and competition-based pricing (competitive bidding). The method a firm uses is chosen according to the nature and degree of competition in the markets it operates in.

Companies must be aware of the laws that affect pricing strategy. Any violation of laws could lead to serious financial consequences. Some areas that are cause for concern include price claims and improper quoting of sale prices, bait and switch tactics, price fixing, double ticketing and bar code price variances, and predatory pricing practices.

A company may also barter its goods and services with goods and services from another company. In the case of bartering, a value is placed on the product or service provided in the exchange. Another new pricing alternative is to offer items for sale by auction. In online auctions, consumers bid against each other and drive the price of the auctioned item up—sometimes higher than its fair value.

KEY TERMS

auction   266
bait and switch   264
bartering   265
break-even analysis   260
chain markup pricing (forward pricing)   260
competitive bidding   261
competitive pricing   256
corporate barter company   265
cost reductions   254
cost-based pricing   257

demand-minus pricing (backward pricing)   261
double ticketing   264
elastic demand   251
fixed costs   257
full-cost pricing   258
inelastic demand   251
law of supply and demand   249
manufacturer's suggested list price (MSLP)   262
monopolistic competition   249
monopoly   251

oligopolistic market   250
predatory pricing   264
price   248
price elasticity of demand   251
price fixing   265
profit maximization   255
pure competition   249
rain cheque   264
retail barter exchange   265
sales volume maximization   255
target pricing   260
variable costs   258

1. Briefly explain how operating in (a) an oligopoly and (b) a monopolistic competition market affects the pricing activity of an organization.
2. What are the differences between elastic demand and inelastic demand?
3. What is the difference between a profit maximization pricing objective and a sales volume maximization pricing objective?
4. Briefly describe the importance of the competition to a firm's pricing strategy.
5. Explain the concept of competitive pricing. Provide some new examples of companies or brands that practise "above competitor" pricing and "below competitor" pricing.
6. Explain the difference between fixed and variable costs.
7. What is the difference between demand-minus (backward) pricing and chain markup pricing?
8. Briefly explain the usefulness of break-even analysis.
9. In terms of pricing, explain the tactics of bait and switch.
10. What is predatory pricing?
11. Briefly explain the concept of bartering.

1. Given the following information, calculate the unit price, using the cost-plus pricing method:

   Fixed Costs = $350 000
   Variable Costs = $65.00 per unit of production
   Profit Objective = $29 500 based on a production level of 600 units

2. Calculate the break-even point in units and dollars, given the following information:

   Fixed Costs = $300 000
   Variable Costs = $0.75 per unit
   Selling Price = $2.50 per unit

3. A book publisher determines that the consumer will pay $29.95 for a reprint of a classic bestseller. It estimates that marketing expenses and profit margin will consume 60 percent of the selling price. Using the demand-minus pricing method, calculate how much the publisher can spend on producing the book.

4. Visit a few fast-food restaurants in your area (e.g., McDonald's, Burger King, Wendy's) and assess from the menu the pricing strategies that each restaurant offers. Briefly analyze the pricing strategies for effectiveness. Are their strategies appropriate? Are there other pricing strategies that they should consider?

5. Ace Manufacturing produces refrigerators. The fixed costs amount to $250 000, and the variable costs are $175 for each unit produced. The company would like to make a profit of $20 000 on the production of 200 units. What selling price must the company charge?

6. A manufacturer has total fixed costs of $54 000. Variable costs are $2.50 per unit. The product sells for $8.00. What is the break-even point in units?

7. A manufacturer of dress belts estimates that consumers will pay $22.00 for its belts. The company sells the belts through wholesalers that in turn sell to retailers. The manufacturer takes a markup of 25 percent in selling to wholesalers, and the wholesalers take a markup of 15 percent in selling to retailers. What price will the wholesalers and retailers pay for the belts? Use the chain markup pricing method to arrive at a solution.

8. A manufacturer produces blank videotapes for $1.50. It adds a 60-percent markup on cost to establish a selling price to wholesalers. Wholesalers then add a 40-percent markup in setting the price that retailers will pay. If the retailer charges consumers $4.99 for the blank videotapes, what will its markup be?

9. The Baltic Manufacturing Company built a new plant at a cost of $12 500 000. Its target return on investment is 15 percent. The standard volume of production for the year is 25 000 units. The average total cost of each unit is $500, based on the standard volume of 25 000 units. What is the selling price? Use the target-pricing formula to arrive at a solution.

10. Rather than increase prices year after year, many firms are evaluating cost-reduction alternatives. Conduct some secondary research and provide some new examples of companies and brands that are following a cost-reduction strategy. What are the risks associated with this strategy?

E-ASSIGNMENT

In this assignment, you will be doing some comparative shopping. Your goal is to make a rational buying decision based on all the information you uncover. You have decided that you would like to buy a new car in the $15 000 to $20 000 price range—some kind of entry-level car. You have also decided that you want a Japanese car. From the Yahoo! website, request a search for online auctions. When you arrive at the auction page, click on "Automotive Auction." On the next page, click on "Yahoo! Autos." Now you can begin to compare some makes and models. Plug in the makes from the menu and select the price range. On the basis of the information you have found, what car will you buy? Why? What are the benefits and drawbacks of buying a car online? If you wish, repeat the exercise using another online service.

ENDNOTES

1. Ian Karleff, "Food makers choking on rising costs," *Financial Post*, April 7, 2004, pp. IN1, IN2.

2. Stuart Laidlaw, "Makers shrinking products to expand their bottom line," *Toronto Star*, December 4, 2001, pp. D1, D11.

3. Practices Branch, Consumer and Corporate Affairs Canada, *Misleading Advertising Bulletin*, 1984, p. 34.

4. Ibid.

5. Marina Strauss, "Forzani probed on sales policy," *Globe and Mail*, January 8, 2004, pp. B1, B6.

6. "Consumers to Be Reimbursed by John Deere Limited—Competition Bureau Settlement Results in $1.19 Million in Rebates," press release, October 19, 2004, Industry Canada, www.ic.gc.ca.

7. Zena Olijnyk, "Wal-Mart finishes first in scanner test," *Financial Post*, November 26, 1998, p. C1.

8. Lauren Foster, "Trouble in toyland," *Financial Post*, September 20, 2004, p. FP16.

9. John Geddes, "The dilemma of predatory pricing," *Financial Post*, September 23, 1991, p. 3.

10. Greg Keenan, "Competition Bureau orders Toyota Canada to revamp pricing," *Globe and Mail*, March 29, 2003, p. B3.

11. Grant Buckler, "Tough times boost barter," *Globe and Mail*, September 27, 2002, p. B15.

Alan Marsh/firstlight.ca

Steven Senne/CP Photo Archive

CHAPTER

11

Price Management

After studying this chapter, you will be able to

1. Describe the various pricing policies practised by Canadian marketing organizations.

2. Outline the various discounts and allowances offered to customers by marketing organizations.

3. Characterize the alternative pricing strategies used in the course of the product life cycle.

4. Explain the role and benefits of leasing as a pricing strategy in the marketplace.

This chapter will focus on the management of pricing activity. The various pricing policies a firm may adopt are discussed, and the types of discounts that are commonly offered in the marketplace are explained. The influence of the product life cycle on price management is also presented. Discussion in this area centres on the pricing of new products and the pricing changes that are implemented throughout the product life cycle. Finally, the use of leasing as an alternative to selling goods is examined.

Pricing Policies

Pricing policies are the basic rules about pricing that enable a firm to achieve its marketing objectives. The policy options available are classified into four primary categories: psychological pricing, promotional pricing, geographic pricing, and flexible pricing. A firm may use one or any combination of these price policies, depending on the objectives established for the product or the nature of the market that the product competes in.

1. Describe the various pricing policies practised by Canadian marketing organizations.

PSYCHOLOGICAL PRICING

In the case of **psychological pricing**, the organization appeals to tendencies in consumer behaviour other than rational ones. It is a practice used more often by retailers than by manufacturers. Psychological pricing influences the purchasing patterns of the final consumer. There are several types of psychological pricing strategies, as described below.

psychological pricing

PRESTIGE PRICING **Prestige pricing** is the practice of setting prices high to give the impression that the product is of high quality. This practice is strongly associated with luxury goods. The fact that the price is high contributes to the image of the product and the status of the buyer. For example, there is a chronic one-year waiting list for the Porsche 911 turbo in Canada even though the price starts at $135 000. The pursuit of prestige is quite expensive, it seems, but buyers of these cars don't seem to care. To purchase a limited-edition Ferrari Enzo, a customer must submit an application that is vetted by head office in Italy. Ferrari carefully gauges suitability of ownership of its vehicles—now *that's* prestige! No need to inquire about price here![1] Refer to Figure 11.1 for an illustration

prestige pricing

ODD–EVEN PRICING For psychological reasons, an odd number is more effective with consumers than a rounded-off number. Thus, a colour television is priced at $499 because it is then not perceived as costing $500. Research has shown that consumers register and remember the first digit more clearly than they do subsequent ones (in this case the 4, which puts the price in the $400 range).[2] Setting prices below even-dollar

PEOPLE DO NOT DECIDE TO
BECOME EXTRAORDINARY.
THEY DECIDE TO ACCOMPLISH
EXTRAORDINARY THINGS.

On May 29, 1953, at 11:30 a.m., Sir Edmund Hillary and Sherpa Tenzing Norgay became the first men to stand on the summit of Mt. Everest. But the top of the mountain was just the beginning of Sir Edmund's journey. More than half a century later, his perpetual pursuit of things once imagined has resulted in the construction of schools, hospitals, medical clinics, bridges and freshwater pipelines for the people of the Himalayas. He may have left his footprint on a mountain, but he put his indelible imprint on the world. Proving once again that some people are simply destined to rise to the top.

OYSTER PERPETUAL EXPLORER · WWW.ROLEX.COM

ROLEX

For the name and address of your nearest official Rolex jeweller, please contact Rolex Canada Ltd.,
50 St. Clair Avenue West, Toronto, Ontario M4V 3B7, 416-968-1100

Courtesy of Rolex

amounts is called **odd–even pricing**. It is popular with retailers and explains the widespread use of such prices as $19.95, $99.95, and $199.95. The sales tax in most provinces and the Goods and Services Tax (GST) put the price into the next range—over the "even barrier"—but do not have a major influence on purchases because consumers are accustomed to these mandatory additions to most of the items they purchase.

The number 9 seems to play a key role in odd–even pricing. To illustrate its strength, consider the case of an association that was marketing a book but didn't know the exact price to charge. Price points of $23, $25, $27, and $29 were tested. To the delight of the association, the $29 price point got the highest response. Consumers simply didn't perceive a difference between $23 and $29. Studies have shown that prices ending in "9" can be more attractive to buyers than lower numbers within the same range.[3]

PRICE LINING   **Price lining** refers to the adoption of price points for the various lines of merchandise a retailer carries. Thus, in the case of a clothing store, the retailer establishes a limited number of prices for selected lines of products rather than pricing the items individually. For instance, price ranges for business suits could be set in the $300 range ($399), the $500 range ($599), and the $700 range ($799). Customers entering the store are directed to the assortment of suits that fall within their price range, once it is known. In each range, the retailer may have purchased suits from different suppliers at different costs but is satisfied with an average markup within each price range because it saves the consumer any confusion over price. Assuming the retailer understands the needs and expectations of its customers and how much they are willing to pay, it can establish its price lines (price ranges) accordingly.

CUSTOMARY PRICING   **Customary pricing** is the strategy of matching prices to a buyer's expectations; the price reflects tradition or is a price that people are accustomed to paying. For example, chocolate bars of average size and weight are expected to have the same price, regardless of the different brand names. Other examples are the prices of daily newspapers, which increase only marginally from time to time, and transit fares for buses and subways. In the candy business, consumers started some years ago to balk at the continual price increases of chocolate bars, and the industry was faced with flat sales. As an alternative to increasing price, manufacturers decided to shrink the product by reducing the weight of the bars. This option was more acceptable than raising the price—and less fattening! The concept of cost reductions was discussed in Chapter 10.

customary pricing

UNIT PRICING   **Unit pricing** is a policy adopted by retailers, particularly grocery retailers, of listing the cost per standard unit of a product to let shoppers compare the prices of similar products packaged in different quantities. Typically, posting bar code price tags on shelf facings does this. The bar codes allow consumers to determine per-gram prices in different-sized containers. In the case of food items, a shelf sticker states the retail price, the size or weight of the item, and the cost per unit of measurement (e.g., cost per gram, cost per millilitre). Although unit prices were originally designed to assist low-income groups, research has shown that well-educated income groups of the middle and upper-middle classes refer to them most often.[4] With consumers being very value-conscious today, comparison shopping has become more common than ever before. Unit pricing in retail stores facilitates brand comparisons. The shopper gets to see which brand offers the best value without having to do the math.

unit pricing

PROMOTIONAL PRICING

Promotional pricing is defined as the lowering of prices temporarily to attract customers (i.e., offering sale prices). In a retail environment, the objective of this practice is to attract people to (build consumer traffic in) the store; retailers know that while the customers are in the store, they could purchase other merchandise at regular prices. Common types of promotional pricing used by retailers include loss leaders and multiple-unit pricing strategies.

promotional pricing

Loss leaders are products offered for sale at or slightly below cost. The consumer recognizes the item as a true bargain and is attracted to a store by the offer. Honest Ed's department store in downtown Toronto is famous for daily "door-crasher" specials. So successful are these door crashers that people line up hours before the store opens to get a shot at the specials, a phenomenon that occurs with unusual regularity.

loss leaders

When **multiple-unit pricing** is followed, items are offered for sale in multiples (pairs are quite common), usually at a price below the combined regular price of each item. Such a practice is quite common when selling goods in supermarkets and discount department stores. Stores such as Safeway, Super Value, Sobeys, and A&P offer such

multiple-unit pricing

deals in their weekly flyers (e.g., soup at 2/$0.99). Other variations include such deals as "two for the price of one" specials or "buy one get one free" or "buy one at regular price and get the second at half price." These types of offers are more frequent in other segments of the retailing industry, such as clothing and hardware stores.

In a manufacturing environment, companies offer a variety of price incentives to attract new users (often users who purchase competing brands). For example, when branded items are on sale in a supermarket or drugstore, it is likely the result of a discount being offered to the retailer by the manufacturer of the product. These price incentives may also be used to place ads in retail advertising flyers (about sale prices) and to encourage displays in the stores. They are designed to build sales of the item in the short term. (For more information, see the section on "Source Pricing and Offering Discounts" in this chapter.)

GEOGRAPHIC PRICING

geographic pricing

Geographic pricing is a pricing strategy based on the answer to the question, "Who is paying the freight?" Does the seller pay the freight costs of delivering the merchandise to the buyer, or does the buyer absorb these charges? Are freight charges averaged to all customers and included in the price? These are geographic pricing questions, and their answers are largely based on the practices of the industry in which the firm operates. In some industries the seller customarily pays, while in others the buyer generally pays. A choice by a seller not to pay the costs in an industry where the sellers usually do pay would have an adverse effect on sales, even though the product might otherwise be the preferred choice. Several geographic pricing possibilities exist, including F.O.B. pricing (free-on-board pricing), uniform delivered pricing, and zone pricing (Figure 11.2).

F.O.B. PRICING   Under this classification are two subcategories for pricing based on who pays the freight.

F.O.B. origin

F.O.B. Origin (Plant)   In an **F.O.B. origin** arrangement, the seller quotes a price that does not include freight charges. The buyer pays the freight and assumes title (ownership) of the merchandise when it is loaded onto a common carrier—a truck, a train, or an airplane. This practice is satisfactory to local customers, but distant customers are disadvantaged. Under such a pricing system, a customer in Vancouver would pay much more for merchandise shipped from Montreal than would a customer in Toronto.

F.O.B. destination

F.O.B. Destination (Freight Absorption)   To counter the impression that distant customers are being penalized, the seller under the terms of **F.O.B. destination** agrees to pay all freight charges. How much of the charges the seller actually absorbs is questionable,

FIGURE
11.2

Who Pays the Freight?

F.O.B. Origin, or Plant	*Buyer*	The buyer takes title when the product is on a common carrier (e.g., a truck).
F.O.B. Destination, or Freight Absorption	*Seller*	The seller pays all freight necessary to reach a stated destination.
Uniform Delivered Price	*Buyer*	The buyer's price includes an average freight cost that all customers pay regardless of location.
Zone Pricing	*Buyer*	All customers within a designated geographic area pay the same freight cost.

however, since the freight costs are built into the price that the buyer is charged. In any event, the title does not transfer to the buyer until the goods arrive at their destination— the buyer's warehouse. Such a strategy is effective in attracting new customers in distant locations.

UNIFORM DELIVERED PRICING   In the case of **uniform delivered pricing**, the price includes an average freight charge for all customers regardless of their location. To develop a uniform delivered price, a firm calculates the average freight cost of sending goods to the various locations of its customers. This practice is more attractive to distant customers than to nearby customers, who pay more than they would under a different pricing system. Local customers pay **phantom freight**, or the amount by which average transportation charges exceed the actual cost of shipping for customers near the source of supply.

ZONE PRICING   In the case of **zone pricing**, the market is divided into geographic zones and a uniform delivered price is established for each zone. For these purposes, the Canadian market is easily divided into geographic zones: the Atlantic Provinces, Quebec, Ontario, the Prairies, British Columbia, and the Territories. Each of these zones may be subdivided further. The Ontario zone could be divided into Northern Ontario, Eastern Ontario, South-Central Ontario, and Southwestern Ontario. For an illustration of geographic pricing strategies and calculations, see Figure 11.3. Air freight carriers, such as Federal Express and UPS, use zone pricing. The distance a parcel travels determines the rate charged. For example, one price is charged for 0 to 599 kilometres, another for 600 to 1199, and so on.

FLEXIBLE PRICING

Flexible pricing means charging different customers different prices. While such a practice initially seems unfair, its actual effect is to allow buyers to negotiate a lower price than that asked by the sellers. It means that the price is open to negotiation. Such negotiations are typical in the purchase of something expensive, say a house or an automobile. In the case of a house purchase, the buyer submits an "offer" and then back-and-forth negotiations begin. In the case of a purchase of a car, negotiations are commonly referred to as "dickering." The salesperson and the buyer dicker back and forth until a mutually agreeable price is arrived at, usually a price well below the sticker price.

According to the Automobile Protection Association, price dickering is one of the most hated aspects of buying a new car. It is an unpleasant experience and a major reason why people resist buying. Both manufacturers and car dealers are taking steps to remedy the situation. The Saturn subsidiary of General Motors, for example, does not negotiate prices. The price is set and that's what the customer pays. Consumers are also finding a higher level of comfort by buying an automobile online.

PRODUCT MIX PRICING

When a product is part of a larger product mix, setting prices is more difficult. The goal in this situation is to set prices so that profits are maximized for the total mix. Some products may be priced low while others are high. On balance, profit objectives are achieved and customers are generally satisfied with the price they pay.

Product mix pricing embraces the following situations.

Optional-Feature Pricing   This involves offering additional products, features, and services along with the main product. Specific option packages are often offered with local phone plans. As more options are added, the price of the plan will increase.

uniform delivered pricing

phantom freight

zone pricing

flexible pricing

FIGURE 11.3 Geographic Pricing Strategies

F.O.B.	Maritimes	Quebec	Ontario	Prairies	B.C.
F.O.B. Origin (Toronto)	$10.00	$10.00	$10.00	$10.00	$10.00
Add: Profit Margin and Freight to Each Customer	2.75	1.75	1.10	2.00	3.25
Customer Pays	12.75	11.75	11.10	12.00	13.25

Uniform Delivered Price:

	Maritimes	Quebec	Ontario	Prairies	B.C.
Zone Price	16.50	15.50	15.00	16.50	17.00
Multiply by: Volume Importance of Each Region	5%	25%	40%	15%	15%

Uniform Delivered Price $15.72

Zone Price:

	Maritimes	Quebec	Ontario	Prairies	B.C.
F.O.B. Origin (Toronto)	$10.00	$10.00	$10.00	$10.00	$10.00
Add: Profit Margin (40%)	4.00	4.00	4.00	4.00	4.00
	14.00	14.00	14.00	14.00	14.00
Add: Average Freight to Each Region	2.50	1.50	1.00	2.50	3.00
Zone Price for Each Customer	16.50	15.50	15.00	16.50	17.00

Product-Line Pricing   Companies normally develop product lines rather than single products. For example, Sony offers flat-screen televisions in various sizes: 27-inch, 31-inch, 35-inch and so on. Corresponding prices might be $699, $899, and $1099.

Captive-Product Pricing   Some products require the use of ancillary—or captive—products. If so, a company must price the captive product appropriately in order to encourage use. Rogers Communications or Bell Mobility may sell a telephone at a relatively low price to attract customers and perhaps not make any money. They will make their money from the monthly fees and on the frequency with which the customer uses the phone.

Fixed-Variable Pricing   Service firms commonly offer two-part pricing consisting of a fixed fee plus a variable usage fee. Fees charged for basic and long distance telephone service by firms such as Bell work this way, as do fees for companies providing Internet access. In the case of Internet access the base fee is for a certain number of hours with additional charges for extra hours.

Product-Bundling Pricing   In this situation the seller bundles its products and features at a set price. Both Bell and Rogers Communications practise this option when selling their digital bundles. Bell, for example, offers Sympatico, ExpressVu, and Mobility in one bundle. When the price of this bundle is compared to other bundles (two options only) it looks very enticing to potential customers. And that's the idea! Refer to Figure 11.4 for an illustration.

Source Pricing and Offering Discounts

Part of price management involves offering discounts to customers. The firm first establishes a **list price**, which is the rate normally quoted to potential buyers. Then, a host of discounts and allowances that provide savings off the list price are commonly offered to customers. In effect, price discounts and allowances become part of the firm's promotional plans for dealing with trade customers—wholesalers, for example—who, in turn, pass on all or some of the savings to the retailers they supply. Very often, it is the combination of allowances that convinces customers to buy in large volumes. In business buying situations, the buyer rarely pays the list price. Typically, a buyer is eligible for some of the discounts given by a manufacturer. Various types of discounts exist.

list price

FIGURE

11.4

Bell bundles its digital services to attract potential customers

Pick the right match. Get the right bundle.

Digital Bundle

Sympatico + Mobility	Sympatico + ExpressVu	ExpressVu + Mobility	Sympatico + ExpressVu + Mobility
Bundle price from	Bundle price from	Bundle price from	Bundle price from
$54.95/mo.	$59.95/mo.	$64.95/mo.	$89.95/mo.
Save $10.00/mo.	Save $9.98/mo.	Save $10.03/mo.	Save $14.98/mo.

No matter which **Digital Bundle** from Bell* you decide on, and how you choose to customize it, your savings are guaranteed every month. Starting with a $25 bill credit for each new service.**

Create your own bundle. They're flexible. Choose from a selection of services from **Mobility**, **Sympatico**™ or **ExpressVu**™. It's up to you. Plus, it's all on one bill.♦ Simple. Easy.

Limited-time
$25
credit on each
new service

Call **1 888 268-8588**
Visit **www.bell.ca/bundle4**
or a **Bell World** store

Bell is a proud sponsor of
the Canadian Olympic team.

Bell
Making it simple.™

*Bell services are available to residential customers where access and technology permit. To be eligible for the Digital Bundle from Bell, you must be a Bell Canada long distance subscriber. Customers who do not subscribe to Bell Canada's local service or other tariffed services are eligible for the Digital Bundle from Bell. Minimum 24-month contract required for each service. Purchase and professional installation fees for the ExpressVu system may apply. Early termination fees apply. Taxes extra. The Digital Bundle is only available with selected ExpressVu, Mobility and Sympatico services and programming plans. Other conditions and restrictions apply. Visit www.bell.ca/bundle or call 1 866 802-0601 to find out if you are eligible for the Digital Bundle from Bell and for full details. Prices/offer subject to change/cancellation without notice. **Offer ends July 10, 2004, and is available only to Digital Bundle subscribers who subscribe to and activate new, eligible Digital Bundle services. $25 credit will be applied towards the rates and charges for the new, activated service and will appear on your monthly invoice 6 to 8 weeks after activation of the applicable service, which must occur no later than July 31, 2004. ♦One Bill does not include services from Mobility. ♥Savings based on a price comparison with the full current rates/charges for the same applicable services if subscribed to individually. Sympatico is a trade-mark of Bell Canada; ExpressVu is a trade-mark of Bell ExpressVu, L.P.

® Official Mark of the Canadian Olympic Committee   BUND3-GNM

CASH DISCOUNTS

cash discounts

Cash discounts are granted when a bill is paid promptly, within a stated period. An example is "2/10, net 30." In this case, the buyer may deduct 2 percent from the invoice price if the charge is paid within 10 days of receipt of the invoice. The account is due and payable within 30 days at invoice price. While this discount appears to be small, it adds up to considerable savings for such mass merchandisers as Canadian Tire, Wal-Mart, and The Bay.

QUANTITY DISCOUNTS

quantity discounts

Quantity discounts are offered on the basis of volume purchased in units or dollars and can be offered non-cumulatively (i.e., during a special sale period only) or cumulatively (i.e., so that they apply to all purchases over an extended period, say, a year). Normally, eligible purchases are recorded in an invoicing system, and a cheque from the supplier is issued to cover the value of the discounts earned by the buyer at the end of the discount period. Refer to Figure 11.5 for an illustration of a quantity discount schedule.

The supplier establishes quantity discounts but they are sometimes negotiable. For example, Holiday Inn or any other major hotel chain may offer corporations a 25-percent discount if they commit to 5000 room nights a year (the total number of rooms booked by all employees). If Holiday Inn is anxious to attract new business it may offer a slightly higher discount to get the business. On the other hand, smart buyers who know that Holiday Inn may have lots of empty rooms may use such knowledge to negotiate a better discount. It is common for a corporation to pool the travel of employees in all subsidiaries in order to earn a better discount.

TRADE OR FUNCTIONAL DISCOUNTS

There are several types of trade discounts.

slotting allowance

SLOTTING ALLOWANCES   A **slotting allowance** is a discount offered by a supplier to a retail distributor for the purpose of securing shelf space in retail outlets. These allowances are commonly offered with the introduction of new products. Since shelf space is scarce, it is often difficult to motivate distributors to carry new products. Given the number of new products that are introduced each year, retailers can be selective and are more receptive to suppliers that offer discounts to help defray the costs associated with getting a new product into their system (e.g., warehousing costs, computer costs, and redesigning store shelf sections).

The practice of offering and accepting slotting allowances is a controversial issue. Critics argue that such a practice puts small suppliers at a disadvantage, since they cannot afford them, and therefore getting a new product into distribution is difficult for

FIGURE 11.5

A Quantity Discount Schedule

Schedule Based on Volume Purchased over One Year

Volume		Discount
Units	Dollars	
100–1000	200 000–2 000 000	10%
1001–2000	2 000 001–4 000 000	15%
2001–3000	4 000 001–6 000 000	20%
3001–4000	6 000 001–8 000 000	25%

them. Large suppliers do not necessarily like to offer these allowances, but since retailers have control in most markets (oligopolies exist in most cases) over the channel of distribution, the alternatives are few if guaranteed distribution is the goal.

OFF-INVOICE TRADE ALLOWANCES An **off-invoice allowance** is a temporary allowance applicable during a specified time period and is deducted from the invoice at the time of customer billing. The invoice indicates the regular list price, the amount of the discount, and the volume purchased. Consider the following example:

Product (24 units in case)	$36.00 per case
Off-Invoice Allowance	$7.20 per case
Net Price	$28.80 per case
Volume Purchased	10 cases
Amount Due	$288.00
Terms	2/10, Net 30

off-invoice allowance

Manufacturers offer an off-invoice allowance to distributors as an incentive to purchase in greater volume in the short term, and to encourage distributors to pass on the savings to their customers. In the example above, as much as $0.30 per unit ($7.20/24 units) could be passed on. Instead of allowing for such discounts on the invoice, a manufacturer sometimes offers them on the basis of a **bill-back**, in which case the manufacturer keeps a record of the volume purchased by each customer and issues cheques at a later date to cover the allowances earned over the term of the offer.

bill-back

PERFORMANCE (PROMOTIONAL) ALLOWANCES A **performance allowance** is a price discount given by a manufacturer to a distributor that performs a promotional function on the manufacturer's behalf. These discounts are frequently made available in conjunction with off-invoice allowances. When the discounts are combined, a wholesaler that purchases in larger volumes will achieve greater savings. The performances that qualify for the allowances may take some or all of the following forms:

performance allowance

1. There is guaranteed product distribution to all stores served by the distributor (e.g., Canadian Tire or Loblaws agrees to ship a certain quantity of the product to each of its stores in a certain region), rather than a system whereby the distributor waits for individual stores to place orders.
2. In-store displays are set in a prominent location (see Figure 11.6).
3. The product is mentioned in retail advertising flyers or in newspaper advertisements that announce weekly specials.

Performance allowances are usually negotiated between a manufacturer and a distributor, and an agreement is signed. The distributor is paid on proof of performance at the end of the term of the offer. Refer to Figure 11.7 for an illustration of promotional discount calculations that a manufacturer may use to promote its product and of their effect on the price customers pay.

SEASONAL DISCOUNTS

Seasonal discounts apply to off-season or pre-season purchases. They are typical of products and services that sell strongly only in a certain season or during certain times. For example, downtown hotels are busy during the week with business travellers but require family package plans to attract customers on weekends. Summer resorts and vacation retreats often offer 20- to 30-percent discounts before and after their prime season. Television viewing is much lower in the summer months. Therefore, networks such as CTV and CBC offer discounted rates to advertisers during this period.

seasonal discounts

FIGURE
11.6

Performance allowances encourage product displays at point of sale

Dick Hemingway

REBATES

rebates

Rebates are temporary price discounts that take the form of a cash return made directly to a consumer, usually by a manufacturer. Periodically, car and appliance manufacturers offer cash rebates to customers who buy their models. Frequently, the rebate program becomes the focal point of advertising campaigns. Such programs are commonly used to reduce inventories or to stimulate sales in traditionally slow selling seasons, or at times when the economy is weak. For more insight into rebates, read the Marketing in Action vignette **Price Incentives: The Crack Cocaine of the Auto Industry** on page 282.

TRADE-IN ALLOWANCES

trade-in allowance

A **trade-in allowance** is a price reduction granted for a new product when a similar used product is turned in. Trade-ins are common in the purchase of automobiles, industrial machinery, and various types of business equipment. If a supplier wanted a company to

FIGURE
11.7

List Price and Discount Calculations

Information:

Cost of Product	$40.00 per case
Trade Discount	$4.00 per case
Quantity Discount	2% for each 100 cases
Performance Allowance	5%
Cash Discount	2/10, n30
Customer Purchases	500 cases

Calculation of Price to Customer:

List Price	$40.00
Less: Trade Discount (10%)	4.00
	36.00
Less: Quantity Discount (2% ×5)	3.60
	32.40
Less: Performance Allowance (5%)	1.62
	30.78
Less: Cash Discount (2%)	.62
Net Price	30.16
Total Discount	9.84
Total Percentage Discount ($9.84/40)	= 24.6 %

trade up to a more sophisticated photocopying machine, that supplier might have to offer a high trade-in value on the buyer's existing equipment. Trade-in allowances are a means of providing customers with a better price without adjusting the list price of the item.

An automobile manufacturer offers rebates, and its dealers offer "trade-ins." In the case of a trade-in, the dealer establishes a value for the customer's current car and deducts this amount from the price negotiated for the new car.

THE LEGALITIES OF OFFERING DISCOUNTS

Marketing organizations must be careful about how they offer discounts and allowances to channel customers. Customers must be treated fairly; that is, if discounts are offered, the same offer must be made to all customers. For example, if cereal is offered at $20 off per case for a four-week period, all customers must receive the discount. In the case of a volume discount, the rate is graduated to accommodate both small and large customers (refer to Figure 11.5). In this situation, a manufacturer, such as Kellogg or General Mills, offers a higher discount to Safeway or Sobeys than it does to a local independent grocer because the national chain stores buy in much greater quantity. Customers are usually categorized by size on the basis of the volume of product purchased from the manufacturer. The volume discount scale is in proportion to the size of each customer or buying group. Discounts of this kind are legal.

Discounts vs. Value Pricing

As stated earlier, a common practice is to quote a list price and then offer a distributor a series of discounts. Typically, the marketing objective of most discounts is to increase sales volume during the period of the discount. Since distributors have so many discounts available from so many suppliers at any given time, it is difficult for distributors to meet the marketing demands of the suppliers. For this reason, manufacturers are rethinking how they offer discounts, while others are moving in another direction entirely. **Value pricing,** or **everyday low pricing** (EDLP), is becoming a popular alternative.

value pricing, or everyday low pricing (EDLP)

Price Incentives: The Crack Cocaine of the Auto Industry

In the automotive industry, price incentives are a huge hit with consumers. They get customers into the showroom and they help keep the industry running from one end to the other. Let's take a closer look at the auto industry and see what the real benefits are. What happens when the incentives are removed? Will the industry come to a grinding halt?

To put things into perspective, economic cycles have a dramatic impact on consumer purchase intentions. As well, North American manufacturers are slowly but steadily losing market share to Japanese and European makes and models. In 2003, for example, sales of domestic automobiles produced by General Motors, Ford, and Chrysler fell 11 percent, while the sales of Japanese models increased 1.2 percent.

One of the ways to combat a decline in sales and loss in market share is to offer incentive packages—including cash-back offers, low- or no-interest financing, and bundling option packages at no extra charge. In recent years these types of programs hit frenzy levels. Cash-back offers as high as $4000 (Ford) and $5000 (General Motors) have been offered. And no-interest financing deals can save buyers between $4000 and $6000 in borrowing costs over four years.

Five years ago, some industry watchers predicted that the road ahead is full of potholes for car companies as they try to wean customers off profit-eroding deals. Their view was simple: incentives could lose their impact and they could ultimately destroy the brand image of a car, an image that has been built over an extended period. These observers were partially right.

Car buyers did take advantage of the program initially, but now consumers are looking more at quality than at price. Consumers seeking quality are looking at the long-term situation (a car lasting five or six years) as opposed to short-term price savings. A company like Toyota has dabbled in the incentives arena but chosen to use it as a strategy of last resort. Their strength is their quality, and that's what brings the people in.

On the other hand, some consumers have grown so accustomed to having rebates that they will postpone purchase until a suitable offer comes their way. These consumers are not brand loyal—they play one manufacturer's offer off against another, and ultimately choose the best deal available. Therefore it's proven to be extraordinarily difficult for domestic carmakers to abandon the strategy, which has been described by some as "the crack cocaine of the auto industry."

So bad is the present situation that some brand-new models were introduced to the market with incentives already on them. "What this does is create a long-term disincentive to ever pay proper retail price for a new vehicle." It seems that the only real winner in this scenario is the consumer.

To sell cars, another solution is needed. Rather than increase prices each year and follow with incentive programs to lower price, the car manufacturers should be looking for cost savings on parts by striking more lucrative contract deals with suppliers. This practice is good in theory, but lowering the quality of parts will affect the overall quality of the vehicle. So that's not a solution either. The other option is to simply build a quality product (as foreign manufacturers do) and charge a fair and reasonable price for it. Car companies are in a tough situation, but it is a situation they have created. Do you have any ideas to correct the problem?

Adapted from Chris Sorensen, "Brands devalued as share erodes," *Financial Post*, August 28, 2004, p. FP4; Richard Bloom, "Incentives blamed for slow car sales," *Globe and Mail*, January 7, 2004, p. B3; and Steve Erwin, "GM reduces incentives—will others follow?" *Driver Source*, April 7, 2002, p. 14.

Dick Hemingway

When a value pricing system is used, the manufacturer or retailer establishes a fair everyday price that is attractive to consumers and profitable for the company. Typically, the price will be lower than a regular price but not as low as a sale price under the discount system. Wal-Mart, for example, uses such a strategy. The price of goods remains constant for long periods of time. In contrast, competitors like Zellers and Sears rely more on sale merchandise to attract shoppers.

The frenzy to be priced right has been driven by Wal-Mart. "The Wal-Mart attitude has worked its way through Canadian society," says Karl Moore, a professor of management strategy at McGill University. Wal-Mart's success at the lower end of the market has forced retailers in the middle to adopt a similar tactic. Sears now keeps its prices for a majority of products at "everyday" price levels. This is a departure from their strategy of using sale prices to attract customers. According to Mark Cohen, CEO of Sears, "35 percent of store sales are pegged to value prices, covering exclusive merchandise and essentials such as underwear." Other stores such as Shoppers Drug Mart and Canadian Tire are following suit.[5]

For the manufacturers of products who supply these retailers, everyday low pricing eliminates the need for short-term price-based promotions. It evens out consumer demand for products and provides an opportunity for a manufacturer to even out production runs, thereby creating efficiencies at the point of manufacture. Such a practice is welcomed by manufacturers such as Kraft and Procter & Gamble, which are accustomed to offering discounts on a regular basis. If they can reduce spending on price discounts the funds saved can be channelled into long-term brand-building opportunities. The manufacturer will have more control over the destiny of its brands.

Prominent retail leaders such as Loblaws (supermarket retailing) and Shoppers Drug Mart (pharmacy retailing) can exercise a lot of control over their suppliers, and they pressure suppliers for deeper and more frequent discounts. Essentially these and other retailers purchase products under a system known as forward buying. **Forward buying** is the practice of buying deal merchandise in quantities sufficient to carry a retailer through to the next deal period offered by the manufacturer. In effect, the retailer never buys goods at the regular price. In such cases, even though the item was bought at a discount it doesn't mean the retail price will be lower for the item. Simply stated, the retailer may pocket the discount—it boosts their profit margin on every item sold!

For additional insight into value pricing, read the Marketing in Action vignette **EDLP and the Sizzle of Sale Prices**.

forward buying

Pricing and the Product Life Cycle

Pricing a new product presents unique challenges for a marketer. Equally challenging is how to adjust prices throughout the life cycle of a product. There are basically two strategies for pricing a new product: skimming and penetration. Which strategy is used depends on the objectives established by the firm at the introduction stage and at subsequent stages of the product life cycle. Generally, higher prices are associated with the early stages, when the firm is trying to recover product-development costs quickly; lower prices are associated with the latter stages, when more competition exists (Figure 11.8). These generalizations are simply guidelines, however. Throughout any given product's life cycle, there could be a lot of experimentation with price.

3. Characterize the alternative pricing strategies used in the course of the product life cycle.

PRICE SKIMMING

A **price-skimming** strategy involves the use of a high price when a product enters the market, which enables a firm to maximize its revenue early. Some of the conditions that encourage the use of a skimming strategy include the following:

price-skimming

EDLP and the Sizzle of Sale Prices

Some critics say Wal-Mart has killed off some venerable Canadian department stores because of its everyday low pricing policy. Other critics say the price competition has been good for Canadians because competitors that are left have had to lower their prices in order to compete. No matter how you look at it, the lower prices are good for customers. And if customers are buying, retailers should be happy.

Wal-Mart has built its empire around its value-oriented pricing policy. As McGill university professor Karl Moore states, "We see the Wal-Martization of the lower-priced end of the market and it drags down the middle segment also." Competitors in the middle segment have reacted and they too are now adopting the value-oriented pricing policy.

Traditionally, Sears and The Bay relied heavily on constant markdowns and scratch-and-save–style promotions to attract customers. They were constantly changing prices and as a result were always incurring additional administration, labour, and marketing costs. Where's the profit? Sears no longer shifts prices up and down. It keeps prices at what it considers a reasonable "everyday" level. This policy is employed on items that are exclusive to Sears and on merchandise that is classified as "essential"—products like underwear and socks. Sears continues with "sale" items as well. After all, if it's out of season, it has to be sold!

At the Hudson's Bay Company, Zellers moved to everyday low prices but retained a "special deal" wrinkle to add a little sizzle to the marketing mix.

Their view is clear: the consumer still likes to think they are getting a good deal. The Bay took a slightly different approach to value pricing. The Bay changed its product mix by bringing in more moderately priced goods and fewer premium priced goods—a wise decision considering the middle-income clientele it serves. Customers who want pricier goods can shop at specialty stores. They were shopping there anyway!

Both Sears and The Bay admit that implementing value pricing has hurt financially in the short term but they see bright prospects in the long term. Everyday low prices allow the retailer to concentrate on its marketing budget and the merchandise it carries rather than worrying about price cuts and price increases. A greater portion of the budget can be allocated to marketing activities that build image and generate more traffic into the stores. Once they are there they get "everyday low prices."

Adapted from Marina Strauss, "Merchants aiming to bag more sales with everyday low prices," *Globe and Mail*, May 2, 2003, p. B9.

Moira Welsh/CP Photo Archive

1. The product is an innovation or is perceived to be significantly better than competing products. Such a situation justifies a higher price.
2. If competing products exist, they are few in number and are generally weak. New products that carry strong and popular brand names face little risk in using a skimming strategy.
3. The product is protected by patent; the resulting lack of direct competition allows a product to recover its development costs quickly by using this strategy.

FIGURE
11.8

**New-Product Pricing
Alternatives**

Price	Skimming	Price Penetration
Strategy	High entry price	Low entry price
Objective	Maximize revenue, and recover research, development, and marketing costs quickly	Gain market acceptance fast, expand the market, and build market share
Suitable Market Characteristics	Inelastic demand and markets where customers are less price sensitive	Elastic demand and markets where customers are price sensitive

A skimming strategy should be used only in cases where the marketing organization has a thorough understanding of the target market's behaviour; that is, they know that price is not a key influence on a purchase. If price is important, a high price will not encourage new buyers to try a product, and the adoption and diffusion process will be slow. A possible hazard of skimming is that competitors who see a product enjoying high profit margins, mainly due to the lack of competition and a skimming pricing strategy, are likely to bring similar products to the market very quickly. Users of a skimming strategy recognize that it is easier to lower prices than it is to raise prices during the life cycle of a product.

To illustrate the concept of price skimming, consider Apple's launch of the iPod digital music player. Apple was first to market such devices and entered with a price of $499. The iPod was an instant hit! It controls 40 percent of the portable digital player market and generates 18 percent of Apple's total revenue. Other brands entered the market with prices below those of Apple. Sensing an even higher degree of competition from new-product launches by Sony and Digital Networks North America (Rio is their player brand name), Apple decided to voluntarily slash prices by 25 percent. The price for a 40-gigabyte player dropped from $499 to $399. Other smaller capacity models were reduced in price accordingly. Apple is the market leader and the company is going to defend its position by managing prices wisely. Apple's pricing strategy placed added pressure on the competitors to compete and make a profit.[6]

Apple iPod
www.apple.com/ipod

PRICE PENETRATION

A **price penetration** strategy establishes a low entry price in order to gain wide market acceptance for the product quickly. The objective of price penetration is to create demand in a market quickly, to build market share, and to discourage competitors from entering. Generally, low prices are attractive to a larger number of customers, so demand and market-share objectives are achieved more rapidly. Potential competitors who analyze the market situation may think twice about entering it if they see that the profit margins of existing competitors are low and their market shares are large. Under such circumstances, the opportunity to recover development costs, especially in a short time, diminishes. Certain conditions are favourable to the use of a penetration strategy:

price penetration

1. The market or market segment is characterized by elastic demand; that is, demand that goes up if prices are low—buyers tend to be price sensitive.
2. The marketing organization has the ability to keep production costs down. Either costs are low initially, allowing a satisfactory profit margin to be achieved with the low-price strategy, or the firm banks on improved production efficiency—resulting from the volume selling encouraged by the strategy—to reduce costs.

3. The market is clearly divided into segments on the basis of price, and the low price or economy segment is large enough to justify entrance or accommodate competition among several brands.

The shortcoming of a penetration strategy is that it generally takes a long time to recover the costs of development and marketing, including the high costs of introducing products, because a high volume of sales is necessary in order to do so. If volume sales are not produced as quickly as anticipated, the realization of any profit may be delayed.

To illustrate the concept of penetration pricing, consider what Research In Motion did when it launched the "BlueBerry," a smaller version of the successful BlackBerry (a handheld email, Internet, and telephone device). Officially called the BlackBerry 6200 and 6210, the new models sold for US$300. Regular BlackBerry units sell for US$500 and were primarily aimed at corporate customers. The reduced price is RIM's attempt to penetrate the "prosumer" market, which consists of small and medium-sized business users. As well, the lower price makes the new unit an attractive option for consumers wanting a handheld device that has a phone, user-friendly Web browser, and personal digital assistant.[7]

4. Explain the role and benefits of leasing as a pricing strategy in the marketplace.

Leasing as a Pricing Option

lease

A **lease** is a contractual agreement whereby a lessor (owner), for a fee, agrees to rent an item (e.g., equipment, house, land) to a lessee over a specified period. In recent years, certain industries have increasingly used leasing in place of buying and selling. When considering the purchase of expensive capital equipment, buyers now frequently assess the lease option.

Expensive capital equipment such as computers, farm equipment, manufacturing machinery, office equipment and furnishings, and automobiles are often purchased on a lease agreement. Colleges and universities, for example, often lease computer equipment so that they have access to the latest technology when a lease expires. The leasing industry in Canada has grown significantly in the past few years. As of 2004, it is estimated that the value of assets under management by equipment finance companies is $67 billion in Canada. The value of the consumer vehicle leasing portfolio is estimated to be $39.7 billion. Vehicle leases now account for 40 percent of all new-car sales in Canada.[8]

Most print ads you see in magazines and newspapers today for expensive goods such as automobiles and computers actively promote the lease option. The main advantage of the car lease is that one pays only for the use of the vehicle versus the entire car. This can mean payments of 20 to 30 percent less than bank financing payments. This is due to an equity benefit remaining in the car belonging to the leaseholder at the end of the term. Generally, the more "high-tech" a piece of equipment is, the more likely it is that companies will lease it. Another standard guideline: if it appreciates, buy it; if it depreciates, lease it.

operating lease

There are two types of leases. An **operating lease** is usually short term and involves monthly payments for the use of the equipment, which is returned to the lessor after a specified period. The lessee does not pay the full value on the equipment, so after the lease term is up the residual value belongs to the lessor. This is a standard arrangement if a consumer is leasing an automobile. A **full-payout lease** is a longer-term lease, and

full-payout lease

the lessor recovers the full value of the equipment's purchase price through monthly payments. It operates much like a bank loan, with the leased goods as collateral. In effect, it is like 100-percent financing with no down payment. This type of lease is more common for items classified as capital goods (e.g., heavy construction equipment, manufacturing equipment).

Leases provide advantages for buying organizations and marketing organizations. For the buying organization, a lease preserves working capital for other ventures, and it allows the company to keep pace with technology (e.g., trade up to new equipment at the end of the lease period). This is a good option for companies that want to keep pace with computer technology, a market in which products become obsolete quickly. Payment schedules are usually lower than those financed by a standard bank loan. For the marketing organization, a lease provides a sale that otherwise would have been lost if the purchaser had to buy it. Financially, the same amount of money is collected, but over a longer period. This helps the cash flow in the marketing organization.

SUMMARY

An organization's pricing policies are the rules it establishes for setting prices that will enable it to achieve marketing objectives. Price policies are generally divided into four categories: psychological pricing (pricing concerned with tendencies in consumer behaviour), geographic pricing (pricing that takes into account freight and shipping costs and whether the seller or the buyer is to absorb such costs), promotional pricing (pricing concerned with the availability of discounts and allowances for attracting potential customers), flexible pricing (charging different prices to different customers), and product-mix pricing (establishing low and high prices for various combinations of product offerings so that on balance profits are maximized).

In managing price strategy, an organization starts with a list price and then offers discounts and allowances to potential buyers. The discounts commonly offered to distributors include cash discounts for prompt payment; slotting allowances for securing distribution of new products; quantity discounts, which are meant to encourage volume purchases; performance allowances that are paid to customers for performing a promotional function; seasonal discounts; rebates, which are temporary discounts intended to stimulate demand; and trade-in allowances.

As an alternative to offering discounts, some firms are moving to value pricing, whereby everyday low prices become the norm instead of the cyclical system of offering regular prices followed by sale prices.

When a firm introduces a product, it chooses between price skimming and price penetration. Price skimming involves the use of a high entry price, which maximizes revenue and recovers development costs as quickly as possible. It is a strategy suitable for innovative products or for products perceived as offering better value. In the case of price penetration, the organization employs a low price in order to gain wide market acceptance for a product and to discourage potential competitors from entering the market.

Implementing price strategies can be a problem for an organization, which must be careful to stay within the laws. In advertising price, an organization must make fair and reasonable representations or suffer the consequences of court decisions. All discounts offered must be made available to all competing distributors and must be offered, where applicable, on a proportionate basis; that is, distributors must be treated fairly in accordance with their size.

Finally, leasing is becoming a popular pricing strategy in the Canadian marketplace. Certain industries—computer, automobile, and aircraft, for example—now frequently use leasing in order to generate new business. For the marketer, the primary advantage of leasing is that it preserves a sale that would have been lost had the lease option not been available. Leasing enables the lessee to avoid the debt load that would result from buying.

KEY TERMS

bill-back   279

cash discounts   278

customary pricing   273

F.O.B. destination   274

F.O.B. origin   274

flexible pricing   275

forward buying   283

full-payout lease   286

geographic pricing   274

lease   286

list price   277

loss leaders   273

multiple-unit pricing   273

odd–even pricing   272

off-invoice allowance   279

operating lease   286

performance allowance   279

phantom freight   275

prestige pricing   271

price lining   272

price penetration   285

price-skimming   283

promotional pricing   273

psychological pricing   271

quantity discounts   278

rebates   280

seasonal discounts   279

slotting allowance   278

trade-in allowance   280

uniform delivered pricing   275

unit pricing   273

value pricing (everyday low pricing; EDLP)   281

zone pricing   275

REVIEW QUESTIONS

1. Identify and briefly explain the various types of psychological pricing.
2. What is a loss leader, and what role does it play in pricing strategy?
3. Briefly explain the difference between uniform delivered pricing and zone pricing. Under what conditions is one option better than the other?
4. Briefly explain the nature of the following product-mix price policies
   a) Optional-feature pricing
   b) Captive-product pricing
   c) Fixed-variable pricing
   d) Product-bundling pricing
5. Briefly explain the nature and role of (a) quantity discounts, (b) trade discounts, and (c) performance allowances.
6. Briefly contrast a price-skimming strategy with a price-penetration strategy. Under what conditions is one option better than the other?
7. Explain the concept of price lining. What are the advantages of this type of pricing strategy?
8. What objectives do the following types of allowances achieve: (a) slotting allowance, (b) off-invoice allowance, and (c) performance allowance?
9. Briefly explain the concept of value pricing.
10. What is the difference between an operating lease and a full-payout lease?

DISCUSSION AND APPLICATION QUESTIONS

1. Visit a car dealer in your area. Select a particular model of car and examine the pros and cons of leasing the car versus buying the car. Which method is best, and why?
2. Refer to the Marketing in Action vignette "Price Incentives: The Crack Cocaine of the Auto Industry." Evaluate the dilemma that automobile manufacturers find themselves in. Are there other marketing solutions that you can offer?
3. Is it fair to charge different customers different prices? Discuss.
4. Which pricing strategy (penetration or skimming) is best suited to the following new-product introductions?
   a) A new line of deodorant and antiperspirant (brand name: Trust) for the unisex market
   b) A new plasma screen HDTV set from Sony
   c) A new, low-cholesterol margarine that looks and tastes just like butter
   d) A new tire whose tread design repels water, keeping it away from the tire in rainy conditions.
5. Conduct some secondary research on everyday low pricing (EDLP). How is it being implemented in Canada and what companies are involved with it? What effect has EDLP had on the sales and profits of the companies involved? Have consumers reacted positively to it?

E-ASSIGNMENT

In this assignment, you will assess the discount programs offered by various rental car companies. Visit the websites of at least two companies in this industry. Select from Hertz, Budget, Thrifty, or another popular brand name. Surf the sites to determine the nature and extent of the discounts that each company offers. Very often, price incentives of the car rental company are tied in with incentives from other travel companies. This marketing strategy may influence a rental decision. At each site, take the steps indicated to secure rates for a typical reservation (e.g., a weekend rental). Which site offers the best rate? (Beware of hidden charges or charges contained in fine print.) Are prices and price incentives clearly communicated to the customer? Is there a reason why you might rent a vehicle from one company and not from the other? Is your decision based on price, or is some other aspect of marketing more important? State your position on the basis of your experience in visiting the websites.

ENDNOTES

1. Deirdre McMurdy, "Take a number," *Financial Post*, May 29, 2004, p. IN1.
2. Gabrielle A. Brenner and Rauven Brenner, "Memory and markets, or why you pay $2.99 for a widget," *Journal of Business*, vol. 55, no. 1, 1982, pp. 147–158.
3. Paul Hunt, "Analyzing the psychology of pricing," *Marketing*, February 25, 2002, p. 27.
4. Bruce McIlroy and David A. Hacker, "Unit pricing six years after introduction," *Journal of Retailing*, Fall 1979, pp. 45–47.
5. Marina Strauss, "Merchants aiming to bag more sales with everyday low prices," *Globe and Mail*, May 2, 2003, p. B9.
6. Connie Guglielmo and Dana Cimilluca, "Apple cuts price on latest iPod music player," *Financial Post*, July 20, 2004, p. FP4.
7. Robert Thompson, "RIM to roll out new mass market BlackBerry," *Financial Post*, March 12, 2003, p. FP1, FP6.
8. Canadian Finance & Leasing Association, www.cfla.acfl.ca/about.cfm.

Distribution

6

This section shows the role of distribution in the marketing mix. Key topics include distribution planning, physical distribution and marketing logistics, wholesaling, and retailing.

Chapter 12 presents the structure of distribution channels and how they are managed, the concept of integrated marketing systems, and the nature of physical distribution and logistics management.

Chapter 13 describes the various types of wholesalers and retailers and the functions they perform. Emphasis is placed on new forms of retailing on the Canadian scene.

Distribution Channels and Physical Distribution

CHAPTER

12

distribution

The third element of the marketing mix is place or distribution. **Distribution** involves all the functions and activities related to the transfer of goods and services from one business to another or from a business to a consumer. Given the competitive nature of the market today, business organizations constantly strive to improve the efficiency of their distribution systems. Very often, the goal of an organization is to reduce the costs of distribution to improve profit margins or to find new channels of distribution to gain competitive advantage.

1. Define distribution planning and the basic role of intermediaries in the distribution channel.

Distribution Planning

distribution planning

Distribution planning is "a systematic decision-making process regarding the physical movement and transfer of ownership of goods and services from producers to consumers."[1] The physical movement and transfer of ownership include activities such as order processing, transportation, and inventory management. These activities are carried out among members of the channel of distribution, which comprises organizations and people commonly referred to as wholesalers, retailers, agents, and brokers. In marketing terminology, these organizations are called channel members, intermediaries, or middlemen.

BASIC ROLE OF INTERMEDIARIES

intermediary

An **intermediary** offers producers the advantage of being able to make goods and services readily available to target markets. A manufacturer located in Winnipeg, Manitoba, would have difficulty contacting retail customers in all parts of Canada if it did not have a direct sales force of its own, and even if it did have such a sales force, it would not be able to contact its customers frequently. To address this difficulty, the manufacturer sells to a wholesaler that, in turn, contacts retail customers and supplies the product to them (Figure 12.1). In option A of this figure, 16 transactions occur when four different manufacturers attempt to reach four consumers. In option B, where an intermediary is used, the transactions are reduced to eight. Option B provides a more economical transfer of goods.

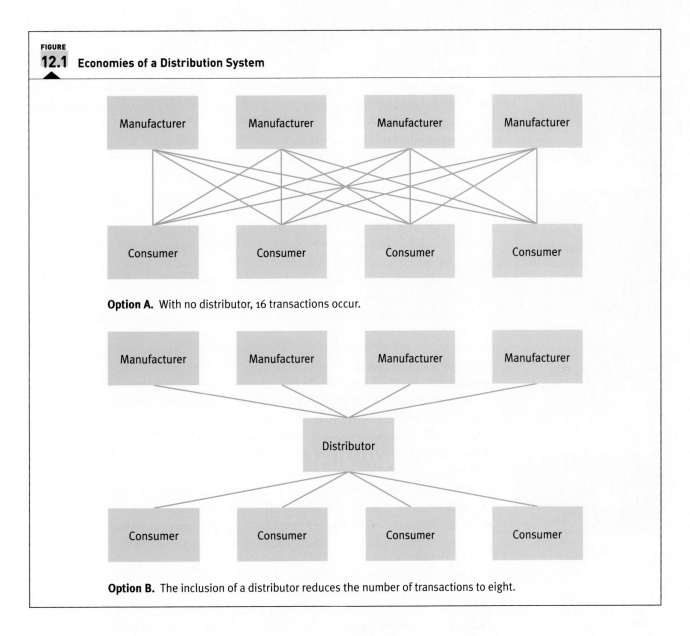

12.1   **Economies of a Distribution System**

Option A. With no distributor, 16 transactions occur.

Option B. The inclusion of a distributor reduces the number of transactions to eight.

Intermediaries provide assistance to manufacturers in the sorting process. The **sorting process** includes the accumulation, allocation, sorting, and assorting of merchandise. Sorting is necessary because manufacturers and consumers have different objectives. Manufacturers like to produce and market limited variety in large quantities, whereas consumers want a large selection of brands, colours, sizes, and price ranges. Sorting reconciles these basic differences. Let us examine each stage of the sorting process.

Accumulation involves wholesalers purchasing and storing quantities of merchandise that come from many producers. The wholesalers redistribute the merchandise in small quantities among the retailers they serve.

Allocation is a function provided by wholesalers and retailers that involves dividing the goods available from a producer among the various wholesale and retail customers. In times of great supply, customers can order the quantity they need and be confident of receiving the required amount. In times of high demand and short supply, a producer would have to allocate goods among its various wholesalers, who, in turn,

sorting process

accumulation

allocation

would do the same for the retail customers. This situation could occur during a labour strike, when goods may not be readily available, or when there is unprecedented demand for a product (e.g., a fad item such as a hot toy product).

Sorting involves separating merchandise into grades, colours, and sizes. For example, fruit is graded "choice" or "fancy" for the purposes of labelling canned goods. Eggs are graded as "grade A small," "medium," "large," and "extra large." The function of **assorting** involves making sure that the merchandise is available to consumers in an adequate variety of brand names, features, and price ranges.

sorting

assorting

The Structure of Distribution Systems

2. Describe the structure of distribution channels, outlining the difference between direct and indirect channels.

direct channel

indirect channel

TYPES OF DISTRIBUTION CHANNELS

Channels of distribution are either direct or indirect. A **direct channel** is a short channel, one in which goods move from producers to consumers without the use of intermediaries. Organizations that use the Internet to market goods are employing a direct channel. An **indirect channel** is a long channel, one in which goods are moved through a series of intermediaries before reaching the final customer (Figure 12.2).

MANUFACTURER TO CONSUMER   The manufacturer-to-consumer channel of distribution is a *direct* channel, in which manufacturers themselves contact and distribute to the final users. It may take the form of a business-to-business transaction, or a transaction in which a business sells directly to a consumer. Software companies, for example, sell their products directly to consumers online and then distribute the products electronically. Financial services companies, such as Canada Life and London Life, sell directly through their head office or regional branch offices to consumers, using their own sales force.

The growth of online marketing is changing the nature of direct distribution. Organizations that traditionally did not sell directly to consumers are finding ways to do so via the Internet. Dell Computer Corporation is an innovator in this area. Dell built its entire business on direct distribution strategies initially through toll-free 1-800 num-

Dell Computer Corporation
www.dell.com

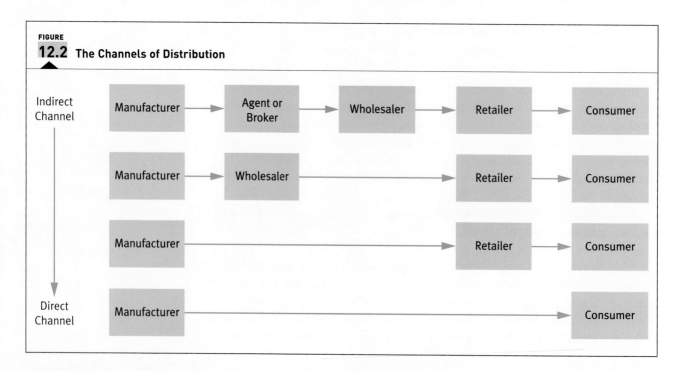

FIGURE
12.2 **The Channels of Distribution**

Indirect Channel

| Manufacturer | → | Agent or Broker | → | Wholesaler | → | Retailer | → | Consumer |

| Manufacturer | → | Wholesaler | → | Retailer | → | Consumer |

| Manufacturer | → | Retailer | → | Consumer |

Direct Channel

| Manufacturer | → | Consumer |

bers. For Dell, the Internet was simply a logical extension to this strategy. Today, Dell operates one of the highest-volume Internet commerce sites in the world and it generates more than half of its total annual business.[2]

MANUFACTURER TO RETAILER TO CONSUMER   The inclusion of a retailer makes the channel somewhat indirect. The retailer provides consumers with convenient access to goods. Apparel manufacturers such as Levi Strauss (blue jeans and leisure wear) and Nike (sport shoes and leisure clothing) sell directly to retail buyers of department stores and corporate chain stores. Retailers often store the merchandise in their own central warehouses so that it can be distributed to retail stores at a later time. Sometimes the manufacturer will open its own stores to sell goods. Sony, for example, operates a chain of Sony Stores to sell its consumer electronics products.

Direct channels are employed when a company wants to maintain control of its marketing programs and have close contact with customers. Such retailers do not have to be bricks-and-mortar retailers. Mail-order prescription drug pharmacies are doing a booming business in Canada shipping orders to the United States. American customers email or fax their original prescription along with a detailed medical history, which is reviewed by pharmacists for accuracy before being sent to a Canadian physician for another review and approval. The entire ordering process can take up to 21 working days.[3] Canadameds and MediPlan Pharmacy are examples of this kind of distributor.

Canadameds
Canadameds.com

MediPlan Pharmacy
www.mediplanhealth.com

MANUFACTURER TO WHOLESALER TO RETAILER TO CONSUMER   The addition of channel members increases the number of transactions and makes the channel indirect. The addition of a wholesaler is common in industries where products are ultimately sold through numerous types of retail outlets—convenience goods such as food, household cleaning products, personal-care products, and pharmaceuticals fall into this category (Figure 12.3). A manufacturer such as Colgate-Palmolive (personal-care products) or S. C. Johnson (waxes and household cleaning products) ships its goods to wholesalers, who in turn ship to retailers they serve. Sobeys Inc., for example, operates

FIGURE
12.3 An Indirect Channel of Distribution in the Grocery Industry

Products ordered by Sobeys Inc. from suppliers are delivered to regional distribution centres. The distribution centres perform the wholesaling function and redistribute products to company-owned and -operated retail outlets. This is an example of corporate vertical marketing integration.

its own wholesaling division in the form of four distribution centres strategically located across Canada. The wholesaling division is responsible for the redistribution of products to all Sobeys retailers, which include Sobeys, IGA, IGA Extra, Price Chopper, Marche Bonichoix, Foodland, and Food Town, among many others.[4]

CHANNELS THAT INCLUDE AGENTS AND BROKERS   The inclusion of agents and brokers makes the channel very long. Typically, an agent or a broker represents a host of small manufacturers who do not have the resources to sell through the channel themselves. In this system, the agent or broker represents the manufacturer to the wholesale and retail trade or to the final consumer and earns a commission based on the sales generated. In the grocery business, agents and brokers commonly represent small manufacturers. Independent general insurance brokers represent numerous companies when they are selling automobile insurance. On the basis of their customers' needs, these brokers search among their insurance providers for the best price. Since the manufacturer is not in direct contact with the customer, it has less control in marketing its product.

Refer to Figure 12.2 for an illustration of the channels available to marketing organizations. Generally speaking, consumer goods tend to use indirect channels, while industrial goods tend to use shorter channels. Industrial marketers use shorter channels because of the geographic concentration of customers, the limited numbers of customers, and the specific design of products to suit unique customer needs. Service channels tend to be shorter due to the intangibility of services and the need for personal relationships in the marketing process.

CHANNEL LENGTH AND WIDTH

When trying to develop an appropriate channel, a producer must consider two characteristics: length and width. **Channel length** refers to the number of intermediaries or levels in the channel of distribution. As indicated earlier, channels are direct (short) or indirect (long). As products increase in price, sell less frequently, and require more direct forms of communication to keep customers informed, the channels become shorter and contain fewer intermediaries. The direct communication of accurate, often technical, product information between a seller and a buyer is more important under these conditions.

As channels become longer, control shifts from the producer to others in the channel. In this situation the producer of the good often implements "pull" strategies (advertising and promotional messages directed at final users) to assist in moving a product through the channel.

Channel width refers to the number of intermediaries at any one level of the channel of distribution. The width of the channel depends on how widely available a producer wants its product to be. Convenience goods, such as milk, bread, tobacco, candy and gum, toothpaste, and deodorant have wide channels of distribution at both wholesale and retail levels. Shopping goods, such as clothing, furniture, and appliances, require a narrower or more selective list of retailers to sell to consumers. Wholesalers may or may not be used in these markets. Specialty goods are generally available in only a limited number of locations for any particular geographic market. For example, a market the size of Regina (Saskatchewan) or Kitchener (Ontario) would need only one Mercedes-Benz dealer. A market the size of Vancouver has seven dealers.

Traditional models, such as those just mentioned, are changing. Business-to-business companies, manufacturers of consumer goods, and retailers are moving toward using the Internet as a means of generating customer contact and ultimately as a means of distributing goods. What is emerging is a model referred to as **multi-channelling**.

channel length

channel width

multi-channelling

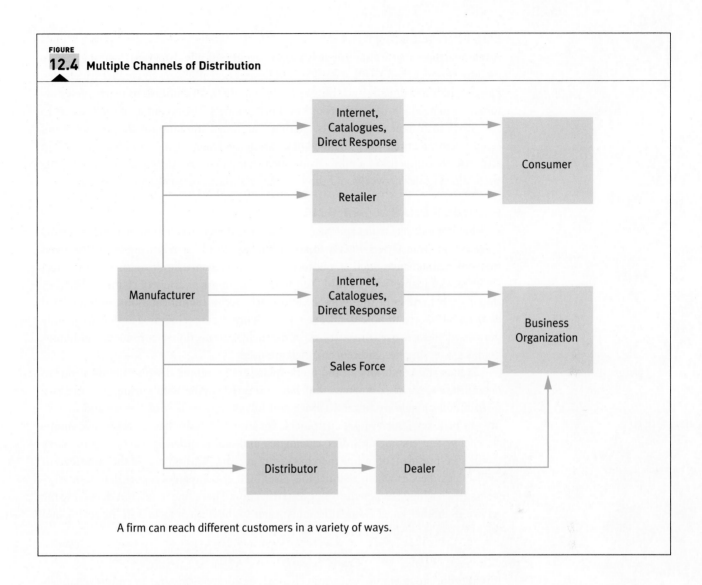

FIGURE
12.4 **Multiple Channels of Distribution**

A firm can reach different customers in a variety of ways.

Multi-channelling involves using different types of intermediaries at the same level of a channel to reach various customer groups. See Figure 12.4 for an illustration.

In a retail context, multi-channelling involves online integration with existing retail store operations.[5] In a manufacturing context, multi-channelling may involve marketing through traditional distributor networks (dealers), directly with customers online through e-commerce initiatives, and even through manufacturer-owned retail locations. Apple, for example, has opened its own retail stores, and Dell is experimenting with kiosks in Canadian shopping malls.[6] Apple's decision to open its own stores could create some conflict with independent Apple dealers. Channel conflict is discussed in more detail later in this chapter.

Factors Influencing Channel Selection

Which type of channel a firm uses depends on which markets it would like to reach and what objectives are to be achieved. A number of questions must be answered: What levels of customer satisfaction are necessary? What functions will intermediaries perform? What degree of coverage is desired? Organizations consider the following characteristics when making channel decisions.

3. Describe the factors considered in selecting channels of distribution.

CUSTOMER LOCATION

A manufacturer that wants to reach a large, geographically dispersed customer group requires indirect channels; the costs would be excessive if it were to contact widely dispersed customers directly and transport goods to them. In contrast, to reach a few customers who need lots of service requires short channels. The potential of the Internet to sell goods to distant customers is altering traditional thinking on this matter. Until recently, customers always purchased new cars at car dealerships. Now, Ford and GM, in response to competition online from such companies as Autobytel, are examining streamlined dealer networks and the Internet as a means of retaining customers.

PRODUCT CHARACTERISTICS

Perishable goods like fruits and vegetables require direct channels or channels whereby the goods are transferred quickly to avoid spoilage. Products requiring installation and frequent maintenance, such as photocopiers and plant machinery, also require direct channels. Companies such as IBM, Xerox, and Canon use a variety of channels, but they ship directly to other business organizations. The technical information communicated by their sales force to potential buyers necessitates the direct approach. For frequently purchased, inexpensive convenience goods, such as confectionery products and household cleaning supplies, indirect channels are used.

Trends and conditions in the marketplace are reshaping distribution decisions in organizations. Many companies that have ventured online with various e-commerce distribution models are finding service and follow-up—or lack of service and follow-up—to be a key issue among customers. For example, Sears has an aggressive multi-channel system embracing stores, catalogues, and online ordering. According to Garry Smith, vice-president of online merchandising at Sears, "Customers get the same level of service regardless of which channel they use."[7] Other companies report that poor service results in a high level of customer dissatisfaction. That's fine to say, but delivering the service is another issue. Companies must cater to the human factors in the selling and buying process, or they will fail.[8]

COMPETITION

It is appropriate to employ the same channels as competitors, and to employ channels that are common to a particular industry, but a firm gains a competitive advantage by developing a new channel of distribution. For example, having a product available in a non-traditional location could result in purchases by new consumers. Earlier it was mentioned that Dell has started selling computers in kiosks at shopping malls. The company believes that by staffing the kiosks with knowledgeable employees, Dell can sell its products to consumers who normally wouldn't shop by telephone or on the Internet.

Well-known retailers looking for a competitive edge are also expanding into non-traditional areas. Tim Hortons' products are available in Esso stations across Canada; Harvey's is setting up shop in Home Depot stores; and Starbucks is selling its famous coffee in grocery stores. In the case of Starbucks, coffee shop customers can now brew their own Starbucks coffee at home, and at-home customers may be sufficiently motivated to visit Starbucks coffee shops. Starbucks has also struck a contractual agreement with Madison Square Gardens and Radio City Music Hall in New York City to be their sole supplier of coffee beverages. Contract distribution is discussed in more detail later in the chapter.

COMPANY RESOURCES

Size and financial resources determine which marketing functions a firm can or cannot handle. Small firms with customers located from coast to coast generally need to transfer the distribution function to intermediaries who can perform the task with greater efficiency. For example, small manufacturers of food products that do not have their own sales force rely on food brokers to contact wholesalers and retailers on their behalf. Thomas, Large & Singer Inc. is an example of a broker that calls on retail grocery stores, food-service establishments, and industrial buyers. This broker serves these market segments through its own sales force and a full-service warehouse.

Large companies have more flexibility and can employ their own direct sales force or use a combination of direct and indirect channels, depending on the customer segments they are going after. The Internet is proving to be a cost-efficient way for small and large businesses to reach customers.

Thomas, Large & Singer
www.thomaslargesinger.com

INTENSITY OF DISTRIBUTION

A producer has to consider what sort of coverage of the market is needed. The degree of market coverage or the availability of a product can be intensive, selective, or exclusive (Figure 12.5).

1. An **intensive distribution** strategy is used by a company that wants to reach as much of the population as possible. This usually applies to low-priced, frequently purchased, branded, convenience goods requiring no service or limited service. Producers continually search for new wholesale and retail outlets to sell through so that the product is convenient for the customer to purchase. It is a strategy directed at the largest number of consumers. Part of Tim Hortons' success is attributed to distribution. At one time in Kingston, Ontario, there were only three Tim Hortons outlets serving a population of 115 000. Today, there are 15 strategically located outlets to serve the same population. Similar situations exist in other cities across Canada. Competitor establishments such as Country Style and Coffee Time are few and far between.

    intensive distribution

2. A **selective distribution** strategy is suitable for medium-priced shopping goods that are purchased less frequently. With this type of distribution, the product is available in only a few outlets in a particular market. Selective distribution is often appropriate for consumer shopping goods and for industrial accessory equipment, where consumers may have preferences for particular brand names. In this situation,

    selective distribution

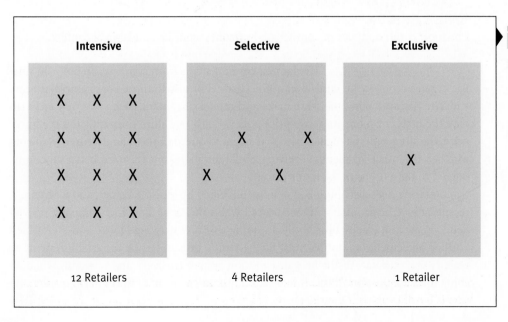

FIGURE 12.5

Intensity of Distribution

limiting the number of retailers allows the marketing organization to reduce total marketing costs while establishing better relationships with channel members. The number of Ford or GM dealerships in a city is an example of selective distribution. Typically, dealerships—for example, GM dealerships—are strategically located to battle competing dealerships (Ford, Chrysler, Toyota, and others) instead of their own dealerships.

exclusive distribution

3. An **exclusive distribution** strategy is sought for high-priced shopping or specialty goods that offer the purchaser a unique value. Typically, the product is purchased infrequently and is associated with prestige and status. In any given geographic area, only one dealer or retail outlet exists—a circumstance that helps protect the producer's image. Typically, the producers and retailers cooperate closely in decisions regarding advertising, promotion, inventory carried by the retailers, and prices. The producer's goals are to present a prestigious image and maintain channel control. High profit margins on every unit sold compensate for lower-volume sales. Such is the case for luxury categories like the premium watches and upscale jewellery sold in high-end retailers such as Birks.

Channel Conflict and Control

4. Outline the nature of conflicts that exist in a channel of distribution and the strategies available to reduce conflict.

All channel members have the same basic objectives of making a profit, providing efficient distribution, and keeping customers satisfied. However, the strategies used by the different members in a channel often lead to problems or conflict between members. Potential sources of conflict often revolve around disagreements on distributor functions or a desire to retain control by a particular member of the channel.

In today's Canadian marketplace, the balance of control or power in some markets has shifted from manufacturers to retailers due to the convergence and consolidation of retailing empires. In Canada right now, five large grocery distributors led by Loblaw Companies control about 80 percent of food store sales—and, therefore, they control the most valuable commodity in retail marketing: shelf space. If your product is not available in their stores, you're dead! "Manufacturers will tell you the big grocery retailers have them by the short and curlies," says the president of one company.[9] Such control breeds conflict.

TYPES OF CONFLICT
The most common types of conflict are horizontal conflict and vertical conflict.

horizontal conflict

HORIZONTAL CONFLICT **Horizontal conflict** stems from competition between similar organizations at the same level in the channel of distribution. For example, if Sears and The Bay are selling the same make and model of camera, each store may strive to have the better or more attractive price policy. But if one store constantly has the lower price, the store with the higher price may begin to question the manufacturer, inquiring whether the other retailer is receiving preferential treatment. Were better discounts offered to the store with the lower price?

Brick Brewing Company: Red Cap
www.brickbeer.com/html/brick005.html

Ontario's beer distribution system is controlled by Molson, Labatt, and Sleeman. A recent case of horizontal conflict surfaced when the Brick Brewing Company revived Red Cap ale in a stubby beer bottle. In doing so Brick Brewing violated an established bottling agreement (all bottles must be the same), thus upsetting the establishment. At issue is the efficiency of the beer distribution system (delivery and retrieval) when all companies use the same bottle.[10] Red Cap captured 1 percent of the Ontario market; the case is now before the Ontario courts.

VERTICAL CONFLICT   **Vertical conflict** occurs when a channel member believes that another member at a different level is engaging in inappropriate conduct. For example, if wholesalers do not pass on discounts that are offered by manufacturers to retailers, friction between the wholesaler and retailer will develop. A manufacturer may pressure a wholesaler or retailer to keep prices at a certain level, but the action desired by the manufacturer may be contrary to the profit objectives of the distributors; conflict is the result.

Conflict is common between suppliers and retailers in situations where retailers have control of the channel. Wal-Mart is known to place considerable pressure on suppliers to keep prices down. If suppliers cannot meet the price demands, they risk losing Wal-Mart's business. Some manufacturers have been forced to outsource production to countries where labour rates are lower, simply to meet Wal-Mart's price demands. Such a tenuous relationship between a supplier and a retailer has serious ramifications for suppliers, especially if the contract is terminated.

Similarly, manufacturers who establish their own retail stores (e.g., Nike has its Nike Town stores and Apple has its Apple stores) or set up their own Internet store to deal with consumers directly risk conflict with other independent retailers that sell their merchandise. The question remains: should manufacturers own and operate their own retail stores in direct competition with dealers that also distribute the same products? For more insight into this issue and the conflict it can create, read the Marketing in Action vignette **Should Manufacturers Be Retailers?**

vertical conflict

> 5. Describe how various members of a channel of distribution attempt to control the channel.

CHANNEL CONTROL

A **channel captain** is a leader that integrates and coordinates the objectives and policies of all other members. The manufacturer is usually the first link in the channel but is not always the one that controls the channel. Depending on the circumstances, leadership and control may be held by the manufacturer, the wholesaler, or the retailer.

channel captain

MANUFACTURER CONTROL   When the manufacturer is in control, the channel is usually a direct one. Goods are distributed directly to the industrial user or to consumers, or they are distributed through a company-owned or -sponsored retail outlet (e.g., a dealer). Microsoft controls the sale and distribution of its computer operating systems. General Motors and Ford control the distribution of their automobiles through a dealer network in which each dealer must meet and maintain certain standards of operation. Both companies are in the process of streamlining their North American dealer networks to achieve greater efficiency and better pricing policies for consumers. New distribution strategies are essential given the new forms of competition from mega dealers that sell a host of different brands (e.g., Car Canada and AutoNation) and from online distributors (e.g., autobytel.com and edmunds.com). The goal for both companies is to regain control of the channel by having fewer "super dealerships" replace smaller, local-market dealerships. Refer to the illustration in Figure 12.6.

Autobytel
Autobytel.com

WHOLESALER CONTROL   When a group of wholesalers controls the channel, the only way for manufacturers to gain access to retailers is through the wholesaling operation. For any product to be sold in Loblaws, Zehrs, No Frills, Your Independent Grocer, Valumart, Fresh Mart, Fortino's, Atlantic SaveEasy, Atlantic Superstore, or Atlantic SuperValue, it must pass through one wholesaling operation: Loblaw Companies East Distribution. Loblaw Companies Limited owns all these retail distributors. For a manufacturer to obtain distribution in any particular retail outlet, it must market its lines to Loblaws' central buying office. Once the product is listed and approved for sale, the wholesaler acts as a coordinating body and service operation for the retailers it supplies.

MARKETING IN ACTION

Should Manufacturers Be Retailers?

John Forzani, the CEO of one of Canada's largest sports retailing companies, doesn't favour suppliers that set up retail operations. Given his position, perhaps his view is a bit biased! As an indication of his beliefs, Forzani recently bought a $3500, 30-inch Sony television at Sounds Around, a local consumer electronics store—he avoided the Sony Store.

In justifying his position, Forzani states, "It's a conflict. It makes it extremely difficult to compete with them." This point of view is shared by many a retailer. In the worldwide Sony system, Canada is unique. Canada is one of the few countries where Sony operates a national chain of stores, 72 outlets and counting. Its flagship store in the Toronto Eaton Centre is a haven for gadget-seekers who see interactivity as a key influence in the buying decision.

The degree and nature of competition is the real issue. The existing dealer network represents Sony effectively and does a good job selling its goods. When a supplier becomes a retailer, existing dealers stand to sell less of the same products. Sporting goods manufacturer Nike Inc. is the latest company to join the retail fray. As an added threat to existing retailers, Sony, Nike, and other companies are setting up websites to sell their goods directly to consumers.

In defending their position, Sony says, "We're not about stealing market share from our dealers. The Sony stores are a showcase for the brand, and in most cases, shoppers compare prices elsewhere before they buy." To its credit, Sony does not undercut dealers' prices.

Dealers seem resigned to competing with Sony. The Future Shop is one of those dealers. Future Shop sees a benefit to Sony's retail presence: Sony displays products so well that it's a kind of advertisement for the goods. The stores have a polished look, and that has pushed Future Shop to sharpen its merchandising, display, and pricing practices.

Sony stores have not always been profitable. In fact, they lost money until 1999. Their turnaround was helped by consumers' rush in recent years to acquire the latest home electronics toys. Stores are being relocated to more fashionable malls and revamped to blend entertainment with technology. It's quite a shopping experience.

Sony uses database marketing to build its business. It recently mailed out $10 gift certificates to its 60 000 best customers and ran a contest that offered prize values up to $10 000 on Sony merchandise in Sony stores. Now that's marketing that would scare the heck out of the existing dealer network!

Adapted from Marina Strauss, "Competition heats up as suppliers become retailers," *Globe and Mail*, November 3, 2000, p. M1.

Dick Hemingway

All merchandising and promotion activity is funnelled through the wholesaler. (Refer to Figure 12.3 for a visual portrayal of the control held by wholesalers in the Canadian grocery trade). Sobeys Inc. is one of five wholesaler/retailer companies that control 80 percent of grocery store sales in Canada. It is also an example of vertical market integration, a concept discussed later in this chapter.

Reprinted by permission of Autobytel.com

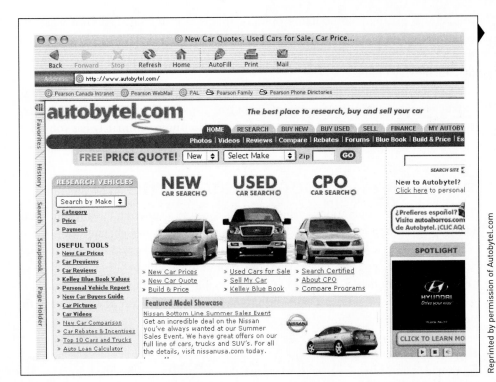

FIGURE
12.6

Online automobile distributors have forced traditional dealers to evaluate and alter their distribution strategy

RETAILER CONTROL   Sometimes one retailer or a select group of retailers controls the process of selling to consumers a wide variety of manufacturers' products. Leading retailers with significant market share fall into this category. Wal-Mart's control over suppliers from a pricing perspective was mentioned earlier in the chapter.

The distribution of movies in Canada is a form of retailer control. First-run movies are controlled by two retail organizations: Famous Players and Cineplex Odeon. A much smaller independent operation, Les Cinemas Guzzo (Montreal), has complained to the Competition Bureau that Famous Players and Cineplex Odeon use their size to pressure distributors to keep blockbuster films out of their theatres, and that they split the movie market to shut out competitors. Guzzo competes with the big chains by offering lower prices but wants access to the same films that the dominant chains get.[11]

Prominent grocery retailers such as Sobeys and Loblaws control a major portion of the volume of merchandise sold through retail outlets in their market segment. In such cases retailers may place added pressure on manufacturers to provide greater price discounts in order to retain distribution and shelf space in their stores. Not wanting to lose any distribution, manufacturers often succumb to the demands of powerful retailers. Shoppers Drug Mart actually requested that all private-label product suppliers remit a "preferred vendor" charge equivalent to 20 percent of the value of their business. Once the demand was made public, however, the public relations backlash forced Shoppers to withdraw the demand.[12]

Some of the examples described under wholesaler control and retailer control appear to be similar. This is done intentionally to demonstrate that if true control is the goal, a company will operate on several levels of the channel of distribution. In the grocery business in Canada, the dominant wholesalers and the dominant retailers are one and the same.

It should be noted that online marketing and e-commerce have changed the power equation. Now, consumers have unprecedented access to information about products, competitive pricing, and sourcing options. If they are not satisfied with what one e-business offers, a competitor is just a mouse click away. Attracting e-shoppers and then retaining them requires a different mindset for traditional marketing organizations that are moving online.

Controlling the channel is a battle over who owns the consumer. If you're Wal-Mart (a retailer), you have a certain amount of control. If you're Coca-Cola (manufacturer), you have a certain amount of control. Perhaps the consumer ultimately has control. If consumers aren't getting what they want, they will take their business somewhere else.

Encouraging Cooperation in the Channel

To illustrate how cooperation is achieved, let us consider a situation in which the manufacturer is the channel captain. The channel captain motivates channel members to accomplish specific objectives or perform certain tasks by providing good service, attractive pricing policies, advertising and promotional support, and sales training (Figure 12.7). Another factor that has helped establish cooperation in the channel of distribution is the adoption of relationship marketing practices, to be discussed in the next section.

SERVICE

To provide good service—that is, to ensure dealers' orders can be filled quickly—the manufacturer maintains adequate inventory. In many cases, for example, car dealers in Canada can obtain original replacement parts within one day of a request. Advancing computer technology has certainly assisted in processing orders; they can now be accepted, processed, and delivered much more quickly than before.

PRICING POLICIES

Manufacturers recognize that every member of the channel must maintain a fair and competitive profit margin. Therefore, they establish list prices and offer discounts and allowances that permit members to make a reasonable profit. Movement of merchandise is a concern to intermediaries; therefore, manufacturers must allow for higher margins on slow-moving items and lower margins on fast-moving items so that, on balance, the intermediary maintains a reasonable level of profit.

FIGURE
12.7

Conflict and Cooperation in Channels

Types of Channel Conflict

Horizontal

Conflict and competition between similar organizations at the same level of the channel

Vertical

Conflict between channel members at different levels of the distribution system

Channel Cooperation

A manufacturer encourages cooperation by:

1. Providing distributors with adequate and proper service in all facets of marketing and distribution support.

2. Providing fair and equitable pricing policies to all distributors.

3. Providing advertising and promotional support to encourage reselling and merchandising support.

4. Providing all dealers and retailers with adequate sales training so that all will benefit.

ADVERTISING AND PROMOTION

Another way to coordinate the different objectives of channel members is through **cooperative advertising**, which involves the sharing of advertising expenses between manufacturers and distributors and the manufacturer providing copy and illustrations to be integrated into the distributor's advertising. This arrangement allows the manufacturer to promote its product while giving the distributor the opportunity to promote itself. Incentives such as sales contests and dealer premiums can also spark interest in a manufacturer's products, at least temporarily, and help gain distributors' support in increasing sales or in acquiring new accounts.

cooperative advertising

SALES TRAINING

Manufacturers who train their distributors in how to sell the product gain the interest of their distributors. Any training provided, particularly to the distributor's sales staff, encourages cooperation. Companies such as Hewlett-Packard and Apple spend time training the sales staff in dealers' computer stores. Detailed training in hardware and software, which provides crucial product knowledge, is the key to success at this stage in the distribution process. The training is mutually beneficial; without it, dealers might be unable to persuade consumers or businesses to buy, and the dealer and the manufacturer would both suffer.

Adoption of the Relationship Marketing Concept

As discussed in Chapters 1 and 5, relationship marketing involves the partnering of organizations in a chain of distribution, from supplier of raw materials to the ultimate consumer who purchases the end product, who then conduct business in such a way that all participants benefit. In the context of distribution strategy this relationship is often referred to as supply chain management. A **supply chain** is a sequence of companies that perform activities related to the creation and delivery of a good or service to consumers or business customers. **Supply chain management** refers to the integration of information among members of the supply chain to facilitate efficient production and delivery of goods to customers. Electronic commerce technology is fuelling the rise in sophisticated supply chain management programs in all kinds of industries. It is creating a seamless system between the original source of supply and the end user (see Figure 12.8, next page).

supply chain

supply chain management

The formation of electronic online relationships between distributors and suppliers is a means of improving efficiency and reducing conflict. It is a flexible system that advocates teamwork and cooperation among all organizations. The implementation of supply chain management in distributing goods is discussed in more detail in the section on Physical Distribution in this chapter.

Integrated Marketing Systems

In order to gain control of a channel of distribution or to foster cooperation among its members, a firm develops a planned integrated marketing system. There are two categories of integrated marketing systems: vertical marketing systems (or vertical integration) and horizontal marketing systems (or horizontal integration).

6. Explain the concept of integrated marketing systems.

VERTICAL MARKETING SYSTEM

In a **vertical marketing system (VMS)**, channel members are linked at different levels in the marketing process to form a centrally controlled marketing system in which one

vertical marketing system (VMS)

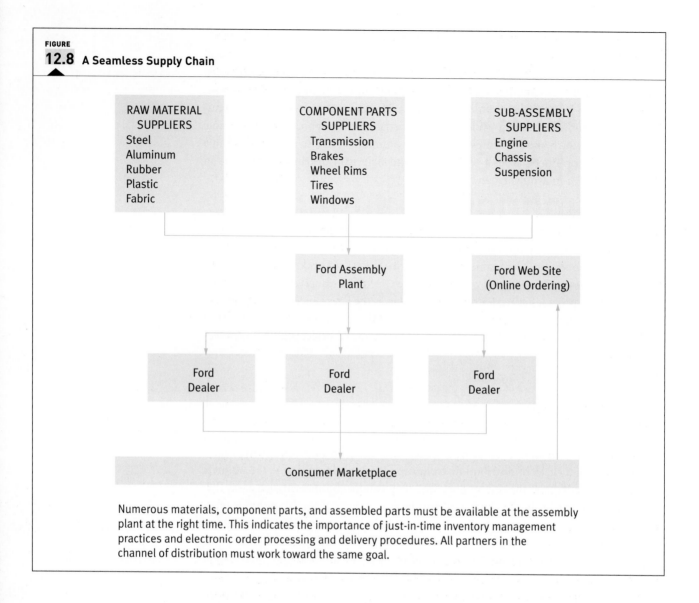

FIGURE
12.8 A Seamless Supply Chain

RAW MATERIAL
SUPPLIERS
Steel
Aluminum
Rubber
Plastic
Fabric

COMPONENT PARTS
SUPPLIERS
Transmission
Brakes
Wheel Rims
Tires
Windows

SUB-ASSEMBLY
SUPPLIERS
Engine
Chassis
Suspension

Ford Assembly
Plant

Ford Web Site
(Online Ordering)

Ford
Dealer

Ford
Dealer

Ford
Dealer

Consumer Marketplace

Numerous materials, component parts, and assembled parts must be available at the assembly plant at the right time. This indicates the importance of just-in-time inventory management practices and electronic order processing and delivery procedures. All partners in the channel of distribution must work toward the same goal.

member dominates the channel. A channel captain has control in a vertical marketing system, whether the captain is the manufacturer, the wholesaler, or the retailer. There are three types of vertical marketing systems: administered, contractual, and corporate.

administered VMS

ADMINISTERED VMS   In an **administered VMS**, the organization with the greatest economic influence has control. This firm plans the marketing program, and identifies and coordinates the responsibilities of each member. For example, category management systems implemented by grocery distributors (e.g., Safeway, Sobeys, and Loblaws) put the wholesaler/retailer in control of the channel. Suppliers such as Procter & Gamble and Kraft have to manage their brands within the shelf space they are allocated. As discussed in the pricing chapters, these retailers can place undue pressure on suppliers for discounts—a form of control. Companies like Wal-Mart and Canadian Tire also have control, since they contract with suppliers for a large portion of the suppliers' output. Canadian Tire, for example, arranges marketing agreements with manufacturers to supply its Mastercraft and Motomaster product lines.

contractual VMS

CONTRACTUAL VMS   As implied by the name, this contractual is governed by a legal agreement that binds the members in the channel. Three forms of contractual vertical marketing systems are possible: retail cooperatives, wholesale-sponsored voluntary chains, and franchises.

Retail cooperatives are composed of independent retailers that join together to establish a wholesaling operation (e.g., a large distribution centre). It is a system that is initiated by retailers and is designed to allow them to compete successfully with chain stores. Each retailer owns a share of the operations and benefits from the economies of scale in terms of buying and marketing goods. For example, lower prices are available to members in the form of discounts and allowances due to the higher volume of goods purchased collectively. Calgary Co-op is a key player in the Alberta grocery industry with 18 stores in the Calgary area. It has more than 380 000 members and annual sales in excess of $730 million, making it one of the largest grocery cooperatives in North America.[13] Home Hardware is another example of a retail cooperative.

retail cooperatives

A **voluntary chain** is initiated by the wholesaler and consists of a group of independent retailers organized into a centrally controlled system. Retailers agree to buy from the designated wholesaler. As in the case of the retail cooperative, the increased buying power results in lower prices for all retailers. Voluntary chains were originally established by independent grocers to compete more efficiently with large chains. IGA (Independent Grocers Alliance) and Western Auto are examples of voluntary chains. The voluntary chain implements inventory management programs and merchandising and advertising programs that benefit all members.

voluntary chain

In a **franchise agreement**, the franchisee (retailer), in exchange for a fee, uses the franchiser's name and operating methods in conducting business. The success of franchises is based on the marketing of a unique product or service concept and on the principle of uniformity, according to which franchisees conduct business in a manner consistent with the policies and procedures established by the franchiser. Typically, franchise dealers receive a variety of marketing, management, technical, and financial services support in return for a fee. Regardless of their location, franchise operations, such as McDonald's, KFC, Second Cup, Budget Rent-A-Car, and Midas Muffler, offer goods and services as well as a quality level that customers are familiar with.

franchise agreement

CORPORATE VMS   A **corporate VMS** is a tightly controlled arrangement in which a single corporation owns and operates in each level of the channel. The ownership and control of the channel can be located at either end; that is, manufacturers may own wholesalers and retailers, or retailers may own the source of supply. In Canada, George Weston Limited (one of Canada's largest bread and dairy products producers) is at the helm of a corporate VMS using forward integration. Weston is both a manufacturer and distributor of the products it makes. Its various manufacturing divisions include Weston Bakeries (makers of Wonder, D'Italiano, Country Harvest, and Weston breads) and Neilson Dairy (the largest milk producer in Ontario under the Neilson and Neilson Trutaste brand names). Weston also operates seafood and frozen food divisions. The products produced by these companies are readily available in all the distribution outlets owned by Weston. Among the retail distributors are Loblaws, No Frills, Atlantic Superstore, Fortinos, Zehrs, Provigo, Real Canadian Superstore, and Your Independent Grocer.

corporate VMS

George Weston Limited
www.weston.ca

Regardless of the type of vertical marketing system, the direction of control is forward or backward. In **forward integration**, manufacturers have control; in **backward integration**, retailers have control. Wholesalers can integrate either forward or backward.

forward integration
backward integration

To illustrate the forward integration concept, Coca-Cola licenses bottlers (wholesalers) in various markets to buy Coca-Cola syrup concentrate; the bottlers then carbonate, bottle, and sell the finished product to retailers in local markets. Production and marketing of the beverage must meet the specifications established by Coca-Cola. As indicated earlier in the chapter, the grocery industry is controlled by a small number of companies that operate a multitude of retail stores across Canada. This is an example of backward integration (refer to Figure 12.3). Manufacturers must constantly meet the demands of these few retailers or they may incur losses in distribution.

HORIZONTAL MARKETING SYSTEMS

horizontal marketing system

In a **horizontal marketing system**, many channel members at one level in the channel have the same owner. In the Canadian hotel business, Choice Hotels operates under a variety of banners: Comfort, Quality, Sleep, Clarion, Rodeway, Econo Lodge, and Mainstay Suites. Choice Hotels is a leader in the value segment of the hotel industry. In the convenience store industry, Alimentation Couche-Tard Inc., a large Quebec-based convenience store chain, is the largest convenience store chain in Canada, operating stores under the following banners: Mac's, Beckers, Mike's Mart, Winks, and Daisy Mart. Couche-Tard recently acquired the Circle K chain in the United Sates, making the company the fourth largest convenience store operator in North America, with annual sales of $4.2 billion.[14]

Exploiting New Distribution Strategies

The identification and pursuit of new channels of distribution is now the battleground for companies wishing to expand. Several other practices are changing the nature of distribution strategy. These include the sale of products through direct marketing and electronic marketing techniques, multi-level marketing techniques, and contract marketing, which guarantees exclusive availability of a product line in a particular establishment. Let us examine each of these practices.

DIRECT MARKETING AND ELECTRONIC MARKETING

In the pharmaceutical market, Glaxo, a prominent manufacturer, launched a 1-800 information line for migraine sufferers to call and request information about Imitrex, its migraine medication. To fuel sales, it wanted to plant information with the ultimate user, who will request it when consulting a doctor. Pfizer Canada Inc. has done the same thing with Viagra, a drug designed to cure male impotence. Their print and television ads encourage men to talk to their doctor about the problem. Both companies believe that if consumers ask for the product, doctors will prescribe it. Another example of direct marketing in the pharmaceutical industry involves the distribution of prescription drugs through mail-order pharmacies or from online pharmacies. In such a channel, it is possible to bypass traditional retail pharmacies and offer consumers lower prices.

Advancing technology makes marketing by mail, telephone, and the Internet very efficient. In all cases, the traditional channel of distribution is bypassed. For example, Amazon.ca buys books from publishers and markets them directly to consumers. No bricks-and-mortar stores are needed. Dell Computer has built its entire business around direct marketing, first by telephone and now by the Internet and telephone. Orders received online by Dell now account for about half of the total business. In both cases, consumers are opting for convenience when buying online, an important factor that manufacturers must consider when developing a marketing strategy.

The issues of direct marketing and electronic marketing are discussed in detail in Chapters 15 and 17.

MULTI-LEVEL MARKETING

multi-level marketing (network marketing)

Multi-level marketing, or **network marketing**, as it is often referred to, is a distribution system in which independent business owners become associated with a parent company in a contractor-like relationship. Owners receive money for shopping within their own business, for selling products and expanding their network of people doing the same. An owner receives a percentage of the profits generated by the network of all owners introduced to the system by him or her. Among the largest and most successful network marketing companies are Amway, Mary Kay, NuSkin, and Tupperware.[15] Amway currently has more than 3 million distributors selling personal-care products, homecare products, nutrition products, and commercial products. The company's success is based largely on customer loyalty.[16]

This form of marketing has an image problem, because it is difficult to distinguish from an illegal practice called pyramid selling. A pyramid scheme is a non-sustainable business model involving an exchange of money for recruiting other people into the scheme, often without any product or service being delivered. Success hinges completely on the exponential growth of new members.

In assessing whether to get involved with such a practice, a consumer should be aware of exaggerated claims of earning potential, the nature of inventory management expectations (e.g., how much an individual has to stock), product return policies, and required purchases as a condition of entry into the system. According to recent laws, measures can be taken against companies that set up unrealistic expectations of earning potential, and if claims are made they must be the average of all participants.

CONTRACT MARKETING

In business-to-business marketing, selling via a contract is normal practice. A typical contractual agreement covers price policies, conditions of sale, territorial rights, service responsibilities, and contract length and termination conditions. More specifically, a supplier agrees to provide goods at certain prices or with certain discounts, and at a quality level that is guaranteed. Further, policies and procedures for returned merchandise are established. If geographical area of operation is an issue, that too must be established (e.g., exclusive territories for a Harvey's or KFC franchise). Usually, the buyer limits the duration of such a contract in order to maintain control. They also specify conditions that could lead to the termination of the contract.

Levi Strauss and Wal-Mart Canada recently struck a contract marketing arrangement involving a new line of Levi's jeans. It is an extension of an existing relationship that has proven to be profitable in the United States. The new line, priced at or under $39, is exclusive to Wal-Mart stores in Canada. Such an arrangement is likely to exert some downward pressure on the price of jeans in Canada.

In some cases, contract marketing presents risk for the producing company. When Air Canada became insolvent in 2003 it terminated its food contract with Cara Operations Limited, the supplier of in-flight meals. Air Canada was Cara's largest customer, accounting for $155 million in sales, or 13.7 percent of the company's gross revenue.[17] Such a direct hit is hard to digest!

Many companies rely heavily on contractual arrangements with Wal-Mart. Wal-Mart currently accounts for 25 percent of Clorox company products and 40 percent of Fruit of the Loom underwear sales. What happens if Wal-Mart does not renew the contract? Wal-Mart does not want to be the sole source of survival for a company, and in recent years has been shortening the length of its contracts with suppliers.[18]

7. Explain the various components of physical distribution and logistics management.

Physical Distribution and Logistics Marketing

Physical distribution or **logistics marketing** involves planning, implementing, and controlling the physical flow of materials, finished goods, and related information from points of origin to points of consumption to meet customer requirements at a profit.[19]

physical distribution (logistics marketing)

Technology is changing the nature of logistics marketing. Traditionally, producers of goods would evaluate and then implement the most efficient method of delivering goods to customers. Today, however, it is the customer, not the producer, that is the centre of the distribution universe. Essential planning starts with the customer and works backward in the channel to the manufacturer and even to the suppliers of raw materials and parts. This method of planning is called supply chain management and it embraces the efficient flow of materials, information, and finances as they move in process from supplier to manufacturer to wholesaler to retailer to consumer. It involves coordinating and integrating these flows both within and among companies.[20]

In a supply chain management system there are *outbound distribution* decisions involving the movement of goods from the point of manufacture to customers, and *inbound distribution* decisions involving the movement of goods from suppliers to the point of manufacture. See Figure 12.9 for an illustration. From a marketing perspective, there are specific goals for a supply chain management system. An efficient system will serve customers better by providing lower prices and better service when goods are delivered or returned. An efficient system will also provide cost savings that trickle down to the bottom line—improved profit margins. Finally, the use of sophisticated planning software from companies such as Geac and Oracle and other technologies such as point-of-sale scanners, satellite tracking devices, and electronic data interchanges provide for efficient ordering, delivery, and payment of goods.

In a supply chain management system, the key logistical components include order processing, warehousing, inventory management, transportation and transportation coordination, and customer service (Figure 12.10).

ORDER PROCESSING

order processing

Essentially, **order processing** involves accepting an order from a customer, ensuring that sufficient stock is available, and then shipping the order through established procedures. Sometimes, not all items that a customer orders are available for shipment. This situation is referred to as a **stockout**. Customers must be advised of stockout situations so that they will know if the item will be shipped automatically at a later date or if a new order must be placed for the item. As indicated above, much of today's ordering, delivery, and billing processes are fully automated with information electronically flowing among distributors, manufacturers, and suppliers.

stockout

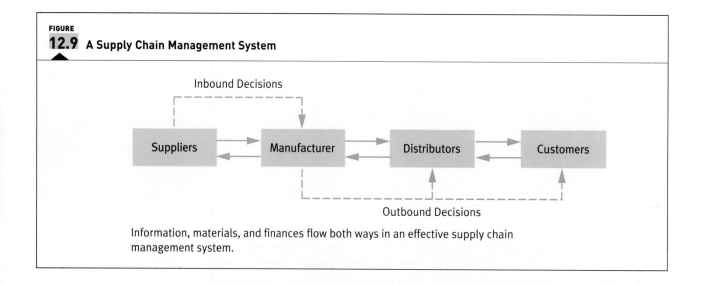

FIGURE 12.9 A Supply Chain Management System

Information, materials, and finances flow both ways in an effective supply chain management system.

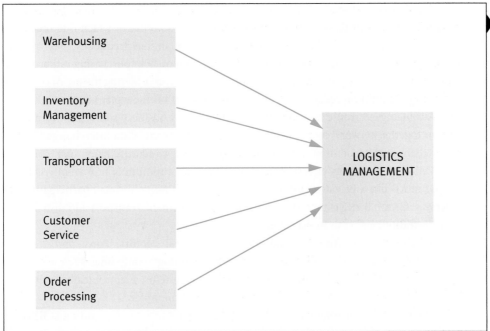

FIGURE
12.10
**Logistical Components
of a Supply Chain
Management System**

WAREHOUSING

The role of a **warehouse** is to receive, sort, and redistribute merchandise to customers.
There are two types of warehouses: storage warehouses and distribution warehouses. A
storage warehouse holds products for long periods of time in an attempt to balance
supply and demand for producers and purchasers. Generally, these facilities are not
specialized; they handle a variety of items, such as tires, equipment, appliances and other
hard goods, and case goods. Very often, a storage warehouse stores manufacturer inventory
that the manufacturer cannot handle in its own storage facilities.

warehouse

storage warehouse

A **distribution warehouse**, or **distribution centre**, assembles and redistributes
merchandise, usually in smaller quantities and in shorter periods of time. A variety of
goods ordered by a customer are assembled into a truckload by the distribution centre
for shipment to the customer. Sobeys warehouses, for example, receive shipments from
a variety of manufacturers (refer to Figure 12.3). These warehouses store, assemble, and
redistribute the same merchandise in smaller quantities to their retail locations. The
success of many organizations, including Wal-Mart and Canadian Tire, has been built
on the efficiency of their distribution centres.

distribution warehouse
(distribution centre)

Modern warehousing operations are very sophisticated; some are fully automated,
with orders being placed electronically. The use of hand-held scanners to place orders is
commonplace in many retail operations. Orders are then processed from a fully automated warehouse that can read computerized orders, determine the correct quantity of
each product, and move them in desired sequence to the loading dock. The automated
system then determines how much stock is needed from producers. Automated warehouses are extremely expensive, but in the long term they provide for cost efficiency in
large-volume distributors, such as grocery and hardware chains.

8. Explain how technology-
based supply chain
management systems are
improving operational
efficiencies in the channel
of distribution.

INVENTORY MANAGEMENT

Inventory management is a system that ensures a continuous flow of needed goods by
matching the quantity of goods in inventory to sales demand so that neither too little
nor too much stock is carried. It is the system of balancing supply with demand in such
a way that the costs of carrying inventory are kept to a minimum while enough inventory is maintained to meet the demands of customers.

inventory management

just-in-time (JIT) inventory
system

Many firms in Canada and the United States have adopted a system of Japanese origin called the **just-in-time (JIT) inventory system**, the objective of which is to reduce the amount of inventory on hand by ordering small quantities frequently. Past practice involved ordering large quantities at low costs to save money in purchasing rather than in storing. A JIT inventory system is more feasible than ever, considering the use of computer technology in inventory planning and in other forms of business planning.

electronic data interchange (EDI)

Advancing electronic technology has brought many businesses in a channel of distribution together to work cooperatively through an **electronic data interchange (EDI)**—an exchange of structured information, by agreed standards, from one computer application to another by electronic means and with a minimum of human interaction.[21] Acting much like a private communications channel among business participants, EDI offers significant benefits in terms of inventory management, transport and distribution, administration, and cash management.

All three North American automakers—General Motors, Ford, and Daimler-Chrysler—as well as durable-goods and high-technology companies such as General Electric and IBM, use electronic data interchange systems. Electronically exchanging data among companies online is becoming more commonplace.

RFID (radio frequency
identification)

The next wave of intelligent technology to impact inventory planning is **RFID,** or **radio frequency identification**. RFID tags will be placed on goods so they can be instantly tracked anywhere in the world. Wal-Mart has requested that its top 100 suppliers have the tags on their shipments by January 2005 and all other suppliers by 2006 if they want to continue the business relationship. This technology will allow Wal-Mart to improve inventory management: it will know what goods are in stock and where they are located at all times.[22] The use of RFID offers several benefits: improved forecast accuracy, increased shelf availability, reduced order cycle times, automatic replenishment, and enhanced collaboration between supplier and customer. With efficiency there will be incremental profits.[23]

Leading retailers such as Wal-Mart and Canadian Tire are examples of companies that have been quick to react to new electronic technology. Both organizations share information with suppliers electronically that they never did before. As a result, buyers no longer have to worry about calculating required inventory. Instead, they can focus on buying the correct merchandise, determining product mixes, and keeping up with the latest trends in the marketplace—in short, providing a better selection of merchandise to keep their customers satisfied.

For more insight into the important role that logistics management plays in an organization today, read the Marketing in Action vignette **Supply Chain Management Is Key to Success**.

TRANSPORTATION

Transportation tends to be the most costly item in physical distribution. The goal of a transportation system is to be efficient so that the producer has a competitive advantage. Hence, a logistics manager evaluates the basic modes of transportation available for the delivery of goods and the location of the customer, and then selects the most efficient. The modes of transportation are trucks, railways, air carriers, waterways, and the Internet.

Trucks are used to make small shipments over short distances. Deliveries within a local area or a certain region are made by truck. Truck transportation is also used for very long hauls, when time is not a consideration. The main advantages of truck delivery are that it can serve a number of locations, particularly distant and remote locations that other modes cannot reach. On the negative side, damages to goods do occur when

MARKETING IN ACTION

Supply Chain Management Is Key to Success

In the channel of distribution, efficient distribution is the modern-day mantra. Fail to deliver a few too many times and you could become a *former* supplier. From a manufacturer's perspective there has been a shift from cutting costs to improving quality, and now the shift is toward efficient distribution.

Delivering goods seems like such a simple process. Products come into a distribution centre, dealers order the products, and products are picked up and shipped to their destination. "Most delivery problems stem from chronic supply problems," says John Gordon, a Queen's University operations management professor. He often cites the 1990 launch of the Gillette Sensor razor as an illustration in delivery mismanagement.

Gillette spent hundreds of millions of dollars on a multimedia advertising campaign that worked so well the company could not meet the pent-up demand for the new product. Gordon says people in sales and marketing frequently underestimate the lead time needed to close a deal.

Today, large organizations use information technology to avoid transportation and logistics problems. Demand-planning software, for example, looks at past delivery history, projects demand activity, reduces chaos, and streamlines operations.

As an alternative, companies are outsourcing logistics planning and are employing companies such as Purolator and UPS to deliver the goods. Purolator recently formed a joint venture with PBB Global Logistics to add customs clearance and trade and regulatory services to its corporate offerings. Purolator president Robert Johnson saw a need for such a service. He says "corporate customers today demand one-stop shopping when it comes to trans-border shipments, full compliance and ease of movement." His company meets that demand!

By calling upon external logistics experts, companies are finding there is a competitive advantage to having a superior supply chain. Apparently, a hassle-free delivery system allows a manufacturer more time and money to build other areas of the business. To put it another way, every time you see a FedEx cargo plane, you're seeing product from a company that couldn't deliver its own order on time!

Adapted from Paul Baker, "Get time on your side," *Financial Post*, October 27, 2003, pp. FP10, FP11.

Rene Johnston/CP Photo Archive

using trucks. Truck transport is significant. Approximately 70 percent of Canada's two-way merchandise trade with the United States moves by truck (80 percent export and 60 percent import).[24] ***Railways*** are the most efficient mode of transporting bulky items over long distances (e.g., farm equipment, machinery, steel, and grain). From Ontario and Quebec, new automobiles are shipped to destinations all over Canada and the United States. Trains can carry a wide range of products, and they serve a large number of locations. The frequency of shipments is, however, low.

Air carriers commonly carry expensive items that can absorb the high freight costs (e.g., technical instruments and machinery). It is also common to ship perishable goods and urgently needed goods by air. The appeal of this method lies in its speed and in the number of markets it serves, particularly major urban markets in Canada and around the world. Its high cost is its major disadvantage.

Shipping by *waterways* involves moving goods by ocean tankers and inland freighters. In Canada, waterway shipping through the St. Lawrence Seaway and the Great Lakes is common. The use of water transportation is widespread for bulky items, such as coal, iron ore, grain, chemicals, and petroleum products. High-value finished goods from overseas are also shipped by water. For example, automobiles from Japan and South Korea arrive in Vancouver by water carrier.

Water transportation is attractive because it allows a wide range of products to be moved at low cost, with only a small amount of loss or damage. On the other hand, movement by water is slow; water carriers can reach only certain places; and shipments tend to be infrequent.

*The **Internet*** is an invisible distribution system that will continue to grow and play a larger role in delivering goods and services. The electronic delivery of computer software, music, and media content from newspapers, magazines, and television, for example, is now commonplace. Refer to Figure 12.11 for an illustration.

TRANSPORTATION COORDINATION

containerization

intermodal transportation

To increase efficiency, more and more firms are employing a combination of transportation modes to ship their products. When several modes of transportation are used, containerization plays a key role. **Containerization** entails the grouping of individual items into an economical shipping quantity that is sealed in a protective container for intermodal transportation to a final customer. **Intermodal transportation** involves two or more modes of transportation, with goods being transferred from one mode to another (e.g., air to truck or rail to truck).

FIGURE
12.11

CTV News digitally delivers the news to Canadians

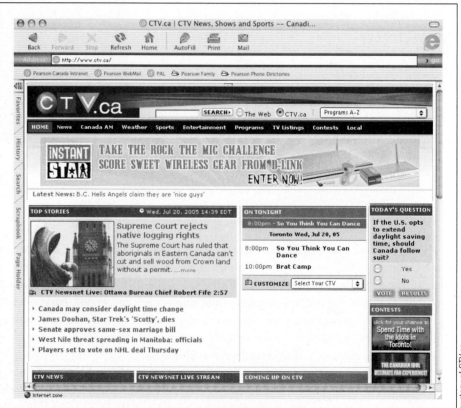

Courtesy of CTV.ca

The most common form of intermodal transportation is piggybacking. **Piggy-** piggybacking **backing** is a system in which the entire load of a truck trailer is placed in a rail flatcar for movement from one place to another. The railway performs the long haul, and the truck performs the local pickup and delivery. Other combinations for intermodal transportation are possible, such as the combination of trucking and water. For example, ferries are used to transport goods from Vancouver Island to the mainland, and trucks are used to complete the delivery of goods.

The combination of air and truck transportation is common for cargo carriers, such as UPS (United Parcel Service) and Federal Express. These companies combine truck fleets for ground travel with air cargo for overnight delivery to distant locations. Due to the growth of online marketing, business has been booming for third-party cargo carriers such as UPS. Companies that have embraced the Internet as a means of marketing goods require the specialized services that UPS and others provide. See Figure 12.12 for an illustration. As well, courier companies are now very active in larger shipments, reflecting the just-in-time demands of today's supply chain: smaller, more

FIGURE
12.12

Delivery specialists now play a more important role in the delivery of manufacturers' goods

frequent shipments that have helped eliminate inventory—and in many cases entire warehouses—from the distribution system.

Coordinating the transportation activities of a large company is a challenge, and sophisticated electronic technology is changing the way in which transportation alternatives are evaluated. Consequently, many firms are now looking at outsourcing their logistics management systems. It seems that companies would prefer to spend more time on what they do best, which is the manufacture and marketing of a product. Distribution and related issues are left to experts such as Ryder Integrated Logistics, a full-service trucking operation that specializes in just-in-time delivery.

CUSTOMER SERVICE

Determining how much customer service to provide and how much to spend on this service are the major considerations for a company that is developing a physical distribution strategy. To provide good service, suppliers of goods develop an order-processing system designed to maximize frequency (how often orders are received), speed (the time it takes to process orders), and consistency (the correct and punctual filling of orders). They also provide warehousing when necessary and develop emergency shipping policies.

In providing good distribution service, a firm evaluates costs against opportunities. Usually, the alternatives with the lowest costs are preferable to the organization, but not to the customer. Therefore, to encourage sales, firms may choose higher-cost options. A producer might want to ship by rail, but loading and unloading at various points might slow down delivery. The customer might want prompt, direct shipment by truck transport, a method that could cost the producer more. To meet the service needs and expectations of customers, the firm may decide to ship by truck despite the extra expense.

SUMMARY

Distribution planning entails making decisions regarding the physical movement of merchandise and its transfer between producers and consumers. A channel of distribution comprises organizations known as intermediaries, middlemen, or channel members. The role of such intermediaries as wholesalers, agents, brokers, and retailers is to facilitate the transfer of merchandise in an efficient, economical manner.

Since manufacturers ship large quantities, while retailers and consumers purchase in small quantities, wholesalers provide a sorting function. Sorting refers to the accumulation, allocation, classification, and assorting of merchandise.

Channels of distribution are either direct (short) or indirect (long). Short channels are commonly used to distribute expensive capital goods under circumstances in which communications between the producer and buyer are crucial. For goods that are less valuable and purchased more frequently, long channels of distribution are used.

With the Internet emerging as a means of delivering goods, many firms are adopting a multi-channel model. Such firms are examining all possible avenues for distributing goods to customers rather than relying on traditional channels.

The elements a firm considers when designing channel strategy include customer location, product characteristics, competition, company resources, and the stage in the product life cycle. Usually, a company that wants to maintain control over marketing programs and customer contact will use direct channels. Companies that are more flexible about control will use indirect channels.

Channel length refers to the number or levels of intermediaries in the channel of distribution. Channel width is the number of intermediaries at any one level of the channel.

Usually, a channel becomes wider as the product moves toward the point-of-purchase (i.e., the retail level where consumers buy). Distribution can be intensive, selective, or exclusive, depending on the marketing objectives of the producing firm.

Within any channel, conflict between members may occur. Conflict can be horizontal (i.e., between similar members at the same level) or vertical (i.e., between members at different levels). The channel captain implements strategies that encourage cooperation between channel members. These strategies include providing good service, fair pricing policies, advertising and promotional support, sales training programs, and the adoption of relationship marketing principles.

Integrated marketing systems are a means of gaining increased control over channel operations. Basically, two types of integrated marketing systems exist. In a vertical marketing system, a manufacturer, wholesaler, or retailer could be in control. These vertical systems are (1) administered, in which case the member with the most economic influence holds control; (2) contractual, in which case control is maintained through a legal agreement; and (3) corporate, in which case one company operates at each level of the channel. In a horizontal marketing system, one firm has many members at one level of the channel.

The pursuit of new channels of distribution is now a hotly contested battleground among competing companies wanting to expand sales. Both manufacturers and retailers are adding direct marketing and Internet strategies as a means of serving consumers whose shopping habits are changing. Other popular alternatives include multi-level marketing systems and contract marketing.

Today, customers are the centre of the distribution universe. Effective supply chain management is crucial. Supply chain management involves the efficient flow of information, materials, and finances among channel members. The use of planning software and independent logistics experts facilitates effective supply chain management. Physical distribution refers to the activities involved in the delivery of merchandise. The major components of physical distribution include customer service, transportation, warehousing, inventory management, and order processing.

KEY TERMS

accumulation   293
administered VMS   306
allocation   293
assorting   294
backward integration   307
channel captain   301
channel length   296
channel width   296
containerization   314
cooperative advertising   305
contractual VMS   306
corporate VMS   307
direct channel   294
distribution   292
distribution planning   292
distribution warehouse (distribution centre)   311

electronic data interchange (EDI)   312
exclusive distributionn   300
forward integration   307
franchise agreement   307
horizontal conflict   300
horizontal marketing system   308
indirect channel   294
intensive distribution   299
intermediary   292
intermodal transportation   314
inventory management   311
just-in-time (JIT) inventory system   312
multi-channelling   296
multi-level marketing (network marketing)   308
order processing   310

physical distribution (logistics marketing)   309
piggybacking   315
retail cooperatives   307
RFID (radio frequency identification)   312
selective distribution   299
sorting   294
sorting process   293
stockout   310
storage warehouse   311
supply chain   305
supply chain management   305
vertical conflict   301
vertical marketing system (VMS)   305
voluntary chain   307
warehouse   311

REVIEW QUESTIONS

1. What is the basic role of intermediaries in the channel of distribution?

2. What is the role of the sorting process in the distribution of goods? Briefly describe the basic elements of the sorting process.

3. What is the difference between a direct channel and an indirect channel? Under what conditions would a company select one option or the other?

4. Briefly describe the factors a firm considers when designing a channel of distribution.

5. What is the difference between channel length and channel width?

6. Under what conditions are the following types of distribution appropriate?
   a) Intensive
   b) Selective
   c) Exclusive

7. What is the difference between horizontal conflict and vertical conflict in the channel of distribution?

8. What is a channel captain, and what role does the channel captain play in the distribution channel?

9. Identify the factors that encourage cooperation among members of a channel of distribution.

10. What are vertical integration and horizontal integration? Provide a new example of each concept.

11. Briefly explain the concept of supply chain management and explain the terms "outbound distribution" and "inbound distribution."

12. Briefly describe the various functions of physical distribution.

DISCUSSION AND APPLICATION QUESTIONS

1. What type of channel of distribution would you recommend for:
   a) A daily newspaper
   b) A cellular telephone
   c) A Rolex watch

2. What degree of distribution intensity is appropriate for each of the following?
   a) *Maclean's* magazine
   b) Toyota Lexus car
   c) Calvin Klein blue jeans
   d) Lever 2000 soap
   e) Rolex watches

3. Review the Marketing in Action vignette "Should Manufacturers Be Retailers?" Examine the facts presented in the vignette and answer the question posed in the title. Is competition from the manufacturer fair to the existing dealer network? Conduct some additional research on this issue before arriving at a conclusion.

4. Conduct some secondary research on contract marketing (contract distribution) in North America. Identify some markets and companies that have been successful in implementing this strategy. Is it fair to block out competition in this manner? What is your opinion?

5. Assume you are going to open a coffee shop in your local market. Would you pursue a franchise opportunity, or would you open up your own independent shop? For cost details on franchises you may wish to consult the *Franchise Annual,* which should be available in the reference section of your school library. If you were contemplating buying a franchise, which one would you select? Defend your selection.

E-ASSIGNMENT

In this assignment, you will assess the channel strategy being employed by Chapters bookstores. Chapters traditionally sold books in "big box"–style stores located in major Canadian cities. More recently, Chapters opened Chapters Online to capitalize on the trend of online book buying. Amazon.com from the United States was doing a brisk business in Canada. Conduct some Web-based research to determine the success of Chapters' online venture. In the long term, what effect will the online business have on Chapters' bricks-and-mortar business? Are multiple channels the route for Chapters to follow? Are there other distribution strategies Chapters should be considering in the short term and the long term?

ENDNOTES

1. Joel Evans and Barry Berman, *Marketing,* 3rd edition (New York: MacMillan Publishing Company, 1987), p. 234.

2. Michael Dell, "Growing with the Internet: Worldwide and Direct" (speech), November 3, 2000, www.dell.com/us/gen/corporate/speech.

3. Leonard Zehr, "Mail-order drug supplier under gun," *Globe and Mail,* February 8, 2003, pp. B1, B6.

4. www.judsonfoods.com/English/Our)Company/corp.

5. Kevin Marron, "Multi-channel route pays off for retailers," *Globe and Mail,* October 25, 2002, p. B11.

6. Shownei Chu, "Dell to sell PCs in kiosks in Canadian shopping malls," *Globe and Mail,* October 26, 2002, p. B4.

7. Kevin Marron, "Multi-channel route pays off for retailers," *Globe and Mail,* October 25, 2002, p. B11.

8. Mark Evans, "The push to pull buyers online," *Globe and Mail,* August 19, 1999, pp. T1, T2.

9. Scott Gardiner, "A wall of silence around retailers' growing clout," *Marketing,* May 28, 2000, p. 16.

10. John Heinzl, "Brick granted bottle reprieve," *Globe and Mail,* February 15, 2003, p. B2.

11. Phinjo Gombu, "Clash of the movie titans," *Toronto Star,* February 1, 2003, pp. H1, H13.

12. Hollie Shaw, "Shoppers Drug Mart Charging Key Suppliers," *Financial Post,* January 18, 2005, pp. FP1, FP2.

13. AC Nielsen, www.acnielsen.ca/Insights/In the news/March/2003.

14. Alimentation Couche-Tarde Inc., www.hoovers.com/fere/co/factsheet.

15. http://en.wikipedia.org/wiki/Multi-level_marketing.

16. Amway Corporation, www.hoovers.com/free/co/factsheet.

17. Rick Westhead, "Air Canada kills Cara deal," *Toronto Star,* November 11, 2003, p. C1.

18. Jack Neff, "Wal-Mart weans suppliers," *Advertising Age,* December 1, 2003, pp. 1, 33.

19. Philip Kotler and Gary Armstrong, *Principles of Marketing,* 10th Edition (Upper Saddle River, NJ: Prentice Hall, 2004), p. 419.

20. searchCIO.com Definitions, www.searchico.techtarget.com/Definitions.

21. http://en.wikipedia.org/wiki/Electronic_Data_Interchange.

22. Barbara Duckworth, "Follow that cow," *National Post Business,* April 2004, pp. 51, 52.

23. Christian Stephan, "Tag, you're it: Meeting the RFID challenge," An Information Supplement for Supply Chain and Logistics Canada, *Globe and Mail,* April 19, 2004, p. B9.

24. "Quick facts about trade and trucking," advertising supplement in *Canadian Business,* February 2002.

Dick Hemingway

Wholesaling and Retailing

Wholesaling and Its Functions

Wholesaling is the process of buying or handling merchandise and subsequently reselling it to organizational users, other wholesalers, and retailers. It is big business in Canada. In 2003, the total value of transactions by wholesalers across all trade groups was $421.3 billion. The largest categories of wholesalers are food products ($76 billion) and motor vehicles ($70 billion). Other large categories include machinery and equipment and building supplies.[1] As discussed in the previous chapter, the wholesaling role is performed either by manufacturers themselves or by independent channel members. Not all independent wholesalers, however, perform every wholesaling function, so when wholesalers are required, a company will select one that meets its needs. The following list describes the basic functions performed by wholesalers.

1. *Providing Market Coverage*—Manufacturers produce and market their goods from one or a few locations, or goods could be imported and stored in a distribution warehouse. Since customers tend to be geographically dispersed, a wholesaler provides the means to efficiently reach them. The wholesaler takes possession of the goods for redistribution to retail customers. In distributing goods, a wholesaler's sales force can complement a manufacturer's own sales force.

2. *Holding Inventory*—In many cases, the title to the merchandise is transferred to the wholesaler, who then holds the goods in inventory. For the manufacturer, this reduces the financial burden of carrying inventory and improves its cash flow to other operational costs.

3. *Order Processing*—Wholesalers represent many manufacturers of similar products. Unlike manufacturers, wholesalers ship small quantities of a variety of merchandise to their customers. Wholesalers not only process orders for the manufacturers' products, but also spread the costs of the order processing across all the manufacturers' products that they represent.

4. *Performing Market Intelligence*—Since wholesalers are in frequent contact with their customers, they have a good understanding of customer needs (e.g., product requirements, service expectations, price). This information is passed on to manufacturers to assist in improving marketing strategies.

5. *Providing Service*—After goods have been transferred to the next level in the channel—to another wholesaler, retailer, or organizational customer—the wholesaler can address any problems that arise. Such service takes the form of returns or exchanges, installations, adjustments, general repairs, technical assistance, and training users in how to use equipment.

1. Define wholesaling and identify its functions.

wholesaling

6. *Providing Assortment*—Wholesalers carry a wide variety of manufacturers' products. The amassing of various items is called assortment. The assortment function simplifies customers' ordering tasks. In certain cases, customers can order from one wholesaler instead of many. A few general-line wholesalers can provide customers with most of the products they need.

7. *Breaking Bulk*—Breaking bulk refers to the delivery of small quantities to customers. Very often, customers do not meet the minimum-shipping-weight requirement established by the transportation companies that deliver the goods. Therefore, wholesalers buy in large quantities from manufacturers and break the "bulk" orders into small quantities so that their customers may buy in the quantities they need.

Types of Wholesalers

Within Canadian industries, wholesalers belong to one of three main categories: manufacturer wholesaling; merchant wholesaling; and agents and brokers (Figure 13.1).

MANUFACTURER WHOLESALING

In the case of **manufacturer wholesaling**, the producer undertakes the wholesaling function because the firm believes that it can reach customers (retailers and organizational customers) effectively and efficiently through direct contact. Direct contact may

2. Characterize the three main categories of wholesaling and the types of wholesaling firms that operate in each category.

manufacturer wholesaling

FIGURE

13.1

Types of Wholesalers

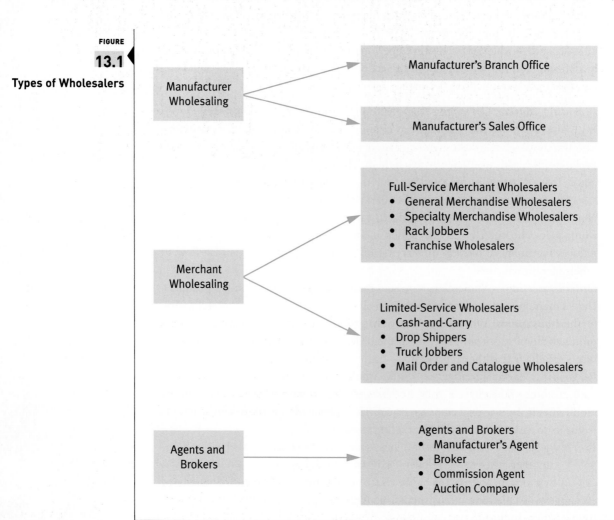

Manufacturer Wholesaling
- Manufacturer's Branch Office
- Manufacturer's Sales Office

Merchant Wholesaling
- Full-Service Merchant Wholesalers
  - General Merchandise Wholesalers
  - Specialty Merchandise Wholesalers
  - Rack Jobbers
  - Franchise Wholesalers
- Limited-Service Wholesalers
  - Cash-and-Carry
  - Drop Shippers
  - Truck Jobbers
  - Mail Order and Catalogue Wholesalers

Agents and Brokers
- Agents and Brokers
  - Manufacturer's Agent
  - Broker
  - Commission Agent
  - Auction Company

be necessary due to the fact that the product requires complex installation or servicing. Examples of such firms include technology-based companies, such as IBM and Xerox, that may ship directly to other organizational customers; and snack-food and beverage manufacturers, such as Hostess Frito-Lay and Pepsi-Cola, that use their own delivery trucks to ship directly to retailers. In each case, the manufacturer itself stores the merchandise in a warehouse and delivers it directly to retail customers.

Manufacturers often conduct wholesaling activities through a branch office or a sales office. Let us distinguish them from one another. A **branch office** is a company office in a specified geographic area, which usually includes a warehouse facility, from which goods are delivered to customers in the area. For example, the Prairie region may be served by a branch office (e.g., located in Regina) of a national company. A sales office is usually located near the customers, but it does not carry inventory. A **sales office** accepts orders that are processed elsewhere (e.g., a branch office or regional warehouse). In Canada, it is quite common for a manufacturer, such as Procter & Gamble or General Mills, to have centralized production and warehousing facilities and regional sales offices in key areas, such as the Atlantic Provinces, Quebec, Ontario, the Prairies, and British Columbia.

branch office

sales office

MERCHANT WHOLESALING

Merchant wholesalers perform the traditional functions of wholesaling. They buy goods and take both title to and possession of them, then resell them to other customers in the channel. The two classifications of merchant wholesalers are full-service wholesalers and limited-service wholesalers. The difference between the two classifications lies in the number and extent of services each provides.

merchant wholesaler

A **full-service merchant wholesaler** assembles an assortment of products in a central warehouse and offers their customers a full range of services, including delivery, storage, credit, and support in merchandising and promotion and in research and planning. They usually employ their own sales force, which regularly calls on retail customers. Full-service merchant wholesalers, who work closely with the manufacturers they represent, are common in certain industries: apparel and dry goods, plumbing and heating equipment, farm machinery and supplies, drug and tobacco products, and hardware supplies.

full-service merchant wholesaler

A **limited-service merchant wholesaler** is selective about the functions it performs. The different types of limited-service merchant wholesalers perform different roles. For an explanation of each type of full-service and limited-service wholesaler, refer to Figure 13.2.

limited-service merchant wholesaler

AGENTS AND BROKERS

Agents and *brokers* perform a variety of wholesaling functions but do not take title to the goods that are sold. They represent the seller in the transaction and work for commissions paid by the selling organization. The main difference between an agent and a broker is in the relationship with the seller. An agent is more likely to be used on a permanent basis, whereas a broker is usually used on a temporary basis. The main types of agents and brokers are manufacturers' agents, brokers, commission merchants, and auction companies.

MANUFACTURERS' AGENTS   A **manufacturers' agent** carries and sells similar products for non-competing manufacturers in an exclusive territory. Such agents are commonly associated with particular industries: electronics, automotive parts, clothing, and food. The commission arrangements for these wholesalers are attractive to small manufacturers that

manufacturers' agent

Full-Service Merchant Wholesalers	
General Merchandise Wholesalers	Offer a full line or wide assortment that serves virtually all customers' needs (e.g., Auto Sense Auto Parts)
Specialty Merchandise Wholesalers	Offer a limited number or narrow line of products but an extensive assortment within lines offered (e.g., frozen food wholesalers)
Rack Jobbers	Sell and stock merchandise in their own retail display racks. Merchandise is sold on a consignment basis; retailer pays when items are sold (e.g., suppliers of magazines and stationery supplies)
Franchise Wholesalers	Supply a complete range of merchandise to a network of franchisees that operate in accordance with a contractual agreement (e.g., National Grocers supplies Valu-Mart and Your Independent Grocer)
Limited-Service Wholesalers	
Cash-and-Carry	Offer a range of products in small quantities to small retailers such as convenience stores and corner stores; cash payment only; no additional merchandising support is provided
Drop Shippers	Wholesaler buys but does not take possession of merchandise; carload quantities of goods are assembled for delivery to customers; common in resource industries such as lumber and building supplies
Truck Jobbers	Distribute branded lines of semi-perishable and perishable goods such as breads, dairy products, and snack foods (e.g., Voortman Cookies and Betty Bread delivered fresh in a scheduled manner)

cannot afford the cost of directly contacting the same customers themselves. The agents' primary task is selling, on the basis of pricing policies established by the manufacturers they represent.

broker

BROKERS   A **broker** plays a key role in the negotiations between buyers and sellers. Depending on the industry and the nature of the selling situation, the broker's relationship with the supply organization can be permanent or temporary. Brokers are common in the financial services industry and the food industry. In financial services, licensed stockbrokers advise business clients and buy and sell stocks on their behalf. Food brokers represent suppliers (usually small manufacturers) to the wholesale and retail food trade. In both of these markets, the relationship between broker and client is usually a long-term one. Food brokers are paid a commission (5 percent is common), and their agreement with the supplier is usually outlined in a contract that clearly defines the length and terms of the arrangement.

Temporary relationships are commonly found in the real estate industry, where brokers are used for individual transactions. The broker may represent many different vendors (sellers) at any one time, but the relationship with each one ends when the sales transaction is complete. Canadian firms doing business in foreign markets frequently employ the services of an export broker.

COMMISSION MERCHANTS   A **commission merchant** works with small manufacturers or suppliers that require representation to reach customers in centralized markets. The merchant receives and sells goods on consignment. Typically, the supplier lacks marketing resources, so the commission merchant arranges shipment of the product to a market, completes the sale, and returns the collected funds (less the commission earned) to the supplier. Dairy and produce farmers rely on merchants to sell their products in urban markets, since the farmer cannot accompany each shipment of goods to the city.

commission merchant

AUCTION COMPANIES   An **auction company** brings buyers and sellers together at a central location to complete a transaction. The supply and demand for the merchandise at auction time determines the selling price. Auctions play a key role in markets, such as those for livestock, tobacco, and used automobiles. In Canada, one of the more famous auction companies is the British-based Sotheby's, which specializes in Canadian art and related products. Auction companies are usually paid a flat fee or a commission for the service provided.

auction company

3. Explain what retailing is and what its functions are.

Retailing and Its Functions

Retailing refers to those activities involved in the sale of goods and services to final consumers for personal, family, or household use. It is the last stage in the channel of distribution. In Canada, overall retail sales have increased steadily. In 2003, the latest year statistics were available for the writing of this book, retail sales in Canada amounted to $330.5 billion. The largest categories of retailers include new-car dealers ($68 billion) and supermarkets ($54 billion).[2]

retailing

The landscape of retailing has been changing in recent years. Traditional department-store retailers that appeal to a wide cross-section of the population have been losing ground to specialized retailers and discount retailers. The specialists include warehouse outlet stores such as Costco and Sam's Club (Sam's has four superstores in Toronto, and many more to come elsewhere). Wal-Mart, a price discounter that arrived in Canada in 1994 and now owns 54.7 percent of the department-store market,[3] is now the leading department store in Canada and attracts shoppers with a serious eye on value. Off-price retailers such as Winners (designer brands at popular prices) are also taking business away from traditional retailers.

The growth of discount retailing illustrates the changing values of shoppers today. More than ever before, retailers must understand how, when, and why customers buy the products they do. For example, time-pressed consumers now view the Internet as an acceptable alternative for personal shopping. The movement to online shopping has been gradual but steady and has created new challenges and opportunities for big and small retailers alike.

Generally, retailers perform four main functions (Figure 13.3):

1. Retailers are part of the sorting process: the store buys an assortment of goods and services from a variety of suppliers and offers them for sale.
2. They provide *information* to consumers through advertising, promotion, and personal selling.

FIGURE
13.3

**The Functions of a
Retailer**

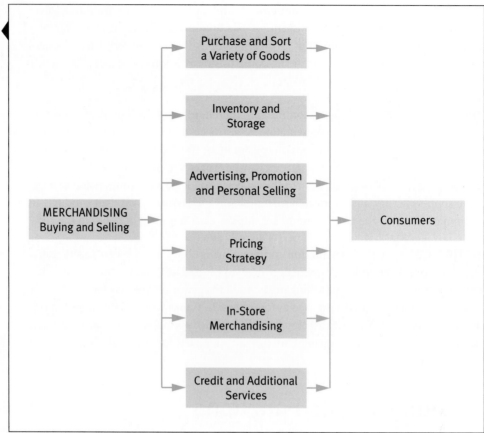

3. They *market* goods by storing merchandise, establishing selling prices, and placing items on the sales floor. They may also ship goods directly to consumers who make purchases online.

4. They complete a *transaction* by offering credit terms, convenient hours, and store locations, and other services such as debit card and credit card purchasing and delivery.

When shopping for goods at retail, the consumer usually has a number of retailers to choose from. A retail store is chosen on the basis of such factors as store image, hours of operation, availability of parking, quality of products carried, additional services provided, store location, and the environment of the store. In planning a strategy, retailers consider these factors and develop a **retailing marketing mix** to attract customers to the store. Retail marketing strategies are discussed in detail in the final section of the chapter.

As discussed elsewhere in the text, mid-market retailers such as the traditional department store are faltering because consumers are trading up or out to specialty stores, or trading down to discount outlets. Successful retailers are adapting to changes in consumer shopping tendencies and revising their marketing strategies accordingly. These retailers remain focused on what they do best. For example, Wal-Mart is focused on lower prices for a range of popular products, while Starbucks charges high prices for an enjoyable customer experience. Refer to Figure 13.4 on the next page for more examples.

retailing marketing mix

4. Describe the different types of retailing operations categorized by ownership, products and services offered, and method of operation.

Retailer Classifications

Canadian retailers are classified into groups according to form of ownership, products and services offered, and method of operation. The different types of stores have different characteristics and, therefore, diverse marketing strategies.

In a changing retail environment the companies that will succeed are those that understand consumer needs and realize they can't be all things to all people.

Successful retailers are the ones that focus on only a few core strengths. All consumer transactions can be reduced to five elements—**price, product**, **service, access,** and **experience**. The best retailers understand this and devote their resources to the one or two elements where they feel they can compete. Here are a few examples:

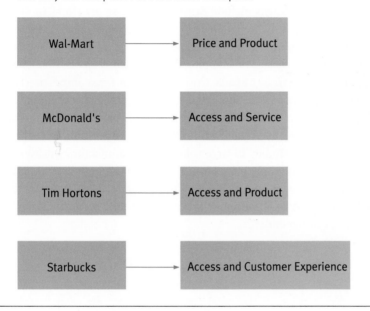

FIGURE
13.4

Understanding Consumers Pinpoints Strategic Focus for Retailers

Source: Adapted from Elizabeth Church, "Retailers don't listen, consumer study says," *Globe and Mail*, August 16, 2001, p. B3.

OWNERSHIP

In terms of ownership, there are three prevalent forms: chain stores, independent retailers, and retail franchises (see Figure 13.5).

CHAIN STORES   A **retail chain store** is an organization operating four or more retail stores in the same kind of business under the same legal ownership. Chain stores are a dominant and growing presence in the Canadian retail marketplace. Examples of large chain stores include specialty stores, such as Fairweather and Mexx (women's fashions), Tip Top Tailors and Moore's (men's fashions), The Brick and Future Shop (consumer electronics), and Sears and The Bay (department stores).

retail chain store

Type of Store	Description	Example
Chain Store	National in scope; four or more stores in chain	The Brick, Future Shop, Tip Top Tailors
Independents	Locally owned stores	S&R Department Store (Kingston), Playful Minds Toy Store (Toronto)
Retail Franchises	Locally owned stores operating to franchisor specifications	Harvey's, A Buck or Two, Mr. Lube, Druxy's

FIGURE
13.5

Retail Stores by Ownership

As mentioned earlier, the trend in shopping behaviour is toward discount department stores, warehouse outlets, and price clubs, and away from traditional chain stores. Costco, for example, a relatively new price club operation, is Canada's largest mass merchandiser, with annual sales of $7.6 billion. That sales volume exceeds The Hudson's Bay Company, Canadian Tire, and Sears.[4] Refer to Figure 13.6 for details. Let us distinguish among these new types of retail outlets.

warehouse outlet (big-box store)

price club

Warehouse outlets are no-frills, cash-and-carry outlets that offer consumers name-brand merchandise at discount prices. They are commonly referred to as **big-box stores**. Examples of warehouse outlets include Brico (building supply stores in Quebec) and Rona and Home Depot (building supply stores throughout Canada). **Price clubs** are essentially the same as warehouse outlets, except consumers must pay an annual fee (usually $40 to $50) for the privilege of shopping there. Costco is an example of a very successful price club operation in Canada. Costco will soon face competition from Sam's Club, Wal-Mart's version of a warehouse outlet, which is gradually expanding in Canada.

Warehouse outlets and price clubs are somewhat hybrid operations; they actually perform many wholesaling and retailing functions in one operation, since their size and buying power allow them to buy in large volume and manufacturers deliver directly to each outlet. They carry anything from Mont Blanc pens to Pirelli tires to Bounty paper towels, so they are competing with all kinds of traditional retailers. Typically, these stores offer limited selection and a minimum of services—but their prices are lower, and that's what brings the customers in!

FIGURE
13.6

Canada's Top Merchandisers and Food and Drugstores

Source: "Financial Post 500 Canada's Largest Corporations," *National Post*, June 2004, pp. 142, 144.

Rank	Retailer	Revenues
Top Merchandisers		
1	Costco Wholesale Canada	7 583 397
2	Hudson's Bay Co.	7 400 051
3	Canadian Tire Corp.	6 552 800
4	Sears	6 222 700
5	Liquor Control Board of Ontario	3 119 240
6	Rona Inc.	2 710 268
Top Food and Drug Retailers		
1	Loblaw Cos. Ltd.	25 220 000
2	Empire Co. Ltd.	10 624 200
3	Katz Group Inc.	6 000 000
4	Canada Safeway Ltd.	5 666 200
5	Metro Inc.	5 567 300
6	Shoppers Drug Mart Corp.	4 415 200

Notes: Empire Co. Ltd. includes Sobeys supermarkets, and the Katz Group includes drug stores under the Rexall, Pharma Plus, Medicine Shoppe, Guardian, and IDA banners and supermarkets under the Payless and Herbies banners.

Wal-Mart revenue figures are not separated from Wal-Mart U.S. in the *National Post* rankings of companies, so they do not appear on the list above.

In response to the growth of warehouse stores, some mass merchandisers and supermarkets, such as Canadian Tire and Loblaws, are opening their own warehouse stores and are adding new and non-traditional product lines. Loblaws, for example, is now the second largest seller of barbecues and patio furniture in Canada, and has aggressive plans to further expand the non-food side of its business.[5] With Loblaws and other stores now carrying such diverse product lines, the nature of competition is getting blurred. For more insight into how competition is intensifying among retailers, read the Marketing in Action vignette **Big Retailers Playing the Same Game**.

INDEPENDENT RETAIL STORES   An **independent retailer** is a retailer operating one to three stores, even if the stores are affiliated with a large retail organization. Independent retailing is dominant among dealers of domestic and imported cars, pharmacies, automotive parts, and locally owned food stores.

Independent retailers contrast greatly with chain stores. Competing with large chains is difficult. The chain store is a large-scale operation, and because it buys in large quantities, it can offer customers lower prices than the independent retailer can (although chains do not always choose to offer low prices). The risk of financial loss is also spread across many stores in a chain operation; successful stores compensate for the unsuccessful. To survive as an independent requires adequate financial resources and good management skills.

RETAIL FRANCHISING   A **retail franchise** is a contractual agreement (a franchise) between a franchisor (a manufacturer, wholesaler, or service sponsor) and a franchisee (the independent business person). In a franchising arrangement, the franchisee purchases the right to own and operate a certain line or brand of business from the franchisor for a specific location. Further, the franchisee agrees to subscribe to a certain set of rules and business practices—a franchisor requires that the product be prepared in a certain way, and management practices and accounting systems must be consistent among all franchisees. Some of the more common names in franchising include Canadian Tire, McDonald's, Pizza Pizza, Tim Hortons, Choice Hotels Canada (Comfort, Quality, Clarion, and Sleep Inns), and Budget Rent-A-Car Canada.

The typical franchise arrangement requires that an initial franchise fee and a percentage of sales (a royalty) be returned to the franchisor. Some franchisors also require that a percentage of sales be returned in order to build a fund for advertising, from which all franchisees benefit. For example, an A&W franchise (630 locations and $475 million in revenue in Canada) has an initial franchise fee of $50 000 and requires a total investment of between $125 000 and $250 000. A&W provides six weeks of in-store training and periodic training thereafter. In addition, the franchisee pays to the franchisor a royalty fee of 2.5 percent of sales and an advertising fee of 2.5 percent of sales.[6]

The advantages of owning and operating a franchise are similar to those associated with being part of a large chain. Franchises have a great buying capability, and each franchisee benefits from the image of the total franchise system. Knowing when to enter into a franchise agreement is crucial. There are risks associated with joining a new franchise early. A large investment could be wasted. Also, in a franchise there is little scope for innovation for the franchisee.

A fairly recent trend in franchising is **co-branding**. This involves two or more separate franchise operations in one facility. In theory, co-branding works best when stores offer complementary products. Couche-Tard, Canada's largest operator of convenience stores, has truly evolved the convenience store concept by adding space for other retail operations such as Timothy's coffee and Subway sandwich counters. Some of these new

independent retailer

retail franchise

co-branding

Big Retailers Playing the Same Game

There was a time when Loblaws competed with Safeway and Sobeys; Wal-Mart competed with Zellers and department stores such as The Bay and Sears; and Shoppers Drug Mart competed with London Drugs and PharmaPlus. There were clear dividing lines between retail categories, and various chains competed directly with each other. That was yesterday! Now the nature of competition is changing. It seems that all big retailers are competing with each other in one form or another.

Perhaps it all started with Wal-Mart's entry to Canada in 1994. Wal-Mart struck fear into the collective management mindset of traditional Canadian retailers. Wal-Mart had such a devastating impact that retailers such as Kmart and Eaton's went out of business. Wal-Mart started as a discount department store, but has gradually added product lines to compete with other retailers.

Wal-Mart's full-scale pharmacies offering prescription services pose a threat to Shoppers Drug Mart, London Drugs, and any other drugstore chain. The addition of groceries poses a serious threat to Loblaws, A&P, Safeway, and any other grocery chain. Next up is Sam's Club, a Wal-Mart operation that combines traditional Wal-Mart stores with a full-scale supermarket.

To survive, Canadian retailers are reacting. They too are adding unrelated product lines. According to John Torella, a prominent retail consultant, "Everybody is in everybody else's business and nobody is protected." They are expanding their business to get extra dollars out of time-pressed shoppers. Loblaws, for example, now sells clothing, soft home goods, cosmetics, office supplies, and electronics. Like Wal-Mart, it wants to provide the

best possible assortment of products. It also wants to keep people out of Wal-Mart!

Canadian Tire has also eyed new territory. In its newer, more shopper-friendly stores, lines such as housewares, home décor, home office products, ready-to-assemble furniture, stationery, and back-to-school goods have been added. Canadian Tire now competes with Ikea, Business Depot, Sears Home Outlets, and Home Outfitters. Strategically, Canadian Tire is positioning itself right between two giants: Wal-Mart and Home Depot.

Will these strategies work? John Torella believes Loblaws is on the right track. He says, "The perception of Loblaws hasn't changed—it's evolved." In fact, he thinks the Loblaws product strategy has taken a lot of confusion out of the marketplace. If customers have confidence in the Loblaw and President's Choice brands, they will save time and effort by shopping there for other things. There is a problem, though: other big companies are adopting the same strategy. Will we all end up shopping in a few mega-stores?

Adapted from Sara Minogue, "Blurring the boundaries," *Strategy*, June 30, 2003, p. 13.

Dick Hemingway

stores have enough seats and tables for 55 patrons. The convergence of fast-food and convenience stores is emerging rapidly. More than 300 Esso gas stations now include On the Run convenience stores, which share space with a Tim Hortons outlet.[7] See Figure 13.7 for an illustration.

FIGURE 13.7 Co-branding of franchised outlets is a popular strategy

Jay LaPrete/CP Photo Archive

PRODUCTS AND SERVICES OFFERED

Stores are also classified based on the extent of products carried and services offered. Essentially, a store offers a full range of services, a limited range of services, or is a self-serve operation.

PRODUCT LINES   Stores classified by product line are determined by the variety of different items they carry and the assortment of each item. A **specialty store** carries a variety of products for a single product line; for example, Aldo carries shoes, and Old Navy carries casual clothing. A **limited-line store** carries a large assortment of one product line or a few related lines of goods (e.g., SportChek sells a variety of sporting goods equipment and a variety of leisure sportswear; Ikea sells home furnishings and household goods).

The concept of warehouse outlets (big-box stores) was mentioned earlier. Prominent big-box retailers have taken hold of numerous product categories—Toys "R" Us (toys and children's accessories), Staples Business Depot (office equipment and supplies, and Rona (home renovation and repairs). There is a spectrum of sizes among big-box stores. Chapters, for example, is 12 times the size of a traditional book store, and Staples Business Depot is 5 times the size of a traditional office supplies store.[8]

Finally, a **general-merchandise store** offers a wide variety of product lines and a selection of brand names within these product lines. Stores such as Sears and The Bay fall into this classification.

specialty store

limited-line store

general-merchandise store

self-serve store

full-serve store

limited-service store

SERVICES OFFERED   In a **self-serve store**, the retailer provides minimum services. The stores rely heavily on in-store displays, merchandising, and reasonable prices to attract customers. Warehouse stores, such as Costco, are self-serve operations, as are supermarkets, hardware stores, and drugstores. In contrast, a **full-serve store** offers customer assistance and a greater variety of in-store service that includes fitting rooms, delivery, installations, and alterations as part of the service mix. Traditional department stores, such as The Bay and Sears, and specialty stores, such as Holt Renfrew and Harry Rosen, are full-serve stores. Discount stores, such as Zellers and Wal-Mart, offer some personal services but their goal is to keep services minimal so that they can maintain lower prices for shoppers. Stores like these can be classified as **limited-service stores**. For a summary of stores by product line and services offered, see Figure 13.8.

Within each of these categories of stores are different types of stores. There are convenience stores, supermarkets, superstores, variety stores, department stores, and discount department stores. Descriptions such as these suggest the nature of products carried and services offered. For a description of these stores and a few examples, refer to Figure 13.9.

METHOD OF OPERATION

The previous sections described retailing in the traditional sense; that is, the purchase of goods in retail stores. There are other ways a retailer can market goods to consumers. In today's market, there is a trend toward marketing to consumers directly. Such retailing includes vending machines, direct home retailing, direct selling, catalogues, temporary display of merchandise, and electronic retailing (e-tailing).

VENDING MACHINES AND AUTOMATED MERCHANDISING   We do not usually think of a vending machine as a form of retailing, but it is. Vending machines often sell cigarettes, soft drinks, coffee, and confectionery products. These machines generate annual sales of approximately $712 million (2002) each year.[9] The machines are usually owned and operated by the retail stores, restaurants, and service stations where they are

FIGURE
13.8

Retail Stores by Products and Services Offered

Type of Store	Description	Example
Product Line		
Specialty Store	Variety of products for a single product line	Sony, La Senza, Roots
Limited-Line Store	Large assortment of one product line or a few related lines	Future Shop, Golf Town
Big-Box Store	Segment specialist; diverse product lines in segment	Staples Business Depot, Chapters, Toys "R" Us
General Merchandise Store	Wide variety of product lines and brand names	The Bay, Sears
Services Offered		
Self-Serve	Minimum of services	Costco
Limited-Serve	Selection of services important to operations	Canadian Tire, Zellers, Wal-Mart
Full-Serve	Wide variety of in-store services	Sears, The Bay

FIGURE
13.9

Retail Stores by Type of
Operation

Type of Store	Description	Example
Convenience Store	Small, food-oriented stores in local communities	Mac's, 7-Eleven, Couche-Tard
Supermarket	Departmentalized food stores (dairy, meat, produce, frozen and packaged food)	Safeway, Sobeys, A&P
Discount Supermarket	Limited-line supermarket offering fewer services and lower prices	Food Basics, No Frills, Save-On
Superstore	Diversified supermarkets carrying a broad range of products	Atlantic Superstore, Real Canadian Superstore
Department Store	General-line retailers offering a variety of products in many price ranges	The Bay, Sears
Discount Department Store	Full line of products at popular prices (fewer services than department stores)	Wal-Mart, Zellers

located. In other arrangements, space in retail locations may be leased by vending machine operators, or the retailer and vending machine operator may strike a deal to share profits in return for the space granted by the retailer.

Vending operators are expanding their traditional lineup of chocolate bars, hot and cold drinks, and other snack foods. Specialty coffees, such as cappuccino and espresso, have been added to the vending menu. Manufacturers are looking at vending machines as a way of increasing market penetration and brand recognition. Nestlé Canada, for example, uses vending machines to sell some of its top-selling brands (Nescafé coffee, Stouffer's entrées, Kit Kat and Smarties chocolate bars). See the illustration in Figure 13.10.

DIRECT SELLING   Direct selling occurs in a variety of forms. Consumers may buy directly based on information received in an infomercial or some other direct-response commercial. An **infomercial** is an extended commercial in a television show format that continuously sells a particular product or service. A **direct-response commercial** is usually a 30-second commercial promoting the availability of goods and services through a 1-800 telephone number. The commercial encourages consumers to call the number to place an order. These concepts are discussed in detail in Chapter 15, "Direct Response and Interactive Communications."

infomercial

direct-response commercial

DIRECT HOME RETAILING   **Direct home retailing** is the selling of merchandise by personal contact in the home of the customer. Several variations of direct home selling exist, covering a wide variety of product lines from cosmetics to vacuum cleaners, newspapers, and toys. Some of the selling alternatives include cold canvass, referrals, and party selling. When the **cold canvass** technique is used, a salesperson in search of customers knocks without notice on doors in a neighbourhood. Electrolux and other vacuum cleaners are sold in this manner. *Telemarketing* campaigns such as those conducted by Bell Canada to sell additional services are another form of cold canvass selling.

direct home retailing

cold canvass

Dick Hemingway

referral

party selling

Tupperware
www.tupperware.com

Holt Renfrew
www.holtrenfrew.com

If **referrals** are used, visits with customers are planned. A salesperson secures names of potential customers from satisfied customers and makes an initial contact by telephone to arrange a time for a face-to-face meeting. A company such as Avon or Amway operates in this way.

In a **party selling** situation, one person acts as a host and invites friends to his or her home for a sales demonstration. Tupperware products are the merchandise best known for being sold on a party-plan basis, though Tupperware has expanded into mail order and telemarketing programs more recently.

The direct selling and direct home retailing market in Canada currently generates about $1.7 billion in sales annually and is an industry expected to grow in importance in the years ahead. It offers strong appeal to time-pressed consumers, who are spending much less time in shopping malls. In fact, the amount of time people spend in shopping malls has fallen by half in the last 15 years, from 110 minutes a week to 45 minutes.[10]

CATALOGUE MARKETING   The distribution of catalogues is another aspect of retailing that is expanding in Canada. In Canada, Sears is probably the largest organization selling goods directly, through its Sears Catalogue. Holt Renfrew, the upscale women's fashion retailer, uses an in-house shopping magazine called *Holt's* to communicate with its customers. *Holt's* includes editorial and advertising features on the store's latest lines. People read the publication with the purpose of buying the sharply edited product selection. According to Barbara Atkin, Holt Renfrew's fashion director, "It's perfect for the time-pressed. It takes a lot of the guesswork out of the process for the reader, making it easy to shop for the hottest items."[11]

TEMPORARY DISPLAYS AND KIOSKS   Traditional retailers are showing interest in concepts such as temporary carts and kiosks as alternatives to opening stores in malls or standalone locations. Peoples Jewellers, for example, recently launched Peoples II, a concept involving a handful of mall carts designed to attract the young, hip impulse buyer. The plan is to start slowly—Peoples tested four locations prior to the 2004 Christmas season. The company believes the cart concept has the potential to add $10 million in sales to its $175-million annual sales in Canada.[12]

Telecommunications companies such as Rogers, Telus, and Bell also utilize kiosks in shopping malls in an attempt to stop busy shoppers passing by. In some cases a store and a kiosk are located in the same mall. It's simply a matter of making the buying situation more convenient for consumers. See the illustration in Figure 13.11.

E-TAILING   The retailing experiment with perhaps the best promise for the future is selling merchandise online. While online shopping remains a tiny fraction of total personal expenditures, Canadians are using the Web in increasing numbers to buy everything from airline tickets to books to lingerie. In 2003, more than 2.8 million Canadian households spent $3 billion for goods purchased online, an increase of 25 percent from 2002.[13]

FIGURE
13.11 Kiosk locations provide added convenience for time-pressed shoppers

Dick Hemingway

In terms of popularity among consumers and direct application by retailers, adoption of online retailing has been relatively slow. Slower adoption is partly attributed to our underdeveloped catalogue market, from which online retailing strategies are a natural extension. The issue of Internet security is also a major concern expressed by consumers. Retailers must address the security issue by implementing better consumer education programs.[14]

The transition to electronic retailing has been relatively easy for Sears. Sears was an established catalogue retailer, so an operational infrastructure that included an automated warehouse and distribution system facilitated the transition to online retailing. Sears.ca is consistently one of the top sites in Canada for online traffic. For that reason, Sears refers to itself as "Canada's online merchant."[15] Other popular Canadian online retailers include Canadian Tire, Future Shop, and Chapters Indigo. All of these retailers are satisfied with their online activities. While each retailer offers stress-free shopping—no parking, no jostling, and no lines—they acknowledge that making the online venture profitable is difficult.

Companies like Sears and Canadian Tire have profitable online divisions because they treat the venture seriously, rather than as sideline of their main business. In the past (namely, the dot-com bust of 1999–2000), many upstart online retailers went under because they didn't have the depth of experience required. Recent history shows there is much more to successful online retailing than having a flashy website. Future Shop executives firmly believe a bricks-and-mortar presence helps customers feel more

FIGURE

13.12 Sears effectively combines e-tailing with traditional retailing

Dick Hemingway

© Sears Canada, Inc., 2005

comfortable with online buying: if something goes awry in cyberspace there is a physical presence they can go to. As well, people want to shop online with a brand they know and trust. Future Shop actually offers more products online than it does in the stores.[16] Refer to the illustration in Figure 13.12.

Ironically, Canada's largest retailer—Wal-Mart—has a corporate presence online but does not sell goods online. It's all about making money, and to date Wal-Mart sees all kinds of companies encountering losses. The Sam's Club division of Wal-Mart, which sells groceries and other household merchandise, does sell online. Perhaps Wal-Mart's rather cautious approach remains the best approach.

Sam's Club
www.samsclub.com

The Retailing Marketing Mix

5. Outline the major elements of retail planning.

When devising a marketing strategy, retailers consider numerous elements—all of which have an ultimate impact on consumers. The challenge is to select and integrate the right combination of elements that will bring the customers in! The major considerations in retail marketing planning are location, brand identity, atmosphere, merchandise assortment, merchandise control, and marketing communications strategy (Figure 13.13).

LOCATION

Many experts suggest that three factors contribute to the success of a retail operation: *location, location, and location!* Traditional thinking suggests that a good location in a high-traffic area gets people into a store. Once they are inside, the quality of the product and the service will determine whether and how often the customers will return. Consumers today, however, are willing to travel greater distances to obtain better value for their shopping dollar. The popularity of warehouse stores in large cities, outlet malls on major roadways outside of cities, and mega-malls that attract customers from hundreds of kilometres away support the "shopping for value" notion. The ability to buy online from anywhere in the world is another factor that suggests location will be less

FIGURE
13.13

Elements of Retail Planning

Consideration	Concerns
Site Location	Deciding where to locate (e.g., downtown, suburbs, regional shopping mall, power mall, etc.)
Brand Identity	Presenting brand banner (logo) in association with other marketing strategies affects consumers' perceptions of store
Atmosphere	Implementing physical characteristics required to create an enjoyable shopping experience (e.g., store layout and design, in-store displays, lighting, open space, etc.)
Merchandise Assortment	Determining the breadth and depth of product lines, and the relationship between product lines and stock balance
Merchandise Control	Implementing controls to measure actual performance against planned performance (e.g., analyzing stock turnover)
Marketing Communications	Communicating effectively with consumers to build store image, attract shoppers, and encourage loyalty

important in the future. This section outlines the various locations where retailers tend to place themselves.

central business district

The **central business district** is normally the hub of retailing activity in the heart of a downtown core (i.e., in the main street and busy cross-streets of a central area). The area usually contains the major financial, cultural, entertainment, and retailing facilities of the city. In Toronto, Bloor Street between Yonge Street and Avenue Road is now considered one of the great shopping avenues in the world. It is a street where those with money can find something to spend it on. The Eaton Centre in Toronto, Rideau Centre in Ottawa, and Pacific Centre in Vancouver, all downtown malls, are among the busiest shopping centres in their respective markets. The downtown location is a deterrent for many shoppers, though—the traffic congestion and lack of parking keep them away.

suburban mall

A **suburban mall** is located in built-up areas beyond the core of a city. In Toronto, for example, malls are geographically dispersed. In the east end of the city, there is the Scarborough Town Centre, and the west end has Sherway Gardens and the Woodbine Centre. In Burnaby, British Columbia, there's the Metro Town Centre. These malls draw most of their customers from those who work or live in the immediate area.

Malls located in the central business district or in suburbia contain as many as 100 or more shops and several large department stores. The stores carry shopping goods and include established retail specialty chains, such as HMV, Athlete's World, Northern Reflections, Aldo, and Radio Shack. Department stores usually anchor the mall.

outlet mall

Outlet malls have become popular in the past decade. An **outlet mall** contains factory outlet stores for well-known brands such as American Eagle, Esprit, Mexx, Nike, Buffalo, and La Senza. Outlet malls are usually located at a key intersection of a major highway. They attract value-conscious customers from distant locations.

mega-mall

The West Edmonton Mall, one of the world's largest indoor malls, is an example of a **mega-mall**. The mall has an area equivalent to 115 football fields, and includes more than 800 stores and services, 110 eating establishments, and 5 amusement areas, including a wave pool and rides for the children, a hockey rink, and many other attractions. A brand-new suburban mega-mall, Vaughan Mills, recently opened north of Toronto. Vaughan Mills combines the regional mall concept with the outlet mall concept. More than half of the stores are outlet versions of the regular retailers mentioned above, while another quarter of the stores are value-priced retailers such as Winners, Designer Depot, Payless, and H&M. The mall also features a bowling-alley-cum-nightclub with a restaurant and art gallery, a go-kart theme park, and other entertainment venues.

power mall (power centre)

A **power mall** or **power centre** is a mall that houses a number of category-killer superstores in one area. It is a concept that capitalizes on consumers' expressed interest in shopping in superstores where value is perceived to be greater. Stores that frequently locate in power malls include Home Depot (household products), Future Shop (electronics), Moore's (men's wear), Sears Home Furnishings (furniture, appliances, and bedding) and SportChek (sporting goods). See Figure 13.14.

lifestyle mall

Faced with rising costs and waning interest in large, traditional enclosed malls, developers have begun experimenting with a "lifestyle" mall concept. The **lifestyle mall** is a smaller, open-air shopping centre featuring clusters of 20 to 30 upscale stores, each with its own entrance onto a main street of the centre along with offices and residential units. The first lifestyle mall in Canada, the Village at Park Royal, recently opened in Vancouver. It features a new-concept Home Depot store spread over two storeys with a heavy emphasis on décor.[17] In Toronto, the Don Mills Shopping Centre was converted to a lifestyle mall and renamed the Don Mills New Town Centre. It features two-level stores with some overhead offices, restaurants, and entertainment venues opening onto landscaped streets with sidewalk cafés. Don Mills is an affluent suburb community.

FIGURE
13.14 Power malls are gaining in popularity

A **strip mall** is usually a small cluster of stores that serve the convenience needs of the immediate residential area. Such a shopping district is generally composed of a supermarket, a drugstore, a variety store, a dry cleaner, a bank, a hair stylist, and other similar service operations.

A **freestanding store** is an isolated store usually located on a busy street or highway. The nature of the business often influences the location of such a store. Consumers will travel beyond their immediate area for the products and services these stores provide. Examples include factory outlets, garden supply stores, discount department stores (e.g., Wal-Mart), and category killers (such as Home Depot and Staples Business Depot). The problem facing these types of retailers is that they must attract their customers without assistance from other retailers.

Research surveys indicate that people are shopping at traditional-style malls less frequently than they used to.[18] New alternatives such as outlet malls, power malls, and now lifestyle malls offer stronger appeal to shoppers and for a variety of reasons: they are time-pressed, tired of fighting traffic, and frustrated with parking problems and waiting in lines. Consequently, locations offering convenience and efficient service will continue to gain market share, while traditional malls will continue to lose ground.

For more insight into the criteria retailers use to determine best locations, read the Marketing in Action vignette **Best Chance to Succeed**.

strip mall

freestanding store

Best Chance to Succeed

To demonstrate the importance of location, let's examine how KremeKo Inc. chose the location for its first Krispy Kreme outlet in Canada. Located in Mississauga, just west of Toronto, the new store occupies a corner of a huge parking lot bordered by three four-lane roads and two expressways, and a stiff walking distance from an established power centre. The process started with a huge map of the Greater Toronto Area.

The company needed to build a bakery and retail outlet with 4500 square feet of space. It had to contain a doughnut machine 39 feet long, the centerpiece of the shop, as well as counters, tables, and 150 staff, the minimum needed to fry fresh doughnuts and display them behind glass cases. The company also needed an acre of parking space to handle the thousands of customers that would visit each day.

According to Chris Tarrant, vice-president of real estate for KremeKo, "The key to a successful outlet is a population base that is big enough to keep the operation bubbling along." Krispy Kreme looks for areas with 100 000 households within a short drive of each store. Ranking second in importance is high traffic flow. At the Mississauga location, 55 000 cars pass by each day—the bare minimum they look for is 35 000 cars. Third in importance is convenience. Coffee shop operators can only expect their customers to stop for a minute or two—the experience can't be too disruptive.

After studying the map of the GTA, Tarrant realized he would not be locating in the city. There was no space available at a cost the company could afford. All potential locations were in the suburbs and satellite communities. KremeKo subsequently opened a second outlet in Richmond Hill, a suburb community just north of Toronto.

Ironically, and despite the effort that KremeCo puts into its location decisions, the company suffered dramatic declines in sales and profits in 2004 and 2005. The low-carbohydrate craze that swept North America hit Krispy Kreme hard. It shows there's definitely more to retailing than location!

Other retailers in the fast-food industry factor in technology before making critical location decisions. Census data is mixed with a host of other information—credit card records, magazine subscriptions, driver's licences—and connected to postal codes to pin the information down to the nearest building or block. With the help of real estate experts, a fast-food hamburger chain should be able to predict with uncanny accuracy how many burgers it will sell, how many coffees it will sell, and how many salads it will sell in a prospective location.

Demographic data are critical to selecting fast-food locations. With good information, a company can predict how many stay-at-home mothers live in the area, how many kids and how many retired people there are, and how many will still be there in 10 or 15 years. Knowing how many teenagers are in the area is important, because they are the prime drivers of the fast-food industry. Stay-at-home moms are in demand, because they drop in with the kids during slow times of the day.

Education level is also a location factor for fast-food restaurants. Apparently high school dropouts eat more fast food than postsecondary students. The ratio of blue-collar to white-collar workers is also a factor. Fast-food restaurants need schools, factories, and offices nearby to provide their core customers.

So, the decision about where to locate a doughnut shop or hamburger restaurant is more complicated than one might think. Of all of the marketing factors that will affect the potential success or failure of the business, it really does boil down to the old real estate mantra of location, location, location. The right location gives the store its best chance to succeed.

Adapted from Oliver Bertin, "Sweet ideas behind doughnuts," *Globe and Mail*, October 8, 2002, p. B10.

Dick Loek/CP Photo Archive

BRAND IDENTITY

In today's marketplace, a retailer must think more like a brand marketer. Effective branding strategies will affect the perceptions consumers hold of a retailer. For example, applying a store banner to a premium-quality program will enforce a premium image for the store. To demonstrate, Harry Rosen is not just another men's wear retailer. Successful marketing strategies have separated Harry Rosen from its competitors. The Harry Rosen brand name suggests such attributes as quality, reputation, contemporary fashion, and personalized service. This shows that a powerful brand identity can be a retailer's most valuable asset.

The brand name and how it is presented to consumers is the one visual element that, without exception, must be consistently applied to all packaging, advertising, and promotions. To illustrate, one of Canada's hottest retailers is La Senza, a lingerie retailer operating under the names La Senza and Silk & Satin. The brand is the store and the store is the brand (see Figure 13.15). La Senza is one of a chosen few retailers—think Gap and Roots—to have a brand that customers immediately identify and understand. La Senza is not a Canadian version of Victoria's Secret. It is a store that walks the fine line between how men see lingerie—racy and exotic—and the way women view it, as something that should be pretty but comfortable. La Senza is successful at selling lingerie in a boutique setting. The name La Senza roughly translates from Italian into "little nothings," an appropriate expression for what it sells.[19]

FIGURE
13.15 The La Senza brand image

ATMOSPHERE

In retailing, **atmosphere** refers to the physical characteristics of a retail store or of a group of stores that are used to develop an image and attract customers. The image of a store has an impact on the type of customer who shops there, so retailers give their stores looks that will attract the sort of patrons they want. Image is created by a combination of elements: exterior appearance, interior appearance, store layout, and interior merchandising and display practices.

To demonstrate, one of the latest trends in retail design is minimalism. *Minimalism* refers to a very simple yet rigidly aesthetic design technique and a devotion to that aesthetic as a lifestyle principle. Style and fashion magazines have adopted the minimalist approach, and retailers have jumped on the trend. The Gap, for example, displays its merchandise in a neat and clean format that allows for a lot of open space in its stores. Bata introduced the "power-wall" of sneakers—a strategy copied by most of its competitors. When you walk by a store and see a wall of sneakers, you know exactly what the store sells. The minimalist approach cuts away the clutter and lets the merchandise speak for itself.

Despite its popularity, the minimalist approach presents challenges for retailers. Telus, for example, employs a very stark style of advertising that emphasizes the brand's blue and green colour scheme and lots of white space. While that look worked well in advertising, it was very sterile in a retail setting. Customers walked into an empty-looking store. There was nothing there to connect the product with the customer.[20]

Among electronics retailers another trend is emerging—the *demonstration centre*. With technology becoming more sophisticated, some retailers are showing shoppers how everything works right on the retail floor. Sony, for example, discovered many of its customers bought expensive equipment but were paralyzed when it came to getting maximum use from it. The company re-engineered its stores to have more of a "solution-oriented" look. Shoppers learn on-site how to retrieve a print from their digital camera via a personal computer—a strategy that removes the mystery and fear from making buying decisions.

Best Buy also discovered that educating its customers was more important than before. Best Buy established "tech-zones" and "discovery clinics" that deal with digital photos, movies, music, living rooms, and wireless technology. Best Buy staffers are also being trained to be experts on technology. Sales in tech-zone stores are 10 percent higher than average.[21] The goal, therefore, is to create an environment conducive to a better shopping experience for customers.

A recent innovation to improve the atmosphere of department stores is the introduction of the boutique. A **boutique**, also referred to as a **shop-in-shop**, is a store-within-a-store, a scaled-down version of a freestanding store within a larger department store. Fashion boutiques for clothing lines such as Ralph Lauren, Tommy Hilfiger, and Nautica are found in The Bay and other department stores. Canadian Tire recently acquired Mark's Work Wearhouse and is incorporating Mark's boutiques in designated Canadian Tire stores. Both the Canadian Tire and Mark's banners will appear outside the stores.

MERCHANDISE ASSORTMENT

Merchandise assortment refers to the product mix; it is the total assortment of products a retailer carries. To ensure that an adequate supply of goods is available to meet customer demands, retailers take into account three merchandising components: breadth and depth of selection, assortment consistency, and stock balance.

The **breadth of selection** concerns the number of goods classifications a store carries. For example, a department store carries fashion apparel, furniture, appliances, toys, sporting goods, home furnishings, fashions for men and women, linens, dry goods, and many more sorts of goods. A drugstore stocks cough and cold remedies, personal-care products, cosmetics, confectionery goods, and a mixture of general merchandise.

The **depth of selection** is the number of brands and styles carried within each classification. A drugstore sells numerous brands of toothpaste in a variety of sizes (50, 100, 150 mL) and flavours (regular, mint, berry). The type of retailer an operation is (e.g., department store, convenience store, or variety store) and the needs of the customers it serves determine the breadth and depth of product assortment.

depth of selection

Assortment consistency refers to product lines that can be used in conjunction with one another or that relate to the same sorts of activities and needs. An example of such consistency is a store such as SportChek, which carries various lines of sporting goods—baseball, hockey, basketball, and running, for example—as well as clothing and accessories to complement these sports.

assortment consistency

Some retailers adopt a strategy of assortment inconsistency. Called **scrambled merchandising**, it arises when a retailer begins to carry products and product lines that seem unrelated to the products it already carries. As indicated earlier in the chapter, many large retailers that are firmly established in their respective categories are adding unrelated lines in order to compete better with Wal-Mart and the anticipated presence of Sam's Club stores (a division of Wal-Mart) in the near future. Loblaws has aggressively expanded its non-food product mix by opening "mall-in-one" stores offering a wide variety of merchandise including kids' clothes, recreational products and outdoor furniture, and services such as full-service pharmacies, fitness centres, photo developing, dry cleaners, and gas bars.[22]

scrambled merchandising

In Canada, Canadian Tire is the most-shopped retailer, attracting more than 90 percent of consumers at one time or another.[23] What is it that attracts so many shoppers to Canadian Tire? According to Wayne Sales, CEO of Canadian Tire, "Successful retailers have the ability to adapt, evolve, and execute" and that's exactly what Canadian Tire does to attract customers.

Canadian Tire just recently introduced a merchandising strategy it refers to as "Concept 20/20." The goal is to increase store sales by 20 percent through increasing selling space by 20 percent. Concept 20/20 incorporates new product categories, bigger and better displays, brighter lighting, demonstrations and presentations, and new signage. Four distinct sections (Living, Playing, Fixing, and Driving) showcase apparel, footwear, home, and recreational products.[24] Progressive and aggressive product and merchandising strategies keep Canadian Tire in the forefront of Canadian retailing despite intense competition from Wal-Mart, Rona, and other hardware and hard goods retailers. Canadian Tire is a company that is very comfortable with change.

Stock balance is the practice of maintaining an adequate assortment of goods that will attract customers while keeping inventories of both high-demand and low-demand goods at reasonable levels. This is not an easy task, but such factors as profit margin, inventory costs, and stock turnover have a direct impact on cash flow and profitability. In addition, the retailer must know the market and tailor the product mix accordingly. Thus, decisions are made regarding what assortment of name brands and private-label brands to stock, what variety of price ranges to offer, and what mix of traditional (established) products and innovative (new) products to stock. Since reordering of goods is now so automated, retail buyers can spend more time making decisions about what goods and what brands to stock.

stock balance

MERCHANDISE CONTROL

There is a direct link between merchandise planning and merchandise control. The best of plans can go awry if proper controls are not implemented to measure the relationship between actual performance and planned performance. The concept of inventory turn or inventory turnover is a key measure of retail control. **Inventory turn** is the number of times during a specific time period that the average inventory is sold. The period for calculating inventory turn is usually one year. Inventory turn is calculated by dividing retail sales at cost (the value of the inventory) by the average inventory. Therefore, if sales at cost were \$100 000 and the average inventory was \$20 000, the inventory turn would be 5 (\$100 000 divided by \$20 000). If a retailer determined that this was a poor inventory turn rate, new marketing strategies would be considered to try to improve the situation.

Knowing the inventory turn rate allows the retailer to plan inventory (i.e., to match supply with demand) effectively. It also enables the retailer to compare the current turnover with past turnovers, to compare one department with another, and to compare the turnover (performance) of different stores in a chain operation. Inventory turn is a guideline for planning. In large retailing organizations, where advanced information technology is the norm, much of the mystery has been removed from inventory control and balancing supply and demand. Electronic point-of-sale equipment triggers the entire reordering system.

MARKETING COMMUNICATIONS STRATEGY

Survival today depends on the retailer's ability to build brand loyalty, because consumers are suffering from "time starvation" and shopping at fewer stores. Further, consumers are thinking of stores the way they do brands, so it follows that stores to which they are extremely loyal will succeed and stores for which they feel little loyalty will fail. In response to this trend, Canadian Tire's philosophy, for example, is to "think like a brand, act like a retailer." Canadian Tire is therefore building bigger and better stores that provide consumers with a pleasant shopping experience, adding new product lines, and employing creative advertising campaigns to build its image. Canadian Tire's branding campaign, "It all starts here," is one of the best examples of retail branding in Canada. It is an established position that customers readily identify with.[25]

The customer experience is increasingly becoming just as important as the products the customer actually buys. Consequently, retailers are getting more sophisticated in how they look at their entire business. According to Dianne Brisebois, president and CEO of the Retail Council of Canada, "It's not just having great visual merchandising, great customer service or great lighting. It's about how all these elements come together and how communications drives traffic to the stores."[26] In an attempt to differentiate themselves retailers are now concentrating on the emotional side of the brand experience, for they know consumers now want to do business with retailers that understand them better.

In Ontario, the LCBO (Liquor Control Board of Ontario) attributes much of its success to an emotional in-store experience and effective marketing communications. For example, displays for wine are often accompanied by different recipes to show customers how they can enjoy the wine. A strong communications visual is a key aspect of the product display. Colin Beaton, managing director of Watt International (a store design consulting company) says, "The LCBO has taken wine and alcohol categories and made them into a fashion and a lifestyle."

SUMMARY

This chapter introduces some of the key elements of whole-saling and retailing activities. Wholesaling involves buying and handling merchandise and reselling it to organizational users, to other wholesalers, and to retailers. The functions of a wholesaler include providing direct sales contact, holding inventory, processing orders, offering sales support, enabling assortment, and breaking bulk.

There are three main categories of wholesalers. In a manufacturer's wholesaling operation, product is sold directly to customers through branch offices and sales offices. Merchant wholesaling consists of full-service wholesalers and limited-service wholesalers. Full-service wholesalers include general-merchandise wholesalers, specialty-merchandise wholesalers, and franchise wholesalers. Cash-and-carry outlets, drop shippers, truck jobbers, and mail-order wholesalers are limited-service wholesalers. The agent and broker categories encompass manufacturers' agents, brokers, commission merchants, and auction companies.

Retailing is the activity involved in selling goods and services to final consumers. The primary function of a retailer is assortment (i.e., bringing together a wide selection of merchandise to one location to meet the needs of customers). Many types of retail operations exist in Canada, and the businesses fall into various classifications depending on form of ownership, product and services offered, and method of operation.

When retailers are classified based on ownership, stores are categorized as retail chain stores, independent stores, or retail franchise stores. When classified according to products and services offered, there are specialty stores, limited-line stores, warehouse outlets, and general merchandise stores. In terms of services provided, there are full-serve stores, limited-serve stores, and self-serve stores. Non-store retailing is an alternative for selling goods. This category of retail operations includes vending machines, direct selling, direct home retailing, catalogue marketing, temporary displays and kiosks, and online retailing.

The diversity of competition and several emerging trends in retailing are creating challenges and opportunities for retailers. Among these trends are the growth of large-format warehouse outlets, big-box stores located in power malls, and steady growth in online retailing. Traditional retailers must adapt to the changes or suffer the consequences. Many retailers are launching websites that will help build brand image and drive shoppers to retail locations. Others are integrating e-commerce directly with bricks-and-mortar stores.

Key aspects of retail marketing strategy include selecting a good location, building a brand identity that resonates with targeted consumers, creating an atmosphere conducive to a pleasant shopping experience, carrying an appropriate selection of merchandise and offering appropriate services, and communicating with customers in a meaningful manner.

KEY TERMS

1. Describe the basic functions associated with wholesaling.
2. What is the difference between a manufacturer wholesaling system and a merchant wholesaling system?
3. Identify and briefly describe the types of full-service merchant wholesalers.
4. Identify and briefly describe the types of limited-service merchant wholesalers.
5. Under what circumstances are agents and brokers likely to be used by a manufacturing organization?
6. What are the basic functions of a retailer?
7. How do warehouse outlets differ from traditional retail stores?
8. Explain the concept of retail franchising and identify the advantages of owning a franchise.
9. In the context of retail franchising, what is piggybacking?
10. Identify and briefly explain the various forms of non-store retailing.
11. Briefly describe the difference between a power mall, a mega-mall, and a lifestyle mall.
12. How important is atmosphere in the retail marketing mix? Briefly explain.
13. Briefly explain the concept of a merchandise assortment.
14. What is scrambled merchandising?
15. Explain the importance of inventory turnover for a retailer.

DISCUSSION AND APPLICATION QUESTIONS

1. Provide a few examples of each of the following types of retailers. Do not include examples mentioned in the textbook.

   a) Discount supermarket
   b) Convenience store
   c) Specialty store
   d) Chain store
   e) Retail franchise
   f) Discount department store
   g) Warehouse outlet

2. Visit a department store in your local market, then present a brief analysis of your perception of the store's image as conveyed by the atmosphere considerations discussed in this chapter. Do the same analysis for a warehouse outlet.

3. What is the best location for the following types of stores in the market nearest your college or university? Explain your choice.

   a) Photography equipment and supply store
   b) Leisure sportswear store
   c) Upscale specialty dress shop
   d) Japanese car dealership

4. Considering the trends in retailing that were presented in this chapter, what is your assessment of the future direction of retailing? For example, will consumers opt for convenience and flock to warehouse outlets, power malls, and the Internet, or will they retreat to neighbourhood shops, where personalized service is more important? What is your opinion?

5. Review both the Marketing in Action vignette "Best Chance to Succeed" and the discussion about location decisions in the chapter. Assume you are going to open a Country Style doughnut shop in your local market. Where would you locate the store? Provide proper justification for your decision.

6. Select a retailer in your local market or a national chain retailer operating in your market. Conduct some secondary research on that retailer to determine the nature of its marketing strategy. What elements of the retail marketing mix are given priority? Are there any areas the retailer could improve upon?

E-ASSIGNMENT

Visit the websites of a few of the retailers listed at right. Compare and contrast the websites for their ability to build image and market goods and services. Are some sites easier to navigate than others? Is it easier to buy on some sites than others? What are the characteristics of a good retail website? Some websites to visit include:

- Canadian Tire
- Sears
- The Hudson's Bay Company
- La Senza
- Future Shop

ENDNOTES

1. www.statcan.ca/english/Pgdb/trad200.html.
2. www.statcan.ca/english/Pgdb/trad15a.html.
3. Jacqui McNish and Marina Strauss, "Pressure on HBC's Heller as equity, hedge funds circle," *Globe and Mail*, March 12, 2005, p. B5.
4. "Financial Post 500 Industry Leaders," *National Post Business*, June 2004, p. 144.
5. "Loblaw plans to take a bite out of healthy foods market," *Globe and Mail*, December 6, 2004, p. B6.
6. "Marketplace," *Franchise Canada*, May/June 2004, p. 72.
7. Jason Chow, "Milk is not enough," *National Post Business*, December 2004, p. 50+.
8. Ken Jones and Michael Doucet, *"The Impact of Big-Box Development on Toronto's Retail Structure,"* Research Report, 1999, p. 1, Ryerson Polytechnic University.
9. "Non-store retailers," *The Daily*, Statistics Canada, May 25, 2004.
10. Dana Flavelle, "Traditional mall now a harder sell," *Toronto Star*, September 21, 2004, p. D2.
11. Mary Pompili and Janet Eger, "Power Tools," *Marketing*, April 19, 2004, p. 23.
12. Marina Strauss, "Peoples takes shine to new retail concept," *Globe and Mail*, October 12, 2004, www.globeandmail.com.
13. "Online shopping leaps 25%, but we're slow to embrace it," *Toronto Star*, September 24, 2004, www.thestar.com.
14. "AC Nielsen Study Finds Continued Growth in Online Purchasing," press release, March 12, 2003, www.acnielsen.ca/News/ContinuedGrowthinOnlinePurchasing.
15. Philip Quinn, "All in favour of online shopping, say 'I'," *Financial Post*, May 23, 2001, p. E2.
16. Peter Brieger, "Online comeback," *Financial Post*, February 3, 2004, p. FP6.
17. Dana Flavelle, "Traditional mall now a harder sell," *Toronto Star*, September 21, 2004, p. D2.
18. "Malls losing popularity with shoppers," *Marketing News*, May 26, 1998, p. 10.
19. Zena Olijnyk, "Va va va boom," *Canadian Business*, May 13, 2002, pp. 49–52.
20. Sara Minogue, "Why minimalism works," *Strategy*, June 30, 2003, pp. 11, 15.
21. Lisa D'Innocenzo, "In store for the future," *Strategy*, September 2004, pp. 30, 32.
22. Hollie Shaw, "Loblaw to expand sales of non-food items," *Financial Post*, May 1, 2003, p. FP7.
23. Peter Brieger, "Chapters shoppers' favourite store, survey shows," *Financial Post*, June 30, 2004, p. FP3.
24. Cathy Gulli, "Canadian Tire Corp. Ltd.," *National Post Business*, July 2004, p. 55.
25. Sara Minogue, "Blurring the boundaries," *Strategy*, June 30, 2003, p. 13.
26. Rebecca Harris, "The New Rules of Retail," *Marketing*, July 26/August 2, 2004, p. 11.

Integrated Marketing Communications

This section examines the roles of the various elements of the integrated marketing communications mix. Integrated marketing communications embrace numerous forms of communication: advertising, public relations, direct response, interactive communications, sales promotion, personal selling, and event marketing and sponsorship.

Chapter 14 introduces the concept of integrated marketing communications and describes briefly the major components that comprise the marketing communications mix. The chapter then moves into more specific discussion of two components of the marketing communications mix: advertising and public relations.

Chapter 15 focuses on direct forms of communication by discussing various forms of direct response and interactive advertising opportunities.

Chapter 16 discusses related elements of the communications mix: sales promotion, personal selling, and event marketing and sponsorships.

PART

7

Advertising and Public Relations

Learning Objectives

After studying this chapter, you will be able to

1. Describe the marketing communications process and the role of the various elements of the integrated marketing communications mix.

2. Identify the factors that influence the size of a marketing budget and list the methods for determining a budget.

3. Describe the strategic decisions involved in developing the creative component of an advertising campaign.

4. Differentiate between creative strategy and creative execution in advertising.

5. Describe the key elements involved in planning a media advertising campaign.

6. Differentiate between media objectives, media strategies, and media execution.

7. Describe the various types of public relations activities.

8. Explain what role public relations has in the communications process.

9. Assess the usefulness of a variety of public relations tools.

---

1. Describe the marketing communications process and the role of the various elements of the integrated marketing communications mix.

integrated marketing communications

advertising

The Integrated Marketing Communications Mix

Integrated marketing communications involves the coordination of all forms of marketing communications in a unified program that maximizes the impact on consumers and other types of customers. It embraces a variety of communication methods: advertising, public relations, direct response and interactive advertising, sales promotion, event marketing and sponsorships, and personal selling (see Figure 14.1).

Several trends have contributed to the growth of integrated marketing communications. First, the use of database management techniques resulting in more effective customer relationship management programs has forced marketers to use non-traditional media along with traditional mass media. Marketers can now reach their targets collectively and individually. Second, advancing technology such as the Internet, cell phones, and personal digital assistants has opened up new means of communication. These technologies offer interactive capabilities that enhance the relationship with customers. Finally, managers today are working with fewer financial resources in an environment where more accountability is required. With spending efficiency a must, marketing managers are looking at "total solutions" to their business problems. Integrated marketing communications play a key role in achieving that goal.

Strategically, managers evaluate how to best utilize the various components of the communications mix. Rarely are all components used at the same time. Instead, they are selected based on the situation at hand: the manager considers the nature of the problem; the availability of appropriate information about the target market (e.g., demographic, psychographic, and geographic information); and the budget available.

Let's start the discussion about integrated marketing communications by clearly explaining the fundamental nature of each form.

ADVERTISING

Advertising is a persuasive form of marketing communication designed to stimulate a positive response from a defined target market. Typically, the role of advertising is to

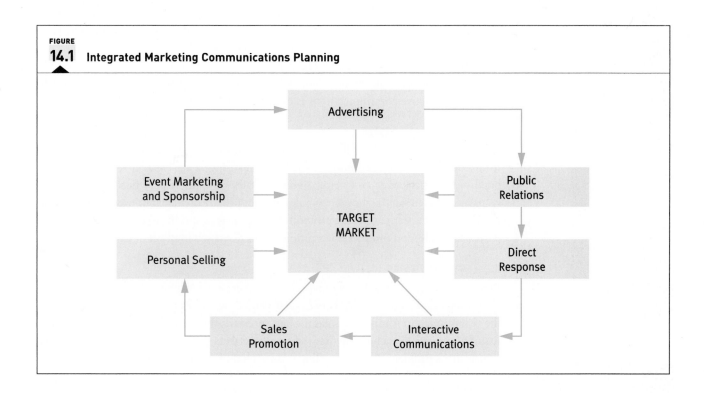

FIGURE 14.1   Integrated Marketing Communications Planning

create positive impressions in the customer's mind that eventually lead to action—the purchase of the advertised product. Advertising can be divided into two primary areas: development of the message (creative planning) and selection of appropriate media to deliver the message (media planning). These concepts will be discussed in detail later in this chapter.

PUBLIC RELATIONS

Public relations is a form of communication designed to gain public understanding and acceptance. Modern-day public relations practices play a significant role in the launch and development of new products and services. A good public relations program gets the sponsor's message into the media without costs being incurred. In effect, public relations can generate "free" exposure. Something as simple as a press release about a new product or service could wind up a news story in every daily newspaper across the country. Such exposure offers legitimacy that advertising does not have. A more complete discussion of public relations occurs later in this chapter.

public relations

DIRECT RESPONSE

Direct response involves the delivery of a message to a target audience of one. As the term implies, "direct" means direct from the marketing company to a current or new user. Direct mail, direct response television (DRTV), telemarketing, and catalogues comprise direct response communications. This segment of the communications industry is growing much faster than traditional forms of advertising. Technology and database marketing techniques are the resource around which direct response communications programs are developed. These forms of communications are discussed in detail in Chapter 15.

direct response

INTERACTIVE COMMUNICATIONS

Interactive communications encompass online advertising and Web-based communications; cell phones and other personal communications devices; and CDs, DVDs, and

interactive communications

electronic kiosks. The new emphasis by organizations on customer relationship management and their ability to manage internal databases is forcing organizations to move into interactive communications. This form of communicating is particularly important for reaching younger consumers who have grown up with computers and cell phones. Interactive communications is discussed in detail in Chapter 15.

SALES PROMOTION

sales promotion

Sales promotion involves offering special incentives to stimulate immediate reaction from consumers and distributors. Whereas advertising is strategic in nature—it helps build brand image over an extended period—sales promotion is tactical in nature and helps increase sales in the short term. Sales promotions are divided into two primary areas: consumer promotions and trade promotions. Each plays a specific role in achieving short-term sales goals for a product. Sales promotion is discussed in detail in Chapter 16.

PERSONAL SELLING

personal selling

Personal selling is the delivery of a personalized message from a seller to a buyer. From the selling organization's perspective, personal selling brings the human component to the communications mix. The sales message presents the features, attributes, and benefits of a product in such a way that the product meets the customer's needs or resolves a customer's problem. Personal selling is presented in more detail in Chapter 16.

EVENT MARKETING AND SPONSORSHIP

event marketing

sponsorship

Event marketing involves planning, organizing, and marketing an event that supports the strategic marketing direction of a brand or company. **Sponsorship** simply means that a company provides money to an event in return for specified advertising privileges associated with the event. Investment in event marketing is escalating rapidly and for good reason: an event reaches a specific target audience in a receptive state of mind at one location. Events and sponsorships are discussed in detail in Chapter 16.

Marketing Communications Planning

marketing communications planning

Marketing communications planning is the process of making systematic decisions regarding which elements of the communications mix to use in marketing communications. In making these decisions, objectives and strategies for the plan are outlined. A company develops its marketing communications plans in accordance with the direction provided by corporate plans and marketing plans. The marketing communications plan complements other marketing mix plans, such as those for pricing, product, and distribution, and together they form the company's marketing plan or a marketing plan for a specific product or service.

MARKETING COMMUNICATIONS OBJECTIVES

Like other elements of the marketing mix, communications activity must complement the total marketing effort. Thus, each element of the mix is assigned a goal on the basis of what it is capable of contributing to the overall plans. Some typical marketing communications goals might be:

· To create, maintain, or build a company or brand image
· To position or reposition the perception of a product in the customer's mind
· To stimulate trial purchase of a product
· To create a perception of competitive advantage
· To defuse a potentially damaging situation

Therefore, depending on the objectives of a marketing communications campaign, any combination of marketing communications components could be utilized in the plan. As well, specific objectives are established for each component of the marketing communications mix. To illustrate how objectives at various levels of planning within an organization are linked, refer to Figure 14.2.

MARKETING COMMUNICATIONS STRATEGY

Strategy is the battle plan that outlines the means of achieving the objectives. While objectives state what is to be accomplished, strategy describes how it is to be accomplished. Therefore, strategic decisions are made regarding which component of the marketing communications mix to employ, a total budget is determined, and funds are allocated across the various activities.

When making strategy decisions the manager assesses who the customers are and then decides on the marketing communications components to employ. The manager must evaluate end users as well as customers who take title to products in the channel of distribution. Programs are devised and funds are allocated to activities that pull and push the product through the channel.

PULL STRATEGY   In a **pull strategy**, the organization creates demand by directing its efforts at consumers or final users of a product (i.e., a consumer purchasing a shampoo brand in a Shoppers Drug Mart, or a purchasing manager responsible for buying supplies and equipment for a company). Pull strategies tend to rely on mass media advertising, online communications, public relations, consumer promotion activities, and event marketing and sponsorships. These activities cause consumers to search for the product in stores or to buy products directly from the manufacturer. This strategy "pulls" the product through the channel of distribution.

pull strategy

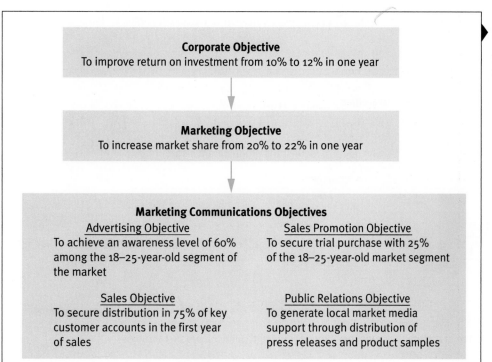

FIGURE
14.2

The Relationships of Objectives at Different Levels of Planning

Corporate Objective
To improve return on investment from 10% to 12% in one year

Marketing Objective
To increase market share from 20% to 22% in one year

Marketing Communications Objectives

Advertising Objective
To achieve an awareness level of 60% among the 18–25-year-old segment of the market

Sales Promotion Objective
To secure trial purchase with 25% of the 18–25-year-old market segment

Sales Objective
To secure distribution in 75% of key customer accounts in the first year of sales

Public Relations Objective
To generate local market media support through distribution of press releases and product samples

push strategy

PUSH STRATEGY   In a **push strategy**, the organization creates demand for a product by directing its efforts at distributor intermediaries, who, in turn, advertise and promote the product among consumers. Push strategies tend to rely on a mixture of personal selling and sales promotion techniques to create demand. An organization will direct marketing activities in the form of discounts and allowances at managers responsible for buying goods for retail establishments—say, for example, buyers responsible for purchasing all shampoo brands stocked at Shoppers Drug Mart. Such discounts encourage the buyers to make the initial purchase and to support the brand's merchandising efforts as time goes on. This strategy helps "push" the product through the channel of distribution. See Chapters 11 and 16 for more details on specific discounts and trade promotions.

See Figure 14.3 for a visual illustration of pull and push marketing strategies.

BUDGETING FOR MARKETING COMMUNICATIONS

In order to develop a marketing communications budget, the manager responsible analyzes several factors, each of which has an impact on the amount of funds required.

> 2. Identify the factors that influence the size of a marketing budget and list the methods for determining a budget.

THE CUSTOMER   Managers must consider what type of customer is targeted when they decide on the nature of the communications activity and the size of the marketing budget. In consumer goods marketing, products directed at a wide cross-section of the population rely on advertising. In contrast, business-to-business marketing involves products with a more narrowly defined and geographically centred audience. Consequently, personal selling, sales promotion, and event marketing (e.g., trade shows) play more prominent roles in the purchase decision process. Budgets are allocated for activities when a company determines the most effective means of reaching its targets.

DEGREE OF COMPETITION   A firm monitors the amount of money its competitors invest in communications programs as well as the effectiveness of these investments. How much its competitors spend provides a useful guideline when a firm is planning a budget. Firms that do not keep pace with others risk a loss in sales. For instance, in markets where two products or two firms dominate (Crest versus Colgate toothpaste or

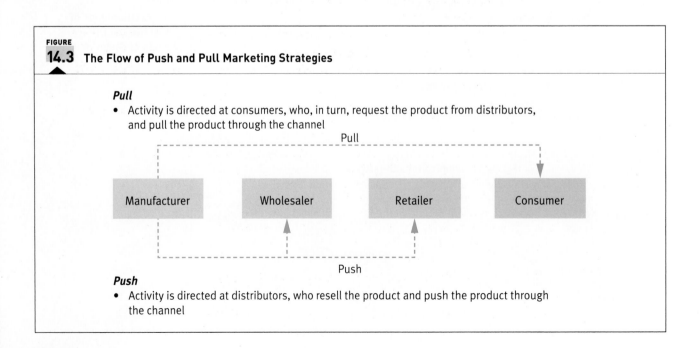

FIGURE
14.3 **The Flow of Push and Pull Marketing Strategies**

Pull
- Activity is directed at consumers, who, in turn, request the product from distributors, and pull the product through the channel

Pull

| Manufacturer | Wholesaler | Retailer | Consumer |

Push

Push
- Activity is directed at distributors, who resell the product and push the product through the channel

Coca-Cola versus Pepsi-Cola soft drinks), industry analysts project that the battle for market share between the rivals could be won or lost by the amount of communications support they offer. Competitive pressure, therefore, causes brands like Coca-Cola and Pepsi-Cola to invest heavily in communications to protect and build market share.

STAGES IN THE PRODUCT LIFE CYCLE   The amount of money required for support varies with each stage of the product life cycle. In the ***introductory stage*** the objective is to create demand, along with product and brand awareness. In relation to sales, the investment in marketing communications will be extremely high. Since the objective is brand development, it is common for a budget to exceed the projected return in sales. Initial losses on a brand are tolerated, as long as the brand is expected to provide adequate profit in the long term.

In the ***growth stage*** competition is present, so the competitors' budgets enter the picture. A manager is concerned about two objectives now: continuing to build awareness, and creating brand preference in the customer's mind. Accomplishing both objectives costs money. Building market share in a competitive environment is challenging and requires a budget that will attract users of competitive brands. Consequently, the brand may wind up spending more on communications in this stage than it would like to.

The focus in the ***mature stage*** shifts from brand development to profit maximization. Rather than spending money on communications, there is a conscious effort to preserve money wherever possible. A brand at this stage is in a maintenance position, so the budget should be just enough to sustain market share position while maximizing bottom-line profit. If life cycle extension strategies such as product modifications, new packaging, and new varieties occur, the level of communication support could increase in the short term (e.g., to create awareness during part of a year).

In the ***decline stage***, profit motives take priority. Since new products have taken over the market, marketing budgets for old products are cut significantly or withdrawn entirely. Profits that are generated from brands in this stage are allocated to brands that are in their developmental stages.

An organization can use a variety of budgeting methods to determine a budget: percentage of sales, industry averages, arbitrary allocation, and task or objective. For a summary of these methods, refer to Figure 14.4.

Method	Procedure
Percentage of Sales	Manager allocates a predetermined percentage of forecasted sales to marketing or marketing communications.
Industry Averages	Manager allocates a budget of the average amount (current or forecasted) spent on marketing or marketing communications by all brands in a market.
Arbitrary Allocation	Manager relies on judgment and experience to assess costs and profit trends and assigns an arbitrary amount to cover marketing communications expenses.
Task (Objective)	Manager defines the objective to be achieved, determines the activities (strategies required) to achieve the objective, and associates a cost with the activities.

FIGURE
14.4
Budgeting Methods

Advertising and Its Role

advertising

Advertising is a paid form of nonpersonal message communicated through the media by an identified sponsor.[1] The media referred to in this definition could be the print, broadcast, or electronic media. Advertising is persuasive and informational, and is designed to influence the thought patterns of the target audience in a favourable manner. Once a favourable attitude develops, the role of advertising is to motivate purchase of a specific brand of product.

Prior to discussing advertising, it is imperative the reader understand the nature of communications process (see Figure 14.5). The process begins with a sender (the advertiser) who develops a message to be transmitted by the media (TV, radio, Internet, magazine, newspaper, etc.) to a receiver (the consumer or business customer).

In the communications process, competing products also send messages to the same target market; meanwhile, the target market may be doing things that distract them from all messages being sent to them. Competing messages and distractions are referred to as *noise*. Advertisers take steps to try to break through the clutter of competitive advertising and make an impact on consumers. Typically, breakthrough messages produce positive attitudes and higher rates of purchase (a form of positive feedback) than do dull or misunderstood messages.

When deciding what products to buy, a consumer passes through a series of behaviour stages. Advertising can influence each stage. The various stages are described as *awareness, comprehension, conviction,* and *action.*

- *Awareness*—In this stage, the customer *learns of something for the first time.* Obviously, the learning can occur only if he or she is exposed to a new advertisement. Awareness can also come from word of mouth, a situation that is beyond the control of the organization.

- *Comprehension*—By this stage, *interest* has been created. The individual perceives the message as relevant, and the product, judged from the information presented, is considered useful. The product becomes part of the customer's frame of reference.

- *Conviction*—The customer evaluates the product benefits presented in the advertising. The product is viewed as satisfactory, and has gained *preference* in the customer's mind. The customer may be sufficiently motivated to buy it when needed.

- *Action*—In this stage, the desired active *response* occurs. For example, a car advertisement motivates a customer to visit a dealer or a website; a coupon motivates a reader to clip it for use in an initial purchase.

Simply stated, the goal of advertising is to link the benefits of a product to the needs of a target market. By doing so, an advertiser starts to influence customer perceptions

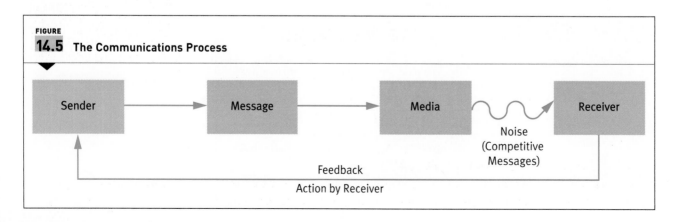

FIGURE
14.5 **The Communications Process**

Sender → Message → Media →〜〜 Noise (Competitive Messages) → Receiver

Feedback
Action by Receiver

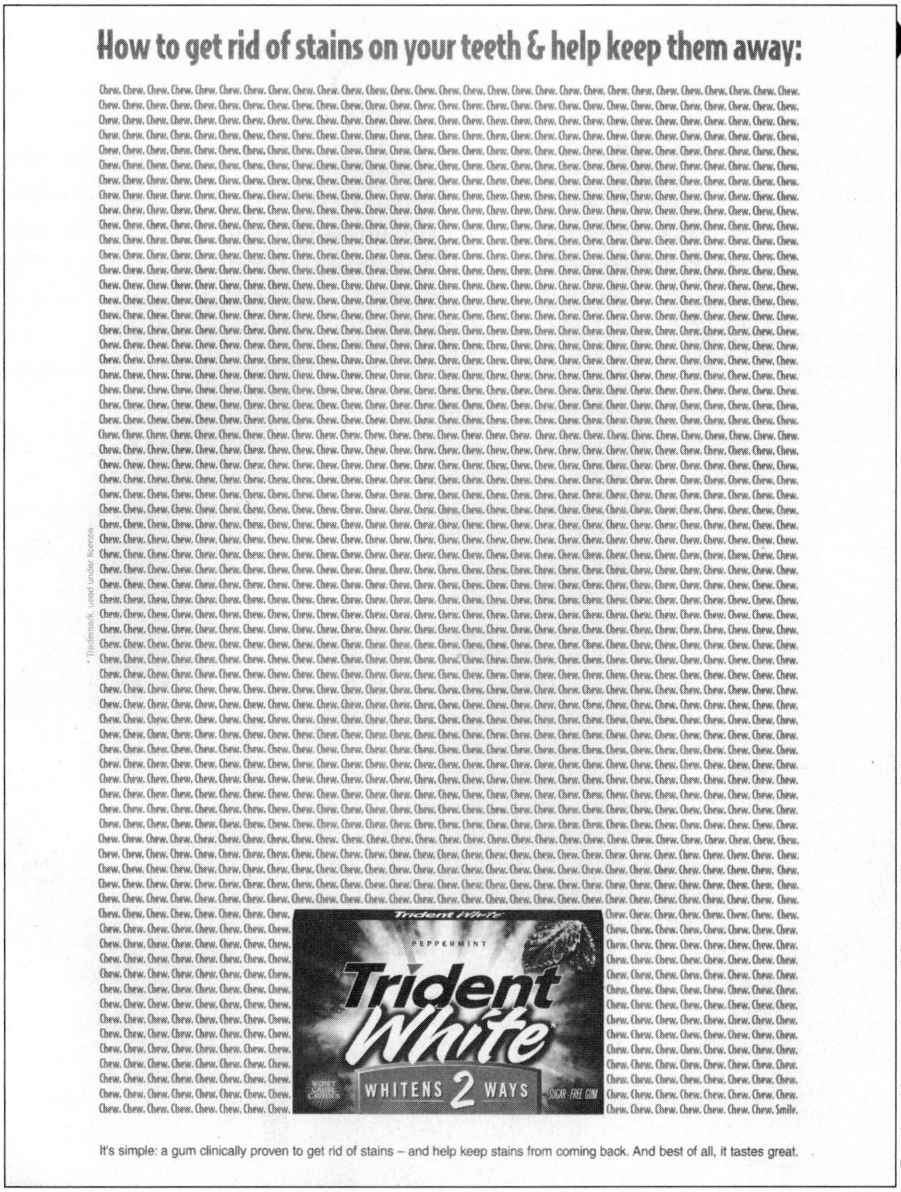

How to get rid of stains on your teeth & help keep them away:

It's simple: a gum clinically proven to get rid of stains – and help keep stains from coming back. And best of all, it tastes great.

Reprinted by permission of Cadbury Adams Canada Inc.

FIGURE 14.6

Trident White gum effectively matches a key benefit to the needs of the target market

and hopefully creates preference over competitive alternatives. For example, Trident White (gum) offers a unique solution to an age-old problem—maintaining white teeth. All you have to do is chew. The challenge for Trident is to make consumers believe that chewing gum helps whiten teeth. Refer to the illustration in Figure 14.6.

Advertising: Creating the Message

The task of developing an advertising campaign is usually handled by an advertising agency. **Advertising agencies** are organizations responsible for creating, planning, producing, and placing advertising messages for clients (the advertisers). The development of an advertising campaign can be divided into two basic parts: creative (message) and media. Creative decisions focus on what to say to customers and how to say it.

CREATIVE OBJECTIVES: WHAT TO SAY

The first step in creating a message is to clearly define the creative objectives. **Creative objectives** state what information is to be communicated to a target audience. For

3. Describe the strategic decisions involved in developing the creative component of an advertising campaign.

advertising agencies

creative objectives

example, the message for Energizer batteries is focused on long-lasting reliability; Head & Shoulders shampoo on the elimination of dandruff; and Old Spice High Endurance Body Wash on a scent that allows regular guys to date women who are out of their league (so the ads say!).

Typically, what to say in an ad is summarized in a **key-benefit statement**, which conveys the most important idea or benefit the advertiser is promising the consumer. Supporting body copy and illustrations help substantiate the promise. The ad in Figure 14.7 serves as a good illustration. The promise or benefit offered by Old Spice High Endurance Body Wash is the emotional response the opposite sex will have to the scent. The headline "Date women out of your league" captures the essence of the message. Television commercials showing males and females interacting (the attraction of the scent) are also part of this advertising campaign.

key-benefit statement

FIGURE 14.7

Old Spice High Endurance Body Wash appeals to basic male instincts

CREATIVE STRATEGY: HOW TO SAY IT

The **creative strategy** specifies how a message is to be communicated to the target audience. It pinpoints the personality and image that an agency should strive to create for the product or service being advertised. Strategy considerations involve decisions about theme (continuity of message across all media) and the appeal techniques that will be employed in the ads. For example, an ad for a perfume may appeal to a customer on the basis of sex or love, whereas an ad for a food product may use a taste comparison with a competitor to show superior taste benefit.

This section examines some of the more common appeal techniques used in advertising today.

HUMOUR   In humorous advertisements, the promise and proof are presented in a light-hearted manner. The now-famous "Bud Light Institute" campaign for Bud Light beer offers a good example. The fictitious institute is dedicated to providing ingenious solutions to everyday chores and responsibilities so that guys 25 to 35 years old can get out with their buddies more often. In the commercials, a rather naïve significant other always falls for the excuses. Effective advertising has helped build the Bud Light brand in Canada. A light-hearted or humorous approach can also work in a print ad. See the Ex-lax ad in Figure 14.8 for a good example.

COMPARISON   In comparative advertisements, the promise and proof are shown by means of comparing the attributes of a given product with those of competing products—attributes that are important to the target market, usually the primary reason why they

4. Differentiate between creative strategy and creative execution in advertising.

creative strategy

FIGURE

14.8   **A light-hearted approach aptly portrays the primary benefit of Ex-lax**

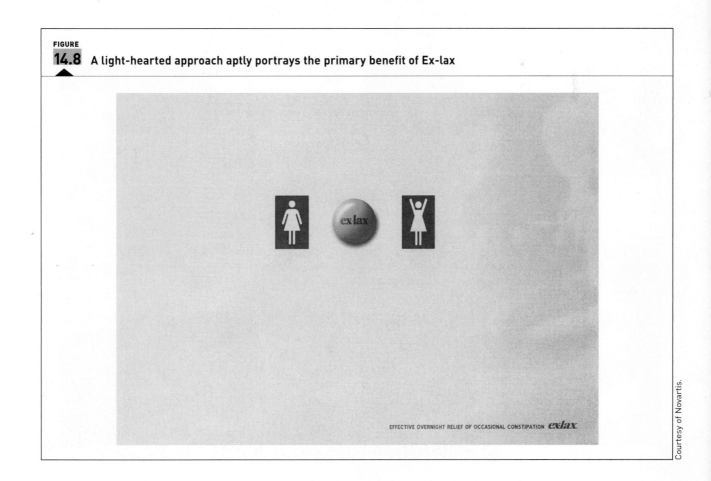

EFFECTIVE OVERNIGHT RELIEF OF OCCASIONAL CONSTIPATION *ex-lax*

Courtesy of Novartis.

buy the product. Comparisons can be direct (e.g., the other brand is mentioned) or indirect (e.g., there is reference to another brand but it is not identified). Charmin Ultra (a toilet paper) claims it is softer and more absorbent than the leading national competitor. The impact of such a subtle comparison is questionable. Brands such as Energizer and Duracell take a more direct approach by making real claims about which brand lasts longer.

Comparative campaigns present an element of risk for the initiator, so it must ensure that any claims of superiority can be supported by marketing research data. Any claims that mislead the public could be challenged by the market leader via legal proceedings.

EMOTION   Emotional advertisements concentrate on creating a mood and conveying the message in a manner that arouses the feelings of the audience or shows that psychological satisfaction is gained by using the product. Mazda uses emotional appeals in its "Zoom-zoom" television campaign. *Zoom-zoom* is a phrase children use when they imitate the sound of a car engine. It expresses a fascination with motion. Mazda conveys this feeling in its products. "The spirit of a sports car is built into every car [they] make," and Zoom-zoom captures the feeling perfectly. Mazda delivers exciting and exhilarating driving experiences for customers who still have that childlike fascination with motion.[2] This is the emotional connection Mazda seeks with its customers. Refer to the illustration in Figure 14.9.

FIGURE 14.9   Mazda connects emotionally with its customers

Courtesy of Mazda Canada Inc.

LIFESTYLE   Some advertisers attempt to associate their brand with the lifestyle of a certain target audience. The key to success in this type of campaign is in the association. If an individual feels a part of the lifestyle, then he or she is likely to view the product favourably.

A company like Labatt Breweries effectively uses psychographic information about its target market to develop lifestyle campaigns. Labatt Blue's most recent campaign, "Cheers. To friends," uses the lifestyle of young urban males to its advantage. A series of television commercials depicts realistically what guys do when they hang out with their friends. Real groups of friends (not actors) show guys doing everything from tipping over an occupied outhouse, to filling a guy's car with golf balls, to leaving another guy tied to a chair in an elevator wearing only his underwear and two hockey sticks. The core message is intended to reflect the attitude of Blue's target market.

Knowing that people wish to associate with particular situations and lifestyles, the ads put people in those situations. The Honda ad in Figure 14.10 appeals to young males living an urban lifestyle.

FIGURE
14.10

An advertisement appealing to young urban male lifestyles

The 2005 Civic Reverb. Alloy wheels. Skirt kit. Rear spoiler. Chrome exhaust tip. And an MP3 compatible, 6 disc in-dash CD changer with auxiliary input and EQ. There's a lot to look at for just $19,100. Get in at civicnation.ca

TESTIMONIAL In the case of testimonial advertising, a typical user of the product or an apparently objective third party describes the benefits of the item. In the toothpaste market, Colgate Total incorporates the phrase "Colgate Total is the only dentifrice to earn the Canadian Dental Association seal of approval for gingivitis reduction and for the prevention of tooth decay." Such a tactic is quite common in automobile advertising, where comments about a car by an influential car magazine are incorporated into an ad. Such an endorsement by a third party enhances the credibility of its message.

CELEBRITY ENDORSEMENT An endorsement is a testimonial by a celebrity whose popularity the advertiser attempts to capitalize upon. Stars from television, movies, music, and sports form the nucleus of celebrity endorsers. Tiger Woods appears frequently in television ads for Buick automobiles and American Express. Hockey star Jarome Iginla of the Calgary Flames recently appeared in television commercials for CIBC. Iginla's fee for appearing in the spot would be a minimum of several hundred thousand dollars.[3] Is it worth it?

Advertisers must be careful about whom they select to present their product. Among the techniques deemed unbelievable by consumers, endorsements rank the highest (72 percent of respondents in a recent survey).[4] And, of course, should the celebrity publicly stumble, as in the case of Kobe Bryant, a brand's image could also suffer due to the association with the celebrity.

CHARACTER PRESENTER What character is closely associated with Kellogg's Frosted Flakes? You are right if you said Tony the Tiger. Character presenters help differentiate one brand from another and play a leading role in producing a positive image for a brand. Over time, there have been many popular brand icons, among them the Pillsbury Doughboy, the Energizer Bunny, and Ronald McDonald (see Figure 14.11).

Character presenters may also be human characters, like the idle Maytag Repairman and the Man from Glad. And, of course, there's the Listerine Action Hero guy—a forty-something man sporting a big blue bottle costume and a venturesome personality.

Colgate-Palmolive Canada
www.colgate.ca

FIGURE
14.11

Advertising Icons

Energizer Bunny courtesy of Eveready Battery Company Inc.; Ronald McDonald used with permission from McDonald's Corporation.

Before the Action Hero campaign (1999), Listerine had a 35-percent market share. After five years with the Action Hero as the central character in Listerine advertising, market share has risen to 49 percent—a clear indication of the Action Hero's effectiveness![5]

SEX   The use of sexual appeal in certain product categories has become increasingly popular in recent years. For such product categories as cosmetics, perfumes, and lingerie, sex is used as an effective motivator. As long as core customers don't find the use of sex offensive, an advertiser may be onto something. Others believe that the use of sexual imagery is now so ubiquitous in advertising campaigns that it has lost the power to shock us. It is no longer engaging our interest, so if it is used it won't make anyone pick up the box, let alone buy it.[6] Of course, the persuasiveness of a message always lies in the eyes of the beholder.

A recent award-winning print campaign for Jergens skin lotion effectively uses the female body form in a sexy, smart, and simple way. The sensuous pictures and minimal copy aptly portray the usefulness of the product. In a variety of executions, lines of lotion suggest clothing on an otherwise nude woman's body, sparking consideration of that most worn undergarment—your skin. Is using Jergens Ultra Care Lotion a potentially sensual experience? View the ad in Figure 14.12 and judge for yourself.

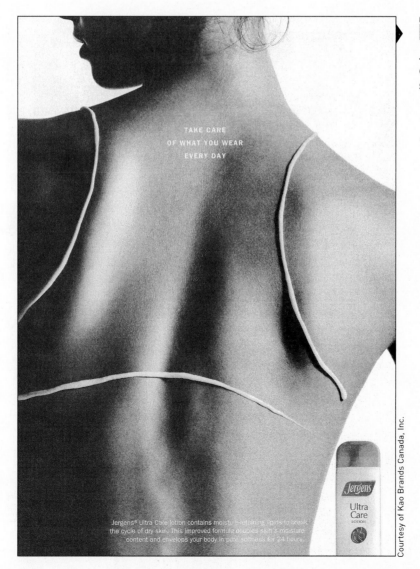

FIGURE
14.12

Jergens Ultra Care Lotion communicates a potential sensual experience

Courtesy of Kao Brands Canada, Inc.

PRODUCT DEMONSTRATIONS

The use of a demonstration to show how well a product performs is quite common in advertising. Several execution options are available. For example, a "before-and-after" scenario is common for diet-related products and exercise equipment, where the message implies usage by the presenter. A second strategy is to simply show the product at work—a technique commonly used in advertising for household products, such as paper towels, cleaners, and floor wax. Remember Bounty towels—the quicker picker-upper!

Some advertisers take their demonstrations to extremes by subjecting the product to exaggerated punishment to dramatize a key benefit. The visual illustration in Figure 14.13 uses an exaggerated technique to portray the safety benefits of an automobile.

For more insight into the nature of advertising messages and how the ideas for ads are developed, read the Marketing in Action vignette **Effective Campaigns Need Time to Evolve**.

FIGURE
14.13

An exaggerated demonstration aptly portrays a safety benefit

Honda Canada Inc.

MARKETING **IN ACTION**

Effective Campaigns Need Time to Evolve

Rightly or wrongly, there is a tendency among marketing decision makers to pull an advertising campaign too soon. There is a management mindset that says, "Give it a year and if it isn't clicking, move on to something different." Such thinking is partly due to the constant turnover of brand managers who don't allow for long-term thinking when creating a campaign. They want results now, but it rarely happens.

In this industry many observers believe that a long-term outlook is needed. Devise a good strategy, a good theme, and then generate new and different executions of it. Be consistent in your approach and let people become familiar with what you are doing.

Perhaps it is the exception rather than the rule, but most successful campaigns do stay on course for an extended period. One such campaign that has proven successful is the Telus Mobility campaign that uses the tagline "The future is friendly" and features really unique animals. Over the years Telus has used frogs, pigs, and penguins—and, most recently, an aqua-coloured chameleon—to entice prospects to its telephones.

According to Alan Middleton, professor of marketing at York University, "The key to Telus' campaign is the human, or in this case animal, touch." High-tech companies usually focus on the rational side of things to get people to buy, but Telus has factored in the emotional side. Says Middleton, "When the difference between competing brands is so little, the real insight is the human connection."

The objective of this campaign is to attract customers through the wonders of nature rather than gizmo geek talk. It is modelled after another successful company that takes an anti-technology approach to communications—Apple Computer Inc. Like Apple,

Telus wants the public to perceive its products to be easy to use, and that is why the tagline "The future is friendly" is at the heart of the campaign.

There are several reasons why the campaign is successful. The ads are distinctive and the animals are cute (in a weird kind of way!). And Telus has stuck with it, letting the campaign evolve. The intent has never been to select an animal spokesperson; rather, a theme is chosen and then an interesting animal is selected that is out of the ordinary but reflects the theme. In a recent commercial, the chameleon actually changes from its natural colour of aqua blue to red as it walks (with the help of some special effects, of course).

The campaign may also have some spin-off effect on society. In the commercials there is a startling juxtaposition between high technology and nature's wonders. As we embrace more and more technology, perhaps this campaign will make us think more about preserving some of the natural wonders of the world. Who knows!

Adapted from Aparita Bhandari, "Cellphone corral," *Toronto Star*, December 20, 2004, pp. C1, C3.

Dick Loek/The Toronto Star

CREATIVE EXECUTION

creative execution

Creative execution refers to the formation of more precisely defined strategies for presenting the message. In this stage, strategies are converted into a physical presentation that expresses the desired image, mood, and personality. The goal is to find the best or most convincing way to present a product so that the customer will be motivated to take the desired action.

The two basic illustrating devices are photography and drawn (or painted) illustrations. In the case of a four-colour medium such as magazines, logic suggests that colour photography be used, but the end product will, of course, be similar to numerous other ads in the same publication. An artist's drawing—even a black-and-white drawing—may command a higher level of attention through contrast. The opposite is true of newspapers. Generally, a good photograph will be most effective in conveying realism, emotion, or urgency. But there are benefits to using drawings. Drawings allow artists to create the desired impression in their own style. The end product can exaggerate or accentuate in ways a photograph cannot often match. In Figure 14.14 a drawing is very effective in communicating the benefits of Charmin—softness: a true benefit for a sensitive area of the body.

Advertising: Selecting the Right Media

5. Describe the key elements involved in planning a media advertising campaign.

The media department of an advertising agency is responsible for planning and arranging the placement of advertisements; it schedules and buys advertising time (broadcast and electronic media) and space (print media). The media department prepares a document that shows all the details of how a client's budget is spent to achieve advertising objectives. In scheduling, it strives to achieve maximum exposure at the lowest possible cost.

FIGURE
14.14

An ad using drawings as a primary means of illustration

Courtesy of Procter & Gamble

MEDIA OBJECTIVES

Media planning begins with a precise outline of media objectives, a media strategy, and the media execution, and culminates in a media plan that recommends how advertising funds should be spent to achieve the previously established advertising objectives.

media planning

In defining **media objectives**, media planners consider how, when, where, and to whom the message will be sent. The first consideration is the target market. The target market is defined in terms of demographic, psychographic, and geographic variables. Careful consideration is given to the media habits of the target audience. As discussed in the creative section, the nature of the message has an impact on what media to use. For example, factual messages necessitate using print media, while messages that include visual demonstrations or comparisons require television. Next, geographic market priorities are established, with decisions being influenced by the size of the media budget. The final thing to be considered is the best time to reach the target: the best time of day, the best day of the week, or the best period of weeks during the year.

media objectives

6. Differentiate among media objectives, media strategies, and media execution.

MEDIA STRATEGY

A **media strategy** describes how the media objectives will be accomplished: how many advertisements or commercials will run, how often, and for what length of time they will appear. A media strategy presents recommendations regarding what media to use and details why certain media are selected and others rejected.

media strategy

MATCHING THE TARGET MARKET   Essentially, the task of an advertising agency's media department is to match the advertised product's target-market profile with a compatible media profile, such as the readership profile of a magazine or newspaper, or the listener profile of a radio station. Three common target-market media strategies are as follows:

1. In the case of **profile matching**, the advertising message is placed in media where the profile of readers, listeners, or viewers is reasonably close to that of the product's target market. For example, advertising in the *Globe and Mail*'s *Report On Business* reaches one type of person; an advertisement in *Chatelaine* reaches another.

profile matching

2. In the case of a **shotgun strategy**, general-interest media are selected to reach a broad cross-section of a market population. For example, television may be chosen to make contact with diverse age groups; say, all adults aged 18 to 49 years old. If so, an advertiser might place a commercial on a popular situation comedy in prime time; a print ad in daily newspapers would also be effective, since it would reach a similar audience profile.

shotgun strategy

3. In the case of a **rifle strategy**, the target market is defined by a common characteristic, such as participation in a leisure activity or participation in a particular industry. Media that appeal specifically to this common characteristic are then used. For example, *Snowboarder* magazine is a logical choice to reach youthful snowboarders, and *Hotel & Restaurant* magazine to reach people in the hospitality industry.

rifle strategy

REACH, FREQUENCY, AND CONTINUITY   The organization must decide on the reach, frequency, and continuity needed to fulfill the media objectives for an advertising message. These factors interact with one another. **Reach** refers to the total audience potentially exposed, one or more times, to an advertiser's schedule of messages in a given period, usually a week. It is expressed as a percentage of the target population in a geographically defined area. Assume a television station is seen by 30 000 households in a geographic area of 150 000 households. The reach would be 20 percent (30 000 divided by 150 000).

reach

Frequency refers to the average number of times an audience is exposed to an advertising message over a period, usually a week. The airing of a television commercial three times on a station during a week would represent its frequency. In media planning, a balance must be struck between reach and frequency. A common dilemma faced by a media planner is whether to recommend more reach at the expense of frequency, or vice versa. Overexposing a target to a message can be a waste of money!

Continuity refers to the length of time required to ensure a particular medium affects a target market. For example, an advertiser may schedule television commercials in eight-week flights three times a year, thus covering a total of 24 weeks of the calendar year, or a magazine campaign may run for consecutive months. A **flight,** or **flighting**, refers to the purchase of media time and space in planned intervals, separated by periods of inactivity.

MARKET COVERAGE **Coverage** refers to the number of geographic markets where the advertising is to occur for the duration of a media plan. In deciding the extent of coverage, the advertiser could select national, regional, or particular urban markets, depending on its marketing and advertising objectives. Such factors as budget, sales volume by area, and level of distribution by area affect the selection.

TIMING In determining the best time to reach a target market, marketers may focus on the time of the day, the week, or the year. The best time to advertise a product or service is the time at which it will have the most impact on the consumer's buying decision. For example, the decision to buy a snowmobile is probably made in the fall. Therefore, if advertising is scheduled for the winter, the message will be delivered too late. Sometimes an advertiser plans its advertising in bursts. A **blitz strategy**, for example, involves spending a large amount of money in a short space of time and then tapering off considerably. In contrast, a **build-up strategy** starts out slowly and gradually builds over a longer period of time. Both alternatives are appropriate for launching new products.

ASSESSING MEDIA ALTERNATIVES In conjunction with other strategic factors, the advantages and disadvantages of the various media are considered (Figure 14.15). An advertiser can rarely use all the media. Specific media are chosen in keeping with budget constraints and in consideration of the habits of the target market and of such variables as reach, frequency, and continuity. Television, newspaper, magazine, radio, and outdoor (transit and posters) are among the **traditional mass media**. Automobile advertising, for example, is concentrated in television and print (magazines and newspapers). Television creates awareness and a sense of excitement about an automobile, while print creates awareness and gives readers more specific details about the automobile and where they can buy it. In contrast, fashion retailers and major department stores utilize television, outdoor, and print as primary media in their media mix.[7]

There is also a variety of nontraditional media or new media alternatives available to advertisers. Among these alternatives are various forms of direct-response advertising and the Internet (see Chapter 15), sports and stadium advertising, theatre-screen advertising, and elevator advertising, to name only a few.

Smart marketers are also looking at a new concept called product placement to deliver their message. **Product placement** refers to the visible placement of branded merchandise in television shows, movies, or media programming. Other terms commonly used to describe this form of advertising include *product integration* and *sponsor integration*. The popular Steven Spielberg movie *Minority Report*, starring Tom Cruise, featured brands such as Lexus, Gap, Reebok, Guinness, and American Express. In other situations a brand name is woven right into the storyline of a show. This is referred to

Advantages	Disadvantages
Television	
1. Impact—sight, sound, and motion; demonstration	1. Cost—high cost of time and commercial production
2. Reach—very high among all age groups	2. Clutter—commercials are clustered together, reducing impact
	3. Fragmentation—audience has many stations to choose from
Radio	
1. Targeting—reaches a selective audience based on type of music	1. Retention—short, single-sense messages
2. Reach and Frequency—reaches the same audience frequently	2. Fragmentation—many stations in large markets reduces impact
Newspaper	
1. Coverage—good local market reach	1. Life Span—short, a one-day medium
2. Flexibility—the message can be inserted quickly and altered quickly	2. Target Market—reaches a broad cross-section; not specific target
Magazine	
1. Target Marketing—specialized magazines reach defined demographic groups	1. Clutter—each issue contains too many advertisements
2. Environment—quality of editorial content enhances the advertising message	2. Frequency—low message frequency (monthly publication)
Outdoor and Transit	
1. Reach and Frequency—frequent message sent to same target audience (based on daily travel patterns)	1. Message—small size in transit; short messages in outdoor
2. Coverage—available on a market-by-market basis	2. Targeting—reaches the broad cross-section of a market's population
Direct Mail	
1. Targeting—reaches a preselected and defined audience	1. Image—low (e.g., junk mail) image; hard-sell approach required to solicit orders
2. Control—expenditure can be evaluated directly for effectiveness	
Internet	
1. Targeting—reaches a specific audience (tracking capabilities of medium)	1. Consumer Frustration—constant barrage of unsolicited emails and unexpected pop-up ads
2. Interactive—two-way communication of detailed content	2. Behaviour—surfers avoid ads (low click rates)

FIGURE 14.15

Media Selection Considerations

as **branded content**. Entire episodes of *The Apprentice* have revolved around brands such as Mars, Crest, and Home Depot.[8] In Canada, L'Oreal has been a major sponsor of *Canadian Idol*. Specific segments within the show itself feature the idols in the makeup room with L'Oreal specialists.

Since many advertisers firmly believe that 30-second television commercials aren't as effective as they once were, networks have responded by presenting "sponsor integration opportunities." On TSN's SportsCentre news show, various highlights segments are sponsored. Vector cereal sponsors the Performer of the Week, and the SportsCentre Top 10 Highlights is sponsored by Molson Canadian's "I AM Canadian."

branded content

MEDIA EXECUTION

Media execution is the final stage of media planning. It is the process of fine-tuning media strategy into specific action plans. Such action plans are divided into the following areas: evaluating cost comparisons so that one particular medium may be selected over another; scheduling specific media in a planning format (i.e., establishing a media calendar of activity); and developing budget summaries that show how advertising funds are to be spent. For example, if magazines are the chosen medium, the decision regarding which magazines to use and how often advertisements will appear in the magazines is made. To reach a business executive, an advertiser, such as Mercedes-Benz or Jaguar, may decide to use a combination of magazines, such as the *National Post*'s *Business* magazine, the *Globe and Mail*'s *Report On Business* magazine, or *Canadian Business*. Depending on the budget available, these advertisers could use all or any combination of the magazine alternatives.

Media-selection decisions are often made based on how efficient a particular medium is at reaching the target audience. For example, each magazine mentioned above would be compared on the basis of CPM. **CPM (cost per thousand)** is the cost incurred in delivering a message to 1000 individuals. It is calculated by dividing the cost of the ad by the circulation of the publication in thousands. Therefore, if an ad cost $30 000 and the circulation was 750 000, the CPM would be $40 ($30 000 divided by 750). The publication with the lowest CPM is the most efficient at reaching the target. CPM calculations are also used to compare the efficiencies across different media. For example, the CPM of reaching a television audience could be compared to the CPM of a newspaper audience.

Public Relations

Public relations consists of a variety of activities and communications that organizations undertake to monitor, evaluate, and influence the attitudes, opinions, and behaviours of groups or individuals who constitute their publics. There are two different publics: *internal publics* and *external publics*. **Internal publics** involve those who the organization communicates with regularly. These parties are close to the day-to-day operations of the organization and include employees, distributors, suppliers, shareholders, and regular customers. **External publics** are not close to the organization and are usually communicated with infrequently. They include the media, governments (all levels), prospective shareholders, the financial community, and community groups.

The word "relations" is important, for it signifies the organization is involved in a relationship with its publics, and that relationship should be a positive one. Positive relations are the result of open, honest, and forthcoming communications with an organization's publics.

It is important to understand the difference between advertising and public relations. Advertising is usually concerned with brand image, whereas public relations tends to focus on corporate image. Public relations will spread good news about an organization and helps remedy problem situations when they arise. Advertising is bought and paid for by an organization, so it controls the content of the message. In contrast, public relations messages are controlled by the media; they are not paid for by the sponsoring organization. Organizations, however, can and often do include paid advertising as part of their public relations activity.

The Role of Public Relations

The role of public relations is varied but generally falls into eight key areas: corporate communications, reputation management, community relations and social responsibility, public affairs and lobbying, publicity generation, product seeding, media relations, and fundraising.

CORPORATE COMMUNICATIONS

As suggested earlier, public relations can play a vital role in building and protecting the image of a company. It doesn't take much for a company's image to come tumbling down if a crisis situation is handled improperly.

On the positive side of the ledger, an organization takes a stand on issues that directly or indirectly affect its operations. Referred to as **issue management**, activities deliver to the public a message that shows exactly where the company stands on a particular issue. For example, a company's stance on environmental issues may be of utmost importance. Is the company taking a proactive stance on protecting the environment? If it is, then a loud and clear message should be sent to the public.

These kinds of messages can be delivered to the public by paid advertising or through public relations. **Corporate advertising** is advertising designed to convey a favourable image of a company among its various publics (consumers, shareholders, business customers, suppliers, and so on). It may attempt to create or improve a company image by showing how the resources a firm has solve customers' problems, by promoting goodwill, or by demonstrating a sense of social responsibility. Shell Canada, for example, is a strong supporter of economic progress while showing concern for the environment.

Advocacy advertising is any kind of public communication paid for by an identified sponsor that presents information or a point of view on a publicly recognized, controversial issue. The objective is to influence public opinion. The Shell Canada ad in Figure 14.16 provides an example of corporate advertising and advocacy advertising in one ad.

REPUTATION MANAGEMENT

Public relations plays a vital role when a company faces a crisis. The final outcome of such a crisis often depends on how effectively a firm manages its public relations activity. For instance, a drug manufacturer may face an angry public when a drug it markets is linked to certain unexpected health problems. When the press acquires such a story and informs the public, a company has to be instantly ready to go into crisis-management mode. Such was the case when Merck & Co. discovered that its wonder drug Vioxx, an anti-inflammatory widely used by arthritis sufferers, increased the risk of heart attack and stroke. Merck reacted swiftly and positively by withdrawing the drug from the market worldwide. Merck's stock value immediately dropped 27 percent.[9]

A much-publicized public relations disaster in 2004 involved the CIBC bank and its wayward faxes to a scrapyard dealer in Virginia. Over a period of three years, the bank had been inadvertently faxing to the dealer confidential account information about customers. The scrapyard dealer advised the bank of the situation but the faxes did not stop—so he went public to alert Canadian customers to the situation. From that point on, CIBC mishandled the situation. The blunder was the subject of national television and newspaper reports for several days.[10]

Many PR experts were surprised by the under-response by the bank. It was slow and defensive rather than quick and responsive. Rather than immediately apologizing to its customers and offering them reassurance, the bank sought legal action against the scrapyard dealer. Many experts believe that when the reputation challenge is serious enough the CEO must step forward—and that was not happening. Eventually, the CEO of the bank, John Hunkin, made a public apology through the *Globe and Mail* and then took out ads in daily newspapers, but considerable time had elapsed. From the public's

issue management

corporate advertising

advocacy advertising

perspective, the incident hit a nerve. People are very concerned about what happens to their personal information when it falls into the hands of large corporations. Violation of privacy is a big issue today.[11]

These incidents indicate the need for a company to be ready when crisis situations arise. They must take control of the communications agenda early and ensure that messages are credible from the outset. Company presidents and high-level executives must be ready to meet the demands of a more sophisticated and more demanding consumer audience, or suffer the consequences of its wrath.

COMMUNITY RELATIONS AND SOCIAL RESPONSIBILITY

In an era of social responsibility, companies are placing high value on programs that foster a good public image in the communities in which they operate. Many companies encourage their employees to give back to the community; some even provide a few hours of work time each week to get involved. Sponsoring community events and teams is part of being a good corporate citizen. Tim Hortons is involved with numerous community programs: it supplies team jerseys to local soccer and hockey teams, sponsors free ice skating for families in local communities during the Christmas holidays, and sends thousands of children to camp each year through the Tim Hortons Children's Foundation.[12] These activities help build Tim Hortons' image in the community.

In an era of social responsibility, marketing companies are becoming more philanthropic in nature. In fact, companies are engaging in **strategic philanthropy** by supporting opportunities that benefit both company and society. RBC Financial Group donates $40 million to charities annually. One of its initiatives is the RBC After-School Grants Program, which encourages kids to stay in school. To receive grants, schools must offer an environment that provides what RBC has termed the "3 S's": safety, social skills, and self-esteem.[13]

PUBLIC AFFAIRS AND LOBBYING

Public affairs involve strategies to deal with governments. To communicate with governments involves lobbying. **Lobbying** involves activities and practices that are designed to influence policy decisions of governments. Naturally, a company or an industry wants government policy to conform to what's best for business. Governments, however, must balance economic well-being with social and environmental well-being, and therein lies the conflict among business, governments, and special-interest groups.

To understand the role of public affairs and lobbying, consider the battle going on between Canadian online pharmacies and pharmaceutical manufacturers. CanadaMeds is an online pharmacy providing discounted Canadian prescription drugs to customers in the United States and other foreign countries. Discounted drugs have become extremely popular with American customers, particularly those on limited incomes. In the United States the cost of prescription drugs has almost doubled in the past five years.

GlaxoSmithKline, a leading pharmaceutical manufacturer in the United States, is lobbying the American government to prevent cheap Canadian drugs from entering the United States. Many believe this action is intended solely to protect the firm's substantial profits. CanadaMeds and other online pharmacies have formed a coalition and are lobbying both the Canadian and American governments to protest this punitive and harmful ban. One of the lobby groups will eventually win this battle.

PUBLICITY GENERATION

Publicity is news about a person, product, or service that appears in the print or broadcast media. Essentially, publicity must be newsworthy. Unfortunately, what seems like news to a company may not be news to the media. Opportunities to communicate newsworthy information include launching a new product, revealing new information based on research evidence (e.g., a discovery), securing a significant contract that will generate new jobs, and achieving significant sales and profit results.

Being creative is a key to generating product publicity. A simple news story issued through a press release can be buried quickly by a news editor. In contrast, consider the approach taken by Scott Paper when it launched Cashmere, a new brand of toilet paper. To elevate and differentiate the new brand, Scott Paper hosted a fashion show called the White Cashmere Collection. The fashions allowed Scott to equate softer-than-soft white cashmere to its bathroom tissue. The show was an overwhelming success, attracting 27 journalists—including those from female-targeted media like *Canadian House & Home* magazine and broadcaster Fashion Television.[14]

PRODUCT SEEDING

A more recent phenomenon to generate publicity is seeding. **Product seeding** involves placing a new product with a group of trendsetters who in turn influence others to purchase the new product. While the product is in the hands of the trendsetters, they are

Tim Hortons
www.timhortons.com

strategic philanthropy

public affairs
lobbying

Canadameds
www.canadameds.com

publicity

product seeding

buzz marketing

creating buzz for the brand by chatting it up whenever they can. Consequently, product seeding is often referred to as **buzz marketing**, though there are other ways of creating a buzz.

Seeding has strong appeal among marketers because it is cheap—it can save significant sums of money normally spent on television commercials and print ads. Marketers know that buzz has strong appeal among the desirable twenty-something target market, a target that has become immune to traditional mass advertising.[15] To demonstrate, when Sony Ericsson launched a cell phone that took pictures, it used an undercover campaign called "Fake tourists." Sixty actors took to the streets in 10 cities. They were irresistibly innocent looking, and they were seeking a small favour: "Excuse me, would you mind taking a picture of us?" It was an easy way to initiate a discussion about the product without the other person feeling like it was a pitch for a new product. The campaign did create buzz![16]

For more insight into the effectiveness of product placement and product seeding, read the Marketing in Action vignette **Creating Buzz**.

MEDIA RELATIONS

media relations

Media relations specialists are employed by public relations companies, and their primary responsibility is to develop unique and effective relationships with the media that cover the particular industry in which they specialize (e.g., financial information, computer hardware and software, automobiles, retailing). Their role is to get industry analysts on board so they will communicate favourable information about a company or brand. The relationship between a media relations specialist and a reporter is important and is something that develops over time. It is predicated on characteristics such as respect, honesty, accuracy, and professionalism.

FUNDRAISING

In the not-for-profit market sector, public relations plays a key role in fundraising. A national organization like the United Way faces a huge challenge each year. Some people perceive the organization to be a big "money hole" and wonder where all of the donations go. To change this perception, public relations is used to educate the public about how the funds are used, to predispose people to give, to solicit commitment, and to make people feel good about giving. The goal of the United Way's campaign (or any other similar campaign) is to create a positive image and secure support by sending a message to the public that clearly states what the organization is all about.

The Tools of the Trade

9. Assess the usefulness of a variety of public relations tools.

The tools available to execute public relations programs are diverse. There are those that are used routinely to communicate newsworthy information and those that are used periodically or on special occasions only. This section discusses those vehicles that are used routinely.

PRESS RELEASE

press release

A **press release** (news release) is a document containing all of the essential elements of the story (who, what, when, where, and why). News editors make quick decisions on what to use and what to discard. Copies of the release are mailed to a list of preferred editors (e.g., established and reliable contacts based on past relationships) and it can also be distributed by a national newswire service and posted on the company website. News releases are distributed at news conferences or sent to the media directly by mail, fax, and email. An example of a press release appears in Figure 14.17.

MARKETING IN ACTION

Creating Buzz

One of the latest trends in marketing is a thing called buzz marketing. Loosely defined, buzz is using the power of word-of-mouth communications to create excitement and awareness and stimulate sales of a product. There are some variations on the buzz-marketing theme. Some refer to it as guerilla marketing, while others call it stealth marketing. Regardless of the name, it refers to unconventional ways for spreading news about a product.

Carefully planned and executed events can catapult brands onto the front pages of newspapers and into the national spotlight of TV news. Such was the case when a throng of scantily clad men and women flashed their underwear emblazoned with the phrase "Booty Call" in front of Grand Central Station in New York City. Pedestrians and car drivers whipped out their digital cameras, and photos posted on the Internet soon drew viewers from all over the world. The skivvy sighting had nothing to do with self-expression. It was part of a campaign by the New York Health and Racquet Club to promote a butt-building class for J.Lo wannabes. The racquet club estimates the stunt generated a half a million dollars' worth of publicity.

In the wake of changing demographic trends, consumer preferences, and lifestyles, marketers are shifting their way of thinking in order to be relevant to consumers. Consumers are spending less time with the media (they are time-poor), so public relations and buzz are taking on a new role in building and protecting a brand.

Reebok Canada offers another good example of buzz marketing. When it launched the U-Shuffle DMX shoe for women, a trendy black and red sneaker with no laces, the company gave 90 young women from across Canada a free pair ($150 value) and asked them to wear them around town. Reebok's goal was to get the funky cross-trainer on the feet of suburban trendsetters, who in turn would influence others to purchase the new product. It worked! The trendsetters were asked all kinds of questions about the shoes and women wanted to know where they could buy them. The word-of-mouth network was soon in high gear!

Buzz marketing offers several advantages. The biggest advantage is the low cost—it's nowhere near the cost of an ad campaign to launch a new product. It also has the capability of reaching a narrowly defined target, as in the case of Reebok. If the seeding works it will attract the attention of the media and next thing you know there is a complete story in the newspaper!

There are a few disadvantages as well. The spreading of buzz cannot be controlled. It will spread but it cannot be moulded, directed, or stopped. It grows, gains momentum, and eventually melts if it is not refuelled. As well, the message cannot be controlled. The message is distorted and filtered by every transmitter and receptor of buzz. Potentially, the communications could have negative implications on the brand or company.

Do buzz marketing and word-of-mouth communications really work? The jury is still out on this issue, but one thing is certain. It is gaining in popularity because consumers are more connected than ever due to cell phones and the Internet. While some marketing managers remain skeptical about its effectiveness, they realize that finding innovative ways of breaking through the clutter of competitive activity is essential for success.

Adapted from Krysten Crawford, "Gotcha! Ads push the envelope," *CNN Money*, August 17, 2004; Karl Moore, "Gotta get that buzz," *Marketing*, July 5, 2004, p. 9; Judy Lewis, "Building buzz," *Marketing*, January 28, 2002, p. 17; and John Heinzl, "If the shoe fits, sell it," *Globe and Mail*, September 7, 2001, p. M1.

A. Linden/Zefa/MaXx Images

FIGURE

14.17

Sample Press Release
Issued to the Media

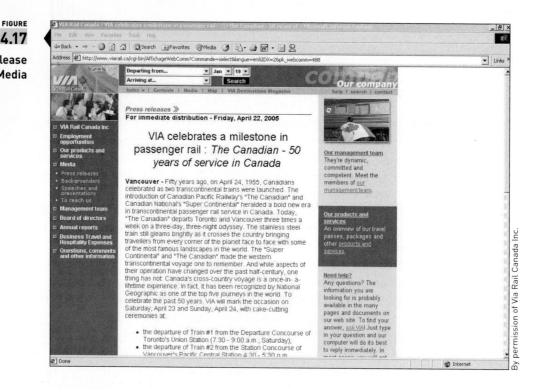

PRESS CONFERENCE

press conference

A **press conference** is a gathering of news reporters invited to witness the release of important information about a company or product. Because the conference is time consuming for the media representatives, it is usually reserved for only the most important announcements. Handling a crisis situation, for example, is usually done by a press conference. A press kit is usually distributed at a conference. The **press kit** includes a schedule of conference events, a list of company participants including biographical information, a press release, photographs, copies of speeches, videos, and any other relevant information.

press kit

WEBSITES

Since the purpose of the website is to communicate information about a company it can be an effective public relations tool. Visitors to a website quickly form an impression about a company based on the experience they have at the site. In fact, a corporate website can be the primary contact point for potential stakeholders. Therefore, the site must download quickly and be easy to navigate. Providing some kind of entertainment or interactive activity also enhances the visit. The Mazda website includes colourful brochures and multimedia presentations (360-degree virtual tours and videos of the cars in action) to show how "the soul of a sports car" is built into every vehicle.

Mazda
www.mazda.ca

The website provides an opportunity to inform the public of an organization's latest happenings. Content can vary from financial information to product information to games and contests. It is now quite common to post all press releases about the company and its products on the corporate website. In large companies it is common to have dedicated web pages for specific brands.

blog

Blogs or weblogs now have an impact on public relations activity. A **blog** is a frequent, chronological publication of personal or corporate thoughts on a Web page that can be updated on a daily basis. In recent years blogging (the process of updating and maintaining a blog) has become popular among individuals who publish their own blogs about topics of interest such as politics, news, and technology.

In 2005 corporations started using blogs to communicate with their stakeholders. It is a new medium for delivering both corporate and brand messages. According to one public relations expert, blogs have the potential to push the news media out of their central role in public relations. Richard Edelman, president and CEO of Edelman Public Relations Worldwide, has said that as practitioners rely less on the media to get messages out, they need to act more like journalists. "Companies now have the ability to post information on the Web and people are reading it and accepting it as truth, therefore, the information should be of journalistic quality."[17]

Traditionally, public relations focused on persuading the media to tell a company's story. Now, more time can be spent speaking directly to the public or trying to influence people who maintain blogs. Blogs and chat rooms are effective in shaping public opinion because the storytellers are average people. That thought throws a scare into many corporations, however!

PUBLICATIONS

A publication or **house organ** is a document that outlines news and events about an organization and its employees. It can be distributed internally to employees or externally to suppliers, distributors, shareholders, and alumni. A house organ can be in the form of a newsletter, newspaper, or magazine. The objective of the house organ is to generate goodwill and build positive public opinion about the organization. Most colleges and universities have an alumni publication that is well received by former students. They like to know what's going on at the alma mater.

house organ

POSTERS AND DISPLAYS

Posters and displays are a common form of internal employee communications. They communicate vital information regarding safety, security, employee benefits, and special events. Displays and exhibits are a portable and mobile form of communications. An exhibit typically provides the history of an organization, product displays and information, and future plans (e.g., plant expansion, new product innovations, etc.). Exhibits are appropriate for shopping malls, colleges, and universities. Internally, bulletin boards are a useful vehicle for keeping employees informed about news and events. Email is now a quick and convenient way to communicate important information to employees.

SUMMARY

Marketing communications is any means of communication used by marketing organizations to inform, persuade, or remind potential buyers about a product or service. To fulfill these tasks, an organization employs an integrated marketing communications mix comprising advertising, public relations, direct response, interactive communications, sales promotion, personal selling, and event marketing and sponsorship. Integrated marketing communications involves the coordination of all forms of marketing communications in a unified program that maximizes the impact of messages on consumers and other types of customers.

There are two basic types of marketing communications strategy: pull and push. In the case of a pull strategy a firm directs its efforts at final business users or consumers; with a push strategy, the firm directs its efforts at channel members or intermediaries. Often, a firm will use a combination of pull and push strategies.

In developing a budget, a business considers many factors, including the characteristics of the customers and the activities that motivate their purchase decisions, the degree of competition that exists, and the stage of the product life cycle the product has reached. Several different methods of determining the actual size of a budget are available to the firm.

The primary role of advertising is to influence the behaviour of a target market in such a way that its members view the product, service, or idea favourably. In developing print and broadcast messages, the creative team (copywriter and art director) considers the behavioural stages an individual passes through prior to making a purchase decision. These behaviour stages are awareness, comprehension, conviction, and action.

In advertising planning, there is a clear division between creative and media functions. On the creative side, creative objectives (what to communicate) are established, and a creative strategy (how to communicate) is developed. In communicating messages, a company uses a variety of techniques, including humour, comparison, emotion, lifestyle, testimonial, celebrity endorsement, character presenter, sex, and product demonstration.

The media plan is divided into three sections: media objectives, media strategy, and media execution. A well-conceived media plan will use the right media to gain maximum exposure for the message developed by the creative department. The media plan will consider such factors as reach, frequency, continuity, market coverage, timing, and which medium is appropriate for delivering the message. All media decisions are influenced by the amount of budget available. Since budgets tend to be scarce, new alternatives such as product placement (also called branded content and sponsor integration) are being added to the media mix.

Public relations refers to the communications a firm has with its various publics. Controlled by the media, it is a form of communication for which the organization does not pay, but it is based on information supplied by the organization. Public relations plays a role in developing an organization's image and is an important means of communication in times of crisis. At the product level various activities are undertaken to generate publicity for brands or the company. Product seeding has become a popular means of generating brand publicity in recent years.

The most commonly used tools of the public relations trade include press releases, press conferences, websites, publications, and posters and displays. Just recently, blogs have become part of the public relations communications arsenal.

KEY TERMS

REVIEW QUESTIONS

1. Briefly describe the elements that comprise the integrated marketing communications mix.

2. Briefly explain the difference between a push strategy and a pull strategy.

3. When devising an advertising budget, what factors must a manager evaluate?

4. Explain the difference between percentage of sales budgeting and industry average budgeting.

5. Explain the significance of the following behaviour stages in terms of developing an advertising message: awareness, comprehension, conviction, and action.

6. What is the difference between a key benefit statement and a support claims statement?

7. In the context of message development, what is the difference between creative strategy and creative execution?

8. What is virtual advertising?

9. In what situations would the following target market media strategies be used: shotgun strategy, profile matching strategy, and rifle strategy?

10. Explain the following media strategy concepts: reach, frequency, and continuity.

11. Briefly explain the concept of "product placement" in television programming.

12. Identify and briefly explain two different roles of public relations.

13. What is product seeding and how does it work?

14. What is the difference between a press release and a press conference?

DISCUSSION AND APPLICATION QUESTIONS

1. Provide examples of commercials or campaigns that use the following creative appeals:

   a) Humour
   b) Emotion
   c) Lifestyle
   d) Testimonial
   e) Comparison
   f) Sex

2. Is virtual advertising a distortion of the truth? Does it breach any ethical advertising standards?

3. Assume you are the marketing manager for Powerade, and you are considering using a celebrity to present your product in advertising. What type of celebrity would you select? Would you select a rising star or an established star? Justify the position you take.

4. Which media are best suited to a profile-matching strategy, for example, a shotgun strategy? Provide some specific examples.

5. Assume you are responsible for devising a media plan for the Apple iPod music player or a Harley-Davidson motorcycle. Define the primary target market and then identify the primary medium you would recommend to reach the target. Provide justification.

E-ASSIGNMENTS

1. Your task is to conduct an Internet-based secondary research investigation to find information that will verify the effectiveness or ineffectiveness of a particular creative strategy. Pick a strategy from among the following: humour, comparison, emotion, lifestyle, testimonial, celebrity endorsement, character presenter, sex, and product demonstration. Prepare a brief report based on your findings.

2. Visit the website for a few of the following companies (or others you may visit frequently). Evaluate the site as a vehicle for public relations activity. Does the site provide worthwhile information that will create goodwill for the company? Does it present a positive image? Make appropriate recommendations for changes where necessary. Prepare a brief report for each company you select.

Volkswagen	vw.com
Nike	nike.com
Levi Strauss	levi.com
Apple	apple.com
Disney	disney.com

ENDNOTES

1. Betsy-Ann Toffler and Janet Imber, *Dictionary of Marketing Terms*, Barron's Business Guides, 1994, p. 13.

2. www.mazda.com/mnl/200204/zoom-zoom/html.

3. Susan Heinrich, "A sporting life: CIBC steps out of the shadows," *Financial Post*, September 27, 2004, p. FP4.

4. Jo Marney, "Credibility and advertising," *Marketing*, June 3, 1998, p. 22.

5. Natalia Williams, "Robertson to the rescue!" *Strategy*, September 2004, p. 17.

6. Matthew Lynn, "Sex is losing sales appeal," *Financial Post*, November 12, 2004, p. FP3.

7. "Nielsen Media Research Spend: Apparel Manufacturers and Retailers," *Media in Canada*, www.media incanada.com/articles, March 24, 2005.

8. Evelyn Nussenbaum, "Television treks onto brand placement trail," *Financial Post*, September 7, 2004, pp. FP1, FP4.

9. Carolyn Abraham, "Death of a wonder drug," *Globe and Mail*, October 1, 2004, www.globeandmail.com.

10. Sinclair Stewart, "CIBC board deals with fax fallout," *Globe and Mail*, December 2, 2004, p. B3.

11. Gordon Pitts, "Get me legal on one, PR on two," *Globe and Mail*, November 30, 2004, www.globeandmail.com.

12. www.timhortons.com.

13. www.rbc.com/community/donations/after-school.

14. Chris Daniels, "Runway PR," *Marketing*, October 24, 2004, p. 4.

15. Melanie Turner, "The new buzz in marketing," www.ifinancialmarketing .com/NewsletterStories.

16. "Undercover Marketing Uncovered," *60 Minutes*, www.CBSNews.com/ stories/2003/10/23/60minutes.

17. Keith McArthur, "Online era leaves media out of loop: PR expert," *Globe and Mail*, March 21, 2005, p. B5.

© Peter M. Fisher/CORBIS

Direct Response and Interactive Communications

Learning Objectives

After studying this chapter, you will be able to

1. Describe the various types of direct response advertising.

2. Explain the advantages and disadvantages of various forms of direct response advertising.

3. Assess the strategies for delivering effective messages via direct response techniques.

4. Describe the various elements of online and other interactive forms of communications.

5. Evaluate the various online advertising models available to marketing organizations.

6. Assess the potential of the Internet as an advertising medium.

Direct response advertising in a variety of forms and interactive communications in a variety of forms are the next two components of the integrated marketing communications mix to be discussed. The targeting capabilities of direct and interactive communications separate them from the traditional forms of mass advertising that were discussed in Chapter 14.

Direct mail remains the most common means of delivering direct response messages, but other forms of direct communication such as direct response television, catalogues, and telemarketing now play a more significant role. The Internet allows organizations to reach prospects in their own environment with a message that is active and interactive in nature compared to passive, traditional forms of advertising. When managers consider the time that people are spending online, it becomes readily apparent that online communications will play a much larger role in the future. Younger target audiences are spending considerable time using cell phones, and this phenomenon has spawned an interest in text messaging and video messaging among advertisers with youthful targets.

Direct Response Advertising

Direct response is rapidly becoming a vital component of the integrated marketing communications mix and it plays a key role in influencing buying behaviour. Simply stated, the glamour days of marketing management are over. Managers cannot rely solely on traditional forms of communications, particularly 30-second television commercials, and expect to get the job done. Managers are making decisions in an era where accountability (for money invested in communications) is paramount, so the media used must deliver bottom-line results.

Direct response communications are going to be more important in the marketing communications mix. There are four primary forms of direct response communications: direct mail, *direct response television, catalogues,* and *telemarketing.* Both direct mail and direct-response television advertising are growing steadily from year to year. In fact, direct mail currently accounts for $1.6 billion, or 15 percent of all advertising revenues in Canada. Among all media, direct mail ranks third behind television (26 percent of revenues) and daily newspapers (16 percent of revenues).[1] It is an essential medium to a good many companies and not-for-profit organizations.

There are good reasons beyond the accountability factor that explain why direct-response advertising is growing. Most important is a company's desire for immediate returns on advertising dollars spent. With direct response, results can be measured quickly. Also, direct response advertising is an appropriate medium for marketers wanting to implement individualized marketing programs that result from the use of sophisticated database management techniques. In short, companies want to build relationships with customers, and direct response provides an efficient means to do so.

Prior to discussing some of the direct response communications techniques, some distinctions should be made between the following marketing terms, which are often confused with each other. Students should first recognize that direct response advertising is a subset of direct marketing. Second, students should understand that the objective of direct response communications is to encourage action immediately. Direct response communications delivers an offer to customers.

1. **Direct Marketing**—A marketing system fully controlled by the marketer that develops products, promotes them directly to the final consumer through a variety of media options, accepts direct orders from consumers, and distributes products directly to the consumer.
2. **Direct Response Advertising**—Advertising through any medium designed to generate an immediate response by any means (such as mail, television, telephone, or online communications) that is measurable. If traditional mass media are used, the message will include a 1-800 telephone number, mailing address, or website address where more information can be secured.

Direct mail is currently the primary medium for delivering direct response advertising messages; however, due to advancing electronic technology, it is expected that direct response television and a variety of online communications will play a much stronger role in the communications mix in the future.

DIRECT MAIL

Direct mail is a form of advertising communicated to prospects via the postal service. The use of mail is widespread due to its ability to personalize the message (the name can be included in the mailing), the need to send lengthy messages (e.g., copy-oriented sales messages along with reply cards and contracts that are returned by prospects), and its ability to provide a high degree of geographic coverage economically (e.g., the mailing can be distributed to designated postal codes anywhere in Canada). There are numerous options available.

SALES LETTERS   The most common form of direct mail, the **letter**, is typeset, printed, and delivered to household occupants or to specific individuals at personal or business addresses. Letters are usually the primary communication in a mailing package, which typically includes a brochure, reply card, and postage-paid return envelope.

LEAFLETS AND FLYERS   **Leaflets** and **flyers** are usually standard letter-sized pages (8.5-inch × 11-inch) that offer relevant information and accompany a letter. Leaflets expand on the information contained in the letter and generate a response (i.e., the recipient takes action).

FOLDERS   **Folders** are sales messages printed on heavier paper, and often include photographs or illustrations. They are usually folded, and are frequently designed in such a way that they can be mailed without an envelope. **Postage-paid reply cards** are an important component of a folder. See Figure 15.1 for an illustration.

2. Explain the advantages and disadvantages of various forms of direct response advertising.

direct mail

letter

leaflets
flyers

folders

postage-paid reply cards

FIGURE
15.1

**A folder with a postage-paid
reply card makes it easy to
respond to an offer**

Courtesy of Canadian Geographic.

bounce backs

STATEMENT STUFFERS   Statement stuffers, or **bounce backs** as they are often called, are advertisements distributed via monthly credit card statements (such as those one receives from Sears, The Bay, or Visa). Capitalizing on the ease of purchasing by credit, such mailings make it very convenient to take action. In this case, one order leads to another, and the prospect is reached at very low cost. Usually, the credit card number is the only information the seller requires.

CD-ROM AND DVD COMMUNICATIONS   Organizations now send serious prospects information by more sophisticated means. A CD or DVD is now a popular means of demonstrating how a product works, how nice a resort destination looks, or how well an automobile performs. In business-to-business markets a CD or DVD is useful for presentation purposes (when combined with personal selling practices) and for letting customers review things on their own time. They can aptly portray how a product works. As well, technical information about a product that is difficult to communicate in hard copy is easily accessed on a disk. CDs and DVDs can be part of a direct mail campaign or a follow-up to a direct mail campaign (e.g., for those who requested more information from the original mailing).

DIRECT MAIL STRATEGY

Essentially, an organization has the option of delivering a mail piece by itself and absorbing all of the costs associated with such a mailing, or delivering an offer as part of

3. Assess the strategies for delivering effective messages via direct response techniques.

a package that includes offers from other companies. The latter option is far less costly. This is the difference between solo direct mail and cooperative direct mail.

SOLO DIRECT MAIL   **Solo direct mail** or **selective direct mail** refers to specialized or individually prepared direct mail offers sent directly to prospects. Solo direct mail pieces are commonly employed in business-to-business communications, supplementing the messages frequently communicated via traditional business publications. Due to the degree of personalization, response rates to this type of mailing tend to be much higher than for a cooperative mailing. Refer to Figure 15.2 for an illustration of a solo direct mail piece.

solo direct mail (selective direct mail)

COOPERATIVE DIRECT MAIL   **Cooperative direct mail** refers to envelopes containing special offers from non-competing products. Consumer-goods marketers commonly employ this method. A typical mailing would contain coupons for a variety of grocery,

cooperative direct mail

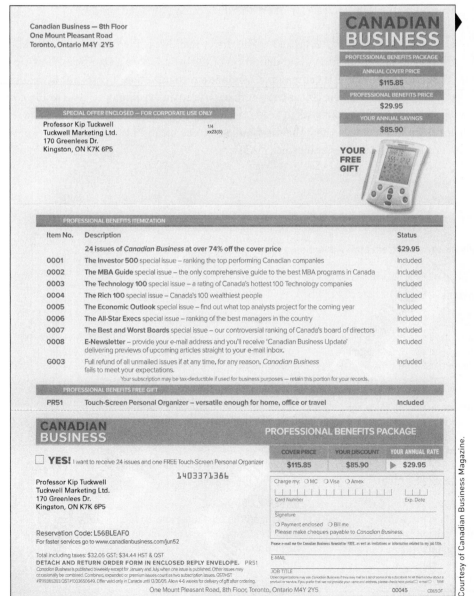

Courtesy of Canadian Business Magazine.

FIGURE
15.2

Contents of a typical solo direct mail campaign

drug, and related products, magazine subscription offers, pre-printed envelopes offering discounted rates for film processing, and so on. The Val-Pak envelope—which is distributed nationally, but contains ads for local businesses—is an example of a cooperative direct mailing. Cooperative direct mailings are frequently used by marketing organizations to achieve trial purchase of a good.

Direct mail marketing strategies are now commonly implemented by leaders in all kinds of industries. They are particularly popular among packaged-goods companies, financial institutions such as banks and life insurance companies, and automobile manufacturers. Contemporary marketing managers clearly see how effective direct mail strategies can be at establishing and building solid customer relationships. For a summary of the advantages and disadvantages of direct mail as an advertising medium, refer to Figure 15.3.

INFORMATION IS KEY TO SUCCESS

Embarking upon a direct mail marketing campaign involves three basic steps: obtaining a proper prospect list; conceiving and producing the mailing piece, which involves developing the right message or offer; and distributing the final version.

OBTAINING DIRECT MAIL LISTS The direct mail list is the backbone of the entire campaign. Both the accuracy and definition of the list can have a significant bearing on the success or failure of a campaign. Companies recognize that it costs about six times as much to acquire a new customer as it does to keep an existing one.[2] As a result, companies are compiling databases to keep track of existing customers and are forming relationships with them through the mail and electronic means. Lists are secured from two sources: internal sources and external sources.

FIGURE
15.3 Advantages and Disadvantages of Direct Mail Advertising

Advantages	Disadvantages
Audience Selectivity Precise targets can be reached in terms of demographic and geographic variables. House lists are a good starting point, along with lists from brokers.	**High Cost per Exposure** Costs can be higher than other print alternatives when costs of producing the mailing, renting lists, mailing, and fulfilling orders are considered.
Message Flexibility There is an opportunity to include a lengthy message (tell more, sell more) and incentives to stimulate action.	**Absence of Editorial Support** Direct mail stands alone; it must grab the receiver's attention quickly.
Exclusivity Mail does not compete with other media when it arrives in a household.	**Image** Consumers perceive it to be "junk" mail, so it may be promptly discarded.
Measurability Based on historical conversion patterns, sales results can be accurately forecast. Traditional media can only measure for awareness and interest.	**Delivery Delays** Relying on the postal service and third-class mail could result in delivery delays; timing of a delivery may be important.

Internal Sources   There is no better prospect than a current customer. Therefore, a company's internal database must be monitored and updated routinely. For example, Shoppers Drug Mart accumulates considerable data about the buying behaviour of its customers who have an Optimum Rewards card. Shoppers recently started sending out customized mail offers to clients based on what it knows. For example, clients who buy diapers regularly will receive a Shoppers' offer for Huggies, a leading brand of diapers.[3] The Hudson's Bay Company also collects a mountain of data from its Hudson's Bay Rewards Program card.

Data mining techniques allow these companies to determine who their heavy customers are, what they buy, how much they buy, and how often they buy. For companies placing value on repeat business, this information can be used to develop new offers that will be of interest to current customers. Today, banks and financial institutions are the most frequent users of internal-database-driven direct mail techniques. In direct mail terms, an internal customer list is referred to as a **house list**.

house list

As an alternative, companies can take steps to form lists of potential customers. Such customers are referred to as prospects. As Figure 15.4 illustrates, Jaguar Canada is collecting information about customers that it can use in the future. This information-oriented postcard appeared in a national magazine with a full-page ad for a Jaguar automobile.

External Sources   People who have a history of responding to mail offers tend to be attractive prospects for new offers. Buying by mail is part of their behaviour. Therefore, the challenge is to find prospects that have a demographic profile, and perhaps a psychographic profile, that mirrors the profile of current customers. A **list broker** can assist in finding these prospects. The marketing manager provides the broker with the profile of the target customer, and the broker supplies a list of possible prospects on a cost-per-name basis.

list broker

Generally, a high-quality list is developed through a **merge/purge** process on a computer, whereby numerous lists are purchased, combined, and stripped of duplicate names. ICOM Information & Communications Inc. is an example of a Canadian list broker. ICOM compiles lists based on interests and demographics. Some of the sub-categories of the interest list include mail order buyers, hobbyists, sports enthusiasts, pet owners, investors, automotive enthusiasts, donors to causes, and travellers. Demographic sub-categories include age of household members, household income, size of household, marital status, and housing type.

merge/purge

ICOM Information & Communications
www.i-com.com

Names are typically purchased on a CPM (cost per thousand) basis. As the quality of a list becomes more sophisticated or specialized (e.g., more demographic or geographic factors are added), the rate per thousand increases. ICOM charges a base rate of $110/M and then adds $10/M for each interest or demographic selection that is added. The minimum order is 5000 names, and the list can be used only once by the renter.[4]

Canada Post also supplies information vital to the accurate targeting of messages. For example, a postal code can isolate a small geographic area—say, a city block—and can then be combined with census data to provide relevant statistics regarding the ages and incomes of homeowners in the area, and whether children are present in the households.

A few types of lists are available: response lists, circulation lists, and compiled lists.

RESPONSE LISTS   A **response list** is a list of proven mail-order buyers. Such lists include book-of-the-month-club buyers, tape and CD music buyers, or people who order from cooperative direct mailing firms. Because these lists include proven mail order buyers, they tend to cost more.

response list

FIGURE
15.4
A reply card that collects valuable information about potential customers

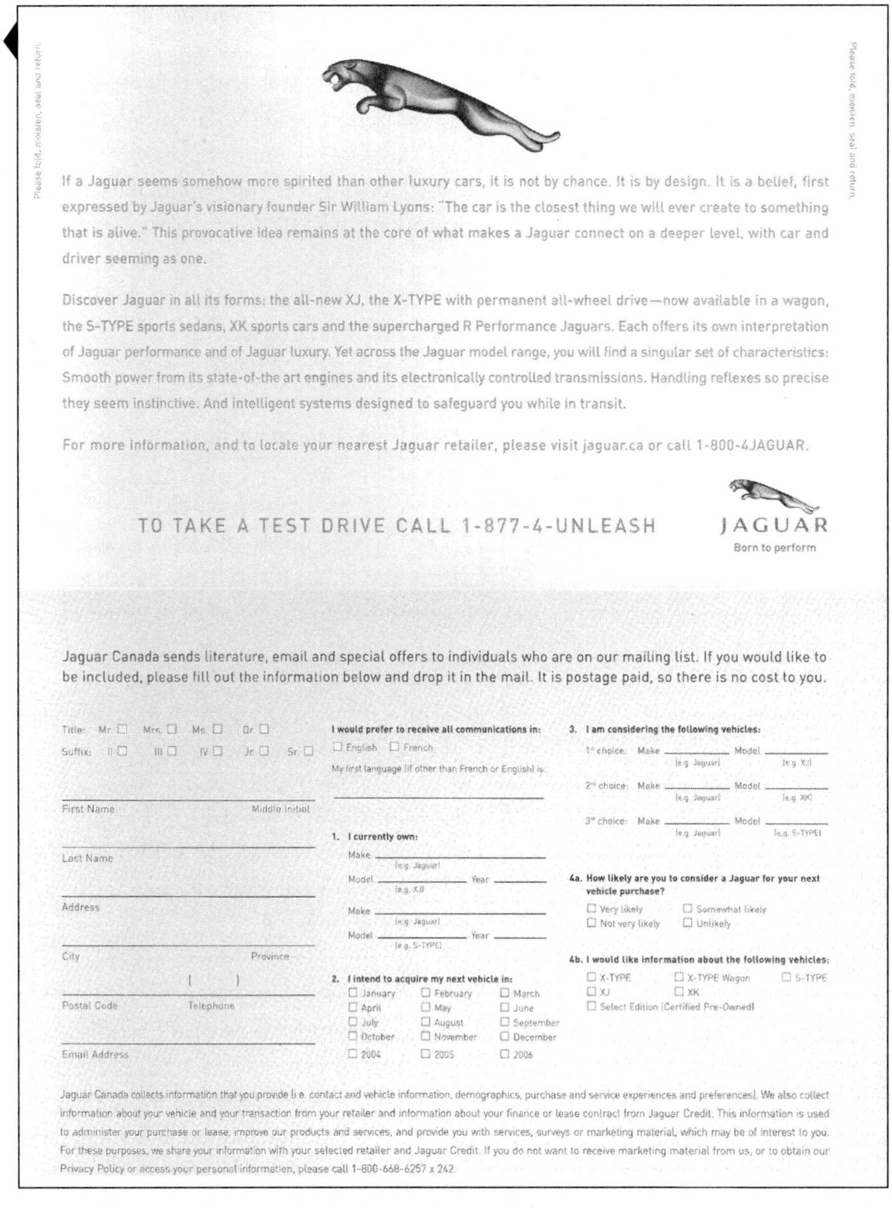

Please fold, moisten, seal and return.

If a Jaguar seems somehow more spirited than other luxury cars, it is not by chance. It is by design. It is a belief, first expressed by Jaguar's visionary founder Sir William Lyons: "The car is the closest thing we will ever create to something that is alive." This provocative idea remains at the core of what makes a Jaguar connect on a deeper level, with car and driver seeming as one.

Discover Jaguar in all its forms: the all-new XJ, the X-TYPE with permanent all-wheel drive—now available in a wagon, the S-TYPE sports sedans, XK sports cars and the supercharged R Performance Jaguars. Each offers its own interpretation of Jaguar performance and of Jaguar luxury. Yet across the Jaguar model range, you will find a singular set of characteristics: Smooth power from its state-of-the art engines and its electronically controlled transmissions. Handling reflexes so precise they seem instinctive. And intelligent systems designed to safeguard you while in transit.

For more information, and to locate your nearest Jaguar retailer, please visit jaguar.ca or call 1-800-4JAGUAR.

TO TAKE A TEST DRIVE CALL 1-877-4-UNLEASH

JAGUAR
Born to perform

Jaguar Canada sends literature, email and special offers to individuals who are on our mailing list. If you would like to be included, please fill out the information below and drop it in the mail. It is postage paid, so there is no cost to you.

Title: Mr. ☐ Mrs. ☐ Ms. ☐ Dr. ☐
Suffix: II ☐ III ☐ IV ☐ Jr. ☐ Sr. ☐

First Name ______ Middle Initial
Last Name ______
Address ______
City ______ Province
Postal Code ______ Telephone ( )
Email Address ______

I would prefer to receive all communications in:
☐ English ☐ French
My first language (if other than French or English) is: ______

1. I currently own:
Make ______ (e.g. Jaguar)
Model ______ (e.g. XJ) Year ______
Make ______ (e.g. Jaguar)
Model ______ (e.g. S-TYPE) Year ______

2. I intend to acquire my next vehicle in:
☐ January ☐ February ☐ March
☐ April ☐ May ☐ June
☐ July ☐ August ☐ September
☐ October ☐ November ☐ December
☐ 2004 ☐ 2005 ☐ 2006

3. I am considering the following vehicles:
1st choice: Make ______ (e.g. Jaguar) Model ______ (e.g. XJ)
2nd choice: Make ______ (e.g. Jaguar) Model ______ (e.g. XK)
3rd choice: Make ______ (e.g. Jaguar) Model ______ (e.g. S-TYPE)

4a. How likely are you to consider a Jaguar for your next vehicle purchase?
☐ Very likely ☐ Somewhat likely
☐ Not very likely ☐ Unlikely

4b. I would like information about the following vehicles:
☐ X-TYPE ☐ X-TYPE Wagon ☐ S-TYPE
☐ XJ ☐ XK
☐ Select Edition (Certified Pre-Owned)

Jaguar Canada collects information that you provide (i.e. contact and vehicle information, demographics, purchase and service experiences and preferences). We also collect information about your vehicle and your transaction from your retailer and information about your finance or lease contract from Jaguar Credit. This information is used to administer your purchase or lease, improve our products and services, and provide you with services, surveys or marketing material, which may be of interest to you. For these purposes, we share your information with your selected retailer and Jaguar Credit. If you do not want to receive marketing material from us, or to obtain our Privacy Policy or access your personal information, please call 1-800-668-6257 x 242.

Please fold, moisten, seal and return.

Reprinted by permission of Jaguar Canada.

circulation lists

CIRCULATION LISTS **Circulation lists** are magazine subscription lists that target potential customers by an interest or activity. A magazine publishing company, for example, sells its list of subscribers to any other business that is interested in a similar target. Cornerstone List Management (a list brokerage) is responsible for managing and renting all Rogers Media consumer publication lists, which include publications such as *Chatelaine*, *Maclean's*, *Canadian Business*, *Profit*, *L'actualité*, and *MoneySense*. The *Maclean's* list, for example, reaches well-educated men and women concerned about today's issues and trends. Cornerstone rents the list (217 000 names available) for $130/M, with additional costs for demographic selections.[5]

Cornerstone List Management
www.cstonecanada.com

compiled lists

COMPILED LISTS **Compiled lists** are prepared from government, census, telephone, warranty, and other publication information. These are the least expensive of the lists and are not always personalized. For example, a business firm may be identified on the list but not the appropriate contact person within the firm. Names of business prospects are compiled from print sources such as *Frasers Canadian Trade Index* or *Scott's Industrial Index*. Provincial and national associations such as the Canadian Medical Association commonly provide mailing lists of their physicians, or, in the case of other associations, lawyers, teachers, and accountants.

For more insight into how companies employ direct mail to their advantage, read the Marketing in Action vignette **Marketing Budgets Go Direct**.

DIRECT RESPONSE TELEVISION

Direct response television (DRTV) is a sales-oriented commercial that encourages viewers to buy immediately. The buying response is usually by telephone or online. There are two types of direct response television ads: short form and long form. Short-form DRTV spots typically air for 60 or 120 seconds. Long-form DRTV typically runs for an extended period and is referred to as infomercials. An **infomercial** is a 30-minute commercial message that is program-like in nature and presents the benefits of the product or service in great detail.

direct response television (DRTV)

infomercial

Direct response television commercials are classified into two categories:

1. *Traditional*—An infomercial that stresses the "buy now, limited-time offer." It tries to sell as much as possible at the lowest cost per order.
2. *Corporate/Brand*—An infomercial that establishes leads, drives retail traffic, launches new products, creates awareness, and protects and enhances the brand image.

As marketers move more and more toward direct response commercials they must appreciate the differences between DRTV and traditional brand advertising. Brand commercials create awareness and build an image in the hope that the customer will buy at a later date. DRTV spots are designed to motivate the viewer to respond immediately. As a result, where brand television ads focus on one key benefit, DRTV spots give the viewer all of the information they need to make a purchase decision. Most DRTV spots also include a special time-sensitive offer designed to induce immediate purchase.[6]

The nature of direct response television advertising has changed over time, and from a quality perspective most brand-based DRTV commercials are indistinguishable from traditional brand-based commercials. Today, many blue-chip companies in the pharmaceutical, banking, automotive, and not-for-profit sectors have produced highly informative commercials. Mainstream marketing organizations such as Ford, Bell, Royal Bank, TD Bank, and ING Direct have embraced direct response television. As a further indicator of how popular DRTV is becoming, consider that 16 percent of all commercials shown on the 2004 Super Bowl (a show where all kinds of new commercials are shown) employed the use of a 1-800 telephone number as a response mechanism, and 63 percent of commercials used an Internet address as a response mechanism.[7]

CATALOGUES

Catalogues are reference publications, usually annual, distributed by large retail chains and other direct marketing organizations. Typically, catalogues would be mailed to current customers whose names are stored in a company database. A catalogue can be general in nature, as is the case of the Sears catalogue and the Canadian Tire catalogue, or it may contain specialized merchandise that is targeted at a specific audience based on some kind of interest (e.g., sporting goods, leisure sportswear, or computers and computer accessories). At the present time, Sears is the largest catalogue marketing organization in Canada with direct sales approaching $1.5 billion annually.

catalogues

MARKETING IN ACTION

Marketing Budgets Go Direct

The trend toward direct mail marketing and direct response marketing has been steadily building. Marketing managers are attracted to better targeting capabilities, sophisticated measurement techniques, and the ability to account for every dollar spent. With so many benefits, why shouldn't it be popular!

Budgets used to be divided 95 percent traditional advertising and 5 percent direct. It moved to 90/10 and now it's about 80/20 and climbing. Loosely translated, that means that 20 cents out of every marketing dollar is now devoted to direct response activities. The Hudson's Bay Company has progressively increased its direct response budget over the past few years and will continue to increase it as long as the return on investment stays positive.

Since Shoppers Drug Mart's introduction of the Optimum loyalty card, it too has shifted more in the direction of direct mail and direct response communications. Where it once used mass advertising to support the loyalty program, it now relies solely on direct mail and email. Shoppers sends out about one million direct mail pieces each month.

According to Marshall Warkentin, manager of Shoppers Optimum, "We've seen a huge increase in vendor activity. Last year (2003) we did mailings on behalf of vendors such as Crest, L'Oreal, and Gillette. Now we're at the point where we've quadrupled that activity."

Companies such as Procter & Gamble and Unilever see great value in tapping into Optimum's lucrative, mostly female customer database through cooperative campaigns targeted at special-interest consumers—new mothers, adults with a host of personal-care needs, allergy sufferers, and so on. L'Oreal did a direct mail piece in conjunction with Shoppers Drug Mart. The mailing piece for Visible Results, a women's skin care product, included beautiful beauty shots, a compelling promise, and, of course, a sample.

How does the Shoppers Optimum system work? Very simply! Shoppers can cross-reference transaction data electronically and tailor offers to specific customers by direct mail or email. Once buyers of certain types of products are known, they become a valuable commodity for the manufacturers of those products. Direct access to a real buyer is a compelling reason why competitors such as Procter & Gamble and Unilever get involved with such programs.

Adapted from Bernadette Johnson, "Dollars to Direct," *Strategy Direct + Interactive*, August 25, 2003, pp. 10, 11; and Michael McGovern, "The precise art of direct marketing," *Marketing*, March 22, 2004, p. 23.

Courtesy of Shoppers Drug Mart

The Sears catalogue is distributed to more than 4.1 million Canadian households. Each year, Sears publishes two general catalogues (Spring/Summer and Fall/Winter), along with a Christmas Wish Book and a series of sale catalogues (see Figure 15.5). Sears is now a fully integrated marketing and marketing communications organization. It accepts orders by fax, by email, and through its website. The company's 1-800 number is the most frequently called toll-free number in Canada.[8]

Reprinted with permission of Sears Canada Inc.

FIGURE
15.5

Sears integrates catalogue buying with online buying

Canadian Tire is another aggressive catalogue marketing organization. Says Mark Foote, president of Canadian Tire's retail division, "We make sure virtually every Canadian household has a catalogue. Eight out of ten Canadians keep it for a full year, until the new one arrives."[9]

Sears and Canadian Tire recognize that catalogue and online activities will cannibalize some sales at stores, but the shift is necessary because they have to respond to customers' wants, and ordering items for home delivery is one of them. Customers are into multi-channel shopping. Both companies effectively combine media advertising (television, print, and flyers) with nontraditional marketing communications (Internet, direct mail, and catalogues).

TELEMARKETING

Telemarketing involves the use of telecommunications to deliver a sales message. Communications via telemarketing is a booming business in North America even though it is considered one of the most irritating forms of marketing communications by consumers. Telemarketing communications are often directly linked to direct response television campaigns. Working together, they are a potent combination for achieving all kinds of marketing objectives.

Most telemarketing activity is conducted at call centres. A **call centre** is a central operation from which a company operates its inbound and outbound telemarketing programs. **Inbound telemarketing** refers to the reception of calls by the order desk,

telemarketing

call centre

inbound telemarketing

customer inquiry, and direct response calls often generated through the use of toll-free 1-800 or 888 numbers. **Outbound telemarketing**, on the other hand, refers to calls that a company makes to customers in order to develop new accounts, generate sales leads, and even close a sale. In Canada, it is estimated that telemarketing campaigns generate in the neighbourhood of $16 billion in sales revenues annually.[10]

Call centre operations will continue to expand in the future. As more and more marketing companies embrace database marketing techniques and customer relationship management programs, there will be a stronger desire to communicate with customers more directly and more frequently.

Since individual companies do not have the capability to handle call centre operations, it is an activity that is commonly outsourced to experts. Experts can effectively manage both inbound and outbound calls with precision so that returns on investment are maximized. Canadian-based call centres are the focal point of North American operations for many companies. The industry has a strong presence in Canada due to our strong telecommunications infrastructure, the capability of operators to speak several languages, and currency exchange rates between Canada and the United States.

The primary advantage of telemarketing is that it can complete a sale for less cost than using such techniques as face-to-face sales calls or mass advertising. However, to be effective, training and preparation of telemarketing representatives needs to be as comprehensive as it is for personal selling. Planning the message is as important as the medium itself.

A drawback to telemarketing is the fact that consumers react negatively to it. A Canadian research study conducted by Ernst & Young revealed that 75 percent of Canadians consider marketing calls unwelcome and intrusive; they are ranked as one of the least liked sales techniques.[11] People frequently react to them by hanging up. Despite this behaviour, organizations see advantages such as call reach and frequency and cost-efficiency outweighing the disadvantages.

Canadian Marketing Association
www.the-cma.org

4. Describe the various elements of online and other interactive forms of communications.

Consumers who do not like telemarketing calls can have their names removed from the lists used by the 800 member companies of the Canadian Marketing Association by filling out a form on the CMA website. The federal government is considering a do-not-call list that would offer one-stop relief for consumers who are fed up with telemarketers. Such a list exists in the United States and it is working effectively.

Interactive Marketing Communications

Advancing technology has thrust upon us new and innovative media that are revolutionizing how companies look at communications strategy, and certainly how they allocate money among the various media. The Internet now plays a significant role in the marketing communications mix, but beyond the Internet are options such as instant text messaging via wireless devices; a booming market for cell phones is fuelling interest in on-the-spot communications with people.

Online communications offer a high degree of personalization, and because personalization is one of the cornerstones of customer relationship management programs the Internet is now an attractive medium to marketers. Since the medium is relatively new, companies are still trying to determine how to best utilize it. One company that has figured things out is General Motors, the leading advertiser in all media in North America. General Motors rethought its marketing communications budget and placed more money into relationship-oriented communications, including the Internet and sponsorships. GM is looking for better ways to target prospects and finds it much easier to do so when they visit the company's various websites.[12]

Strategically thinking, marketing managers now realize that online and other inter-active communications are complementary to traditional media and, when used together, improve awareness levels and stimulate more action. Further, these new media are providing progressive companies with a means of reaching what was once thought to be an unattainable goal: a personal, one-to-one relationship with customers involv-ing continuous interaction in the pre-transaction, transaction, and post-transaction phases of a purchase. The Internet seems to offer unlimited communications potential.

ONLINE ADVERTISING

The Internet provides access to customers all over the world and delivers information in ways that traditional print and broadcast media cannot. Traditional media are passive by nature. In contrast, communications on the Internet goes both ways—it is an inter-active medium. The potential offered by the Internet in terms of communication leaves little doubt that it will become an important medium among advertisers looking to reach large numbers of people in a cost-effective manner.

5. Evaluate the various online advertising models available to marketing organizations.

As an advertising medium, the Internet is now growing at a significant rate. In Canada, online advertising revenues are expected to reach $300 million by the end of 2004, a 68-percent increase in just two years.[13] The increase in online revenues is a response to people spending more and more time online. In fact, a survey conducted by SRI Knowledge Networks found that the Internet now ranks third in "share of voice"— behind television and radio, and ahead of newspapers and magazines. Further, con-sumer media habits across all demographics are changing rapidly. A poll by Forrester Research indicated that 21 percent of consumers now watch less television, 10 percent listen to the radio less, and 13 percent spend less time reading newspapers and maga-zines.[14] Given these trends, what choice does an advertiser have but to shift more money into online advertising?

SRI Knowledge Networks
www.knowledgenetworks.com

Forrester Research
www.forrester.com

Online advertising is defined as the placement of electronic communication on a website, in email, or over personal communications devices (e.g., personal digital assis-tants and cell phones) connected to the Internet. While the ultimate goal of most forms of advertising is to motivate the purchase of a brand, online advertising is useful for:

online advertising

· Creating brand awareness
· Stimulating interest and preference
· Providing a means to make a purchase
· Providing a means to contact an advertiser
· Acquiring data about real/potential consumers

Based on these objectives, the essential role of the Internet is to communicate vital information about a company and its products. When a company quotes a website address in other forms of communications, it finds that interested buyers start to visit its site for new information. Such behaviour could eventually translate into a purchase. Therefore, organizations shouldn't neglect traditional forms of advertising. Very often, the best way to advertise a Web-based company is through traditional media.

It's important to understand some basic terminology prior to examining the vari-ous online advertising alternatives. All terms relate to how Internet ads are measured for effectiveness:

Impressions (Ad Impression)—An ad request that was successfully sent to a visitor. This is the standard way of determining exposure for an ad on the Web.

Clicks (Clickthroughs)—This refers to the number of times that users click on any banner ad. Such a measurement allows an advertiser to judge the response to an ad. When viewers click the ad they are transferred to the advertiser's website or to a special page where they are encouraged to respond in some way to the ad.

Clickthrough Rate—The *clickthrough rate* indicates the success of an advertiser in attracting visitors to click on its ad. For example, if during one million impressions there are 20 000 clicks on the banner, the clickthrough rate is 2 percent. The formula is clicks divided by ad impressions.

Visitor—Any individual who accesses a website within a specific time period.

Visit—A sequence of page requests made by one user at one website. A visit is also referred to as a *session* or *browsing period*.

A site's activity is described in terms of visits and visitors, the former always being larger than the latter because of repeat visitors. A site that can report, for example, that it had 8 million page views, 100 000 visitors, and 800 000 visits last month would be doing very well. It means that the average visitor returns to the site 8 times each month, and views 10 pages on each visit. That's incredible "stickiness" (most sites don't do that well)! **Sticky content** refers to the notion that the website has a compelling reason for users to frequently come back.

TYPES OF ONLINE ADVERTISING   There are a variety of choices available to online advertisers: banner advertising, pop-up and pop-under ads, interstitials and rich media ads, superstitials, sponsorships, websites, and email advertising.

Banner Advertising (Display Advertising)   A **banner ad** usually refers to third-party advertising on a website. In terms of design, it stretches across a page in a narrow band. Its appearance is much like that of an outdoor poster or a banner ad that stretches across the bottom of a newspaper page. This style of banner is static in nature and the content is minimal. Smaller versions of the banner (e.g., one-half the width, smaller rectangles, and squares) are referred to as **buttons**. Banner advertising is also referred to as **display advertising**.

Banner ads are available in a choice of sizes. Advertising research conducted by the Interactive Advertising Bureau has concluded that larger formats are more visible and more effective than smaller, standard-sized banners. Some of the larger sizes include the skyscraper and large rectangle. A **skyscraper** is a tall, skinny oblong that appears at the side of a Web page. The **rectangle** is a larger box; it is not as wide as a banner but offers more depth. In addition to being more effective, the sheer size of the ad provides an opportunity for advertisers to be more creative with their ads—many advertisers now integrate some animation in order to attract more attention. Refer to Figure 15.6 for an illustration.

Given the interactive nature of the medium, and the behaviour of Internet users who like to avoid ads if at all possible, the results achieved from banner ads have been short of expectations. Consequently, advertisers are experimenting with more animated forms of advertising, television-style online advertising, sponsorships, and email advertising.

Pop-up and Pop-under Ads   A **pop-up** or **pop-under ad** appears in a separate window on top of or beneath content already on a computer screen. Pop-under ads remain concealed until the top window is closed, moved, resized, or minimized. Advertisers that employ pop-ups or pop-unders do so at their own peril. A recent PlanetFeedback survey found pop-ups lead all ad forms in levels of annoyance and distrust. Despite the consumers' distaste for pop-ups, advertisers like them because the clickthrough rates and conversion rates are 13 to 14 times higher, respectively, than for standard banner

---

sticky content

6. Assess the potential of the Internet as an advertising medium.

banner ad

buttons
display advertising

Interactive Advertising Bureau
www.iabcanada.com

skyscraper
rectangle

pop-up or pop-under ad

FIGURE
15.6

An illustration of a standard size banner ad and a larger rectangular ad

ads.[15] Negative feedback by consumers, however, has led some Web publishers to ban pop-ups and pop-unders. The consumer remains in control in terms of what's appropriate and inappropriate with online advertising!

Rich Media: Interstitials and Superstitials   **Rich media** is a form of online communication that includes animation, sound, video, and interactivity. An **interstitial** is a rich media message that is contained in a pop-up window while the requested content loads in the background. It is an intrusive message that is delivered automatically without being requested by the user. A **superstitial** is similar to an interstitial but is more elaborate, usually incorporating multimedia and interactive elements. A superstitial is displayed in the active browser window. Viewing such ads requires special software such as Flash and Shockwave.

A superstitial closely resembles a television commercial and is delivered by a process called streaming media. **Streaming media** involves the continuous delivery of small, compressed packets of data that are interpreted by a software player and displayed as audio or full-motion video. The similarity to television advertising makes it attractive to advertisers using traditional media. As well, the creativity aspect of rich media options makes online advertising more sexy, fun, and something new to try.

ESPN.com now runs Web commercials in a video format bundled with video content the user has requested. The TV-style ads are embedded in sports highlights clips that are readily available at the website. Viewers see the video clip followed by an ad

rich media

interstitial

superstitial

streaming media

followed by another video clip, and so on. The strategy ensures the ad is viewed. Generally speaking, the clickthrough rates for rich media ads are higher than for static banner ads. The rate for rich media averages 3.5 percent, whereas banners are only 0.5 percent.[16]

For more insight into the use of TV-style ads online and their growing popularity, read the Marketing in Action vignette **Online TV Commercials Attract Advertisers**.

Sponsorships   An online sponsorship is a commitment to advertise on a third-party website for an extended period. Advertisers are attracted to sponsorships on the basis of Web content. If the content is of interest to the advertiser's target market, visitors are likely to visit the site regularly. For example, a young male target audience frequents the TSN.ca website for up-to-the-minute sports scores, highlights, and breaking news. So, Molson Canadian sponsors the site's Fantasy Sports Network (an interactive section devoted to forming fantasy sports teams and leagues). Similarly, Nissan Canada sponsors a Ski Report on the Weather Network—two of Nissan's sport utility vehicles, the Pathfinder and the Xterra, are positioned to suit outdoor lifestyles, so the sponsorship is strategically sound. Nissan is also involved with other sponsorships involving skiing in Canada.

Websites   Most websites are commercial in nature. For example, a company website delivers important information about the company and/or its products to visitors. It also provides a means of collecting information about visitors (e.g., through contests and surveys). If managed properly, the Internet is one component of a database management system. The information collected at a website can be used to identify prospects and better market products in the future.

The nature of the information communicated will vary from one organization to another. For example, news and information organizations such as the *Globe and Mail, Maclean's,* CNN, and others use the Internet to disseminate information. Each medium offers an online version of its content. Entertainment companies like Disney and Universal Studios build pre-release excitement for new movies through online promotions and giveaways and by broadcasting movie trailers at their websites. Using the Internet in this manner can create demand in a less expensive way than using traditional forms of advertising.

Traditional media communications and other forms of online communications encourage users to visit a company website. Click on a banner ad, for example, and you are there! A website provides companies with an opportunity to really tell a story. A company cannot tell or show as much through traditional media as inexpensively as it can on the Internet. Research evidence indicates that people do their research online before making purchasing decisions. Therefore, advertising in the traditional media should always provide a website address and encourage customers to contact the site for additional information.

Automobile companies typically include website addresses with their media advertising and have elaborate sites with bold and vivid visuals, virtual tours, and all kinds of technical information about the latest makes and models (see Figure 15.7). For companies such as General Motors, Ford, Toyota, and many others, websites play a key role in building brand awareness and brand preference. Marketing research conducted by the Internet Advertising Bureau found that media combinations that included television, print, and websites generate higher awareness and preference levels than just television and print.[17]

Websites also play a key role in business-to-business marketing communications. A research study by Nielsen//NetRatings found 50 percent of business decision makers saying that a website influenced them to make a purchase or obtain a service for their business. Related information also indicated that reference to media such as television, newspapers, and magazines had declined.[18]

The Sports Network
www.tsn.ca

The Weather Network
www.weathernetwork.com

Internet Advertising Bureau
www.iab.net

MARKETING IN ACTION

Online TV Commercials Attract Advertisers

How effective is any form of online advertising? General Motors, Canada's largest advertiser, has discovered it is quite effective when used in conjunction with traditional media. When online advertising and television advertising were used together in a GM campaign versus television alone, there was a 28-percent increase in brand awareness among the sample group.

GM has long been a believer in the value of online advertising, but the research study that produced the above awareness scores helped the company further understand the synergies between the media and provided actionable ways to better plan creative, media allocations, and scheduling. Canadians are changing their media habits, so marketers must follow their customers.

Very likely, GM will start to cash in on the latest craze in online advertising—video advertising. TV-style ads delivered over the Internet are exploding in popularity. Canadian advertisers already using video ads are Rona Inc. and Alliance Atlantis Communications. The ads appear in small windows or full screen. Some are user initiated, while others are interspersed within video content or appear on screen when users surf from page to page.

The TV-style ads offer several benefits to advertisers. They can minimize their creative costs, as they can simply convert commercials into digital files for the Web. Couple that with the high level of broadband Internet adoption in Canada and you've got an appealing

format. At the very least, it gives advertisers that are skeptical about the effectiveness of Web advertising an incentive to at least dabble in it.

Inevitably, there will be a downside to video ads. For starters, Web surfers have notoriously short attention spans. Advertisers also risk a backlash against unexpected video from online users who are still fuming about persistent pop-up ads. And with people now paying less attention to television ads, it stands to reason that TV-style ads online will eventually get the same response from consumers. However, since consumers are spending more and more—and more—time online, and less time with other media, advertisers have little choice but to jump on the online video ad bandwagon.

Adapted from Tessa Wegert, "On-line video ads grow more popular," *Globe and Mail*, November 11, 2004, p. B10; and Carl Bialik, "TV Commercials Go Online, But Will Surfers Tune In?" *Yahoo! Finance*, July 8, 2004, www.yahooo.com.

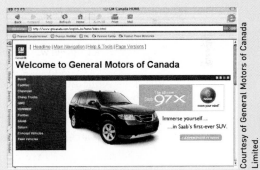

Courtesy of General Motors of Canada Limited.

Webcasting (Internet Infomercials) A recent online innovation is webcasting. **Webcasting** involves the production of an extended commercial or infomercial that includes entertainment value in the communications. While consumers are using digital video recorders to skip television ads they don't like, they are using the Internet to tune in to spots they want to see—an interesting phenomenon!

As a relatively small competitor in the shaving market, Schick Canada used webcasting to differentiate itself from Gillette. A series of eight "webisodes" under the title of "Close Shaves" featured Pistol Pete Madigan, the cartoon host of a radio show for guys, who rants about such topics as why he hates golf, and why facial hair makes people look like they eat out of garbage cans. In one segment Pistol Pete wears a Shick Quattro

webcasting

397

FIGURE

15.7

Websites provide essential information to prospective automobile buyers

t-shirt and talks approvingly about how the company is using girls on Harleys to promote its product. James MacIntosh, director of marketing for Schick, says "We're doing something unique to break through. The product needs to be edgier to stand out."[19]

While the number of potential viewers of a webcast can't match a television ad, MacIntosh likes the fact that viewers are there for a reason—to view the episode. The behaviour of people watching a commercial on the Web is much different from that of people watching a television commercial.

Email Advertising   Email advertising is very similar to direct mail advertising in terms of how it operates. The keys to a successful campaign are also similar: having the right list, having the right message or offer, and then designing the creative that will address the audience in the right way. The response rates for email are very similar to those for direct mail, with the average between 0.2 percent and 5.0 percent (e.g., up to five purchases for every mailing). The real benefit of email is the lower production and distribution costs. Sending an email offer costs only between 1 and 3 cents, whereas a direct mail piece will range from 70 cents to $2.[20]

Thanks to an unbelievable deluge of spam, email marketing is quickly becoming a mistrusted—even dreaded—medium for consumers. **Spam** is unsolicited email that people do not expect to get. On the other hand, legitimate or permission-based email seems quite acceptable. **Permission-based email** is sent to recipients who agree to receive that information in that form. In most cases, people will actually subscribe to receive the email because it is about something that is of interest to them. Users may subscribe and unsubscribe as they wish.

spam

permission-based email

Email marketers can also access lists from list brokers. An opt-in email list is rented from a list broker the same way a direct mail list is. An **opt-in list** contains the names of people who have agreed to have their information included.

In the age of database marketing, the compilation of an in-house list is essential. Sending email to customers and prospects who specifically request it will almost always work better than using a rented list. Many marketers firmly believe that the key objective of email is to establish and maintain a relationship with customers, which will ultimately generate sales. Blue Mountain, an Intrawest-owned ski destination, routinely sends email to all of its past customers—the goal of which is to encourage patrons to return to Blue Mountain instead of another ski destination. In many cases, the email message will include special offers or other promotional incentives to spur action. See Figure 15.8 for an illustration.

opt-in list

Text Messaging   **Text messaging** refers to the transmission of short, text-only messages on wireless devices such as cell phones and personal digital assistants (PDAs). As the penetration of cell phones continues, more and more marketers will look at this medium more seriously. Currently, text messaging is a popular means of reaching a young target audience. According to a Trendscan study, 52 percent of Canadian youths have their own cell phones. Sharp marketing managers wanting to reach this elusive target are already using text messaging.[21] Teens and young adults have been attracted to text messaging because of its portability and low cost. In contrast, palm devices are too expensive and laptop computers are inconvenient. Email is too slow—kids are into instant messaging.

text messaging

Trendscan
www.trendscan.de

FIGURE
15.8   Blue Mountain's email campaigns help form relationships and build loyalty with past customers

BLUE MOUNTAIN RESORTS LIMITED | R.R. #3 | COLLINGWOOD, ON | L9Y 3Z2

The application of text messaging was paramount in the hit reality show *Canadian Idol.* Following each show, cell phone users could—at their own expense—vote for their favourite contestant. On *Canadian Idol,* a total of 7.5 million text messages were sent during the 2004 season.

Over the next few years, cell phones will become capable of handling colour pictures, video, and hi-fi sound, so the anticipated flow of multimedia messages will contribute to the growth of the medium. The person-to-person link that marketers will have with individuals wherever they may be is an undeniable advantage of cell phone communications. There is also great potential to access vast databases of user profiles; for example, the database information that supermarkets, retailers, and mail-order companies have created for their customers. With a mere phone number a marketer could deliver millions of personalized messages, some of which could be tailored to a user's location and the time of day.[22]

For a summary of the advantages and disadvantages of online marketing communications, refer to Figure 15.9.

FIGURE 15.9　**Advantages and Disadvantages of Online Advertising**

Advantages	Disadvantages
Targeting Capability	**Effectiveness Is Low**
Technology in the form of cookies (electronic identification tags) allows ads to be targeted to Web site visitors based on their browsing behaviour. Database information enhances the quality of the online advertising effort.	While more than half of Canadians have access to the Internet, a majority of users do not perceive it to be an advertising medium. Consequently, ads are avoided or simply go unnoticed.
Timing	**Selective Reach**
The Internet is a 24/7 operation so ads are delivered anytime, anywhere. Content of the message can be changed quickly if need be.	In terms of reaching prospects at home, the Internet remains the domain of middle- to upper-class target markets. The cost of participation for consumers is high.
Interactivity and Action	**Privacy Concerns**
There is an opportunity to interact and develop a relationship with visitors to a Web site. Sufficient information and proper interaction can motivate a customer to take action.	Consumers are concerned about how information collected about them is used. Consumers are concerned about the intrusiveness of advertising (some ads can't be avoided). Their privacy is being invaded.

SUMMARY

Direct response advertising is one of the largest advertising media in Canada. The major forms of direct response advertising are direct mail, catalogues, direct response television, and telemarketing. Interactive advertising includes various forms of online advertising and text messaging.

Direct mail is the most prominent form of direct response advertising. A direct mailing usually includes a sales letter, leaflet or flyer, folder, and statement stuffer. Advertisers choose between solo direct mail and cooperative direct mail. Solo distribution is much more expensive than cooperative distribution.

The primary advantages of direct mail for advertisers are its audience selectivity, high reach potential, and geographic flexibility. Disadvantages include the absence of editorial support and poor image. The success of any direct mail campaign largely depends on the quality of the list the advertiser uses. Lists are available from list brokers on a cost per thousand basis, and from other secondary sources such as directories and trade indexes. The types of lists available include response lists, circulation lists, and compiled lists.

Advancing technology has spurred growth in direct response television and telemarketing. Whether it's a 60-second commercial or a 30-minute infomercial, direct response television is becoming popular with traditional advertisers. It is used to establish leads, build image, and launch new products. It's effective in communicating information that involves a lot of details.

The catalogue industry in Canada is underdeveloped and is largely controlled by Sears. Catalogues do cannibalize sales from stores, but in today's market customers are demanding alternative and convenient ways to shop. Consequently, retailers like Sears and Canadian Tire are establishing a catalogue and online presence.

Companies are attracted to telemarketing (inbound and outbound) because of the relatively low cost. Quite simply, telemarketing is far less expensive than face-to-face communications or mass advertising. A drawback is the negative perceptions people have about this communications technique.

The Internet appears poised to be a strong media alternative in the future, largely based on its efficiency in reaching consumers. Marketing managers now realize that online communications are complementary to traditional media, and when used together can improve awareness levels and stimulate more action. The Internet as an advertising medium is growing in popularity among advertisers because customers are spending less and less time with the traditional media. Media habits are changing.

A variety of options are available to online advertisers: banner ads, pop-ups and pop-unders, and interstitials and superstitials. Banner ads and pop-ups are static in nature, while interstitials and superstitials include audio and video components. They appear on-screen much like a television commercial. Additional online opportunities include sponsorships, company-owned websites, and webcasting. Webcasting involves the production of an extended commercial much like an infomercial. It includes some entertainment value.

Permission-based email represents significant opportunities for advertisers. Using rented lists or lists generated from in-house databases, email represents a cost-effective way to reach prospects and current customers. Text messaging is just starting to grow in popularity among advertisers, and the future for communicating with customers through cell phones is quite promising. As technology advances, cell phones will be capable of handling more colour pictures, video, and hi-fi sound. It will be an attractive medium for reaching consumers wherever they may be.

KEY TERMS

banner ad   394
bounce backs   384
buttons   394
call centre   391
catalogues   389
circulation lists   388
compiled lists   388
cooperative direct mail   385
direct mail   383
direct response television
(DRTV)   389
display advertising   394
flyers   383
folders   383

house list   387
inbound telemarketing   391
infomercial   389
interstitial   395
leaflets   383
letter   383
list broker   387
merge/purge   387
online advertising   393
opt-in list   399
outbound telemarketing   392
permission-based email   398
pop-up or pop-under ad   394
postage-paid reply cards   383

rectangle   394
response list   387
rich media   394
skyscraper   394
solo direct mail
(selective direct mail)   385
spam   398
sticky content   394
streaming media   395
superstitial   395
telemarketing   391
text messaging   399
webcasting   397

1. What are the major forms of direct response advertising?

2. What is the difference between direct marketing and direct response advertising?

3. What is the difference between a solo direct mail campaign and a cooperative direct mail campaign?

4. What are the advantages and disadvantages of direct mail advertising for a business-product advertiser (e.g., a manufacturer of business equipment)?

5. Explain the differences between a response list, a circulation list, and a compiled list.

6. Explain the following terms as they relate to direct response advertising:
   a) bounce backs
   b) house list
   c) list broker
   d) merge/purge
   e) infomercial
   f) inbound telemarketing versus outbound telemarketing

7. What is the difference between a traditional infomercial and a corporate or brand-oriented infomercial?

8. Explain the following terms as they relate to advertising on the Internet:
   a) click
   b) clickthrough rate
   c) impressions
   d) visit

9. What is banner advertising and how does it work?

10. Identify and briefly explain the various types of banner ads.

11. Briefly explain how an online advertising sponsorship works.

12. Briefly explain the following Internet communications terms:
   a) permission-based email
   b) opt-in
   c) spam
   d) rich media
   e) streaming media
   f) opt-in list

13. What is webcasting and how does it work?

14. Identify and briefly explain two advantages and two disadvantages of Internet-based advertising.

DISCUSSION AND APPLICATION QUESTIONS

1. "The dollars an advertiser invests in direct mail advertising are wasted owing to the poor image of the medium." Discuss.

2. Catalogues seem to be the reserve of big retail organizations such as Sears and Canadian Tire. How should smaller retail organizations, with less financial resources, compete with bigger retailers? What direct response strategies should they adopt, and why?

3. "Persistent invasions of consumer privacy will be the undoing of Internet-based advertising." True or false? Conduct some online secondary research to update the status of this issue. Report on your findings.

4. "Direct response television will play a more prominent role in future television advertising campaigns for traditional advertisers such as banks, automobile manufacturers, and insurance companies." Is this statement true or false? Discuss.

5. Conduct some online secondary research on the advertising applications of text messaging. Will it continue to develop as an effective medium for reaching consumers, or will consumers react negatively to persistent messages from advertisers? Defend your position.

E-ASSIGNMENTS

1. Visit the websites of two direct competitors in a particular market (e.g., automobiles, soft drinks, newspapers, television sports networks, and so on). Compare and contrast the sites to determine if they effectively build brand/company image and if they communicate relevant information to prospective customers. Is one competitor more effective than the other with its online communications?

2. Placing third-party advertising on a company website can produce additional revenue for an organization. Google encourages this practice through a program called AdSense. Visit the Google AdSense (**www.google.com/adsense**) Web page and evaluate whether an organization should take advantage of this opportunity. What are the pros and cons of this practice?

ENDNOTES

1. Canadian Media Directors' Council *Media Digest* 2004/05, p. 10.

2. Franzi Weinstein, "Short, sweet and smarter creative," *Marketing*, April 29, 1996, p. 17.

3. Susan Heinrich, "Direct marketing gets Xerox makeover," *Financial Post*, November 15, 2004, p. FP4.

4. ICOM Information & Communications Inc., www.i-com.com.

5. Cornerstone List Management, www.cstonecanada.com.

6. Ian French, "A primer on DRTV," *Marketing*, August 25/September 1, 2003, p. 16.

7. 800 Response, www.800response.com/studies/resources/superbowl.

8. "Sears Canada this year's directors' choice," *Strategy Direct Response*, November 22, 1999, p. 10.

9. Stephen Theobald, "Canadian Tire flyer grows up," *Toronto Star*, March 15, 2001, p. E1.

10. Sue Bailey, "Do not call registry under study," *Toronto Star*, September 20, 2004, www.thestar.com.

11. Mary Gooderham, "Level of antipathy a wake-up call for telemarketers," *Globe and Mail*, May 7, 1997, p. C11.

12. "GM shows way toward the new mix," *Advertising Age*, January 20, 2003, p. 20.

13. "Canadian Interactive Marketplace Grows 68% in Two Years," November 2, 2004, press release, Interactive Advertising Bureau of Canada, www.iabcanada.com/newsletters.

14. Scott Meyer, "Web found to drive off-line sales," *Mass Market Retailers*, August 23, 2004, www.massmarketretailers.com/articles.

15. "Pop-ups Annoy, But Generate Business," Research Brief, Centre for Media Research, July 2, 2003.

16. Pamela Parker, "Branding Beyond Intuition," Streaming Media 101, Part V, www.turboads.com/richmedia_news/2001rmn/rmn20010822. shtml>(November 2003).

17. Tobi Elkin, "Net advantages," *Advertising Age*, February 10, 2003, p. 29.

18. Toby Elkin, "Study: Net best to get business," *Advertising Age*, September 9, 2002, p. 24.

19. Keith McArthur, " Webisodes are the new frontier of Internet ads," *Globe and Mail*, June 4, 2004, www.globeandmail.com.

20. Rebecca Harris, "E-mail delivers," *Marketing*, September 6, 2004, p. 14.

21. Karen Whitney-Vernon, "How to target teenage textualists," *Financial Post*, June 28, 2004, p. FP6.

22. Stephen Baker, "A marketer's dream: Your cell phone," *Business Week Online*, July 27, 2004, www.businessweekonline.com.

CHAPTER

16

Sales Promotion, Personal Selling, and Event Marketing and Sponsorships

Learning Objectives

After studying this chapter, you will be able to

1. Describe the various types of consumer and trade promotion activities.

2. Describe the roles of sales representatives and the types of selling that occur in a business organization.

3. Outline the steps in the selling process.

4. Explain the role and importance of event marketing and sponsorships in contemporary marketing.

5. List the unique considerations involved in planning event marketing programs.

This chapter examines the three remaining elements of the marketing communications mix: sales promotion, personal selling, and event marketing and sponsorships. These activities, along with advertising and public relations, and direct response and interactive communications, complement one another and work together to help achieve the marketing and business objectives of an organization.

Sales Promotion

Sales promotion is any activity that provides special incentives to bring about immediate action from consumers, distributors, and an organization's sales force; in other words, it encourages the decision to buy. The expression "advertising appeals to the heart and sales promotion to the wallet" shows the distinction between the two types of activity. Advertising tells us why we should buy a product, whereas sales promotion offers financial or other incentives (e.g., a cents-off coupon, a free sample, or a sale price) to purchase a product.

Sales promotion strategies play a key role in attracting new customers to a brand or retailer and also play a role in developing loyalty between the customer and the brand or retailer. The availability of customer information through database marketing techniques allows companies to target their best customers with sales promotions that generate additional business over the long term.

Two principal kinds of sales promotion exist: consumer promotion and trade promotion.

CONSUMER PROMOTION

Consumer promotion is any activity that promotes extra brand sales by offering the consumer an incentive over and above the product's inherent benefits. These promotions are designed to pull the product through the channel of distribution by motivating consumers to make an immediate purchase. The objectives of consumer promotions are as follows:

1. *Trial Purchase*—When introducing a new product, marketers want customers to make a first purchase right away so that product acceptance can be secured quickly. Something as simple as a coupon will accomplish this goal.

2. *Repeat Purchases*—Marketers protect loyalty to an established product by offering incentives for consumers to buy the item repeatedly. Including coupons with a product that can be redeemed on the next purchase is a way of holding loyalty, as are loyalty cards where points are accumulated for future use.

sales promotion

1. Describe the various types of consumer and trade promotion activities.

consumer promotion

405

Direct-to-Consumer	2002	2003	2004
Quantity Distributed	2.32	2.60	2.93
Quantity Redeemed	110 million	97 million	99 million
Average Face Value Coupons Redeemed	$1.25	$1.23	$1.55
Consumer Savings	$118 million	$105 million	$118 million

Note: Distribution in billions

3. *Multiple Purchases*—Promotions of this nature "load the consumer up." For example, a contest may be run to spur many entries and purchases, or cash refunds may offer savings that increase with each additional purchase of an item. For instance, a $1.00 refund may be available on one purchase and a $3.00 refund on two purchases.

The major types of consumer promotion are coupons, free samples, contests, cash refunds, premiums, frequent-buyer programs, and delayed-payment incentives.

coupon

COUPONS   A **coupon** is a price-saving incentive to stimulate quicker purchase of a designated product. In Canada, coupons are distributed in mass quantity. As of 2003, the total number of coupons distributed by packaged-goods manufacturers amounted to 2.93 billion. Of that total, 99 million were redeemed (Figure 16.1). With the average face value of coupons distributed being $1.19, consumers saved $118 million on purchases.[1]

The objectives of a coupon promotion affect the way that coupons will be delivered. These objectives are often related to the stage in the product life cycle that the item has reached. In the introduction and growth stages, a key objective is to get the target audi-

media-delivered coupons

product-delivered coupons

ence to try the product. Therefore, **media-delivered coupons** are common since they reach new users. As a product moves into maturity, **product-delivered coupons** are frequently distributed to prompt current customers to continue purchasing the product. Ensuring brand loyalty helps preserve market share. When the objective is to make competitive users switch to one's own brand, coupons can be delivered by the media or by in-store distribution where the product is available. See Figure 16.2 for an illustration of an in-store delivered coupon.

The free-standing insert is the most common medium for delivering coupons (62 percent of all coupons distributed, but only 11 percent of all coupons redeemed). In-store coupons are the most important medium in terms of redemption, accounting for 44 percent of all coupons redeemed. The effectiveness of a brand-specific coupon

redemption rate

campaign is determined by the **redemption rate**, or the number of coupons returned to an organization expressed as a percentage of the total number of coupons in distribution for a particular coupon offer. A high redemption rate indicates the coupon offer had significant impact on the target market.

Savvy shoppers now look to online sources for valuable money-saving coupons. A consumer can select specific goods and services, survey the discounts offered, and obtain the coupon from online sources. Save.ca and Coupons.com offer marketers the opportunity to provide coupons online. According to Wayne Mouland, Director of Analytical Services, Resolve Corporation, and a leading expert on coupon trends in Canada, "More marketers are using online coupons but this media still represents a little less than one percent of all coupons, both distributed and redeemed."[2]

FIGURE
16.2 **An in-store coupon helps achieve trial purchase objectives**

Courtesy of Reckitt Benckiser

For a summary of the various types of coupons and their primary objectives, refer to Figure 16.3.

FREE SAMPLES   A **free sample** is a free product distributed to potential users, either in a small trial size or in its regular size. Sampling is commonly practised when a company is introducing a new product, a line extension of a new product, or a product improvement,

free sample

FIGURE
16.3

Methods of Distributing Coupons

Method	Explanation and Objective
Product-Delivered Coupon	
In-Pack Self	Coupon redeemable on the next purchase of the same product. This coupon encourages brand loyalty.
On-Pack Self	Coupon redeemable on next purchase of same product. This coupon encourages loyalty. Redemption is lower than in-pack as coupon is less convenient to clip.
Instantly Redeemable	Coupon affixed to the package but easily removed at point-of-purchase. The objective is trial purchase and loyalty as it appeals to new and current users.
Cross-Ruff	In-pack or on-pack coupon redeemable on a different product. It encourages trial purchase of that product.
Media-Delivered Coupons	
On-Page Newspaper and Magazine	Coupon redeemable on the next purchase of a new or established product. The primary objective is trial purchase. It also encourages brand switching.
Direct Mail	Coupon delivered in a cooperative mailing envelope with other similar but non-competing offers. The objective is trial purchase.
Free-Standing Insert	Pre-printed advertisement and coupon in single or multiple-page format inserted loose in daily newspapers. The objective is trial purchase.
In-Store Delivered Coupons	
Product Displays, Demonstrations, Shelf Pads, and Booklets	Coupon immediately redeemable on purchase. The objective is trial purchase by new users; it also encourages brand switching.

such as a new flavour, taste, blend, or scent (see Figure 16.4). Offering samples is an effective way of getting trial usage because it eliminates the financial risk associated with a new purchase. In comparison to coupons, the sample is less efficient in converting trial users to regular users, and it is an expensive proposition because of the costs of the product and its packaging and distribution.[3]

The most frequently used method of sample distribution is in-store. There are several variations of in-store sampling: product demonstrations and sampling, saleable sample sizes (small replica-pack sizes of the actual product), and cross-sampling. Samples distributed in stores are an attempt to influence the consumer's decision at the point-of-purchase. Packaged-goods companies, such as Kraft and General Mills, frequently employ this type of sampling, as do retailers who promote their private-label brands. **Cross-sampling** refers to an arrangement whereby one product carries a sample of another product (e.g., a regular-sized box of Cheerios cereal carries a small sample package of Count Chocula cereal).

Companies are discovering new ways of delivering samples while at the same time generating positive publicity for the brand involved in the promotion. Some refer to it as **on-site sampling**; others call it **experiential marketing**. For example, Procter & Gamble completely revamped a public washroom at the Canadian National Exhibition

cross-sampling

on-site sampling

experiential marketing

so that consumers could sample several of its products. The washrooms included treats such as aromatherapy, potted plants, soothing music, uniformed attendants, and wall-mounted ads for Charmin Ultra. Charmin Ultra paper was available in the stalls, Ivory liquid hand soap was at the sinks, and people dried their hands with Bounty towels.[4]

Retailers have also ventured into on-site sampling by establishing in-store setups that allow shoppers to actually use or experience products before deciding on a purchase. Music stores permit shoppers to listen to CDs, and Maytag retail outlets allow shoppers to bring in a load of laundry to try out their washers and dryers. According to Paul Bognar, general manager of Maytag, "Appliances are usually a grudge purchase. People buy because they have to. We're trying to make it fun, or a more enjoyable experience."[5]

Maytag Canada
www.maytag.ca

Marketing managers employ sampling programs for good reason. A recent survey shows that consumers perceive sampling programs favourably: 94 percent of respondents view sampling as a risk-free way of trying a new product, and 83 percent see a demonstration as a way of increasing the comfort level when buying the product.[6]

The Internet has spawned another form of sampling. Software suppliers can now download demonstration copies of their programs directly to interested customers for a trial period of 30 to 60 days. If satisfied, the customer can order the complete version at the end of the trial period and download it directly over the Internet.

CONTESTS   Contests are designed to create short-term excitement about a product. A contest usually provides an incentive to buy an item, requiring, for example, the submission of a product label or symbol and an entry form that is included with the product. Consumers are encouraged to enter often and thereby improve their chances of winning a prize. This results in many purchases. While contests tend to attract the current users of a product, they are less effective in inducing trial purchases than are coupons and samples. Consequently, contests are most appropriate in the mature stage of the product life cycle, when the aim is to retain the present market share. Sweepstakes and instant wins are two major types of contests.

A **sweepstakes** contest is a chance promotion involving the giveaway of products and services of value to randomly selected participants who have submitted qualified entries. Prizes such as cash, cars, homes, and vacations are given away (see Figure 16.5). Consumers enter sweepstakes by filling in a blank entry form, usually available at the point-of-purchase or through print advertising, and submitting it along with a proof of purchase to a central location where a draw is held to determine the winners.

sweepstakes

FIGURE 16.5   A Gillette sweepstakes contest involves a variety of Gillette products

Courtesy of The Gillette Company.

game (instant-win contest)

A **game** (or **instant-win contest**) is a promotional vehicle that includes a number of predetermined, pre-seeded winning tickets in the overall, fixed universe of tickets. Packages containing winning certificates are redeemed for prizes. Variations of this type of contest include collect-and-wins, match-and-wins, and small-prize instant-wins combined with a grand-prize contest. These types of contests are commonly used by quick-serve restaurants. The annual "Roll Up the Rim" promotion at Tim Hortons is a prime example.

In the age of database marketing, companies have integrated contests into their websites. Potential customers are encouraged to visit sites through traditional forms of advertising, but when they arrive there they want to be entertained. A contest is one way of doing that. It also provides an opportunity to collect valuable demographic information about the potential customer.

Contests are governed by laws and regulations and any company that runs one must publish certain information: how, where, and when to enter; who is eligible to enter the contest; the prize structure, value, and number of prizes; the odds of winning and the selection procedure; and conditions that must be met before a prize is awarded (e.g., a skill-testing question must be answered). Contest details are made available at point-of-purchase and at the sponsor's website. Since provincial laws governing contests vary from province to province, sponsors must be very careful about how details are communicated to consumers.

cash refund (rebate)

CASH REFUNDS (REBATES)   A **cash refund,** or **rebate** as it is often called, is a predetermined amount of money returned directly to the consumer by the manufacturer after the purchase has been made. For companies in the packaged-goods industry, cash refunds are useful promotion techniques in the mature stage of the product's life cycle, for such activity reinforces loyalty. The most common type of refund is the single-purchase refund in which consumers receive a portion of their money back for the purchase of a specified product. However, refunds are designed to achieve different objectives; hence, they can be offered in different formats. Refunds encourage consumers to make multiple purchases and stock their pantries. For example, the value of the refund may escalate as the number of items purchased increases. An offer could be structured as follows:

- Buy one and get $1.00 back
- Buy two and get $2.50 back
- Buy three and get $5.00 back

slippage

In this case, the refund is greatest when the consumer takes maximum advantage of the offer. In refund offers where multiple purchases are necessary, slippage generally occurs. **Slippage** happens when a consumer starts collecting proofs of purchase for a refund offer but neglects to follow through and submit a request for the refund. In effect, the manufacturer does not pay for the purchases induced by the promotion. Slippage is a significant factor. In a survey of grocery shoppers, it was found that one-half of all refund participants sometimes neglect to submit a request for a refund even after they have bought the product with the intention of using the refund offer.[7]

Rebates are very popular in durable-goods markets such as automobiles, appliances, and electronics equipment. Automobile incentives such as $1000 or $2000 cash back combined with low-cost financing programs will boost sales in the short term, but in the long term they have made the cost of an automobile higher and have affected the profitability of domestic manufacturers.

Data compiled by Resolve Corporation (formerly NCH Watts Promotional Services) show that not every eligible consumer will claim a mail-in rebate, even rebates

Resolve Corporation
www.resolvecorporation.com

with a $100 value. Apparently, there is a tendency for time-pressed consumers to simply forget about the rebate.[8] HP Canada (Hewlett-Packard) data show that about 40 percent of their customers, for whatever reason, do not bother applying for mail-in rebates on their computer printers. HP rebates average $50. This unclaimed money is pure gravy for the manufacturer.[9]

PREMIUMS   A **premium** is an item offered free or at a bargain price to consumers who buy another specific item or make a minimum purchase. The goal of a premium offer is to provide added value to new and repeat purchasers.

premium

A good premium offer will help differentiate one brand from another at a crucial point in time—the time when consumers decide to buy. Some premiums produce a huge spike in sales, as was the case with Labatt Blue's "NHL Crazy Coldie Program." Throughout the 2002 NHL playoffs, Labatt's Double Blue 24 cases included one of 30 NHL insulated bottle holders shaped like a team jersey. The combination of hockey (the number-one sport among beer drinkers in Canada) and the Coldie's ability to keep the beer cold was an instant hit with consumers. Market share grew 300 percent during the promotion period and sales were double the original forecast. The promotion was supported with media advertising.[10]

The use of premiums achieves several objectives: they increase the quantity of brand purchases made by consumers; they help to retain current users; and they provide a merchandising tool to encourage display activity in stores. Hallmark recently implemented a value-added offer called "Butterflies are free." Customers who purchased a card at a Gold Crown store received a free wind-up butterfly to place in it. When the card is opened the butterfly flutters out. During the promotion, transactions in stores increased by 10 percent. For additional insight into the effectiveness of this sales promotion offer in building sales, read the Marketing in Action vignette **Hallmark Promotion Builds Sales**. Also see the illustration in Figure 16.6.

FIGURE
16.6

Hallmark's "Butterflies are free" premium offer increased sales by 10 percent during the promotion period

Hallmark Promotion Builds Sales

Advertising builds a brand in the long term and sales promotions give sales a short-term boost. Is this statement true or false? If the success of a recent Hallmark promotion is any indicator, it has to be true. In 2003 Hallmark Canada launched a promotion called "Butterflies are free," and greeting card transactions increased 10 percent, card unit sales 14 percent, and sales by 13.5 percent, the highest percentage gains for any summer promotion undertaken by the company.

How did Hallmark do it? The company was searching for a simple way to reward customers for choosing Hallmark and to develop a campaign that would generate incremental sales during the promotion period. At the time several stores were selling butterfly inserts for greeting cards. When a card is opened, a life-like butterfly pops out.

Hallmark quickly realized the butterfly was perfect for delivering an element of surprise and delight to those who would receive cards. The mechanics of the promotion were simple. Buy a greeting card and get a free butterfly—there's nothing more appealing to a shopper than getting something for free! The butterflies had been selling for $2.95, so there was a high perceived value associated with the offer.

Six different butterflies were designed for the first campaign, and the promotion was communicated to shoppers by point-of-purchase display cards, banners, staff buttons, and mobile butterflies. In-store representatives were told to communicate the offer to shoppers and to demonstrate how the butterflies worked. Television spots increased awareness during the promotion period.

The promotion was an overwhelming success—more than 1.8 million butterflies were released. All retailers of Hallmark cards loved it and more than 80 percent of them said the promotion increased store traffic. The campaign was repeated in 2004 with new butterfly designs and colours, and the company is looking ahead to 2005 as well.

Adapted from Paul Berto, "Butterflies are free," *Marketing*, August 6/13, 2004, p. 30.

Courtesy of Hallmark Canada.

LOYALTY (FREQUENT-BUYER) PROGRAMS Canadian retailers and a variety of service industries, such as airlines and hotels, have made loyalty or frequent-buyer programs popular. In fact, almost two-thirds of Canadians have at least one loyalty card in their wallet or purse.[11] A **loyalty (frequent buyer) program** offers the consumer a small bonus, such as points or "play money," when they make a purchase. The bonus accumulates with each new purchase. The goal of such an offer is to encourage loyalty, and that's what a program like Shoppers Drug Mart's Optimum rewards program does. In this program, shoppers accumulate points that are redeemable on future purchases.

loyalty (frequent buyer) program

The card is an integral component of Shoppers' new customer relationship management program. The retailer can electronically cross-reference transaction data and tailor offers and services to specific customers by email. The company has more than one million names in its database.[12]

Canadian Tire's program is perhaps the best-known and longest-running (more than 43 years) frequent-buyer program in Canada, and indeed has become engrained as Canada's second currency. It rewards regular shoppers who pay for merchandise with cash or a Canadian Tire credit card with Canadian Tire "money" worth up to 4 percent of the value of the purchase. Canadian Tire customers now collect virtual money on the company's house credit card, its website, and its affiliate MasterCard. Canadian Tire money captures the essence of a rewards program, because customers really can purchase something for free. With a program like Air Miles, it takes a considerable length of time before rewards kick in.

Technology is the driving force behind loyalty programs. Today, retailers can slice and dice databases to find out who their best customers are and then send them incentives to encourage them to purchase more often. The Gap values it best customers and has found a way to reward them by direct mail. One mailing included coupons offering 20 percent off their next purchase of $100 or more in November, 15 percent off $75 or more in early December, and then 10 percent off $50 or more in late December. The incentives gave a boost to Christmas sales.[13]

DELAYED-PAYMENT INCENTIVES   In a **delayed-payment incentive promotion**, a consumer is granted a grace period during which no interest or principal is paid for the item purchased. Once the purchase is made from the retailer, a finance company assumes the agreement and charges interest if full payment is not made by the agreed-upon date.

Leon's Furniture pioneered the delayed-payment concept in Canada under promotions called the Don't Pay a Cent Event and the No Money Miracle. "Consumers search the market for incentives and credit arrangements are merely part of an overall package that will motivate buying decisions" says Terry Leon, executive vice-president at Leon's. The Don't Pay a Cent promotion accounts for 40 to 60 percent of the company's business, depending on the time of year.[14] This innovative technique has spread to other hard-goods retailers in the household furnishings and consumer electronics markets.

COMBINATION OFFERS   In order to maximize the effectiveness of a promotion, marketers often combine the consumer promotion techniques discussed in this chapter. For example, when a free trial sample is given away in a store or distributed through a direct mailing, it is common to include a coupon. Assuming the consumer is satisfied with the trial usage, the coupon provides an added incentive to make the first official purchase of the product. Coupons and contests are another frequent combination. The coupon attracts the user for the initial purchase, and the contest encourages additional purchases. The illustration in Figure 16.7 is an example of a combination offer.

TRADE PROMOTION

Trade promotion is promotional activity directed at distributors to push a product through the channel of distribution; it is designed to increase the volume purchased and encourage merchandising support for a manufacturer's product. Along with trade discounts and performance allowances (discussed in Chapter 11), the most commonly used trade promotion activities are cooperative advertising, performance allowances, in-ad coupons, dealer premiums, collateral materials, dealer display materials, and trade shows.

delayed-payment incentive promotion

trade promotion

> **FIGURE**
> **16.7** **A combination promotion offer that includes a coupon and contest**

cooperative advertising

COOPERATIVE ADVERTISING   In the case of **cooperative advertising**, manufacturers allocate funds to pay a portion of a retailer's advertising. For example, a predetermined percentage (say, 3 percent to 5 percent) of the dollar volume purchased by a distributor accumulates in an account with the company selling the goods. When the selling company wants to run a promotion with the distributor, it draws upon the accumulated funds to pay a portion of the retailer's advertising.

The advertisements by major supermarket chains showing weekly specials, for example, are partially paid for by the manufacturers participating in the advertisements in any given week. In some cases, the manufacturer may agree to pay half of the retailer's cost of advertising, and frequently the manufacturer provides advertising illustrations and artwork that are integrated into the retailer's advertising message.

performance allowance

PERFORMANCE ALLOWANCES   A **performance allowance** is an additional discount (over and above a trade allowance) offered by manufacturers to encourage retailers to perform specific merchandising functions (e.g., display the product at retail, provide an advertising mention in a flyer, or offer a lower price for a period of time). Before paying the allowance, the manufacturer requires proof of performance from the retailer. Over the years, trade monies devoted to performance allowances have become an expectation by distributors rather than a promotional vehicle. Many manufacturers believe they have been shortchanged in the process and are making stronger demands for proof of performance.

Manufacturers are trying to shift their marketing mix away from trade spending (a short-term, sales-boosting tactic) and more toward brand efforts such as advertising (a long-term, brand-building strategy). As recently as 2003, trade spending comprised an average of 54 percent of a packaged-goods brand's marketing budget.[15]

retail in-ad coupon

RETAIL IN-AD COUPONS   A **retail in-ad coupon** is a coupon printed in a retailer's weekly advertising, either in the newspaper or in supplements inserted in the newspaper. These coupons are redeemable on national brands and are usually paid for by the manufacturer. Retailers pay for coupons redeemable on private-label brands. The programs for national brand products are negotiated between manufacturers' sales representatives and retail buyers. Usually, the funds to cover such coupons are derived from a trade-promotion budget; thus, they are included as a trade-promotion activity.

dealer premium

DEALER PREMIUMS   A **dealer premium** or dealer loader is an incentive offered to a distributor by a manufacturer to encourage a special purchase (e.g., a specified volume of merchandise) or to secure additional merchandising support from a distributor. Premiums are usually offered in the form of merchandise (e.g., a set of golf clubs, or other forms of leisure goods or sporting goods); the value of the premium increases with the amount of product purchased by the retailer.

Their use is often controversial. Some distributors forbid their buyers to accept premiums because they believe only the individual buyer, rather than the organization, benefits. Such a situation, often referred to as "payola," may lead the buyer to make unnecessary purchases and ignore the objectives of the distributor. The other side of the argument is that the purchase of the goods at significant savings (through allowances and premiums) offers direct, tangible benefit to the buying organization. These practices are perceived by many to be unethical, and they should not occur. Nonetheless, some dealings do happen under the table, so students should be aware of it.

COLLATERAL MATERIALS   To help itself in the personal-selling process, the sales force uses **collateral materials** supplied by the manufacturer to provide information to customers. These materials include price lists, catalogues, sales brochures, pamphlets, specification sheets, product manuals, and audio-visual sales aids prepared by the manufacturer. In the age of digital marketing it is now common for such materials to be available in CD-ROM format or on a company's website. From a buyer's perspective, sales information can be reviewed at a more leisurely pace and perhaps at a more convenient time.

collateral materials

DEALER-DISPLAY MATERIALS   **Dealer-display material,** or **point-of-purchase material,** consists of self-contained, custom-designed merchandising units, either permanent or temporary, that display a manufacturer's product. It includes posters, shelf extenders (tray-like extensions that project outward from the shelf to extend shelf display), shelf talkers (small posters that hang from shelves), channel strips (narrow strips containing a brief message attached to the channel face of a shelf), advertising pads or tear pads (tear-off sheets that usually explain details of a consumer promotion offer), display shippers (shipping cases that convert to display bins or stands when opened), and permanent display racks. The use of such displays and materials is at the discretion of the retailers whose space they occupy. The role of a manufacturer's sales representative is to convince the retailer of the merits of using the display. Refer to the illustration in Figure 16.8.

dealer-display (point-of-purchase) material

TRADE SHOWS   **Trade shows** are typically organized by an industry association each year to demonstrate the latest products of member manufacturers. There are, for example, toy shows, automobile shows, computer shows, and appliance shows. Trade shows are the fastest way to reach a large number of targeted customers in a fixed time frame, where you can talk, show, and impress them with the latest wizardry while getting leads for the future. A show also provides an opportunity to collect valuable information about prospective customers—information that can be added to a database for future follow-up by sales representatives or for direct mail or email offers designed by marketing managers.

trade shows

A recent research study shows the value of trade show participation. The average cost to close a lead (make a sale) obtained through field sales is $1140, versus $705 to close a lead from a trade show.[16] Trade shows are a cost-effective way of doing business.

Personal Selling

Personal selling is a personalized form of communication that involves a seller presenting the features and benefits of a product or service to a buyer for the purpose of making a sale. It is an integral component of the marketing communications mix, for it

personal selling

FIGURE
16.8

In-store displays attract attention and end encourage impulse purchases

is the activity that in many cases clinches a deal, and does so based on the human touch the sales representative brings. Advertising and sales promotion creates awareness and interest for a product. Personal selling creates desire and action. In creating that desire and action, the interaction between the seller and buyer is crucial. While the purpose of selling is to make the sale, the role of the sales representative goes beyond this task.

THE ROLE OF THE CONTEMPORARY SALESPERSON

2. Describe the roles of sales representatives and the types of selling that occur in a business organization.

GATHERING MARKET INTELLIGENCE   In a competitive marketplace, salespeople must be attuned to the trends in their industry. They must be alert to what the competitor is doing, to its new-product projects, and to its advertising and promotion plans, and they must listen to feedback from customers regarding their own products' performance. Competitive knowledge is important when the salesperson faces questions involving product comparisons. Data collected by a salesperson can be reported electronically to the company's head office. Managers can retrieve the information and use it appropriately at a later date.

PROBLEM SOLVING   The only way a salesperson can make a sale is to listen to what a customer wants and ask questions to determine his or her real needs. Asking, listening, and providing information and advice that is in the best interests of the customer is what consultative selling is all about. The seller must demonstrate a sincere concern for the customer's needs.

LOCATING AND MAINTAINING CUSTOMERS   Salespeople who locate new customers play a key role in a company's growth. A company cannot be satisfied with its present list of customers because aggressive competitors attempt to lure them away. To prevent shrinkage and to increase sales, salespeople actively pursue new accounts. Their time is divided between finding new accounts and selling and servicing current accounts.

FOLLOW-UP SERVICE   The salesperson is the first point of contact should anything go wrong or should more information be required. Maintenance of customers is crucial, and very often, it is the quality of follow-up service that determines if a customer will remain a customer. Since the salespeople are the company's direct link to the customer, it cannot be stressed enough how important their handling of customer service is. The sale is never over. Once a deal has been closed, numerous tasks arise: arranging for delivery, providing technical assistance, providing customer training, and being readily available to handle any customer problems that emerge during and after delivery. The personalized role of the sales representative is instrumental in building relationships.

TYPES OF SELLING

BUSINESS-TO-BUSINESS SELLING   Business-to-business salespeople either sell products for use in the production and sale of other products, or sell products to channel members who in turn resell them. For example: a Xerox sales representative sells photocopiers to another business for use in its daily operations; a representative from Nike may sell a new line of running shoes to the head office of a group of specialty retailers, such as Foot Locker or Athlete's World, who in turn distribute the running shoes through their retail locations.

RETAIL SELLING   Retail selling is the sale of merchandise or services to final customers for personal use. These salespeople are often referred to as sales clerks or associates and are employed by department stores, specialty stores, and other types of retailing firms. Wal-Mart, for example, uses the term "associates" for its sales and service employees. Anyone employed by these types of stores and who is in contact with a customer has a direct or indirect influence on the sale of merchandise or the level of customer satisfaction and, therefore, should have some basic training in sales and customer service.

DIRECT SELLING   There are several types of direct selling. **In-home selling** uses a network of local people to sell products in their communities, often at home "parties." These selling practices take advantage of the social environment of a home party, and as such there is less pressure to buy. Companies that operate in this way include Mary Kay (cosmetics), Avon (perfumes, cosmetics, and a variety of personal-care products), and Tupperware (plastic goods for the household).

in-home selling

Telemarketing involves the use of a telephone as an interactive medium for marketing response. It employs highly trained people and database marketing techniques to seek and serve new customers. Telemarketing improves productivity because it reduces direct-selling costs. Telemarketing is useful for screening and qualifying incoming leads, generating leads from directories and mailing lists, and calling current customers to secure orders, offer additional services, sell products to new customers, or determine the level of customer satisfaction.

telemarketing

Online selling refers to the use of websites as a vehicle for conducting business transactions. Consumers who are looking for convenience as part of their shopping experience now look to the Internet for a solution. Websites are capable of accepting and processing orders, receiving payment, and delivering goods and services directly to businesses and consumers. Since all transactions are electronically recorded, companies are accumulating huge databases of information that can be used for marketing purposes in the longer term. The concept of e-marketing is discussed in detail in Chapter 17.

TYPES OF SALESPEOPLE

Salespeople are classified by the nature of the tasks they perform, including processing orders and being creative sellers and missionary sellers.

ORDER PROCESSORS

Order processing is common at the wholesaling and retailing levels and is essential in maintaining current customers. In wholesaling, the order taker processes an order over the telephone or from mail orders. Such a job is a good training position, as it is a good means of learning about a company and its products and how to deal with customers. In retailing, the order taker is the retail clerk, a person responsible for responding to customers' questions, preparing invoices, checking credit, handling complaints, and completing the sale.

CREATIVE SELLERS

When selling creatively, the primary responsibility is to pursue an order aggressively. This requires extensive knowledge about the product, competing products, and the sales-communication process. It is a process in which the seller explains and demonstrates to the customer how a product will satisfy his or her needs. This is a challenging type of selling that involves all of the steps in the selling process (discussed in the following section). Creative sellers play an essential role in business-to-business marketing environments and in building customer relationships.

MISSIONARY SELLERS

Missionary selling is an indirect activity dedicated to selling the goodwill of a company. It is a supplement to creative selling. For example, a missionary—or merchandiser, as they are often referred to—will contact retailers to check stocks, arrange displays, and provide basic information about new products. Many leading packaged-goods companies, such as Procter & Gamble, Nestlé, and Neilson Cadbury, have added merchandisers and reduced the number of sales representatives in their sales forces. In an industrial environment, a missionary is responsible for technical assistance or training to ensure that customers get maximum usage from the products or services they have purchased.

3. Outline the steps in the selling process.

THE STEPS IN THE SELLING PROCESS

PROSPECTING

Seven steps are commonly associated with personal selling (Figure 16.9). The first step is **prospecting**, which is a systematic procedure for developing sales leads. If salespeople do not allocate enough time to finding new customers, they risk causing a decline in sales for their company. If their income is geared to the value of the business they produce, they risk the loss of personal compensation as well. Potential customers, or prospects, are identified by means of published lists and directories, such as *Scott's Industrial Directory, Frasers Canadian Trade Directory*, and *Canadian Key Business Directory*. A **referral** is a prospect that is recommended by a current customer. Other sources of leads include names obtained from trade shows, advertising, direct-response communications, telemarketing and online communications, and channel members.

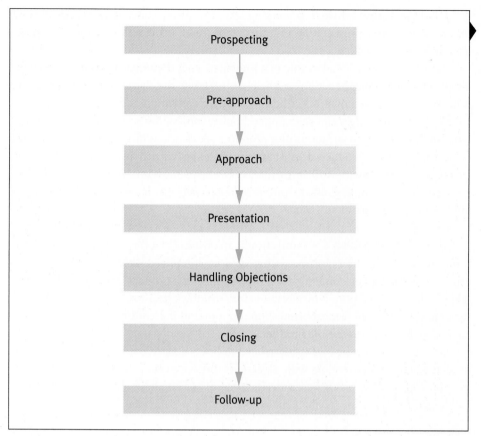

FIGURE
16.9

Steps in the Selling Process

Prospecting

Pre-approach

Approach

Presentation

Handling Objections

Closing

Follow-up

PRE-APPROACH   The **pre-approach** involves gathering information about potential customers before actually making sales contact. During the pre-approach stage, customers are *qualified*, which is the procedure for determining if a prospect needs the product, has the authority to buy it, and has the ability to pay for it. There is little sense in pursuing customers who lack the financial resources or have no need to make the business relationship successful. The seller also gains insights into the customer that can be used in the sales presentation: information such as the buyer's likes and dislikes, personal interests and hobbies, buying procedures, and special needs and problems.

pre-approach

APPROACH   The **approach** is the initial contact with the prospect, usually a face-to-face selling situation. Since buyers are usually busy, little time should be wasted in the approach. In the first few minutes of a sales interview, the salesperson must capture the attention and interest of the buyer so that an effective environment is created for the presentation of the product's benefits.

approach

PRESENTATION   The actual sales **presentation** consists of a persuasive delivery and demonstration of a product's benefits. An effective sales presentation shows the buyer how the benefits of the product satisfy his or her needs or help resolve a particular problem. In doing so, the seller focuses on the benefits that are most important to the buyer. Critical elements usually focus on lower price, the durability of the product, the dependability of supply, the performance of the product, and the availability of follow-up service.

presentation

It is at this stage that asking proper questions and listening attentively are most important. A salesperson listens to and analyzes what buyers are saying, then uses what he or she has discovered when presenting the appropriate benefits. Being flexible and making changes to a presentation in mid-stream could be the difference between making a sale and not making a sale.

demonstration

Demonstrations play a key role in a presentation. A **demonstration** is an opportunity to show a product in action and helps substantiate the claims that the salesperson is making. A good demonstration holds the buyer's attention and creates interest and desire. Laptop computers and changing technology now allow for multimedia presentations and precise demonstrations of a product's attributes. While technology helps put the spotlight on the product, it is important not to get carried away with presentation technology—the content of the presentation is what is most important.

Lengthy and complex information should be available on a website or a CD-ROM for customer reference at any time.

objection

HANDLING OBJECTIONS   An **objection** is an obstacle that the salesperson must confront and resolve if the sales transaction is to be completed. Prospects almost always express resistance when contemplating the purchase of a product. An objection is a cue that the buyer wants more information before making a decision. The seller must view the objection as useful feedback and should respond to it accordingly. It gives the seller another opportunity to sell the product.

Typical objections involve issues related to price, quality, level of service, and technical assistance. When dealing with objections the salesperson should ask questions of the buyer to confirm his or her understanding of the situation, answer the objection, and then move on to the next benefit or attempt to close the sale.

closing

CLOSING   Does the buyer voluntarily say "Yes, I'll buy it"? The answer is, no! Getting the buyer to say yes is the entire purpose of the sales interview, but this task is accomplished only if the salesperson asks for the order. **Closing** consists of asking for the order, and it is the most difficult step in the process of selling. Salespeople are reluctant to ask the big question, even though it is the logical sequel to a good presentation and demonstration. In fact, a good salesperson attempts a close whenever a point of agreement is made with the buyer. If the buyer says no, the close is referred to as a **trial close**, or an attempt to close that failed. The salesperson simply moves on to the next point in the presentation.

trial close

Timing a close is a matter of judgment. Good salespeople know when to close—it is often referred to as the "sixth sense" of selling. The salesperson assesses the buyer's verbal and non-verbal responses in an effort to judge when he or she has become receptive, and at the right moment asks the big question. When the time to close arrives, the seller may employ one of these commonly used techniques:

1. *Assumptive Close*—In the case of this close, the salesperson assumes the prospect has already decided to buy. The representative makes a statement, such as, "I will have this model delivered by Friday," or asks a question, such as, "What is the best day for delivery?" An agreement or answer confirms the assumption that the customer has chosen to buy.
2. *Alternative-Choice Close*—Here the seller also assumes that the sale has been made and simply inquires which option is preferable. For example, the representative may ask, "Would you prefer the metallic blue or cherry red colour?"
3. *Summary-of-Benefits Close*—The salesperson using this close summarizes the key benefits that the buyer acknowledged during the presentation, such as the favourable credit terms, the dependability of the product, the availability of frequent service, and the prompt delivery. When the summary is complete, the representative then

poses a direct closing question, such as "Do we have a deal?" or "When would you like delivery?"

4. ***T-Account Close***—In this case, the prospect evaluates the pros and cons of the purchase. The salesperson lists the positive and negative points in a manner suggesting that the positive points outweigh the negative. In doing so, he or she leads the prospect to the decision that now is the time to buy.

FOLLOW-UP   There is an old saying: "The sale never ends." There is truth to this statement, for a new sale is nothing more than the start of a new relationship. Keeping current customers satisfied is the key to success. Effective salespeople make a point of providing **follow-up**; that is, they keep in touch with customers to ensure that the delivery and installation of the goods are satisfactory, that promises are kept, and that, generally, the expectations of the buyer are met. When problems do occur, the salesperson is ready to take action to resolve the situation.

follow-up

In today's competitive business environment, good follow-up strategies help reduce customer attrition and help solidify customer relationships. Companies realize that a satisfied customer is a long-term customer. As famous retail clothier Harry Rosen states, "We don't look at a person in terms of an immediate sale. We look at him in terms of potential lifetime value."[17]

To be successful in selling requires dedication, determination, and discipline. What separates the successful salesperson from the unsuccessful one usually boils down to how well an individual follows an established set of principles. While the wording of these principles may vary from one source to another, the intent behind them is consistent. See Figure 16.10 for some pointers on what separates the professionals from the average salespeople.

FIGURE

16.10 Tips for Successful Selling

Tips for Successful Selling

1. **Selling Is a Skill, Not a Talent**
    Successful salespeople develop skills in asking questions, listening attentively, identifying customer needs, and developing product benefits that satisfy those needs. Knowledge of the product, the customer, and the competition is essential.

2. **You Are the Most Important Product of All**
    Successful salespeople sell themselves. If the customer isn't sold on you, he or she won't buy your product.

3. **Relationships, Emotions, and Feeling Are Important**
    Successful salespeople not only have all the facts, they also have the ability to create positive emotions about themselves and their products.

4. **Effective Prospecting Is Crucial**
    Organizing and managing your time when not selling is important. Discipline is required to contact prospects to request appointments. Proper follow-up is essential to keep a customer.

5. **A Sales Call Is a Performance**
    Be prepared! Begin with a bang that will get the prospect's attention and interest. Encourage participation so the customer discovers the benefits for himself or herself.

6. **Develop Negotiation Skills**
    A successful salesperson closes a profitable sale by developing and using negotiation skills. It is important to package together all points of agreement and use them to your advantage.

7. **Use Objections to Advantage**
    A successful salesperson encourages the prospect to raise concerns. Solving those concerns leads to agreement and opportunities to close the sale.

8. **Always Be Closing**
    Closing begins at the start of a presentation. The challenge is to build agreement and help the prospect decide how to buy, not whether to buy. When the prospect agrees, ask for the order!

SALES MANAGEMENT

The sales manager is the link between the sales force and the company. Sales managers are responsible for numerous managerial functions, including recruitment and selection, training, organization, supervision, motivation, compensation, and evaluation and control. Typically, a company will have a national sales manager, who is ultimately responsible for the activities and performance of all the salespeople. Below the national manager may be a group of regional sales managers, each responsible for a different geographic area (e.g., Maritimes, Quebec, Ontario, Prairies, and British Columbia). The sales manager represents the needs of the customers and the sales representatives to senior management.

In some markets, particularly business-to-business markets, sales management functions are allocated by industry or market segment. As discussed in the chapter on business-to-business marketing, companies are altering their organizational structures so that they can reach and serve those segments with the greatest sales potential more efficiently. By focusing on specific industries, marketing and sales programs can be tailored to industry-specific needs.

4. Explain the role and importance of event marketing and sponsorships in contemporary marketing.

Event Marketing and Sponsorships

Event marketing and sponsorships are fast becoming important elements of the marketing communications mix. **Event marketing** is the process, planned by a sponsoring organization, of integrating a variety of communication elements behind an event theme (e.g., Molson's coordination of advertising, public relations, and sales promotion activities for the Molson Indy car race).

event marketing

event sponsorship

Event sponsorship is the financial support of an event (e.g., an auto race, theatre production, or a marathon road-race) by a sponsor in return for advertising privileges associated with the event. Usually, an event marketer offers sponsorships on a tiered basis. For instance, a lead sponsor or sponsors would pay a maximum amount and receive maximum privileges. Other sponsors would pay less and receive fewer privileges.

Event sponsorship is big business! According to IEG Consulting, a Chicago-based sponsorship measurement firm, the North American sponsorship market (2004) is valued at $11.1 billion and the annual rate of growth is in the 10-percent range. Sports events attract the lion's share (about 70 percent) of sponsorship revenue.[18] Sponsorships in Canada could be worth as much as $1.1 billion annually.

Investment in event marketing and sponsorships is mainly divided among three areas: sports, entertainment, and cultural events. Visa, for example, is involved in all three areas—it sponsors the Olympic Games, the Visa Triple Crown (a series of thoroughbred horse races), Canadian film festivals, and the Dubai Shopping Festival, among many other sponsorships.

SPORTS SPONSORSHIP

Sports sponsorship occurs at amateur and professional levels and can be subdivided into classifications from local events to global events (Figure 16.11). Sports sponsorships tend to be dominated by certain industries and manufacturers. For example, the automobile industry is well represented by General Motors and Ford; the brewing industry by Molson and Labatt; and the financial industry by Royal Bank and Bank of Montreal, and VISA and MasterCard.

ambush marketing

A recent phenomenon associated with event marketing and sponsorships is the practice of ambush marketing. **Ambush marketing** is a strategy used by non-sponsors to capitalize on the prestige and popularity of an event by giving the false impression of

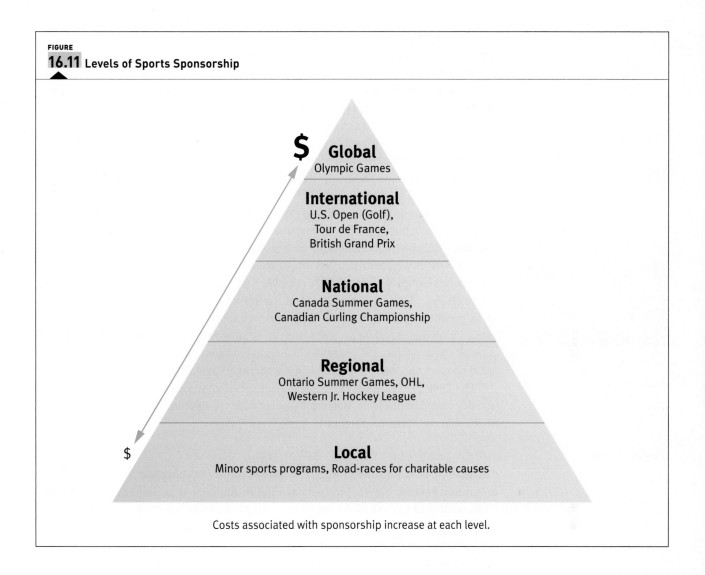

FIGURE
16.11 Levels of Sports Sponsorship

$ Global
Olympic Games

International
U.S. Open (Golf),
Tour de France,
British Grand Prix

National
Canada Summer Games,
Canadian Curling Championship

Regional
Ontario Summer Games, OHL,
Western Jr. Hockey League

Local
Minor sports programs, Road-races for charitable causes

$

Costs associated with sponsorship increase at each level.

being a sponsor. An ambusher borrows the prestige of the property—for example, the Olympics—without spending any money in support of amateur sport. During the 2004 Summer Olympic Games in Athens, the Canadian Olympic Committee identified numerous ambushers including Air Canada, LG Electronics, and Volkswagen Canada. Air Canada ads during the Olympics featured various athletes in challenging situations who devise humorous and creative solutions. The ads boasted that Air Canada was a proud sponsor of the broadcast. Air Canada did pay to place its ads on the CBC, but it was not an official sponsor of the Olympics.[19]

Venue marketing, or **venue sponsorship**, is another form of event marketing. Here, a company or brand is linked to a physical site such as a stadium, arena, or theatre. In Canada, there is the Corel Centre (Ottawa Senators), the Air Canada Centre (Toronto Raptors and Toronto Maple Leafs), and GM Place (Vancouver Canucks). Inside the Air Canada Centre there's the Sears Theatre, and inside GM Place there's the Air Canada Club. Pre-eminent title positions like these break through the clutter of other forms of advertising, but this prominence does come at a hefty cost. Air Canada spent $20 million on a 20-year agreement for the naming rights to the Toronto Maple Leafs' home rink. Hummingbird, a software development company, paid a flat fee of $5 million to have its name on a performing arts theatre in Toronto.[20]

venue marketing (venue sponsorship)

Organizations that are contemplating sports sponsorships can do so at much lower costs if they consider *grassroots* participation. Local participation at much lower cost can produce attractive results. Tim Hortons, for example, is actively involved in community sponsorships through its Timbits hockey and soccer programs. The company provides team jerseys to youth leagues.

Tim Hortons is now associated with curling on a national and community level. As of 2005, Tim Hortons will be the title sponsor of the Brier, Canada's national men's curling championship. There are also plans to initiate a national (community by community) "Timbits Little Rock" program for young curlers. Bill Moir, executive vice-president of marketing, says, "The sport of curling, similar to the Tim Hortons brand, has a unique Canadian identity and community appeal. It's a great fit for us."[21]

How effective is investment in sports sponsorship? A key indicator of success is awareness and association and how participation contributes to the building of a brand. Bell Canada has committed an unprecedented $200 million to the Vancouver Organizing Committee (VANOC) for the 2010 Winter Olympic Games. In doing so, Bell effectively locks out all other telecommunications companies during the games. Michael Sabia, president of Bell, considers the money well spent on branding at a time when telcom services are increasingly being seen as commodities. "If we increase our market share by 1% in satellite TV, it adds $300 million in shareholder value." Sabia believes Bell will do better than that through the Olympics brand association.[22]

The Olympic Games are the grandest of sports sponsorships. For insight into the benefits and drawbacks of Olympic sponsorship programs, read the Marketing in Action vignette **Olympic Dreams!**

ENTERTAINMENT SPONSORSHIPS

Canadian corporations invest huge amounts of money to sponsor concerts and secure endorsements from high-profile personalities in the hope that the celebrity–company relationship will pay off in the long run. Companies such as Molson, Coca-Cola, and PepsiCo, which are interested in targeting youth and young adult segments, use entertainment sponsorship as a vehicle for developing pop-music and youth-lifestyle marketing strategies.

Film festivals are enticing to sponsors because they reach a cross-section of adult targets. At film festivals a sponsor can capitalize on the status of the celebrities who attend. For two prominent film festivals, the Toronto International Film Festival and the Festival des Films du Monde in Montreal, there are waiting lists for platinum sponsorships. Sponsorship revenue at the Toronto Film Festival reaches $4 million, with top-sponsor spots taken by Bell, AGF, the *National Post,* and Visa. Visa leverages its sponsorship by offering exclusive ticket packages to Visa cardholders, providing access to "Visa Screening Rooms": posh branded lounges where purchasers of special passes can enjoy a relaxing environment and refreshments before a screening. Visa entertains its best corporate clients at film festival events.[23]

CULTURE AND THE ARTS SPONSORSHIPS

Arts and cultural event opportunities embrace dance, literature, music, painting, sculpture, and theatre. What separates cultural events from sports and many entertainment events is the audience size. Depending on the sponsor, this is an advantage or a disadvantage. A company such as Molson prefers the mass audience reach of a sports event, whereas Infiniti or BMW may prefer to reach a more selected and upscale audience through an arts event. Perhaps only 2500 people attend the cultural event, but those people can be powerful. Typically, their education level would be above average, as would their income. Such an audience profile would be a good match for promoting a new luxury car.

MARKETING IN ACTION

Olympic Dreams!

Is sponsorship of the Olympic Games a wise investment? A select group of global companies including McDonald's, Coca-Cola, and Visa, along with some Canadian companies such as Labatt and Bell, make a point of closely associating themselves with the Games. There must be something to it!

Visa has been a long-term sponsor of the Olympics. Brenda Woods, vice-president of consumer products marketing for Visa Canada, sees the Olympic sponsorship as a brand-building program, the fruits of which materialize in the long term. Rick Burjaw, vice-president of marketing for Pepsi-Cola Canada, is intrigued by the games and said that if Coke ever relinquished its rights to the Olympics, Pepsi would take a hard look at the opportunity. Coke isn't likely to surrender its grip any time soon.

The investment in the Olympics is huge, and for some companies it will be the single biggest investment in a marketing activity ever. Bidding for the Canadian rights for the next eight years has already begun, with funds raised going to the Vancouver Organizing Committee (VANOC) to prepare for the Vancouver 2010 Winter Olympic Games.

Price tags are estimated to be in the $60 million range for tier-one sponsors. And that's a fraction of what it will cost the winners to leverage those rights through advertising and promotion. To put things into perspective, RBC Financial Group's entire marketing budget for a year is approximately $20 million. RBC is an Olympic sponsor.

Despite the high costs, there is expected to be keen competition for rights among company leaders in various categories: General Motors versus DaimlerChrysler; CIBC versus RBC; Telus versus Bell; and WestJet versus Air Canada. The battle could be so heated that these corporations could overpay for rights. VANOC estimates the cost of the 2010 Games to be $1 billion, and it hopes to raise 25 percent of that from Canadian sponsors. International

sponsors such as McDonald's and Coca-Cola would provide additional sponsorship monies.

For such an investment, there had better be some brand building. Unlike traditional media advertising, where there are some metrics available for calculating return on investment, the calculus of brand building through sports marketing is difficult. It is possible to calculate the "impressions" sponsorship generates—how many times consumers are reminded of the connection between the Olympics and the sponsor, either through advertising or public relations. In some categories, the impressions could be worth $15 million to $30 million over the eight-year period.

RBC views the Olympic connection in more qualitative terms. "It's a unique property because it combines sports and emotions. It draws people who aren't necessarily sports fans and it reaches all demographics. RBC also uses the Olympic association inside the company to demonstrate its core values: personal responsibility for high performance, diversity, teamwork, innovation, and integrity. Athletes at the games (with few exceptions) demonstrate similar values.

Adapted from Rick Westhead, "Canada's First Olympic Sponsor," The Business of Sports, special supplement in *Canadian Business*, 2004, pp. S10, S12; Keith McArthur, "Pepsi and MasterCard do hockey, leave Olympics to Coke and Visa," *Globe and Mail*, September 3, 2004, pp. B1, B2; and Keith McArthur, "Squaring off over sponsorships," *Globe and Mail*, August 21, 2004, p. B4.

Mike Sturk/CP Photo Archive

The primary benefit these companies gain by sponsoring the arts is goodwill from the public. Most firms view this type of investment as part of their corporate citizenship objectives (e.g., being perceived as a good, contributing member of society). They do want to get some marketing mileage out of it, however. One way to do this is to add value to the event experience. Bell Canada, a long-term sponsor of the Stratford Festival, enhanced attendees' experience though unique signage in the lobbies. Using two giant screens donated by Panasonic, Bell looped information about the festival along with sponsorship recognition. The screens gave Bell an opportunity to showcase its technology. Attendees were treated to on-screen interviews with the actors who performed at the festival. Activities like this produce more meaningful relationships between an event and its sponsors.[24]

Some of the other cultural events sponsored by Bell include the Shaw Festival, the International Film Festivals in Toronto and Vancouver, and the Just for Laughs Festival in Montreal. Bell has always invested in the communities it serves, and has a varied sponsorship portfolio including major cultural and sporting events that enable it to be present in the community throughout the year. An illustration of Bell's commitment appears in Figure 16.12.

FIGURE
16.12

A corporate ad that communicates Bell's commitment to the community

Courtesy: Bell Canada

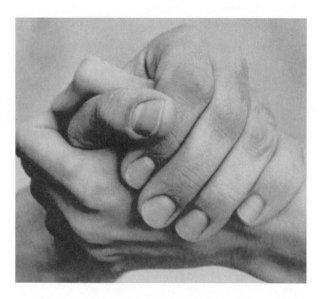

Communication makes the world a better place.

At Bell we are committed to enriching the lives of Canadians and the communities we live in. One of the ways we do this is by contributing millions of dollars each year to support charitable programs that connect people, technology and knowledge in new ways. Because we believe in the power of communication to change the world.

Imagine A Caring Company

CONSIDERATIONS FOR PARTICIPATING IN EVENT MARKETING

Companies enter into sponsorships in an effort to create a favourable impression with their customers and target groups. For this to be accomplished, the fit between the event and the sponsor must be a good one. For instance, Nike sponsors national and international track and field events as well as community-based events such as fun runs. Much of the company's success has been based on event sponsorship and the distribution of merchandise that bears Nike's trademark logo—the swoosh. The most effective sponsors adhere to the following principles when considering participation in event marketing.

5. List the unique considerations involved in planning event marketing programs.

1. *Select Events Offering Exclusivity*—The need for companies to be differentiated within events they sponsor calls for exclusivity, meaning that direct competitors are blocked from sponsorship. Also, a concern among sponsors is the clutter of lower-level sponsors in non-competing categories that reduce the overall impact of the primary sponsor.

2. *Use Sponsorships to Complement Other Promotional Activity*—The role that advertising and promotion will play in the sponsorship must be determined first. Sponsorship of the proper event will complement that company's other promotional activity. For example, Nextel (a telecommunications company) is the title sponsor of Nascar racing in the United States. Effective communications between the pit and the driver are critical for successful racing; Nextel technology is used trackside. This sponsorship is a natural fit for Nextel, and the association can be built into the company's advertising and promotion strategies.

3. *Choose the Target Carefully*—Events reach specific targets. For example, while rock concerts attract youth, symphonies tend to reach audiences that are older, urban, and upscale. As suggested earlier, it is the fit, or matching, of targets that is crucial.

4. *Select an Event with an Image That Sells*—The sponsor must capitalize on the image of the event and perhaps the prestige or status associated with it. A luxury car, such as the Mercedes M-Class Sport Utility Vehicle, may be a suitable sponsor for a significant arts or cultural event or a major national golf championship (e.g., the Mercedes Open in Hawaii). The prestigious image and status of such events have an impact on the sale of products that project a comparable image (in this example, the image and status that come with ownership of a Mercedes-Benz automobile).

5. *Establish Selection Criteria*—In addition to using the criteria cited above, companies evaluating potential events for sponsorship should consider the long-term benefit such sponsorship offers compared with the costs in the short term. For example, being associated with an event that is ongoing, popular, and successful is wise, as there is less risk for the sponsor. Before committing financial resources to an event, a company should conduct a cost–benefit analysis. The benefits must outweigh the costs (see the next section for details).

MEASURING THE BENEFITS OF SPONSORSHIP

With sponsorships, large sums of money are spent at one time for a benefit that may be short-lived. For the manager making the decision, trying to determine the return on investment is extremely difficult. The basic appeal of event marketing is that it provides the sponsor a means of connecting more personally with its target market. Communications occur in an environment where the target market is comfortable. The following indicators, many of which are obtained from research, are used to measure the benefits of sponsorship.

1. *Awareness*—How much awareness of the event within each target group is there, and how well do people recall the brand or product name that sponsored the event?

2. *Image*—What change in image and what increase in the consumer perception of leadership or credibility resulted from the sponsorship?

3. *New Clients*—How many new clients were generated as a result of the company's sponsoring an event? Entertaining prospective clients in a luxury box at an event goes a considerable way in building a relationship.

4. *Sales*—Do increases in sales or market share occur during post-event periods? Be aware that the real sales benefit may take years to build—it takes time for a sponsor to become closely associated with an event.

5. *Specific Target Reach*—Do the events deliver constituency? Carefully selected events reach specific targets that are difficult to reach by conventional communications. For example, pre-teens and teens are difficult to reach through conventional media but can be reached effectively through sponsorship of rock concerts and music tours.

6. *Media Coverage*—What value was derived from editorial coverage? Did the sponsorship result in free publicity for the sponsor? The industry benchmark for sports sponsorship is currently 4:1, meaning $4 in exposure (e.g., free air time) for every $1 spent on sponsorship and its marketing support.

For sponsorships to be successful they must be integrated seamlessly into corporate marketing and marketing communications plans. An organization has to make a financial commitment above and beyond the rights fees. A general ratio for spending should be three to one. In other words, for every $1 spent on securing the rights, $3 should be spent to promote the relationship to the event.[25]

SUMMARY

Sales promotion plays a key role in influencing purchase behaviour and helps boost sales in the short term. Sales promotion activity can be divided into two categories. The first is consumer promotions. These are designed to pull the product through the channel of distribution and prompt purchases (trial, repeat, or multiple) of the product. Such promotions may take the form of coupons, free samples, contests, cash refunds, premiums, frequent-buyer programs, and delayed-payment incentives.

Trade promotions, the second kind of sales promotion, are designed to push the product through the channel of distribution and secure product listings among distributors, build sales volume, and gain merchandising support. Cooperative advertising, performance allowances, in-ad coupons, dealer premiums, collateral materials, dealer display materials, and trade shows are among the types of trade promotion that occur.

Personal selling refers to personal communication between sellers and buyers. The role of the salesperson is to locate customers whose needs can be satisfied or whose problems can be resolved through the use of a company's products or services. The selling process involves seven distinct steps: prospecting, pre-approach, approach, presentation, handling objections, closing, and follow-up. The nature of personal selling today relies on direct communications and the establishment of enduring relationships between buyers and sellers. If partnerships are formed between the two organizations or between the organization and the final consumer, both will prosper financially. Technology is changing the nature of the creative salesperson. Less time is now spent on personal content, while more time is devoted to electronic contact and activities designed to service and retain customers.

Event marketing and sponsorship programs are now an important element of a firm's marketing communications mix, particularly among large Canadian corporations. Sponsorship is concentrated in three popular areas: sports events, entertainment events, and cultural and arts events. Sports attract the lion's share of the sponsorship pie. Prior to getting involved with sponsorships, an organization should establish specific criteria for participation. Factors to consider include product category exclusivity, relationships with other marketing communications programs, and the image-building potential offered by an event. Once a sponsor has established an association with an event, the expectations turn to improving image, attracting new clients, and building sales.

KEY TERMS

REVIEW QUESTIONS

1. What are the objectives of consumer promotions and trade promotions?

2. Explain how the product life cycle affects the use of media-delivered coupons and product-delivered coupons.

3. Briefly explain the following free-sample terms: (a) cross-sampling; (b) on-site sampling or experiential marketing.

4. In the context of a mail-in refund or rebate, what is slippage?

5. Briefly explain the nature of a loyalty (frequent buyer) program.

6. How is cooperative advertising different from other forms of advertising?

7. How does a manufacturer of a product benefit from offering a performance allowance to a distributor?

8. List and briefly describe the seven steps in the selling process.

9. What is the difference between event marketing and event sponsorship?

10. What is ambush marketing? Briefly explain.

11. Briefly describe the main benefits of event marketing participation.

12. What are the basic factors an organization should consider prior to participating in event marketing and sponsorships?

DISCUSSION AND APPLICATION QUESTIONS

1. Identify which consumer promotion activities are best suited to meet the following marketing objectives:

    a) Trial purchase

    b) Brand loyalty

    c) Multiple purchase

2. "The use of dealer premiums is an unethical practice in contemporary marketing." Discuss this statement.

3. If you were the marketing manager for Nike or BMW, what events would you sponsor? What benefits would you derive from these sponsorships? Be specific.

4. Assume you are the marketing manager for Apple Computers in Canada. Your market share is about 4 percent and you rank as the number 6 brand. Hewlett-Packard with 6.5 percent share and Toshiba with 5 percent share are just ahead of you. Your goal is to move ahead of at least one of these brands. What promotion recommendations do you have to build Apple's market share? Justify your recommendations. Conduct some secondary research on the computer market to familiarize yourself with competitive activity.

5. Assume you are a brand manager for Maxwell House coffee (a mature brand leader). The primary marketing objective is to encourage brand loyalty. What promotion recommendations do you have? Be specific, and justify your recommendations.

6. "Advances in communications technology will dramatically change the role and nature of selling." Discuss and provide examples of changes that are already having an influence on selling strategies.

7. Read the vignette "Olympic Dreams!" Is Olympics sponsorship a wise investment or a waste of money? Conduct some additional secondary research on the issue and present a case for or against such an effort.

8. Assume you are an executive member for a local sports organization in your community. How would you go about finding sponsors for your league?

E-ASSIGNMENT

Select an actual contest campaign (visit a supermarket or drugstore for ideas) that is being advertised in the mass media (television, radio, newspaper, and magazines) or on packages and point-of-purchase material. Visit the website for the company or brand and evaluate how the Internet was integrated into the campaign. Is the Internet a viable vehicle for implementing sales promotion activities?

ENDNOTES

1. Wayne Mouland, "Coupons Take Off," press release, Resolve Corporation, February 2005.

2. Ibid.

3. Jo Marney, "The basics of promotion," *Marketing*, February 6, 1989, p. 28.

4. Alanna Mitchell, "Lavatory luxury a new Ex-perience," *Globe and Mail*, August 21, 2004, p. A9.

5. Marina Strauss, "Take the washer for a spin (cycle) first," *Globe and Mail*, August 3, 2004, pp. B1, B2.

6. Geoff Dennis, "Sampling growth spurs creativity," *Strategy*, May 20, 2002, p. 1.

7. NCH Promotional Services, *A Marketer's Guide to Consumer Promotion*, 1990, p. C4.

8. Wayne Mouland, "Mail-In Rebates Boost Retail Sales," press release, Resolve Corporation, October 2004.

9. David Menzies, "Mail-in rebates gravy train for manufacturers," *Financial Post*, October 2, 2004, p. IN2.

10. Michelle Halpern, "Labatt's big PROMO! Score," *Marketing*, October 6/13, 2003, p. 28.

11. Danny Kucharsky, "Consumers drawn to loyalty rewards, *Marketing*, May 6, 2002, p. 3.

12. "Shoppers launches creative loyalty program," *Marketing*, December 18/25, 2000, p. 21.

13. Dina El Boghdady, "Giving Discounts Where It Counts," *Washington Post*, December 19, 2003, p. E01.

14. Daniel Girard, "Rarity in rugged retail field Leon's keeps profits rising," *Toronto Star*, June 12, 1993, pp. C1, C2.

15. Stephanie Thompson, "Nestle warns stores: Prove it or lose out," *Advertising Age*, September 13, 2004, pp. 1, 52.

16. Barry Suskind, "Trade shows work—it's all about the numbers," *Small Business Canada Magazine*, March/April 2002, p. 43.

17. "Relationship Marketing," *Venture* (Canadian Broadcasting Corporation), broadcast on April 7, 1998.

18. "Sponsorship spending to see big rise in five years," IEG Sponsorship Report, www.sponsorship.com.

19. Keith McArthur, "COC sets sights on Air Canada sports ads," *Globe and Mail*, August 20, 2004, p. B2.

20. "Your name here," *Report on Business Magazine*, May 2002, p. 31.

21. "Tim Hortons to Sponsor Brier and Trials," press release, March 11, 2004, www.timhortons.com.

22. Stan Sutter, "Olympic Gamesmanship," *Marketing*, November 1, 2004, p. 2.

23. Terry Poulton, "Basking in the starlight," *Strategy*, September 9, 2002, pp. 21–24.

24. Sara Minogue, "Enriching the event," *Strategy*, September 8, 2003, p. 15.

25. Wendy Cuthbert, "Sponsors pump ROI with experimental approach," *Strategy*, March 12, 2001, p. B7.

Emerging Directions in Marketing

PART

8

The marketplace is constantly changing, and the practice of marketing must change right along with it. This section presents some of the emerging areas of contemporary marketing, along with the special marketing considerations necessary for its success.

Chapter 17 presents the fundamental activities associated with online marketing. The chapter describes the role of online marketing and examines how this new and exciting way of doing business will improve the effectiveness and efficiency of business operations.

Chapter 18 examines the unique characteristics of the services and not-for-profit marketing environment, and shows how marketing strategies are adapted to serve customers in these markets.

Chapter 19 emphasizes the importance of analyzing global market opportunities and strategies for pursuing global markets.

CHAPTER

17

Internet Marketing

Learning Objectives

After studying this chapter, you will be able to

1. Describe the fundamental activities associated with online marketing.

2. Explain the opportunities for marketing, sales, and customer service presented by the Internet.

3. Describe the role and importance of online marketing today and in the future.

4. Describe the role the Internet can play in marketing research.

5. Demonstrate how the various elements of the marketing mix apply to Internet marketing.

Introduction to E-Commerce

1. Describe the fundamental activities associated with online marketing.

Today's business climate can be summed up in three words: Everything is changing. And much of the change is directly related to technology. "Technology is like a steamroller. You are either on top of it or under it." This expression sums up the rapid pace of Internet growth: the Internet has been accepted more quickly than any other form of communications technology. At the end of 2003, 7.9 million of Canada's 12.3 million households, or 64 percent, had at least one member using the Internet regularly, either from home, work, school, public library, or another location. However, the level of growth in Internet use that had been surging throughout the 1990s began to level off in 2003. It seems that the bulk of Canadians who want to be online are already there.[1]

The growth and acceptance of electronic business practices have fuelled organizational interest in electronic marketing. Prior to getting into a discussion of Internet marketing, a few basic business terms should be clarified.

E-commerce refers to buying and selling goods online and the transfer of funds through digital communications (e.g., Amazon.ca sells a book or Expedia.com sells an airline ticket and the consumer pays online via credit card). The growth of electronic business and electronic commerce is like an ocean rising. Each day more and more companies are joining the online world and more and more consumers and businesses are getting more comfortable with online transactions. In 2003, total e-commerce sales in Canada amounted to $18.6 billion. Business-to-business transactions accounted for $13.1 billion, and business-to-consumer sales accounted for $5.5 billion.[2] Electronic commerce spending by consumers represented only a tiny fraction of the $688 billion in total personal expenditures in 2003.[3]

e-commerce

E-business is defined as conducting business on the Internet—not only buying and selling, but also servicing customers and collaborating with business partners. It embraces activities such as the electronic transfer of information between companies in order to facilitate the production and distribution of goods, and billing and payment processes in a virtual environment. A research study conducted by Visa Canada (2004) estimates that by 2008 one-third of business transactions will be e-purchased, e-billed, and e-paid.[4]

e-business

As indicated by the statistics above, the online B2B market is much bigger than the B2C market, but much growth is anticipated in B2C as consumers get more comfortable buying and paying for goods online. On average, e-commerce households are spending $956 annually online. Paradoxically, many shoppers indicate concerns about security aspects of the Internet, but they seem willing to use their credit cards online.[5] This is very good news for Canadian retailers contemplating a website with e-commerce capability. Companies such as Sears, Canadian Tire, and Chapters-Indigo have effectively combined e-marketing and e-commerce with their traditional methods of conducting business. Others must follow. Many retailers resist the temptation to go online for fear they will cannibalize their own in-store sales. In the end, they will have to go online and eat their own business before a competitor does it for them.

The transition to electronic business is well underway as large established companies in traditional industries, such as steel, forestry, and automobile manufacturing, are taking advantage of the online world. At the same time, new upstart companies are aggressively trying to dislodge the old order. Amazon was one such company. As one of the first Internet retailers, it had a dramatic and negative effect on bricks-and-mortar book retailers.

Internet Penetration and Adoption

INTERNET USER PROFILE

There are some common characteristics among the 7.9 million Canadian households that use the Internet regularly. These households tend to have medium to high incomes, members active in the labour force, children living at home, and people with higher levels of education. These households are in the forefront of Internet adoption.

Being more specific, 82 percent of households in the highest income group (the top quarter of households based on income) had a member using the Internet from home. Education plays a key role in adoption. The higher the level of education achieved, the more likely someone at home is accessing the Internet. By geographic location the highest rates of usage are in British Columbia, Alberta, and Ontario, where roughly 6 out of every 10 households are connected to the Internet. All other provinces are below the national average of 55 percent.[6]

From the above data it appears the Internet is an ideal medium for reaching mid- to upper-income households and households with post-secondary education. The Internet is taking on mass media status and as such can be effectively integrated into targeted marketing programs. It should play a vital role in future marketing activity.

On the horizon is the full-scale emergence of wireless communications. The adoption of cell phones with Internet capabilities, laptops with wireless links, and the small hand-held devices (personal digital assistants) that are being developed by such companies as Nokia, RIM, and Motorola, will make wireless communications in all forms the preferred method to connect to the Internet in the longer term. Wireless networks will enable consumers to shop anytime and anywhere.

INTERNET BEHAVIOUR

Technology is changing consumer behaviour. Specifically, the Internet has altered people's entertainment and media habits. An organization's website must transfer important company and product information—information that people will benefit from and perceive to be relevant.

While customers actively seek information online, the existence of company websites is not a given. Large companies have adopted e-business and e-commerce much more quickly than have small and medium-sized businesses.[7]

Internet users are information-oriented and more demanding by nature. They expect instant information, lower prices, and incentives such as free shipping. Organizations, therefore, must provide information on the assumption it will create goodwill, brand interest, and, in the future, some form of purchase (online or offline).

The Internet Presents Marketing Opportunities

The Internet offers three significant opportunities. First, it will be the medium of choice for communicating detailed information about goods and services. This is particularly true among 18- to 34-year-olds (a desirable target market of new buyers), who account for 24 percent of the population and 40 percent of all Web pages viewed.[8] Many businesses, including newspapers and magazines, specialize in the delivery of information. As well, companies that have embraced the Internet publish all kinds of information about themselves so that customers can make more informed buying decisions.

The second opportunity is the capability to sell goods online. Online storefronts—such as those for Sears and Canadian Tire—fall into this category, as do the electronic communications systems established among business-to-business buyers and sellers.

The third opportunity deals with the concept of mass customization. **Mass customization** refers to creating systems that can personalize messages and ultimately products to a target audience of one. Dell Computer Inc., for example, builds a computer to unique customer specifications once the order is received online.

mass customization

As one of the leading makers of desktop and laptop computers, Dell's business was founded on the basis of direct marketing techniques. The transition to online marketing was smooth for Dell (see its website in Figure 17.1). Today, Dell operates one of the highest-volume e-commerce sites in the world. Via the Web, Dell has 82 country sites in 21 languages and transactions are conducted in 40 currencies.

Dell understands how the Internet can impact a business. In 2003, Dell's sales revenues amounted to US$41 billion. A significant portion of that revenue is generated

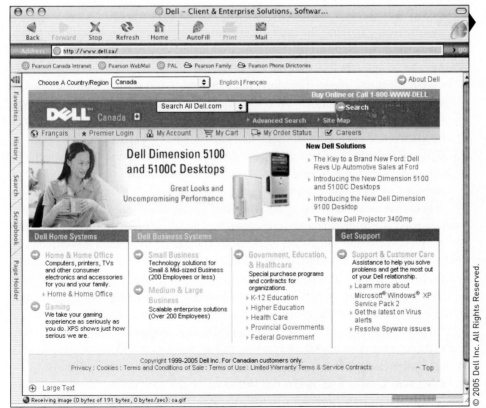

FIGURE
17.1

The Dell website is one of the busiest commercial sites on the Internet

from online sales. In the U.S. Dell generates $30 million a day in computer sales alone, and the company has surpassed Compaq Computer Corp. to become the leading brand in the U.S.[9] Dell has proven that selling computers online is a more effective method than selling by traditional means.

For more insight into Dell's Internet success, read the Marketing in Action vignette **Dell Leads the Way**.

3. Describe the role and importance of online marketing today and in the future.

Internet Marketing Performs Important Roles

The challenge for marketing organizations is to determine how the Internet fits in with traditional marketing models. The Internet is not a replacement for traditional activities but rather an additional tool that can assist the organization in achieving its marketing objectives. The success of Internet activities still relies on traditional marketing techniques, such as advertising, promotion, and public relations, for these activities draw attention to a company's Internet operations. More importantly, the Internet is used as a vehicle for most traditional marketing activities: advertising, sales promotions (e.g., delivering coupons), public relations, and pre- and post-sale customer service. Some of the key marketing functions the Internet can perform include:

1. *Creating Company and Brand Awareness*—Through a company website essential information can be communicated about the company and its brands. Such information may have a financial orientation to help attract potential investors, or it may focus on the unique features and benefits of its product lines. In contrast to traditional media, online communications can be much more detailed. An organization can also place advertising in a variety of forms on other Internet sites. (Refer to Chapter 15 for additional details.)

2. *Branding and Image Building*—Branding is the responsibility of marketing communications activities. The intent is to have the public perceive a brand in a positive manner. Since consumers actively seek information about products at company websites, it is important that the site project an image that is in keeping with the overall company image. Therefore, the appearance and style of communications should be consistent between the traditional media and online media. Any advertising that is done online (e.g., at another website) should project a similar look and image about the company or brand being advertised.

3. *Offering Incentives*—Many sites offer discounts for purchasing online. Electronic coupons, bonus offers, and contests are now quite common. Such offers are intended to stimulate immediate purchase before a visitor leaves a website and encourage repeat visits. Canadian Tire offers special deals online as a means of getting people comfortable with online buying. Companies can also distribute online coupons to consumers. Save.ca identifies offers that are available, takes requests for the coupons from consumers online, and then mails the coupons to consumers.

4. *Lead Generation*—The Internet is an interactive medium. Visitors to a site leave useful information behind when they fill in boxes requesting more information (e.g., name, address, telephone number, and email address). A site may also ask for demographic information that can be added to the company's database. Such information forms the basis for efficient market segmentation and the development of customer relationship management programs.

5. *Customer Service and Relationship Management*—In any form of marketing, customer service is important. Satisfied customers hold positive attitudes about a

MARKETING IN ACTION

Dell Leads the Way

Michael Dell is a very rich man. He is currently ranked the 18th richest man in the world, with about US$11 billion in assets. Not bad for a guy who started making and selling personal computers in a college dormitory. He never did finish college. Today, at only 40 years of age, Michael Dell is the chief executive of the world's largest personal computer company.

So what is Dell's competitive advantage? It has to do with the way the company makes and markets personal computers. Unlike all of its competitors, Dell was built on direct marketing techniques, so integrating the Internet into the direct model was a natural extension of its way of doing business.

What Dell does well is cut out the middleman. To buy a Dell you pick up the telephone or visit the company's website. It doesn't matter if you are buying one computer or a thousand computers. Dell doesn't need stores, so it doesn't pay any rent. The company doesn't retain a large inventory because its computers are not manufactured until they have been sold. It doesn't need resellers and distributors, so the price tag doesn't swell. Dell is a unique company!

Michael Dell used the direct mail model back at college. The same direct marketing concept exists today but it is supported by an advanced made-to-order system and order-placement through the Internet. Today the company sells about half of all its computers over the Web.

Dell started out in 1984. In the first 8 years the company grew by 80 percent annually; in the next 6 years by 60 percent annually; and in the past 3 years by 40 percent annually. This business model is really about direct relationships with customers—big corporations, governments, or individual consumers. Dell's business model provides accountability, higher quality, more responsive support, and certainly lower cost.

Dell understands how the Internet can impact a business. In fact, while GDP in North America is only about 3 to 4 percent online, the GDP for Dell is about 50 percent online. Over US$40 million of sales in a seven-day week occur online, and of the roughly US$33 billion in revenue generated in the latest year, about US$20 billion will be transacted online.

Dell's climb to market leadership is the result of a persistent focus on delivering the best possible customer experience by directly selling products and services based on industry-standard technology and by introducing relevant technology more quickly than competitors. Dell is moving beyond computers and is now marketing flat-screen televisions online. With such an enviable reputation for delivering online, it can be safely predicted that Dell will one day become a leader in this market as well.

The question has to be asked. Why can't other companies duplicate what Dell is doing?

Adapted from Tyler Hamilton, "That $18 billion smile," *Toronto Star*, April 2, 2002, pp. C1, C13; www.dell.com/us/en/gen/corporate/factpack; and www.dell.com/us/gen/corporate/speech/speech_2000-04-07-tor. © 2000 Dell Computer Corp.

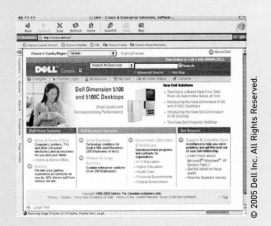

FIGURE
17.2

An illustration of
permission-based email
marketing

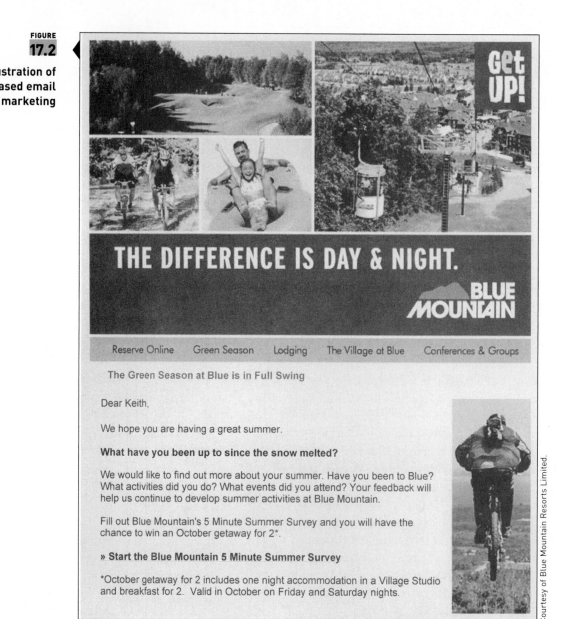

company and are apt to return to buy more goods. The Internet can perform a host of customer service activities but is perceived to be a weak link in the marketing loop. Companies must pay close attention to customer service, inbound sales, order tracking, order problems, out-of-stock issues, deliveries, and returns. Leading courier companies such as FedEx and UPS offer a service that allows customers to track where their packages are and when they will arrive. Such a service enhances the relationship between an organization and its customers.

6. *Email Marketing*—Firms retain visitor information in a database. Emailing useful and relevant information to prospects and customers helps build stronger relationships. As discussed in Chapter 15, permission-based email is quite acceptable to Internet users. Other mail applications include distributing information about promotional offers, customer newsletters, and viral marketing techniques (encouraging customers to forward the email to a friend). See the illustration in Figure 17.2.

7. ***Selling Online***—Currently, the business-to-business market is booming with business transactions. Firms in the supply chain are linking together to form what's called a B2B exchange. The goal of the exchange is to achieve efficiencies in the buying–selling process. For example, The Hudson's Bay Company links hundreds of The Bay, Zellers, and Home Outfitters vendors to buying groups for the interchange of electronic procurement documents.

As indicated earlier in the chapter, consumers do their research online before making important purchase decisions. So, if the consumer does not buy online, the Internet will play an influencing role in purchases that are made in stores. The Internet will drive sales in traditional channels. In the automobile market, three of ten people who configure a car online end up sending the specifications to a dealer. Consequently, Ford shifted a considerable portion of its marketing budget out of traditional media and into Internet marketing activities. The Internet now accounts for 20 percent of the budget allocation. Ford sees the Internet as a living brochure. At the website, a customer can build their car and then receive a price quote. They are then guided to the nearest dealer, who manages the purchase and after-sales support.[10]

Marketing Research Applications

As discussed in Chapter 3, marketing organizations access data to make more informed marketing decisions. Secondary data on the Internet are usually more current because the medium does not face the long lead times associated with the print media. The data can be accessed quickly and inexpensively. Primary data are collected primarily through online email and Internet surveys.

> 4. Describe the role the Internet can play in marketing research.

SECONDARY DATA COLLECTION

The primary advantage of Internet information is the speed at which the information is available. Data are readily accessible 24 hours a day, 7 days a week, from all over the world, and in a matter of seconds. Secondary information can be gathered from public and private sources. The major weakness of the data secured is similar to that of other secondary sources—it rarely solves an organization's specific marketing problems and it can become outdated rather quickly. Sites such as Hoovers, for example, provide useful financial information about a company along with links to a company's primary competitors. Therefore, another company could quickly develop a profile of industry participants by visiting such a site.

Hoovers
www.hoovers.com

Marketing organizations conduct online and offline investigations to ensure they stay on top of trends that will affect the direction of marketing strategies. Updated information on demographic trends, social and cultural trends, lifestyle trends, technological trends, and competitor activity trends is essential. The Statistics Canada website is a good source of information on social, demographic, and economic trends.

Statistics Canada
www.statcan.ca

Research organizations such as Angus Reid and consulting companies such as Deloitte & Touche often publish the results of their generic surveys on the Internet. Company websites are another source of information—very often, a good source of information for students doing marketing projects! It is now common practice for a company to publish its annual report online along with press releases that contain the latest news about the company.

PRIMARY DATA COLLECTION

The most common types of online research include focus groups, observations, and surveys.

1. *Focus Groups*—A traditional focus group collects qualitative data from 10 to 12 participants who are brought together at a central location. An online focus group brings people from diverse geographic areas together in a virtual environment. Participants respond to questions independently and as a result are less intimidated by others while expressing their views (a factor that influences regular focus group opinion). The advantage of online focus groups is that they are quicker and less expensive to operate than traditional groups. There are several drawbacks: the body language of the participants cannot be observed, and the authenticity of the respondent can be questionable (e.g., a teenager could pose as a 35-year-old and vice versa).

2. *Observations*—The technology is available to observe visitor behaviour automatically. The most common form of observation is to record and analyze viewing patterns at a website. A visitor's entry point, clicks, and time spent on a page are recorded in a log file. Periodically, the log file is analyzed to determine the most popular aspects of the site. It allows managers to adjust the arrangement of the site in order to best serve the customer. At a site such as Amazon.ca (a seller of books and music), where a user registers before using the site, data about purchases are captured in a database. Based on historical ordering of items, Amazon can make recommendations to customers by sending email to them at a later date.

3. *Surveys*—In an online survey, respondents usually indicate their response by selecting from a drop-down list, placing a checkmark in a box, or clicking a button. Online surveys offer several advantages: they are fast and inexpensive compared to traditional survey methodologies (e.g., focus group, personal interview, mail); participants respond immediately, results can be tabulated instantaneously, and there are no fees for personal contact or return mailings; and no data-entry errors occur—the respondent fills in the information and it is fed directly to a database with no possibility of coding or input errors. Finally, some researchers have discovered that respondents answer questions more openly and honestly when an interviewer is not present.

Some researchers do not like the fact that respondents are not selected by an established research procedure. For now, it is common for the respondents to come to the researcher. Because of this bias, an organization must be careful when interpreting data. Another disadvantage is the concern about respondent authenticity. People can disguise themselves very easily on the Internet. Children can pose as adults, men can pose as women, and so on. These situations bias the survey results.

All things considered, however, online research is quickly taking off. Marketing managers like the speed with which information can be gathered, analyzed, and used in making decisions. For more insight into the burgeoning role of online research, read the Marketing in Action vignette **Online Research: Faster, Easier . . . Better?**

Online Marketing Strategies

5. Demonstrate how the various elements of the marketing mix apply to Internet marketing.

How to integrate Internet marketing with traditional forms of marketing is a challenge that all companies now face. Due to the newness and uncertainty of the Internet, some companies have chosen to take bold steps and are excelling, while others are moving slowly and perhaps failing. Yet others jumped in immediately and are now out of business. There is a learning curve associated with Internet marketing, along with a lot of experimentation to figure out what does and doesn't work.

How a company uses technology seems to be the key to success. Scanning devices at the point of sale and the electronic observation techniques employed online are producing

Online Research: Faster, Easier ... Better?

Is it possible to test commercial messages online and get results similar to traditional forms of marketing research testing? Early results from a new technique that tests television commercials for effectiveness suggest it is possible.

AskingMedia, a broadband-based research technology developed by Delvina Interactive (Toronto), allows advertisers to show television shows, 3D images of products, and commercials to consumers and record results in real time. The process is faster and cheaper than traditional methods.

AskingMedia can recruit a client-specific sample from all across the country within 24 hours. The traditional procedure is to use focus groups that are usually a sampling from one geographic area or city. Online consumers view the commercials twice and then record their likes and dislikes by simply sliding their mouse. Once viewing is completed, participants are given a standard online questionnaire to complete.

Millward Brown Goldfarb, a research company, tested the online research procedure with two of its clients: Nissan and Expedia.ca. Traditional focus groups were run parallel to the online method and the results of both methods were found to be the same. Researchers have some reservations about online research. Apparently people tend to score emotional factors higher when they are reacting to another

person, as is the case in a focus group. Stephen Popiel, a Millward Brown Goldfarb research consultant, offers a different view based on his test experience. "Since the pattern of responses over the whole questionnaire is the same, it's easy to adjust online scores with an algorithm for comparison with off-line databases."

The cost of online ad testing using a national sample is about the same as for offline testing by traditional means and in only one location. Given the diversity of the sample and time saved in the research process, it seems almost certain that online research will become the way of the future.

Adapted from Paula Baker, "Online Research," *Strategy*, October 4, 2004, p. 25; and Adam Froman, "Real Time Research," *Marketing*, June 7, 2004, p. 15.

© Kathleen Finlay/ Masterfile.

goldmines of data. As mentioned in the chapter on marketing research, organizations have to invest in data-mining activities if they are to exploit the full business potential of the Internet.

This section briefly examines the components of the marketing mix—product, price, distribution, and marketing communications—in the context of online marketing strategy.

PRODUCT STRATEGIES

The Internet is proving to be a viable means of creating awareness and securing orders for a variety of products. An organization's website plays a key role in the successful online marketing of a product. Such attributes as effective site navigation, quick download speed, site organization and attractiveness, secure transactions, and user privacy must be considered. User-friendliness is probably the most important attribute a website can offer.

Some goods and services lend themselves to online marketing and sales, while others do not. Personal computers (refer to the Marketing in Action vignette about Dell) are among the products that sell easily. Other top sellers include clothes (16 percent of online sales), toys and video games (11 percent of sales), and consumer electronics (10 percent of sales). These figures exclude services, such as online travel bookings through companies such as Expedia, Travelocity, and Orbitz.[11] Reading materials such as books, magazines, and newspapers are also popular online purchases. The numbers of households ordering music online is increasing, while the number downloading music for free (an illegal activity) is declining.[12]

The Internet has changed how some products get into the hands of consumers. For example, media companies have had to re-examine the way they distribute information. Since time spent online by consumers is increasing each year, they are spending less time with traditional media. Therefore, traditional media, such as newspapers, magazines, radio, and television, have established their own websites. All the important news stories from the *Globe and Mail* or CBC Newsworld are readily available at their respective websites. To many people, the physical product (e.g., going out and buying the newspaper) is redundant. Refer to Figure 17.3 for an illustration.

When the sales of online products are analyzed, it can be seen that successful online products share certain attributes that make them attractive for online sales. Popular sellers online tend to be:

1. *Nonperishable*—The items can be shipped by common carrier without spoiling in transit. They are classified as shopping goods and include such items as toys, books, music, and information. They tend to be "low touch" products and can be sampled directly online before purchase.
2. *Of High Relative Value*—Computers, consumer electronics products, and software tend to be expensive. These items are a serious purchase, and information is usually collected about the product before making a decision. Computer software is a natural for online selling because the product is delivered electronically.
3. *Information Intensive*—The items require research before making a purchase decision, and that research can be conducted online. For example, people will research extensively when planning a vacation, contemplating buying an automobile, or making an investment decision online.
4. *High-Tech in Nature*—The Internet's current users have a strong interest in technical products, so within a market segment purchasing computer hardware or consumer electronics products and conducting online banking transactions are popular practices. In fact, 57 percent of households using the Internet at home had someone accessing online banking services.[13] The popularity of online banking indicates that consumers are becoming more confident in the security aspects of electronic commerce.

BRANDING STRATEGIES   In a traditional marketing environment, companies use family brand names or individual brand names along with symbols to create an image for the brand in the minds of customers. Names such as Tim Hortons and Coca-Cola, and symbols such as the classic shape of the Coke bottle become registered trademarks of the company and are legally protected from imitation. A good brand name, symbol, and the experience a customer enjoys with the product often create a deep emotional bond with consumers.

Companies going online face numerous brand decisions. What domain name should be used for the site? Should the name be an existing brand name, or should new

Reprinted with permission from *The Globe and Mail*.

FIGURE
17.3

Traditional media adapt to an electronic format

brand names apply if the product is new? Popular brands such as Nike or Dell use their corporate name as the domain name, for the products and the company are one and the same. Customers searching for specific information can browse through these sites once they arrive at the home page. In the case of a packaged-goods company like Procter & Gamble or Colgate Palmolive, the company name is the domain name. There are specific brand pages at the company site. Companies often establish separate websites for new brands, line extensions, and sales promotions (e.g., Coca-Cola established a unique website for its iCoke card, when it was launched). See Figure 17.4 for an illustration.

Other companies use acronyms or shortened versions of their company name as part of their domain name. Such use presumes widespread awareness of the acronym. Canadian Pacific, Canadian National, and the Canadian Broadcasting Corporation are examples of this strategy. These companies' site names already have meaning for consumers based on marketing activity that has preceded the Web-based marketing. For example, people refer to the Canadian Broadcasting Corporation as the CBC.

Choosing the right domain name is important because it can influence the amount of traffic at a website. The length of the name is another factor to consider. Names that are too long can be misspelled, and the user will have trouble finding the site. Whatever the decision, the name should be consistent with the company or brand's marketing communications strategy. As mentioned earlier, domain names should always appear in all other forms of marketing communications to increase awareness of the website.

The image a brand projects online should be identical to the image it projects offline. Brand names, symbols, and slogans that appear in print and television advertising should play a role in online advertising and on company or brand websites.

"Coca-Cola" and "iCoke.ca" trademarks appear courtesy of Coca-Cola Ltd.

FIGURE 17.4

Companies often establish separate websites for new brands, line extensions, and sales promotions

With reference to Figure 17.5, note that the design and layout of the home page of the Delta Hotels website are the same as what appears in print advertising. The packaging of information at a website plays a role in creating and enhancing an image in the browsing public's mind.

PRICING STRATEGIES

In business-to-consumer transactions, intermediaries (such as wholesalers and retailers) are eliminated in the distribution of goods. In traditional channels, when intermediaries are eliminated there are fewer markups to be taken in the channel, so prices to consumers are lower. When purchasing goods online consumers are buying directly, but new intermediaries have entered the scene—meaning that prices are not necessarily cheaper. The consumer perception that you will find a better price online is not necessarily true.

There are several factors that tend to increase prices and several factors that decrease prices. Things tend to balance out. Factors that have a tendency to increase online prices include the following:

1. **Direct Distribution**—Online retailers have to ship to each customer individually. Therefore, the costs of shipping are added to the price of the product, and shown in the total price quoted to customers. Though all reputable online retailers disclose shipping costs upfront, customers usually don't think about shipping costs until they see them added to their total at the end of the checkout process. At that point, many customers may decide that shipping costs outweigh the other benefits of shopping online.

2. **Auctions**—In an auction, prospective customers bid on items they wish to buy. Items are posted on a Web page and a time for the auction is set. Interested customers can return to the auction page at any time to monitor the progress of their item. The winner of the item is notified by email and put in contact with the seller.

FIGURE
17.5

An Illustration of Consistent Design between Traditional Advertising and Website

In some cases, bidding can drive the price higher than fair market value (similar to a traditional auction) or it could be lower—it's a function of supply and demand. Customers should be aware of fair market value before entering into an auction.

3. *Website Development*—Establishing and maintaining a site is expensive. An organization must consider initial development costs along with the ongoing costs (hardware, software, and Internet connection costs) associated with managing and maintaining the site. All costs must be factored in to prices charged for goods sold online.

4. *Marketing Costs*—The cost of directing Internet traffic to a site is very high. Typically, a company will have to advertise in the mass media to create initial awareness of its online existence. According to consulting firm McKinsey & Co., the average e-commerce company spends US$250 on marketing and advertising to acquire one customer. Customer relationship management programs have to be implemented to ensure repeat business from that customer, and there are additional costs associated with that.[14] There are also new costs associated with 24/7 service and the development of customized products for customers.

Factors that have a downward influence on price include the following:

1. *Competition*—Consumers can search the Internet worldwide (global rather than local sourcing) for the best possible price. Therefore, the identification and knowledge of competitors is not as clear as it once was. Knowing that consumers will conduct product searches to compare prices, it is important to keep prices as low as possible. In the travel market a site like Expedia.ca will find shoppers the best possible prices for air travel. Expedia and its competitors can offer amazing last-minute specials on flights and holiday packages, assuming there is some flexibility on the part of the customer (e.g., where and when they wish to travel).[15]
2. *Product Life Cycles*—The rate of change is so rapid that life cycles of products in some categories are not that long. Therefore, the high price that is usually associated with first-entry advantage does not last very long, either.
3. *Streamlined Order Processing*—In business-to-business situations where partnerships have been formed in the channel of distribution, automatic reordering and delivery systems save money for all partners. Savings can be passed on to customers. Customer relationship management programs involving channel members encourage efficiency in purchasing goods so that all members benefit from lower prices.
4. *Location*—Online retailers such as Amazon that do not operate traditional stores do not need to rent expensive retail space in high-traffic locations. Their inventory can be stored in warehouses that are located in low-rent and low-tax areas. The result is lower prices for the products they sell. In contrast, retailers such as Chapters-Indigo, Future Shop, and Canadian Tire are all divisions of a bricks-and-mortar operation that have much higher overhead costs.

Online firms are struggling with their pricing strategies. They are under pressure from customers to offer lower prices online than offline, yet in consumer products such as books, where profit margins are razor-thin, it becomes nearly impossible for the company to turn a profit. Lower distribution costs ease the situation somewhat, but the fact remains that a lot of online companies are losing money.

PRICING ALTERNATIVES

Online pricing strategies are different from those in offline markets. In an era of value consciousness, consumers tend to shop for the best possible deals. Value pricing is popular in a bricks-and-mortar environment, so why should it be any different online? It seems as though customers have been conditioned—possibly because of Amazon.com, the first online retailer—to believe that prices online must be cheaper. Given the consumers' perceptions about the direct nature of the distribution channel that was discussed earlier, a **price skimming strategy**—setting a high price initially—does not seem appropriate. On the Internet, even time-pressed consumers have time for comparison shopping. This behaviour forces prices down and ultimately makes price less important as a differentiator.

price skimming strategy

The objective for an online company is to be competitive while offering value to potential customers. The perception of added value (e.g., convenience of ordering and delivery) offers a company some leeway in increasing prices.

A **penetration strategy** involves charging a low price for a good or service for the purpose of gaining market share. It is an appropriate strategy to get someone to try something for the first time, but not a good strategy to pursue in the long term. Too much discounting by brands in the same market in order to remain competitive with each other can impact profits negatively. Consider what happens in the hotel market. Before the Internet, a price cut by one hotel would be seen by relatively few customers, so there wasn't much of an incentive for competitors to follow. But a price reduction advertised in cyberspace is now quickly matched by other hotels, a situation that leads to less profit for all competitors. Similar situations exist in the airline, car rental, and wireless industries.[16]

Price leadership is generally an issue in offline marketing, and it usually refers to the brand with the highest price—typically the brand leader in a market. On the Internet, **price leadership** refers to the company charging the lowest price. As discussed in the previous section, such a strategy is feasible only if costs are kept as low as possible. In an offline environment, the largest producer usually has the economies of scale and the lowest prices. On the Internet, however, small companies may have much lower operating costs, so ultimately the small company could have the lowest price and be the price leader. Theoretically, the playing field is more level on the Internet. Small firms can compete better with big firms, at least on price—a definite argument for small businesses to start marketing online.

DISTRIBUTION STRATEGIES

The traditional functions of distribution were discussed in Chapters 12 and 13. The value of the various functions changes when they become Internet-based. This section briefly examines the influence of the Internet on distribution functions.

In terms of performing a *marketing intelligence* function, information is obtained in a more timely fashion (e.g., from a computer in an office). In general, collecting information from distributors and consumers online saves an organization time and money and allows a company to react faster to changes in the environment.

Marketing communications with channel members and consumers is performed quickly—information is sent directly to literally millions of people simply by hitting a "send" button. Assuming the information is sent only to those who requested it, or who subscribed to receive updates, it will be well received. In comparison to traditional methods, such as direct mail (which requires paper, envelopes, and postage), the cost of delivering an online message is lower.

The Internet provides an additional means of *buyer contact*. Unlike traditional forms of advertising, a dimension of interactivity is added. Teens, especially, are moving toward interactivity in their daily communications with friends through such software programs as ICQ. Interactivity adds value, since information can be targeted directly (e.g., it can be customized for each individual). Further, people can access websites for information any time or any day of the week. Accessing the Internet through cell phones enhances this capability.

Matching products to suit consumers' needs is easier on the Internet. Comparison shopping sites such PriceScan allows consumers and companies to compare prices and features in product categories. By altering price or feature requirements while visiting this site, the consumer can identify a product source where value is the greatest. Some of the more well-established online retailers use filtering software to analyze what combinations

penetration strategy

price leadership

PriceScan
www.pricescan.com

of products people buy, then use this data to "suggest" to customers what product they might like. Amazon is one company using this technology. In doing so, Amazon provides value-added opportunities that create a pleasant shopping experience for customers.

On the Internet, **physical distribution** is replaced by electronic distribution for some products. It is an ideal medium for distributing text, graphics, and audio and video content. Apple has become the leader in portable music, a market once dominated by Sony and its Walkman products. For a fee, consumers can download music through Apple's iTunes service directly to their iPods. This venture has helped reverse the fortunes of Apple. In the print media, newspapers (www.globeandmail.com), news (www.cbc.ca), and sports reports (www.tsn.ca) are available online.

For goods that require physical delivery, existing specialists can play a key role. Sears, for example, has an established warehousing and distribution system for its catalogue operations. The same system is used for online marketing and distribution activities. Sears offers its heir facilities and expertise to other companies that want to go online but do not have the expertise or financial resources to build their own infrastructure. Companies working with Sears are then capable of offering their customers the convenience of online shopping. Sears is now handling the online business for Roots, starting with a Roots boutique within the Sears.ca site.[17]

Receive goods directly, pay for them directly—that is the mantra of the Internet. In the business-to-business market, where cooperative working relationships have been established between buyers and sellers, the **financing** aspect of e-commerce transactions has been widely accepted. As indicated earlier in the chapter, consumers are also becoming more responsive to paying for their purchases online. Security issues are gradually being eliminated.

As mentioned in the pricing strategy section, *price negotiation* is available to online shoppers. Submitting bids at auction sites is a form of price negotiation. Consumers can select products from a wide cross-section of suppliers and bid for the goods that are available. In theory, a wide supply of products should produce lower prices for bidders. In business-to-business markets, online buying groups are better able to negotiate lower prices due to the high volume the group purchases.

CHANNEL STRATEGIES   Any form of direct marketing, such as direct mail, telemarketing, and online marketing, involves a direct or short channel of distribution. In traditional or longer channels, intermediaries provide specialized services and functions that are beyond the capability of the source manufacturer.

On the Internet, some intermediaries have disappeared but their functions have not. The Internet has gone through a process of disintermediation and reintermediation. Refer to Figure 17.6 for an illustration. **Disintermediation** refers to the disappearance of intermediaries in the channel of distribution. As intermediaries disappear, costs are reduced, so theoretically prices of goods and services bought by consumers should be lower. Initially, it was thought that disintermediation would take hold on the Internet. Granted, traditional channel members, such as wholesaling specialists and retailers, have been eliminated, but in many cases, they have been replaced by Internet equivalents.

The replacement of old intermediaries with new and different intermediaries is referred to as **reintermediation**. For example, online distributors such as Cars4U.com and MSN CarPoint now play a key role in providing car buyers with information. MSN, which is owned by Microsoft Corp., operates MSN Autos Canada, a Canadian car buying site. At the website, consumers can compare models with various features and prices. They are then referred to the nearest dealer if they wish to buy the car. See the illustration in Figure 17.7.

disintermediation

reintermediation

MSN Autos Canada
www.autos.msn.ca

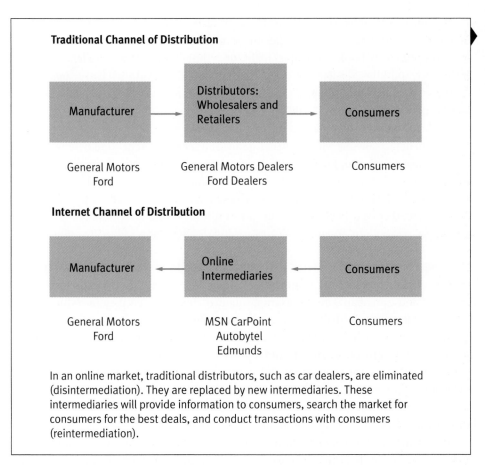

FIGURE

17.6

The Process of Disintermediation and Reintermediation

In an online market, traditional distributors, such as car dealers, are eliminated (disintermediation). They are replaced by new intermediaries. These intermediaries will provide information to consumers, search the market for consumers for the best deals, and conduct transactions with consumers (reintermediation).

FIGURE

17.7

New intermediaries such as MSN Autos Canada allow buyers to compare prices

Reprinted by permission of MSN.

A similar situation exists in the travel industry. Online intermediaries such as Expedia.com and Travelocity.com offer the same services that traditional travel agents do. Both sites can book an airline flight or a hotel room for travellers. Expedia, Travelocity, and other similar sites are given discounted rooms to sell by various hotels. For the services they provide, they mark up the room rates accordingly. Expedia actually sold 11 million room nights in 2002.[18]

In the disintermediation and reintermediation process, costs have not been reduced very much. In fact, anyone who purchases goods and services online should be aware that they will now pay for shipping charges that were once buried in the channel of distribution. If goods are purchased in the United States and delivered to Canada, appropriate taxes and duty fees are added. All things considered, potential cost savings disappear. Therefore, marketing organizations must invest resources into activities that will change consumers' perceptions about the advantages and disadvantages of buying online.

CHANNEL MANAGEMENT AND CONTROL   In Canada, powerful retailers control the channel of distribution (e.g., in grocery retailing and general merchandise retailing). Wal-Mart and Canadian Tire, for example, gained control when they introduced electronic reorder systems that simply advised suppliers how much merchandise they required. Suppliers who thought they were in control of the buying-and-selling situation had to adjust to a new way of thinking.

The Internet is customer-centric, and, despite the fact that markets are broadened, the availability of information and the ability to search shifts a lot of the power advantage to the consumer. Also, the advent of shopping agents who rank sources of supply by price on spreadsheets gives buyers a lot of flexibility as to where and from whom they buy.

In business-to-business situations, the Internet has facilitated further use of EDI systems. **Electronic data interchange** (EDI) refers to computerized transfer of information among business partners. Such an automated system produces efficiency in the ordering and delivery systems among partners in a distribution channel. EDI systems are expensive to install since all partners had to be linked in order to share data.

On the Internet, EDI has changed. Most organizations have an intranet. An **intranet** is an internal website that only employees can access. An intranet facilitates the transfer and manipulation of company information internally. In the context of distribution, EDI uses an extranet. An **extranet** is a system that connects the intranets of individual companies together through private communications lines. All partners in a supply chain can be connected by an extranet, a completely paperless environment. It is now possible to use the public Internet system to link companies. The information is encrypted so that other people on the public Internet can't see the communications.

Grand & Toy, one of Canada's leading business supply companies, recently introduced an Internet-based strategy to serve its business-to-business customers. G&T has been an active database marketer and has leveraged that strength to its Net strategy. Customer segmentation, customer promotions, and personalization features are incorporated into the site to help convert existing customers to the e-commerce environment. They have made it easy for customers to transact with them. See the illustration in Figure 17.8.

The site also features opt-in, permission-based email marketing, and to grease the wheel the company launched an online newsletter to provide customers information on subjects to help them with their daily office routines—everything from ergonomics to nutrition. According to Mike Duggan, director of commercial marketing and e-commerce at Grand & Toy, "G&T hopes to expand its overall volume of business with its online presence and the goal is to generate 50 percent of its business through the Internet."[19]

electronic data interchange (EDI)

intranet

extranet

FIGURE
17.8

An e-business and
e-marketing strategy drives
Grand & Toy's business

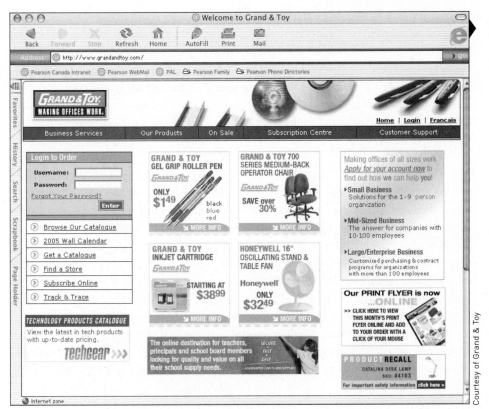

Courtesy of Grand & Toy

MARKETING COMMUNICATIONS STRATEGIES

The nature of Internet-based marketing communications was presented in Chapter 15, as it is an important component of integrated marketing communications strategies. Therefore, this section will simply review some of the important communications concepts.

The Internet seems to offer unlimited communications potential. It is a medium that reaches vast numbers of potential customers in a cost-effective manner, so it will play a more prominent role in a company's comprehensive marketing strategy in the future.

The objective of online and offline advertising is to get the viewer to the company or product website, where detailed information is provided. The Internet must be seen as a supplement to traditional forms of advertising; it is by no means a replacement. In fact, generating traffic to a company's website involves advertising the existence of the site in all media, including the Internet.

All aspects of marketing communications can be implemented online. The most common alternatives include online advertising, sponsorships, email advertising, sales promotion, public relations, and websites.

ONLINE ADVERTISING   Response rates for standard banner ads are low, so advertisers have started using more advanced banners that include animation and video. When audio and video components are included the quality of the ads is much like that of a television commercial. The ability to show the same message online as on television is attractive to advertisers.

The Internet's strength in terms of advertising is its direct response capability and its ability to be measured. Interactive two-way communications combined with online transaction capabilities at a website means a user can complete the entire purchase decision cycle simply by clicking on an ad. The gap between grabbing one's attention and generating action can be closed quickly.

SPONSORSHIPS   An Internet **sponsorship** occurs when an advertiser commits to an extended relationship with another website. To illustrate, Colgate-Palmolive, the maker of Mennen Speed Stick, implements a seasonal promotion (the Speed Stick Basketball Challenge) on the Canoe website to leverage Mennen Speed Stick among its target audience of males aged 16 to 29. The interactive format of the fantasy sports pool that runs during the long basketball season allows for a more extensive branding effort than a banner campaign. The cost of the sponsorship is incredibly cheap for the degree of exposure the brand receives.

EMAIL ADVERTISING   Using email to deliver an advertising message is the equivalent of direct mail in traditional mass advertising. The most effective way to communicate with customers is to encourage them to subscribe to receive information. To secure permission to send email an incentive is usually required (e.g., free information, a free sample, or a discount on the first purchase) in exchange for the customer's registration. Once a company has a list of subscribers it can begin to send offers by email. This is referred to as *permission-based email*. There are software systems that can be used to send messages, monitor responses and failures, track whether the recipient clicked on a link in a message, and even reply automatically.

Permission-based email provides several benefits to a company. It can send customers newsletters containing new information about the products and services offered, and also can send incentives that will help stimulate additional purchases. Refer to the illustration in Figure 17.9.

SALES PROMOTION   The Internet is capable of distributing coupons and samples to prospective customers. Retailers such as Canadian Tire distribute e-coupons through their e-flyer, which is available online. There are also some independent coupon sites such as Coupons.com that distribute coupons on behalf of national manufacturers of all kinds of goods and services.

Some sites allow users to sample their products prior to purchase. A packaged-goods company like Kraft, for example, will offer consumers free samples online in exchange for demographic, psychographic, and geographic information about cosumers. Such information accumulates in a database for later marketing use. Consumers tend to provide information more freely online than they would by other means—this is ironic yet favourable behaviour for marketing organizations!

Many software companies allow a free download of a demonstration version of their software. Once the demonstration period expires (30 to 60 days), a timer built into the download displays a message that you must purchase the software and instructs you how to do so.

Contests have proven to be another effective online tool for creating interest in a brand. Wrigley's Excel gum recently ran an integrated marketing campaign to help launch the new Cherry Chill flavour. As part of the campaign, advertising was purchased on Canada.com. Customers could visit the site and guess what day would be the coldest day of the year (The Weather Network would verify the coldest day). A grand prize of $20 000 was awarded to the winner.[20]

PUBLIC RELATIONS   An organization can use the Internet to communicate information to a variety of publics in a timely and inexpensive manner. Many different publics will visit a corporate site: shareholders, prospective employees, suppliers, customers, and the media, to name just a few.

FIGURE

17.9 An incentive offered by email encourages additional purchases

----- Original Message -----
From: Blue Mountain
To: KTUCKWELL@COGECO.CA
Sent: Thursday, October 20, 2005 5:07 PM
Subject: Only 5 Days Left!

The information provided must be meaningful and representative of what the company is about. One of the primary objectives of public relations is to improve the image of the company and its products. The mere existence of the Internet encourages people to seek out information about a company. Therefore, visiting a company website should be an enjoyable experience. Visitors should be able to navigate the site quickly, and information should be presented in an interesting and interactive format. Information should always be kept up to date, and all recent press releases about the company should be readily available. The website is an effective PR tool for building interest and credibility with the various publics that visit the site.

THE WEBSITE The Internet provides a new and exciting means of gaining additional exposure for a company. Since consumers' attention is becoming a scarce economic resource, marketers must understand the true value of a website. A website usually holds a browser's attention for two to five minutes, and while there the browser is in an attentive frame of mind.[21] Compare that behaviour to the viewing of a 30-second television spot that is interrupted by channel surfing, or the speed with which someone turns a magazine or newspaper page.

The website should deliver qualified leads, because visitors are expressing interest simply by being there. In effect, the website is lining up qualified buyers at an electronic showroom and giving them enough relevant information to make a buying decision. Since the information is always there, the Internet is a less expensive and more expansive medium than the traditional mass media. If the site has e-commerce capabilities it can also generate a sale immediately.

It is not the quantity of people attracted to a site that is important, but rather the quality of their experience while interacting at the site that counts. A small number of loyal customers are much more valuable than millions of hits by people who will not return. A person's experience at a site is important. Some experts describe the experience in terms of **flow**. They say the experience should integrate the active and the passive to absorb and immerse customers in a memorable and enjoyable experience that makes them want to come back again and again.[22]

flow

Customer Relationship Management

Online customer service strategies go well beyond post-sale activities. The Internet provides a vehicle for a company to develop a true customer relationship management program. Online marketers must be able to do three things well. They must predict the changing needs, wants, behaviours, and expectations of e-consumers; they must pursue an e-marketing strategy that is relevant to each e-consumer; and they must identify high-value e-consumers and repeatedly satisfy them better than competitors can.

Organizations must acknowledge that the Internet is a "product pull" individual-user medium, not a "product push" mass-marketing medium. Therefore, if the 80/20 rule of business applies to the Internet, 20 percent of customers will be in the high-value category and will generate 80 percent of profits. These high-value and tech-savvy customers must be part of an effective and efficient customer relationship management program. If they are not, they will do business with other companies.

When FedEx first put up its website in 1995 it estimated a savings of $1 million per day, because customers would be able to check the status of their package online rather than having to call. Today, "chat" is a technology that allows customer service representatives to speak to customers in real time over the Web. It seems that the opportunities for companies to better serve their customers, to reduce costs, and to build relationships is one of the most important uses of the Internet to marketing.

SUMMARY

Due to the rapid pace of change in technology and the growing willingness by businesses and consumers to conduct transactions electronically, organizations are integrating e-marketing techniques into their marketing strategies. Currently, the business-to-business segment of e-commerce is much larger than the business-to-consumer segment.

Internet penetration has grown more rapidly than any other medium ever has. Mid- to higher-income households and households with higher education levels are in the forefront of Internet adoption. Future growth of online commerce between companies and consumers is dependent on technology being more readily available to and accepted by lower-income households. Among current Internet users, the most popular activity is communications (email, instant messaging, chat rooms). That is followed by general browsing and shopping.

For marketers, the Internet offers three opportunities: it is a medium to communicate with customers, it allows a company to conduct transactions online, and it permits mass customization. Online marketing complements other marketing strategies as it can help build awareness and image, offer incentives to stimulate sales, generate leads, improve customer service, and allow transactions to be conducted without the use of intermediaries. If programs are implemented effectively, cost efficiencies in distributing goods are achieved and prices are lowered for consumers.

The Internet is an effective medium for conducting marketing research. Consumers and companies can access secondary data and information quickly and conveniently. Online primary research in the form of focus groups, electronic observation, and surveys also provides a lower-cost, accurate, and speedier means of collecting information from consumers. Certain research biases such as sample misrepresentation can influence the credibility of information collected, but researchers generally acknowledge that online research is the future of research.

Consumers shopping online do so based on the perception that prices are lower than offline prices. For a variety of reasons, including the cost of developing and maintaining a website and the cost associated with marketing strategies to attract visitors to the site, that is not the case. Unlike the offline environment, small companies can compete effectively with large companies online. Since their overhead costs are lower, theoretically, they should be able to offer lower prices to consumers.

The Internet performs all distribution functions, but in a different manner. The primary benefit for online companies is their ability to communicate with channel members and consumers in an interactive manner. As well, some goods can be delivered directly online. The response time between ordering a product and having it delivered by an independent carrier is shortened due to the directness of the channel. Although the Internet is still in its infancy, the distribution channel has already gone through a process of disintermediation and reintermediation. New distributors in the online market have replaced distributors that are key members of the channel in the offline market.

In terms of marketing communications, the Internet provides a new and effective means of reaching consumers and business customers. In addition to a variety of forms of banner advertising, companies can pursue sponsorship opportunities online along with email marketing strategies. Permission-based email marketing programs are proving to be very effective. The Internet also presents opportunities to offer sales promotion incentives that attract visitors and develop loyalty (return visits). As a public relations tool, a company website is an ideal medium to communicate information about a company and to build goodwill that will directly or indirectly provide benefits in the long term. The quality and quantity of information that can be delivered by a website is far beyond that of the traditional media.

KEY TERMS

disintermediation   448
e-business   433
e-commerce   433
electronic data interchange
(EDI)   450

extranet   450
flow   454
intranet   450
mass customization   435
penetration strategy   447

price leadership   447
price skimming strategy   446
reintermediation   448
sponsorship   452

REVIEW QUESTIONS

1. What is the difference between e-business and e-commerce?
2. The Internet has presented three significant opportunities for business organizations. What are those opportunities?
3. Explain the concept of mass customization. Provide an Internet illustration of this concept.
4. Identify and briefly explain some of the key marketing functions that can be conducted on the Internet.
5. Briefly explain how primary marketing research can be conducted online.
6. Assess the benefits and drawbacks of conducting focus groups and surveys in an online environment.
7. Identify the profile of successful products marketed on the Internet.
8. Identify the basic elements that contribute to a successful online branding strategy.
9. Identify and briefly explain two factors that tend to increase the price of merchandise bought online, and two factors that tend to decrease the price.
10. In the context of online marketing, what does "price leadership" mean?
11. In the context of online marketing, explain the concepts of disintermediation and reintermediation.
12. What is the difference between an intranet and an extranet? What impact have extranets had on electronic data interchange (EDI)?

DISCUSSION AND APPLICATION QUESTIONS

1. What is your assessment of Internet marketing over the next 5 to 10 years? Will it be as significant as industry forecasters believe it will be? Conduct some secondary research on Internet marketing trends and prepare a position on the issue.

2. Is consumers' concern for security and privacy valid? Conduct some online secondary research and present an opinion on these issues.

3. Conduct some Internet-based research to determine the extent to which small business is adopting e-commerce business and marketing models. Is there positive movement in terms of adoption? Are small businesses successful when they adopt e-commerce? Cite specific examples.

E-ASSIGNMENTS

1. Visit a travel website such as Expedia.ca or any of its competitors, as well as the website for a hotel chain of your choosing (Holiday Inn, Westin, Sheraton, etc.). Go through the procedure of booking a room for the hotel you have selected at the travel site without actually booking it. Do the same thing at the hotel's own website. How do the prices compare? Do online intermediaries offer better deals than the hotels? What observations can you make about using intermediaries compared to dealing directly with the source?

2. Visit mySimon.com and conduct a search for the purchase of an item of your choosing. What is your assessment of the effectiveness of mySimon's service? Are you satisfied with the results of the search, or are there better deals to be had offline?

3. Visit Ford.ca and spec out a car of your choice (e.g., select a make, model, options packages, etc.). What is your opinion of this process? Are you satisfied with the information provided? Would you buy a car online? Why or why not? Do you have any suggestions for Ford on how to improve the buyer's online experience?

ENDNOTES

1. Simon Avery, "Net not just for wealthy, Statscan says," *Globe and Mail*, July 9, 2004, p. A10.

2. "Canadian E-Commerce Statistics," Industry Canada, http://e-com.ic.gc.ca.

3. "E-commerce: Household Shopping on the Internet," Statistics Canada, *The Daily*, September 23, 2004, www.statcan.ca/daily.

4. Peter Wilson, "Full e-biz implementation 5 years off: study," *Financial Post*, June 23, 2004, p. FP6.

5. "E-commerce: Household Shopping on the Internet," The Daily, Statistics Canada, September 23, 2004, www.statcan.ca.

6. "Household Internet Usage Survey," 2003, Statistics Canada, www.statcan.ca.

7. "Canadian E-commerce Statistics," Industry Canada, http://e-com.ic.gc.ca.

8. "Buying the Future," *The Economist*, February 2005, pp. 15-16.

9. Chet Dembeck," Online PC Sales Push Dell Past Compaq in U.S.," E-Commerce Times, January 19, 2005, www.ecommercetimes.com.

10. "Motoring Online," *The Economist*, April 2, 2005, pp. 11, 12.

11. "Buying the Future," *The Economist*, April 2005, p. 15.

12. "E-commerce: Household Shopping on the Internet," *The Daily*, September 23, 2004, www.statcan.com.

13. "Household Internet Use Survey," 2003, Statistics Canada, www.statcan.com.

14. Troy Young, "Delivering customer service online," *Business Sense*, January/February, 2001, p. 38.

15. Sarah Staples, "Hits but mostly misses," *Financial Post Money*, March 1, 2003, p. IN3.

16. Michael Kahn, "Is the Internet killing profits?" *Toronto Star*, April 22, 2002, p. C7.

17. Sean Hart, "Canadian retailers piggyback smaller players," *Strategy Direct + Interactive*, May 21, 2001, p. D5.

18. Motoko Rich, "Orbitz taps hotel market," *Globe and Mail*, March 3, 2003, p. B11.

19. Bernadette Johnson, "Grand & Toy forges ahead with full-fledged Net Strategy," *Strategy Direct + Interactive*, January 29, 2001, pp. D1, D4.

20. "Win a Cool $20,000 with CANOE.ca and Excel Cherry Chill Gum," Canoe Network press release, January 7, 2002, www.2.cdn-news.com.

21. "Motoring Online," *The Economist*, April 2005, p. 12.

22. Frank Feather, *Future Consumer.com* (Toronto: Warwick Publishing, 2000), p. 272.

Services and Not-for-Profit Marketing

Services Marketing

The service industry in Canada is divided into four primary categories: leisure and personal services; food and beverage services; accommodation; and business services. The services industry includes some of Canada's largest employers as it embraces banks and other financial service companies, telecommunications companies, professional firms of accountants and management consultants, real estate companies, advertising agencies, and hotel and food-service businesses.

In Canada, the period since the Second World War has been marked by a steady shift away from the production of goods toward more emphasis on services. More than 7 out of 10 employed Canadians now work in the service industry. Much of Canada's employment growth in the past decade has come from the service industries, and this trend is expected to continue in the next decade as we move further into the technology and information era. Because of the high-tech nature of certain service sectors, growth in services will more than compensate for declines in the manufacturing sector.

FACTORS CONTRIBUTING TO GROWTH IN SERVICES

Several factors have influenced growth in services. Among them are technology, the adoption of a marketing and customer-service orientation by service providers, the changing characteristics of consumers, and outsourcing.

TECHNOLOGY   Technological developments have spurred the service sector. Advancing technology and the shift to online business models has actually created a new industry, that of online consulting. Companies that wish to build customer relationships and take advantage of the latest telecommunications technology to build their business seek out the expertise of consultants in the telecommunications industry (see Figure 18.1). Other companies have simply repositioned themselves as services industry providers. IBM, for example, has completely repositioned itself in the business-to-business market by becoming an innovative business-solutions business (i.e., a service). Part of the repositioning involved selling off its microcomputer manufacturing operations to a Chinese computer manufacturing company.

MARKETING AND CUSTOMER-SERVICE ORIENTATION   Professionals in the service sector have become aware of the usefulness of marketing. In order to differentiate themselves from competitors, service providers, such as banks, accountants, lawyers, and management consultants, are adopting a marketing philosophy to attract new business

FIGURE
18.1

Service providers advertise to inform clients how they help solve business problems

(Figure 18.1). These and other service suppliers are adopting a brand orientation for their marketing strategy and are seeking the services of marketing communications specialists (another service industry) to develop programs to attract and retain customers.

CHANGING CUSTOMER CHARACTERISTICS In the consumer market, the key issue is time. Dual-income households are time-pressed to even do the smallest of chores. Consequently, there is a rising demand for a variety of household services, such as maid and cleaning services, lawn and garden care, and home decorating and renovations. In the business-to-business market, customers want greater value (more services included for what they pay) when contemplating travel and accommodation decisions. Hotels, for example, are doing considerable retooling of their services offerings to keep customers happy. Much of their marketing strategy revolves around the extent of services offered.

OUTSOURCING   Manufacturing firms have been going through the rationalization process (e.g., the process of downsizing and the search for cost-saving strategies), and many have decided to contract out services previously done in-house. Advertising, legal, payroll, and computer systems services, among others, fall into this category. Such a transfer of responsibility has contributed to growth in the service business sector.

CHARACTERISTICS OF SERVICES

A **service** is defined as work done by one person (organization) that benefits another. In a business-to-business context, one business sells assistance and experience rather than a tangible product.[1] There are four characteristics that distinguish services from products: they are intangible, they are inseparable, they vary in quality, and demand for them is perishable.

INTANGIBILITY   **Intangibility** is the quality of not being perceivable by the senses (i.e., a service cannot be seen, heard, tasted, smelled, or touched). For example, a life insurance policy may be worth $500 000, but its true benefit is the security it imparts, and security cannot be seen or touched. This type of product is quite different from something like coffee, whose aroma can be smelled and whose flavour can be tasted.

A marketer deals with the intangible issue by trying to express the value of the service in tangible terms. In this regard, branding and advertising play a key role. For example, all car rental companies could be perceived by consumers as relative equals—they all provide the same type of service. However, a unique brand name such as Budget Rent-A-Car and Discount Car and Truck Rentals suggest price savings and differentiates those brands from competitors.

INSEPARABILITY   **Inseparability** refers to the equating of the provider of the service with the service itself. People feel this way about their doctor, their financial planner, or even their hairstylist. While apparent substitutes are available, the buyer feels more comfortable with his or her preferred and regular source of supply. A close relationship, or inseparability, exists between the service supplier and the customer.

A service organization must therefore train all employees to perform the service at the desired level. Hotels implement training programs dealing with guest satisfaction—a crucial aspect of achieving repeat business from a customer. Once the desired level of service is in place it must be communicated to the customer. In the Crowne Plaza Hotel advertisement shown in Figure 18.2, the unique selling point is the special services that collectively provide the business traveller a good night's sleep. For new customers who cannot judge the quality of service prior to purchase, corporate advertising promoting image, reputation, and value-added services is helpful.

VARIABILITY IN QUALITY   To customers, a quality service is one that meets their expectations, is available when needed, and is administered in a consistent manner. Can a services provider meet this challenge? **Quality variability** refers to the variations in services offered by different individuals, even within the same organization. For example, all London Life insurance agents perform the same service, but they each approach and deal with their customers differently, and some are much more attentive to their clients' needs than others. This is a challenge for marketers.

---

2. Outline the characteristics of services marketing and distinguish between service and product marketing.

service

intangibility

inseparability

quality variability

FIGURE
18.2

An ad stressing value-added services to attract business customers

Like inseparability, quality variability can be controlled through standardization programs. The growth of franchises and their acceptance by consumers is a result of their ability to offer uniform quality throughout the franchise system. McDonald's motto of quality, service, and value and the intensive training program that all its employees and managers must undergo demonstrate how food can be prepared and delivered in a standardized way. The quality of service offered in franchise operations can be monitored via customer feedback surveys.

PERISHABILITY OF DEMAND   The demand for services is **perishable**; that is, demand for them varies over a given period. Demand for a service may diminish, but the facilities offering the unwanted service still remain. To understand the concept of uneven demand, consider that hotel rooms sit idle during weekends, when business travel is less frequent, and that theatre seats are often vacant on weekdays and full on weekends. In both cases, the building must be large enough, or have sufficient rooms or seats, to accommodate the crowds during peak demand.

perishable

Hoteliers counter perishability of demand by offering reduced rates for hotel rooms on weekends; movie theatres offer lower prices on Tuesday evenings; and phone companies offer reduced rates in non-business hours. Such measures encourage the use of services during times of low demand.

BUYING BEHAVIOUR IN SERVICES

In marketing services, an organization should be aware that there are some differences in consumer behaviour between services and goods. Differences exist in attitudes, needs and motives, and basic decision-making behaviour.

ATTITUDES   When deciding whether to purchase a good or a service, customers are obviously influenced by their own attitudes. Since services are intangible, the impression that a customer has of the service and of the supplier is a strong influence on his or her decision to purchase the service. It is also much easier for a customer to express dissatisfaction with a service because of the personal nature of a service offering.

Since customer attitudes are important, a service organization must take steps to ensure that the quality of services offered remains high so customers are satisfied. A recent report about the airline industry revealed that lower-paying passengers flying Air Canada were treated in a hostile, rude, indifferent manner.[2]

NEEDS AND MOTIVES   Both goods and services satisfy needs and motives, often the same ones. Thus, one could satisfy the need to repair a roof either by buying shingles and laying them oneself or by hiring a contractor to provide and lay the shingles. Purchasing the goods and purchasing the service both address the same requirement. The provider of the service offers the customer convenience and expertise in getting the task performed. Yet, in addition to satisfying the need for a repaired roof, the service could also cater to another need of the customer—the need for personal attention. People often feel that the personal touch is lacking in their hurried, hectic lives. Customizing the service for individual customers with unique needs gives them the satisfaction of receiving personal attention.

PURCHASE BEHAVIOUR   A customer must decide what to buy, when to buy it, and from whom. The purchase of many services is seasonal. Household improvements are commonly made in the spring and summer, retirement plans sell heavily in the winter, and vacation travel peaks in the summer months. Whatever the time of year, selecting a service takes longer than choosing goods because it is difficult for a buyer to assess the quality and value of a service due to its intangibility.

Buyers of services are influenced more by information provided by potential suppliers in their marketing communications programs. They pay more attention to advertising and surf the Internet for detailed information and visuals that aptly portray the service. Buyers of services also value the opinions of other people—friends, neighbours, or relatives—more than do buyers of tangible goods. To illustrate, consider a couple planning a winter ski vacation. Once the information search is complete (e.g., pamphlets, brochures, and Internet search) and potential destinations are identified, a person will then seek references from acquaintances that have used the facilities. Then, a decision is made.

THE SERVICES MARKETING MIX

SERVICES AS A PRODUCT   The elements of the marketing mix for services are the same elements as those found in the mix for tangible goods. As a "product," however, a service differs from other products because the selling attributes are intangible

3. Describe the elements of the services marketing mix.

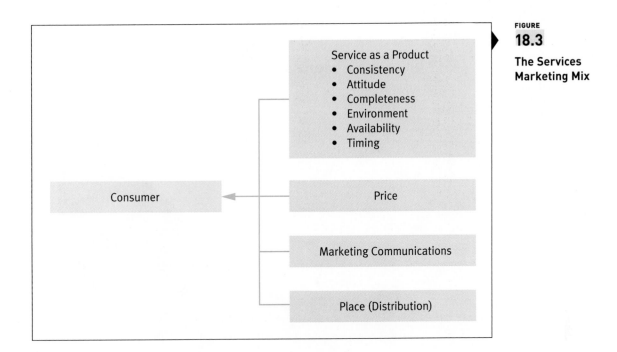

FIGURE
18.3

**The Services
Marketing Mix**

(Figure 18.3). With services, the customer is less interested in ownership or physical qualities and more interested in certain conveniences, such as timing, availability, and consistency. Following is a list of some of the intangible qualities that sell a service:

1. *Consistency*—Purolator Canada, a courier service, uses the slogan "Where business is going" in its advertising. Their television commercials show the promptness with which packages are delivered (a buyer's primary need) and state that Purolator delivers for more businesses in Canada than any other courier. Purolator illustrates consistency by delivering the goods on time, all the time.

2. *Attitude*—The attitude of those providing the service may be a selling point. Equally important is the degree of personalization between the supplier and the customer. Taking a personal approach and addressing key customers by name and then asking if the quality of the service they received was satisfactory leads to the formation of a relationship with the customer.

3. *Completeness*—Some organizations provide a range of conveniences to attract customers. For business travellers, a hotel may offer an express check-in/check-out service, fully stocked rooms with online capabilities, and meeting rooms with the latest telecommunications technology. Business travellers basically need an office when they are away from the office, and that's the level of service they expect from hotels today.

4. *Environment*—A clean, comfortable environment is an essential component of a service offering. Travelling on an airline or train can be an uncomfortable experience, so many airlines have taken steps to incorporate more comfortable seats that electronically convert to beds. Trains now offer better seating and more leg room to make the travel experience more comfortable. See the illustration in Figure 18.4.

5. *Availability and Timing*—An airline or bus line that offers frequent and convenient departure times or ease of entry and accessibility for the disabled is selling availability. Being available at the time it is needed is a selling attribute for a service. For example, availability and timing (e.g., the promise of next-day delivery) are crucial product service elements in the parcel-delivery business.

Courtesy of VIA Rail Canada Inc.

6. ***Supplementary Services***—A company will often market a primary service and then supplement the basic offering with peripheral services. For example, the primary service supplied by a luxury hotel is clean, comfortable lodging. Yet a hotel can distinguish itself from competitors by offering additional services. W Hotels, an ultra-chic and urban hotel (a division of Starwood Hotels), promises customers stylish design, sensual comfort, and sublime services. In fact, it offers a "whatever/whenever" service tailored to the fantasies of its guests, where every desire is satisfied "so long as it's legal and ethical."[3] Such an intriguing services mix distinguishes W Hotels from other upscale competitors.

     The addition of peripheral services does increase the amount that a firm must invest in its operations; however, consumers like to choose among services that are clearly differentiated, just as they do with tangible products. Differentiating the service through the service mix can ensure that the service attracts its target market. In the case of the hotel, consumers can compare room rates and additional services before selecting the one that meets their needs.

PRICING   The various types of services require various pricing strategies from the supplier. Prices can be determined by regulation, tradition, or negotiation.

1. *Regulated Pricing*—In the case of utilities, telephone service, and cable television, the services provided are regulated by government agencies. The suppliers of the service must present and defend rate increases to the agency prior to changing prices.
2. *Traditional Pricing*—Some services have prices that are established or have become traditional. It could be an established hourly rate for a service provided by an auto mechanic, electrician, or plumber, or a set rate of commission for a real estate agent or financial planning broker.
3. *Negotiated Pricing*—Fees for the services of lawyers and marketing research and management consultants are often negotiated. Typically, these companies will submit bids based on specifications supplied by the client. The client then selects a supplier from among the bids, often after further decreases in price have been negotiated.

A buyer's ability to negotiate is often critical and can save a company considerable sums of money. For example, corporations will strike deals with hotel suppliers and car rental companies largely based on price negotiation, and they demand the best possible price before committing their business. Traditionally, corporate discounts for hotel rooms are in the 20- to 25-percent range, but sharp negotiation skills can earn a company higher discounts. Consumers can also negotiate a better room rate if they possess the right negotiation skills. Don't accept the first rate that is quoted to you! It is now possible to compare prices associated with travel and other services online. With price comparisons available so quickly, goods and services providers must sharpen their pencils regarding the prices they charge.

DISTRIBUTION

In the service sector, where the relationship between the supplier and the client is close, the distribution channels tend to be direct. Because services are intangible and cannot be stored, there is often no need for intermediaries. Even if intermediaries are used, and in some businesses they commonly are (e.g., numerous small insurance companies are represented by independent insurance agents), their role is to create demand rather than perform the traditional functions of a distributor.

At one time, it was generally thought that personal contact was the key to marketing services, particularly in such industries as insurance, financial investments, and travel planning. The acceptance of online marketing by consumers has changed this way of thinking, and these and other industries have had to react. Stockbrokers are being eliminated by discount brokers, or e-brokerages such as E*Trade. Tech-savvy investors are making their own investment decisions instead of listening to the advice of their former stockbrokers. Traditional travel agents (bricks and mortar) have lost considerable business to online travel sites such as Travelocity.com and Webflyer.com.

MARKETING COMMUNICATIONS

Marketing communications strategies focus on the primary service, detailing what it is and what it does for the customer. In today's competitive market, it is imperative that service companies use all elements of the communications mix. Courier service companies such as UPS and Purolator spend a great deal of money on advertising to create awareness of and interest in the services they provide (see Figure 18.5). To secure new business, they also employ personal selling and direct response techniques. Information-rich websites reinforce messages from the mass media and provide the details that help convert a prospect into a customer.

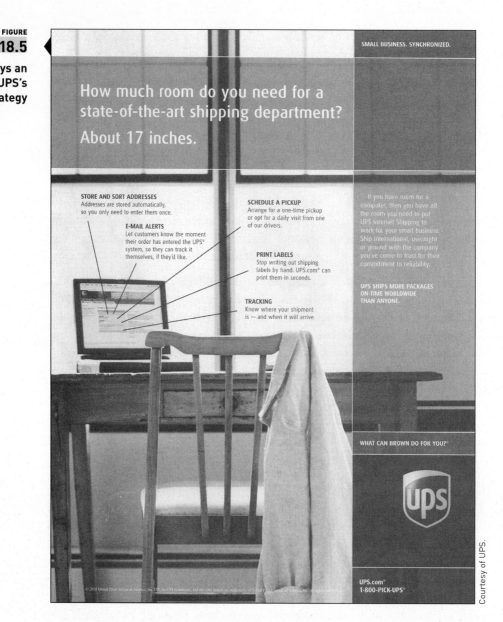

Explaining the extent of services offered by a service company is often difficult when using traditional forms of marketing communication. A print ad, for example, may simply pique the interest of a prospective customer without communicating important details. Additional essential and more detailed information is communicated to the customer from the company website. In the ad that appears in Figure 18.6 on page 468, TD Canada Trust promises customers a convenient and easy-to-use online banking service. Complete details are only a computer keystroke away.

For more insight into the changing nature of services marketing and the need to keep pace with change, read the Marketing in Action vignette **Hotels Woo Customers with Innovative Services**.

4. Explain the nature, scope, and characteristics of not-for-profit marketing.

Not-for-Profit Marketing

not-for-profit marketing

Not-for-profit marketing refers to the marketing effort and activity of not-for-profit organizations. These organizations operate in the best interests of the public or champion

MARKETING IN ACTION

Hotels Woo Customers with Innovative Services

The Canadian hotel industry was hit hard in the post-9/11 era, and hotels in Toronto were hit hard again in the wake of the SARS outbreak of 2003. Business and leisure travel was way off! To woo customers back, many of the big hotel chains have invested fortunes on upgrades and added new and innovative services.

To accommodate business travellers' needs, the InterContinental Toronto Centre Hotel spent $2.2 million to create two state-of-the-art boardrooms, each featuring side-by-side plasma screens, high-speed and wireless Internet access, and drop-down LCD projectors. The boardrooms were part of a $30-million renovation that included bigger and more comfortable beds in all rooms, Internet access in all rooms (at no additional cost), and WiFi Internet access in common locations such as lobbies, bars, and restaurants. A keen eye on the nature and quality of services offered is helping bring back the customers.

Niche services are helping out at other hotels. The hip Drake Hotel in Toronto and the upscale W Hotel in Montreal are promoting fantasy as "just a concierge call away." These upscale hotels are piggybacking on the twin pillars of sex and consumption in order to generate new business.

The Drake, a boutique hotel frequented by artists, actors, and businesspeople, now offers customers discreet access to its "pleasure menu," which includes massage oils, velvet restraints, condoms, how-to videos, and vibrators. Drake spokesperson Jeff Stober says, "We're simply augmenting the hotel's cultural programming. Sex, exhibitionism and romance have always played key roles in democratic society. All we're doing is reinterpreting and embracing that freedom of expression."

Similar services are offered at Montreal's uber-chic W Hotel. There, a guest can enjoy in-room massages, voyeur showers, and peekaboo windows in the bathrooms. According to W Hotels, "W is more than a hotel. It is a place to escape from the routine and become part of all that is 'now.' A paragon of service, a temple of ambience and design. A world where anything can happen." The additional service offerings of the Drake and W Hotels are intriguing new marketing ideas to say the least! Perhaps they are on to something.

Adapted from Sandra Martin, "Putting out the welcome mat," *Financial Post*, November 26, 2004, pp. FP1, FP6; and Misty Harris, "Hotels add fantasies to room service," *National Post*, November 5, 2004, p. A2.

Courtesy of W Hotels.

a particular idea or cause, and they do so without seeking financial profit. The goals and objectives of these groups are quite different from those of profit-based enterprises.

NATURE AND SCOPE OF NOT-FOR-PROFIT MARKETING

Not only do not-for-profit organizations market goods and services, but they also market people, places, ideas, and organizations. One major goal of not-for-profit marketing is to promote a social consciousness. The use of marketing to increase the acceptability of social ideas is referred to as **social marketing**. Examples of social marketing include programs dealing with ecological concerns, recycling, the preservation and conservation

social marketing

FIGURE
18.6

Service organizations often rely on print ads for awareness; complete details of services offered are available at a website

of natural resources, and spousal abuse, to name a few. Many of these programs are financially supported and promoted by profit-based organizations. For an illustration, refer to Figure 18.7.

Not-for-profit organizations that use marketing strategies effectively include colleges and universities, political parties and politicians, the Canadian Armed Forces, the Humane Society, the Canadian Cancer Society, and the YMCA of Canada. This brief listing of organizations indicates that marketing achieves different objectives. It is used to recruit personnel, to raise funds to support causes, and to encourage the public to volunteer time and to make other contributions to worthwhile causes.

CHARACTERISTICS OF NOT-FOR-PROFIT MARKETING

There are many similarities between marketing in a not-for-profit environment and marketing in a profit-oriented environment. In both situations, the customer must

FIGURE
18.7

An illustration of social marketing

choose between competing organizations. A person must decide which charitable groups to support and how much support to give, just as he or she must determine which car to buy and how much to pay for it.

However, there are some differences between not-for-profit and profit-based marketing, especially in the areas of philosophy, exchange (what is exchanged), objectives, benefits derived, and target groups.

PHILOSOPHY   Not-for-profit marketing is concerned with the promotion and support of people, causes, ideas, and organizations. It raises funds to support a cause or promote a concept. In the case of profit-based marketing, the goal is to generate a financial return on investment. An illustration of the not-for-profit philosophy is included in Figure 18.8.

EXCHANGE   In profit-based marketing, money is exchanged between buyers and sellers for the goods or services provided. While money may exchange hands in not-for-profit marketing, it does so under different circumstances. What people receive for their money cannot be quantified; they give, for example, for the psychological satisfaction of supporting a cause they believe in. In the political arena, the exchange may take the form of a vote given in return for the promise of a better government.

FIGURE
18.8

An advertisement encouraging support of a worthwhile cause

United Way of Greater Toronto

When you give to United Way, you're providing abused women and their children with safe shelter and counselling that will help them start new lives free of violence. With United Way funded agencies helping so many in our community, making a difference is easier than you think. Please give generously. Visit www.unitedway.ca

WITHOUT YOU, THERE WOULD BE NO WAY

Courtesy of United Way of Greater Toronto.

OBJECTIVES   Profit-oriented companies establish objectives in terms of sales, profit, return on investment, and market share. In not-for-profit organizations, the objectives are not always quantifiable and measurable. They establish targets for fundraising, but these are subordinate to other non-financial objectives. The Canadian Cancer Society attempts to find a cure for a disease, as do similar organizations. Other groups like MADD—Mothers Against Drunk Driving—attempt to change the public's attitudes or to get the public to agree with a certain position.

BENEFITS DERIVED   In an exchange made for profit, a buyer benefits directly from the good or service supplied by the selling firm. In a not-for-profit environment, only a small portion of "buyers," or supporters, ever receive any material benefits from the supported association or institution. For instance, funds to aid health organizations are solicited from the general population, but only a relatively small portion of the population contract a particular disease and use the services of any given health clinic each year.

TARGET GROUPS   Not-for-profit organizations must serve two groups: clients and donors. Clients are those to whom the service is provided. Donors are those from whom the resources are received. The resources they donate may be in the form either of money or of time. Donors are concerned about the availability of goods and services, about whether or not the resources they provide are spent well in the provision of services, and, generally, about receiving recognition for their contribution.

TYPES OF NOT-FOR-PROFIT MARKETING

There are four categories of not-for-profit marketing: organization marketing, people marketing, place marketing, and idea marketing.[4]

ORGANIZATION MARKETING   **Organization marketing** is marketing that seeks to gain or maintain acceptance of an organization's objectives and services. Colleges and universities engage in such marketing; they turn to fundraising campaigns as a survival tactic in the wake of government restraints on funds for education, and to attract prospective students to their institutions. The organizations want the public not only to accept their goals but also to use their services. Colleges and universities promote the concept of life-long learning, and they seek to have organizations use their facilities for business training, seminars, and conferences.

PEOPLE MARKETING   **People marketing** refers to a process of marketing an individual or a group of people in order to create a favourable impression of that individual or group (e.g., politicians, political parties, sports and entertainment celebrities) among a target group.

Politicians, aware that their career is created or destroyed by their image, call upon image-makers to fine-tune their personal and presentation style. In preparing for political debates on television, all participants are carefully prepared by consultants, so that their strengths, and not their weaknesses, will show in the heat of battle.

High-profile celebrities frequently appear in advertising campaigns for a commercial product or a not-for-profit cause. Celebrities employ agents and marketing consultants who seek and secure contracts for them. Wayne Gretzky is one of Canada's more popular spokespersons, appearing in ads for Ford and McDonald's. His imprint on a product or service or support of a worthy cause has a dramatic impact on how the public perceives and supports that cause. Gretzky's contribution to worthwhile causes is less known than his commercial exploits. He recently worked with TransAlta Corp., an Alberta-based company, on its Project Planet Challenge, a contest for school kids to create projects to improve the environment.[5]

PLACE MARKETING   **Place marketing** draws attention to and creates a favourable attitude toward a particular place, be it a country, province, region, or city. Places are marketed in much the same way as products. The benefits and advantages of the location are the focal points of advertising and promotion campaigns. Themes and slogans are developed for long-term use to provide continuity in advertising (see Figure 18.9). Provincial governments, for example, use catchy slogans such as "A World Away" (Newfoundland and Labrador), "More to Discover" (Ontario), and "Super, Natural" (British Columbia). In place marketing, advertising is the principal strategy, for it creates the image for the destination. Specific details that are essential for planning vacations and travel are available on information-rich websites.

IDEA MARKETING   **Idea marketing** encourages the public to accept and agree with certain issues and causes. It is often referred to as **cause marketing**. The campaigns

5. Describe the types of not-for-profit marketing and the role of the marketing mix in not-for-profit environments.

organization marketing

people marketing

place marketing

idea marketing

cause marketing

FIGURE 18.9

Vivid pictures and catchy slogans promote tourism in Canada

aimed at convincing people of the need to wear seatbelts, to avoid drinking and driving, and to exercise regularly are instances of idea marketing. Idea marketing is social marketing, and its ultimate objective is to induce the majority of the population to accept a given idea, cause, or way of thinking (refer to Figures 18.7 and 18.8).

advocacy advertising

Advocacy advertising is a form of idea marketing practised by corporations and associations that are concerned about issues or legislation that affect them. It is designed to communicate a company's position on a particular issue. A pulp and paper company may use this form of advertising to tell the public what it is doing about restoring forests, for example. It is common for consumer groups who disagree with a corporation's position to advertise the opposite point of view.

MARKETING STRATEGY IN A NOT-FOR-PROFIT ORGANIZATION

A comprehensive marketing strategy is crucial to the success of any not-for-profit group today. As suggested earlier, communications plays a prominent role, but all elements of the mix are given due consideration. The charitable marketplace today is just as competitive as any commercial marketplace. Consequently, not-for-profit marketing managers think of their organizations as brands and develop their strategies accordingly. This section briefly examines the contribution of product, price, distribution, and marketing communications to the strategic market planning of not-for-profit organizations.

PRODUCT   Product strategy in a not-for-profit organization is virtually the opposite of the strategy employed by a firm driven by the profit motive. Profit-based organizations start by trying to discover what needs the consumer has and then formulating a concept—a product or a service—to satisfy those needs. Not-for-profit bodies, on the other hand, believe from the start that they provide what the public needs. Very often, they feel that others only have to be made aware of a certain viewpoint regarding an idea, cause, person, or place for it to become widely accepted. Campaigns for such causes as the Heart and Stroke Foundation or the Alzheimer's Society exemplify this strategy. Contemporary not-for-profit organizations are like companies that operate for a profit, in that they find it effective to develop a product mix that includes identification (e.g., logos), a package (membership cards to acknowledge contribution), and other product variables. For additional insight into the brand strategies of not-for-profit organizations, read the Marketing in Action vignette **Doing Good Requires Effective Marketing Strategy**.

PRICE   In a not-for-profit organization, money is not necessarily the only form of exchange. Sometimes no money changes hands; instead, time or expertise is volunteered in return for the psychological satisfaction of helping others or the knowledge that society will be made better. Even if money is involved, the nature of the exchange is different from an exchange made for material profit. While long-term profit is the goal of the profit-based organization, a short-term gain is all a not-for-profit organization seeks. Special events are frequently a means of generating revenue for not-for-profit organizations. The annual "Run for the Cure" (for breast cancer research) is a major fundraising event that is supported financially by Canadian corporations and the public.

DISTRIBUTION   Because not-for-profit entities deal in intangibles, channels tend to be direct; that is, the organization tends to work directly with the donors. If intermediaries—professional fundraisers, for example—are used, they act on behalf of the organization. They do not assume any responsibility or control.

MARKETING COMMUNICATIONS   Communications is the most visible aspect of not-for-profit marketing. Advertising and various direct response techniques, including the mail and telephone, form the nucleus of an organization's effort, particularly for fundraising programs (refer back to Figures 18.7 and 18.8). Public-service announcements, a low-cost form of advertising, may be used to point out the benefits of contributing to a cause or charitable foundation.

Mass advertising plays a bigger role in people marketing. Think of all those ads you see in a federal election campaign. Their role is to create and maintain an image for a person or party. Very often, a charitable organization will use a known personality as its spokesperson. Michael J. Fox, for example, has Parkinson disease and is a primary spokesperson for the Parkinson Foundation.

Personal selling is also common: the Heart and Stroke Foundation, and many other worthwhile causes, use local residents to solicit funds door-to-door in their own neighbourhoods. Such campaigns are undertaken annually and are supported by advertising to build awareness of the fundraising project.

Doing Good Requires Effective Marketing Strategy

With so many charitable organizations seeking funds from the public to support myriad causes, is it any wonder that competitors are turning to tried and true brand marketing strategies to get the job done? Alison Gordon, the marketing director of Rethink Breast Cancer, says, "If we don't push the envelope, we're the Foundation with less money."

In the wake of government cutbacks, charitable organizations now speak in terms of market share and target audiences—and they are now among the best in terms of mainstream marketing strategies and tactics. Instead of focusing on doing good work and creating ideas to raise money, they now think of themselves as brands. And good brands are always building!

To understand this concept, consider the image of an organization like Unicef. Unicef does wonderful things for children around the world—but even after six decades of helping, most adults associate Unicef only with the boxes their kids carry for coin donations at Halloween. A re-branding strategy was needed.

The re-branding strategy introduced a simple tagline, "For every child," to replace the scattered messages Unicef had been using. "People are bombarded with so many messages each day. Brands are a tool to help people understand an organization better in a very simple way," says Nicole Ireland, director of communications for Unicef.

Another example involves the recent launch of a new brand-building campaign for the YWCA by a prominent Toronto ad agency—the campaign is intended to communicate how the YWCA helps women at critical times in their lives, such as when leaving an abusive relationship. Andy Macaulay, the founding partner of the agency, puts the need for the campaign into perspective: "If you don't clearly understand what the organization is about, why should you give it your money or your time to help it succeed?"

Macaulay's view aptly demonstrates why charitable and cause-related organizations need more effective marketing programs.

Adapted from Keith McArthur, "Just doing good deeds no longer does it," *Globe and Mail*, September 6, 2004, pp. B1, B5.

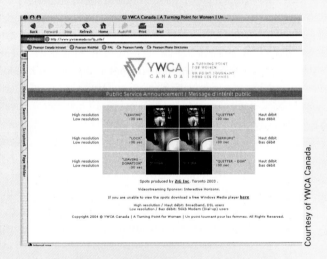

Courtesy of YWCA Canada.

SUMMARY

The service sector in Canada is a rapidly growing segment of the economy and includes many large corporations in a cross-section of markets. Advancing technology, the use of modern marketing strategies by service companies, and the growing number of time-starved consumers have contributed to the expansion of this sector.

Services have certain characteristics that distinguish them from products. A service is intangible; it cannot be seen, heard, or touched. It is inseparable from the source of supply, since each supplier is unique, despite competitive attempts to imitate a service. The quality of a service also varies, even within a single organization, where different people perform the same service in different ways. Finally, demand for certain services is perishable; in other words, demand is uneven, in some cases seasonal, and this creates a problem for marketers of services.

Since services are intangible, their price is derived more from the value they provide consumers than from direct costs. The channels of distribution are direct, and promotional efforts are aimed directly at the final user. Service marketers do employ all elements of the marketing mix, but the main planning concern is that the firm understands exactly what it is that the customer is buying. Once it establishes what the primary service is, a firm develops a complete service mix. A service mix includes those additional elements that differentiate one service from another in the minds of consumers. Service organizations market themselves much like brands do.

Not-for-profit marketing is used by organizations whose goals do not centre on financial gain. Such organizations operate in the best interests of the public or advocate a particular idea or cause. Not-for-profit groups have unique characteristics and different objectives. Their objectives are to promote (1) people, by fostering certain attitudes toward particular persons; (2) ideas, by gaining acceptance for a way of thinking; (3) places, by encouraging visits to a country, province, or city; and (4) organizations, by raising funds, cultivating an image, or persuading people to use the facilities. Rather than aiming for financial targets, not-for-profit bodies attempt to change attitudes. In doing so, they must consider two distinct targets: the clients who use and derive the benefits of the organization, and the donors who provide the organization with resources.

Not-for-profit organizations face intense competition in trying to access the public's support. These organizations think and act like brand marketers, have a clear brand strategy, and use all elements of the marketing mix to help reach their goals.

KEY TERMS

advocacy advertising   472
cause marketing   471
idea marketing   471
inseparability   460
intangibility   460

not-for-profit marketing   466
organization marketing   471
people marketing   471
perishable (perishability of demand)   461

place marketing   471
quality variability   460
service   460
social marketing   467

REVIEW QUESTIONS

1. What factors have contributed to the growth of the service economy in Canada?
2. Briefly describe the basic characteristics of services.
3. How important a role do customers' attitudes play in their decisions to purchase services?
4. "A service is an attribute or series of attributes offered to consumers." What does this statement mean?
5. How is pricing a service different from pricing a tangible product? What are the different pricing strategies used in services marketing?
6. Briefly describe the various types of not-for-profit marketing.
7. Describe the basic differences between marketing for profit-oriented and not-for-profit organizations.

DISCUSSION AND APPLICATION QUESTIONS

1. If you were in the home-decorating business (painting and wallpapering), how would you convince do-it-yourselfers to use the service?

2. Review the concept of perishability of demand in the service industry. If you were in charge of marketing for the following businesses, what strategies would you recommend to overcome perishability of demand?

   a) Air Canada Centre (or any other major arena)

   b) Holiday Inn Hotels

3. Assume you are in charge of marketing for the following companies. Describe the quality of service offerings that would be given priority in order to attract and maintain customers.

   a) Air Canada

   b) Budget Rent-A-Car

   c) McDonald's

   d) Cineplex Odeon Theatres

   e) Tripeze.com

4. You are the Director of Marketing for the Toronto Blue Jays. The average attendance at games is in the 15 000 to 20 000 range in a stadium that seats about 50 000. These seats used to be filled. What do you do to resurrect interest in this troubled baseball franchise and get people back into those seats?

E-ASSIGNMENTS

1. Visit the website for a popular hotel chain (e.g., Sheraton, Holiday Inn, Delta, or another of your choice). On the basis of the information you gather from the site, analyze the hotel's primary services in terms of the various characteristics of services: intangibility, inseparability, quality variability, and perishability of demand. What influences will these characteristics have on the marketing strategies employed by the hotel? Discuss.

2. Assume you are booking a rental car for a weekend excursion (choose your own destination). Visit the websites for two competing car rental companies (e.g., Enterprise, Hertz, Budget, Discount, and so on) and go through the process of finding the best price for a return trip to that destination. Evaluate the pricing strategies of the companies. Will your decision to pick one company over the other be based solely on price, or will other elements of the marketing mix have an influence? Discuss.

ENDNOTES

1. *Dictionary of Marketing Terms*, Barron's Business Guides, 1994, p. 479.

2. www.cbc.ca/stories/2002/04/18/Consumers/travelcomplaints.

3. Misty Harris, "Hotels add fantasies to room service," *National Post*, November 5, 2004, p. A2.

4. Philip Kotler, *Principles of Marketing* (Upper Saddle River, NJ: Pearson Education, 2004), p. 282.

5. Carol Howes, "Still scoring in ad game," *Financial Post*, June 5, 2000, pp. C1, C14.

© David H. Wells/CORBIS

CHAPTER

19

Global Marketing

The first decade of the 21st century will be a challenging one for Canada and Canadian businesses as a new era of global marketing beckons. Domestically, many prominent companies operate in industries where growth potential is flat or marginal at best. Consequently, these companies look at expansion in foreign countries as a viable alternative for growth. More than a decade ago, top executives at Toyota commissioned detailed demographic studies that confirmed their fears: Japan was aging rapidly and the population would start to shrink by 2007. In contrast, the U.S. market was young and growing due to a steady flow of Hispanic and Asian immigrants. Toyota made North America a priority market, and as a result of sales growth there the company is about to become the third largest automotive company worldwide (behind General Motors and Ford).[1]

Many prominent Canadian companies are global marketing organizations. Four Seasons Hotels, Fairmont Hotels, Bombardier (aircraft and mass-transit vehicle manufacturer), Nortel (telecommunications), and Alcan (aluminum manufacturer) are among them. Growth-oriented companies like these have a careful eye on expansion beyond Canadian borders and are looking at four key regions for growth: North America (through the North American Free Trade Agreement, or NAFTA); the European Union; Eastern Europe and Russia; and the Pacific Rim (China, Japan, Malaysia, Indonesia, and Thailand, among others). The Four Seasons (an upscale luxury hotel chain) sees growth opportunities in the Middle East, India, and China. In the Middle East alone there are plans to open hotels in Beirut, Damascus, Qatar, and Kuwait.[2]

Canadian International Trade

For Canada, the importance of international trade is significant. In 2003 (latest year that statistics were available), exports to foreign countries amounted to $380.8 billion while imports were $335.8 billion, for a positive trade balance of $45 billion. Canada's largest trading partner by far is the United States, which accounts for 86 percent of exports and 64 percent of imports. Other important trading partners include China, Japan, and Mexico. Refer to Figure 19.1 for statistical information on Canada's international trade position.

Canada's five leading merchandise exports are automobiles and light-duty motor vehicles, motor vehicle parts, computer and peripheral equipment, oil and gas extraction, and engine parts. Canada's leading imports are similar and include automobiles and light-duty motor vehicles, oil and gas extraction, aerospace products and parts, paper mill products, and petroleum products. Clearly, the health of the Canadian automobile industry has a significant impact on the economy.

FIGURE
19.1

Canada's Trade Balance Trends and Major Trading Partners, 2003

Source: Adapted in part from the Statistics Canada website http://www.statcanca/trade/scripts/trade_search.cgi

Trade Balance Trends
$ Million

	2001	2002	2003
Total Exports	404 085	396 379	380 846
Total Imports	343 127	348 718	335 806
Trade Balance	60 958	47 661	45 040

Major Trading Partners
$ Million

Country	$ Exports	% of Exports	$ Imports	% of Imports
United States	326 700	85.7	203 622	60.6
Japan	8 144	2.1	13 818	4.1
United Kingdom	6 086	1.6	9 208	2.7
China	4 766	1.3	18 570	5.5
Germany	2 881	0.7	8 637	2.6
Mexico	2 210	0.6	12 186	3.6

The World Trade Organization (WTO) governs international trade. The WTO has six basic functions: administering WTO agreements, handling trade disputes, being a forum for trade negotiations, monitoring national trade policies, providing technical assistance and training for the developing countries, and facilitating cooperation with other international organizations. Its primary objective is to ensure that trade flows as smoothly, predictably, and freely as possible between nations. At the heart of the WTO system are the basic ground rules for international commerce. Essentially, they are contracts guaranteeing member countries important trade rights. They also bind countries to keep their trade policies within agreed-upon limits, to everybody's benefit.[3] International trade is very important to the well-being of Canada. Among the factors that show the importance of trade are the following:

**World Trade Organization (WTO)
www.wto.org**

1. One-quarter of our national wealth is derived from international trade.
2. One-third of our jobs depend on international trade.
3. Nine thousand new jobs result from every $1 billion of additional exports.
4. Nearly half of Canada's manufacturing output is exported.

THE MOVEMENT TO GLOBAL MARKETS

There are several reasons why companies are moving toward global marketing. First, most opportunities have been exhausted in domestic markets. Molson, for example, owns 45 percent of the Canadian beer market, a market characterized by flat growth from year to year. Molson is expanding in the United States, Brazil, and China in order to grow. Second, the formation of common markets or trading blocs has influenced how companies approach world trade. For example, NAFTA (North American Free Trade Agreement), which encourages open trade among Canada, the United States, and Mexico, affects other countries and companies wanting to trade with these three nations.

2. Describe the reasons why a growing number of firms are active in seeking global market opportunities.

European countries have combined forces to form the European Community, a trading union that features a common currency known as the euro. This union presents challenges for North American companies wanting to trade there. Other areas of opportunity include the Pacific Rim and Eastern Europe. Currently, the Asia–Pacific region represents 60 percent of the world's population, 50 percent of the world's production, and 40 percent of the world's consumption. China and Japan are the countries that marketing organizations are targeting.

When deciding to market in a foreign country, certain advantages must exist. These are described as absolute advantage and comparative advantage.

absolute advantage

ABSOLUTE ADVANTAGE   **Absolute advantage** occurs when only one country provides a good or service, or when one country produces a product at significantly lower cost than others. Asian countries, for example, have labour rates much lower than in North America (some critics say they are so low that North American companies are simply exploiting the workers). These countries manufacture products such as toys, clothing, and electronic goods much less expensively than in North America. As a result, goods can be sold in North America at prices lower than those of similar, domestically produced products. Many North American–based companies have shifted their manufacturing to nations where labour rates are lower.

comparative advantage

COMPARATIVE ADVANTAGE   **Comparative advantage** occurs when a country can produce and market an item more efficiently or abundantly, as well as more cheaply, than other countries. Such an advantage could be based on the resources available, specialization, technology, and geography (e.g., climate). Countries attempt to exchange goods in which they have an advantage for those in which they have a disadvantage.

Canada, for example, is a market leader in forestry products because of its comparative advantage (plentiful resources) in this natural resource–based industry. Some Canadian companies that are international leaders in their respective fields include Nortel (telecommunications), Quebecor (multimedia), Alcan (mining and metal manufacturing), and Bombardier (high-tech manufacturing). Japan and the United States are leaders in technology; hence, both enjoy comparative advantage in certain markets: computers, automobiles, electronics, and aircraft. Popular consumer electronics companies and brands such as Sony, Panasonic, and Hitachi all hail from the Far East.

NORTH AMERICAN FREE TRADE AGREEMENT

The North American Free Trade Agreement (NAFTA) is a trilateral agreement between Canada, the United States, and Mexico. The agreement changed the competitive environment in North America and presented new opportunities for companies in all three countries to gain a competitive advantage. For example, current trade patterns among the three countries strongly indicate that Mexico will replace Canada as the largest trading partner with the United States. Lower labour costs in Mexico are attractive to manufacturers, particularly in the automotive sector, and more vehicle production is occurring there. Mexico surpassing Canada in terms of automotive vehicle production is imminent.

The open North American market has encouraged Canadian businesses to expand manufacturing facilities and improve the efficiency of their operations in order to supply the volume of products necessary to meet the needs of a much larger market. The elimination of tariffs presents an opportunity for companies to increase their market share. The positive trade balance that Canada has with the United States and Mexico suggests that free trade has been helpful in spurring Canada's economy (refer to Figure 19.1). The agreement has encouraged U.S.–based businesses to make further investments in their Canadian operations so that these operations can be expanded to serve the North American market.

The full implications of NAFTA remain uncertain at this time. What *is* certain, however, is that companies both here and in the U.S. will continue to rationalize operations and make decisions that will have both positive and negative effects on employment in Canada. General Motors, for example, has already closed American and Canadian manufacturing facilities in favour of production in Mexico.

Analyzing Global Marketing Opportunities

3. Outline the factors that an organization considers when planning to enter foreign markets.

When a firm is determining if it should enter a foreign market, it analyzes the same set of external environments that it does in the case of domestic markets. These are the economic environment, the consumer environment, the political environment, the legal and regulatory environment, the technological environment, and the competitive environment.

ECONOMIC ENVIRONMENT

From nation to nation, economies vary considerably. The economic character of any country is shaped by variables that include its natural resources, population, income distribution, employment, system of education, and the way its goods are marketed. There are four basic types of economies: subsistence, raw materials exporting, industrializing, and industrialized.[4]

1. *Subsistence Economy*—A subsistence economy is based on land and agriculture and consumes most of what it produces, a circumstance that leaves the country few opportunities for trade. A number of nations in Africa and Asia are in this category. The level of literacy and technology in such countries usually is low. What is available after satisfying its own needs is generally used for bartering. **Bartering** is a system of exchange whereby something other than currency or credit is used as a form of payment.

   bartering

2. *Raw-Material Exporting Economy*—Countries with this sort of economy usually have one rich natural resource or a few natural resources whose exports contribute significantly to the economy. For example, Saudi Arabia has oil, Chile has tin and copper, and Colombia has coffee. These economies are attractive to companies that export equipment, technology, and transportation and communications expertise—all products that can be used in the extraction of the natural resource.

3. *Industrializing Economy*—These countries have a skilled or semi-skilled workforce and a growing manufacturing base. Education and technology are rising and labour rates are lower than in industrialized nations. Their populations are shifting into middle and upper classes. Several Latin American countries, the Philippines, and Mexico have economies of this kind. Such countries import the goods and services needed to facilitate their industrial development.

4. *Industrialized Economy*—These countries have a highly skilled workforce and a strong manufacturing and technological base. They export manufactured goods, services, and investment funds. Their extremely large middle class makes them a good target for imported consumer goods. Canada, the United States, Japan, Australia, and members of the European Community are all industrialized nations. Much of Canada's economic development is in the area of automobile and recreational vehicle manufacturing, automobile parts manufacturing, telecommunications, and services.

CONSUMER ENVIRONMENT

In assessing the consumer environment, a company will look at how culture, language, and differences in needs and motivation will affect the development of global marketing strategies. Needless to say, there are significant variations from one part of the world to another. How a company interprets these differences is another matter.

CULTURE   Segmenting markets on the basis of culture is important in global marketing, since the values and beliefs people hold vary from nation to nation. While businesses must think globally, they must act locally. Failing to recognize cultural differences has resulted in marketing blunders by even the biggest corporations. The Chinese government, for example, banned a Nike television commercial that featured basketball sensation LeBron James. In the commercial James is seen in a video game defeating a kung fu master and a pair of dragons, an important symbol of traditional Chinese culture. "All ads must uphold national dignity and interest, and respect of the motherland's culture," according to regulations established by the Chinese government.[5]

It is critical that a marketer understand an audience's values, norms, and customs. But because of huge differences from one part of the world to another it is easy to see why marketing organizations sometimes invite disaster. China, for example, comprises two dozen distinct markets sprawling across 2000 cities. The values and language of the Chinese population vary from one province to another. Therefore, it is very difficult to use humour and sexual appeals in advertising in China—techniques that are quite common in North America. However, based on cultural values it is a good idea to place a high emphasis on group and family values. Even when directing messages at teens, advertisers should show a healthy respect for parental authority. Using the number four—a homonym for "death" in China—could spell death for the product.[6] For certain, marketing communications strategies must be adapted to local customs and preferences if the company is to be successful in a foreign market.

LANGUAGE   Language is the most obvious barrier to a global marketing program. A product name chosen to appeal to an English-speaking market must be replaced with something that will have greater effect in non–English speaking countries. In North America, for example, Lever markets a fabric softener under the brand name Snuggle. The brand name has connotations that Lever wanted to carry over into other markets. For this reason, the brand name has been changed to Fa Fa in Japan, and Cajoline in France. The packaging, the positioning, and the teddy bear mascot remain the same everywhere.

Very simple mistakes in judgment however, or carelessness in checking out local interpretations of names and phrases, have proven costly for many firms. Volkswagen's Vento went over well in Germany, but in Italy it had people holding their noses. To them, Vento means fart. During the summer Olympics in Sydney, Australians giggled at the Roots apparel worn by Canadian athletes. In Aussie slang, to root is to have sexual intercourse.[7] Roots will have to deal with brand-name issues if it ever expands to Australia.

Symbols are also a factor in communications, and they too pose problems for global marketing organizations. In China, the following symbols signify death: shooting stars, upright chopsticks, odd numbers, the number four, white handkerchiefs, and clocks and watches. These symbols should be excluded from any form of marketing communications.[8]

NEEDS AND MOTIVATION   Differences in consumers' needs and motivation for buying products make it difficult to establish marketing strategies that work globally. For example, McCain Foods Limited, a prominent Canadian-based company and global marketer, ran into all kinds of trouble trying to market frozen vegetables in South

Africa. Marketing Director Heather Partner put it this way: "White people have nannies or maids and they don't need to come home and grab something from the freezer. And black people don't eat frozen foods." There is a cultural distrust based on unfamiliarity with prepared foods among black South Africans. As well, about 30 percent of South Africans, virtually all of them black, live in communities without access to electricity.[9] Clearly, McCain's management misjudged South African consumers.

In contrast, numerous North American fast food restaurants such as McDonald's, KFC, and Pizza Hut have been readily accepted in Far East countries due to their understanding of local market needs and motivations. Their approach is to give local needs priority over global needs. McDonald's is a master at adapting itself to the idioms and mores of different climes. You can eat McFelafels in Egypt, an egg-topped McHuevos burger in Uruguay, and a McLuks salmon burger in Finland.[10] Rarely can a product be positioned uniformly around the world. Perhaps the Gillette Sensor razor is one of the exceptions (see Figure 19.2). Gillette Sensor has followed a common positioning strategy that emphasizes the technical features of the product (e.g., the razor senses and adjusts to the contours of an individual's face, providing a safe, comfortable shave) that should be important to men everywhere.

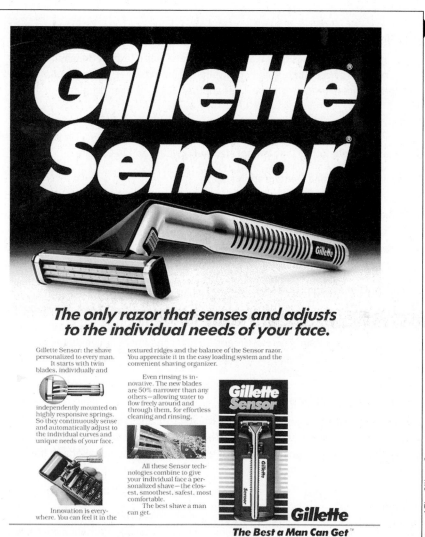

FIGURE
19.2

Global advertising strategy for the Gillette Sensor Razor

Courtesy of The Gillette Company.

For additional details and idiosyncrasies about the culture, language, and needs of global consumers, see Figure 19.3.

POLITICAL ENVIRONMENT

The political environment in a foreign country can shape trading policy and have a dramatic impact on a company's profitability. For example, a change in government could alter how a North American company operates in a foreign country. Such was the case for Coca-Cola in India in the late 1970s. A new government ordered Coca-Cola to dilute its investment in its Indian subsidiary and to turn over its secret formula. It was unthinkable that Coke would reveal its formula! Coke pulled up its stakes and quit India. One of its Indian bottlers then developed a cola-type product and called it Thums Up. The product caught on immediately and became a top seller in India.

In 1993, when the Indian government liberalized its economy and encouraged foreign investment, Coke returned and gained a commanding lead in the market by acquiring Thums Up. Coca-Cola was re-introduced in India as well, but to this day lags behind Thums Up in market share. Pepsi-Cola is the leading cola in India.[11] The politics in India over the years have had a harmful effect on the performance of Coca-Cola.

FIGURE
19.3

Some Facts and Oddities about Global Marketing

Market Segmentation

Heineken beer is positioned everywhere in the world (except Holland) as a premium-priced, high-quality brew. In its home market, it is a popular-priced brand and is perceived to be "just another beer" by beer drinkers.

Product and Package

In Britain, you can buy cold milk in cans in vending machines. Do you think that canned milk (other than evaporated milk) would sell in Canada?

Psychographics and Demographics

In most countries, psychographic analysis can be more revealing than demographics. Lifestyle-based research provides valuable insights into target-market opportunities. For example, Volvo designed a small, sporty coupe specifically for the European career woman. Is Canada ready for a sporty Volvo? Is this your image of Volvo?

Quality, Quality, and More Quality

Consumers around the world rate goods made in Japan, Germany, and the United States tops in quality, in that order. Canada ranks sixth behind both France and Britain. The poll among 20 000 consumers suggests the existence of "nation equity" or the perceived quality that countries' goods enjoy. (Source: Gallup Worldwide Poll, 1994)

Making Generalizations

Marketers cannot generalize about the Asia-Pacific region. Even within a country, consumers are not alike. In China, there are 60 different ethnic groups and 300 different dialects spoken. The northern Chinese tend to be taller and have long faces. Southern Chinese tend to be shorter and have rounder, fuller faces.

Know Your Customer

Doing business in China revolves around personal relationships. Getting to know your customer means getting to know them personally. Without a personal relationship, there is no business relationship.

TRADE BARRIERS   The purpose of a **trade barrier** is to protect a country from too much foreign competition within its borders. Canada and the United States, for example, believe that the automobile industry needs some form of protection. Consequently, only so many foreign-produced cars are allowed into these countries each year. Such a belief protects employment domestically. **Protectionism** is a belief that foreign trade should be restricted so that domestic industries can be preserved. The WTO disagrees with North America's view on protectionism as it applies to the automobile industry. Several cases are currently before international courts.

Even Canada and the United States have their trade disagreements in spite of the free trade agreement. The dispute between the two nations regarding Canadian softwood lumber shipments is a good example. Believing that Canadian government subsidies have lowered the price of our lumber below that of the United States, the U.S. government imposed a tariff (27.2 percent) on our exports to the U.S. Canada's position on the issue is clear: if we have a free trade agreement then we should be free traders.

To restrict trade, governments use tariffs, quotas, embargoes, and local content laws. A **tariff** is a tax or duty imposed on imported goods. In Canada, prices for domestically produced goods and services tend to be high, due to the high costs of labour, raw materials, and parts. In comparison, goods from Asian countries in such markets as toys, clothing, and electronics are produced at a much lower cost. To balance the price differences between imported and domestic products in these industries, Canada imposes a tariff on incoming foreign goods. The advantage of a tariff is that it can be specific in nature and protect particular industries, when needed (for example, see the Canada–U.S. dispute about software lumber described above).

A **quota** is a specific limit on the amount of goods that may be imported into a country. In Canada, precise quotas are placed on Japanese automobiles each year to restrict their penetration of the domestic market. In the late 1980s, several Japanese producers built Canadian production facilities as a means of circumventing quotas. Canada reacted and introduced local content laws. A **local content law** is another way of protecting local industry and employment. In this case, a foreign-based manufacturer is required to use a specified amount of locally produced components (car parts). Such a law could spur employment in the domestic auto parts industry.

An **embargo** disallows entry of specified products into a country. Concerns related to politics, health, and morality are frequently cited as the reasons for imposing embargoes. Canada Customs Agency is responsible for screening various products—pharmaceutical, chemical, food, and many others—as they enter the country. Products that do not meet standards are rejected. For example, toys from abroad that do not meet Canadian safety standards are rejected at the border.

Non-governmental organizations and groups can also impose embargoes in the form of a boycott. A **boycott** is an organized refusal to buy a specific product. Nike Watch, an organization supported by Oxfam Community Aid Abroad, encourages people to not buy Nike products because of the company's labour practices. Nike promotes healthy living, but the lives of the workers who make their shoes and clothes in Asia and Latin America are anything but healthy. Research indicates workers live in poverty and suffer stress and exhaustion due to overwork.[12] There is also a boycott against the IAMS Company, maker of IAMS and Eukanuba dog and cat foods. Apparently dogs and cats in company laboratories have suffered painful experiments to the point of death in the name of nutrition research.[13] Animal testing is a common practice in many companies (what are the alternatives?), but it remains a practice that many people object to.

trade barrier

protectionism

tariff

quota

local content law

embargo

boycott
Oxfam: Nike Watch
**www.oxfam.org.au/
campaigns/nike**

LEGAL AND REGULATORY ENVIRONMENT

Marketing organizations must know what they can and cannot do with a product in a foreign country. Awareness of local laws and regulations for packaging and advertising is crucial. In the Middle East, for example, advertisements can only show the product; in Austria, children cannot be used in advertisements.

Canada and the United States have their own idiosyncrasies that foreign marketers must deal with or that apply when the two countries are trading with each other. For instance, packaging in Canada must be bilingual. A firm manufacturing in the United States must develop separate packaging if it wishes to pursue the Canadian market. Canadian food companies must have separate packaging if they sell their products in the United States. The regulations that govern ingredient lists and nutritional guides vary in each country. Marketing a product—in either direction—is not as easy as simply sending shipments across the border.

TECHNOLOGICAL ENVIRONMENT

The technological environment in a country is influenced by the type of economy it has. For instance, a company that plans to organize a technologically based manufacturing operation in a non-industrialized country must do so with caution, for the available workforce may not have the education and skills required to run it. The foreign firm may have to commit to extensive training and development, which adds to the cost of operations. When the Japanese and South Korean automobile manufacturers built facilities in Canada, they had to deal with this situation to a certain extent. While Canada was knowledgeable in automobile manufacturing and its labour force was skilled, the foreign firms had to educate their Canadian employees in their management style and their way of doing business. Such integration of Canadian and foreign influence allowed the foreign organization to learn about Canadian culture, trade, consumers, and ways of doing business.

Of concern to Canadian companies is the increasing sophistication of technology, the speed at which technology is developed, and the fact that new technology, like competition, can originate from many places. Technology advancements in the Far East tend to be ahead of North America, so these countries will have a significant impact on Canada as we move further into the 21st century. To illustrate, a large majority of Japanese consumers currently use hand-held personal digital assistants (multi-purpose devices), whereas Canadians and Americans are only at the early growth stage with this technology. Japan and other Asian countries are well ahead of North America in moving to a wireless communications world.

COMPETITIVE ENVIRONMENT

Firms that market globally are aware of the developments that affect the global economy generally. These influences include cartels, orderly market agreements, and common markets.

cartel

A **cartel** is a group of firms or countries that band together to conduct trade in a manner similar to a monopoly. The purpose of a cartel is to improve the bargaining position of its members in the world market. One of the world's most influential cartels in recent times is the Organization of Petroleum Exporting Countries (OPEC), which comprises 13 oil-producing nations from around the world. OPEC countries can restrict the supply of oil, a resource that is in high demand in other nations, thereby forcing the price up. The higher prices affect the economy of an importing country, because any increase in oil price is added to the cost of manufacturing in that country. This means that consumers ultimately pay more for the products they purchase.

Organization of Petroleum Exporting
Countries (OPEC)
www.opec.org

An **orderly market agreement** is an agreement by which nations share a market, eliminating the trade barriers between them. The free trade agreement among Canada, the United States, and Mexico (NAFTA) is an example of an orderly market agreement because it allows the markets to become open to industries on both sides of the border.

A **common market** is a regional or geographical group of countries that agree to limit trade barriers among members and apply a common tariff to goods from non-member countries. The European Union, referred to earlier in this chapter, is an example of a common market. Gradually, the trade barriers that had existed between its members were removed and all countries agreed to a common currency—the euro. Unique marketing strategies will be needed for Canadian companies wanting to do business in this region.

Strategies for Entering Global Markets

Companies pursuing international opportunities must decide how to enter the various markets. Some of the strategies for doing so include direct investments and acquisitions, joint ventures, and indirect and direct exports (Figure 19.4).

DIRECT INVESTMENT AND ACQUISITIONS

Direct investment refers to a company's financial commitment in a foreign country whereby the investing company owns and operates, in whole or in part, the manufacturing or retailing facility in that foreign country. In many cases a company will acquire an existing business instead of investing in startup operations. Jean Coutu, a leading drugstore chain based in Quebec, recently acquired more than 1500 Eckerd drugstores in the U.S. from J.C. Penny at a cost of US$2.4 billion. Coutu is now the largest drugstore chain in Canada and the fourth largest in the United States. Several prominent Canadian retailers have failed in the United States: Canadian Tire, Shoppers Drug Mart, and Marks Work Wearhouse are among them. Drugstore growth in the U.S. of 35 percent over the past five years (twice that of the retail sector generally) got Coutu's attention.[14]

Acquisition strategies allow a firm quick entry into a foreign market. As well, a company will avoid the cost of developing new products and the need to invest heavily in marketing to create an awareness of new products in that country. Coutu plans to retain the Eckerd brand name but has new ideas to improve marketing and merchandising strategies.

orderly market agreement

common market

4. Describe the business strategies commonly used by firms entering foreign markets.

direct investment

FIGURE 19.4

Strategies for Entering Global Markets

Export	Joint Ventures	Direct Investments
Direct	Licensing	Manufacturing Facilities
Indirect	Contract Manufacturing	Assembly Facilities
	International Franchising	

Risk
Commitment ————————————→
Control

Risk, commitment, and control increase as a marketing organization moves from simply exporting goods to a foreign country to actually manufacturing the goods in a foreign country.

JOINT VENTURES

In a global context, a **joint venture** is a partnership between a domestic company and a foreign company. Such an arrangement allows a company to produce and market in a foreign country at a lower cost and with less risk to itself than would be the case if it undertook a venture on its own. Even the largest of companies are pursuing joint ventures to reduce the costs of expansion. The partnership of General Motors and Toyota, producing small cars in a California production facility, is an instance of a joint venture between two large multinational corporations. The foreign partner, in this case Toyota, can take advantage of the domestic company's knowledge of the country's culture, lifestyles, and business practices.

Krispy Kreme expanded into Canada through a joint venture. Krispy Kreme usually takes a 35-percent stake in the joint venture, with foreign franchisees investing 65 percent.[15] The luxurious Four Seasons Hotel chain, a Canadian company, has expanded through joint ventures. The hotel retains a small equity position in its properties but has numerous long-term partners including Quinlan Private, an Irish property and investment fund.[16]

Other options for shared enterprises are licensing, franchising, and contract manufacturing.

LICENSING **Licensing** is the granting of a temporary agreement allowing a company (the licensee) to use the trademark, patent, copyright, or manufacturing process of another company (the licenser). In this type of agreement, the licensee assumes most of the financial risk. In return for the licence, the source company is paid a royalty. Labatt Breweries of Canada has been marketing Carlsberg beer (a Danish beer) in Canada under licence for 15 years. Carlsberg recently decided not to renew the agreement, stating it wanted to establish a stronger presence in Canada. Carlsberg will market the beer while contracting out the brewing to Moosehead Breweries Ltd., another Canadian brewery.[17]

INTERNATIONAL FRANCHISING International franchising is the same as domestic market franchising, except that it is done in other countries. Major fast-food chains, such as McDonald's, Burger King, and Wendy's, have franchise networks in many nations. In many cases, the products have to be adapted to conform to local tastes if the company is to be successful. In other cases, consumers in foreign countries gradually accept the taste of the original food. The Second Cup, a coffee chain owned by Cara Operations Limited (a Canadian company) expanded to the Middle East through franchise agreements. Cara signed a master franchise agreement with Binhendi Group, a Middle Eastern food and fashion retailer. Second Cup has opened outlets in Saudi Arabia, Egypt, Bahrain, and Syria.[18]

For insight into how a Calgary-based bakery expanded into Asia, read the Marketing in Action vignette **Cinnzeo Heads East, Far East**.

CONTRACT MANUFACTURING **Contract manufacturing** occurs when a manufacturer stops producing a good domestically, preferring to find a foreign country that can produce the good according to its specifications. Typically, the original firm will seek a nation where labour and raw material costs are lower. In most cases, such initiatives are taken because the costs of manufacturing in the domestic country are too high. Even though the good is produced elsewhere, the same brand name appears on the product. Nike and Levi Strauss, for example, are prominent U.S. companies that produce their goods in the Far East. Often accused of sweatshop production practices, both companies have to defend their respective positions on where and how goods are produced via public relations programs.

joint venture

licensing

The Second Cup
www.secondcup.com

contract manufacturing

MARKETING IN ACTION

Cinnzeo Heads East, Far East

The likelihood of a Calgary-based bakery becoming an international franchise operation seems improbable if not impossible. But that's just what happened to Cinnaroll Bakeries Ltd. In just five years, it has expanded from a handful of cinnamon retail outlets in Western Canadian malls to the world's second largest cinnamon roll franchisor.

Founding partners Brian Latham and Barry Wolton now face the daunting challenge of developing and implementing a marketing strategy to guide their fast-growing cinnamon bun empire, Revenues at the end of 2002 were $20 million. There are more than 150 franchise outlets, with the most recent openings being in Beirut, Saudi Arabia, Qatar, and Kuwait.

The basic expansion strategy involves working with master franchisees. On this basis, Cinnzeo has commitments to open 130 new outlets in the Middle East, China, Southeast Asia, California, and Texas. There are also plans to expand eastward in Canada. You would think that Cinnzeo would have developed the Canadian market first, but their second franchise was actually in Manila—and that's what started the international ball rolling.

How did it all happen? Latham and Wolton owned 18 franchises of another chain called Cinnabon. Seeing significant potential in terms of expansion, they sold out and opened their own chain called Cinnzeo. Once established in the West, the plan was to gradually move eastward—in Canada, that is.

Out of the blue, they received a letter from a group of Filipino businessmen who had seen a franchise in Vancouver. So impressed were they with what they saw, they wanted the franchise rights for the Philippines. Skeptical at first, the partners trekked east and soon discovered a country of 68 million people with the world's largest middle class—an opportunity they couldn't pass up. Other franchise food businesses were flourishing there. In fact another Canadian bakery, Saint Cinnamon, was already there.

In negotiating a franchise deal, the Filipino partners wanted a different look for the stores. In Canada, the indoor mall locations called for a small, functional design and a rather spartan look. In the Philippines, it would be street-front locations, a Starbuck's café environment, and a design and look that would include comfortable seating and piped-in music. The product would remain the same.

Today, Cinnzeo is the leading cinnamon bun maker in the Philippines. Latham credits its strategy of "adapting its franchise to local market needs" for its success. In terms of marketing, they haven't done much—they have relied on word of mouth and their website. The company supports the brand with slogans, uniforms, and a consistent store décor: colours, wood, and brass. Specific advertising campaigns are left to franchisees.

The Cinnzeo empire is expanding quickly—as are the waistlines of some of its customers. Experts admire the company's strategy of working with local market master franchisees. "International business people are well-traveled and they know what opportunities will work at home." They often succeed where many traditional franchises that do everything on their own have failed. Second Cup, for example, met with failure while trying to expand in the U.S.

For now, Cinnzeo continues to get franchise inquiries from all over the world—a sure sign of success!

Adapted from Norma Ramage, "Battle of the buns," *Marketing*, September 2, 2002, pp. 10, 11; and Norma Ramage, "Canadian cinnamon buns savoured in Asia," *Marketing*, May 15, 2001, p. 6.

Courtesy of Cinnaroll Bakeries Limited.

The contract manufacturing option saves the company money. It avoids any direct investment in the producing nation, while capitalizing on, for example, its low labour rates.

INDIRECT AND DIRECT EXPORTING

There are two forms of exporting available to a company: direct and indirect. The difference is in the distribution strategy each form entails. A company using **indirect exporting** employs an intermediary or trading company that specializes in international marketing to establish a distribution system for its goods in the foreign country. Generally, the intermediary works for a commission. In terms of control, the foreign company has very little. This is usually an attractive option for firms that are new to the global market scene.

A company using **direct exporting** usually strikes agreements directly with local market companies, which would be responsible for distribution in that country. Basically, the company itself performs the role of the intermediary. An export division or export sales force often becomes part of an organization's structure and is responsible for developing the distribution network. The foreign company faces a greater risk than does a company pursuing indirect exporting, but it has greater control over the distribution process.

Global Marketing Strategy

Does a firm develop specific strategies for each country, or does it use a common strategy in all countries where its products are available? In the past, the tendency was to specialize by giving consideration to the unique characteristics and tendencies of local markets. Then, in the 1980s and 1990s, there was a movement toward the use of global marketing strategies, a trend that is expected to continue.

In its purest sense, **global marketing strategy** is taking one brand and marketing it exactly the same way around the world. The growing popularity of global marketing strategies suggests that advancing technology in communications and distribution has created markets for standardized products; everyone everywhere wants the same things. The global approach enables a company to enjoy economies of scale in production and marketing expenditures, particularly in the areas of advertising, distribution, and management. BMW (luxury automobiles), and Nike (sporting goods and accessories), for example, are global brands because they stand for the same things in every country.

If a firm uses a **country-centred strategy**, it develops a unique marketing strategy for each foreign market it enters. It does so because of the unique needs, values, and beliefs of consumers in that market. Such an approach does add to the marketing costs of an organization.

A more common practice is referred to as **glocalization**—the creation of products and services intended for the global market but customized to suit a local culture. In other words, it does not completely use one marketing strategy or the other. Cadbury is a leading brand of chocolate around the world. It uses all of the usual marketing tools to promote its confectionary brands while acknowledging local tastes. "We run our business on a regional not global basis and tailor our products and marketing strategies to the local markets." Cadbury has been particularly successful in markets such as Russia and China, where chocolate preference is less established.[19]

When determining which strategy to use, answers are required for three basic questions:

indirect exporting

direct exporting

5. Describe the nature of marketing strategies used by firms seeking global market opportunities.

global marketing strategy

country-centred strategy

glocalization

1. How does market development differ from one country to another?
2. Do the needs of consumers vary from country to country?
3. Are the characteristics of the target-market profile different?

The Kellogg's experience with bran flakes serves as an example to show the importance of these questions. Kellogg's attempt to market bran flakes in Asia was a futile one because the customer expects to have rice-based products for breakfast. As well, hot cereal is preferred over cold cereal. Kellogg's had not considered the needs and values of the Chinese market.

In contrast, Starbucks has been a huge success in Asia, where it has 250 stores in 10 countries—countries that, traditionally, are better known for tea drinking. The Starbucks brand carries a cachet of wealth, success, and status that is attractive to an emerging Asian middle class willing to pay a premium price for a cup of coffee. The chain's chic interiors and sturdy wooden tables—the decor is nearly identical to that in North America—is a sharp contrast to familiar tea stalls and smoky cafés.[20]

PRODUCT

When it comes to global product strategy, a company has three options: to market a standardized product in all markets, to adapt the product to suit local markets, or to develop a new product.

Using **standardized products** in all markets can be a successful strategy. Products such as cell phones, digital cameras, and even automobiles can be essentially the same regardless of the country they are marketed in. Even fast-food marketers such as McDonald's and KFC find that many foreign markets are accepting of American fare. They do, however, add local dishes to their menus to round out their offerings.

Adapting a product to local tastes and preferences is common in the fast-food industry. Different ingredients may be used to make a fairly uniform product more attractive to local customers. Coca-Cola's formula is a secret, but there are about a dozen versions of it around the world. Did you know that the Canadian formula is seven calories sweeter than the U.S. version?[21] In Indonesia, KFC serves rice with its chicken meals, which Indonesians prefer to mashed potatoes, and all of its food is certified *halal,* or prepared in accordance with Islamic dietary law.[22]

The final alternative, **developing a new product**, is the most costly. A company employs such a strategy only when its market analysis indicates the existence of a sizable market opportunity. This strategy presents a high degree of risk, because the company may not fully understand the needs and customs of the local market in different countries. The assistance of local marketing consultants is essential to ensure that development heads in the right direction.

In the packaged-goods arena, the cost of building a brand is very high so the value of an existing brand name is important. If a brand can be extended to foreign markets, the development and marketing costs are spread over a larger market. Strong brands should be used in as many markets as possible and weak brands should be replaced if a stronger name is available. In Canada, for example, PepsiCo eliminated the Hostess potato chip brand in favour of its Frito-Lay brand name, one that is popular in the United States and other countries. The impact of U.S.–based marketing programs for Frito-Lay can be seen and heard by customers in Canada. For more insight into what constitutes a truly global brand name, refer to Figure 19.5.

PRICE

Among the factors affecting price are local competition, dumping, tariffs, and the value of currency. McCain Foods Limited of Florenceville, New Brunswick, the world's biggest

FIGURE
19.5

**Characteristics of Truly
Global Brands**

Source: Adapted from "The Top 100
Brands," *Business Week*, August 2, 2004,
www.businessweek.com.

The Top 10 Global Brands

The top brands globally have a decidedly North American bent, with only Finland's Nokia and Germany's Mercedes making it into the elite group.

Rank	Brand	Value US$ Billions	Origin
1	Coca-Cola	$70.5	U.S.
2	Microsoft	$65.2	U.S.
3	IBM	$51.8	U.S.
4	GE	$42.3	U.S.
5	Intel	$31.1	U.S.
6	Nokia	$29.4	Finland
7	Disney	$28.0	U.S.
8	McDonald's	$24.7	U.S.
9	Marlboro	$22.2	U.S.
10	Mercedes	$21.4	Germany

The characteristics of great global brands are many; here are a few. A strong global brand

- Has leadership at home
- Is associated with its country of origin
- Has a compelling platform that propels it beyond domestic borders
- Is ever-renewing and is tailored to local markets
- Is obsessed with innovation
- Makes money

producer of frozen french fries, found that it had to lower prices in order to penetrate the American market. The sheer size and reputation of McCain meant nothing to food service customers.

Dumping is the practice of selling goods in a foreign market at a price lower than they are sold for in the domestic market. Used as a means of penetrating foreign markets, it is judged by most countries to be an unfair practice, since it can undermine domestic companies and the workforce they employ. To protect themselves against such undermining and to maintain a reasonable level of competition between foreign and domestic marketers, countries impose *tariffs* (see earlier discussion).

The value of the Canadian dollar in relation to foreign currencies also has an impact on the level of demand for Canadian goods. When its value is low in relation to the American dollar, the prices for our goods are more attractive to American buyers; therefore, demand for Canadian goods increases, and exports to the United States increase. Conversely, if the Canadian dollar rises in relation to the American dollar, the prices of our goods are less attractive than those of American products or other foreign products; therefore, demand for Canadian goods decreases. The present value of the Canadian dollar in relation to the American dollar has a significant impact on our positive trade balance with the United States.

Mars Inc. used a unique pricing strategy when it entered the Russian market. The disintegration of the Soviet Union threw open a vast Russian market hungry for consumer goods. Without government subsidies Russian factories sat idle, and there was

dumping

no production of chocolate at all. Despite a volatile political landscape, Mars forged ahead into Russia with Mars Bars, Milky Way, and Snickers. While many Western companies offer goods only for hard currency, Mars sold its products for rubles. Each bar cost about 300 rubles (US30¢). For Russians, chocolate bars were among the most affordable Western status symbols.

MARKETING COMMUNICATIONS

While a product may be suited for worldwide distribution, it is very difficult to promote it in a uniform manner everywhere. In similar markets, such as the Canadian and American markets, a uniform promotion can be successfully implemented, but regional differences will often dictate that alternative strategies be used. Since organizations like to protect their brand image, it is common for standard communications to be made available for foreign markets. Regional or local managers often decide if and how such communications are employed.

On a more worldly scale, marketing communications is not that simple. Because of the differences in language and culture around the world, companies often adapt a communications strategy to meet local tastes. Standardized advertising is effective only if consumers think, act, and buy in the same manner.

Language poses the main challenge to global advertising. When KFC entered China it wanted to use the famous slogan "Finger-lickin' good"—which, when translated to Chinese, read as "So good you will eat your fingers off." Ouch! Perdue Chickens, entering the Mexican market, attempted to translate the phrase "It takes a tough man to make a tender chicken." The result: "It takes a virile man to make a chicken aroused." So much for that idea![23] Today, there is a movement toward globalization in the advertising industry, since most large advertising firms now have offices or subsidiaries around the world to help multinational clients adapt their advertising to local ways. Appropriateness is the key element of the global advertising equation.

The Philips ads that appear in Figures 19.6 and 19.7 are executions of a global advertising strategy that is designed to inform consumers that Philips is more than a home electronics company. The ad includes a new theme line—"Sense and simplicity"—which replaces the longstanding theme of "Let's make things better." For more insight into this global campaign, read the Marketing in Action vignette **Philips's Global Ad Campaign Repositions Company.**

DISTRIBUTION

Firms generally secure distribution in international markets in two ways. They either use existing channels employing intermediaries, or they introduce new channels; their choice depends on the needs of the marketing organization. If it chooses existing channels, a firm may employ a trading company in the home country, making it responsible for distributing goods to other distributors and to final users in the foreign country. Wal-Mart's expansion into Hong Kong, China, and Japan would not have happened had it not formed a partnership agreement with a trading company in Hong Kong and existing department stores in China and Japan.

A company may also decide to use a specialized sales force of its own that sells directly to existing foreign-market agents, distributors, or final users (Figure 19.8). On the other hand, new channels of distribution can be developed. To illustrate, two North American fast-food outlets, McDonald's and KFC, have successfully extended their distribution strategies into the European and Asian markets. The acceptance of superstores (stores selling groceries and general merchandise under one roof) in the United States and Canada is an example of European distribution systems working in North America.

Philips's Global Ad Campaign Repositions Company

Royal Philips Electronics N.V is a huge company based in the Netherlands. The company offers a diverse range of products in several market segments: consumer electronics, lightbulbs, electric shavers and other personal-care appliances, picture tubes, semiconductors, and medical systems. Consumer electronics and appliances account for about a third of the company's sales. Worldwide sales (2003) amount to $36.5 billion, with net income being $873 million.

The general perception the public holds about Philips is that it is a consumer electronics company: its brand name is well known. The primary objective of Philips's new advertising campaign is to alter perceptions held and make the public aware of the other markets the company is involved in. Philips allocated 80 million euros (US$97.5 million) toward the effort.

The new campaign employs a new theme line, "Sense and simplicity," which replaces the longstanding "Let's make things better."

According to Andrea Ragnetti, chief marketing officer, "The brand campaign will help us tell the world we are a different company than most of our observers think." She says "We are too well known for consumer electronics, there are other businesses to grow."

In the United States alone Philips employs more than 20 000 people, but it is a region of the world where awareness of the Philips brand is by far the lowest. It is a brand better regarded in Europe and Asia. Currently, Philips markets high-end televisions in the U.S. under the Philips name and low-priced models under the Magnavox name.

Lee Garfinkel, chairman and chief creative officer at DDB, the agency that developed the campaign, says "We set out to create a more human connection, to keep the message basic, keep it real, and keep it sensible." One of the initial television commercials, for example, shows a box being opened by an assortment of hands from off-screen, while voiceovers take turns saying things like, "I see technology that is humanity," and "I see technology that doesn't make me feel inadequate," The spot concludes with the line, "I see technology as simple as the box it comes in."

Most of the products and markets that Philips competes in are featured in the pool of advertisements. Another commercial features flat-screen televisions and promotes a model that projects a colourful glow on the wall that matches the colours on the screen. This unique technology was the brainchild of two Philips divisions: consumer electronics and lighting.

Strategically placed, all of the ads run together in a short period so that people will know about Philips on many different levels. The campaign is aimed primarily at affluent business executives, 35 to 55 years old, who make purchase decisions for their companies.

The "Sense and simplicity" line is one element of a much broader campaign, but is an accurate reflection of a company that has both widened its product range while streamlining its products to meet consumer needs. The company wants to simplify things for customers who say the world is "too complex." Two of the company's ads appear in Figures 19.6 and 19.7.

Adapted from Nat Ives, "Philips widens its product range," *The New York Times*, September 18, 2004, www.nytimes.com.

Courtesy of Philips Electronics Ltd.

Courtesy of Philips Electronics Ltd.

FIGURE 19.6

An execution of Philips's global advertising strategy

FIGURE
19.7

**A second execution of
Philips's global advertising
strategy**

Since shipping overseas involves water transportation, the port facilities of foreign-market destinations are an important consideration in distribution planning. For instance, some ports are unequipped to load and unload containerized ships, a circumstance that makes water transportation impractical for some countries. Distribution capabilities must be evaluated when a company is considering marketing products in other countries.

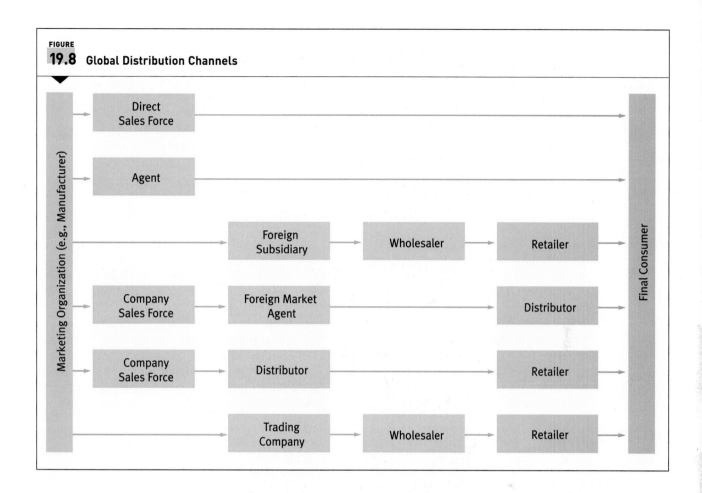

FIGURE 19.8   Global Distribution Channels

SUMMARY

As Canadian businesses move into the new century, more and more emphasis will be placed on regional marketing and global marketing. Such factors as the North American Free Trade Agreement, the European Union, and the development in Pacific Rim countries represent new challenges for Canadian marketing organizations.

To analyze global market opportunities, a marketing organization considers a host of factors, including the economy, culture, language barriers, varying consumer needs, politics, laws and regulations, technology, and competition in countries where potential markets exist. Before entering a foreign market, a firm must understand that market if it is to develop appropriate marketing strategies for penetrating it.

Several options are available to a firm that is going into an international market. Among the more common strategies are direct investment and acquisition, and such joint ventures as partnerships, licensing agreements, franchising, and contract manufacturing. Exporting goods indirectly through intermediaries or directly by the company are other options.

As it does in domestic marketing, a company that is developing a marketing strategy for a foreign market employs the elements of the marketing mix: product, price, marketing communications, and distribution. The company can either use a global strategy, in which, a standardized product is marketed in a uniform manner in all markets where it is available, or a country-centred strategy, in which case the marketing mix is tailored to the specific needs of individual countries. Often, a firm combines the best elements of both and implements a strategy referred to as glocalization.

KEY TERMS

REVIEW QUESTIONS

1. What is the difference between an absolute advantage and a comparative advantage?
2. How does knowledge of a nation's stage of economic development assist a global marketer?
3. Why do countries impose trade barriers?
4. What is the difference between the following trade barriers?
   a) Tariff
   b) Quota
   c) Embargo
5. What is the difference between a cartel and an orderly market agreement?
6. What is a joint venture, and what benefits does it provide participants?
7. Distinguish between licensing and contract manufacturing as strategies for pursuing global market opportunities.
8. What is the difference between a global marketing strategy and a country-centred marketing strategy?
9. What does glocalization refer to? Briefly explain.

DISCUSSION AND APPLICATION QUESTIONS

1. "Because of the cultural differences that exist from nation to nation, marketing communications strategies must be tailored to each country." Discuss the validity of this statement.
2. Are Canadian corporations likely targets for takeover by foreign-based companies? Conduct some secondary research about acquisition strategies by foreign companies prior to reaching any conclusions. Present your views on this statement.
3. If you were marketing a soft drink, such as Pepsi-Cola or 7-Up, in Latin America, what factors would you consider when developing a marketing strategy?

E-ASSIGNMENT

In this exercise, you will conduct a Web-based secondary investigation to determine the market potential of entering a foreign country.

Situation: You are the brand manager for a specific product (conduct some research and pick one) at one of the following Canadian companies:

McCain Foods
Roots
Maple Leaf Foods

Your first task is to identify relevant aspects of the marketing strategy used in Canada. In other words, develop a brief profile for product strategy, price strategy, marketing communications strategy, and distribution strategy. Also identify what the primary target market is.

The second task is to conduct appropriate secondary research to assess the potential of marketing your product in a foreign country (a country of your choice). You must identify the challenges and opportunities that exist and then identify relevant factors that will influence your marketing strategy. What elements of the Canadian marketing strategy will be retained, and what elements will have to change? Present your findings in a brief report.

ENDNOTES

1. Norihiko Shirouzu and Todd Zaun, "Japanese car firms focus on U.S." *Globe and Mail*, January 6, 2003, pp. B1, B9.

2. Matthew Garrahan, "Four Seasons looks east," *Financial Post*, November 26, 2004, p. FP6.

3. www.wto.org/wto/inbrief.

4. Philip Kotler, Gordon McDougall, and Gary Armstrong, *Marketing*, Canadian Edition (Toronto: Prentice-Hall Canada Inc., 1988), p. 424.

5. Geoffrey Fowler, "Cultural evolution," *Financial Post*, December 8, 2004, p. FP7.

6. "Two Chinas," *Advertising Age*, August 16, 2004, pp. 1, 22.

7. John Heinzl, "Brand names that can't cross the border," *Globe and Mail*, December 22, 2000, p. B12.

8. Ronnie Lipton, "Symbols to avoid like death," *Strategy*, September 23, 2002, p. 24.

9. Stephanie Nolan, "McCain learns tough lesson of culture in S. Africa," *Globe and Mail*, October 21, 2004, www.globeandmail.com.

10. Jeet Heer and Steve Penfold, "Fast Food Celebrates Regional Differences," *National Post*, February 15, 2003, pp. B1, B4.

11. Manjeet Kripilani and Mark Clifford, "Finally, Coke gets it right," *Business Week*, February 10, 2003, p. 47.

12. www.oxfam.org.au/campaigns/nike/.

13. www.iamskills.com/index.shtml.

14. Bernadette Marotte, "Coutu takes on fortress Retail, USA," *Globe and Mail*, September 4, 2004, p. B5.

15. Betty Liu, "Sugarles donut for Krispy Kreme?" *Financial Post*, March 16, 2004, pp. FP1, FP14.

16. Matthew Garrahan, "Four Seasons looks east," *Financial Post*, November 26, 2004, p. FP6.

17. Rob Ferguson, "Labatt, Carlsberg hoist last brew," *Toronto Star*, December 2, 2003, www.thestar.com.

18. Hollie Shaw, "Second Cup chain expands to the Mideast," *Financial Post*, July 26, 2002, p. FP7.

19. Stephanie Margolin, "The Chocolate Market Unwrapped," www.brandchannel.com, May 5, 2003.

20. Ginny Parker, "Starbucks finds Asia a vast, thirsty market," *Globe and Mail*, May 29, 2000, p. B6.

21. Murray Campbell, "Asterix promoting McBurgers in France," *Toronto Star*, January 24, 2002, p. A3.

22. Cris Prystay, "KFC puts focus on values," *Globe and Mail*, April 3, 2003, p. B11.

23. John Heinzl, p. B12.

The Financial Implications of Marketing Practice

The objective of this appendix is to illustrate the financial implications of marketing decisions. Readers must recognize that marketing actions and results are measured quantitatively. It can be said that marketing actions directly affect the financial well-being of an organization.

This appendix presents some of the key financial areas for marketing managers; namely, the operating statement and the balance sheet (plus the various ratios obtained from these) and markups and markdowns.

Operating Statement

One of the major financial statements of an organization is the operating statement, often referred to as an income statement or a profit-and-loss statement. It shows whether a business achieved its primary objective—earning a profit. A profit or net income is earned when revenues exceed expenses (losses occur when expenses exceed revenues).

Revenues are inflows of cash or other properties received in exchange for goods or services provided to customers. Expenses are goods and services consumed in operating a business. From the various figures included in an operating statement, ratios are calculated and reviewed so that the financial performance of the firm can be assessed. For the purposes of analysis and control, the marketer can relate each component of an operating statement to sales. Operating statements are used for comparative purposes. For example, the ratios on the latest statement can be compared with past ratios or with planned ratios for a given period. The analysis of ratios indicates problems that management may try to correct through marketing and financial decisions.

Important Components of the Operating Statement

SALES

The top line of any operating statement is sales; in the sample statement for KJT Enterprises, the top lines are gross sales and net sales. The level of sales is influenced by numerous marketing decisions, such as pricing strategy and the budget allocated to generate sales. Returns and allowances must be deducted from gross revenues, as net sales are the actual revenues received by the firm. Returns and allowances include returned merchandise (i.e., faulty or damaged products) and partial refunds or rebates to the customer. Since customer service is an important element of the marketing process, an organization should not view returns and allowances negatively. How product returns are handled has a direct impact on the level of customer satisfaction.

COST OF GOODS SOLD

The cost of goods sold in a manufacturing organization includes the costs of work in process and the inventory costs of raw materials and finished goods. In a retailing environment, cost of goods sold refers to the value of inventory offered for sale. Firms attempt to minimize the cost of goods sold, wherever possible. The lower the cost of goods sold, the higher is the gross profit.

OPERATING EXPENSES

These expenses are costs other than the merchandise costs and inventory costs cited in the cost-of-goods-sold explanation. Typically, operating expenses include marketing or selling expenses (advertising, sales expenses, and other related expenses), general expenses (rent, salaries, utilities, telephone, and so on) and interest expense. The objective of the firm is to control such expenses as much as possible, thereby improving profitability.

Let us assume that the operating statement for KJT Enterprises, Inc. is as follows:

Operating Statement
as at December 31, 200X

	$ Value	% of Net Sales
Gross Sales	820 000	102.5
Less: Returns and Allowances	20 000	2.5
Net Sales	800 000	100.0
Less: Cost of Goods Sold	480 000	60.0
Gross Profit	320 000	40.0
Less: Operating Expenses	200 000	25.0
Net Profit before Tax	120 000	15.0
Income Tax	40 000	5.0
Net Profit after Tax	80 000	10.0

THE OPERATING STATEMENT AND RATIO ANALYSIS

These ratios are worthy of explanation:

1. *Gross Profit Percentage*—This percentage indicates the average profit margin on all merchandise sold during a period. Such information can be compared with past results, with a plan for the year, or with industry averages, if such information is known. If margins are too far above or below industry averages, it may indicate a cost problem or a pricing problem in the firm.
2. *Operating Expense Ratio*—This ratio is needed to control individual expense categories and to evaluate performance. Ratios in this area have a direct relation to marketing activity, since marketing budgets are included in operating expenses. The challenge for managers is to minimize operating expenses (lower the ratio) while maximizing sales.
3. *Net Profit Percentage*—This is a ratio that takes into account prices, costs, and all other expenses and is, therefore, a reflection of the firm's bottom-line profit. Since the bottom-line profit is often used to determine the objectives of the firm, it is a figure scrutinized very closely by managers, shareholders, and potential investors. The net profit percentage clearly relates the quality of a firm's decisions to the revenue it generates. Decisions that reduce costs and expenses while maintaining or increasing sales revenue have a positive effect on the net profit percentage.

The ratios for the sample operating statement for KJT Enterprises are calculated by means of the following formula:

Operating ratio $= \dfrac{\text{\$Value of Component}}{\text{Net Sales}} \times 100\%$

Each ratio compares a particular component with sales, the actual amount of revenue received by KJT Enterprises.

Therefore,

Cost of Goods Sold	=	$\dfrac{\text{Cost of Goods Sold}}{\text{Net Sales}} \times 100\%$
	=	$\dfrac{480\ 000}{800\ 000} \times 100\%$
	=	60%
and, Gross Profit	=	$\dfrac{\text{Gross Profit}}{\text{Net Sales}} \times 100\%$
	=	$\dfrac{320\ 000}{800\ 000} \times 100\%$
	=	40%
and, Operating Expenses	=	$\dfrac{\text{Operating Expenses}}{\text{Net Sales}} \times 100\%$
	=	$\dfrac{200\ 000}{800\ 000} \times 100\%$
	=	25%
and, Net Profit before Tax	=	$\dfrac{\text{Net Profit before Tax}}{\text{Net Sales}} \times 100\%$
	=	$\dfrac{120\ 000}{800\ 000} \times 100\%$
	=	15%
and, Net Profit after Tax	=	$\dfrac{\text{Net Profit after Tax}}{\text{Net Sales}} \times 100\%$
	=	$\dfrac{80\ 000}{800\ 000} \times 100\%$
	=	10%
	=	27.9%

KJT Enterprises would compare the above ratios with those of a plan or those of past years to determine if the financial results are satisfactory.

Balance Sheet

The purpose of a balance sheet is to show the financial position of a business on a specific date. The financial position is shown by listing the assets of the business, its liabilities or debts, and the equity of the owners. The balance sheet of an organization allows an organization to evaluate its earnings in a given period against the amount of money invested in the organization. Managers, therefore, assess ratios from both the profit-and-loss statement and the balance sheet.

Assume that the balance sheet for KJT Enterprises is as follows:

BALANCE SHEET
as at December 31, 200X

Assets	
Cash	$200 000
Accounts Receivable	100 000
Inventory	100 000
Facilities	200 000
Equipment	50 000
Total Assets	650 000
Liabilities	
Accounts Payable	120 000
Long-term Liabilities	100 000
Total Liabilities	220 000
Owner's Equity	
Capital	330 000
Retained Earnings	100 000
Total Owner's Equity	430 000
Total Liabilities and Owner's Equity	650 000

THE BALANCE SHEET AND RATIO ANALYSIS

RETURN ON INVESTMENT (ROI) This ratio compares earnings directly against investment in a particular year. Return on investment is calculated using the formula:

$$\text{ROI} = \frac{\text{Net Profit (Net Income)}}{\text{Average Assets}} \times 100\%$$

AVERAGE ASSETS Therefore, following the sample statements of KJT Enterprises, Inc., the calculation would be:

$$\text{ROI} = \frac{120\ 000}{650\ 000} \times 100\%$$

$$= 18.5\%$$

For the purposes of this calculation, the net profit before taxes was compared with the value of the firm's assets at the end of the period. Another way to look at the 18.5 percent ROI percentage is to say that for every dollar of assets held by the firm, there was a return of 18.5 cents. These figures, like those derived from the operating statement, can be compared with past years, plans, or industry averages.

RETURN ON EQUITY (ROE)   This ratio compares the firm's earnings directly with the amount of money an owner has invested in the business, an amount called owner's equity. Return on equity is calculated using the formula:

$$\text{ROE} = \frac{\text{Net Profit}}{\text{Owner's Equity}} \times 100\%$$

OWNERS' EQUITY   Therefore, using the sample statements of KJT Enterprises, Inc., the calculation would be:

$$\text{ROE} = \frac{120\ 000}{430\ 000} \times 100\%$$

$$= 27.9\%$$

This figure can be used by the organization to assess the worth of the investment. If the return on equity is below that of potential returns on bank deposits and certificates, the firm would question the value of being in business. On the other hand, if the ratio is very high, effort could be put into growth and expansion plans for the business.

Markups and Markdowns

Markups and markdowns are a form of financial analysis commonly used by members of a channel of distribution (wholesalers and retailers).

MARKUPS

A markup involves adding a predetermined amount to the cost of a product to determine a selling price. If a product costs $10.00 and sells for $14.00, the difference between the two prices is the markup. Markup is the difference between selling price and the cost. Markups can be expressed as:

$$\text{Markup} = \text{Retail Price} - \text{Cost}$$
$$\text{or}$$
$$\text{Cost} + \text{Markup} = \text{Retail Price}$$

Markups should be high enough to cover operating expenses and desired profit. The percentage markup can be computed in two ways (i.e., by markup on cost or by markup on sales).

$$\text{Markup (MU) on Cost} = \frac{\text{Dollar Markup}}{\text{Purchase Cost}} \times 100\%$$

$$\text{Markup (MU) on Sales} = \frac{\text{Dollar Markup}}{\text{Selling Price}} \times 100\%$$

SELLING PRICE   To illustrate these formulae, let us assume the following figures. The product has a cost of $200.00 and the desired profit is $80.00. Therefore,

$$\text{Markup (MU) on Cost} = \frac{80}{200} \times 100\%$$

$$= 40\%$$

and, Markup (MU)   = $\dfrac{80}{280} \times 100\%$
on Sales

                         = 28.6%

Both these figures are used in many ways by wholesalers and retailers. Markup on cost is a method of setting prices. In the example above, the cost was $200.00 and the desired markup was $80.00, resulting in a selling price of $280.00.

MARKDOWNS

A markdown refers to a downward adjustment in selling price. For example, if a $30.00 jacket is marked down $5.00, the new selling price is $25.00. Retailers express the markdown as a percent of the new selling price. To compute the markdown percent, the following formula is used:

$$\frac{\text{Markdown}}{\text{New Selling Price}} = \text{Markdown Percentage}$$

$$\frac{\$5.00}{25.00} = 20\%$$

When a retailer offers a price reduction (e.g., for an item on sale), the markdown is expressed as a percentage of the original selling price for the consumer's benefit. The markdown formula in this case would be:

$$\frac{\text{Markdown}}{\text{Old Selling Price}} = \text{Markdown Percentage}$$

$$\frac{\$5.00}{30.00} = 16.66\%$$

Internally, the markdown is usually based on a net sales figure rather than the original sales figure. To illustrate the offset of markdowns on a larger scale, consider an example where the total value of the markdowns is $60 000. The calculation for markdown would be as follows:

Markdown Percentage   = $\dfrac{\text{Markdown on \$}}{\text{Net Sales}} \times 100\%$

NET SALES Therefore, if net sales are $240 000 and the markdown in dollars is $60 000, the calculation would be:

Markdown Percentage   = $\dfrac{60\,000}{240\,000} \times 100\%$

                        = 25%

In the example, the markdown represents 25 percent of net sales. Wholesalers and retailers frequently use markdowns to promote sale items, to reduce inventories of certain goods, or to balance out sales volume over a period. The results of such marketing decisions can be viewed in light of previous years' activities.

Canadian Marketing Cases

These cases can be found in the Instructor's Resource Manual and on the *Canadian Marketing in Action* Companion Website at **www.pearsoned.ca/tuckwell**. For your reference a complete list is shown below.

Glossary

Absolute advantage A situation in global marketing when only one country provides a good or service or when one country produces a product at significantly lower cost than others.

Accessory equipment Items that are usually not part of a finished product.

Accumulation The purchase by wholesalers of quantities of goods from many producers for re-distribution in smaller quantities to retailers they serve.

Acquisition strategy A corporate strategy in which a company decides to acquire other companies that represent attractive financial opportunities.

Administered VMS A cooperative system where the organization with the greatest economic influence has control of planning the marketing program and identifies and coordinates the responsibilities of each member.

Adoption A series of stages a consumer passes through on the way to purchasing a product on a regular basis.

Advertising Any paid form of non-personal message communicated through the media by an identified sponsor.

Advertising agencies Service organizations responsible for creating, planning, producing, and placing advertising messages for clients.

Advocacy advertising Any kind of public communication, paid for by an identified sponsor, that presents information or a point of view on a publicly recognized, controversial issue.

Allocation The division of available goods from a producer among the various wholesale and retail customers.

Ambush marketing A situation whereby non-sponsors of an event give a false impression through marketing communications that they are sponsors of an event.

Animated banner A form of online banner advertising that includes movement or action.

Approach The initial contact with the prospect, usually a face-to-face selling encounter.

Assorting Making sure that the merchandise is available to consumers in an adequate variety of brand names, price ranges, and features.

Assortment The variety of products that meet a retailer's target market needs.

Assortment consistency Product lines that can be used in conjunction with one another or that all relate to the same sorts of activities and needs.

Atmosphere The physical characteristics of a retail store or group of stores that are used to develop an image and attract customers.

Attitudes An individual's feelings, favourable or unfavourable, toward an idea or object.

Auction (online) A method of sale whereby an object for sale is secured by the highest bidder.

Auction company A commission merchant who brings together sellers and buyers at a central location to complete a transaction.

B2B e-commerce Online communications and business transactions between two or more organizations.

B2C e-commerce The retailing component of online selling; retailers selling their goods online to consumers.

Backward integration A situation in which retailers have control of the channel.

Bait and switch A situation in which a company advertises a bargain price for a product that is not available in reasonable quantity; when customers arrive at the store they are directed to another product, often more highly priced than the product advertised.

Banner ad A rectangular ad in the shape of a narrow band that stretches across a portion of a page on an Internet site.

Bartering The practice of exchanging goods and services for other goods and services rather than for money.

Behaviour response segmentation The division of buyers into groups according to their occasion for using a product, the benefits they require in a product, the frequency of use, and their degree of brand loyalty.

Beliefs The strongly held convictions on which an individual's actions are based.

Bid A written tender submitted in a sealed envelope by a specific deadline.

Big box (category killer) A product-specific megastore that offers a huge selection of low-priced merchandise.

Bill-back A discount in which the manufacturer records sales volume purchased by a customer and then pays the customer the total accumulated discount at the end of a deal period.

Blended family A family structure created by separation or divorce; two separate families merge into a single household as spouses remarry.

Blitz strategy A media strategy in which there is a heavy concentration of spending in a short period of time.

Blog A frequent, chronological publication of personal or corporate thoughts on a Web page that can be updated on a daily basis.

Bounce back An offer that rides along with a product shipment or with an invoice from a previous order.

Boutique A store-within-a-store concept (e.g., designer label boutiques in large department stores).

Boycott An organized refusal to buy a specific product.

Branch office A company office in a specified geographical area, which usually includes a warehouse facility from which goods are delivered to customers in the area.

Brand A name, term, symbol, or design, or some combination of them, that identifies the goods and services of an organization.

Brand acceptance wall (BAW) A barrier that stops most products from further consumer acceptance.

Brand equity The value a consumer derives from a product over and above the value derived from the physical attributes.

Brand insistence At this stage, a consumer will search the market extensively for the brand he or she wants.

Brand loyalty The degree of consumer attachment to a particular brand, product, or service.

Brand manager An individual assigned responsibility for the development and implementation of effective and efficient marketing programs for a specific product or group of products.

Brand name That part of a brand that can be vocalized.

Brand preference The stage of a product's life at which it is an acceptable alternative and will be purchased if it is available when needed.

Brand recognition Customer awareness of the brand name and package.

Branded content A situation where the brand name of a product or service is woven into the storyline of a movie or television show.

Brandmark (logo) That part of a brand identified by a symbol or design.

Breadth of selection The number of goods classifications a store carries.

Break-even analysis Determining the sales in units or dollars that are necessary for total revenue to equal total costs at a certain price.

Breaking bulk The delivery of small quantities, usually below the weight requirement established by transportation companies, to customers.

Broker A sales agent who represents suppliers, usually small manufacturers, to the wholesale and retail trade in a particular industry.

Build-up strategy A media strategy where the spending pattern or intensity of media weight gradually builds over a period of time.

Business analysis A formal review of some of the ideas accepted in the screening stage, the purpose of which is again to rank potential ideas and eliminate those judged to have low financial promise.

Business goods Products purchased by business, government, institutions, and industries that facilitate the operations of an organization.

Business-to-business advertising A business advertising its products, services, or itself to other businesses.

Business-to-business market Individuals in an organization who are responsible for purchasing goods and services that the organization needs to produce a product or service, promote an idea, or produce an income.

Button A small circle, square, or rectangular-shaped banner ad.

Buying centre An informal purchasing process in which individuals in an organization perform particular roles but may not have direct responsibility for the actual decision.

Buying committee A formal purchasing process involving members from across a business organization who share responsibility for making a purchase decision.

Buzz marketing Marketing activities designed to generate publicity about a new product. Such activities may embrace street-level activities, product seeding, sales promotions, and other activities that generate positive word-of-mouth about the brand.

Call centre A central operation from which a company operates its inbound and outbound telemarketing programs.

Canadian Marketing Association (CMA) A not-for-profit association comprising a cross-section of industry members.

Cannibalization (rate) The rate at which a new product reduces the sales of an existing product.

Capital items Expensive goods with a long lifespan that are used directly in the production of another good or service.

Cartel A group of firms or countries that band together and conduct trade in a manner similar to a monopoly.

Cash discounts Discounts granted for prompt payment within a stated period.

Cash refund Predetermined amount of money returned directly to the consumer by the manufacturer after the purchase has been made.

Cash-and-carry outlet A limited-service merchant wholesaler who serves small independent retailers who come to the wholesaler to purchase small quantities of goods.

Catalogue A reference publication distributed by large retail chains and other direct marketing organizations that promote the sale of goods.

Catalogue showroom A form of discount retailer that lists its merchandise in catalogues and displays selected lines of merchandise in a showroom where customers come to place their orders.

Category killer (big box) A product-specific megastore that offers a huge selection of low-priced merchandise.

Category manager An individual assigned the responsibility for developing and implementing marketing activity for a group of related products or product lines.

Cause marketing See *Social marketing.*

Census Metropolitan Area (CMA) An area that encompasses all rural and urban areas that are linked to a city's urban core, either socially or economically.

Central business district Normally, the hub of retailing activity in the heart of the downtown core (i.e., the main street and busy cross-streets in a centralized area).

Chain store (retail chain store) An organization operating four or more retail stores in the same kind of business under the same legal ownership.

Chain-markup pricing In this method, the firm considers the profit margins of its distributors.

Channel captain A leader that integrates and coordinates the objectives and policies of all other members.

Channel length Refers to the number of intermediaries or levels in the channel of distribution.

Channel width Refers to the number of intermediaries at any one level of the channel of distribution.

Circulation lists Moderately priced magazine subscription lists that target potential customers by an interest or activity.

Clicks (clickthroughs) In Internet marketing, the number of times that users click on any banner ad.

Clickthrough rate A calculation that determines the effectiveness of an ad in generating clicks; clicks divided by impressions is the clickthrough rate.

Closed bid A written, sealed bid submitted by a supplier for review and evaluation by the purchaser on a particular date.

Closed-end lease An agreement in which the lessor (leasing company) assumes financial responsibility for the difference between the depreciated value of the item and its actual cash value at the end of the lease.

Closing The point in the sales presentation when the seller asks for the order.

Co-branding Occurs when a company uses the equity in another brand name to help market its own brand-name product or service (two brand names on a product). This term also applies to two organizations sharing common facilities for marketing purposes (e.g., two restaurants in one location).

Cognitive dissonance An individual's unsettled state of mind after an action he or she has taken.

Cold canvass A type of selling where a sales representative in search of customers knocks on doors without notice.

Collateral material Literature and promotional materials used by a company's sales force to help sell a product (e.g., pamphlets, bulletins, price lists, and specifications sheets).

Commercialization The full-scale production and marketing plan for launching a product on a regional or national basis.

Commission merchant A wholesaling merchant who receives and sells goods for suppliers in centralized markets on consignment.

Common market A regional or geographical group of countries that agree to limit trade barriers among their members and apply a common tariff to goods from non-member countries.

Community shopping mall A medium-sized mall that serves an immediate geographic area; a community shopping mall contains convenience goods as well as shopping goods operations.

Comparative advantage A situation in global marketing in which one country produces and markets an item more efficiently or abundantly, as well as more cheaply, than other countries.

Comparative testing Used in direct marketing, it is the altering of one component of the proposed campaign to judge the effect of the change on the acceptability of the offer.

Competition Act Replaced the original Consumer and Corporate Affairs Act; it has three purposes.

Competitive bidding A situation in which two or more firms submit written price quotations to a purchaser on the basis of specifications established by the purchaser.

Competitive pricing Placing of prices above, equal to, or below those of competitors.

Compiled lists Lists prepared from public sources of information.

Component parts Goods used in the production of another product but which do not change form as a result of the manufacturing process.

Concept test The presentation of a product idea in some visual form, with a description of the basic product characteristics and benefits, in order to get customers' reactions to it.

Consultative selling In personal selling, the process of asking questions, listening attentively, and providing information and advice that is in the best interests of the customer.

Consumer analysis The monitoring of consumer behaviour changes (tastes, preferences, lifestyles) so that marketing strategies can be adjusted accordingly.

Consumer behaviour The acts of individuals in obtaining goods and services, including the decision processes that precede and determine these acts.

Consumer goods Products and services ultimately purchased for personal use.

Consumer promotion Activity promoting extra brand sales by offering the consumer an incentive over and above the product's inherent benefits.

Consumerism A social force within the environment designed to aid and protect the consumer by exerting legal, moral, and economic pressure on businesses.

Containerization The grouping of individual items into an economical shipping quantity that is sealed in a protective container for intermodal transportation to a final customer.

Contingency plan The identification of alternative courses of action that can be used to modify an original plan if and when new circumstances arise.

Continuity The length of time required to create an impact on a target market through a particular medium.

Contract manufacturing A situation when a manufacturer stops producing a good domestically, preferring to find a foreign country that can produce the good according to its specifications.

Convenience goods Those goods that consumers purchase frequently, with a minimum of effort and evaluation.

Convenience store A food and general merchandise store, situated in a busy area of a community, selling limited numbers of lines over long hours.

Cookie An electronic identification tag sent from a Web server to a browser to track a person's surfing patterns.

Cooperative advertising Funds allocated by a manufacturer to pay for a portion of a retailer's advertising.

Cooperative direct mail Mail envelopes containing special offers from non-competing products.

Copyright The exclusive right to reproduce, sell, or publish the matter and form of a dramatic, literary, musical, or artistic work.

Corporate advertising Advertising designed to convey a favourable image of a company among its various publics.

Corporate barter company A company that takes possession of goods and redistributes them among barter exchange members.

Corporate culture The values, norms, and practices shared by all the employees of an organization.

Corporate objectives Statements of a company's overall goals.

Corporate plan Identifies the corporate objectives to be achieved over a specific period.

Corporate planning Planning done by top management that includes three variables: a mission statement, a statement of corporate objectives, and a statement of corporate strategies.

Corporate strategies Plans outlining how the objectives are to be achieved.

Corporate VMS A tightly controlled arrangement in which a single corporation owns and operates in each level of the channel.

Cost reductions Reductions of the costs involved in the production process.

Cost-based pricing A type of pricing whereby a company calculates its total costs and then adds a desired profit margin to arrive at a list price for a product.

Cost–benefit analysis Used in the evaluation of price by a customer in a purchase situation, it is a procedure whereby all associated costs of the product are measured against the benefits of the product.

Countertrading (bartering) A system of exchange in which something other than currency or credit is used as a form of payment.

Country-centred strategy The development of unique marketing strategies for each country a product is marketed in.

Coupons Price-saving incentives offered to consumers by manufacturers and retailers to stimulate purchase of a specified product.

Coverage The number of geographic markets where advertising is to occur for the duration of a media plan.

CPM (cost per thousand) The cost of reaching 1000 people with a message; it is a quantitative measure for comparing the effectiveness of media alternatives.

Creative boutiques Specialist advertising agencies that concentrate on the design and development of advertising messages.

Creative execution The formation of more precisely defined strategies for presenting a message to a target market.

Creative objectives Statements of what information is to be communicated to a target market.

Creative strategy Statements outlining how a message is to be communicated to a target market.

Cross-elasticity of demand The degree to which the quantity demanded of one product will increase or decrease in response to changes in the price of another product.

Cross-marketing A strategy in which two independent organizations share facilities and/or resources to market their goods and services to similar customers. Also referred to as *co-branding*.

Cross-ruff An in-pack or on-pack coupon valid on the purchase of a different product.

Cross-sampling Distribution of free samples by using another product as the means of distributing them.

Cross-tabulation Comparison and contrast of the answers of various sub-groups or of particular sub-groups and the total response group.

Cult brand A brand that captures the imagination of a small group who spread the word, make converts, and help turn a fringe brand into a mainstream brand.

Culture Behaviour learned from external sources, which influences the formation of value systems that hold strong sway over every individual.

Customary pricing The strategy of matching prices to a buyer's expectations: the price reflects tradition or is a price that people are accustomed to paying.

Customer relationship management (CRM) The partnering of manufacturers with members of a channel of distribution to produce efficient operations so that all partners benefit.

Cyberspace The world of online computer networks.

Damage control techniques Sales support systems that companies employ to ensure that a customer remains a customer, such as toll-free 1-800 numbers, recall notices, liberal refund policies, intensive staff training, training of customer service personnel, warranties and extended warranties, and repair and maintenance reminders.

Data analysis The evaluation, in market research, of responses on a question-by-question basis, a process that gives meaning to the data.

Data interpretation Relating accumulated data to the problem under review and to the objectives and hypotheses of the research study.

Data mining The analysis of information so that relationships are established between pieces of information and more effective marketing strategies can be identified and implemented.

Data transfer a process whereby data from a marketing research questionnaire is transferred to a computer.

Database A customer information file that is continuously updated by a company.

Database management system (DMS) See *Management Information System (MIS)*.

Database marketing The process of analyzing customer and prospect data contained in a database to identify new markets and selling opportunities and to prepare marketing programs targeted to people most likely to buy.

Dealer premium An incentive offered to a distributor by a manufacturer to encourage a special purchase (i.e., a specified volume of merchandise) or to secure additional merchandising support.

Dealer-display material See *Point-of-purchase material*.

Decision support system An interactive, personalized marketing information system, designed to be initiated and controlled by individual decision makers.

Decline stage At this stage in the product's life cycle, sales begin to drop rapidly, and profits are eroded.

Delayed-payment incentive Incentive allowing the consumer a grace period during which no interest or principal is paid for the item purchased.

Demand-based pricing A pricing strategy whereby the firm calculates the markup needed to cover selling expenses and profits and determines the maximum it can spend to produce the product; the calculations work backwards, since they initially consider the price the consumer will pay.

Demand-minus (backward) pricing An organization determines the optimum retail selling price that consumers will accept and then subtracts the desired profit margin and marketing expenses to arrive at the cost at which the product should be produced.

Demarketing Reducing demand to a level that can be reasonably supplied.

Demographic segmentation The division of a large market into smaller segments that are based on combinations of age, gender, income, occupation, education, marital status, household formation, and ethnic background.

Demographics The study of the characteristics of a population.

Demonstration An opportunity to show a product in action; it helps substantiate the claims that the salesperson is making.

Department store A large general-product line retailer that sells a variety of merchandise in a variety of price ranges.

Depression A long and harsh period of decline.

Depth of selection The number of brands and styles carried by a store in each product classification.

Derived demand Demand for products sold in the business-to-business market is actually derived from consumer demand.

Differential advantages The unique attributes of a product.

Diffusion The manner in which different market segments accept and purchase a product between the stages of introduction and market saturation.

Diffusion of innovation The gradual acceptance of a product from its introduction to market saturation.

Direct channel A short channel of distribution.

Direct competition Competition from alternative products and services that satisfy the needs of a common market.

Direct exporting A form of international distribution whereby the exporting company itself strikes agreements with local market companies that would be responsible for distribution in the foreign country.

Direct home retailing The selling of merchandise by personal contact in the home of the consumer.

Direct home shopping A shopping service provided by cable television stations, whereby products are offered for sale by broadcast message (e.g., Canadian Home Shopping Network).

Direct investment A company's financial commitment in a foreign country, whereby the investing company owns and operates, in whole or in part, the facility in that country.

Direct mail A form of direct advertising communicated to prospects through the postal service.

Direct marketing An interactive marketing system, fully controlled by the marketer, who develops products, promotes them directly to customers through a variety of media, accepts orders directly from customers, and distributes products directly to consumers.

Direct response advertising Messages that prompt immediate action, such as advertisements containing clipout coupons, response cards, and order forms; such advertising goes directly to customers and bypasses traditional channels of distribution.

Direct response television (DRTV) A sales-oriented television commercial message that encourages people to buy right away, usually through 1-800 telephone numbers.

Directory database A commercial database that provides quick information about a company (e.g., size, sales, location, and number of employees).

Discount (junior) department store A store that carries a full line of merchandise at low prices while offering consumers limited customer service.

Discount supermarket (or warehouse store) A supermarket offering limited lines, a limited assortment of brands, few services, low margins, and low prices.

Disintermediation In an Internet marketing context, the disappearance of intermediaries in the channel of distribution.

Display advertising See *Banner advertising*.

Disposable income Actual income after taxes and other expenses; it is income available for optional purchases.

Distribution All activities related to the transfer of goods and services from one business to another or from a business to a consumer.

Distribution planning A systematic decision-making process regarding the physical movement and transfer of ownership of goods and services from producers to consumers.

Distribution strategy The selection and management of marketing channels and the physical distribution of products.

Distribution warehouse A warehouse, or distribution centre, that assembles and redistributes merchandise, usually in smaller quantities and in shorter periods of time.

Diversification strategy (corporate) A situation where a company invests its resources in a totally new direction (e.g., a new industry or market).

Divesting Removing an entire division of a company through sale or liquidation.

Double targeting Devising a single marketing strategy for both sexes.

Double ticketing A situation in which more than one price tag appears on an item.

Drop shipper A merchant wholesaler who purchases goods from manufacturers, then contacts customers and puts together carload quantities of goods that can be delivered economically.

Dumping The practice of selling goods in a foreign market at a lower price than they are sold in the domestic market.

Durable goods Tangible goods that survive many uses.

Early adopters A large group of opinion leaders who like to try new products when they are new.

Early majority A group of consumers representing the initial phase of mass market acceptance of a product.

E-business Conducting business on the Internet, not only by buying and selling, but also by servicing customers and collaborating with business partners.

E-commerce The buying and selling of goods online and the transfer of funds through digital communications.

E-coupon (electronic coupon) Coupons that are printed directly from websites for use by consumers.

E-procurement An Internet-based business-to-business marketplace through which participants are able to purchase goods from each other.

Economic order quantity (EOQ) The size of an order of goods that will strike the best balance between the cost of ordering goods and the cost of carrying goods in inventory.

Editing In marketing research, a stage where completed questionnaires are reviewed for consistency and completeness.

Elastic demand A situation in which a small change in price results in a large change in volume.

Electronic data interchange (EDI) The computerized transfer of information among business partners in order to facilitate efficient transfer of goods.

Embargo A trade restriction that disallows entry of specified products into a country.

Emergency goods Goods purchased immediately when a crisis or urgency arises.

Encryption A set of complex algorithmic codes that ensure network privacy; in online business transactions, messages are encrypted in both directions.

End-product advertising Advertising that promotes an ingredient of a finished product.

Event marketing The process, planned by a sponsoring organization, of integrating a variety of communication elements behind an event theme.

Event sponsorship A situation in which a sponsor agrees to support an event financially in return for advertising privileges associated with the event.

Evoked set A group of brands that a person would consider acceptable among competing brands in a class of product.

Exchange The transfer of something of value from an organization in return for something from the customer so that both parties are satisfied.

Exclusive distribution The availability of a product in only one outlet in a geographic area.

Execution (tactics) Action plan that outlines in specific detail how strategies are to be implemented.

Experiential Marketing A type of marketing that creates awareness for a product by having the customer directly interact with the product (e.g., distributing free samples of a product at street level is a form of experiential marketing).

Experimental research Research in which one or more factors are manipulated under controlled conditions, while other elements remain constant, so that respondents' reactions can be evaluated.

Exploratory research A preliminary form of research that clarifies the nature of a problem.

External Publics Publics that are distant from an organization and are communicated with less frequently (e.g., media, governments, and prospective shareholders).

Extranet A system that connects the intranets of individual companies together through private communications lines.

F.O.B. destination pricing A geographic pricing strategy, whereby the seller agrees to pay freight charges between point of origin and point of destination (title does not transfer to the buyer until the goods arrive at their destination).

F.O.B. origin pricing A geographic pricing strategy, whereby the price quoted by the seller does not include freight charges (the buyer assumes title when the goods are loaded onto a common carrier).

Fact gathering The compilation of already discovered data, originally published for reasons that have nothing to do with the specific problem under investigation.

Fad A product that has a reasonably short selling season, perhaps one or a few financially successful seasons.

Family brand The use of the same brand name for a group of related products.

Family life cycle A series of stages a person undergoes, starting with being a young single adult, progressing to marriage and parenthood, and ending as an older single individual.

Fashion A cycle for a product that recurs through many selling seasons.

Fixed costs Costs that do not vary with different quantities of output.

Fixed-response questioning Questionnaire used for a large sample that contains predetermined questions and a selection of answers that are easily filled in by the respondent or interviewer.

Flexible pricing Charging different customers different prices.

Flight (flighting) The purchase of media time and space in planned intervals, separated by periods of inactivity.

Flyers See *Leaflets*.

Focus group A small group of 8 to 12 people with common characteristics, brought together to discuss issues related to the marketing of a product or service.

Folders A direct response sales message printed on heavier stock paper; typically, they can be mailed without an envelope.

Follow-up An activity that keeps salespeople in touch with customers after the sale has been made, to ensure that the customer is satisfied.

Forward buying The practice of buying deal merchandise in quantities sufficient to carry a retailer through to the next deal period offered by the manufacturer.

Forward integration A situation in which manufacturers have control of the channel.

Franchise agreement A franchisee (retailer) conducts business using the franchiser's name and operating methods in exchange for a fee.

Franchise wholesaler Retailers affiliate with an existing wholesaling operation and agree to purchase merchandise through it.

Free sample See *Sample*.

Freestanding insert (FSI) A pre-printed advertisement in single- or multiple-page form that is inserted loose into newspapers.

Freestanding store An isolated store usually located on a busy street or highway.

Freight forwarder A firm that consolidates small shipments—shipments that form less than a carload or truckload—from small companies.

Frequency The average number of times an audience is exposed to an advertising message over a given period, usually a week.

Frequency distribution In a survey, the number of times each answer was chosen for a question.

Frequent-buyer program Offers the consumer a small bonus when a purchase is made.

Full-payout lease A type of lease where the lessor recovers the full value of the goods leased to a customer.

Full-cost pricing A desired profit margin is added to the full cost of producing a product.

Full-serve store A retailer that carries a variety of shopping goods that require sales assistance and a variety of services to facilitate the sale of the goods (such services may include fitting rooms, delivery, and installations).

Full-service agencies Advertising agencies that offer a complete range of services to their clients.

Full-service merchant wholesalers Wholesalers who assemble an assortment of products in a central warehouse and offer their customers a full range of services, including delivery, storage, credit, support in merchandising, promotion, and in research and planning.

Full-text database A database that contains the complete text of a source document making up the database.

Funnelling The dividing of a subject into manageable variables so that specifically directed research can be conducted.

Funnelling (of questions) Using general questions initially, then progressing to more specific questions.

Game (or instant-win) contest Promotion vehicle that includes a number of pre-determined, pre-seeded winning tickets in the overall, fixed universe of tickets. Packages containing winning certificates are redeemed for prizes.

General-merchandise store A store offering a wide variety of product lines, and selection of brand names within those product lines (e.g., a department store).

General merchandise wholesaler A wholesaler who carries a full line or wide assortment of merchandise that serves virtually all of its customers' needs.

Generic brand A product without a brand name or identifying features.

Geodemographic segmentation The isolation of dwelling areas through a combination of geographic and demographic information, based on the assumption that people seek out residential neighbourhoods in which to cluster with their lifestyle peers.

Geographic pricing Pricing strategy based on the question, "Who is paying the freight?"

Geographic segmentation The division of a large geographic market into smaller geographic or regional units.

Geographical information systems Mapping software used to help make business decisions and get a competitive edge.

Global management structure Ideas that are developed in one country are considered for another, so that economies of scale are achieved.

Global marketing strategy A marketing strategy whereby a product is marketed in essentially the same way, whatever the country, though some modification to particular elements of the marketing mix is often necessary.

Globalization The idea that the world as a marketplace is becoming smaller and progressive-minded companies are pursuing opportunities for growth, wherever possible.

Glocalization The creation of products and services intended for the global market but customized to suit local needs.

Grey market A market segment based on age and lifestyles of people who are over the age of 65 years.

Gross Domestic Product (GDP) The total value of goods and services produced in a country on an annual basis.

Growth stage The period of rapid consumer acceptance.

Head-on positioning A marketing strategy in which one brand is presented as an equal or better alternative to a competing brand.

Hierarchy of needs The classification of consumers' needs in an ascending order from lower-level needs to higher-level needs.

Horizontal conflict Conflict between similar organizations at the same level in the channel of distribution.

Horizontal integration strategy One organization owns and operates several companies at the same level in the channel of distribution.

Horizontal marketing system A situation in which many channel members at one level in the channel have the same owner.

House list An internal listing of customers.

House organ An internal communications document that outlines news and events about an organization to employees.

Hypotheses Statements of predicted outcomes.

Idea marketing Encouraging the public to accept and agree with certain issues and causes.

Impressions The total audience delivered by a media plan.

Impressions (page views) The number of times a banner image is downloaded to a page being viewed by a visitor.

Impulse goods Goods bought on the spur of the moment, or out of habit when supplies are low.

Inbound telemarketing The reception of calls by an order desk, customer-service enquiry, and direct-response calls, often generated through toll-free telephone numbers.

Income distribution Trends in income among various income groups: upper class, middle class, and lower class.

Independent retailer A retailer operating one to three stores, even if the stores are affiliated with a large retail organization.

Indirect channel A long channel of distribution.

Indirect competition Competition from substitute products that offer customers the same benefit.

Indirect exporting A form of international distribution where a company employs a middleman or trading company to establish a distribution network in a foreign country.

Individual brand The identification of each product in a company's product mix with its own name.

Industrial (business) advertising Advertising by industrial suppliers directed at industrial buyers.

Industrial (business) goods Products and services purchased to be used directly or indirectly in the production of other goods for resale.

Industry Canada Regulates the legal environment for marketing and other business practices in Canada.

Inelastic demand A situation in which a change in price does not have a significant impact on the quantity purchased.

Inflation The rising price level for goods and services that results in reduced purchasing power.

Infomercial Typically a 30-minute commercial that presents in more detail the benefits of a product or service.

Information search Conducted by an individual once a problem or need has been defined.

In-home selling A form of personal selling whereby an individual uses a network of local people to sell products in their communities, often at home parties.

Innovators The first group of consumers to accept a product.

In-pack or on-pack premium A free item placed inside the package or attached to a package and overwrapped for protection and security.

Inseparability The equating of the provider of the service with the service itself.

Installations Major capital items used directly in the production of another product.

Instant bust A product that a firm had high expectations of but that, for whatever reasons, was rejected by consumers very quickly.

Instant wins See *Game contest.*

In-store delivered coupons Coupons distributed by in-store display centres and dispensing machines usually located near the store entrance, or on the shelves from shelf pads.

Intangibility The quality of not being perceivable by the senses.

Integrated marketing communications (IMC) The process of building and reinforcing mutually profitable relationships with customers and the general public by developing and coordinating a strategic communications program that enables them to make constructive contact with the company or brand through a variety of media.

Intensive distribution The availability of a product in the widest possible channel of distribution.

Interactive banner (rich media banner) A banner ad that engages the viewer in some kind of activity (e.g., a game, or providing information).

Interactive Communications A system for communicating that involves the use of the Internet or other mobile communications devices (cell phones).

Intermediary Offers producers of goods and services the advantage of being able to make goods and services readily available to target markets.

Intermodal transportation Moving goods using two or more modes of transportation, with goods being transferred from one mode to another.

Internal publics Those publics that an organization communicates with regularly (e.g., employees, distributors, suppliers and customers)

Internet A network of computers linked together to act as one in the communication of information.

Interstitial An online ad that pops onto a computer screen and interrupts users.

Intranet An internal website that employees can access; a private network on the Internet in which companies can communicate with one another.

Introduction stage The period after the product is introduced into the marketplace and before significant growth begins.

Inventory management A system that ensures continuous flow of needed goods by matching the quantity of goods in inventory to sales demand so that neither too little nor too much stock is carried.

Inventory turn The number of times during a specific time period that the average inventory is sold.

Issue management Public relations messages that deliver a message showing where a company stands on a particular issue.

Joint or shared demand A situation in which industrial products can only be used in conjunction with others, when the production and marketing of one product is dependent on another.

Joint venture In a global marketing situation, a partnership between a domestic company and a foreign company.

Just-in-time (JIT) inventory system A system that reduces inventory on hand by ordering small quantities frequently.

Key-benefit statement Conveys the most important idea or benefit the advertiser is promising the consumer.

Knock-offs Look-alike products that are often a copy of a patented product.

Labels Printed sheets of information affixed to a package container.

Laggards The last group of people to purchase a product.

Late majority A group of consumers representing the latter phase of mass market acceptance of a product.

Law of demand States that consumers purchase greater quantities at lower prices.

Law of supply and demand An abundant supply and low demand lead to a low price, while a high demand and limited supply lead to a high price.

Leaflets (flyers) Standard letter-sized pages that offer relevant information about a direct mail offer; they expand on information contained in a letter.

Lease A contractual agreement, whereby a lessor, for a fee, agrees to rent an item to a lessee over a specified period.

Licensed brand Occurs when a brand name or trademark is used by a licensee.

Licensing One firm legally allowing another firm to use its patent, copyright, brand name, or manufacturing process, for a certain period.

Lifestyle A person's pattern of living as expressed in his or her activities, interests, opinions, and values.

Lifestyle mall A smaller, open-air shopping centre featuring clusters of 20 to 30 upscale stores, each with its own entrance onto a main street of the centre along with offices and residential units.

Limited-edition brand A brand that is on the market only for a short period; it capitalizes on the popularity of an individual or event.

Limited-line store A store that carries a large assortment of one product line or a few related product lines.

Limited-service merchant wholesalers Wholesalers that are selective in the functions they perform.

Limited-service store A type of retailer that only offers a small range of services in order to keep operating costs to a minimum.

Line extension The introduction of a different version of an existing product (e.g., a new flavour, scent, or size) under the same brand name.

List broker A specialist who makes all the arrangements for one company to use the lists of another company.

List price The rate normally quoted to potential buyers.

Lobbying A public relations activity designed to influence policy decisions of government.

Local content law A way of protecting local industry and employment by requiring a foreign-based manufacturer to use a specified amount of locally produced components.

Loss leaders Products offered for sale at or slightly below cost.

Loyalty (frequent buyer) program Offers the consumer a small bonus, such as points or "play money," when they make a purchase; the bonus accumulates with each new purchase.

Mail interviews A silent process of collecting information; reaches a highly dispersed sample in a cost-efficient manner.

Mail-in premiums Items offered free or at a bargain price to consumers who send away for them.

Mail-order wholesaler A wholesaler who relies on catalogues instead of a sales force to contact customers.

Management information system (MIS) People and equipment organized to provide a continuous, orderly collection and exchange of information needed in a firm's decision-making process.

Manufacturer wholesaling When a producer undertakes the wholesaling function, feeling that it can reach customers effectively and efficiently through direct contact.

Manufacturer's agent A sales agent who carries and sells similar products for non-competing manufacturers in an exclusive territory.

Manufacturer's suggested list price (MSLP) The price manufacturers suggest retailers should charge for a product.

Market A group of people who have a similar need for a product or service, the resources to purchase it, and the willingness and ability to buy it.

Market analysis The collection of appropriate information (i.e., information regarding demand, sales volume potential, production capabilities, and resources necessary to produce and market a given product) to determine if a market is worth pursuing.

Market challenger Firm or firms attempting to gain market leadership through aggressive marketing efforts.

Market development A strategy whereby a company attempts to market existing products to new target markets.

Market differentiation Targeting several market segments with several different products and marketing plans.

Market follower A company that is generally satisfied with its market share position.

Market integration Expansion from a single segment into other similar segments.

Market leader The largest firm in the industry and the leader in strategic action.

Market nicher A firm that concentrates resources on one or more distinguishable market segments.

Market penetration A strategy whereby a company attempts to improve the market position of existing products in existing markets.

Market planning The analysis, planning, implementation, evaluation, and control of marketing initiatives to satisfy target market needs and achieve the organization's objectives.

Market segmentation The division of a large market (mass market) into smaller homogeneous markets (targets) on the basis of common needs and/or similar lifestyles.

Market share The sales volume of one competing product or company expressed as a percentage of total market sales volume.

Marketing The process of planning the conception, pricing, promotion, and distribution of ideas, goods, and services to create exchanges that satisfy individual and organized objectives.

Marketing audit A systematic, critical, and unbiased review and appraisal of the basic objectives and policies of the marketing department and of the organization, methods, procedures, and people employed to implement the policies.

Marketing channel A series of firms or individuals that participate in the flow of goods and services from producer to final users or customers.

Marketing communications planning The process of making systematic decisions about which elements of the marketing communications mix to use.

Marketing communications strategy The blending of advertising, sales promotion, event marketing and sponsorship, personal selling, and public relations to present a consistent and persuasive message about a product or service.

Marketing concept The process of determining the needs and wants of a target market and delivering a set of desired satisfactions to that target market more effectively than the competition does.

Marketing control The process of measuring and evaluating the results of marketing strategies and plans and taking corrective action to ensure that marketing objectives are attained.

Marketing execution Planning that focuses on specific program details that stem directly from the strategy section of the plan.

Marketing management The directing of marketing activity on the basis of geography, type of customer, product line, or category of product, depending on the nature of the organization.

Marketing mix The four strategic elements of product, price, distribution, and marketing communications.

Marketing objectives Statement outlining what a product or service will accomplish in one year, usually expressed in terms of sales volume, market share, or profit.

Marketing planning The analysis, planning, implementation, evaluation, and control of marketing initiatives in order to satisfy target market needs and organizational objectives.

Marketing plans Plans that are short-term and specific, and combine both strategy and tactics.

Marketing research A function that links the consumer, customer, and public to the marketer through information—information used to define marketing opportunities and problems; to generate, refine, and evaluate marketing actions; to monitor marketing performance; and to improve understanding of marketing as a process.

Marketing strategies Identify target markets and satisfy the needs of those targets with a combination of marketing mix elements within budget constraints.

Maslow's hierarchy of needs This theory states that needs can be classified in an ascending order.

Mass customization The creation of systems that can personalize messages to a target audience of one.

Mass marketing The use of one basic marketing strategy to appeal to a broad range of consumers without addressing any distinct characteristics among them.

Mature stage The stage of a product's life cycle when it has been widely adopted by consumers; sales growth slows and eventually declines slightly.

Media execution The final stage of media planning; the process of fine-tuning media strategy into specific action plans.

Media objectives Media planning statements that consider the target market, the presentation of the message, geographic market priorities, the best time to reach the target, and the budget available to accomplish stated goals.

Media planning A precise outline of media objectives, media strategies, and the media execution, culminating in a media plan that recommends how funds should be spent to achieve the previously established advertising objectives.

Media relations specialists In public relations companies, responsible for getting industry analysts on board to communicate favourable information about a company or brand.

Media strategy Statements that outline how media objectives will be accomplished; typically, they outline what media will

be used and why certain media were selected and others rejected.

Media-buying service A specialist advertising agency that concentrates on planning and purchasing the most cost-efficient time and space in the media for their clients.

Media-delivered coupons Coupons distributed by advertisers through newspapers and magazines.

Mega-mall A destination mall characterized by its incredibly large size and diversity of stores and services; they include amusements and other attractions that entertain shoppers.

Merchandise assortment The total assortment of products a retailer carries.

Merchant wholesalers See *Full-service merchant wholesalers.*

Merge/purge A procedure in which duplicate names are eliminated from lists that are going to be used for direct mail purposes.

Micro-marketing The development of marketing strategies on a regional basis, giving consideration to the unique needs and geodemographics of different regions.

Mission statement A statement of purpose for an organization reflecting the operating philosophy and direction the organization is to take.

Missionary selling A form of selling that focuses on building goodwill; missionaries contact retailers to check stocks, arrange displays and provide basic information about products.

Modified rebuy The purchase by an organization of a medium-priced product on an infrequent basis.

Monopolistic competition A market in which there are many competitors, each offering a unique marketing mix based on price and other variables.

Monopoly A market where there is a single seller of a particular good or service for which there are no close substitutes.

Motives The conditions that prompt the action necessary to satisfy a need.

Multibrand strategy The use of a different brand name for each item a company offers in the same product category.

Multi-channelling A type of distribution for which different kinds of intermediaries are used at the same level in the channel of distribution.

Multi-level marketing A distribution system in which distributors are stacked on top of each other in a shape resembling a pyramid. Distributors higher up in the pyramid receive commissions from the sale of merchandise by distributors situated below them.

Multinational corporation A firm that operates in several countries and usually has a substantial share of its total assets, sales, and labour force in foreign subsidiaries.

Multiple-unit pricing Offering items for sale in multiples, usually at a price below the combined regular price of each item.

National advertising Advertising of a trademarked product or service wherever the product or service is available.

Nationalization A form of expropriation, whereby the government of a country takes control of the operation of a foreign company operating there.

Need A state of deprivation or the absence of something useful.

Need description In business-to-business marketing, a stage where a buying organization identifies the general characteristics of the items and services it requires.

Needs assessment The initial stage of marketing planning in which a company collects appropriate information to determine if a market is worth pursuing.

Neighbourhood shopping mall This type of mall contains a row or strip of stores, mainly selling convenience items and services. It typically houses a drugstore, a variety store, a hardware store, a bake shop, a hair stylist, and a convenience store.

Network marketing A distribution system in which distributors are stacked on top of each other in the shape of a pyramid. Distributors higher up in the pyramid receive commissions from the sale of merchandise by distributors below them.

New product A product that is truly unique and that meets needs that have been previously unsatisfied.

New-products strategy A corporate strategy that calls for significant investment in research and development to develop innovative products.

New-task purchase The purchase of an expensive product by a business for the first time.

Niche marketing Targeting a product line to one particular segment and committing all marketing resources to the satisfaction of that segment.

Nondurable goods Tangible goods normally consumed after one or a few uses.

Non-probability sample The respondents have an unknown chance of selection, and their being chosen is based on such factors as convenience for the researcher or the judgment of the researcher.

North American Industry Classification System (NAICS) A numbering system that allows a supplier to track down customers who can use its goods and services within an industry category.

Not-for-profit marketing The marketing effort and activity of not-for-profit organizations.

Objection An obstacle that the salesperson must confront and resolve if the sales transaction is to be completed.

Objectives Statements that outline what is to be accomplished in a corporate plan or marketing plan.

Observation research A form of research in which the behaviour of the respondent is observed and recorded.

Odd–even pricing A psychological pricing strategy that capitalizes on setting prices below even-dollar amounts.

Off-invoice allowance A temporary allowance that is deducted from the invoice at the time of customer billing.

Oligopoly A market situation in which a few large firms control the market.

One-on-one interview An in-depth face-to-face interview between a moderator and a respondent.

Online advertising The placement of a commercial message on a website, in email, or over personal communications devices.

Online database A public information database accessible to anyone with proper communications facilities.

Online selling The use of Internet websites as a vehicle for conducting business transactions.

Online surveys A survey conducted via the Internet.

On-site sampling Delivering samples while generating positive publicity for a brand; also called *Experiential marketing*.

Open bid An informal submission by a potential supplier of a price quotation in written or verbal form.

Open-end lease An agreement in which the lessee (customer) assumes financial responsibility for the difference between the estimated wholesale value of the item and the proceeds of its sale at the end of the lease.

Operating lease A short-term lease involving monthly payments for use of equipment, which is returned to the lessor.

Opt-in list Contains the names of people who have agreed to have their information included.

Order and reorder routine In business-to-business marketing, the placing of an order and the establishment of a repeat order process with a supplier.

Order processing A distribution activity that involves checking credit ratings of customers, recording a sale, making the necessary accounting entries, and then locating the item for shipment.

Orderly market agreement An agreement by which nations share a market, eliminating the trade barriers between them.

Organization marketing Marketing that seeks to gain or maintain acceptance of an organization's objectives and services.

Organizational buying The decision-making process that firms follow to establish what products they need to purchase, and then identify, evaluate, and select a brand and a supplier for those products.

Outbound telemarketing The calls a company makes to a customer in order to develop new accounts, generate sales leads, qualify prospects, and close a deal.

Outlet mall Contains factory outlet stores for well-known brands; usually located at a key intersection of a major highway.

Outsourcing The contracting out of services or functions previously done in-house (e.g., a firm contracts out its computer services function).

Packaging Those activities related to the design and production of the container or wrapper of a product.

Partnering See *Relationship marketing*.

Parts and materials Less expensive goods that directly enter another manufacturer's production process.

Party selling A form of selling where a person (a host) invites friends to his or her home for a sales demonstration.

Patent A provision that gives a manufacturer the sole right to develop and market a new product, process, or material.

Penetration strategy (corporate) A corporate strategy that calls for aggressive and progressive action on the part of an organization—growth is achieved by investing in existing businesses.

People marketing The marketing of an individual or group of people to create a favourable impression of that individual or group.

Perceived risk Closely associated with attitudes and beliefs, this risk factor is generally higher for first-time purchases or when the price of any purchase increases.

Perception How individuals receive and interpret messages.

Perceptual map In the context of product positioning, a grid-like diagram in which competing brands are plotted according to certain product characteristics.

Performance allowance Discount offered by a manufacturer to a distributor who performs a promotional function on the manufacturer's behalf.

Performance evaluation Process that determines the effectiveness of a marketing strategy or marketing mix activity and therefore acts as a control mechanism.

Performance reviews The final step in the buying process, where the buying organization establishes a system of obtaining and evaluating feedback on the performance of the supplier's products.

Perishable (perishability of demand) Demand for services varies over a given period.

Permission-based email A situation where consumers agree to accept online messages from commercial sources.

Personal interviews Face-to-face communication with groups or individuals, usually done through quantitative questionnaires.

Personal selling Face-to-face communication involving the presentation of features and benefits of a product or service to a buyer for the purpose of making a sale.

Personality Distinguishing psychological characteristics of a person that produce relatively consistent and enduring responses to the environment in which that person lives.

Phantom freight The amount by which average transportation charges exceed the actual cost of shipping for customers near the source of supply.

Physical distribution (logistics management) The range of activities involved in the flow of materials, finished goods, and related information from points of origin to points of consumption to meet customer requirements at a profit.

Piggybacking A system in which the entire load of a truck trailer is placed in a rail flatcar for movement from one place to another. In retailing, piggybacking also means the sharing of facilities for marketing purposes (see also *Twinning* and *Co-branding*).

Place marketing Drawing attention to and creating a favourable attitude toward a particular place, be it a country, province, region, or city.

Planning The process of anticipating the future business environment and determining the courses of action a firm will take in that environment.

Point-of-purchase material Self-contained, custom-designed merchandising units that either temporarily or permanently display a manufacturer's product.

Population A group of people with certain specific age, gender, and geodemographic characteristics.

Pop-up (pop-under) ad Appears in a separate window on top of or beneath content already on a computer screen.

Portfolio analysis A process of reviewing the business categories or market segments that a firm operates in, based on the fact that the total company can be divided into strategic units.

Positioning Designing and marketing a product to meet the needs of a target market, and creating the appropriate appeals to make the product stand out from the competition in the minds of customers.

Postage-paid reply cards An important component of a sales folder.

Post-testing The evaluation of an advertisement, commercial, or campaign, during or after its implementation.

Power centre (power mall) A mall that houses a number of category-killer superstores in one enclosed space.

Pre-approach Gathering information about potential customers before actually making sales contact.

Predatory pricing A situation in which a large firm sets an extremely low price in an attempt to undercut all other competitors, thus placing them in a difficult financial position.

Premium An item offered free or at a bargain price to customers who buy another specific item or make a minimum purchase.

Presentation The persuasive delivery and demonstration of a product's benefits.

Press conference A gathering of news reporters invited to a location to witness the release of important information.

Press kit The assembly of relevant public relations information into a package (press releases, photographs, schedules, etc.) that is distributed to the media for publication or broadcast.

Press release A document prepared by an organization containing public relations information that is sent to the media for publication or broadcast.

Prestige pricing A situation in the sale of luxury goods in which a high price contributes to the image of a product and to the status of the buyer.

Pre-testing The evaluation of an advertisement, commercial, or campaign to determine the strengths and weaknesses of the message prior to a final creative production.

Price The exchange value of a good or service in the marketplace.

Price clubs Essentially the same as warehouse outlets, except customers must pay a fee (usually $25.00) to shop there.

Price elasticity of demand Measures the effect a price change has on the volume purchased.

Price fixing Competitors banding together to raise, lower, or stabilize prices.

Price leadership In offline marketing, the brand with the highest price; typically the brand leader in a market. On the Internet, the company charging the lowest price.

Price lining The adoption of price points for the various lines of merchandise a retailer carries.

Price penetration Establishing a low entry price in order to gain wide market acceptance quickly.

Price planning Developing a strategy that provides reasonable profit for the firm while making the product or service attractive to the customer.

Price skimming (strategy) Establishing a high entry price so that a firm can maximize its revenue early.

Price strategy The development of a pricing structure that is fair and equitable for consumers and still profitable for the organization.

Primary package The package containing the actual product (e.g., the jar that contains the jam).

Primary research Data collected and recorded for the first time to resolve a specific problem.

Private-label brand A brand produced to the specifications of the distributor, usually by national brand manufacturers that make similar products under their own brand names.

Probability sample The respondents have a known or equal chance of selection and are randomly selected from across the country.

Problem awareness Attempting to specify the nature of the difficulty in the marketing research process.

Problem recognition In the consumer buying process, a stage where a consumer discovers a need or an unfulfilled desire.

Processed materials Materials used in the production of another product but which are not readily identifiable with the product.

Product A bundle of tangible and intangible benefits that a buyer receives in exchange for money and other considerations.

Product Description (Product Specification) In a B2B context, a description of the characteristics of a product an organization requires. The description is used by potential suppliers when preparing bids to supply the product.

Product development A strategy whereby a company markets new products or modified existing products to current customers.

Product differentiation A strategy that focuses on the unique attributes or benefits of a product that distinguish it from another product.

Product item A unique product offered for sale by an organization.

Product life cycle The stages a product goes through from its introduction to the market to its eventual withdrawal.

Product line A grouping of product items that have major attributes in common but may differ in size, form, or flavour.

Product line depth Number of lines in the mix.

Product line width Number of items in the line.

Product manager See *Brand manager.*

Product mix The total range of products offered for sale by a company.

Product placement In public relations, the placement of a product in a movie or television show so that the product is exposed to the viewing audience (e.g., the branded product is a prop in the show).

Product planning Organizations examine ways to design products in line with consumers' expectations.

Product research Produces information about how people perceive product attributes.

Product seeding Placing a new product with a group of trendsetters who in turn influence others to purchase the product.

Product strategy Making decisions about such variables as product quality, product features, brand names, packaging, customer service, guarantees, and warranties.

Product stretching The sequential addition of products to a product line to increase its depth or width.

Product testing In direct marketing, the testing of the viability of a product or service to see how acceptable it is to the target market.

Product-delivered coupons Coupons that appear in or on the package.

Production orientation Occurs when organizations pay little attention to what customers need, concentrating instead on what they are capable of producing.

Profile matching A media strategy whereby the advertising message is placed in those media where the profile of readers, listeners, or viewers is reasonably close to that of the product's target market.

Profit maximization To achieve this, an organization sets some type of measurable and attainable profit objective on the basis of its situation in the market.

Project teams Groups of sales representatives formed to deal with customers' needs more effectively.

Promotion (performance) allowance A rebate or discount offered by a manufacturer or its agent to a distributor who agrees to promote the product purchased under allowance.

Promotion mix The combination of five promotional elements: advertising, sales promotion, personal selling, public relations, and event marketing and sponsorships.

Promotion planning A systematic decision-making process regarding the use of various elements of the promotion mix in marketing communications; the process by which objectives and strategies are outlined.

Promotion strategy The blending of advertising, sales promotion, event marketing and sponsorship, personal selling, and public relations activity to present a consistent and persuasive message about a product or service.

Promotional pricing The temporary lowering of prices to attract customers.

Proposal solicitation A situation where a buying organization seeks and evaluates written proposals from acceptable suppliers.

Prospecting A systematic procedure for developing sales leads.

Prosperity Occurs when growth is sustained at significant levels for an extended period.

Protectionism A belief that foreign trade should be restricted so that domestic industry can be preserved.

Prototype A physical version of a potential product, that is, of a product designed and developed to meet the needs of potential customers; it is developmental in nature and refined according to feedback from consumer research.

Psychographic segmentation Market segmentation based on the activities, interests, and opinions of consumers.

Psychological pricing Pricing strategies that appeal to tendencies in consumer behaviour other than rational ones.

Public affairs A form of communications strategy in which communications activities are focused on various levels of governments.

Public image The reputation that a product, service, or company has among its various publics.

Public relations A variety of activities and communications that organizations undertake to monitor, evaluate, influence, and adapt to the attitudes, opinions, and behaviours of their publics.

Publicity The communication of newsworthy information about a product, service, company, or idea, usually in the form of a press release.

Pull strategy Creating demand by directing promotional efforts at consumers or final users of a product, who, in turn, put pressure on the retailers to carry it.

Pure competition A market in which many small firms market similar products.

Push strategy Creating demand for a product by directing promotional efforts at middlemen, who, in turn, promote the product among consumers.

Qualifying The procedure for determining if a prospect needs the product, has the authority to buy it, and has the ability to pay for it.

Qualitative data Collected from small samples in a controlled environment, the data result from questions concerned with "why" and from in-depth probing of the participants.

Quality variability The variations in services offered by different individuals, even within the same organization.

Quantitative data Collected using a structured procedure and a large sample, the data provide answers to questions concerned with "what," "when," "who," "how many," and "how often."

Quantity discount Offered on the basis of volume purchased in units or dollars.

Quota A specific limit imposed on the amount of goods that may be imported into a country.

Quotation A written document, usually from a sales representative, which states the terms of the price quoted.

Rack jobbers Wholesalers responsible for stocking merchandise-display racks that they own and that display the products they carry.

Rain cheque A guarantee by a retailer to provide an original product or one of comparable quality to a consumer within a reasonable time.

Rationalization The restructuring, downsizing, and, if necessary, the closing of operations that are not economically justified.

Raw materials Farm goods and other materials derived directly from natural resources.

Reach The total audience potentially exposed, one or more times, to an advertiser's schedule of messages in a given period, usually a week.

Real income Income adjusted for inflation over time.

Rebate A temporary price discount in the form of a cash return made directly to the consumer, usually by a manufacturer.

Recall test A message-effectiveness test that measures consumers' comprehension following exposure to a message.

Recession A decline in real output that lasts for six months or more.

Recognition test A message-effectiveness test that determines the level of consumer awareness of an advertisement.

Recovery The initial phase of economic expansion following a decline.

Rectangle An oversized rectangular-shaped banner ad.

Redemption rate The number of coupons returned to an organization expressed as a percentage of the total number of coupons in distribution for a particular coupon offer.

Reference group A group of people with a common interest that influences the members' attitudes and behaviour.

Referrals Occur when a salesperson secures names of potential customers from satisfied customers and makes an initial contact by telephone to arrange a time for a face-to-face meeting.

Refund See *Cash refund.*

Regional Marketing Management The management of marketing activity based on the needs of customers in different geographical locations (e.g., Ontario, Western Canada, Quebec and so on).

Regional shopping mall This is a large mall containing as many as 100 or more stores and several large department stores.

Reintermediation The replacement of old intermediaries with new and different intermediaries in a channel of distribution.

Relationship marketing The formation of integrated ties between customers and suppliers in a channel of distribution so that all parties derive mutual benefit. Also called partnering or database marketing.

Reliability (of data) Refers to similar results being achieved if another research study were undertaken under similar circumstances.

Reorder point An inventory level at which new orders must be placed if normal production operations are to be maintained or demand for finished products to be satisfied.

Repositioning Changing the place a product occupies in the consumer's mind, relative to competitive products.

Research objectives Statements that outline what the research is to accomplish.

Response list A purchasable list that identifies mail order buyers.

Retail advertising Advertising by a retail operation to communicate image, store sales, and the variety of merchandise carried.

Retail barter exchange A buying-selling situation where small companies band together through an exchange agent who facilitates transactions among members for a fee.

Retail chain store See *Chain store.*

Retail cooperatives Retailers that join together to establish a distribution centre that performs the role of the wholesaler in the channel.

Retail franchise A contractual agreement between a franchiser and a franchisee.

Retail in-ad coupon A coupon printed in a retailer's weekly advertising, either in the newspaper or in supplements inserted in the newspaper.

Retailing Activities involved in the sale of goods and services to final consumers for personal, family, or household use.

Retailing marketing mix The plan a retailer uses to attract customers.

Reverse marketing In business-to-business marketing, an effort by an organizational buyer to build relationships that shape a suppliers goods and services to fit the buyer's needs and those of its customers.

Reversification A corporate strategy in which a company sells off unprofitable divisions and retreats to its core areas where profit potential is greater.

RFID (radio frequency identification) The next wave of intelligent technology to impact inventory planning; RFID tags will be placed on goods so they can be instantly tracked anywhere in the world.

Rich media A form of online advertising that incorporates greater use of, and interaction with, animation, audio, and video.

Rifle strategy The selection of media that appeal to a common interest of a particular target market.

Sales office A company that is usually located near the customers but does not carry inventory.

Sales promotion Activity that provides special incentives to bring about immediate action from consumers, distributors, and an organization's sales force.

Sales volume maximization A firm strives for growth in sales that exceeds the growth in the size of the total market so that its market share increases.

Sample (free sample) A free product distributed to potential users either in a small trial size or in its regular size.

Sample population A representative portion of an entire population used to obtain information about that population.

Sampling frame A listing that can be used to access a population for research purposes.

Sandwich generation A generation of parents who are simultaneously caring for children and aging relatives.

Scanner A device that reads the UPC codes on products and produces instantaneous information on sales.

Scientific method A research method comprising awareness of a problem, collecting information, evaluating alternatives, analyzing and interpreting data, and taking action based on the findings.

Scrambled merchandising The addition, in retailing, of unrelated products and product lines to original products.

Screening An early stage in the new product development process where new ideas are quickly eliminated.

Seasonal discounts Discounts that apply to off-season or pre-season purchases.

Secondary data Data that have been compiled and published for purposes other than that of solving the specific problem under investigation.

Secondary package An outer wrapper that protects the product, often discarded once the product is used the first time.

Selective distribution The availability of a product in only a few outlets in a particular market.

Selective exposure Only noticing information that is of interest.

Selective perception Screening out information and messages that are in conflict with previously learned attitudes and beliefs.

Selective retention Remembering only what you want to remember.

Self-concept theory States that the self has four components: real self, self-image, looking-glass self, and ideal self.

Self-liquidating premium A premium offer in which the full cost of the premium is recovered by the purchase price of the offer.

Self-regulation A form of regulation whereby an industry sets standards and guidelines for its members to follow.

Self-serve store A store that is characterized by the limited number of services offered. Such a store tends to rely on in-store displays and merchandising to sell products.

Selling orientation When companies believe that the more they sell the more profit they will make.

Semantic differential Use of opposite descriptions of the attributes of a product or service to describe product or service attributes.

Service mix The particular combination of all services that a supplier offers.

Service quality The expected and perceived quality of a service offering.

Services The activities and benefits provided by an organization that satisfy the buyer's needs without conferring ownership of tangible goods; also, intangible offerings required to operate a business efficiently (e.g., repair or maintenance services).

Shop-in-shop A scaled-down version of a freestanding store within a larger department store; a store-within-a-store.

Shopping goods Goods that the consumer compares on such bases as suitability, quality, price, and style before making a selection.

Shopping mall A centrally owned, managed, planned, and operated shopping facility comprising a balanced mix of retail tenants and adequate parking for customers.

Shotgun strategy The selection of general-interest media to reach a broad cross-section of a market population.

Situation analysis Collecting of information from knowledgeable people inside and outside the organization and from secondary sources.

Skyscraper A tall, oblong-shaped banner ad that usually appears at the side of a Web page.

Slippage A situation in which a consumer starts collecting proofs of purchase for a refund offer but neglects to follow through and submit a request for the refund.

Slotting allowance Discount offered by a supplier to a retail distributor for the purpose of securing shelf space in retail outlets; such allowances are commonly associated with product introductions.

Social class The division of people into ordered groups on the basis of similar values, lifestyles, and social history.

Social marketing Marketing activity that increases the acceptability of social ideas.

Social responsibility An attitude of corporate conscience that anticipates and responds to social problems.

Socially responsible marketing The notion that business should conduct itself in the best interests of consumers and society.

Solo direct mail Specialized or individually prepared envelopes containing offers sent directly to prospects.

Sorting Separating merchandise into grades, colours, and sizes.

Sorting process The accumulation, allocation, sorting, and assorting of merchandise.

Source list A list maintained by the Ministry of Supply and Services that includes the names, products, and services of all companies that have expressed an interest in dealing with the federal government.

Spam The inappropriate use of an online mailing list to deliver a message; it is unsolicited junk mail.

Specialty goods Goods that consumers will make an effort to find and purchase because the goods possess some unique or important characteristic.

Specialty store A store selling a single line or limited line of merchandise.

Specialty-merchandise wholesaler A wholesaler that carries a limited number or narrow line of products but offers an extensive assortment within these lines.

Sponsored email The inclusion of a second message (from a sponsor) when a website mails information to a subscriber.

Sponsorship The financial support of an event by an organization in return for certain advertising rights and privileges associated with the event.

Sponsorship (online) An advertiser committing to an extended relationship with a website unrelated to the company's own site.

Staple goods Products that are needed or used on a regular basis.

Sticky content The notion that the website has a compelling reason for users to frequently come back.

Stock balance The practice of maintaining an adequate assortment of goods that will attract customers while keeping inventories of both high-demand and low-demand goods at reasonable levels.

Stockout Items that are not available when a customer's order is shipped.

Stockturn The number of times during a specific period that the average inventory of a store is sold.

Storage warehouse A warehouse that holds products for long periods of time in an attempt to balance supply and demand for producers and purchasers.

Straight (or full) rebuy The purchase of inexpensive items on a regular basis by an organization.

Strategic alliance A partnering process whereby two firms combine resources in a marketing venture for the purpose of satisfying the customers they share; the firms have strengths in different areas.

Strategic business unit (SBU) A unit of a company that has a separate mission and objective and that can be planned independently of other company business.

Strategic control Long-term control measure common in multi-product, multi-division companies.

Strategic philanthropy Supporting opportunities that benefit both company and society.

Strategic planning The process of determining objectives and identifying strategies and tactics within the framework of the business environment that will contribute to the achievement of objectives.

Strategies Statements that outline how objectives will be achieved.

Streaming media The continuous delivery of small, compressed packets of data that are interpreted by a software player and displayed as audio or full-motion video.

Strip mall A collection of stores attached together in a neighbourhood plaza.

Subculture A subgroup of a culture that has a distinctive mode of behaviour.

Suburban mall Located in built-up areas beyond the core of a city.

Supermarket A departmentalized food store, selling packaged grocery products, produce, dairy, meat, frozen food, and general merchandise.

Superstitial Online ads that include animation, audio, and video; they resemble a television commercial.

Superstore A diversified supermarket that sells a broad range of food and non-food items.

Supplier search A stage in the business-to-business buying process where a buyer looks for potential suppliers.

Supplier selection The stage in the business-to-business buying process where the buying organization evaluates the proposals from various suppliers and selects the one that matches its needs.

Supplies Standardized products that are routinely purchased with a minimum of effort.

Supplies and services Goods purchased by business and industry that do not enter the production process but facilitate other operations of the organization.

Supply chain A sequence of companies that perform activities related to the creation and delivery of a good or service to consumers or business customers.

Supply chain management The integration of information among members of a supply chain to facilitate efficient production and distribution of goods to customers.

Survey research Data that is collected systematically through some form of communication with a representative sample by means of a questionnaire.

Sweepstakes A type of contest in which large prizes, such as cash, cars, homes, and vacations, are given away to randomly selected participants.

SWOT analysis The examination of critical factors that have an impact on the nature and direction of a marketing strategy (strengths, weaknesses, opportunities, and threats).

Syndicated survey A survey where the findings are offered for sale to any organization that has an interest in them.

Tabulation Counting the various responses for each question and arriving at a frequency distribution.

Target market A group of customers who have certain characteristics in common.

Target Market Management System The management of marketing activity based on the requirements of different customer groups (e.g., industry, government, consumers and so on).

Target pricing A pricing strategy designed to generate a desirable rate of return on investment and based on the full costs of producing a product.

Tariff A tax or duty imposed on imported goods.

Telemarketing The use of telecommunications to promote the products and services of a business.

Telephone interviews Communication with individuals via the telephone, usually conducted from central locations.

Test marketing Placing a product for sale in one or more representative markets to observe performance under a proposed marketing plan.

Text messaging The transmission of short, text-only messages on wireless devices such as cell phones and personal digital assistants (PDAs).

Total product concept The package of benefits a buyer receives when he or she purchases a product.

Trade advertising Advertising directed at channel members by a source supplier, such as a manufacturer.

Trade barrier Intended to protect a country from too much foreign competition within its borders.

Trade fair A periodic show or exhibition at which manufacturers in a particular industry gather to display merchandise to prospective wholesalers and retailers.

Trade promotion Promotional activity directed at distributors that is designed to increase the volume they purchase and encourage merchandising support for a manufacturer's product.

Trade shows Shows organized by an industry association each year to demonstrate the latest products of member manufacturers.

Trade-in allowance Price reduction granted for a new product when a similar used product is turned in.

Trademark That part of a brand granted legal protection so that only the owner can use it.

Trading bloc Economic alliance between countries in the same area of the world.

Traditional mass media Television, newspaper, magazine, radio, and outdoor (transit and posters).

Trial close An attempt to close that failed.

Truck jobber A specialty wholesaler operating mainly in the food distribution industry, who sells and delivers goods to retail customers during the same sales call.

Twinning Offering two or more different brands at the same location or adjoining locations (e.g., two restaurants under one roof). See also *Piggybacking* and *Co-branding*.

Undercover marketing See *Buzz marketing.*

Uniform delivered pricing A geographic pricing strategy that includes an average freight charge for all customers regardless of their location.

Unique selling point (USP) The primary benefit of a product or service, the one feature that distinguishes a product from competing products.

Unit pricing The expression of price in terms of a unit of measurement (e.g., cost per gram or cost per millilitre).

Unsought goods Goods which consumers are unaware they need or about which they lack knowledge.

Validity (of data) Refers to a research procedure's ability to actually measure what it is intended to.

Value pricing (EDLP) The establishment of a fair everyday price that is attractive to consumers and profitable for the company (often referred to as everyday low pricing).

Variable costs Costs that change according to the level of output.

Variety store A store selling a wide range of staple merchandise at low or popular prices.

Vendor analysis An evaluation of potential suppliers based on an assessment of their technological ability, consistency in meeting product specifications, quantity, delivery, and their ability to provide needed quantity.

Venue marketing (venue sponsorship) The linking of a brand name (company name) to a physical site such as a theatre, stadium or arena.

Vertical conflict Conflict that occurs when a channel member feels that another member at a different level is engaging in inappropriate conduct.

Vertical integration strategy A corporate strategy where a company owns and operates businesses at different levels of the channel of distribution.

Vertical marketing system (VMS) The linking of channel members at different levels in the marketing process to form a centrally controlled marketing system in which one member dominates the channel.

Video brochure A video presentation of a product.

Viral marketing A situation where the receiver of an online message is encouraged to pass it on to friends.

Virtual advertising The electronic placement of an advertising image into television programs, both live and taped.

Vision statement A statement that defines plans for the future, what the company is and does, and where it is headed.

Visit A sequence of page requests made by a visitor at a website.

Visitor A unique user who comes to a website.

Voluntary chain A wholesaler-initiated organization consisting of a group of independent retailers who agree to buy from a designated wholesaler.

Warehouse a distribution centre that receives, sorts, and redistributes merchandise to customers.

Warehouse outlets (big-box stores) No-frills, cash-and-carry outlets that offer customers name-brand merchandise at discount prices.

Web browser A software program that allows a user to navigate the World Wide Web.

Webcasting The production of an extended commercial or infomercial that includes entertainment value in the communications.

Website An encompassing body of online information for a particular domain name (e.g., an organization or business).

Wholesaling Buying or handling merchandise and subsequently reselling it to organizational users, other wholesalers, and retailers.

World Wide Web The collection of websites linked together on the Internet.

Youth market A market with brand loyalties are in the formative stages.

Zone pricing The division of a market into geographic zones and the establishment of a uniform delivered price for each zone.

Index

Note: Key terms are boldface.